# THE TONI MORRISON
# ENCYCLOPEDIA

# THE TONI MORRISON ENCYCLOPEDIA

Edited by
Elizabeth Ann Beaulieu

GREENWOOD PRESS
Westport, Connecticut · London

**Library of Congress Cataloging-in-Publication Data**

The Toni Morrison encyclopedia / edited by Elizabeth Ann Beaulieu.
    p. cm.
  Includes bibliographical references and index.
  ISBN 0-313-31699-6 (alk. paper)
    1. Morrison, Toni—Encyclopedias.  2. Women and literature—United
States—Encyclopedias.  3. African Americans in literature—Encyclopedias.
I. Beaulieu, Elizabeth Ann.
PS3563.O8749 Z913    2003
813′.54—dc21        2002021617

British Library Cataloguing in Publication Data is available.

Library of Congress Catalog Card Number: 2002021617
ISBN: 0-313-31699-6

First published in 2003

Greenwood Press, 88 Post Road West, Westport, CT 06881
An imprint of Greenwood Publishing Group, Inc.
www.greenwood.com

Printed in the United States of America

The paper used in this book complies with the
Permanent Paper Standard issued by the National
Information Standards Organization (Z39.48-1984).

10  9  8  7  6  5  4  3  2  1

# Contents

# Introduction

If all of Toni Morrison's work could be summed up with just one quotation from one of her characters, it would have to be Pilate's observation, in *Song of Solomon,* "Life is life. Precious." Indeed, Morrison's work overflows with the stuff of life—the examined and the unexamined life, the triumphant and the tragic life, the small, undervalued life and the flamboyant, celebrated life. In reviewing Morrison's work to prepare this volume, it occurred to me that the very imperative which compels Toni Morrison to write is life itself. And what grander subject matter is there?

Around the time I first began reading Morrison seriously, I ran across an interview in which she was defending herself against the allegation that the tales she tells are larger than life. "Life IS large," she retorted, and her work supports that claim vociferously. The irony comes in the stories she chooses to tell; after all, what is the value in hearing the story of a young Black incest victim who wishes for nothing but the blue eyes she believes will grant her society's acceptance and the love she craves? Or the adventures of a materialistic young man with the appropriate surname "Dead," who stoops to rob even his own aunt? Or the harrowing journey of a runaway slave woman whose brief taste of freedom convinces her that killing her children is more just than allowing them to be returned to slavery? Through her novels Morrison forces us to acknowledge that the lives we often overlook and rarely celebrate are perhaps the lives we can learn most from.

As a writer, Toni Morrison personifies courage. She tells stories that we often do not wish to hear. She speaks as a Black woman in a world that still undervalues the voice of the Black woman. She blends the personal and the political—for she feels very strongly that art should have meaning—to depict African American cultural and social history, and she does so in a way that resonates for readers of all ages, races, ethnicities, and genders. Morrison embodies a rare writer's gift: the ability to tell the powerful stories she imagines, employing an equally powerful, yet simultaneously poetic language. One might argue that Morrison herself has become one of the ancestor figures she privileges in her work, guiding her readers to a much-needed understanding of the past in order that they might recognize the urgent promise of the future, and doing so with a wisdom and eloquence unparalleled in American letters.

Toni Morrison was born Chloe Anthony Wofford on February 18, 1931, the daughter of Georgia-born George Wofford, a shipyard welder, and Alabama-born Ramah Willis Wofford. She was the second of four children and spent her childhood in Lorain, Ohio, an ethnically diverse steel town just west of Cleveland where her parents had relocated to avoid the racism of the deep South. Morrison attended an integrated school in Lorain and excelled early on, especially in reading. Even before her formal school years, though, Morrison had absorbed at home a love of stories from her parents, both of whom were storytellers and musicians and who instilled in their children a deep respect for their heritage through the stories they told.

Morrison graduated from Lorain High School with honors in 1949 and enrolled in Howard University, where she majored in English and minored in classics. During her college years she joined a university-affiliated touring repertory company, and also changed her name to Toni, allegedly because so many people had difficulty pronouncing Chloe. Following graduation from Howard in 1953, Morrison attended Cornell University, earning a master's degree in English after writing a thesis on William Faulkner and Virginia Woolf.

In 1955–57 Morrison taught at Texas Southern University, then returned to Howard University to join the faculty in 1957. There she met her husband, Harold Morrison, a Jamaican architect. They married in 1958 and had two children, Harold Ford and Slade Kevin, before they divorced in 1964, the same year Morrison left Howard University. It was during this period that Morrison began writing in earnest, as an antidote to the loneliness she often felt. One of her first projects was a short story about a young Black girl who dreamed of having blue eyes.

In 1964 Morrison began work as an editor for the textbook subsidiary of Random House in Syracuse, New York, and was promoted to senior editor at the company's headquarters in New York City in 1967, where she had the opportunity to work with a number of prominent Black authors. While at Random House, Morrison continued to teach, holding positions at SUNY-Purchase (1971–72) and Yale University (1976–77). She left Random House in 1983 and was named the Albert Schweitzer Professor of Humanities at SUNY-Albany in 1984. Presently Morrison is Robert F. Goheen Professor in the Council of Humanities at Princeton University, the first Black woman to hold an endowed chair at an Ivy League university.

The workshop story that Morrison began in the mid-1960s was published as her first novel, *The Bluest Eye*, in 1970. She maintains that in working on the manuscript she was striving to write the type of literature that she liked to read and that was too often unavailable. This novel, which served as Morrison's introduction to the American literary scene, was followed in 1973 by *Sula*, for which she received the National Book Award nomination in 1975. She published *Song of Solomon* next, in 1977; it garnered a Book-of-the-Month Club selection, the National Book Critics Circle Award, and the American Academy and Institute of Arts and Letters Award. The novel was also a paperback best-seller. *Tar Baby*, released in 1981, landed Morrison on the cover of *Time* magazine, and in 1988 Morrison received the Pulitzer Prize in Literature for what many consider to be her greatest novel, *Beloved*, published in 1987. *Jazz*, Morrison's sixth novel, appeared in 1992.

In 1993, Toni Morrison received the Nobel Prize in Literature, only the eighth woman ever to do so, and the first Black woman. Upon awarding Morrison the prize, the Swedish Academy described her as a writer "who, in novels characterized by visionary force and poetic import, gives life to an essential aspect of American reality." Already a writer with an international reputation in 1993, Morrison's recognition by the Swedish Academy "was the official inscripting of a worldwide recognition and appreciation of the intellectual stimulation and awesome power of her writing," according to Trudier Harris in an essay that appeared shortly after the honor was conferred.

Since becoming a Nobel laureate, Morrison has published *Paradise* (1998), the novel she had in progress at the time of the award. In addition to her seven novels, Morrison has written a significant work of literary criticism, *Playing In the Dark: Whiteness and the Literary Imagination* (1992) and has also edited two collections of essays, *Race-ing Justice, En-Gendering Power: Essays on Anita Hill, Clarence Thomas, and the Construction of Social Reality* (1992) and *Birth of a Nation'hood: Gaze, Script, and Spectacle in the O.J. Simpson Case* (1997).

This introduction, presenting as it does the basic facts of Morrison's life and the salient details of her career, is necessarily brief. Fine interviews and biographies have been published, and studies of her novels abound. Each time a new novel is published, her readers thrill to discover what reading challenge Morrison has designed for them, what new and delicious uses of the English language she has invented, what memorable characters will join the ranks of the Breedloves, the Deads, the Peaces, and the Suggses. And each time her readers are not disappointed. Toni Morrison's contributions to literature are vast—the characters and places she has created, the situations she has imagined, the moral ambiguities, public pronouncements, private agonies and celebrations she has dramatized—all these make up an oeuvre that is unrivaled in American literature.

*The Toni Morrison Encyclopedia* seeks not to document Morrison's work exhaustively, but instead to catalog and interpret for readers some of her most important themes, characters, and places. There are essays on each of her literary works, as well as an "approaches" section designed to offer readers various paths of entry into her work. For the convenience of the reader, entries are arranged alphabetically. They vary in length, with the novels and major themes receiving more in-depth treatment than characters, places, and minor themes. The volume is by no means complete; like Morrison's novels, which offer "gaps" through which the reader can enter and co-create, there is ample room here for individual interpretation and elaboration.

More than fifty scholars from across the country pooled their expertise to produce the entries that make up *The Toni Morrison Encyclopedia*; without them, this volume would not have been possible. When the project was first announced, inquiries from around the world poured in. All of the entries are signed by the critics who contributed them, and many conclude with a list of sources that readers may wish to consult for further reading and research. Finally, the *Encyclopedia* concludes with a selected bibliography that is just that—selected. In 2002 the MLA Bibliography listed well over one thousand books and articles on Toni Morrison and her work; Morrison scholarship has become a virtual industry. What this volume hopes to contribute to that industry is an overview of Morrison's primary concerns and achievements, and a reference point for readers who wish to go beyond Morrison's texts themselves. Like the talking book that "speaks" at the end of *Jazz*, urging readers to consider the manifestation of creativity and love they have, by reading, participated in, I like to think that this volume "speaks," too—testifying to Toni Morrison's gifts and accomplishments, encouraging the creativity of her readers, and reminding us of the many ways that Morrison insists on life.

# Acknowledgments

I wish to thank the following programs and individuals for making this work possible:

- The Frances Holland Black Endowment in Women's Studies at Appalachian State University, for funding a graduate student to assist in the technical preparation of this manuscript.

- Gena Pittman, who had never read Toni Morrison, for spending an entire summer turning hundreds of entries into a book manuscript, and for remaining cheerful and pleasant while she sorted through characters, places, and story lines she surely found, at the very least, bewildering.

- Friends, colleagues, and Morrison aficionados who contributed entries, advice, general support, and much-needed encouragement for a project they insisted was long overdue.

- And finally, my husband, James M. Ivory, for what can only be called his many expertises, and my son, Sebastian Luke Ivory, for all the ways he tried to exercise patience during the many stages of this project.

# A

## Acton (Jazz)

In *Jazz*, Dorcas Manfred's* boyfriend with whom she cheats on the married Joe Trace*. The type of man Joe would call a "rooster," Acton is narcissistic, critical, and unable to empathize with Dorcas, which makes him all the more appealing to her. She tries in vain to please him, losing herself to his self-serving demands. As she lies dying of a bullet wound, he is angry that her blood has soiled his clothing. *See also Jazz*.

Caroline Brown

## African Myth, Use of

Critics such as Henry Louis Gates, Jr., argue that an understanding of African mythology is an important backdrop against which to read African American writing. While elements from biblical and classical Roman and Greek mythology* also exist in Morrison's work, African myths do, indeed, play an especially important role. These mythic elements root the novels in the African tradition and provide a spiritual and cultural bridge between the history of her characters' ancestors and the lives of the characters at the times the novels are set in the United States. The myths also provide a context for understanding the magical realism* that is often such an important aspect of the stories.

In *Song of Solomon**, for example, the novel opens with the flight of a Black insurance agent, Robert Smith*, who jumps off the roof of No

Mercy Hospital* and ends with Milkman Dead*, who, after tracing the roots of his flying African* ancestors, gains the incentive he has needed all along to join them. Many readers have noted elements of the Greek myth of Icarus in this novel. This trait of flying, however, also goes back to the myths of flying Africans that slaves carried with them to the shores and fields of the United States. For example, slaves frequently told stories of the Africans who flew back to Africa rather than be enslaved. The act of flying is believed to result from a realization, often, of one's identity*. While most readers readily suspend their disbelief in this work of fiction, the flying myth grounds the magical realism of the story firmly in African heritage.

*Beloved** is a novel steeped in African spirituality* and myth. One belief is in a collective consciousness of the ancestors that is carried among the living, which often results in ancestor worship. Another feature is that the female often holds a leadership role in this ancestor community, even taking on a goddess-like quality. Burial practices are very important, and improperly or incompletely buried corpses are thought to generate angry ghosts that linger among the living or return to raise havoc among them. The living are believed to be able to communicate quite readily with their dead ancestors.

All of these elements play an important role in *Beloved*, from the abilities as mediums of Baby Suggs*, Sethe Suggs*, and Denver Suggs*, to the poltergeist character, Beloved*. Beloved was murdered, and this violent end causes her soul unrest in Western tradition. However, she was named and received her gravestone in an act of sexual submission by her mother, and this wrongful burial has made her spirit angry and restless in the African mythological tradition. Naming is also important in African mythology, and so are tricksters*. Beloved, as a character whose naming history is clouded, becomes a trickster able to change forms and cause trouble and misfortune among the living. This trickster characteristic is reminiscent of the Signifying Monkey of Yoruba mythology. In this myth, Monkey tells insults to Lion that were supposedly told to him by Elephant, in order to set Lion and Elephant against one another. Beloved's manipulative presence in the household similarly causes conflicts in many of the domestic relationships. Beloved's deeds turn deadly because of the collective weight of the ancestors' experiences of slavery* that she brings upon the living from the dark side.

In the twentieth century, Morrison and other writers began using African myths as a means of bringing Africa closer to those who were stolen away from that continent to America and also closer to their descendants. Through her work, Morrison engages her characters in calling on the wisdom of their African ancestors to help them meditate and rise above the circumstances in which they find themselves, even if this calling is subconscious or complicated with problems. The richness of African mythology and how it is applied in Morrison's work enhances the reading experience for her readers. It also adds to the credibility and authenticity of Morrison's voice. *See also* Ancestor; Flying Africans, Myth of; Oral Tradition.

References: Paula Barnes, *Tradition and Innovation: Toni Morrison and the Flight Motif in Afro-American Literature* (2000); Samuel Burbanks IV, "African Spiritual Culture in *Sula, Song of Solomon*, and *Beloved*," *http://www.timbooktu.com/burbanks/spiritual.htm*; Henry Louis Gates, Jr., *The Signifying Monkey: A Theory of African-American Literary Criticism* (1988); Samuel B. Olorounto, "Studying African-American Literature in Its Global Context," *VCAAA Journal* 7: 1 (Summer 1992); Gay Wilentz, "Civilizations Underneath: African Heritage as Cultural Discourse in Toni Morrison's *Song of Solomon*," in *Toni Morrison's Fiction: Contemporary Criticism*, ed. David L. Middleton (1997).

Connie Ann Kirk

## Ajax (*Sula*)

Alias for Albert Jacks or A. Jacks, the handsome, dark-complexioned young man who loves airplanes and refers to Sula Peace* and Nel Wright* as "pig meat." Years later Ajax becomes Sula's lover, but terminates their relationship when she starts to become possessive. *See also* Sula.

Douglas Taylor

## Albright, Mavis (*Paradise*)

The twenty-seven-year-old Mavis, who arrives in 1968, is the first and most conservative of the Convent* women and title character of one of *Paradise*'s* nine sections. After accidentally suffocating her newborn twins by leaving them in the car, Mavis believes that her abusive husband and three surviving children are trying to kill her. Planning to escape to California, she steals her husband's Cadillac and drives west until she runs out of gas and takes shelter in the Convent. Almost immediately, Mavis begins to hear the laughter of Merle and Pearl, her dead twins, and finds herself staying at the Convent without ever deciding to. With the aging Consolata Sosa* (Connie) to look after, the ghostly presence of the ever-growing twins, and the aggressive, nighttime sexual dream-visits of a strange man, Mavis lives an unhealthy but safe fantasy-family life. It is her guilt over the death of the twins and the fear of abusive men that she must excise through the "loud-dreaming" sessions that Connie begins to lead. Although Mavis leaves the Convent several times throughout the years (to get a look at, but never to talk to, her surviving children), she is there the morning of the assault in 1976 and is one of the three women shot down outside while attempting to escape. After the attack, Mavis appears once more in the novel; she shares a brief meal with her now-grown daughter, Sally, in a country inn restaurant before disappearing into the crowd. *See also Paradise.*

Julie Cary Nerad

## Ancestor

For the Yoruba of Nigeria, in West Africa, ancestors are everywhere: in the earth, in the air, and within one's children. Their presence links souls of the present with souls of the past. Their lessons transcend both time and space—enriching their descendants with a perspective full of other-world wisdom applicable to this world. They are deities or family members who have passed on, yet remain accessible to the living. They are the ancestors.

To understand the definition of the ancestor and, by extension, grasp its function in Toni Morrison's novels, one must first become familiar with the function of the ancestor in West African cosmology. Typically, in Western notions of the spirit, death marks the soul's movement to heaven or some other static afterlife. In contrast, for West Africans, spirits of the deceased remain on earth, dwelling among the living in rivers and trees, and also through their descendants. For the West African, there is no separation between the spiritual and material worlds. The ancestors live on a spiritual continuum between worlds and generations. Therefore, even though an individual's physical body may be gone, s/he remains present as spirit, as ancestor. While anyone has the power to tap into the energies of the ancestors, community elders are the primary link between the people and their ancestors. As repositories of tribal history, the elders ensure that subsequent generations understand the importance of the ancestors as well as modes of access to them. As literary elder, Morrison modifies this use of the ancestor and transforms it into a layered literary device that explores the manifold ways in which characters relate to their ancestors and, by extension, their communities.

Morrison provides some insight into her use of the ancestor in "Rootedness: the Ancestor as Foundation," an essay that, among other things, explains how, within the text, a character's connection with the ancestor determines his or her success in life. Using her own writing as an example, Morrison seeks to debunk the rhetoric of self-reliance as the key to prosperity and instead uses her characters to promote ancestral connections as the linchpin of success. Morrison believes that the relationship between character and ancestor, antagonistic or amicable, directly correlates with that character's success in navigating life.

Morrison is not only concerned with the relationship between character and ancestor; she is also interested in the connection between character and community*, particularly a Black community. For Morrison, Black communities are ancestral legacies that represent a wellspring of culturally inflected information, tropes, and values. The ancestral legacies encountered by Morrison's characters go beyond the return of deceased family members. Her characters may interact with the ancestor as collective history or through ancestral stories. Morrison's writing also invokes a familial ancestral legacy—one fostered by the stories she heard as a young girl. When she was growing up, her grandfather related the story of the family's ascent from the South to the North during the Great Migration, while her father captivated the family with ghost stories*. These legends represent a familial ancestral legacy—a legacy that emerges in Morrison's writing through texts that read with a rhythm and flow reminiscent of the oral narratives she once heard. By using the novel to keep oral history alive, Morrison, in turn, allows the memory of her familial ancestors and others like them to endure. In her novels, Morrison adapts West African views of the ancestor as deceased family member or deity and expand them to include ancestor as familial history, ancestor as collective history, and ancestor as ancestral stories.

Four of Morrison's seven novels—*Song of Solomon**, *Tar Baby**, *Beloved**, and *Jazz**—explore, more explicitly than the others, the different ways individual characters relate to this expanded notion of the ancestor and how this relationship relates to personal, interpersonal, and communal well-being. In *Song of Solomon*, Morrison traces the quest of Milkman Dead* as he searches to reconcile his perception of and experience with both his immediate family* and his ancestors. What begins as a search for gold becomes Milkman's journey into the depths of his ancestry, where he comes to understand his place in the world. Through Milkman, Morrison reveals that disordered existence is part and parcel of fragmented ancestral relationships. In contrast, Pilate Dead*, Milkman's aunt and hearer of voices from beyond the grave, demonstrates the inner strength that exists when one lives a life fully connected to the wisdom and stories of the ancestors.

Morrison continues this interest in ancestral foundations in *Tar Baby*, where, through the impassioned affair between Jadine (Jade) Childs* and Son*, she demonstrates how strained relationships with the ancestors arrest the development of intimate interpersonal relationships. Initially, Jade and Son resist their intense attraction to one another;

eventually, they yield to their desires and form a relationship. Soon after, however, the couple realizes that they have serious ideological conflicts. As they struggle, to no avail, to resolve their opposing ideas on women's roles and what constitutes "success," each is thrust into a confrontation with an ancestral force that had hitherto been denied. For Son, the horsemen of Isle des Chevaliers* symbolize an ancestral force he must connect with to define himself. Similarly, Jade must confront her orphaned distance from her ancestors, the swamp women, to grow. Where *Song of Solomon* explores how a character's conflict with the ancestors affects one personally, *Tar Baby* exposes how strained relationships with the ancestors hinder healthy interpersonal relationships.

With *Beloved*, Morrison invokes the ancestral legacy of her father's ghost stories to present a hauntingly complex story of slavery*, possession, and love. Based on the true story of Margaret Garner*, a runaway slave who, upon being found, attempted to murder her children to keep them from being returned to slavery, Morrison tells the story of Beloved*: the ghost of Sethe Suggs's* murdered child who has returned from the other side. What begins as a haunting of surviving family members within the home transforms into a haunting of the entire community. Beloved's return thrusts her family and the surrounding community into a process of rememory. This act of rememory forces the characters to confront historical ancestral legacies—from the Middle Passage to slavery—even though they do not want to. In addition, during a crucial moment in the novel when Beloved tries to kill Sethe, Baby Suggs* comes to Denver Suggs* as spirit, as ancestor, and encourages her to move past the boundaries of the yard that have held her captive and save her mother. In *Beloved*, the ancestor prompts characters to confront an otherwise unsettling past and provides the emotional grounding needed to do so.

In *Jazz*, Morrison explores the role of the ancestor by analyzing characters' relationships with their forefathers, with whom they must reconcile to grow. *Jazz* examines the characters involved in a bizarre love affair between Joe Trace*, a married man in his fifties, and an eighteen-year-old girl named Dorcas Manfred*. After three months, their affair sours and Joe shoots Dorcas. Then, at Dorcas's funeral, Joe's wife, Violet*, bursts in to seek revenge on her husband's lover by slashing her face. Morrison introduces the presence of the ancestors by tracing the lives of the major characters—Dorcas and Alice Manfred*, Violet and Joe—to reveal the source of their current distress. Each is haunted by memories of the past, a past often riddled with incidents of racist violence*. Several characters set out on a search for their true ancestors and, in doing so, are able to create surrogate families and to mature emotionally. By showing how characters turn on themselves and each other when disconnected from their ancestral stories, *Jazz* demonstrates the need for a healthy connection between ancestor and individual to ensure the psychological health and well-being of the community at large. Taken together, *Song of Solomon, Tar Baby, Beloved,* and *Jazz* demonstrate Morrison's interest in uncovering the function of and possibilities within using the ancestor as foundation. *See also* Ghost Story, Use of; Oral Tradition.

References: Missy Dehn Kubitschek, *Toni Morrison: A Critical Companion* (1998); Toni Morrison, "Rootedness: The Ancestor as Foundation," in *Black Women Writers (1950–1980): A Critical Evaluation,* ed. Mari Evans (1984); Nellie Y. McKay, "An Interview with Toni Morrison," in *Conversations with Toni Morrison,* ed. Danielle Taylor-Guthrie (1994); Marilyn Sanders Mobley, *Folk Roots and Mythic Wings in Sarah Orne Jewett and Toni Morrison: The Cultural Function of Narrative* (1991).

Shanna Greene Benjamin

## Approaches to Morrison's Work: Ecocritical

Ecocriticism, a literary movement that began in the 1970s, does not pretend to solve the world's ecological problems through the study of literature. Rather, it allows both readers and authors to foreground environmental issues in texts so that these themes may be recognized and perhaps even studied scientifically. First coined by William Rueckert in his 1978 article "Literature and Ecology: An Experiment in Ecocriticism," the term "ecocriticism" is based on what Rueckert calls ecology's first law: the belief that all things are interconnected (73). Like ecology itself, ecocriticism is interdisciplinary in nature and borrows not only from literary criticism but also from science, the social sciences, and the humanities in its approach to the study of literature. Cheryll Glotfelty, in the preface to *The Ecocriticism Reader* (1996), further explains that the focus of ecocriticism is the interrelation of nature and culture (xix). This method is particularly useful to the study of Toni Morrison's novels precisely because of its varied character. An ecocritical approach demands not just a scientific envisioning of the environment but also a psychological, sociological, religious, and historical analysis of nature and its manifestations in the work at hand. Morrison weaves all of these strands together to produce a narrative history* of African Americans, a history largely ignored by white society.

For Morrison, nature is inextricably linked with religion, and all of her texts grapple in some way with the interplay between these two seemingly contradictory forces. All of her writings show the connection between the biblical Garden of Eden, the plagues and natural catastrophe of the apocalypse, and the human psyche. From Pecola Breedlove* of *The Bluest Eye**, whose misfortune causes marigolds to die, from *Tar Baby*'s* Jadine Childs*, whose lover is born to her as Adam is, out of the primordial ooze, from *Beloved*'s* Sethe Suggs*, who "falls" from innocence when a tree is carved on her back, to the covey of strange women living at the Convent* in *Paradise**, who finally find their City of God when their home is brutally destroyed, Morrison's characters are both imbued with religious sensibilities and closely linked to nature. For, according to Evan Eisenberg in *The Ecology of Eden* (1998), behind every Western understanding about nature lies a notion of Eden. Since God created the world and proclaimed it good, Morrison asserts through her characters, all is not lost even if the apocalypse seems to some to presage the end of the world. She invokes these biblical images not to proclaim her texts explicitly or even implicitly religious, but rather to make clear the connection between the nature that surrounds us and the inner nature that makes up our psychological world. A scrutiny of the relationship between nature and religion in the novels therefore will help illuminate Morrison's proposals for societal healing from historical wounds.

In addition to the epic religious struggles, Morrison's novels also grapple with American history. The novels foreground nature in their descriptions of the various movements that comprise African American and, indeed, American history. The tree named Brother* in *Beloved* that benignly watches as Black men swing by their necks from its branches, the forlorn parrots that squawk "I love you" in their tiny cages in *Jazz** during the Harlem Renaissance, the wind that cries out a woman's name during the Great Depression in *Song of Solomon**, and the trees whose intertwined silhouette resembles a couple making love during the Civil Rights movement in *Paradise* all tell both of the degradation faced by African Americans during the last two centuries of American history and of their strength. For in the end, though trees do unwittingly shelter nooses, they also bloom and lead Paul D Garner* north in *Beloved*; although trapped by their cages, much like their owner Violet Trace*, who is ensnared by her circumstances, the parrots do eventually fly free. Even though the sound Milkman Dead* hears in the woods leaves him melancholy and mournful, it also alerts him to the murderous presence of Guitar Baines*, who has been driven mad by penury and racial victimization. And despite their isolation from the relative civilization of Ruby, Oklahoma*, the enjoined trees serve to remind *Paradise*'s Deacon (Deek) Morgan* of the hubris in thinking that his town could remain apart from the larger world forever. For it is in connections, Deek learns, that human beings grow and flourish. Without this communion, they wither and die much like the marigolds in *The Bluest Eye*.

It is in *The Bluest Eye* that the connection between nature and racial hatred can perhaps be seen most clearly. Split into four sections named after the seasons, and set in the year before America's entry into World War II, the novel tells the story of Pecola Breedlove, a young girl who has been impregnated by her drunken father and whose greatest desire is to be white. Pecola so longs for blue eyes—which she believes to be the standard by which all beauty is judged—that she eventually comes to conclude that her eyes are indeed blue and that she is therefore worthy of love. She so accepts the white standard of beauty and denigration of her race that everything around her in the natural world seems to die. It is not only Pecola who affirms this standard of beauty, however. Pecola is uniformly despised by other Black children for her too-dark skin, her poverty, and her awkwardness. When Claudia* and Frieda MacTeer's* marigolds refuse to grow, they understand that it is not really the fault of the barren soil, but the fault of the community* to accept Pecola for who she really is and, by extension, to accept themselves.

*Sula** adds to this image of nature as an expression of racial self-hatred a sense of survival. Sula Peace*, one of Medallion, Ohio's* renegade young women, returns to town during a plague of robins. Typically harbingers of spring, these birds presage only gloom and despair for the community. For Sula, despite her status as the granddaughter of the beloved Eva Peace*, harbors no love for its citizens. The town's residents, who view evil as something to be survived much like floods or other natural disasters, project all their troubles onto Sula, the woman they judge to be evil. If the milk curdles, they imagine that Sula must be nearby. If their husbands lose interest in them, they reason that Sula must be involved. For the Black residents of Medallion, Sula comes to represent the rose they see when they look at the rose-shaped birthmark above her eye: she attracts with her beauty and stings with her thorns. And like the rose, she dies young.

Despite their joy at Sula's death, the townspeople soon come to mourn her loss, for the evil they had once projected onto her now comes to wound them. They have lost their focus, and begin to turn their thoughts more and more to the bridge being built over the river that separates them from the white community. When they realize that the jobs promised to them will never materialize, they storm the river and unwittingly destroy the bridge, killing many of their numbers in the process. The polluted river continues to flow between the two halves of town, which have no bridge to connect them. Although this bridge has been the focus of their energies for many years, and its destruction represents a tremendous loss, it also keeps them separate from a people who despise them. The river may not nourish them, but neither does its bridge poison them by allowing self-hatred to invade their community.

Milkman Dead, the protagonist of *Song of Solomon*, knows well the divisions in the Black community. The son of a wealthy landowner, he is unpopular and scorned. What he comes to understand when he returns to the rural Virginia town of his forebears, is that his indolence and haughtiness have caused much of the judgment against him, and not his skin tone or his social standing. Having gone to Virginia to look for a sack of gold he thinks his aunt Pilate Dead* had abandoned there, he soon realizes that the real treasure lies in discovering his ancestry. His plans are nearly foiled, however; as he leans against an old tree, he discovers his friend Guitar Baines* has come to kill him. Part of a messianic group formed to bring about racial justice, Guitar is overcome by greed and attempts to kill his oldest friend to get the gold. When Milkman later runs into Guitar again, the latter is leaning against a persimmon tree, much like the proverbial snake in Eden. The knowledge that Guitar gives him— that love and respect mean nothing compared to vengeance—so disheartens Milkman that he succumbs to Guitar's quest and kills himself rather than be killed. What saves *Song of Solomon* from being a novel primarily about the impossibility of triumph in the unrelenting face of nature and prejudice is that Milkman flies as he jumps off the cliff. Milkman may not be able to sustain his flight, but he is proof that even when befriending figurative serpents, human beings can redeem themselves.

Though *Tar Baby* contains no serpent, the Caribbean island on which much of the novel is set certainly resembles Paradise. Only a few families live amid lush vegetation and beautiful beaches. Those living on the island do not recognize the wonder of the place, however, until Son* rises out of the swamp to rescue them from their torpor and help them connect to their roots. Created, like Adam, out of the mud, Son seems to spring out of nowhere to show the island's inhabitants their true selves. Gradually, as he strips away the veneer covering Valerian* and Margaret Street*, Sydney and Ondine Childs*, and Jadine Childs*, Son himself begins to change. As he demonstrates to the sealskin-clad Jadine how far she is from her roots as a Black woman, he begins to remember the importance of his own roots. As he prods Ondine into revealing Margaret's secret maiming of her child, Son realizes the damage done to his relationship with his own father and vows to repair it. Though it is unclear at the end of the novel whether or not Jadine will return to the world of high fashion that Son exposed as being so false, it is clear that she will remember him and the lessons he taught her. Son breathed life into her, and even though she is afraid of that life, its presence is undeniable.

It is in *Beloved* that Morrison's invocation of edenic and apocalyptic imagery becomes most clear. As in her other novels, this invocation occurs through nature and is closely linked to racial identity*. From the corrupted Eden that is Sweet Home* to the four horsemen of the apocalypse who are schoolteacher* and his posse come to return Sethe and her children to slavery*, the novel is infused with religious imagery. Sethe, whose name resembles Seth, the child Adam and Eve bore to replace Abel after Cain killed him, learns, only after she hears schoolteacher comparing her to an animal, exactly how inherently evil Sweet Home is. Before this moment, she believes that the male slaves really are men, as Mr. Garner* says, and that the Garners really are protecting the slaves from harm. What she discovers is that in the eyes of whites, her husband and friends will never be men, and that no matter how benign on the surface, slavery is always evil. Sweet Home becomes not the Eden of tranquillity and unity, but the place where the serpent not only stripped her of her innocence but also bit her.

Although it is not clear at the end of the novel that Sethe will regain her sanity, it is clear that in uniting to banish the ghost of Sethe's daughter from 124 Bluestone Road*, the community has made strides toward healing the divisions that were threatening to destroy it. Sethe may not have found the City of God, but she has at least survived her own personal apocalypse. Furthermore, Denver Suggs's* success gives hope that with time, the deep wounds created by slavery can begin to heal.

Healing is also central to *Jazz**. When Joe Trace*, the son of a shadowy wild woman who is perhaps Sethe's daughter Beloved*, murders his young lover in a jealous rage, and when Joe's wife Violet slashes the young girl's face as she lies in her coffin, it seems as though their lives, and their love, will be destroyed forever. Violet lets free the birds she has kept for years, thinking that the music* in her life has soured, changing from an upbeat jazz* tune to a mournful blues ballad. The Joe she first met in Virginia, when he fell out of a tree like an apple next to her, seems to have vanished.

When Joe Trace first meets Dorcas Manfred* (Dorcas means gazelle), he becomes, like the lover in the Bible's Song of Songs, sprightly and young again. He tells Dorcas that she is the reason Adam ate the apple, and that she gives him such pleasure, it is as if he is learning everything for the first time. Dorcas, however, quickly becomes bored with Joe and rejects him in favor of a young neighborhood playboy. It is Dorcas's friend Felice* who helps to mend the rift the affair opened in the Trace family's life. By telling Joe that Dorcas's final words were to tell Joe that he was right, that only one apple exists, Felice reminds Joe that the knowledge he acquired by having a relationship with Dorcas did not end with her death. He and Violet can rediscover joy together.

In *Paradise*, Morrison unites the joy found in *Jazz*'s Garden of Eden imagery with the racial self-hatred seen in *The Bluest Eye*. In her description of a small band of freed slaves who form their own community to isolate themselves from the dominant white culture of the United States, Morrison writes a scathing critique of the notion of racial purity. Ruby, Oklahoma—the town founded by the Morgan brothers when their original town, Haven, Oklahoma*, becomes too corrupt—is a community* ruled by tradition. For those who live there, it is a place apart, a paradise isolating them from the corrupt outside world they have rejected. Underneath the tranquil surface, however, lies a world every bit as corrupt and disordered as the world beyond the town's borders.

When strange young women begin to flock to the Convent, an old mansion located seventeen miles outside of Ruby, the town's unrest is given a focus. Much as Sula directs her neighbors' wrath, so does the Convent become the recipient of Ruby's anger. When nine members of the town's founding families gather to rid the Convent of its evil influence, Ruby's barrenness is finally showcased. The intertwined fig trees that grow out of the banks of a dry riverbed will never bear fruit as long as the town clings to one notion of what it means to be Black in America. Accepting change, the kind of change that comes with surviving great difficulty, is the only avenue to peace. Finally freed from their own resistance to change, the Convent's women strive to heal the people they wounded after their figurative deaths in the massacre. Gigi/Grace Gibson* visits her convict father, Seneca* finds her mother, Mavis Albright* comforts her daughter, Sally, over coffee, and Pallas Truelove* returns to her mother for one last visit. While the women may not have discovered Paradise, they have found the new life of the apocalypse.

An ecocritical reading of Morrison's work demonstrates her belief in the interconnectedness of nature, religion, and African American identity. Without such an understanding, Morrison's works seem to tell a disjointed story of disappointment and destruction; when read ecocritically, they offer hope for creating a better future. *See also* Approaches to Morrison's Work: Historical.

References: Evan Eisenberg, *The Ecology of Eden* (1998); Cheryll Glotfelty and Harold Fromm, eds., *The Ecocriticism Reader: Landmarks in Literary Ecology* (1996); Deborah Guth, "'Wonder What God Has in Mind': *Beloved*'s Dialogue with Christianity," *Journal of Narrative Technique* 24: 2 (1994); Lauren Lepow, "Paradise Lost and Found: Dualism and Edenic Myth in Toni Morrison's *Tar Baby*," *Contemporary Literature* 28: 3 (1987); William Rueckert, "Literature and Ecology: An Experiment in Ecocriticism," *Iowa Review* 9: 1 (1978).

Elizabeth Ely Tolman

## Approaches to Morrison's Work: Feminist/Black Feminist

Toni Morrison's novels especially lend themselves to feminist readings because of the ways in which they challenge the cultural "norms" of gender, race*, and class. Many feminist scholars subscribe to the idea that language as we commonly think of it is male-centered, and that language privileges masculinity* because it privileges traits traditionally associated with men. In other words, language, as it has been viewed, is expected to be powerful, decisive, and logical. Women, on the other hand, have been characterized as being incapable of clear verbal expression, and more reliant on emotional, illogical, and incomplete utterances. While agreeing that society has "gendered" traditional language so that it reinforces the dominant position of men, feminist scholars also note that women's ways of communicating only appear to be chaotic because men, from their expectation of what language is and does, fail to comprehend the fluidity, creativity, challenge, and unifying characteristics of women's communication. A woman's approach to language is not meant to overpower or to conquer, but strives to build bridges of understanding and inclusion in a society where her voice, in order to be heard, must resonate with difference.

There is a special woman's way of approaching language and communication. This is not to suggest the existence of a biological essentialism. The uniqueness does not exist because a woman is female. Rather, it exists because she is a woman, a product of a specific cultural environment—a male-dominated society—in which she has created a way of communicating that is characterized by various combinations of words, nonverbal sounds, silences, and secrets, among others. In a feminist approach to reading texts, awareness of these sometimes subversive communicative techniques is helpful since they not only influence many women writers but also help to shape the characters and actions within the texts that these women writers create.

I must take this concept one step further, however, as it applies to Black feminism. Black feminists propose that the Black woman and the Black woman writer negotiate multiple social locations in securing a place in American culture and literature—not only those of gender and class found in all feminist approaches, but that of race as well. As a result, Black women writers have always, out of necessity, had to maneuver outside of the dominant white (including the white woman's) literary system. Their exclusion from the mainstream literary traditions led them to develop and employ alternative means of communicating, drawing upon their own experiences of oppression and resistance to shape their texts and to represent the characters and situations within it. In addition to some of the communicative techniques I list above for the feminist approach, I would add the following that specifically address the Black feminist approach: humor (ironic and otherwise), misdirection, and song. All of these feminist techniques, and more, come into play in Morrison's novels, but my emphasis here is on the polyvocal oppressions resisted through a Black feminist reading of the narratives. Such resistance manifests itself in Morrison's emphasis on the discovery and rediscovery of Black life, especially that of the Black woman, as it has been lived in America.

Morrison's first novel, *The Bluest Eye*\*, concerns itself with the painful acts engaged in by and perpetrated against its Black characters, who are forced to measure themselves in terms of Western standards of beauty. This is particularly true of the Black girls and women in the novel. The now-adult Claudia MacTeer\* tells the story of Pecola Breedlove's\* destruction in a retrospective narration that recollects their childhoods. This woman, as storyteller and "rememberer," shares what she has seen from her Black woman's space along the periphery of society. Her language is distinctly "female," but also relies upon the performance aspects of the African American oral tradition\*, the music\* of gospels and the blues, and the blurring and interplay between poetry and prose. The textual structure of *The Bluest Eye* and Morrison's construction of characters support the woman's unique understanding and use of alternative communicative devices. Just as the novel is an extended blues lyric itself, so it also tells of the life of the blues lived by its women characters. Claudia's mother, Mrs. MacTeer, periodically stops talking (that is, stops using traditional language) and effortlessly moves into singing the blues as she works in the kitchen, merging prose with poetry. The hard, desperate lives of the three prostitutes\*, China, Poland, and Miss Marie, is also summed up in their singing of the blues as they blur the hard lines of "male" language. In addition to representing the racial struggles of these characters, woman's singing also addresses gender oppression and class oppression in *The Bluest Eye*.

Mrs. MacTeer is a poor, struggling Black wife and mother trying to instill a sense of pride in her daughters while still pursuing the "American Dream." She doesn't realize that by reinforcing Western ideals of beauty through the white baby dolls she gives her daughters Claudia and Frieda\* at Christmas, she is compromising their ability to recognize their self-worth. Morrison demonstrates Claudia's recognition of the racially selective nature of the "American Dream" when she depicts Claudia decapitating the white dolls and rejecting the image of Shirley Temple that everyone else, including her sister Frieda and Pecola, adores.

The three prostitutes pretend to be victorious in their battle to defeat efforts to minimize them as Black women by acting hard, by focusing on their material gains, and by laughing at the men they purport to control with their sexuality\*. But without uttering words in the traditional way, they demonstrate through sighs and song their failure and their regret at having to sacrifice their individual selves in order to find a place in this (white) man's world.

The ultimate victim of the novel, Pecola Breedlove, is totally lacking in self-esteem. She cannot claim power from man's language because of her femaleness; she watches and admires the bravado of the prostitutes, but finds herself unable to emulate them because of her poverty, and she cannot inspire the love that the lemon-yellow Maureen Peal receives and that she so desperately wants because of her Blackness—she can never be the blonde, blue-eyed "Mary Jane" whose face stares at her from the label of the candy she devours.

Morrison ridicules the ideal American family by showing, through the Dick and Jane chapter headings, that the Claudias, Friedas, and Pecolas of the world are being socialized into a society which excludes them because of race, gender, and class. Even Pecola's father, Cholly Breedlove*, is used to depict the minimization of women when he is figuratively raped by a flashlight in the hand of a white man. This emasculation, with its accompanying destruction of Cholly's ability to love, is instrumental in his rape of Pecola. Innocent, passive, rejected by the white standards of society, and starving for love, Pecola is the perfect sacrifice. She cannot resist this victimization because every Western ideological concept tells her that she does not have the right to resist—tells her that she, as a Black and as a woman, is nobody. Her insanity brings her partial freedom because through it, she acquires the "blue eyes" that make her acceptable to a society that places such importance and admiration on this endowment.

The story does not end with Pecola's destruction, however; Morrison salvages the Black woman by designating Claudia as the voice of survival. It is the story coming from Claudia's mouth that redeems the Black woman in the end.

*Sula** addresses the special relationship that often develops between women, a relationship so close—as in the case of Sula Peace* and Nel Wright*—that the women are sometimes indistinguishable in the eyes of other characters. The novel is also driven by its depiction of women's nurturing, creative, and destructive powers, powers that at times reach almost godlike proportions.

Eva Peace* is the woman-god of *Sula*. She is the matriarch of the Bottom* (itself a womblike image). In that capacity, she is the mother-creator; when she names people and things, that is what they become. Morrison has Eva naming all the stray boys she takes in "Dewey*"—from the jet black one to the nearly white one. Eventually, no one can tell them apart. Morrison not only deconstructs color here, she reduces the importance of maleness through her codification of these male figures under the control of Eva Peace. But Morrison also shows that the combination of mother and god leads to disaster, "mother" being a feminine force that traditionally represents creation, birthing, and nurturing, while "god," like language, embodies the masculine acts of violence* and destruction. The negative aspects of this combination emerge when Eva, the "mother," plays "god" and sacrifices her son, Plum*, to save him from himself.

Sula and Nel, who are apparent opposites in everything except gender, are actually complements, the one completing the other. While light-skinned Nel is from a middle-class, "proper," nuclear family\*, dark-skinned Sula emerges from a woman-dominated household that is as chaotic, as creative, and as lively as woman's way of communicating. The relationship between Sula and Nel, this Black-woman-to-Black-woman relationship, is built on shared secrets, emotional bonds, and trust. Being neither white nor male, they find strength in the sisterhood they form within an antagonistic society. What destroys the relationship is the intrusion of Western ideology through the lives of both women—Nel's traditional marriage and Sula's travels among and relationships with white men. Nel loses her "self" when she becomes a wife and mother. With Sula's return to the Bottom, however, the Nel who had died begins to resurface. Sula's acquired attitudes about the impersonality of sex, along with her belief that everything between Nel and herself could be shared, leads to her ill-advised relationship with Nel's husband, Jude Greene\*, and the subsequent destruction of the bond between the two women. Laughter, a primary avenue of communication for Black women, had been so deep between Nel and Sula before the "betrayal" that it had scraped their ribs; afterward, when laughter finally returns near the end of Sula's life, it is forced, lacking in genuine emotion. It is some time after Sula's death that Nel is able to reclaim the self that she had been, and she does this by recollecting what she had shared with Sula before marriage molded her into society's expectations of the Black wife and mother. At the end, Nel is able to redeem herself by acknowledging that she wasn't always the good one; what made her "good" was her and Sula together. Thus, their woman's bond reunites their spirits, transcending death.

The male characters in *Song of Solomon*\*, including Milkman Dead\* until he learns to reject the Western ideological valuation of male dominance and material things, are egocentric and self-absorbed; the women emerge as nurturers, teachers, and storytellers. The most powerful of these women is Pilate Dead\*, who serves as a link between the material world (represented by the articles associated with her: rocks, the geography book, and the bones) and the spiritual world as she re-creates history\* and herself based on the bits and pieces of memory\* she carries with her.

Pilate defies traditional "norms" in a number of ways: she literally gives birth to herself, emerging from the womb of her dead mother; she lacks a navel, which gives her an otherworldly characteristic; and she defies the construct of gender through her androgynous appearance—being a woman but dressing like a man, wearing her hair short like a man (or covering it), and displaying traditional masculine behavior. Everything about Pilate supports Morrison's rejection of traditional norms, especially those which limit one based on gender.

Pilate, like Eva Peace in *Sula*, also functions as a "creator." Whereas Eva is not able to separate the creator from the destroyer in her godlike stance, however, Pilate (her name notwithstanding) does, re-creating not only herself but also others (for instance, making Robert Smith* a part of folklore* as the flying man), or setting them on the path to re-create themselves, as she does with her brother, Macon Dead*, and with Milkman.

Morrison establishes her challenge of cultural norms from the beginning of *Song of Solomon*. Pilate's presence at the unexpected birth of Milkman coincides with the unexpected death (at least in body) of Robert Smith. While his flight for freedom is immortalized he, as a member of the Seven Days*, represents male violence and destruction. Milkman, his name suggesting his close attachment to women, is born to replace violence with love and eventually takes on the characteristics of a Christ figure. And when Ruth*, Milkman's mother, goes into labor watching Robert Smith prepare to dive from the roof of the whites-only Mercy Hospital, she inadvertently knocks down the bars of segregation—Milkman arrives the next day, making him the first Black baby born in that facility.

While *Song of Solomon* revolves around a Black man's search for self and ancestral identity*, the power in Morrison's novel rests with the multiple roles of the women who touch his life, making it the story of the Black woman's sacrifice to protect and ensure the community's* ancestral memory.

Son* in Morrison's *Tar Baby** has Jesus characteristics similar to those in the character of Milkman in *Song of Solomon*. But, as in her earlier novel, Morrison again emphasizes the communal power of the feminine—the night women of Son's southern hometown of Eloe* ("Eloe" was allegedly spoken by Christ on the cross and is translated as "godly") and the feminine nature of the Caribbean island itself. Both are fertile, nurturing, sensual, and untamed, representing woman's refusal to be dismissed by white and male dominance.

Streets have no business in an island paradise, and Morrison's use of the name "Street" for the white plantation owner is a criticism of the white-male intrusion into and attempt to dominate this native location. Her inclusion of the alien greenhouse within which Valerian Street* attempts to nurture plants not indigenous to the island, and his failure to do so, speak to Morrison's rejection of the maleness and whiteness* that attempt to categorize, domesticate, tame, and dominate this womblike, Black female environment.

Another juxtaposition is represented by the coldness and sterility of the white-male dominated Street house in comparison with the rich vitality of the earthy female space of the island. Those within the Street home, including the Black servants Sydney and Ondine Childs* and their niece Jadine*, are tainted (and blinded) because of their aspirations toward Western ideals. Their world is shaken and disrupted because of Son's arrival, an arrival that represents salvation and a reaffirmation of the maternal—of the island and of Black women. Spirituality*, history, and cultural recovery are introduced by the Christlike Son, but as provinces of the Black woman. Meanwhile, Jadine battles with the earthiness of the Black women whose powers assault her assumed Western ideologies— the woman in yellow and the women of Eloe. The tensions of race, gender, and class all come together in Jadine's struggle between the Western materialistic life she has led and the mystical, seemingly childlike life of the earth that continually confronts her after the arrival of Son. Son is the catalyst, but the focus of *Tar Baby* is untamed Black womanness.

With *Beloved**, Morrison again sets her narrative in the distant past with its focus on the horrors of slavery*, especially for the enslaved Black mother. The novel is a painful account of the lengths to which the protagonist, Sethe Suggs*, goes in order to keep her children from the chains of slavery. As we saw with Eva Peace in *Sula*, Sethe seems to cross the line, and we are again faced with the problem of trying to reconcile our feelings about the mother (nurturer) who takes the life of her child (murderer) in order to protect it.

As is true in most of Morrison's work, men play peripheral, although important, roles in *Beloved*; however, the focus of the novel is on the survival of women. Various women's voices tell the story; the helping hands of women support and nurture Sethe; and a multitude of communities of women manage, ultimately, to bring Sethe to the point of becoming whole. Just as we are given no explanation of the origins of Son in *Tar Baby*, so we are challenged with the mystical in this novel as well, with the introduction of the character of Beloved*. Another theme that Morrison uses often emerges here: mother/daughter relationships. Sethe had been disconnected from her mother; Sethe gives birth to Denver* (with the helping hand of white Amy Denver*) on her run to freedom; and Beloved attaches herself to the mother she needs and who had killed her, in turn draining the life out of Sethe.

In *Beloved*, it is the women who heal each other, beginning with Amy rubbing life back into Sethe's swollen, dying feet, moving to Baby Suggs's emotional/spiritual healing of Sethe, and ending with the community of thirty women who unite to drive Beloved from 124 Bluestone Road* so that Sethe will finally be free.

Morrison's *Jazz**, like jazz* music itself, is full of movement, twists, and turns. It also addresses the theme of fragmentation—how spirits get broken into little pieces and one's attempt to become whole again. The three main female characters of *Jazz* (again, mother-daughter links) are True Belle*, her daughter Rose Dear*, and Rose Dear's daughter Violet Trace*. They represent memory and history as maintained by the Black woman and as passed on to future generations; as such, they are the nurturers of Black heritage. In *Jazz*, that history starts with the New Negro Jazz Age of Violet, moves back to the slave experiences of her grandmother True Belle, and then to the despair and degradation of her mother Rose Dear, not to mention the various syncopated movements in between and around them.

The mysterious voice telling the story intersects with the voices of the other characters, creating a lyrical narrative that is characteristic of the open-endedness of woman's way of talking. Morrison's experimentation with language and voice in *Jazz* is an example of her rejection of the traditionally masculine style of clarity, logic, and decisive action as the traits associated with the novel. Just as one's memory is disjointed—recalling pieces of life lived out of order and with various degrees of clarity—so is history as told by women in the context of *Jazz*, and so is its text as structured by the author of *Jazz*.

The black women in *Jazz* attempt to reinvent and re-create themselves out of the discordant bits and pieces of their lives—the ragged edges left from slavery that defined them as mammies and/or harlots, the post-slavery disempowerment that forced them to continue in positions of domestic and menial labor, and the social and economic strife that limited their advancement in the urban centers of the North after the Great Migration.* Morrison alternately shows them as victors and as victims throughout the novel, but their ultimate aura of strength is embedded in the fertile, earthy, untamed images of the South. Like Eloe and the Caribbean island in *Tar Baby*, like Shalimar in *Song of Solomon*, and like the Bottom in *Sula*, the nurturing places in *Jazz* are feminine.

The Oven* and the Convent* are the primary images in Morrison's *Paradise*, and they represent the femaleness of the novel. Although the men built the Oven, which was the communal gathering place for the town, its importance is that it was the place where the women baked the bread that sustained the community. Convents have traditionally been situated away from the world of men and have represented havens for women saving themselves for God. In *Paradise*, the Convent represents the last refuge for women trying to find themselves and an escape from the sordid lives society has dealt them. Whereas the Oven early on embodies mystical qualities tied to the nurturing actions of women, it loses this influence as the town of Haven, Oklahoma* (renamed Ruby* after the woman who died on the move to this location), comes to represent the damaging power of the men who embody the physical and emotional destruction of women.

As the power of the Oven declines, the Convent assumes the mystical, mysterious character it once represented as broken and fragmented women find their way to its doors. The raw, primal power of these women is represented in the garden that they maintain, in the potent pepper relish and sauces that they prepare, and in the bread that they bake. Bread is no longer baked in the communal oven of Ruby, but is purchased by the townspeople from the women of the Convent, evidence of the growing power of women who have removed themselves from men.

Not surprisingly, the five women of the Convent come to represent a challenge to male authority, a challenge that the men of Ruby must eliminate. In the end, the major story line within *Paradise* seems to fall along gender lines—the women are good and the men are evil. Morrison uses the brutality of the assault on the women of the Convent as an indication of the emotionless, cold, calculating nature of man in fear of losing his power over woman, and thereby his dominant position in society. The mystical survival of the Convent women, however, moves us from the material world of man to the spiritual world of woman.

A final note: Morrison never specifically identifies the race of any of the women of the Convent. All we know for sure is that the first to be shot was the white girl. Perhaps Morrison's failure to note the race of each damaged woman is her own mysterious way of saying that all women in our patriarchal society risk being broken unless we maintain communities of women to help hold the fragments together.

References: Catherine Belsey and Jane Moore, eds., *The Feminist Reader: Essays in Gender and the Politics of Literary Criticism* (1989); Martin Bidney, "Creating a Feminist-Communitarian Romanticism in *Beloved*: Toni Morrison's New Uses for Blake, Keats, and Wordsworth," *Papers on Language and Literature* 36: 3 (Summer 2000); Kyung Soon Lee, "Black Feminism: *Sula* and *Meridian*." *Journal of English Language and Literature* 38: 3 (Fall 1992); Angelyn Mitchell, "'Sth, I Know That Woman': History, Gender and the South in Toni Morrison's *Jazz*," *Studies in the Literary Imagination* 31: 2 (Fall 1998); Barbara Smith, "Toward a Black Feminist Criticism," in *All the Women Are White, All the Blacks Are Men, But Some of us Are Brave*, ed. Gloria T. Hull, Patricia Bell Scott, and Barbara Smith (1982).

Johnnie M. Stover

## Approaches to Morrison's Work: Historical

In 1974, Toni Morrison edited *The Black Book**, a collection of photos, newspaper articles, patents, advertisements, and other texts about Black life in America. That same year, she published "Rediscovering Black History" in the *New York Times Magazine*, an article describing her process in creating *The Black Book*. These two texts represent the public beginning of Morrison's profound concern with African American history* and its excision from national narratives of our past, a concern that extends into her fiction. Morrison's novels collectively can be seen as a project of historical remembrance and recovery*. They depict the intermingling of the past and the present in what

Morrison terms "rememory," a nod to the African belief that present and past are united, not separate. Yet they also demand a rewriting of past historical narratives to include the ever-present traumas of slavery* and structural racism. Viewing her work from a historical perspective, then, can yield fruitful insights.

Morrison's career is marked by an increasing engagement with history on a thematic and structural level. *The Bluest Eye*\*, her earliest novel, is not directly concerned with historical practice, but it does reflect how the mass culture industry disallows African American history and culture in its drive toward sameness for all under the rule of consumption. Thus, even though it is not a historical novel, Morrison does confront questions of African American history. *Sula*\*, Morrison's next novel, takes the form of a chronicle, with chapters labeled by year. It tells the history of the Bottom*, focusing particularly on Sula Peace* and Nel Wright*. Yet the tale moves beyond them to capture the town as a whole—its rituals, its history. In the interplay between the personal and the communal we find truth.

*Song of Solomon*\* is the story of a search for family history, one made of myths and legends as well as facts and dates. Milkman Dead*, the central character of the novel, is on a quest to recover his past as well as his identity*. In fact, these two are inextricably linked for Morrison; one's past determines one's identity. Milkman demonstrates his understanding of his heritage by singing songs at Pilate Dead's* death. And his final leap at the end of the novel is a figurative leap into the past. His acceptance of his ancestors' flying myths enables him to recover his identity while legitimating alternative histories. As a result, *Song of Solomon* is the most overtly historical of the earlier novels. *Tar Baby*\*, on the other hand, would seem to be the least historical of Morrison's novels. The past is never brought into the present; instead, it is held separate, inaccessible. Yet the continuity of past and present is clear, particularly in the economic dominance established across time. *Tar Baby* represents colonial inequality as a historically based system of racial prejudice.

Morrison's more recent works, however, are historical fictions, more overt explorations of history and its forms. Morrison relates disturbing moments in our past, refusing to look away from the horrors and tragedies that form African American history. Yet she also engages history on a structural level, using folklore*, myth*, oral narratives, and other nontraditional sources as a means for weaving an alternative history that captures what traditional histories leave out. Morrison thus redefines historical methodology as well as content in her later work. For example, her play *Dreaming Emmett*\* was commissioned to celebrate the first federal holiday commemorating the birth of Martin Luther King, Jr. For this occasion, Morrison chose to retell the story of Emmett Till, a Black teenager lynched in Mississippi for allegedly whistling at a white woman. Morrison's innovation was to bring Till alive on stage and let him tell the story of his murder from his perspective. This play inaugurates Morrison's turn toward historical narratives, yet her novels (and this play) blur the lines between history and fiction, truth and lies, reality and imagination.

Perhaps Morrison's most famous novel, *Beloved**, is the exemplum of African American historical fiction. Morrison based the novel on the story of Margaret Garner*, a Kentucky slave who killed her own child when recaptured after escaping to the North. Morrison discovered this story while editing *The Black Book*, but she purposely did not research further, choosing to let her imagination reconstruct the tale. Thus, the novel is far more than a simple retelling of the Margaret Garner story. *Beloved* reenacts slavery*, engaging the reader with the material consequences of this historical institution through a focus on the victims whose histories have been ignored in the dominant culture. *Beloved* relates slavery's trauma* through personal histories, stories, and tales. History is more than facts and dates; it is memories, stories, ghosts, and houses. *Beloved* reinvents historical recovery as an act of imagination. It legitimates alternative sources for history, such as oral stories and myths, because for Morrison, telling history is a survival strategy for African Americans. Her goal is to refigure the past to include other voices, not to be possessed by it.

*Jazz** also is based on an actual event, the case of a Harlem* woman who, shot by her lover, nevertheless refuses to incriminate him so he can escape. Yet once again Morrison goes beyond the specific event to capture a larger panorama. *Jazz* is also about a period (the Jazz Age) and the people who were living then, unconscious of the formative nature of that time. In writing the novel, she invents new ways to relate experience, going beyond traditional history to capture the essence of a community*. *Jazz* alludes not only to the history of the 1920s but also to the most horrific acts of the postbellum period. It references the lynching of Blacks in the nineteenth century and the stealing of Black lands; the 1920s riots in East Saint Louis and Tulsa; the NAACP silent march; the all-Black 369th regiment that Joe Trace* marches with in their victory parade, reminding the reader of the Great War.

In essence, Morrison captures the history of slavery, the Reconstruction, and the Great Migration* leading into the Harlem Renaissance, but she does so from an oblique angle. In so doing, she reveals the larger struggle that exists between white culture's interpretation of Black history and the interpretations woven from the wealth of stories and experiences in the Black community. And just as in *Beloved, Jazz* is an argument for how we should tell history through multiple voices. *Jazz* is a story reconstructed from fragments of memory*, gossip, and news—all are equally useful in telling the story, even if official historical methods decry such subjective forms of communication. Morrison's point is that we must cobble together our story of the past from multiple accounts. This is not to say that all representations are equal; instead, Morrison highlights the active process of narrativizing history. Readers must piece together the story themselves, weighing evidence and constructing events. *Jazz* has as much to do with the structure as the content, a riff on the musical form reimagined in words.

The last novel of Morrison's historical trilogy is *Paradise\**, a novel that tells the story of five murdered women through a collection of subjective accounts. Morrison again questions the construction of a historical narrative while she exposes a violence directed through race* and gender toward women. As in the previous novels, history is a subjective act of experience and imagination, retold in multiple forms. Morrison wants to recognize that the stories embodied in history contain the life of a culture. Her historical text, then, is one filled with gaps and misinformation, an example of life as it is lived, fragmented and incoherent at times, yet rich and vibrant, filled with love and hate, pleasure and pain. History is a creative process for Morrison, always subject to revision through imagination in a search for the truth that lies beyond facts. *See also* Flying Africans, Myth of; Ghost Story, Use of; Oral Tradition.

References: Susan Comfort, "Counter-Memory, Mourning and History in Toni Morrison's *Beloved*," *Lit: Literature Interpretation Theory* 6: 1–2 (April 1995); Henry Louis Gates, Jr., and K.A. Appiah, *Toni Morrison: Critical Perspectives Past and Present* (1993); Jane Kuenz, "*The Bluest Eye*: Notes on History, Community, and Black Female Subjectivity," *African American Review* 27: 3 (1993); Angelyn Mitchell, "'Sth, I Know That Woman': History, Gender, and the South in Toni Morrison's *Jazz*," *Studies in the Literary Imagination* 31: 2 (Fall 1998).

David E. Magill

## Approaches to Morrison's Work: Pedagogical

The most productive critical approach to the novels of Toni Morrison may be debatable, but Morrison leaves no doubt about the most productive pedagogical approach to her fiction. Repeatedly over the years, in essays and interviews, she has explained that she writes for a participatory reader. Our job as teachers of Morrison is clear. We must facilitate the active, involved reading that her novels require. However, as Morrison herself has noted more than once, this is not an easy task today, when, reared on television's undemanding, formulaic plots, students expect narratives to be linear and simple. Therefore, before we can model the participatory reading that Morrison requires, we must open our students to Morrison's aesthetic.

How do we do that? I think the best plan is to go to the source: Morrison herself. Students are greatly assisted by Morrison's also being a teacher, a theorist, a critic, and an editor. Unlike some writers, Morrison—whose sophisticated narrative style often links her to writers like William Faulkner* and Gabriel García Márquez—eloquently discusses her own work. And she has been doing so for years, from her first interviews about *The Bluest Eye** to those regarding her most recent novel, *Paradise**. I urge teachers of Morrison to read Morrison on Morrison. Two excellent sources are Nellie Y. McKay and Kathryn Earle's *Approaches to Teaching the Novels of Toni Morrison* (1997) and Danielle Taylor-Guthrie's *Conversations with Toni Morrison* (1994). One thing readers will find when they read Morrison's critical commentary is that her central issues—thematic and stylistic—have not changed much over the thirty-plus years that she has been writing. Morrison is clear and consistent about her concerns.

The simple act of considering Morrison's novels in light of her commentary is itself participatory. Students can interview the author vicariously, gaining insight into the aesthetic motivating the text. Informed about and familiar with the author, they can return to the text productively. Also, for students who have trouble appreciating the intentionality of the writing enterprise, this kind of textual complement demonstrates more clearly than anything else the art of fiction. It moves them past dismissal of complexity and unresolvedness as flaws, and leads them to seek why the author has made the choices evidenced in the text. And when they find an explanation, even though it may seem enigmatic, they often respond as if a secret has been entrusted to them, bonding with the author and the novel.

Teachers of Morrison would be well advised to develop a bibliography of Morrison on Morrison for this purpose. While she has written a number of helpful essays, one that I find extremely rich is "Memory, Creation, and Writing," which Morrison published in *Thought* in 1984. By this time—after *Tar Baby** and before *Beloved**—her first four books had made her a respected narrative stylist. This essay reads much like the kind of preface or essay literary innovators have felt called to write at various times in history—Hawthorne, James, and Eliot come to mind—in order to create an informed audience for their work. In that, it can be very illuminating. To illustrate, I will discuss a few passages from "Memory, Creation, and Writing" and relate Morrison's assertions there to her fiction. I regret that publishing arrangements for this volume forbid my quoting from the essay, and I wish to assure readers that I have attempted to accurately reflect Morrison's full argument in my paraphrasing. I have also cited the location of each passage being discussed to assist readers who wish to consult Morrison's essay.

In this essay, Morrison explains that she wishes her fiction to encourage readers to participate actively in the nonliterary experience of the text. She wants the experience of reading her novels to be more than merely the detached, passive acceptance of data (387). Knowing that this kind of involvement is the author's goal leads students to better appreciate the epic intensity and complex histories of the Breedloves*, the Peaces*, the Deads*, the Streets*, the Suggses*, the Traces*, and the Morgans*. Further, instead of feeling alienated by Morrison's enigmatic beginnings—those first sentences which arrest and baffle the reader—students enter the narrative as informed participants, teased but not put off.

In this essay, Morrison also declares that she wants to subvert the reader's comfort, leading the reader to a new, less conventional experience (387). Again this information, besides opening the class discourse to consideration of what she means, exactly, and inviting students to provide illustrating instances from the text, allows students to be participatory readers because they know the "rules of the game." Instead of feeling manipulated and teased by information withheld, they enjoy realizing that they, the readers, have been a primary consideration in the creative process. Armed with this awareness, their participation gains a new dimension. They begin to consider their own responses to the language of the text.

In a discussion of *The Bluest Eye*, Morrison makes the following point, which could apply to any of her novels. She explains that as she developed the pieces of that story, she discovered that she preferred them unconnected. She feels that the resulting narrative, with events that relate, but do not flow coherently or directly, best communicates the story of the fractured perceptions resulting from a splintered life (388). These comments are key to linking issues of form and content in Morrison's novels. Fractured narratives result from and reveal the splintered perceptions caused by shattered lives—from the wounded Pecola Breedlove* (*The Bluest Eye*) to the scarred Sethe Suggs* (*Beloved*) to the damaged women of the Convent* (*Paradise*). Morrison's uniting of form and content facilitates her objective of having readers fully experience the text. Like the characters, readers are caught in the confluence of past and present, of conflicting perceptions, of uninformed involvement.

Here Morrison also discusses what she describes as her Black métier and third world cosmology: the presence of flying, ghosts, and magic in her stories. Although students may not have studied the realistic, rational origins of the novel, they have been reared in the Western literary tradition, and operate on its assumptions. Morrison's highlighting of what some have described as elements of magical realism* opens discussion of the literary tradition, canon, and genre.

But Morrison's point is much more specific and illuminating; these magical, supernatural elements in her fiction are integral to their—and her—Blackness. She argues that since her writing confronts a reality unlike the rational worldview of Western culture, it must validate ways of seeing the world that are discredited by the West. This "other" view of reality is dismissed as "lore" or "gossip" or "magic" or "sentiment." Morrison maintains that this dismissal by Western culture is not because these views themselves are false or dangerous, but simply because they are maintained by discredited people (388). With this insight provided by the author, students can move far beyond merely not resisting the nonrealistic elements in her fiction, a big hurdle for many readers. They learn to appreciate it in terms of ideology. The teacher can open discussion of the politics of aesthetics and of the academy.

Morrison has much to say on this subject. One clear lesson that comes from having Morrison help teach Morrison is that she is proudly an African American writer. While her artistry may transcend any limits, it is an artistry focused on telling Black stories in a Black way. This cannot be overstated. Any teacher who downplays Morrison's race* identification out of respect for the transcendent and universal in her fiction is doing both Morrison and the students a disservice. Issues of Blackness in white America must be embraced for productive study of Morrison's art. Anyone who does not believe that needs only to listen to Morrison on the subject. Here, as elsewhere, she clearly states that she wishes to write in a way that is identifiably Black, thematically and stylistically. She sees her creative task as the production of Black art, and she wants her fiction to be assessed in terms of a Black aesthetic, the principles of which she has helped articulate (389).

Morrison as artist is not merely contextualizing her plots. She is shaping her aesthetic and sharing it with readers. She asserts here that if her work is to reflect the aesthetic tradition of African American culture, it must translate its other art forms into print. And she lists some of the qualities which mark that aesthetic—particularly antiphony, collaboration, and functionality. She also makes special note of the element of improvisation and audience participation. And finally she identifies Black art as a critical voice, upholding traditional communal values but also providing moments of individual defiance and even transcendence of group restriction (389). Because these points are so specific, it is not difficult for students to see their presence in the texts once they understand them. So class time is well spent making sure they understand what Morrison means by each one.

That exercise often leads naturally to more learning. For instance, while the logical place to begin understanding antiphony is by defining the term, once students learn that the word describes call-and-response songs and chants, they will be ready for more connection. They will begin to appreciate the history* of this community* rhetoric that connects contemporary African American church liturgy to spirituals rooted in slavery and even further back to African oral traditions*. Then they can consider antiphonal qualities in Morrison's style, which they can easily do—whether they consider the multivoiced narration of her novels or the call of her narratives for a response from the reader.

Or, to provide another example, examination of the term "functionality" can be very productive. Morrison's point is that the literary creation serves the group as an expressive and critical voice. The storyteller, as griot, is powerful. Through understanding this point, students can move from an appreciation for Morrison's novels to an appreciation of the potential power that resides in art, one far greater than entertainment. But Morrison also clarifies what the limits of that power are, explaining that stories should not attempt to solve social problems; rather, they should try to clarify them (389).

This assertion is extremely helpful in clarifying Morrison's narrative goal. Here, too, is a good illustration of why using Morrison's own words can be so helpful. This statement is more than a simple caution against narrative didacticism—to show rather than tell. The teacher can point to the fact that Morrison is not discussing what the storyteller should and should not do, but rather what the story itself should and should not do. Further, she is declaring a narrative ethic by exhorting against any plot that "solves" its problems. For many students, this concept impels a paradigm shift, enabling them to find new pleasure in certain of Morrison's narrative qualities, such as the lack of clear resolution in her plots, which previously might have caused them readerly discomfort.

The Black aesthetic also emphasizes art as a group collaboration. It must be essentially improvisational because it depends on its relationship to the audience. Students pondering these assertions realize that they must actively participate in the interpretive experience to fulfill the author's intent. They are given license by the author to respond to the text from their various social positions and histories. If the powerfully charged stories and their troubling characters ignite confrontation with silenced issues within and among individual readers, the novels are living their promise.

A teacher can also move from Morrison's reference to the individual in relation to group restrictions to draw attention to the many ways her novels focus on the effects of socially and historically constructed identity*. Highlighting this dynamic in the novels creates the need for contextualizing. Each of Morrison's novels is enriched tremendously by knowledge of the social-political-economic conditions of the historic moment, regardless of whether that time and place is Cincinnati, Ohio, in the 1870s; Harlem, New York*, in the 1920s; or Ruby, Oklahoma*, in the 1970s. With this information, students can better understand both the factual circumstance of the novel and the forces on identity determined by race, class, and gender.

I have narrowed this discussion to one of Morrison's essays in order to illustrate how fruitful her own commentary can be. I wish to show how effectively her own discussion—on the human condition, American life, the literary tradition, aesthetics, the writing process, the medium of language—can be used to teach her novels. Teachers will find equally helpful commentary in almost any direct source. Interviews that focus on individual novels can be particularly helpful for studying that specific text. And since 1993, when Morrison was formally recognized as one of the world's great writers with the Nobel Prize for Literature, she has received substantial serious attention in respected journals, such as *The Paris Review* (vol. 35, 1993) and *Modern Fiction Studies* (vol. 39, 1993). Printed interviews with her are usually thoughtful and thorough, and perhaps because Morrison is also a teacher and a scholar, she is amazingly forthright and articulate. Her interviews are not the wily games of catch-me-if-you-can delivered by some authors. Morrison, the author-cum-professor, seeks to communicate.

In their effort to use Morrison to teach Morrison, teachers can also benefit from Morrison's academic lectures, some of which are in print. In Part Three of "Unspeakable Things Unspoken: The Afro-American Presence in American Literature," she focuses on her own novels (*The Bluest Eye* through *Beloved*) to demonstrate the existence of an identifiable Black aesthetic as evidenced in the use of language (*Michigan Quarterly Review*, 1989). As illustration, she explicates the opening lines of each novel, explaining how issues of Blackness (African and African American)—hers and her characters'—are naturally present in the language. Her commentary is both enlightening and provocative. And no teacher should overlook the insights on the American literary tradition that are found in *Playing in the Dark: Whiteness and the Literary Imagination*. As Morrison has explained, this provocative book-length essay from a lecture series at Harvard resulted directly from her perspective as a Black literary scholar. Instructed and intrigued by Morrison's commentary, students can pursue productive close readings of the novels with a focus on the nuances of language. Morrison's explanation enables students to approach her texts as art, giving the thoughtful consideration to the chosen words that every teacher dreams of developing.

In an often-referenced early interview with Janet Bakerman in *Black American Literature Forum* (1978) about her fiction and about the power of her sympathetic imagination to "become" some terribly flawed characters, Toni Morrison explains that all of her writing is about love. I would go further and assert that Morrison writes *with* love. Writing as an act of love is vitally connected to the Black aesthetic she espouses. Her novels have communal efficacy. But for this aesthetic to be fully realized, the reading community must participate. Students cannot read passively for entertainment. They must respond to the call of the text.

Teachers serve a vital role in teaching students how to be the participatory readers necessary for Morrison's novels. When they do participate actively, students discover that Morrison's are healing texts—for Black students who experience noble representation, and for white students who are provided the opportunity to expand their understanding. They also discover the truth of what Amy Denver* tells Sethe in *Beloved*: that nothing can heal without causing pain of the past, which they must confront in Morrison's novels. And certainly many white students wish to distance themselves from what they see as the guilt of their ancestors. And many from both groups wish the classroom to be a place of denial, apart from the racialized world outside. Traditional study of "classic" texts of the Western tradition, with its emphasis on transcendence and universality, has fostered the desire for escape. Clearly, Morrison does not want that, and the teacher of Morrison should not encourage it.

There is a great potential for healing and growth within reading communities of Toni Morrison's novels. This is a precious gift, one that teachers should not take lightly. Nor should they take lightly their role as bearers of the gift. It is up to teachers to extend the act of love begun by Morrison in the writing of her novels, and continued by her in her commentaries. They can develop classroom communities of informed, participating readers, confronting and interacting with Morrison's texts. *See also* Flying Africans, Myth of; Ghost Story, Use of.

References: Nellie Y. McKay and Kathryn Earle, eds. *Approaches to Teaching the Novels of Toni Morrison* (1997); *Modern Fiction Studies*, special issue 39: 3–4 (1993); Toni Morrison, "Memory, Creation, and Writing," *Thought* 59 (1984); Toni Morrison, "Unspeakable Things Unspoken: The Afro-American Presence in American Literature," *Michigan Quarterly Review* 28 (1989); Elissa Schappell and Claudia Brodsky Lacour, "Toni Morrison: The Art of Fiction CXXXIV," *The Paris Review* 35 (1993); Danielle Taylor-Guthrie, ed., *Conversations with Toni Morrison* (1994).

Jane Atteridge Rose

## Approaches to Morrison's Work: Postcolonial

A review of the scholarship reveals that little work has been done on Toni Morrison as a postcolonial writer; this is due in part to the developing history of America as Britain's predecessor as the new Empire. A quick glance at the body of research in American literature reveals similar results; an unscientific look at a literature database indicated that less than 10 percent of the works on postcolonialism are about American literature, and that less than 1 percent are about African American literature.

While the term "postcolonial writer" is often reserved for Anglophone or Francophone writers who are from postcolonial nations, often poorly termed "the Commonwealth" or the "Third World" (e.g., Nigeria, Kenya, and India), this term is an appropriate and important category for writers who are often grouped as simply "African American writers" as if the African American experience were a monolith. Much like the settler colonies/nonsettler colonies quagmire in postcolonial studies, studies of American colonization have yet to adequately address the complex issues of human suffering and denigration resulting from the Middle Passage, slavery*, and the systemic removal of Native Americans. In addressing some of the complexities of what America means to the descendants of the African Diaspora, Toni Morrison emerges as a prominent voice to critically examine the psychological weight of the darkest legacy of the African Diaspora, the Middle Passage.

Postcolonial women writers such as Ama Ata Aidoo, Buchi Emecheta, Jean Rhys, Nadine Gordimer, and Bapsi Sidwa wrestle with the pains of cultural in-betweenness in their themes about motherhood*, sisterhood, and family* viewed through the disrupted and uprooted meanings of "home" within the cultural partition of Empire. Viewed within the context of postcolonial studies, Toni Morrison's novels engage history* in terms where home* is unstable topography between protected private space and vulnerable public space threatened by the American colony's destructive desire to reduce Black bodies to chattel. This has led to Morrison's exploration of identity* and self-worth. For example, in the sexual politics in *Sula**, the public and private space of what might be considered "home" is quite disturbing. And as Sula Peace* and Nel Wright* struggle for self-definition, this self-definition is similar to questions of origin or disrupted origin connected to the disrupted history of American slaves. The final moments of *Sula* emphasize water and fluidity. The song "Shall We Gather at the River" and the rain at Sula's funeral draw a connection between death* and water (the grave and water as Sula's final home). However, this is not T.S. Eliot's "Death by Water," but a historical reminder of the Middle Passage. Nel's final cry reinforces the image; her cry of "girl," which repeats once, then fuses three times to mimic a sound like gurgling or drowning, bonds Sula's memory or absent presence to Nel's desire to move on with the business of living. The novel's final image of circles as a description of sorrow enforces the fluid over the linear.

Morrison's use of fluidity and identity points to her use of the "in-between" found in the traditions of W.E.B. Du Bois's "double consciousness" and Ralph Ellison's *Invisible Man*. Resulting from the Middle Passage and American slavery, this fluid or less stable identity remains paramount in African American literary tradition; Morrison also uses water in *Tar Baby** and *Beloved**. Moreover, this writing style that rejects the "linear" for the "circular" reappears in *Beloved*. The question in *Sula*, whether to reject or embrace "home" within the context of one's sexual identity or otherwise, is a question that individuals face within the postcolonial cultural situation, whether that situation is in England or America. While the circles of sorrow in *Sula* remain a burden for the living, in *Beloved* the circles move concentrically to embrace the living, the dead, the past, and the present.

In Morrison's *Song of Solomon*\*, the myth of the flying Africans\* works to connect the past with the present. The myth of the flying Africans tells of Africans who escaped the slave trade by flying from slave ships during the Middle Passage or back to Africa after arriving in the Americas. The novel both begins and ends with the promise of or hope for flight. And while the theme of flight is obviously connected to issues of a struggle to be free, represented in Milkman Dead\*, the theme of flight as connected to its mythic past in the flying Africans also suggests an effort to reconcile with an African past. As with "rememory" in *Beloved*, we see Milkman's struggle to understand family\* history through the folk song Pilate Dead\* sings at his birth or origin. The final act of the novel indicates reconciling with and reclaiming a lost past or lost African home. The idea of air works to reverse images of suffocation and water connected to the Middle Passage in other novels.

Postcolonial approaches to Morrison's narratives move toward, through, and beyond her Pulitzer Prize-winning novel *Beloved*. Sethe Suggs's\* story about the legacy of slavery mediated through a mother's infanticide\* is not only a story about the tragedy based on the life of Margaret Garner\*; it is the affirmation and reclamation of the millions of voices lost as a result of the Middle Passage. In its affirmation and reclamation of these voices, *Beloved* opens up spaces where a "national" literature about the tragedy of slavery may be more fully articulated, understood, and appreciated. Questions about home are apparent early in *Beloved*. The narratives-within-narratives that describe the ironically named Sweet Home\* address the complexities of the postcolonial figure within the context of home. The idea of home for the descendants of African slaves is one where home is and is not Africa, and home is and is not America: "home" is lost and gained, gained and lost.

The stories in *Beloved*, often about family, marriage, relationships, and/or sexuality\*, produce questions of where the postcolonial African American fits in. Paul D\* wanders for eighteen years before arriving at Sethe's home; the first sentence of the novel reminds readers that the family is home at 124 Bluestone Road\*, but no sooner is this welcome mat put out, than the spiteful relationship to home is introduced. And as Paul D struggles to find a home, Beloved\*, too, struggles to find home; Beloved's status at the novel's opening is one of in-betweenness. She is not of the world of the living or the flesh; however, she will soon emerge from the world of the water to become flesh. Her journey from the water that is grave reverses the ending of *Sula*. And like Sula, Beloved's origin or home is intimately connected to sexuality: her womb/tomb through Sethe as well as her desire for Paul D as she demands that he touch her *and* call her name. The issue of ownership becomes a further entanglement in all their lives.

The meaning of home as a site of origin extends beyond the borders of 124 Bluestone Road. The site of the woman's body has been interestingly politicized within postcolonial studies. The history of England's Britannia and India's "Mother India," along with a number of female religious deities, suggests that the site of women's bodies, mythic or otherwise, is important to the study of culture and cultural conflict. In Morrison's *Beloved* the site for this struggle is Sethe's body—the womb and the tomb. And when Beloved returns to this site, we see an ensuing battle for this "home" between Denver Suggs* and Beloved, a battle in part echoing Sula's and Nel's battle for "home." However, the battle for this site does not end there. The events surrounding Sethe as the site of origin or womb move into what Homi Bhabha has called "reclamation." Through Beloved's death and return, Sethe wishes to reclaim the product of her womb, which she considers her most precious thing. Such ownership functions in much the same way that a formerly colonized nation must reclaim the "culturally dead State" and identify it as its property yet again. Reclaiming this property is also a reclaiming of some form of identity separate from the colonizing nation or the institution of slavery.

In this psychological context, "rememories" are another form of reclamation. In a less gothic fashion than Beloved's desire for Paul D to call her name, Beloved, Sethe, and Denver, according to Bhabha, reclaim and name through their fuguelike monologues. While Sethe's body serves as a site of origin and the formally enslaved body, emblematic of a colonized nation, it is Beloved's body that transgresses the boundaries of life and death, past and present. It is her transgression that opens up questions of identity and historical experience (Who is Beloved?). Therefore, it is through Beloved's agency that Sethe and Denver are able to engage in the project of reclaiming the self. Satya P. Mohanty argues that the "fusion of perspectives" (including Paul D's) is where the act of reclamation must be accomplished.

The issue of reclamation in *Beloved* offers unlimited possibilities within a postcolonial studies context. Within the demands and designs of American slavery, the connection between reclamation of the body and reclamation of land proves fascinating in regard to the promise of "forty acres and a mule" as reparation for the suffering of slavery. Reclamation of the body as "nationhood" is emphasized in Baby Suggs's* forest injunction for Blacks to love themselves. Along with Denver's name (reclaiming the memory or "rememory" of Amy Denver*), names like "Here Boy" (slavery's emasculation) and "Stamp Paid" (ownership of the self) indicate attempts to "reclaim" human dignity. Baby Suggs's sermon asking Blacks to turn self-loathing into self-loving raises another form of reclamation: reclamation of an African American culture.

Colonial conquests often lead to the colonized culture's defamation. Whether in Africa, India, or Ireland, the native culture is defined as inferior or barbaric, and hence must be supplanted by the colonizer's "superior" culture and educational system. From the language to the government, systems are put in place by the colonizer to ensure that its culture will thrive while the culture of the other will wither. Morrison's work, along with that of many other African American writers, reclaims a tradition that had previously been relegated to second-class status. From *The Bluest Eye** to *Paradise**, Morrison celebrates the complexity of the African American experience.

In postcolonial studies, the idea of "home" resides in a space that must be read through its historical loss and mystery. In works by Morrison, the instability or incommensurability of the concept of "home" is represented by the historical gaps in the Middle Passage. While most obvious in *Beloved*, the issues surrounding these historical gaps influence a great deal of Morrison's talents and interest. Within the context of an American literary tradition, Morrison explores issues and attitudes toward the unsettled and unsettling conditions of the legacy of descendants of American slaves. Just as "forty acres and a mule" proved to be an empty dream of home for freed American slaves, so Morrison's novels call into question the ideas of home for those who remain partly "in-between" Africa and the American plantation. Most of the bloody and vile history of the Middle Passage remains locked in the depths of the Atlantic, and home and history remain a space of uncertainty for many African Americans. It is in that tradition that Toni Morrison's work continues to be of interest to postcolonial studies. *See also* Gothic Tradition; History; Sexuality.

References: Homi Bhabha, *The Location of Culture* (1994); Lynda Koolish, "Fictive Strategies and Cinematic Representations in Toni Morrison's *Beloved*: Postcolonial Theory/Postcolonial Text," *African American Review* 29: 3 (1995); Satya P. Mohanty, "The Epistemic Status of Cultural Identity: On *Beloved* and the Postcolonial Condition," *Cultural Critique* 3: 1–2 (Spring 1993); Alan Rice, "Erupting Funk: The Political Style of Toni Morrison's *Tar Baby* and *The Bluest Eye*," in *Post-Colonial Literatures: Expanding the Canon*, ed. Deborah L. Madsen (1999).

James M. Ivory

## Approaches to Morrison's Work: Psychoanalytic

In *Psychoanalysis and Black Novels*, Claudia Tate explains why psychoanalytic theory has largely been avoided by Black intellectuals. Focusing on the dynamics of family* relations while ignoring the social forces that precondition the family environment, the psychoanalytic model "relegates the bleak material circumstances of real lives to the background." Carrying "irritating baggage" with it as it isolates the Black family from the social forces that condition it, psychoanalytic theory "has avoided examining the relationship of social oppression to family dysfunction and the blighted inner worlds of individuals" (16). Thus scholars who study African American literature "shun" psychoanalysis because it effectively "effaces racism and recasts its effects as a personality disorder caused by familial rather than social pathology" (16). Because of the continuation of racial oppression and "the demand for black literature to identify and militate against it," remarks Tate, "black literature evolves so as to prove that racism exists in the real world and is not a figment of the black imagination" (17).

If Toni Morrison, who is acutely aware of the social pathology of racism, examines the social trauma* of racial oppression in her novels, she also focuses sustained attention on the private world of the individual and family as she depicts the African American experience. Thus, even though traditional psychoanalytic models have been viewed with suspicion by many scholars of African American literature, as the comments of Tate reveal, some critics nevertheless have turned to psychoanalytic theories in their investigations of the representation of family and personal relations in Morrison's novels—in particular, *Sula**, *Song of Solomon**, and *Beloved**. Though discussions of *Sula* and *Song of Solomon* center attention on the psychology of the individual and family relations, interpretations of *Beloved*, while placing emphasis on family relations—in particular the mother/daughter relationship—also comment on the connection between the personal and the political in Morrison's novel.

A central focus of critics who have applied psychoanalytic theory to *Sula* is the dynamics of the friendship between Nel Wright* and Sula Peace*. Attempting to explain the deep girlhood bonding between Nel and Sula, Elizabeth Abe,l for example, makes use of object relations theory, in particular Nancy Chodorow's analysis of mother-daughter relationships in *The Reproduction of Mothering*, in which Chodorow describes how the infant daughter's pre–Oedipal attachment to her mother leads, in the developing girl and the adult woman, to a relational mode of identification characterized by a fluidity of self–other boundaries. In Abel's view, the female bonding of Nel and Sula, in which each girl seeks commonality, not complementarity, in friendship, exemplifies a relational mode of self-definition. Analyzing the developmental function of Nel's and Sula's interpersonal identification with an other who represents an essential aspect of the self, Abel argues that friendship, not parental or sexual relations, is "both the vehicle and product of self-knowledge" in *Sula*. Morrison, as she combines "the adolescent need for identification with the adult need for independence" in telling the story of her characters' friendship, "presents an ideal of female friendship dependent not on love, obligation, or compassion, but on an almost impossible conjunction of sameness and autonomy, attainable only with another version of oneself" (429).

Drawing on, but also disagreeing in part with Abel's analysis, Alisha Coleman acknowledges the commonality of Nel and Sula's friendship but also argues that Morrison's characters "complement or rather complete each other." In Coleman's view, the two friends combine to form a whole identity*, for Nel represents the superego or conscience, and Sula the unconscious pleasure and desire of the id (151). Marianne Hirsch, who has a less positive reading of the friendship between Nel and Sula, argues that Morrison's novel, even as it affirms the fusion of the two friends and their pre-separational female past, also insists on the separation of the roles and voices of mothers and daughters. While the plot of female friendship is offered as an alternative to the maternal plot, Morrison's characters are unable to transcend or repeat the plots of their mothers, and thus have "nowhere to go" (184–85).

Whereas *Sula* focuses on the developmental importance of female relationships, *Song of Solomon* depicts Milkman Dead's* development of a masculine identity in the Black patriarchal family. Reading *Song of Solomon* within the framework of Freudian psychoanalysis but also arguing that "the Afrocentric and the psychoanalytic are everywhere in the text," Eleanor Branch states that Morrison "rewrites the traditional Oedipal narrative to highlight what she perceives to be critical issues in the development of Black male identity" (53, 56). Through an analysis of the Oedipal tensions written into the family histories of Milkman's parents, Ruth* and Macon Dead*, Branch illuminates Milkman's negotiations with the Oedipal issues that govern his life: his Oedipal attachment to his mother and his rivalrous and antagonistic relationship with his father. Morrison's refashioning of the resolution of the Oedipal struggle, according to Branch, includes Milkman's reclamation of his African heritage as well as his affirmation of not only the masculine but also the feminine.

For Gary Storhoff, who argues that psychological criticism has tended to oversimplify Morrison's multigenerational novel by focusing too exclusively on Oedipal issues, *Song of Solomon* dramatizes the dangers of parental enmeshment in telling the story of Milkman Dead. Making use of family systems theory, which studies the family as an interpersonal system, Storhoff argues that Morrison's novel "contrasts Macon Dead's and Ruth Foster's families of origin to reveal why they overinvolve themselves in Milkman's life, as they attempt to recapitulate childhood patterns in their own family" (291). Serving as the connective agent of his family, Milkman becomes triangulated into his parents' power struggle and preoccupied with their problems. Fighting to establish his own emotional boundaries, he ultimately is able to affirm family relations while freeing himself from the "anaconda love" of parental enmeshment.

Because psychoanalysis "isolates psychic experience from the diversities of ethnicity and class" and because, in its intense focus on the mother/infant relationship, it ignores the social conditioning forces that impact parenting, some critics have expressed "grave reservations" about the application of psychoanalytic theory to *Beloved* (FitzGerald 669). Yet as psychoanalytic critics have shown, even as *Beloved* emphasizes the private world of the individual and family, it also focuses attention on the social and political forces that impact the family as it points to the horrible psychic costs of slavery*.

In an analysis that shows the connection between intrapsychic and social reality in *Beloved*, Barbara Schapiro draws on the work of object relations theorists like Melanie Klein and D. W. Winnicott, and also on Jessica Benjamin's related intersubjective theory, which argues that the autonomous self is an inherently relational, social self dependent on the mutual recognition between self and m/other as separate subjects. *Beloved*, as it depicts the emotional costs of enslavement, shows the psychic consequences of the slaveowner's denial of the slave's status as a human subject. Finding a "wounded, enraged" baby as the central figure in *Beloved*'s psychic economy—"both literally, in the character of Beloved*, and symbolically, as it struggles beneath the surface of the other major characters"—Schapiro describes the infantile rage she locates in the novel as a "form of frustrated, murderous love" (195, 197). "If from the earliest years on, one's fundamental need to be recognized and affirmed as a human subject is denied, that need can take on fantastic and destructive proportions in the inner world: the intense hunger, the fantasized fear of either being swallowed or exploding, can tyrannize one's life even when one is freed from the external bonds of oppression. … The free, autonomous self, *Beloved* teaches, is an inherently social self, rooted in relationship and dependent at its core on the vital bond of mutual recognition" (209).

Also finding object relations theory useful in interpreting *Beloved* because it offers "a model of how social, cultural and political forces become internalized," Jennifer FitzGerald draws on Kleinian object relations theory in her analysis of the various discourses circulating in the narrative (670). While the discourse of slavery inscribes the characters in *Beloved* as objects, "their unconscious … has an investment in Kleinian discourse, in which pre–Oedipal fantasies are inscribed" (672). Not only can Beloved's obsessive relationship with Sethe Suggs* be described as pre–Oedipal—or like the pre–Oedipal infant described in Kleinian theory, Beloved is symbiotically attached to Sethe and she both idealizes Sethe as the good, loving mother and feels aggression toward Sethe as the bad, abandoning mother—but Beloved also serves as a fantasy figure onto whom others project their own wishes and fears. While Sethe, who is excessively invested in motherhood*, asserts "her position as subject in the discourse of the good mother," she also treats her children* as part of herself, not as separate, and thus makes "life-and-death decisions for them" (677, 678).

In *Beloved* Morrison depicts how slavery undermines the characters' sense of self, and she also, through the character of Baby Suggs*, insists on the importance of the nurturing power of the community* and communal self-love. "*Beloved*'s exposition of communal mothering," FitzGerald argues, "offers an alternative to the individualism and autonomy privileged by classical psychoanalysis." In this revised version, "identity is constructed not within the narrow confines of the hegemonic nuclear family but in relation to the whole community" (683). Through a psychoanalytic reading of *Beloved*, investigators can examine not only the psychic costs of slavery but also its therapeutic alternative—"the cooperative self-healing of a community of survivors" (685).

In yet another analysis of *Beloved*'s representation of slavery and the slave mother, Jean Wyatt uses a Lacanian perspective to investigate what she calls the "maternal symbolic" in the novel. If in Lacanian theory the child's entry into the patriarchal symbolic order of language entails a move from "maternal bodily connection to a register of abstract signifiers" (475), Morrison's *Beloved* challenges Lacan's account of the opposition between bodily presence and abstract signifier. Arguing that Sethe "operates within her own 'maternal symbolic' of presence and connection," Wyatt explains that just as Sethe "declined any mediation between her body and her nursing baby, insisting on presence," so she "refuses to replace that baby with a signifier, to accept the irrevocability of absence by putting the child's death into words" (475, 477). Simultaneously the preverbal baby killed by Sethe, the pre-Oedipal daughter who wants to merge with her mother, and the collective victim of slavery's "unspeakable" horrors, Beloved ultimately remains outside social discourse, and thus outside narrative memory as the "disremembered" whose story should not be retold. While Beloved remains outside the paternal symbolic of language, Denver Suggs* finds, in the end, "a more inclusive replacement for Lacan's paternal symbolic: a social order that conflates oral and verbal pleasures, nurtures her with words, and teaches her that caring is 'what language was made for'" (475). Just as Morrison revises Lacan in describing Denver's entry into the social order of language, so she revises Lacan's assumptions about language by making Sethe's physical contact with Paul D* at the novel's end the necessary grounds for Sethe's "full acceptance of the separate subjectivity required by language systems" (484).

If, again and again, critics have used psychoanalytic theory to examine the relationship between Sethe and Beloved, they also have used the psychoanalytic concept of the "return of the repressed" to explain the novel. Mae Henderson, for example, argues that "psychoanalysis ... is based on the theme which preoccupies Morrison's novel: the return of the repressed." Because the events of Sethe's enslaved past "have become sources of both repression and obsession," she must "'conjure up' her past—symbolized by Beloved—and confront it as an antagonist." Through her communication with Beloved, Sethe is given the opportunity to work through her past. "Thus, the psychoanalytic process becomes, for Sethe, the means by which she must free herself from the burden of her past and from the burden of history" (74). In a similar way Linda Krumholtz views Beloved as "the physical manifestation of suppressed memories." At one and the same time "the pain and the cure," Beloved is, in a sense, "like an analyst, the object of transference and cathexis that draws out the past, while at the same time she is that past. Countering traumatic repression, she makes the characters accept their past, their squelched memories, and their own hearts, as beloved" (400). And for Naomi Morgenstern, Morrison's *Beloved*, while repeating the story of slavery, also insists that "it is only through an account of traumatic repetition that the story of slavery ever gets told" (118).

In their varied investigations of Morrison's novels, psychoanalytically oriented critics have found Freudian or object relations or Lacanian theory helpful in their analyses of the girlhood bonding of Nel and Sula in *Sula*, the Oedipal development of Milkman Dead in *Song of Solomon*, and the mother–daughter relationship of Beloved and Sethe in *Beloved*. Despite the reservations some scholars have expressed about using psychoanalytic theory to discuss the works of an African American author like Morrison, psychoanalytic critics have successfully highlighted the central place of fantasy and the unconscious in Morrison's novelistic narratives as they have investigated Morrison's representation of the complex inner and social worlds of the individual and family. *See also* Memory.

References: Elizabeth Abel, "(E)merging Identities: The Dynamics of Female Friendship in Contemporary Fiction by Women," *Signs: Journal of Women in Culture and Society* 6: 3 (Spring 1981); Eleanor Branch, "Through the Maze of the Oedipal: Milkman's Search for Self in *Song of Solomon*," *Literature and Psychology* 41: 1–2 (1995); Alisha Coleman,

"One and One Make One: A Metacritical and Psychoanalytic Reading of Friendship in Toni Morrison's *Sula*," *CLA Journal* 37: 2 (December 1993); Jennifer FitzGerald, "Selfhood and Community: Psychoanalysis and Discourse in *Beloved*," *Modern Fiction Studies* 39: 3–4 (Fall/Winter 1993); Mae Henderson, "Toni Morrison's *Beloved*: Re-Membering the Body as Historical Text," in *Comparative American Identities: Race, Sex, and Nationality in the Modern Text*, ed. Hortense Spillers (1991); Marianne Hirsch, *The Mother/Daughter Plot: Narrative, Psychoanalysis, Feminism* (1989); Linda Krumholtz, "The Ghosts of Slavery: Historical Recovery in Toni Morrison's *Beloved*," *African American Review* 26: 3 (Fall 1992); Naomi Morgenstern, "Mother's Milk and Sister's Blood: Trauma and the Neoslave Narrative," *Differences: A Journal of Feminist Cultural Studies* 8: 2 (1996); Barbara Schapiro, "The Bonds of Love and the Boundaries of Self in Toni Morrison's *Beloved*," *Contemporary Literature* 32: 2 (Summer 1991); Gary Storhoff, "'Anaconda Love': Parental Enmeshment in Toni Morrison's *Song of Solomon*," *Style* 31: 2 (Summer 1997); Claudia Tate, *Psychoanalysis and Black Novels: Desire and the Protocols of Race* (1998); Jean Wyatt, "Giving Body to the Word: The Maternal Symbolic in Toni Morrison's *Beloved*," *PMLA* 108: 3 (May 1993).

J. Brooks Bouson

## Approaches to Morrison's Work: Womanist

African American women authors like Toni Morrison have worked to clarify and illustrate the principal tenets of womanism, which finds its intellectual roots in Alice Walker's preface to *In Search of Our Mothers' Gardens* (1983). Walker's philosophy foregrounds how racist, classist, and sexist power structures disempower African American women. In womanist works, often structured as bildungsromans, the heroine embarks on a literal or psychological journey during which she confronts physical or psychological enslavement so that she may achieve personal freedom. However, this female's new self-empowerment cannot come at the exclusion or to the detriment of others. Rather, womanism rejects separatism, thereby encouraging men and women to create communities that foster a wholeness which transcends gender, class, and racial lines because, as Patricia Collins argues, "[b]lack women's struggles are part of a wider struggle for human dignity and empowerment" (37). Yet, while womanists seek to challenge oppressive power structures and to create spaces of nondominance, critics like bell hooks claim that womanism "is not sufficiently linked to a tradition of radical political commitment to struggle and change" (182). Furthermore, while Walker advocates anti-separatism, some critics claim that she fosters it. *The Bluest Eye\**, *Sula\**, and *Beloved** function as representative texts that illustrate how Morrison simultaneously embraces and challenges womanist tenets and the criticism womanism elicits. Understanding how Morrison negotiates the most fundamental elements of womanism in these texts will permit fuller explorations of the paradigm in *Song of Solomon**, *Tar Baby**, *Jazz**, and *Paradise**.

Typically the womanist journey toward self-empowerment and wholeness begins with images of Black heroines ensnared in oppressive and hostile environments that impede growth. Echoing late nineteenth-century Naturalist paradigms, Morrison creates settings in which characters must combat social forces (class, race*, and gender oppression) that undermine individual power and free will. In *The Bluest Eye*, Pecola Breedlove's* belief that life would improve if she had blue eyes dies in the abandoned store in Lorain, Ohio*. In marked opposition to the very happy family* that inhabits the very pretty green and white house (references to the Dick and Jane primer), Pecola's experience inside the walls of the ugly storefront represents a microcosm of the violence* and oppression she witnesses and experiences in the larger world. Cholly* and Pauline Breedlove* routinely enact for the children not scenes of love but fierce physical and verbal battles stemming from their life frustrations. After Cholly sets fire to their storefront home, Pecola temporarily escapes the brutal epithets that her parents inflict upon each other and their children when she moves in with the MacTeer family. However, even Mrs. MacTeer, ostensibly more motherly than Pauline, does not fail to voice, quite loudly, her discontent with the "case" who burdens the family budget by drinking so much milk. Thus, even when Pecola resides with the supposedly more nurturing MacTeer family, she is in an environment that deprives her of milk, synonymous with maternal nourishment. Thus, Pecola's displacement (due to fire, and later rape) leaves her with no place to go or to grow. Just as the marigolds die because Claudia MacTeer* plants them too deep, so Pecola cannot blossom because she finds herself planted too deep in non-nurturing soil.

In *Sula*, Morrison subdues the hostile environment's destructive potential by giving her protagonist the power to leave it. From her earliest moment of self-awareness, Sula Peace* wants to create an individual self; however, both the larger community* and her family environment threaten this goal. As a whole, the Bottom* risks stunting Sula's personal autonomy because "[n]o one in the village escapes the violence perpetuated by 'capitalism's joke'" (Cadman 67). Although Morrison geographically separates the Bottom from the white world, she inextricably links this African American community to the oppressive white patriarchy. The Bottom arose out of a design to oppress African Americans because the supposedly rich and fertile earth that the white landowner offered his ex-slave was hilly land on which seeds could not be sown.

Like the seeds that cannot take root on the hillside, Sula's family and neighbors cannot thrive in the Bottom. Furthermore, the violence that permeates the larger community ultimately infiltrates each family environment. Determined to create the identity* that she desires, Sula rebels against the oppressive environment through her escapes into Eva Peace's* quiet attic and Nel Wright's* orderly house, and ultimately in her decision to leave the Bottom. Thus, whereas Pecola can escape her hostile environment only through insanity, Morrison casts Sula as a girl-woman who willfully separates herself from the sterile chaos and frees herself from the Bottom's oppressive conformity.

Morrison creates more complex womanist spaces in *Beloved* as characters, in their quests to find self-worth, struggle between controlling and falling prisoner to the spaces they inhabit. Under schoolteacher's* reign, Sethe Suggs* tries to make Sweet Home* her own by gathering flowers for the kitchen; however, she cannot create safety because schoolteacher has the power to turn Sweet Home into a space that ruptures Sethe's body, mind, and family. Furthermore, Morrison initially suggests that 124 Bluestone Road*, under Baby Suggs's* dominion, would offer Sethe the healing and nurturing community (familial and otherwise) necessary to "remember" herself. However, even though Baby Suggs tries to eradicate slavery's* presence by remodeling 124, neither she nor Sethe can control this space after schoolteacher invades her yard. 124 threatens to destroy its inhabitants with its eighteen years of spiteful baby venom, and again after Sethe recognizes Beloved*. For Sethe, domestic spaces (which in the nineteenth century were held as the safe havens women created) represent sites of crisis and self-destruction. Only nature—Sixo's* and Paul D's* trees, Denver Suggs's* boxwood, and Baby Suggs's clearing—offers characters the possibility for liberation.

Pecola, Sula, Sethe, and Denver represent a range of Morrisonian females whose experiences in such hostile environments inspire journeys (literal and/or psychological) of self-re-creation, a fundamental womanist tenet. Morrison follows in the footsteps of her foremothers (Harriet Jacobs, Frances E. W. Harper, Nella Larsen, Zora Neale Hurston, and Ann Petry) who employ the bildungsroman to chart how their heroines undergo trials in the search of autonomy and self-realization. At each journey's end, heroines such as Linda Brent, Iola Leroy, Janie Mae Crawford, and Celie attain greater autonomy and empowerment while others, such as Helga Crane and Lutie Johnson, find themselves victims of even greater oppression. Morrison's female protagonists reflect this spectrum and affirm that the journey toward empowerment and autonomy does not always proceed as smoothly or end as happily as Celie's journey in *The Color Purple*.

*The Bluest Eye* epitomizes a failed womanist quest because even before Cholly violates his daughter's budding sexuality, Pecola's quest to gain "Shirley Temple beauty" has its locus not in challenging the oppressor but in fundamentally altering herself. Morrison casts Pecola as a counterpart to the sugar-brown Mobile girls who live to obliterate their true selves as they squelch what Morrison terms "funkiness." Similarly, Pecola strives to obliterate the ugliness she has internalized. Like Celie in *The Color Purple*, Pecola tries to efface herself and prays that God will help her disappear. Unable to make herself disappear, Pecola pursues various avenues to attain the external beauty that would make her visible and lovable. Yet because of the nature of Pecola's quest, her efforts prove futile. Mrs. MacTeer thwarts Pecola's quest for blue eyes when she stops providing the milk that Pecola obsessively drinks so that she can resemble Shirley Temple. Mr. Yacobowski's refusal to validate Pecola and the sidewalk crack that causes Pecola's fall threatens to destroy the bliss she attains during her journey to purchase three Mary Jane candies which allow her to devour ideals of white beauty. Louis Junior's offer of friendship and a kitten lures Pecola into a white house, but there she becomes his prisoner and experiences both his violence and Geraldine's crude and inhumane denunciation. Ultimately her journey to Soaphead Church*, who advertises his ability to help the distressed, ends Pecola's quest as she spirals into insanity. This obliteration of the self, evident from her dialogue with the imaginary friend to whom she confides the story of her rape and her belief that she has attained the blue eyes, most forcefully challenges womanist principles which maintain that heroines transcend the physical and psychological matrix of domination.

In *Sula*, Morrison tests the nature of the womanist quest by casting an air of ambiguity around whether or not Sula's journey empowers her. Whereas Morrison dooms Pecola's quest from the start, she seems to instill in Sula a ray of hope. Sula's quest to make herself takes her out of the chaos of her home, into the order of Nel's home, into the mystery of Shadrack's* shack, to college, and to major U.S. cities. However, like Shadrack and Plum*, Sula returns "home" disillusioned with and alienated from the world and from herself. Whereas Celie in *The Color Purple* returns home empowered economically, personally, and creatively (she makes pants), Sula returns to the Bottom when her attempt to create a nurturing heterosexual partnership ends. Without the ability to integrate herself into or positively influence the community, Morrison suggests that Sula's journey leaves her disempowered and purposeless. Sula's death (in the fetal position facing a boarded window) in Eva's bedroom suggests a woman who dies defeated and alone (i.e., *sola*). Yet, Morrison simultaneously gives Sula's journey an empowering, womanist echo because in her death, Sula helps to free Nel. Sula's deathbed words about self-creation ring in Nel's ears for over twenty-four years and, as Stein suggests, ultimately transform her: "Nel, who never left home, makes the terrifying journey into the depths of her soul admitting the guilt she had tried to deny, and recognizing her failure of sympathy for her friend. Nel comes to terms with herself and frees her emotional capacity. Thus, Nel, a cautious, conventional woman, learns the meaning of Sula's life, and survives" (149).

In *Beloved*, Morrison creates a complex web of "quest[s] for social freedom and psychological wholeness" (Bell 8) because, essentially, almost every character goes on a quest. Sethe initiates her literal journey from Kentucky to Ohio not because she desires to attain the white patriarchy's concept of beauty or to escape an African American community's demand for conformity, but because what she earlier perceives as a nonthreatening environment suddenly jeopardizes her children. However, after schoolteacher ruptures the twenty-eight days of freedom she and her children experience at 124 Bluestone Road, Sethe's freedom quest ends. She limits herself to 124's confines and never dares to travel within herself. However, when Paul D and Beloved end their own journeys at 124, they nurture Sethe's (and ironically their own) psychological journey of rememory. Sethe must open the protected space in her mind so that she may learn the truth about Halle Suggs*, understand and give voice to the mother love that led her to commit infanticide*, and recognize Beloved as the angry, crawlingalready? baby made flesh. Likewise, Paul D must look within the tin box that he so carefully allows to rust shut in his heart to reconstruct the manhood that schoolteacher, Mister* (the rooster), and his experience on the chain gang violated. Through each character's struggle to face the past and present, Morrison captures the complex and horrific emotional and psychological journey that these individuals endured to achieve wholeness and empowerment.

In Sethe's children, Morrison illustrates an equally difficult journey for the younger generation who may have escaped slavery's lash, but still suffer its scars. Howard and Buglar Suggs* flee 124 Bluestone Road when they can no longer live with slavery's ghost. Nor can Beloved find peace until she returns from the other side to simultaneously reunite with and destroy Sethe. But in Denver, Morrison invests both conflict and hope. Morrison ties Denver to slavery through her birth on the Kentucky side of the Ohio River, and by having her both drink her sister's blood and live with her ghost (i.e., the violence of slavery). Yet Morrison positions Denver on the path toward empowerment because Denver's birth occurs (with a white woman's help) during Sethe's flight to freedom and her bloody union with her sister occurs when her mother challenges the oppressive slavocracy. Furthermore, seven-year-old Denver journeys daily to Lady Jones's home, where Morrison notes that Denver learns to write the capital *w*, the little *i*, and her name. While Lady Jones's lessons reinscribe Denver in a racial environment in which Denver must remember her place as a "little *i*" and not a "capital *w*" (i.e., White), they also teach

Denver about shaping her identity. However, Denver cannot create an identity separate from her family's history*. Therefore, Nelson Lord, a classmate, forces Denver to reconceptualize her "little *i*" when he asks if Sethe actually killed her daughter.

During her two years of deaf silence and fear, before she finds a level of camaraderie in the baby ghost, Denver protects herself from Sethe in her daily ventures away from 124 to the boxwood, where "Denver nurtures herself, embracing her body and mind within an embrace of trees" (Cadman 61). Baby Suggs also teaches Denver to love her body. These lessons in identity and self-love ultimately save Denver. Cadman correctly argues that Denver remains a prisoner of 124 during her girlhood (63)—and, one would add, during the time she acts as a "slave" to meet Beloved's every need and desire. However, Denver reopens her journey toward empowerment and self-actualization when she realizes that Beloved, ironically, has come to resemble the schoolteacher-like force that originally invaded Baby Suggs's yard, to threaten not her but her mother, whom Denver loves and fears. But Denver can no longer live in fear. Beloved's threat to Sethe's life prompts Denver to seek help beyond 124. Denver's journey into the community not only saves her mother, but also enables her to resume her self-creation. Ironically, Denver encounters Nelson Lord, who, in telling her to take care of herself, awakens Denver to another level of self-worth. Thus, in Denver's journey toward wholeness, Morrison best illustrates one tenet of womanism.

While Morrison upholds, with some variation, the bildungsroman tradition, she simultaneously embraces and questions a central element of womanism: the creation of a female community or sisterhood to counter male dominance. Traditionally, the questing heroine encounters one or more females who assist her during the various trials and facilitate healing; however, as Tuzyline Allan argues, women can oppress each other ("Womanism" 98). In *The Bluest Eye*, Morrison implicates the female community in Pecola's inability to transcend the hostile environment, her negative self image, and the myriad experiences with male domination and abuse. Unlike Shug Avery, who assists Celie on her journey toward self-worth, no one intercedes for Pecola. The most important female for Pecola, Pauline Breedlove, cannot help her daughter overcome her oppression because she, too, lives with a sense of her own ugliness (her lame foot and missing tooth) and loneliness.

Just as Hurston's Janie believes that Joe Starks will save her when he comes whistling down the road, so Pauline believes Cholly will love her, help her feel beautiful (he kisses her lame foot), and end her loneliness. But like Janie's, Pauline's romance ends quickly, especially since she finds no Tea Cake to teach her self-love. Rather than valuing herself, Pauline worships Hollywood's definitions of whiteness, and finds power and meaning in the overflowing cupboards and spic-and-spanness of the

Fisher house, where she works. Furthermore, as a martyr who believes she has been wronged, Pauline abuses her husband and victimizes her children rather than changing her life because she has relinquished hope. Pauline falls victim to seeing white as beautiful and Black (i.e., herself and her own child) as ugly. Her coldness and violence toward her daughter, in contrast to the love and affection she showers on the Fisher child, appears most forcefully when she beats Pecola for accidentally toppling the cobbler in the Fisher kitchen. As opposed to the hard mother love that allows Claudia and Frieda MacTeer* to grow and at least understand their circumstances, Morrison suggests that Mrs. Breedlove (as Pecola calls her mother) teaches Pecola to fear others and life itself. Rather than destroy the legacy of "ugliness" and oppression, Pauline teaches it to Pecola, and as a result practically ensures her child's "death."

Furthermore, Pecola lacks a supportive nonfamilial female community to which she can turn for nurture. For example, Pecola lacks the nonbiological, female support network that Janie Crawford finds in Pheoby; that Selina finds in Beryl, Rachel, Suggie, and Mrs. Thompson; and that Celie finds in Nettie, Shug Avery, and Mary Agnes. Pecola's peers (Maureen, Claudia, and Frieda) try to help her, but they cannot. Similarly, while Claudia and Frieda feel true compassion for Pecola and help her on more than one occasion, they realize they failed her. Nor can the seemingly supportive adult community that Pecola finds in the prostitutes* save her. Having experienced the society that ostracizes them—even the children call China, Poland, and Miss Marie derogatory names—they include the ostracized Pecola in their female community. Morrison suggests that they refer to Pecola fondly, tell her stories of their pasts, give her gifts, and treat her to the movies. She, in turn, loves them, knows their real names, and neither fears them nor labels them disparagingly. Yet, although these women possess a more positive sense of self than many of the other women in the novel, their hatred of men and women alike limits their influence and ability to save Pecola. As Jane Kuenz suggests, China, Poland, and Miss Marie's inability to see the differences between men and women transfers to their inability to see the specifics of Pecola's dangerous life experiences. Thus, while these female characters (unlike Pecola's mother) appear to care, Harris argues that "[t]he patterns of caring and incorporation hinted at in some of the occurrences in the novel never reach [Pecola] strongly enough to reshape her opinion of herself" (73).

In *Sula*, Morrison suggests what can happen when the heroine feels rejected by, and in turn rejects, the female community that theoretically should help her formulate an empowered self-image. The adult female community does not help Sula define a self separate from men—who, Morrison suggests, control the Peace household and the Bottom. Like Pecola, Sula learns that she cannot find an advocate in her mother, whom

Sula overhears stating that while she loves Sula, she dislikes her. Nor does Sula find a nurturing female, as does Denver, in her grandmother. Victoria Middleton argues that Eva and Hannah's absent nurturing empowers Sula by "liberat[ing] Sula from lifelong dependency on others" (374). Yet Morrison suggests the negative consequences of the complete absence of a female community, because not only does Sula develop into a woman independent of men, but she also dismisses women, which explains why she can watch her mother burn, can so easily commit Eva to Sunnydale Nursing Home, and can seduce other women's (including her best friend's) husbands. When Nel, Sula's soulmate, opts to marry Jude Greene*, Sula feels betrayed and concludes that Jude embodies men's tendency to subjugate women and obliterate their identities in order to affirm their own manhood. While Sula may seduce Jude as a way to reunite with Nel, once she does so, Nel abandons Sula even though she realizes the substance of her marriage to Jude had eroded long ago. Nel, a former ally, joins the sisterhood that excludes Sula rather than attempt to understand (until she is ready to do so, twenty-four years later) Sula's autonomous, nonseparatist ideals that could have, in themselves, reformulated the corrosive sisterhood that exists in the Bottom.

In *Beloved*, Morrison strikes a balance between the missing or hostile female community and a healing sisterhood. Like Pecola and Sula, Sethe lacks her mother's support and nurture because, in this case, slavery has violated that bond. Beloved helps Sethe recall the painful memory of her birth, her mother's hanging, and her own feelings of deprivation from her mother's inability to nurse her. Sethe also mourns the absence of a female community at Sweet Home* that could have answered her many child-rearing questions. Yet while this absence of sisterhood hinders Sethe's level of empowerment, Morrison also suggests the female community's oppressive potential. Jealous that Baby Suggs can celebrate the arrival of her daughter-in-law and grandchildren, the community that previously found solace and healing at 124 Bluestone Road not only chooses not to warn of schoolteacher's arrival but also condemns Sethe for the infanticide*. In turn, Sethe isolates herself from the community and the community rejects her. Morrison suggests that this conscious refusal to maintain the sisterhood created at 124 and in the Clearing* perpetuates an air of silent but violent destruction both on the Suggs family and on the Black community.

However, *Beloved* also offers several positive images of female community in which women work together to empower women, much like the women in *The Color Purple*. Both Amy Denver*, Morrison's "brightest ray of hope for black and white sisterhood" (Bell 11), and Baby Suggs help heal Sethe in body and spirit during and after Sethe's escape and journey to 124. Similarly, Beloved initially creates a nurturing female community in 124 by helping Sethe and Denver engage in the difficult process of reconstructing the past. Ironically, when Beloved assumes her quasi-demonic posture, she helps to reestablish a healing female community; Denver turns to the female community for literal and emotional sustenance, and her request for assistance leads to a community's healing. When the female chorus arrives at 124, they not only exorcise Beloved's ghost to save Sethe; they also exorcise their hatred and restructure the community to include those whom they previously renounced. The restoration of a sisterhood devoted to inclusion and healing in *Beloved* suggests Morrison's support of the womanist tenet absent in *The Bluest Eye* and *Sula*.

Finally, Walker's womanist paradigm suggests that true healing comes about not only by using sisterhood to conquer the oppressive patriarchy but also by creating nurturing, nonpower-driven relationships with men. *The Bluest Eye* offers Morrison's most pessimistic womanist stance because it offers no possibility for healthy relationships between men and women. Morrison depicts Cholly, Mr. Henry, and Shadrack as males who inflict on women and children the rage they hold against the racist and classist world that oppresses them. Similarly, in *Sula*, Morrison proffers no image of men and women engaging in mutual love. For example, Nel loses her identity to her husband, Jude, and Ajax* threatens Sula's self-reliance when she falls into a state of possessiveness. However, in *Beloved*, Morrison's creation of Halle Suggs*, Sixo, and Paul D challenges the stereotype of the oppressive males evident in previous novels. Specifically, Morrison makes Paul D essential to Sethe's healing process. His arrival initiates Sethe's healing because he asks her questions and gives her information that forces her to recall the past she has repressed. However, their early relationship is based on illusions. In his attempt to assert his own sense of manhood, slavery repeatedly undermined, Paul D violently banishes the crawlingalready? ghost from the house, thereby making 124 Bluestone Road susceptible to a much more powerful force in Beloved; he asks Sethe to have his child when Beloved threatens his manhood; and he calls Sethe an animal, thereby replicating the slavocracy that taught its members to view slaves as part human and part animal.

Not until Paul D undergoes his own conversion by facing the contents encoded in the tin box that Beloved forces open can he fully understand his own and Sethe's experience. As in *The Color Purple*, Mr.__ becomes Albert and unofficially agrees to a "peace treaty" with Celie, whom he had oppressed, and in doing so, heals himself, so in *Beloved*, Morrison suggests that complete recovery comes from interdependence. Paul D needs Sethe because she affirms his manhood. Similarly, Sethe needs him. Upon Beloved's departure, Sethe relegates herself to the keeping room where Baby Suggs surrendered hope and died. Morrison suggests that Paul D's arrival at 124 saves Sethe. However, for this partnership to succeed, Sethe must know that Paul D will rub her feet rather than count them, and that he will help her recognize her self-worth. In this reunion, Morrison creates the healing partnership womanism endorses.

Critics who find fault with womanism's "[non]radical political commitment" or the "unbridgeable gulf [it creates] between white and black feminist writers" may find fault with Morrison's womanist canon, from *The Bluest Eye* to *Paradise*. In doing so, however, they fail to recognize the political and uniting force inherent in merely telling one's story. *The Color Purple*'s womanist message resides not only in the characters who undergo trials and create nonseparatist communities of healing, but also in Celie's ability to tell her story. Similarly, in *The Bluest Eye*, Morrison offers a ray of hope for overcoming oppression in Claudia MacTeer's ability to speak the unspeakable. Having heard the Breedlove family secrets, Claudia's listeners will know to reject the image of white beauty and oppressive relationships, and as such will not evaluate themselves according to oppressive dictates but, possibly, transcend them. Furthermore, having witnessed the compassion Claudia feels for Pecola may help readers create healthy relationships that will enable them to nurture men and women in ways more productive than Claudia could do as a child praying over magic seeds. For Morrison, as for Walker, the magic occurs when womanism transcends the narrative's boundaries, and in this transcendence achieves its political and unifying force. *See also* Approaches to Morrison's Work: Feminist/Black Feminist.

References: Tuzyline J. Allan, "Womanism Revisited: Women and the (Ab)use of Power in *The Color Purple*," in *Feminist Nightmares, Women at Odds: Feminism and the Problem of Sisterhood*, ed. Susan Weisser and Jennifer Fleischner (1994); Tuzyline J. Allan, *Feminist and Womanist Aesthetics: A Comparative Review* (1995); Bernard Bell, *"Beloved*: A Womanist Neo-Slave Narrative; or Multivocal Remembrances of Things Past," *African American Review* 26 (1992); Deborah Cadman, "When the Back Door Is Closed and the Front Yard Is Dangerous: The Space of Girlhood in Toni Morrison's Fiction," in *The Girl: Constructions of the Girl in Contemporary Fiction*, ed. Ruth Saxon (1998); Patricia H. Collins, "Defining Black Feminist Thought," in her *Black Feminist Thought: Knowledge, Consciousness, and the Politics of Empowerment* (1990); Trudier Harris, "Reconnecting Fragments: Afro-American Folk Tradition in *The Bluest Eye*," in *Critical Essays on Toni Morrison*, ed. Nellie McKay (1988); bell hooks, *Talking Back: Thinking Feminist, Thinking Black* (1989); Jane Kuenz, *"The Bluest Eye*: Notes on History, Community, and Black Female Subjectivity," *African American Review* 27: 3 (1993); Victoria Middleton, *"Sula*: An Experimental Life," *CLA Journal* 28: 4 (1985); Chikwenye Ogunyemi, "Womanism: The Dynamics of the Contemporary Black Female Novel in English," *Signs: Journal of Women in Culture and Society* 11 (1985); Karen F. Stein, "Toni Morrison's *Sula*: A Black Woman's Epic," *Black American Literature Forum* 18: 4 (1984); Alice Walker, *In Search of Our Mothers' Gardens: Womanist Prose* (1983).

Deborah De Rosa

# B

### Baines, Guitar (Song of Solomon).

Milkman Dead's* lifelong friend who witnesses Robert Smith's* suicidal leap on the novel's opening pages. As a young boy, he joins Milkman in his interactions with Pilate Dead*, going so far as to assist him in the attempted robbery of Milkman's aunt's house. As he grows up, he and Milkman drift apart due to their disparate politics. Milkman remains complacent and politically ignorant while Guitar becomes more and more radical. He eventually joins the Seven Days*, a politically motivated group. Guitar also becomes obsessed with finding the missing gold supposedly hidden in Macon Dead's* Virginia homeland. His obsession eventually leads him on a manhunt of Milkman during which he inadvertently kills Pilate. *See also Song of Solomon.*

Fiona Mills

### Baltimore, Maryland (*Jazz*)

City where True Belle* moves with Vera Louise Gray* and Golden Gray* after Vera is exiled by her family. Joe* and Violet Trace* originally plan to move to Baltimore but continue on to Harlem, New York*, instead. *See also Jazz.*

Caroline Brown

## Beloved (*Beloved*)

Beloved is the title character of Morrison's Pulitzer Prize- winning fifth novel, *Beloved*. She is the physical manifestation of the ghost of Sethe Suggs's* daughter, killed some twenty years before the present moment of the story. She calls herself B-e-l-o-v-e-d based on the letters on the headstone for her grave. She is filled with the desire of a young child whose mother terminates its life and, as the ghost of slavery*, she is comprised of the kind of raw, unbridled desire that slavery—as a system of deprivation—nourishes. Because she has the mind of the baby she was when Sethe killed her, she cannot begin to understand that her mother's act was the ultimate act of sacrifice and love. Her all-consuming hunger* makes her grow larger and larger as she feeds on Sethe's guilt, while Sethe becomes smaller and smaller. As raw, unbridled desire, Beloved can be displaced only by love, and the love that exorcises her comes in communal form near the end of the novel. *See also Beloved.*

Lovalerie King

## *Beloved*, Film

As soon as she read Toni Morrison's newly published novel *Beloved*, Oprah Winfrey knew she wanted to turn this book into a film. She immediately called Morrison (tracking down her home phone number through the local fire department) and asked her to think about what price she would ask for movie rights to the work. Although Morrison was skeptical that her novel could be translated into film, she finally agreed to come up with a figure. Winfrey then called her attorney and instructed him to complete the deal. She told him she wanted no dickering—she would pay Morrison's price for the film option no matter how costly—because she would find it highly satisfying to make sure that a Black woman with such talent received top dollar for her work.

Despite Winfrey's haste to procure film rights, it took over a decade to make and release the movie *Beloved*. The first obstacle was translating the novel into a workable movie script, a formidable task. Morrison's *Beloved* is written in a beautifully lyrical narrative voice*, and the story is told with many abrupt shifts in time and place (some occurring midsentence) that slowly, sometimes only suggestively, reveal the repressed memories of the main characters. Hauntingly evocative recurring images provide a backdrop of emotional reference points. All of these traits would prove difficult challenges to the scriptwriters. By the time it was completed, the script had been worked on by at least three writers—actress/author Akosua Busia (who had acted with Winfrey in *The Color Purple*), Richard LaGravenese, and Adam Brooks.

In January 1997, Jonathan Demme (*The Silence of the Lambs*, 1991; *Philadelphia*, 1993) read the script and agreed to direct the film. Winfrey was criticized by some for not choosing a Black director, but she had long known that she wanted Demme for the job. By mid-June the cast was assembled and work on the film began. Winfrey herself would play Sethe Suggs*, her first movie role since her portrayal of Sofia in *The Color Purple* in 1985. Veteran performer Danny Glover, who had also been in *The Color Purple*, was cast as Paul D Garner*, Kimberly Elise as Denver Suggs*, and British actor Thandie Newton as Beloved*. Other cast members included Beah Richards as Baby Suggs*, Albert Hall as Stamp Paid, and Kessia Randall as Amy Denver*. Lisa Gay Hamilton played the young Sethe.

Winfrey put a lot of effort into preparing herself for her role. She read slave narratives and social histories of slavery*, took lessons in nineteenth-century cooking, participated in an enactment of an Underground Railroad escape, and went through an intensive, all-day meditation exercise (blindfolded and in a forest) to help her emotionally regress to the emotionally charged racial atmosphere of the film's 1800s setting. She later said these efforts gave her a comprehension of slavery much deeper than mere factual information about the institution; she claimed her exercises allowed her to gain an emotional understanding of how the lack of free will and of a sense of selfhood could drive a loving mother to kill her children rather than see them become enslaved.

Reviewers by and large praised much of the acting in *Beloved*, especially the performances of Danny Glover and Kimberly Elise. Winfrey was generally applauded for a credible portrayal of the film's protagonist and for making sure that her Sethe projected none of the glamour that television viewers associated with Oprah. Thandie Newton's interpretation of Beloved proved quite controversial, however. Newton, faced with the task of portraying a two-year-old whose mother had sawed her throat open and who now has returned home in the body of an eighteen-year-old, used her voice timbre and her body language to convey a not-entirely-worldly being caught between two ages. She spoke throughout the film in a startlingly gruff, croupy voice and used uncoordinated body movements to suggest Beloved's arrested development. Her head wobbling on her neck was a constant reminder (especially to viewers already familiar with the plot) of why her psyche is driven by such a conflicting blend of anger, insecurity, and insatiable hunger* for her mother's love and attention. Critical responses ranged from those who found Newton's depiction of Beloved riveting, even brilliant, to those who found it bizarre and revolting. *New Yorker* reviewer David Denby unflatteringly compared Newton's performance to Linda Blair's in *The Exorcist*.

Despite a stamp of approval from Toni Morrison herself, the movie was not a critical success. It failed to garner the award nominations and critical acclaim that before its release many had felt were inevitable.

Reviewers complained that only those already familiar with the novel could comprehend the film. The novel's stream-of-consciousness intrusions of the past into the present are handled through flashback scenes, but these are often confusing and left unexplained, and they sometimes occur too quickly to be absorbed. There are no voice-overs, so even though much of Morrison's dialogue is there word for word, the power of the novel's lyrical narrative voice is missing. A few of the side stories are cut to provide more focus, but all the book's major scenes involving Sethe are depicted. This accounts for the film's 172-minute viewing time—a length often criticized in reviews. Ironically, the fact that the movie in most respects remains incredibly faithful to the book became cited as one of its greatest weaknesses: many critics faulted what they saw as the film's homage to the book taking precedence over its attempt to be a movie with its own artistic integrity.

The movie *Beloved* was also a failure at the box office. Its makers knew that noncomic films featuring Black casts usually fail to attract white viewers (even the work of such successful directors as Steven Spielberg have not been able to overcome this disturbing trend—*Amistad*, for instance, was not a commercial success). Still, hopes ran high that *Beloved* would begin a new era for Black films. This was not to be the case. Despite Oprah Winfrey's power to affect public tastes and a $30 million publicity campaign mounted by the Disney Company, the movie was not financially successful. After coming in a disappointing fifth for attendance its opening week, the movie quickly dropped into obscurity. And disappointingly, *Beloved* lacked popularity not only with white moviegoers but with most Blacks as well; only Black women over thirty-five seemed drawn to the film.

It remains to be seen how the failure of the movie *Beloved* will affect Black filmmaking in the future. Almost certainly backers and directors will pause before casting their lot with a big-budget, mass-market Black film project. And the social history* of race* relations in the United States still awaits a time when movies that seriously explore the experience of African Americans in films featuring all or nearly all Black casts can attract enough white viewers to ensure commercial success. *See also Beloved.*

References:"*Beloved* It's Not," *Economist* (November 21, 1998); David Denby, "Haunted by the Past," *The New Yorker* (October 26 and November 2, 1998); Janet Maslin, "'*Beloved*': No Peace from a Brutal Legacy," *The New York Times* (October 16, 1998); Laura B. Randolph, "Oprah and Danny," *Ebony* (November, 1998); John C. Tibbetts, "Oprah's Belabored *Beloved*," *Literature Film Quarterly* 27: 1 (1999); Oprah Winfrey, *Journey to Beloved* (1998).

Grace McEntee

## *Beloved*, Novel (1987)

*Beloved*, Toni Morrison's Pulitzer Prize-winning fifth novel, fits into the subgenre of African American literature known as the neo-slave narrative*. *Beloved* is the type of neo-slave narrative that is set in antebellum America and deals directly with slavery* in a fictionalized manner. Another type of neo-slave narrative, such as Richard Wright's *Native Son* (1940), deals with slavery indirectly, as the cause or impetus for later conditions. In *Beloved*, Morrison combines history*, folklore*, and a wonderfully creative imagination to tell a story about the challenge of loving under severe oppression, and the trauma* it causes.

Set in the free state of Ohio and the slave state of Kentucky, the story is based on the real-life story of Margaret Garner*, an enslaved woman who killed her daughter rather than have her returned to slavery. Morrison came across the story while editing *The Black Book*, a 300-year folk history of African American experience. Garner's story is featured in Steven Weisenburger's *Modern Medea: A Family Story of Slavery and Child-Murder from the Old South* (1998). Modeling her protagonist, Sethe Suggs*, on the real-life Margaret Garner, Morrison tried to imagine and then create the scenario by which historical and personal forces could compel an otherwise loving mother to kill her child. Significantly, Morrison has chosen to use Garner's name as the last name of the owners of the Kentucky plantation where much of the past action of the story takes place. As property, enslaved persons usually took on the last names of their enslavers. Paul D Garner*, his brothers (Paul A and Paul F), Sethe, Halle Suggs*, and Sixo* had at one time comprised the enslaved population at Garner's Kentucky plantation, known, ironically, as Sweet Home*. Sethe came to Sweet Home at the age of thirteen, both to serve as a replacement for Baby Suggs* (whose son, Halle, had purchased her freedom), and also to produce the children who would add to the Garners' property.

*Beloved*'s narrative is comprised of the fragmented recollections of Sweet Home's traumatized survivors. The story belongs first and foremost to Sethe, but her narration and recollections must be considered along with information revealed through the third-person narrator and the voices of other characters. The story is related through several narrative voices* in flashbacks that take us from freedom to slavery and back again. The narrative is, therefore, neither chronological nor linear; set against the linearity of Western history and the prototypical slave narrative, *Beloved*'s narrative meanders forward, slips backward, spirals upward or downward, and then goes forward again. Individual stories complement each other; readers must participate by collecting the partial stories into a whole.

The present moment of the very intimate story at the center of the novel runs from 1873 to 1875; at the beginning, the Civil War has been over for eight years and, thus, slavery has been outlawed. Sethe, her eighteen-year-old daughter Denver*, and the sad, spiteful spirit of Denver's dead sister live at 124 Bluestone Road*, near Cincinnati, Ohio. The ghost's presence in the house is evidenced by a glimmering red light. Sethe's sons Howard and Buglar Suggs*, having tired of living with the anxiety created by the ghost's presence, had left in 1864; Sethe's mother-in-law, Baby Suggs, died not long after. In 1873, no one in the surrounding community comes to visit at 124 Bluestone Road, and Sethe and Denver visit no one. Several events had precipitated a long-standing rift between the community* and the Suggs family. First, the community thought that the party celebrating Sethe's successful escape from Sweet Home back in 1855—depicted as a kind of "loaves and fishes" event—had been overdone, and smacked of pride. Chagrined, they stood mute when they should have sounded the warning that harmful forces were approaching. Finally, they were appalled by Sethe's act of infanticide*, and equally appalled by her aloofness and general air of independence once she was released from imprisonment. Emotionally traumatized, Sethe has managed to physically survive slavery and the havoc it wreaked on her family, but her continued physical survival has been based on her ability to suppress the memory* of past events, including the events that led to the central act of infanticide. Occasionally, however, aspects of her past manage to seep through cracks in her memory, regardless of her efforts to suppress them. In 1873 the past—in the form of Paul D, an old friend from Sweet Home—comes to visit Sethe. Sethe begins to "rememory" certain experiences and events that have long lain dormant.

Paul D and Sethe revisit some very painful memories of slavery and its aftermath. Morrison sifts through their rich memories to reconstruct for us Sweet Home and the people—both free and enslaved—who had resided there. We learn that Sweet Home was anything but sweet for those forced to serve first under Mr. and Mrs. Garner*, and then under the cruel slavemaster known as schoolteacher*, so named by Sethe and the others because he was always asking questions and writing things down. The personification of scientific racism, schoolteacher spent much of his time observing their behavior and listing their attributes under "animal" and "human" subcategories.

Schoolteacher's scientific racism differed only in degree from Garner's patented benevolent form of slavery. While he was alive, Garner had bragged that his slaves were men, that he had perfected the art of creating the perfect environment for producing pacified slaves. Evidence of Garner's success exists in the brothers known as Paul A, Paul D, and Paul F. The names suggest a series of the same model. The Pauls* are all brothers bred (or perhaps manufactured is a better word—since no mention is made of their having parents) at Sweet Home. They had come to adulthood within the confines of Sweet Home. The suggestion is that there must have been Pauls B, C, and E at some point. The Pauls' collective perceptions of themselves vis-à-vis the world were created, conditioned, and honed under Garner's special philosophy of slavery. They had been reared to serve perfectly and contentedly; prior to schoolteacher's arrival, they were not beaten, they had plenty to eat, and Garner had even allowed them to use guns for hunting. He told them that they were men, and they believed him. Garner's death and schoolteacher's new rules turned their "safe" little manufactured world upside down. Paul F is sold for the money needed to keep Sweet Home afloat, and Paul A is hanged during the aborted escape attempt. Paul D is later sold, spends time on a chain gang after trying to kill his new owner, and eventually comes to develop an identifiably separate consciousness. He realizes much later that it had, after all, been Garner who controlled the definition of the term "man" which he chose to bestow on the Pauls and that he could have removed the term whenever he wanted to remove it. We are left to ponder, along with Paul D, whether he and his remaining brother would ever have tried to seek freedom if schoolteacher had not taken over and installed his harsh regime.

We learn also that others did not fit the Sweet Home mold so easily. Sixo, whom we can assume had recently been taken from Africa when he arrived at Sweet Home, is described in the past tense as very dark-skinned and "wild." At Sweet Home, he was the quintessential rebel; he routinely broke the rules by sleeping when he was required to work, by leaving the premises to visit his lover, Patsy* (rather than having sex with farm animals), and by helping himself to forbidden foods. Sensitive and generous-natured, Halle Suggs demonstrated his discontent by working on his free Sundays so that he could earn his mother's freedom. Without ever having experienced freedom, Halle sensed that it was something wonderful; in his most generous gesture, he bestows the gift of freedom on his mother, Baby Suggs. A year after Sethe comes to Sweet Home as Baby Suggs's replacement, she chooses the extraordinary Halle as her future husband. Thus, the plan of escape from Sweet Home is left to Sixo and Halle, the two men not created, developed, and refined at Sweet Home; they were the only two men among the enslaved population who had the routine contact with the outside world necessary to gain information about how to access the Underground Railroad.

During the mass exodus from Sweet Home, Paul A was captured and hanged, Sixo was burned and shot to death, Halle witnessed an atrocious abuse of Sethe and slipped into insanity, and Paul D was captured and sold. Sethe and her children were the only ones to reach freedom. After Sethe lived free for twenty-eight days, daring for the first time to love her children fully and completely, schoolteacher tracked them down at Baby Suggs's 124 Bluestone Road residence. In a moment of desperation,

Sethe decided that she and her children would be better off dead. She succeeded in killing only the older daughter before she was stopped. After serving time in jail for the child's murder (her real-life counterpart had been charged with theft of her master's property), she returned to the house on Bluestone Road to live with her three surviving children and Baby Suggs, and to try to keep the past from consuming her. By the time Paul D arrives in 1873, only Sethe, Denver, and the spiteful ghost remain.

Shortly after his arrival at Bluestone Road, Paul D confronts and drives away the ghost of Sethe's dead daughter—whom Sethe and Denver had accepted as part of their strange existence. Paul D and Sethe work toward establishing a "normal" family life for the first time for either of them. Before long, however, the ghost returns, this time in the flesh of the twenty-year-old young woman Sethe's daughter would have been had she lived. She simply emerges from the water, fully grown and fully dressed. Based on the only word that Sethe could afford to have carved on the child's tombstone, she believes her name to be B-e-l-o-v-e-d.

The human inhabitants of 124 Bluestone Road take Beloved* in, because it is the appropriate thing to do; she is a young woman alone and in need of shelter. Denver is the first to recognize the woman as her sister. She had missed the baby ghost, her only playmate since her brothers fled the strange house almost a decade before. Denver also missed Baby Suggs, and she has spent most of her eighteen years yearning for her absent father, Halle, who is probably also dead. Driven from the school yard and from childhood friends years before by cruel taunts about her unusual family* history, Denver had turned into a genuine recluse; the ghost kept her company. Though Denver welcomes the young woman, Paul D is suspicious from the beginning, and rightly so.

As Trudier Harris and others have noted, Beloved can be seen as a succubus; she is a consuming machine, comprised of all the desire created by the systematic deprivation inherent in the institution of slavery. She is not only Sethe's rebuked child come to claim her due; she also represents—in a larger sense—the unbridled desire that hundreds of years of slavery created. She is not only prepared to suck the life out of Sethe, she is also ready to destroy any opportunity her mother has for real love, since real love displaces desire.

As a first order of business, therefore, she drives Paul D from the house, seducing him in the process. (Harris has treated at length the folkloric implications of Paul D's fear and anxiety about Beloved.) Once Paul D is driven from the house, the well-meaning Stamp Paid administers the final straw when he shares with Paul D a newspaper clipping about Sethe's act of infanticide and subsequent incarceration. Paul D goes to Sethe to hear the story from her own lips. For the first time in the narrative, the details surrounding the child's death are revealed. Paul D makes the mistake of sounding like schoolteacher when he suggests to Sethe that she acted more like an animal than a human being.

Sethe soon recognizes Beloved as her daughter and submits totally to the increasingly demanding ghost. Beloved grows larger as Sethe diminishes in size. Realizing that her mother is being drained of life, Denver—with a little coaxing from the ancestral presence and spirit of Baby Suggs—summons up the courage to go out of the yard in search of assistance. She shares information with members of the community, and that information, once consumed, digested, and passed along, sets them into action.

The community's return to 124 Bluestone Road, after having turned its collective back on the house some twenty years before, is depicted as a parallel to the earlier scenario during which schoolteacher had arrived to return Sethe and her children to slavery. This time it is Mr. Bodwin* who arrives to carry Denver off to her new job, but for Sethe it is that earlier moment all over again. Amid the chanting and praying of the community women, the emotionally and physically emaciated Sethe emerges from the house along with the now enlarged and hideous figure of Beloved. With ice pick in hand, Sethe rushes forth to attack the slave catcher she believes Bodwin to be; the ever-practical Ella* fells her with a strong blow. Sethe is bedridden for a time, but Paul D eventually returns to the house on Bluestone Road and Sethe. The novel's ending suggests that they will have a chance to resume their quest for a love relationship.

*Beloved* thus explores, among other things, the difficulty of loving under the traumatic conditions of slavery and its aftershocks. Paul D's romantic relationship with Sethe (and Denver's personal development) had, in essence, been disrupted by the insistent presence and full weight of the ghost of slavery. In providing the stories about the individual and collective lives of the people who were enslaved at Sweet Home, Morrison takes special pains to focus on the most intimate details of their lives; in doing so, she highlights their humanity under a system that thrived by subjugating that humanity. She imagines many of the details that were routinely left out of slave narratives. For example, that narrator tells us that Sixo felt comfortable near the trees, and that he danced near them at night. Sixo helped Sethe with child care, and it was in knowing Sixo that Paul D understood that Garner did not own the definition of "manhood." Sixo is transcendent in a way that disrupts the system of slavery and that invokes the myth of the flying Africans*.

Of Sethe, we learn that she pilfered bits of cloth to make a special dress for her wedding day. She brought salsify into Mrs. Garner's kitchen in an effort to make it seem more like her own. She took great pride in caring for her children and in providing them with the nourishing milk from her breasts; motherhood* is an important aspect of her self-identity, and she is deeply wounded (both emotionally and physically) when schoolteacher supervises his nephews* in her forced milking—as he would livestock. The violation is, for Sethe, an act of rape and severe deprivation, so severe that it sets in motion a stream of desire that culminates in the appearance of the all-consuming, desire-filled ghost of slavery.

Indeed, the significance of motherhood to self-identity is a central theme in the novel and one of the keys to understanding Sethe's dilemma. Black feminist scholars, in particular, have identified the figure of the outraged mother as a recurring one in Black women's literature, and Sethe is, above all else, an outraged mother. Related issues and themes include the sexual and reproductive exploitation that figured prominently as a part of the system of chattel slavery. We learn, for example, that Halle was the only one of Baby Suggs's eight or nine children that she was allowed to keep. Another character, Ella, had been forced as an adolescent to serve the perversions of a father-and-son team; so horrific was her treatment that she uses the experience as a yardstick by which to measure other atrocities. Sethe's own mother had been forced to mate with a variety of men for the purpose of enriching the slave-owner's supply of free labor. Paul D witnesses the lynching of a Black woman accused of theft for trying to gather ducks she believes to be her lost children. Enslaved women, when they were allowed to keep their children in close proximity, faced the problem of providing proper child care and forming maternal bonds with them because the system made no suitable provision for either. In *Beloved*, Sethe had almost no contact with her own mother beyond the probable two or three weeks of nursing, after which she was turned over to a wet nurse. The myriad issues surrounding motherhood that Morrison addresses in *Beloved* are also addressed in some of the best-known slave narratives, including those by Frederick Douglass and Harriet Jacobs.

Other themes in the novel that mirror those of slave narratives include the quest for identity* (or search for self-knowledge) and the passage from innocence to experience. Such passages are noted early in Douglass's 1845 *Narrative of the Life of Frederick Douglass, An American Slave* and Jacobs's 1861 *Incidents in the Life of a Slave Girl*. Like these two prototypical slave narratives, *Beloved* explores in some depth the question of manhood, especially through the characters Paul D and Sixo. The neo-slave narrative mirrors another primary objective from the earlier tradition by demonstrating how race-based discrimination deforms the human spirit of both the oppressor and the oppressed. One is left with the question, after all, of whether Sethe was any crazier than those who benefited most from the inhumane system. Ultimately, Beloved, like its slave narrative predecessors, must be considered representative—as a composite for the many stories that cannot and will not ever be told. *See also* Approaches to Morrison's Work: Feminist/Black Feminist; Brother; Clearing, The; Ghost Story, Use of; Home; Neo-Slave Narrative.

References: William L. Andrews and Nellie McKay, eds., *Toni Morrison's Beloved: A Casebook* (1999); Trudier Harris, *Fiction and Folklore: The Novels of Toni Morrison* (1991); Missy Dehn Kubitschek, *Toni Morrison: A Critical Companion* (1998); Nellie Y. McKay and Kathryn Earle, eds., *Approaches to Teaching the Novels of Toni Morrison* (1997); David L. Middleton, ed., *Toni Morrison's Fiction: Contemporary Criticism* (2000); Nancy J. Peterson, ed., *Toni Morrison: Critical and Theoretical Approaches* (1997); Barbara H. Solomon, ed., *Critical Essays on Toni Morrison's Beloved* (1998); Steven Weisenburger, *Modern Medea: A Family Story of Slavery and Child Murder from the Old South* (1998).

Lovalerie King

## Best, Patricia

*See* Cato, Patricia Best (*Paradise*).

## *Big Box, The* (1999)

In 1999, award-winning novelist Toni Morrison made her first foray into the world of children's literature. The result is a picture book, *The Big Box*, coauthored by Morrison's son Slade and illustrated by Giselle Potter. A long story poem, the book focuses on three children, Patty, Mickey, and Liza Sue. Each of the children, in turn, has behavior problems and is sent, by parents and other authoritative adults, to live in a big box, a room from which the children cannot escape. They are provided with all the material comforts they could want, but must live isolated in the box, the monotony broken only by weekly visits from their parents. Throughout the book, the children are compared to animals who enjoy the freedom and liberty of the natural world. While the adults maintain that these severe restrictions are for the children's own good, the final page of the book depicts the three breaking down the walls of their box to escape.

As in her fiction for adults, Morrison has created a work of strong social commentary, questioning commonly held beliefs about the rights and responsibilities of our youngest citizens. The three children in this book are portrayed as perfectly normal children—energetic, exuberant, and perhaps a bit mischievous. But none of them is a serious problem child; Patty talks too much in school, Mickey plays handball in his apartment building, and Liza Sue sympathizes with the animals on her family farm. None of them threatens social order. Clearly, the society that would repress children to the extent of eliminating normal childhood is the real threat. Morrison manages to attack our rule-bound society (rules are posted everywhere in the children's world), as well as our intolerance for the inconvenience that we so often associate with children. She also comments strongly on the materialism of contemporary American culture. When these children are put in the box, they are obviously cut off from experience in the natural world; their parents respond by filling their lives (their box) with *stuff*—toys, gadgets, total consumer indulgence.

Unfortunately, Morrison's message is a bit heavy-handed, and the book suffers. Critical response to *The Big Box* has been mixed, at best. Reviewers agree that this picture book holds little appeal or meaning for the traditional picture-book audience: young children. The plot is boring for little people, perhaps even a bit frightening, and the message doesn't really apply to them—children are the victims here, not the oppressors. Adults, on the other hand, are not typically drawn to picture books, nor are older children. So *The Big Book* may be remembered purely because it was written by Toni Morrison, not because millions of children clamored to hear it every night at bedtime.

Lisa C. Rosen

### Birth of a Nation'hood: Gaze, Script, and Spectacle in the O.J. Simpson Case (1997)

In a work that reveals her continuing interest in the American legal system, *Birth of a Nation'hood: Gaze, Script, and Spectacle in the O.J. Simpson Case* presents Morrison's response to the O.J. Simpson phenomenon, resulting from his arrest for the murders of his ex-wife, Nicole Brown Simpson, and her acquaintance Ronald Goldman, his trial, and his acquittal. This collection, coedited by Claudia Brodsky Lacour, was published in 1997 by Pantheon Books. The contributors to the book are notable intellectuals who are both male and female, both Black and white, and include writers (among them Ishmael Reed) and professors from the fields of literature, legal studies, and American studies. While one reviewer of the book suggests that there is little groundbreaking work here on the subject of race* and is disturbed by some of the contributors' insistence on Simpson's innocence, he still applauds the book for its interesting investigation of whiteness*. The result of Morrison's collaboration is a collection of thoughtful examinations or interrogations of what the O.J. Simpson case represents to an American cultural, racialized, and classed consciousness.

Morrison not only edited this collection but also wrote the introduction, "The Official Story: Dead Man Golfing." While the book refers to her contribution as an "introduction," her essay is one more conversation in the think tank of the collection; nowhere in the introduction does Morrison refer to the themes or ideas offered by the other contributors, nor does she mention their names. However, the "misnaming" of Morrison's essay by no means detracts from its interesting exploration of the O.J. Simpson quagmire.

Morrison begins by comparing the Simpson case to Herman Melville's short story "Benito Cereno." Morrison's interest in the story revolves around the themes of deception and contradiction, themes that she sees as equally pervasive in the cultural readings or misreadings of the "character" O.J. Simpson. Rinaldo Walcott, in his review of this collection, begins by arguing that the entire O.J. Simpson case is about "reading practices." Repeatedly, Morrison insists that within the media-generated narratives O.J. Simpson "stands in for" or represents something else, whether that be the whole African American race or other racialized stereotypes or fears heaped upon the backs of African Americans. Additionally, she quotes William Faulkner* as an indication of the complete reduction or dehumanization of African Americans and the perceptions of their thoughts and behaviors. Of course, it is precisely these misperceptions or misreadings of the captain in "Benito Cereno" that lead to the chaos and mutiny: the belief that the Blacks are demure servants incapable of violence* reveals how the captain, and perhaps the readers are shocked out of their comfortable situations through the mutiny. Morrison argues that the inability to classify the abyss of contradictions seen in the alleged actions of an American hero or icon like O.J. Simpson gives rise to a need for culturally sanctioned narratives that not only leave Americans feeling safe but also protect them from the vulnerability that Melville writes about in his story.

For Morrison, one of the most disturbing aspects of the O.J. Simpson case is the manner in which it gives rise to the official story, the national narrative, or a metanarrative. Morrison explores tendencies of the official media to include or exclude particular surveys, opinions, and attitudes that might complicate thinking about the Simpson case. Moreover, she explores theories, conspiracy and otherwise, in an attempt to better understand the culture's desire to simplify the plethora of both legal and societal issues emerging from the Simpson case, including domestic violence, police brutality and abuses of power, sexual assault, equal treatment under the law, freedom of information, and freedom of speech, among others. For Morrison, the result of this metanarrative is a denial similar to that in "Benito Cereno" when the white captain has to discover the "hidden" racism.

Near the conclusion of her essay, Morrison calls on another American narrative driven by the polemics of race. The title for the collection signifies or maybe reracializes the title of D.W. Griffith's famous film *The Birth of a Nation* (1915), which single-handedly, through its heroic portrayal of the Ku Klux Klan, gave rise to a new Klansman, reinvesting post–Civil War America with white rights and supremacy. By adding the "hood" to Griffith's title, Morrison accomplishes two tasks: she reveals the "hidden hood" represented by the hoods worn by the Klansman, hidden racism now recognizable in its more familiar forms, and she questions how the official story manages to re-present O.J. Simpson as an African American Everyman, in a kind of "gentrification" of race in the hood of the media.

Reference: Rinaldo Walcott, "Deceived: The Unreadability of the O.J. Simpson Case," *Canadian Review of American Studies* 28: 2 (1998).

James M. Ivory

## Black Book, The (1974)

During her career as a senior editor for Random House, Toni Morrison worked on a one-of-a-kind project titled *The Black Book*, edited by Middleton A. Harris, Morris Levitt, Roger Furman, and Ernest Smith. In compiling materials for the volume, the editors acknowledge the contributions of a number of people, including Morrison's parents, Ramah Willis and George Wofford. Readers familiar with Morrison's work are no doubt aware that while working on this project she encountered a visual representation (not included in *The Black Book*) and the story of Margaret Garner*, the formerly enslaved Cincinnati woman who killed her daughter rather than have her returned to slavery*. Margaret Garner's story would become the impetus for Morrison's masterwork, *Beloved**.

*The Black Book* is both eclectic and grandly illuminating. Its real value lies in its breadth of coverage, for even the most devoted scholar of Black life and culture is likely to find something revelatory in the volume. Entries—including news items, photographs, recipes, handwritten letters, patent records, and birth records—are generally, but not always, arranged chronologically; the "story" clearly begins with the African, and includes information about Blacks in the New World before the coming of Columbus and the Atlantic Slave Trade as we know it. Salient passages from the writing of Aimé Césaire, Henry Dumas, Langston Hughes, Robert Hayden, Gwendolyn Brooks, and others often accompany the visuals and serve as epigraphs, sometimes encapsulating a specific period or attitude, and other times suggesting the possible interpretation of an individual photograph.

The first almost full-page photograph is of a vibrant, young woman, clearly African. She is standing upright—looking ahead and possibly walking forward; her facial expression suggests wonder, perhaps longing, and some measure of anxiety. Above the photograph, lines from Bernard Dadie speak to witnessing the beginning of a major turning point: "I was there when the Angel/drove out the Ancestor/I was there when the waters/consumed the mountains." Juxtaposed against this opening visual is the final one, featuring an elderly, feeble-looking Black American man, seated, fully dressed in worn clothing—in stark contrast to the sparsely clothed, almost nude subject of the opening photograph. The words of Henry Dumas that accompany this final photo suggest the beginning of a new journey, perhaps toward full citizenship: "We have a journey/to take and little time;/we have ships to name/and crews."

In the volume's short but provocative introduction, celebrated entertainer William H. (Bill) Cosby, Jr., asks us to consider the type of scrapbook a 300-year-old Black man might have put together had he started collecting materials at the age of ten. What he might have included is an assortment of pictures of Black cowboys, a list of colonial enactments aimed at impeding Black progress, and a late nineteenth-century news article about a prize-winning grower and spinner of silk, Miss Ruth Lowery of Huntsville, Alabama. He might have included records of patents relating to all the following items: the fountain pen, a type of clothes dryer, an airship, a typewriting machine, a pencil sharpener, a window cleaner, a cigarette roller, a corn harvester, a street sweeper, a hot comb, a lawn sprinkler, a steam furnace, the antiaircraft gun, a lamp, the telephone, and many more. He might also have included a recipe for scuppernong wine, or the very specific directions for mixing and cooking hoe cake; he might have included a wonderful parody of Joyce Kilmer's famous poem about trees. Surely he would have explained how the "dozens" came to be called by that name, and he would have included posters advertising the public sale of displaced Africans as slaves, such as the one describing "2 likely young Negro wenches," one of whom is missing an eye.

Like the editors of *The Black Book,* in compiling his scrapbook the 300-year-old Black man would have wanted to include testimonials of everyday miracles of resistance and survival alongside more notorious historical events, such as an eyewitness account of John Brown's execution following his raid on Harper's Ferry in 1859. There would be space for a copy of Frederick Douglass's handwritten letter defending his choice for a second wife, and for pictures and news articles representing the horrible period of lynching following the Civil War and extending well into the twentieth century. He would include evidence of religious hypocrisy and moral corruption among the beneficiaries of "the evil institution," and he would make note of the fact that New York's African Aid Society addressed a letter to the king of Dahomey in West Africa, telling him that it would be much more financially lucrative to stop selling enslaved Africans to European traders and instead use their labor at home to boost local production. Indeed, he would be sure to include information about New World Blacks who owned slaves, and information about whites who served as conductors on the Underground Railroad. Certainly he would want people to know that the Empress of the Blues once won the Tennessee roller-skating championship in Chattanooga, and that one of the Fisk Jubilee Singers went to Europe, changed her name to Desireo Plato, and continued to perform concerts.

An incredibly rich and unique source of information about Black American life covering several centuries of Blacks as subjects and participants in the history of the world, *The Black Book* includes all the above information and much, much more.

Lovalerie King

## Bluest Eye, The (1970)

Toni Morrison's first novel, *The Bluest Eye,* is a coming-of-age story that marks painful childhood lessons and the far-reaching effects of those pains in adulthood. It weaves different stories of adolescence and adulthood that, together, come to revolve around the life of the novel's protagonist, Pecola Breedlove*. As readers learn Pecola's story, the novel provides a look into and understanding of the stories of the other characters in the text. More important, the novel illustrates what happens to seeds planted in childhood innocence and watered by racial hatred, social discrimination, and sexual violence*. By forcing readers to interpret the characters' stories in the text, Morrison forces them to reinterpret the stories of their own childhood that have come to shape their adulthood, their existence.

The novel begins with a tale from the popular Dick and Jane series of children's literature. The Dick and Jane stories taught many children how to read through short, simple sentences recounting scenes from, according to the books' portrayals, everyday life of everyday people. The story's text introduces readers to its concept of the *typical* family* unit. This middle-class family is complete with a father, mother, son, daughter, dog, and cat, all housed in a quaint green and white house bordered with a white picket fence. While the family has no name, everybody knows them because, supposedly, they speak the story of childhood in Anytown, USA, and the life lessons learned therein. Every story has some basic, rudimentary elements. The man has ascended to the head of this household, in strength and stature. The woman has fulfilled the dream of homemaker and wife, and happily assumes those roles in her home*. The two children, Dick and Jane, are being groomed in this tradition and learning the bonds of family. More important, each member seems to be learning the lessons of love—the love of family, the love of life. In *The Bluest Eye*, however, the story and its telling become more disjunctive. By mimicking the Dick and Jane story, Morrison creates a poignant par adox for study of the novel. While she reinforces the idea that this story reflects life lessons and childhood experiences, and maintains the earlier tone and structure of the Dick and Jane story in her mimicry, she also reminds the reader that the story and the lessons that come to form those experiences are different for different children and different communities. The simple sentences become a jumble of words, one after the other, with no terminal punctuation and no lines of clear division and borders. Finally, the words become a series of letters running together, and the message and the sense of the earlier story are suddenly and violently disrupted. The story, in essence, turns against itself and falls apart as other stories, which lie buried beneath this mythic portrait of the American Dream, appear and shatter the conventional paradigm.

Set between the fall seasons of 1940 and 1941, it immediately informs the reader that Pecola Breedlove, an eleven-year-old child, is having her father's baby. The happy-go-lucky tenor of the earlier Dick and Jane story, which informs the mind-set of the reader and the characters within the text, is immediately banished for more realistic portrayals of life, living, and love in this alternate story. Immediately, Morrison reminds the reader that the stories other American texts have told are not universal. There are others that lurk in the silences, in the places and hearts that have tried to hide and conceal the ugliness of that existence. The Dick and Jane story frames the novel's central story and implies the novel's central theme. Thus, only by reading the story of Dick and Jane can one understand *The Bluest Eye*. In essence, for readers, learning the rudimentary elements of the frame enables an understanding of the lessons about racial, social, and sexual discrimination to come.

From a distance, the story seems simple. Pecola Breedlove, a foster child, comes to live with a small neighboring family, the MacTeers, in Lorain, Ohio*, after her parents' relationship spirals into a continuous cycle of poverty, discord, and violence*. Particularly, Pecola relocates after her father, Cholly Breedlove*, attempts to burn down the storefront home where they live—the first of his many abuses. The MacTeers' two daughters, Claudia* and Frieda*, bond with Pecola during her stay in their parents' home. While Pecola's presence is unexpected and sudden, both Claudia and Frieda consider Pecola to be family, and want to learn as much as they can about their new friend. As the story continues to unfold, however, Claudia and Frieda learn more about themselves as they learn more about Pecola and the events that bring Pecola to the MacTeer home—and eventually remove her. Claudia and Frieda, ironically, go on their own personal journeys. Eventually, the reader learns that all of the girls are searching for growth and acceptance of themselves in a world that seeks to ignore and discredit their presence.

Claudia narrates Pecola's story and immediately contrasts the archetypal Dick and Jane. Pecola is the daughter of Pauline* and Cholly

Breedlove. The Breedloves, a lower-class family, live in a converted store-front. Here, Pecola learns her basic lessons of childhood and how to *read* the world. While Dick and Jane sleep soundly every night to the sound of a figurative lullaby of love and acceptance, Pecola's lullaby is anger and rejection. As Pecola listens to her mother and father argue each night, she imagines that all except her eyes disappears. In essence, her eyes become the core of her being, her inner self. Her eyes, however, are not the dark eyes that she is born with, but the bluest eyes imaginable. She ultimately believes that if she has blue eyes, not only will she no longer be considered the ugly child, but her parents will not fight, and she will be loved. Pecola's one desire is to learn *how* to get people to love her. Readers, feeling wise, assume that Pecola's flaw is in wanting to know how to be loved. Yet, before readers can feel sorry for Pecola, Morrison takes this sad perversion a step farther and draws not just on Pecola's failings but on the readers' failings as well. The idea that Dick and Jane's parents love them, that Dick and Jane's parents love each other, and that Pecola wishes to have this love is not worthy of pity. Instead, it is Pecola's and the readers' assumption, both within and outside of the text, that only aspects of whiteness*, or products thereof, are beautiful and should be loved. In fact, whiteness, never stated in the story itself, becomes the readers' creation and, automatically, synonymous with being loved and beautiful. Thus, while the Dick and Jane story seems out of place in the novel itself, it has a central place in the story of the characters in the text and the readers of the text who consciously and subconsciously view whiteness, and expressions of it, as synonymous with love.

All of the members of Pecola's family, readers learn, have struggled with the need to be loved, and possess a level of self-loathing for their own being as Black in a white world. Pecola's mother, Pauline (Polly) Breedlove, lost a front tooth through rot and also impaled her foot at age two. This accident left her with a flat, archless foot that flopped around when she walked and the persistent feeling in her childhood that she did not belong anyplace. Though her family prevents her from hearing the taunts of other children, Pauline feels unaccepted, so she creates a world within where she controls her own destiny and experiences love through acceptance in all parts of her community*, not just in the protected space of her family and her home. Love, for Pauline, equals acceptance. As she grows older, Pauline assumes all of the responsibilities of caring for her younger siblings, which makes her feel needed and then accepted. Thus, as an adult, she feels love only in places where she feels acceptance. Her tumultuous relationship with Cholly makes her feel unaccepted in her own home, ugly, and unloved. Yet when she works as a maid in a white family's home, she feels beautiful and loved; she mistakes the white family's *need* for her services as an acceptance of her. Consequently, she bestows more love on the white child for whom she cares than on her own child, Pecola, whom she feels is too Black, dirty, and ugly—ironically, the same way she felt about herself as a child.

Similarly, Cholly Breedlove struggles to find love through acceptance in a white world that sees him only as an uneducated Black brute. He is plagued by a time in his childhood when he bore the brunt of the sexual perversion of three white hunters, who stood over him and watched as he had his first sexual experience. While the experience could have been a beautiful one, instead it was unfulfilling and tinged with hatred both for the white men and for the young girl with whom he had the encounter. When Pauline and Cholly meet, they are two beings longing and needing to be accepted, who view that acceptance as love.

By the spring of 1941, Pecola is back home with her parents. While she is washing dishes at the sink, Cholly comes into the kitchen and returns momentarily to a time of his youth. He remembers his love for Pauline, and the day that Pauline leaned idly on the fence in front of her home and he, Cholly, bent down, laughing, tickling her foot and kissing her leg. He thinks lovingly of his young Pauline in her awkwardness perched over that fence. He reaches out to Pauline and, tickling and kissing that foot and leg again, remembers the love that he felt and so desired. Yet the foot and the leg are not Pauline's, but Pecola's, and the fence is not a fence but a kitchen sink where Pecola attends to one of her daily tasks. The love and laughter that return from the heart of Pauline that sunny day in Kentucky are replaced by the screams and pain of a daughter unable to understand the brutality of this love in a kitchen in Lorain, Ohio. Cholly rapes Pecola and impregnates her. Ironically, the love that he perhaps wanted to show makes her first experience of sex* as painful and devastating as his own.

As Pecola's pregnancy becomes evident, she is expelled from school and scorned by the community. More important, she falls farther and farther from reality. By the fall, Pecola's baby is dead. With the death of her baby, Pecola lapses into madness and develops an imaginary friend who, she exclaims, loves her and her blue eyes.

Critically, Morrison's story reflects several important themes and concepts. The setting of the text in Lorain, Ohio, the place of Morrison's own coming-of-age, gives the reader a backdrop for the pattern of racism and discrimination in America of the 1940s that came to a head in America in the 1960s and 1970s. She reminds the reader that places other than the South were mired in the same racial prejudices, despite being north of the Mason-Dixon Line. Several critics make this connection to the American tradition and Toni Morrison's critique of the traditional values within. Morrison seems to make this connection herself by juxtaposing the concept of the American Dream and American patriotism fostered during U.S. participation in World War II with the hypocritical treatment of the Black community at the war's end. The nationalistic ethic that held the nation together through the bombing of Pearl Harbor in 1941 and the entrance of America into the war shortly thereafter becomes a vague memory* by the 1960s. In fact, the disenfranchisement of millions of Black Americans perpetuated through the 1940s and 1950s, resulting in the activities and events of the 1960s, seems to contextualize the many thematic emphases of this story. While many Black Americans fought for the nation in World War II and helped ensure America's victory, these same persons were discriminated against, rejected, and reviled in their homeland. Claudia's recollection of the events of that fateful year of 1941 is poignant when considering the effect of those racial tensions on her and other people of color, not only as children but also as adults fighting in the Civil Rights movement of the 1960s and 1970s. She does not speak of the war abroad but of the war at home. *The Bluest Eye*, in essence, addresses this tension but, through Claudia, also speaks to the hope of being able to exist regardless of the hatred and bigotry of others. The events of Pecola's story culminate in this nationalistic climate of 1941, and just as her dream is a perverted one, so, too, is this ethic.

On a deeper level, however, the novel, though devoid of white persons as major characters, incorporates whiteness not only as an idea but also as a character. Thus, while there are no visible white characters that come to frame the story's tale, their presence is immediately felt by readers. In essence, all of the characters are struggling against whiteness and trying to accept their Blackness. They define acceptance, however, by the tenets of a white world and, ultimately, many of the characters lose themselves. Pecola has a fascination not only with blue eyes but also with the baby-doll stature of the child star Shirley Temple and the Shirley Temple cup in the MacTeer home. Pecola gorges herself on white milk and drinks the milk only from the Shirley Temple cup so that she can look upon those blue eyes and blond curls and, for a moment, "be" like Shirley and be loved. Claudia's childhood love-hate relationship with white baby dolls and Shirley Temple, icons of whiteness and innocence, stems from the presence of whiteness in her life as well. But Claudia, unlike Pecola, comes to hate white baby dolls and Shirley Temple for the very images of whiteness they possess. She questions why beauty has to be white. More important, by questioning whiteness she questions whiteness's abuses of Blackness. Whiteness is both hated and revered. Some of the characters believe that whiteness brings privilege, and with privilege comes the acceptance of and, more important, the love of self. Claudia is able to understand that love is color-blind, and learning how to love yourself is what is most important in learning how to "be" despite the world's attempt to deny that you exist. Pecola (and all little Black girls like her) searches for the love that she is denied by the world, but finding that love means learning to love herself.

Scholars cite institutional racism and its psychological and physical effects on African Americans and the African American community as another predominant theme. While the Dick and Jane story never mentions the skin color of its characters, the behavior and activities of the characters force many readers to assume that they are white. Whiteness, then, becomes synonymous with beauty and love. Rosemary Villanucci, the neighbor of Claudia, Frieda, and Pecola, though Italian, has white skin, and thus white privilege and "love" associated with that skin. Rosemary's ethnicity, however, speaks something other than the privilege of whiteness that she enjoys. Maureen Peal is a young Black girl, but her light skin, in the minds of the Black community, makes her closer to white than Black and closer to the world of privilege. Thus, even the appearance of whiteness lays claim to privilege. Ironically, however, this appearance leads to ambivalence because it reminds those who cannot pass of their inability to find the acceptance they desire. Color, then, is not just a barrier between different racial groups; color is a barrier within the races as well. Morrison's text not only calls on the white world to consider how they *love*, but on the Black race* to consider what they *call* love.

While the story is a struggle for being African American against the larger American tradition of institutionalized racism, it also uncovers what some scholars have called the identity* of the Black female or the Black female self. The world consumes Pecola. Claudia, however, lives to tell the pains of her existence and to rise above them. She learns that beauty and love are found only through self-acceptance, and once she accepts herself, she finds the love she needs. Both characters reflect the difficulties that confront Black women and the obvious force that threatens them—racism—but they also speak to other intersecting oppressions, like class and gender, that serve as additional, crippling forces. The characters equate acceptance with love in the story. For Black females, by nature of both color and sex, acceptance is further complicated. Pecola and all the members of her family feel uglier than, in reality, they are because they feel outside of the community. The storefront is out of place with the other dwellings in Lorain and marks the family as members of the lower class. Class, like race, breeds acceptance. The MacTeers, though not rich by any stretch of the imagination, possess membership in the higher class and garner acceptance through that membership. The Breedloves' lower-class status garners them pity and disdain.

Yet, within this class story, women are further distanced from self-actualization by virtue of a world that views their worth in terms of the function of their reproductive organs. Pecola's, Claudia's, and Frieda's lives are marked not only by their social experiences with the world but also by their sexual ones—particularly Pecola's sexual experiences. Readers mark the maturation of the girls in the story through Pecola's first menstruation, her rape, her dealings with the prostitutes*, and her danger at the hands Soaphead Church*, a pedophile. Pecola's life becomes marked by her sex, as do the lives of all of the female characters in the text. The prostitutes, for instance, are working girls who earn their living and ascend to their middle-class standing by selling their bodies to men for money. While the community at large rejects them, they entertain many of the "higher" members of that same community in their beds. In addition, the prostitutes are the only people in the story who make Pecola feel beautiful and loved, because they offer the only place where she finds acceptance. With the prostitutes, Pecola is no longer the ugly, too-Black girl who wants blue eyes; she is simply a young girl wanting to belong, and with the prostitutes, she belongs because she learns to accept herself.

So the story comes full circle and dramatizes the unspeakable pain of what it is to be outside of what is accepted. As simple as the lesson may be, beauty and love come from within. Finding the truth of one's own beauty is the only way to avoid the madness, the loss of self. In essence, the text ends as it begins, presenting an alternate story of being, but in this case, that being is not Pecola's, or even Claudia's, but a reminder of the choice we have as individuals to succumb to the madness of racism or to overcome it. *See also* Approaches to Morrison's Work: Feminist/Black Feminist; Motherhood; South, Influence of; Shame; Trauma.

Reference: Elizabeth T. Hayes, "'Like Seeing You Buried': Persephone in *The Bluest Eye, Their Eyes Were Watching God,* and *The Color Purple,*" in *Images of Persephone: Feminist Readings in Western Literature* (1994).

Gena Elise Chandler

## Bodwins, the (*Beloved*)

The Bodwins are a brother and sister who live in Cincinnati and are long-time acquaintances of Mr. Garner*, the onetime owner of Sweet Home* and of the Blacks who live there. The Bodwins lease Baby Suggs* the house at 124 Bluestone Road* when Garner first delivers her to Ohio in 1848. Quakers and abolitionists, the Bodwins are opposed to slavery* in any form. Mr. Bodwin intervenes to save Sethe Suggs* from the gallows after she commits infanticide*. Toward the end of the novel, at Janey Wagon's urging, the Bodwins hire Denver Suggs*. Mr. Bodwin is almost assaulted by Sethe when he arrives at 124 Bluestone Road during the communal exorcism of Beloved*. *See also Beloved.*

Lovalerie King

## Bottom, the (*Sula*)

African American neighborhood in Medallion, Ohio*. Given its name as a "nigger joke" by a white farmer who tricks his slave into performing some difficult chores in exchange for freedom and a piece of land, "the Bottom" is actually located in the hilly, hard-to-farm section of the town. *See also Sula.*

Douglas Taylor

## Breedlove, Cholly (*The Bluest Eye*)

Cholly Breedlove, Pecola's* father, appears at the novel's opening to be the villain. His rape and impregnation of Pecola is the first and lasting memory* that readers receive. However, the complexity of Cholly's character does not stop with this one violent act. Cholly's adult behavior, like that of all of the novel's characters, has roots in a painful childhood. As a young boy, Cholly's first sexual experience was shared under the glaring lights and eyes of three white hunters who stumbled upon Cholly and then forced him to finish the sex* act under their watchful glare. Since that day, Cholly has struck back at the white world that humiliated him. The powerlessness that he experienced as a child, however, does not go away. While he is able to overpower his wife and his child physically, he still cannot overcome the white world and their perception of him as an ignorant, Black brute. His helplessness in the white world manifests in violence* at home. Cholly's ugliness is in his helplessness and his choice to punish those around him for his own inadequacies. His rape of Pecola is just as psychologically violent as it is physically violent, for in his attempt to "breed love" from the world that loathes him, he kills love in the world that needs him. *See also Bluest Eye, The.*

Gena Elise Chandler

## Breedlove, Pauline (*The Bluest Eye*)

Pauline "Polly" Breedlove is the mother of Pecola* and, in a sense, foreshadows Pecola's downfall. "The sins of the mother," it seems, fall on the child and eventually come to destroy her. Pauline's childhood fears, we learn, are much like her daughter Pecola's. A loss of a front tooth and the piercing of her foot with a nail in childhood left Pauline with irreversible scars, threats to her physical beauty, and a fear that she would not gain acceptance. While Pauline's mother attempted to ensure her acceptance in the world, Pauline destroys Pecola's chance for acceptance. In fact, Pauline's lack of acceptance of herself leads her to fall victim to the white world's conception of beauty. She becomes enamored with white movie starlets and resigns herself to ugliness in the face of what is simply her difference. Despite others', including Cholly's, attempts to make her believe that she is beautiful, she chooses to see only ugliness. Transferring her desires to reflect the white images on the screen, she finds pride in cleaning for and taking care of a white family and their child in the Lorain community, but fails to see how she has succumbed to the same racism and oppression that she has been blindly fighting against. Even her name, Polly, reflects her oppression, as she is reduced to a diminutive name given to her by the white child she raises. Her assigning of beauty to race* and social class leaves her feeling ugly and rejected in her own community and yearning for acceptance of herself as she attempts to "breed love" instead of accepting love from those around her. *See also Bluest Eye, The.*

Gena Elise Chandler

## Breedlove, Pecola (*The Bluest Eye*)

Eleven-year-old Pecola Breedlove functions as *The Bluest Eye*'s protagonist. In addition, she comes to signify the novel's central themes and to illustrate how racism can distort and destroy the self. Pecola believes that she can be accepted, and thus loved, only if she has blue eyes. The blue eyes in the text are synonymous with whiteness*, and since Pecola has never found acceptance as a young Black girl, she turns to the only expression of love she has seen: the blond-haired, blue-eyed characteristics of whiteness. Pecola also equates her lack of love with her outward appearance, and thus decides that she is cloaked in ugliness. She sees that ugliness in her Blackness and the brown eyes and features that accompany it, and believes that she can "breed love," as her surname suggests, if she has the things the ones who are loved, the little white children, possess. All she needs are the seeds to grow what was not given to her at birth, to create what was denied her. Pecola misunderstands the problems of accepting these white conceptions of beauty and attempting to find acceptance without when she has not found acceptance within. More important, Pecola's childhood naiveté prevents her from understanding that the blue eyes she covets will never disguise the ugliness of an outside world that senselessly assigns acceptance on the basis of race*.

More painful than Pecola's inability to accept herself is the complicity of her community* in fostering her lack of acceptance, continuously reflecting images of white beauty. All around her, these are the images that people love and admire. There is no positive reinforcement at home telling Pecola that she is just as beautiful and loved as those images, so she seeks to breed the love that she lacks and desires. The rape by her father further compounds her misconception of love. All she truly wants is love and acceptance, and the first place she looks for them is in her home\*. The lack of acceptance and love at home leads her to look for alternative ways and places to receive what she is lacking. When her father rapes and impregnates her, he not only confirms what she views as a lack of love and acceptance, but also ensures that she will feel unloved and unaccepted by the world. The death of her baby, born prematurely, signifies the death of a chance, in essence, for the Black baby. Instead of breeding love, Pecola succeeds in breeding a child of anger and a world of hate. *See also Bluest Eye, The.*

Gena Elise Chandler

## Brother (*Beloved*)

"Brother" is the name given to a giant sycamore tree at Sweet Home\*. The enslaved men at Sweet Home lie under the tree during episodes of male bonding. Brother is a highly symbolic aspect of Paul D's\* meditation on manhood. An African parallel to the role of the giant sycamore can be found in the role of the giant baobab tree under which men in some cultures gathered to make decisions. *See also Beloved.*

Lovalerie King

# C

### Cato, Billie Delia (*Paradise*)

The light-skinned daughter of Patricia Best Cato* and Billy Cato. Although still a virgin in her twenties, Billie Delia has a reputation for sexual promiscuity because at the age of three, she removed her underwear on Main Street one Sunday morning in order to feel the movement of Hard Goods, a horse, against her skin. Having taken refuge at the Convent* after her mother hits her on the head with an iron, Billie Delia is one of the few who befriend the Convent women and is the only character who is not puzzled by their disappearance; she believes the women have left only to return prepared for a battle with Ruby, Oklahoma*, with men, and with all the forces that had haunted them. *See also Paradise.*

Julie Cary Nerad

### Cato, Patricia Best (*Paradise*)

Title character of one of *Paradise*'s nine sections and the daughter of Roger Best and a not-from-Ruby woman light enough to pass as white, Patricia is Ruby, Oklahoma's* light-skinned schoolteacher and unofficial town historian. Distinctly aware of Ruby's inverse color hierarchy (the Black-as-8-rock people disdain those of lighter skin), Pat is discontent with both her own place, and her light-skinned daughter's in the community*, and ultimately destroys her notebooks on Ruby's history* in an attempt to save herself from its oppression. *See also Paradise*.

Julie Cary Nerad

## Chicken Little (*Sula*)

Little boy who slips from Sula Peace's* hands into a river, and drowns. Chicken Little is later found by a white bargeman, returned to the Bottom*, and given a proper burial. Sula and Nel Wright* never admit the role they played in Chicken Little's accidental drowning. *See also Sula*.

Douglas Taylor

## Children

African American children were an integral part of the fight for civil rights. Along with their elders they have borne the albatross of racism. Many lived to tell their stories of courage and strength during a time of national crisis. Ruby Nell Bridges, founder of the Ruby Bridges Foundation, at the age of six integrated the William Frantz Elementary School in New Orleans in 1960. Yolanda, Martin, Dexter, and Bernice King; Attilah, Qubilah, Ilyasah, Gamilah, Malikah, and Malaak Shabazz; Darrell Kenyatta, Reena and James van Dyke Evers—all these children bore up under the assassinations of their fathers. The Shabazz and Evers children witnessed the horror firsthand. Other children, including Emmett Till and four little Sunday school girls—Denise McNair, Cynthia Wesley, Addie Mae Collins, and Carol Robertson—were lynched and murdered, respectively, by white supremacists.

Within the vortex of racial hatred, bigotry, and divides between rich and poor, the African American child became either a witness to or a target of violence* in the dominant culture. In her novels, however, Toni Morrison explores the plight of the African American child within the African American community*. In various works Morrison asks: What intraracial dynamics has the African American child had to bear within its own community? Does s/he survive? If so, how? What is "home"* for the African American child when its own community is in chaos? Are there any happy children in the African American community, and if so, how is happiness defined and how is it maintained?

What is interesting about Morrison's children is that they cannot completely articulate what is happening to them. There are struggles—psychic ones—that compel characters to carry traumatic events which are beyond their control as childhood secrets, as Sula Peace* and Nel Wright* do; to come to terms with mothers whose choices can even *name* you in a community, as in Milkman Dead's* case; to journey from the afterlife to the present in order to make some sense of being murdered by your mother; and to come to terms with adultery and what that means when your "indiscretion" cannot find a seat at the table of girl talk, as Dorcas Manfred* realizes. Morrison's children must possess an inner wisdom to buffer them against the ideologies of racism and bigotry that are bigger and stronger than they are. If this wisdom is arrested, we see the total destruction of the child.

Morrison's first novel, *The Bluest Eye**, is a testament to this arrest of wisdom and lack of inner strength. Pecola Breedlove* is a Black child who yearns for blue eyes. From her birth, Pecola is pronounced ugly by her mother. Blue eyes, Pecola believes, will not only make her beautiful, but these particular organs of sight will bring her acceptance and love. Thus begins her journey to find someone who will give her blue eyes. The MacTeers, school, Geraldine's household, Pauline* and Cholly Breedlove*, the prostitutes* (Poland, China, and Miss Marie) and the church are some of the people and institutions that Pecola unconsciously consults for acceptance. Pecola's position as "the ugly one" in her Black community practically gives other children carte blanche to cast her about without any thought of punishment. Maureen Peale can dare to drop her façade and taunt Pecola; the boys on the playground can freely encircle Pecola and push her around; and Louis can get away with the lie that Pecola harmed the black cat. Interestingly, because Pecola's looks signify to Geraldine, Louis's mother, the Southern ugliness from which she escaped, it is easy for her to believe that Pecola is the culprit. In the end, Pecola is raped by her drunken father and further abused at the hands of religious leader Soaphead Church*. Pecola disintegrates and descends into madness. The members of the community allow it to happen.

Nel and Sula are two child characters who have to live with the secret that one of them unwittingly caused the death of Chicken Little*, their childhood friend. In the novel *Sula**, the twelve-year-olds have participated in the taking of a life, no matter that it was an accident that happened innocently. Even though Chicken Little's fall is dismissed as an accidental drowning, the fact that Nel and Sula agree to make it a memory all their own casts a spell on the friendship. Boundaries are broken, and the relationship becomes fraught with conflict, assumptions, and misunderstandings. Moreoever, it is that summer which welds Nel and Sula into one entity. Therefore, sharing the secret of Chicken Little opens the door for *every* other thing to be shared. This is why the adult Sula feels no remorse in "stealing" Nel's husband because, essentially, Sula cannot steal what she already owns. That childhood secret is why Sula takes no thought for Nel and her love for Jude Greene*: Sula *is* Nel *is* Sula *is* Nel loving Jude. Within the confines of the nursing home, Nel comes to this realization. Her visit with Eva Peace*, Sula's grandmother, jars her memory of the Chicken Little incident. On the way home, Nel calls out to Sula and comes to appreciate that the two were joined in friendship in the very end.

In *Song of Solomon**, Ruth Dead* nurses her son beyond normative time in the privacy of her own home, but is discovered by a passing neighbor who verbally thrusts Ruth's furtive gesture into the street of the neighborhood. Her son, thereafter nicknamed Milkman, must negotiate within a community that knows his mother's secret; fortunately, he finds solace in the wisdom of Pilate Dead*, his aunt. Ultimately Milkman Dead literally disinters his own name in the quest for the truth behind the bag of bones, literally using the songs of nursery-rhyming children.

On one level, Morrison's *Jazz** is a novel that deals with the process of reassembling the self once it is torn from the land of the South* and placed on the concrete sidewalks of the North. Joe* and Violet Trace* are people of the agricultural South who migrate north, and we see their psychological struggle to fit themselves into an environment far removed from their Southern roots. On another level, *Jazz* bows to the genre of Black popular romance, and it is within this framework that Morrison treats teenage love. Dorcas, Joe Trace's teenage lover, removes herself from the relationship because its secrecy and constraints prohibit her from sharing the details with her peers. She chooses Acton*, even though he is no good for her, because she is able to gossip about this relationship. This kind of dialogue creates a bond among girlfriends; it allows the peer group to take sides and develop loyalties (and betrayals). The Dorcas/Joe dyad alienates Dorcas from her peers as she realizes that adult love stifles her interaction with her world. The relationship cuts off communication with her generation, and aligns her with the world of Joe and Violet, which includes the elder couple's past. Dorcas, then, releases herself from the relationship with Joe to reintegrate herself into *her* time and *her* space—a time and space within which she can move without restraint.

In Morrison's *Beloved**, we experience the spiritual unrest of Beloved*, the crawlingalready? baby girl who is killed by her mother, an escaped slave named Sethe Suggs*. Even though Sethe's dreadful act is motivated by her desire to protect her children from being returned to slavery*, Beloved translates it as being abandoned and unloved. Beloved returns from the afterlife to insert herself into the present and into the memory of her sister, Denver Suggs*, and to become a part of her mother's life— to be loved. Beloved, too, is searching for her own stories, stories she hopes will tell her who she was before her life was taken. But her brothers, young Howard and Buglar*, are affected by the legacy as well. They are, literally, the almost-killed children who share, firsthand, the experience of their slain sibling. This psychological trauma* causes them to refuse Sethe's touch after her release from jail. Finally Howard and Buglar run away from the spite of 124 Bluestone Road*.

Morrison's treatment of children reminds us of the legacy that African American children have given to the world. Her novels order us to be cognizant of their presence, to honor them, and to take responsibility for their existence, because they are viable and visible testimony to the survival of the African American community.

Reference: Philip Page, *Dangerous Freedom: Fusion and Fragmentation in Toni Morrison's Novels* (1995).

Kwakiutl L. Dreher

## Childs, Jadine (*Tar Baby*)

One of the main protagonists of *Tar Baby*, Jadine is an orphan who is raised by her uncle and aunt, Sydney and Ondine Childs*, who work as butler and cook to Valerian Street*. A model and art history graduate student at the Sorbonne studying cloisonné, Jadine is Morrison's image of the new Black woman. She is more concerned with herself than with her community* or the past. Her relationship with Son* fails because she is not prepared to give up her independence, her lifestyle, or her values. Some consider her a race* traitor and the tar baby of the title, because she adheres to white cultural values. However, Morrison complicates this view in the conclusion when Jadine declines to marry her white boyfriend, Ryk, and returns to Paris to take on life on her own terms.

Jadine is one of Morrison's most complicated and conflicted characters. Some readers believe she has "sold out" and is a cautionary example of a Black woman out of touch with her "ancient properties." Son accuses her of embracing white values and culture. For him these white values include wanting to get ahead, participating in the consumer society, and remaining apart from "real" Black society. If Jadine rejects Black culture, it can also be said that Black culture rejects her. Son calls her a white girl, Marie-Therese Foucault* and Gideon refer to her as the "yalla," and the woman in yellow spits in her direction. Further, Jadine is tormented by nightmares of being attacked by representations of Black women; she dreams she is attacked by women's hats—a sign for Black women—and dreams of the Black women braggadociously showing her their breasts. Each dream focuses on Jadine's supposed lack of authenticity as a Black woman. If Jadine is not Black enough, according to these criteria, then what is she? Jadine's realization at the end of the novel that she is the tar responsible for holding herself together seems to be in line with

Morrison's previous articulation of individualistic Black female identity*
that she explored in *Sula** and *Song of Solomon**. *See also Tar Baby*.

Nicole N. Aljoe

## Childs, Sydney, and Ondine (*Tar Baby*)

Sydney and Ondine Childs, Jadine Childs's* aunt and uncle, also act as
her surrogate parents. They have been employed as Valerian Street's*
butler and cook for years. They are both Philadelphia Negroes and very
proud of this fact. The Philadelphia Negroes were the basis of an 1897
sociological study by the young W.E.B. DuBois. The first engaged study
of African American society, it became the foundation for his notion of
the "Talented Tenth," the cream of Black American society, that would
uplift the Black race*. Sydney and Ondine are disappointed that Jadine
does not feel obligated to them. Slighted by her return to Paris, they are
not confident that she will return to do her duty as a daughter by taking
care of them in their old age. *See also Tar Baby*.

Nicole N. Aljoe

## Christianity

*See* Spirituality.

## Church, Soaphead/Micah Elihue Whitcomb
## (*The Bluest Eye*)

Though appearing only briefly in *The Bluest Eye**, Soaphead Church
comes to symbolically represent the problems with loving in a racist
world. Soaphead is a self-proclaimed spiritualist and psychic who ministers to the people through false promises, and services his own needs
by molesting little girls. Soaphead considers both his ministry and his
molestations ordained by God; they are expressions of God's love
through him. Soaphead's own perversions illuminate the perversions of
a world driven by race* as a determinant of love. Just as readers find Soaphead's endeavors loathsome, so, too, they should find the world and its
preoccupation with race loathsome. Pecola Breedlove* comes to Soaphead with one request: blue eyes. Despite his earlier crimes against the
community* and his inability to see his ugliness, Soaphead genuinely
empathizes with Pecola because he knows she is in search of the thing
that all of the people he meets, including himself, desire—to be loved.
Soaphead himself is a product of inbreeding and incest, so the need in

Pecola is a need that Soaphead understands and shares. Yet like everyone else, Soaphead abuses Pecola's need and uses her desperation to help alleviate a nuisance in his own life. Pretending to cast a spell, Soaphead mixes a poison and directs Pecola to give the mixture, sprinkled on some meat, to a mangy dog that lies every day on his doorstep. He tells Pecola that the dog's behavior will be a sign that her wish has been granted. When Pecola gives the mixture to the dog, it convulses and dies. Pecola is horrified.

Her rape, compounded with Soaphead's trickery and the community's abuse, causes Pecola to spiral into madness. In her madness, however, Soaphead leaves her with the belief that she has blue eyes. In his own madness, he chastises God in a letter for not bestowing upon Pecola the one thing she desires and assigns a level of greatness to his own person in his ability to give her, and other little girls, the love that they want. Ultimately Soaphead becomes not just a critique of the world but a critique of how the world justifies who and what it loves. *See also Bluest Eye, The.*

Gena Elise Chandler

## Circe (*Song of Solomon*)

The apparition-like, ancient housekeeper and midwife who delivers both Macon Dead* and Pilate Dead*. She possesses supernatural powers and remains alive long after her former employers have died, determined to see their home literally disintegrate around her. Milkman Dead* seeks her out while on his journey to his father's Southern homeland. Circe is indispensable because she provides him with valuable information and stories about his father's family* and history. *See also Song of Solomon.*

Fiona Mills

## Clearing, The (*Beloved*)

The wooded area where Baby Suggs* preaches, urging her followers—members of the free Black community* and escaped slaves—to love themselves, since the dominant culture will not. *See also Beloved.*

Lovalerie King

## Community

Morrison's novels are about triumph and failure in African American communities. Morrison believes that her writing must be about the community and the individual, or it will not be about anything. Thus, her fiction is rooted in the folkways of the African American community. Her novels depict women gathered in kitchens talking together or doing each other's hair; they also show men gathering in pool halls, on the streets, and in barbershops.

Because of its role in creating ritual and determining appropriate behavior, community is as powerful a force in Morrison's novels as any of her characters. Throughout her fiction, Morrison stresses that one's identity* is dependent upon and inseparable from community, even if the community is seriously flawed. For example, since race* and gender are socially constructed, individual identity is inextricably linked to community. Morrison subverts traditional Western notions of self-identity as a reflection of an inner "essence." Instead, she challenges the notion of the self in her novels by creating representations of community which suggest that identity is constructed through social relations. In other words, one's identity is always dependent on community, no matter how dysfunctional the community may be. Self and community are inseparable in the African cosmos. In other words, the individual cannot exist apart from his/her relationships with others.

In Morrison's novels, the values of a community are the measuring stick for an individual's behaviors. Since the community embodies cultural memory*, individuals must be a part of it if they are to be whole. The concept of neighborhood as community through which the characters understand history* is an important one.

Morrison grew up in Lorain, Ohio*, where the entire community took responsibility for raising each child. Her upbringing explains why in her fiction her characters are generally better off when they are close to the community. Community affirms a culture's traditions and beliefs, and it shapes individual character. However, physical proximity to the community is less important than emotional attachment to it. Those characters in Morrison's novels who fail to internalize community, or who reject it, experience tragedy. In fact, Morrison often writes about the theme of the individual against the community. Her novels *The Bluest Eye**, *Sula**, *Beloved**, and *Paradise** all have this theme at their center.

Morrison's fiction contains outlaw or outsider figures. These important characters stand outside of the community and include Sethe Suggs* in *Beloved*, Soaphead Church* in *The Bluest Eye*, and Shadrack* and Sula Peace* in *Sula*. These novels depict families and individuals living on the edges of their communities. In *Beloved*, for example, Sethe lives on the edge of town, and the physical isolation leads to her isolation from the community on the day she kills her daughter. In *Song of Solomon*, Pilate Dead's* house is described as being located barely inside the boundary of the Black community. Such characters are "outdoors," meaning that they are in some way "exiled" from community and lack meaningful connections to it. The community often fears these people, even though it often is marginalized or dispossessed, as is the case in both *Sula* and *The Bluest Eye*. In fact, the community's condemnation of Sula and Pecola Breedlove*, both outsider figures, helps them to define themselves. However, while Sula can handle being "outdoors" because she herself encourages this status, Pecola cannot, and subsequently goes insane. Other characters, such as the prostitutes* in *The Bluest Eye*, find freedom in their outsider status.

Characters who are cut off from the community for whatever reason are frightening to the community, particularly when the community itself is marginalized from mainstream society. The community deals with its fear by treating the "exile" as a scapegoat. We see this in both *The Bluest Eye* and *Sula*. In turn, the isolation that the victims experience eventually may cause them to behave violently or cruelly (as Cholly Breedlove*, Sula, and Soaphead Church do) because of an inability to interact meaningfully with others.

Repeatedly in her fiction, Morrison shows the reader that those who cut themselves off from community experience a feeling of incompleteness, even when the community is not a positive force, as is the case in *Sula*, *Beloved*, and *Paradise*. When faced with small-minded and arrogant communities, individuals must choose between accepting this sense of "wholeness" offered by the community (even though it is restrictive) and rejecting the community in favor of freedom (even though doing so results in incompleteness).

*The Bluest Eye*, Morrison's first novel, is a realistic portrayal of a specific Black community at a specific time—Lorain, Ohio, in the 1940s. At the same time, it shows how the racism and poverty of the wider world have affected this community. This community is out of touch with its history, and that is part of their problem. They collectively experience a sense of dislocation because they are defining themselves by external (white) standards, instead of according to their own heritage. The difference between the white community and the Black community is dramatized by the Dick and Jane chapter headings. Having internalized the racism of the white community, the Black community destroys its weakest members. For example, in the section titled "Winter," Claudia MacTeer* relates the community's idolatry of Maureen Peale, because she is both light-skinned and middle-class. She then shows Maureen verbally attacking Pecola. When Cholly rapes his daughter, he is condemned by the community. However, they also speculate that Pecola must have done something to bring it on. In *The Bluest Eye*, the community treats Pecola badly because they recognize, guiltily, that they cannot live up to society's standard of beauty, either. Pecola becomes the African American community's scapegoat, just as the African American community is the scapegoat for white America.

When Claudia uses the word "we" in *The Bluest Eye*, she is not just referring to herself and her sister, Frieda*; she is simultaneously speaking for the specific community of Lorain, Ohio, and for the world community. All of these communities are complicit in Pecola's breakdown. It is the specific community that placed the Breedloves "outdoors" and looked down on them, and it is the larger community that places such emphasis on white standards of beauty.

In *Sula*, Morrison's focus on place (the Bottom*) demonstrates the ways in which Black communities form their own social structures and cultures. *Sula* concerns the life and death of the community of the Bottom. The novel explores what it takes for a community to be healthy and viable (and, by extension, what it takes to be a healthy individual).

In *Sula*, the community establishes the acceptable attitudes and conventions for the citizens of the Bottom. Nel Wright* and Sula are contrasts in their relationship to this community. Nel assimilates, defining herself according to community standards. Sula, however, rejects the community and defines herself against it.

Sula's rejection of her community is undermined by the novel's structure and narration. First, the novel begins and ends with the Bottom community and is threaded throughout by the stories of Shadrack, Nel, and the Peace family. This structure forces us to read Sula's story as part of the community's story. Ajax* and Sula exist as contrasts to the value the community places on ritual and tradition. However, the community needs Sula as a scapegoat; they unite against her when she rejects them. Despite rejecting the community, Sula is defined by and gets her identity from the community. Morrison does not describe the eighteen years Sula spent elsewhere because she does not exist outside of the Bottom (narratively). Sula, like Shadrack, may reject the community's ways, but both characters need to stay in it in order to exist.

Sula is different from the other characters in the Bottom because she chooses to leave the community. When other members have left, it has not been solely of their own volition. Shadrack and Plum* leave when they are drafted to serve in World War I, and Eva Peace* leaves after Boy-Boy abandons her so that she can find a way to support the family. When they return, each is somehow damaged; Shadrack and Plum suffer psychological damage, and Eva has lost her leg.

However, the community's acceptance of Shadrack and his "suicide day" shows that the African American community is willing to absorb its bizarre characters. A further example of this is Hannah's and Eva's acceptance of the insane, infirm, young, and old into the "big house." Sula's case is different because she refuses to be a part of the community. Still, the community finds a way to allow Sula to coexist with them when she returns. The novel shows that the community needs all of its members if it is to survive. The ending of the novel, which shows the Bottom changing significantly, suggests that such communities are in danger of being lost and, with them, their history and culture.

One of the primary themes in Morrison's fiction is the relationship between the individual and the community. Her third novel, *Song of Solomon**, follows a bildungsroman pattern, but Morrison gives much space (most of the first part of the novel) to Milkman's home* life before he leaves. The inclusion of such details of community underscores Morrison's belief in the community's influence on creating individual character.

Morrison's emphasis on and incorporation of folklore* into her novels further supports this theme, because folklore comes out of and expresses a particular community. In *Song of Solomon*, Milkman Dead achieves a sense of self and discovers his place in community only when he hears the legend of his great-grandfather who could fly. This folktale of the flying Africans* underscores the importance of community to African American identity, because it helps create a group identity.

In contrast to Milkman is Hagar Dead*, whose lack of meaningful connection to community has tragic consequences. If Hagar had a relationship with a community, she would have learned how to cope with being abandoned by her lover. Without such important knowledge, she goes mad and dies.

*Beloved* depicts a community in transition from slavery* to freedom, and the adjustments it will have to make in the process. The community's resentment of Baby Suggs*, for example, demonstrates their reluctance to make a commitment to one of the members, and is one of the legacies of slavery. The community's jealousy of Baby Suggs—for having a prosperous, relatively intact family*—is stronger than their loyalty, indicating slavery's negative impact on communities. As a direct result of this jealousy, they fail to warn Sethe that schoolteacher* has come after her. They also do not help her after she is arrested for the murder of the crawlingalready? baby. It is this betrayal that leads to Baby Suggs's own death.

Due to this lack of community support, Sethe, Denver Suggs*, and Beloved*—at one stage in their relationship—seem to mother each other. However, the same community that alienates Sethe eventually rescues her. Nineteen years after betraying her, the community collectively saves Sethe by driving away Beloved. In this action, the community represents the African American network of care and support.

*Paradise* focuses on the self-governing, all-Black community of Ruby, Oklahoma*. In the novel, Morrison exposes the problems of such "utopias." The Oven* functions as a symbol of the community of Ruby. It was constructed by the townspeople of Haven*, the first all–Black community. From Haven, some of the townspeople later left to start a new community and took the Oven with them. There is an ongoing generational debate about what the Oven's inscription supposedly says. All anyone knows for sure are the words "the Furrow of His Brow." The older generation believes it to say "By the Furrow of His Brow." Younger townspeople, however, think it reads either "Be the Furrow of His Brow" or "Beware the Furrow of His Brow." This debate symbolically represents the deep fissures that exist in this community.

Chiefly, the town ostracizes those whom they deem unworthy. Such "perfect" communities are doomed to fail, because all people are capable of sin and violence*. Morrison undermines the romantic views of communities of African Americans who are completely free of white oppression and governance. Even though Ruby is founded by those who have been excluded from white, mainstream society, the townspeople themselves are quite conservative and practice exclusion. They exclude those who are not dark black, for example. The novel shows two communities at war: the women of the Convent* and the town[smen] of Ruby. The attack on the Convent shows Black men excluding Black women.

Throughout the body of her fiction, Morrison portrays a variety of communities. In *The Bluest Eye* and *Sula*, the community fails the main characters. However, in *Song of Solomon*, the Southern community helps Milkman find his roots. Like *Paradise, Tar Baby** depicts a divided community that cannot provide adequate role models for the younger generation. The community in *Tar Baby* is divided on a number of fronts: gender (Son* v. Jadine Childs*), generation (Jadine v. Ondine Childs*), and class. In *Beloved*, the community initially betrays Sethe but eventually rescues her. *Jazz** portrays a political and artistic community. In all of the novels, the community acts as a kind of character, because it is crucial to the individual's existence. Through her novels, Morrison demonstrates her commitment to preserving Black communities; she communicates cultural values that are in danger of being lost. She maintains that we need stories and novels because they are the rituals by which we create community. *See also* Ancestor.

References: Susan Blake, "Folklore and Community in *Song of Solomon*," *MELUS* 7: 3 (Fall 1980); Toni Morrison, "Rootedness: The Ancestor as Foundation," in *Black Women Writers (1950–1980), ed Mari Evans* (1984); Sandi Russell, "It's OK to Say OK," in *Critical Essays on Toni Morrison*, ed. Nellie Y. McKay (1988).

                                                      Lisa Cade Wieland

## Conjure

"Conjure" is a term used in African American cultures to denote the magical and the mystical. It is often referred to as voodoo, hoodoo, and obeah. Conjure may also be an umbrella term used to identify various spiritual Africanisms in American culture; therefore, practices like the voodoo and Santeria religions may also be considered conjure. Voodoo and Santeria are synthesized religions that mix African religions with Catholicism; however, in the Americas, voodoo, hoodoo, obeah, rootworking, and conjure are sometimes used interchangeably. Add to this list the healing art of midwifery, and the word "conjure" takes on even more nuances. Western culture has often labeled the mysticism and healing rituals of voodoo as magic.

Frequently labeled magical realism*, Toni Morrison's works make use of conjure in various ways. Her narratives accept that magic is real. That women are born without navels, that grown men fly, and that murdered babies return from the dead full grown and willful are natural elements of Morrison's texts. She portrays practitioners of these African-rooted traditions (also known as rootworkers, conjurers, hoodoos and witches) in her fiction and, just as important, relies upon these ancient beliefs and practices to inform and construct her narratives. Three of Morrison's novels utilize conjure overtly: *Song of Solomon**, *Tar Baby**, and *Beloved**, *The Bluest Eye**, *Sula**, *Jazz**, and *Paradise** subtly make mention of conjurers and conjure, but do not use African spiritual elements as controlling images or influences in their texts.

Morrison's first novel, *The Bluest Eye*, mentions a conjurer named Soaphead Church*. He is a sad man who is named as conjurer by the community* but possesses no real magical or mystical powers. The tragic Pecola Breedlove* comes to him in the hope of receiving blue eyes. He performs no magical African ritual to heal Pecola. He only offers her a cruel solution to her problem. Soaphead commands her to feed an annoying neighborhood dog. She complies, not realizing she is feeding the dog poison. Soaphead tells Pecola that by following his command she will receive her blue eyes. This scene, which comes at the novel's conclusion, is the only reference to conjure in the text. Likewise, in *Sula* the only acknowledgments of conjure are the references to Sula* as a witch at the novel's conclusion and to Ajax's* mother as a conjure woman.

*Song of Solomon* offers clear examples of Morrison's reliance on conjure. This world is a world where words create magic, where words create power. As Milkman Dead* embraces his role of family* griot and discovers family secrets and power, he learns of his destiny and his capacity to love through his aunt, Pilate Dead*. Pilate is a true conjurer or conjure woman. Morrison gives Pilate a magical start in the world by describing her as being born without a navel. Pilate is also responsible for Milkman's conception. Macon* and Ruth Dead's* union, long passionless, is temporarily renewed when Pilate creates a mixture to be ingested by her brother Macon. It is Pilate who foresees the powerful coming of Milkman Dead. A woman who lives close to the earth, who births babies, and who believes in ghosts, Pilate is one of Morrison's most important conjurers.

The other important conjure element of *Song of Solomon* is its link to the oral tradition*. Morrison's use of the myth of the flying Africans* is embedded in the text as a real legacy of African magical power. The novel convinces its readers that it is possible to belong to a lost tribe of flying Africans, and it is possible to reclaim this heritage by remembering the power of their stories through language. This connection of power and magic with African American folklore* is also seen in *Tar Baby*. Using the classic African American folktale as a model, Morrison constructs the story of Jadine Childs* and Son*, two people in love but lost to each other. The setting of the novel, a fictional Caribbean island Morrison names Isle des Chevaliers*, is haunted by the ghosts of African horsemen who escaped enslavement and still roam the mountains. When their love affair ends, Son, who is a fugitive from the law after killing his wife, escapes into the mountains to join the ghost band of maroons. *Tar Baby* claims oral folklore, but also makes the imaginative, intangible world of ghosts as real as the African, New World history* it represents.

The most important of Morrison's texts to utilize conjure is *Beloved*. Morrison borrows from ancient African sources to create the ghost child Beloved*. The child called Beloved is hard to recognize because Morrison looks to West African Yoruba culture to help create this character. Even though *Beloved* is a novel about a woman's loss of her child to the brutality of slavery*, it is also about the loss of many enslaved mothers and children*. In the language of the Yoruba, Beloved is an *abiku*, a spirit child who is fated to a cycle of early death* and rebirth to the same mother. These spirits are said to be souls who are seeking to torment their parents by repeatedly returning. Usually a child who is stillborn or dies in infancy is referred to as an *abiku*. After the death of *abiku* children, parents frequently mark the bodies before burial, so if that child returns, it will be recognizable to the parents.

Morrison relies on the *abiku* in several ways. First, Sethe Suggs's* murdered daughter is "born" to the same mother, as signified by the breaking of Sethe's water when she first lays eyes on Beloved. Second, when Beloved emerges from the water, symbolic of amniotic fluid, she has the characteristics of an infant. Third, before killing Beloved, Sethe's fingernails scratch the child's head, and these marks appear on the forehead of the "adult" woman. Finally, the *abiku* appears to torment its parents for some sin. The child ghost wreaks havoc in the lives of the Suggs family, specifically Sethe. In African belief, torment of this nature happens when some crime against the gods or against the universe has been committed; therefore, the torment is punishment. Perhaps Sethe's sin is loving her children too much (enough to kill them), or perhaps it is her willful forgetting.

There are also some important conjurers in *Beloved*. Baby Suggs*, Sethe's mother-in-law, is a healer who assists her bruised and battered people through the harshness of slavery toward wholeness. Sethe's daughter Denver* is also portrayed as a conjurer, for it is she who sees her sister's ghost long before the other characters recognize her. Denver's magic is expressed in her power to see ghosts and in her ability to see the truth of Beloved's intentions clearly.

Finally, *Paradise*'s magic is not specifically related to the African spiritual tradition, but it does contain unique magical elements. *Paradise* is the story of the all-Black town of Ruby, Oklahoma*, and a band of emotionally wounded women who settle in a deserted convent there. These women become a community* of sorts and are perceived as an affront to the patriarchy. Consolata Sosa*, Mavis Albright*, Grace Gibson*, Pallas Truelove*, and Seneca* band together for their own survival and become ostracized as witches, much as Morrison's character Sula is. They are a group of tragic characters whose crimes range from murder to prostitution. The men of Ruby feel compelled to invade the Convent* and kill the women. They believe they have succeeded, only to find that the bodies have disappeared without a trace. Readers are left with the same sense of openness that appears at *Song of Solomon*'s conclusion: Did Milkman fly? How did these women survive such a brutal crime?

Morrison's use of conjure is multilayered and complex, with her influences ranging from Western myth to West African spirituality*. Her body of literature demonstrates a diverse knowledge of cultural traditions synthesized to create an important and ultimately unique contribution to the American canon. *See also* African Myth, Use of; Folklore; Trickster.

Kelly Norman Ellis

## Convent, The (*Paradise*)

Never an actual convent and seventeen miles from Ruby, Oklahoma*, the Convent was originally an embezzler's mansion, decorated throughout with sexually explicit objects: bathroom fixtures, doorknobs, and ashtrays shaped like genitalia; paintings of copulating couples or women in positions of subjugation; dark rooms whose original purposes are unknown. After having thrown one grand orgy in the not-quite-completed mansion, the embezzler was arrested, and the land was leased to the Catholic Church. The Sisters Devoted to Indians and Colored People came to the Convent in 1925 to establish Christ the King School for Native Girls, also known as Sisters of the Sacred Cross School for Arapaho Girls, and quickly destroyed, hid, or painted over the sexually explicit décor. By 1953, the school was closed, and only the aging Mother (Mary Magna*) and Consolata Sosa* stayed on, selling hot pepper jelly and pies to Ruby's citizens and occasional travelers. Beginning in 1968, when Mavis Albright* arrives, the Convent is transformed into a safe haven for wayward women. Regardless of what brings them to the Convent, the women stay without financial obligation or moral restriction. Although—or perhaps because—many of Ruby's citizens visit the Convent in times of trouble, the Convent and its women, who live free of patriarchal restrictions, become the scapegoat for Ruby's growing turbulence. In July 1976, nine of Ruby's leading men attack the Convent and presumably kill the five women living there. The men find signs of the women's lives that they cannot interpret: baby booties hanging above a new, but empty, crib; an unreadable letter written, they believe, in blood; and on walls and floor of the basement, signs and pictures drawn in paint and colored chalk. Although all five women are shot, when Ruby's mortician, Roger Best, returns to the Convent, there are no bodies and the women's car is missing. Later, when Reverend Richard Misner* and Anna Flood visit the Convent to see for themselves that the women are gone, they see, or rather feel, an opening in the air (he sees a door, she sees a window) that leads to some other place. *See also Paradise.*

Julie Cary Nerad

# D

### Dead, First Corinthians (*Song of Solomon*)

Daughter of Macon Dead*, and sister to Milkman Dead* and Magdalena Dead*. She is highly educated, having attending Bryn Mawr and a French university. However, she is overeducated and can find work only as a housekeeper for a poet. This is emblematic of the racism rampant in the Midwest. She eventually falls in love with Mr. Porter, a member of the Seven Days*. *See also Song of Solomon.*

Fiona Mills

### Dead, Hagar (*Song of Solomon*)

Granddaughter of Pilate Dead* and daughter of Reba Dead*; her love affair with Milkman Dead*, her cousin, lasts for seventeen years. Milkman takes advantage of her love and eventually breaks off their relationship with a casual Christmas card. This devastates her and prompts her to attempt to kill Milkman on a monthly basis. She eventually dies from a broken heart. *See also Song of Solomon.*

Fiona Mills

### Dead, Macon (*Song of Solomon*)

Technically named Macon Dead, II, after his father, Macon Dead, Sr., Macon, unlike his namesake, is concerned primarily with making money and owning things and people. Hence his being slumlord in which he rules tyrannically over poor, working-class African Americans. He married his wife, Ruth*, the daughter of a prominent Black doctor, as a means of joining the ranks of the Black middle class. His tyrannical ways extend into his mistreatment and abuse of his wife and his two daughters, Magdalena* and First Corinthians*. He is estranged from his sister Pilate* and her family. *See also Song of Solomon.*

Fiona Mills

## Dead, Magdalena (*Song of Solomon*)

Also called Lena. She is sister to Milkman Dead* and First Corinthians Dead*, and daughter of Macon Dead*. She is a timid, undeveloped woman who, in an isolated moment of fearless rage, vehemently castigates Milkman for informing their father about First Corinthians's relationship with Mr. Porter. *See also Song of Solomon.*

Fiona Mills

## Dead, Milkman (*Song of Solomon*)

The novel's unlikely protagonist. His actual name is Macon Dead III, but he was given the nickname "Milkman" by Freddie, the janitor, after Freddie witnessed Macon nursing at his mother's breast at the ripe old age of four. The novel opens with his birth, notable since he is the first Black child born in Mercy Hospital. The spoiled and selfish youngest child of Macon* and Ruth Dead*, he is estranged from the African American community* and out of touch with his cultural heritage. The novel centers on his eventual acquisition of a sense of his history* and his embrace of the Black community. *See also Song of Solomon.*

Fiona Mills

## Dead, Pilate (*Song of Solomon*)

Sister of Macon Dead*, and Milkman Dead's* aunt. Her most distinctive feature is her lack of a navel. She is the mother of Reba Dead* and grandmother of Hagar Dead*, Milkman's longtime lover. In contrast to her materialistic brother, Pilate is steeped in folklore* and the supernatural. Milkman becomes fascinated by her, much to his father's chagrin, and she is the key to Milkman's discovery and eventual embrace of his African American heritage. *See also Song of Solomon.*

Fiona Mills

## Dead, Reba (*Song of Solomon*)

Pilate Dead's* only child and mother of Hagar Dead*. She is a listless, unfocused woman, unlike her strong and impressive mother. She lives with Pilate. *See also Song of Solomon.*

Fiona Mills

## Dead, Ruth Foster (*Song of Solomon*)

Long-suffering, abused wife of Macon Dead* and mother of Milkman*, Magdalena*, and First Corinthians Dead*. As the daughter of the only Black doctor in town, Ruth enjoyed a life of relative wealth and luxury. She was unnaturally close to her father, as evidenced by the scene Macon witnessed upon her father's death*—Ruth lying prostrate and naked over her father, sucking on his dead fingers. She is a timid shell of a woman and allows Macon and her son to walk all over her. *See also Song of Solomon.*

Fiona Mills

## Death

The reality of death and the ways death affects African American communities haunt Toni Morrison's work. Death and dying are everywhere; slave murders, lynchings, and the deaths ever present in Black American experience (along with multiple specific deaths) grace each novel. But death is not only an inevitability of poverty and pain, something inflicted by white society; death is the truth, a part of life, the connection to ancestors*. Morrison's novels challenge readers to think about the relation between life and death, ensuring that even murders of one Black person by another invoke awareness of community* and the necessity for embracing truth and each other. Death haunts because it is a spiritual challenge, demanding responsibility to the world of meaning and the question of what God has in mind.

Death in Morrison's novels also helps to articulate the responsibility readers and characters, cast in a clearly African American and embodied spirituality*, bear: to life, love, and community. Facing death enables life and consciousness. There is no self-centered guilt in Morrison's characters, no retaliatory solution to deaths caused or experienced. Those who feel false guilt recover; those who cause death learn to live with their actions; those who watch others die respond with curiosity and/or grief. Death is not an ending; it doesn't resolve. Rather, as readers recognize the reality that death carries for people who can get killed simply for being Black, death enables thematic and structural celebration of Black life. As Morrison's characters' particular vulnerability to death comes through, so does an ability to value others while living with, understanding, and surviving the deaths that create the contexts of their lives.

*The Bluest Eye**, for example, tells the story of a young Black girl who wants Shirley Temple eyes. Death in the novel is at first the ultimate loss, something the young narrator Claudia MacTeer* comes to understand as a violation of nature caused by systemic racism: Pecola Breedlove's* baby (by her father) dies, and so do the marigolds, because nothing grows the year that Pecola grows too fast, too much, too soon. Death operates as a semistructural element, signaling racist oppression: in the backwardness of the telling through the seasons, in the madness of impossible identity* goals framed by the Dick and Jane story, in the disturbingly violent death of a cat. But death also becomes the negative positive theme—the realization that her mother's harsh care is about trying to keep Claudia alive. Love made visible by the proximity of death provides the location of the novel's transformative possibilities.

Morrison's second novel, *Sula**, also uses death thematically and structurally. Shadrack*, a returning World War I veteran, decides to manage death's unexpectedness by devoting one day to it every year. The rest of the novel, about a Black community and the friendship between women, shows death not just as the horrors of war but also, inevitably, as unpredictable accident, intention, and result of life's desires, fears, and disappointments. Chicken Little* dies when Sula spins him out over the water and their hands slip. Sula's mother, Hannah, dies after catching fire while canning. Hannah's mother sets her own son on fire. Shadrack's first successful National Suicide Day* results in death when townspeople go to kill the tunnel they are not allowed to build and are killed by its collapse. And Sula dies, leaving Nel Wright*. *Sula's* multiple deaths structure the truth of Medallion, Ohio's* lives while helping characters and readers realize that friendship and community matter.

*Song of Solomon** confronts death as a moral question, both by naming its principal character Milkman Dead* and by having two thematic death threads: Milkman's need to comprehend the losses of his past, and his friend Guitar Baines's* insistence that the killing of innocent Black people be met by the killing of innocent white people. The story opens with an insurance agent leaping to his death—except the word "death" does not appear. Robert Smith* believes he can fly. By the end of the novel, Milkman also can fly, like his ancestor Solomon*. Death, flying, and abandonment articulate the moral condition of Black American men's freedom while the background provides the motivations for such freedom in the deaths haunting Guitar's and Milkman's histories. As the novel explores the question of an appropriate response to the killing white culture, it presents others: what happens in death, when one is left or when one kills? The family* that killed Milkman's grandfather died out while the Dead children survived. Milkman's lover tried to kill him after he left her, and he has to learn that she died of lovelessness. Guitar tries to kill Milkman and kills Pilate Dead* instead. In *Song of Solomon*, facing death consciously becomes a means of flying, of outlasting pain and turning it to love, knowledge, and *responsible* freedom.

*Tar Baby** uses death as a motif framing questions of how and whether Black and white can live together. The novel begins on a Caribbean island with a young Black man trying to escape death (he has killed a white woman) and an old white man waiting for it. But there is also death within culture and in the imagination. When the novel describes Jadine Childs's* sealskin coat, it repeats over and over that ninety baby seals died for that coat. The older characters, Valerian Street* and his servants Ondine and Sydney Childs*, constantly say they are simply living until death. But Valerian Street lives with one kind of personal ghosts, such as his mother, who tells him about her abortions. Isle des Chevaliers* contains other ghosts—Black swamp women and blind horsemen—associated with the natural world. Neighboring Dominique holds dead plantations, an economic and social death brought by white colonists. Death as a phase of cultural history shows the economic source of racial conflict, while reminders of death illuminate the imperative that Jadine and Son* find a way to be born, to live and love in time, without killing their ancestors.

*Beloved** makes another point dramatically clear: when humans are property, everything is a matter of life and death. Even a "good" plantation becomes a killing field when its owner dies, for it leaves slaves. Unable to tolerate this condition, the five Black men and one woman of Sweet Home* risk their lives to escape. Some die, but while he burns, Sixo*, whose lover is carrying his child, laughs—he *will* live. Those who survive have to come to terms with Sixo's kind of death and the fact that they sometimes wished for their own. Sethe Suggs*, faced with the loss of life and freedom for her children*—for thus she sees slavery*—tries to kill them, succeeding only in slashing her toddler's throat. And yet the novel doesn't ask whether Sethe's act is legitimate so much as it explores the causes of the urge for death; why a mother would wrest death away from slaveholders; how this would affect her and her surviving children; and how any of them could continue living. Sethe and her community have to "rememory" stories that are literally unbearable. Thus the slain toddler becomes a living presence, ensuring that *Beloved* doesn't claim death as a simple means of freedom, but rather shows the consequences of appropriating death's power. Readers realize Beloved's* death is not a return to Nature but to history* and the trauma* of the Middle Passage. The rememory of this journey is a necessary step in the development of Beloved's, Sethe's, and their own consciousness.

*Jazz** also explores the question of why one Black person would kill another. Multiple references to horrible deaths and the highlighted death of a young girl emphasize the historical conditions of Black lives—the ever present pain of what had to be borne. Deaths also create the plot, presenting characters with revelatory moral and psychic challenges. *Jazz* wonders how, in the context of the Great Migration* and Harlem*, a good Black man might take a teenage lover and then kill her. The tale, however, is more about living with death than about the legitimacy of murder. *Jazz* most deeply probes how Joe* and Violet Trace*, Alice Manfred* (the aunt), and Felice* (her friend) confront Joe's shooting of Dorcas Manfred* (a reincarnation of Beloved); Violet's slashing of her dead face; and the fact the girl let herself die. As the novel moves beyond why and how, Dorcas's death, like Beloved's, forms a spiritual and communal challenge to consciousness.

Continuing Morrison's historical trilogy, *Paradise* again invokes the stark horror of child death. Mavis Albright* has managed to kill her twin babies by leaving them in a hot car; she now fears she will be killed by her husband and children. Yet death is neither a direct moral question nor a specific plot element; rather, it is a means of examining the two paradises in the novel: the all-Black, male-authorized town of Ruby, Oklahoma*, named after a young dead Black woman and fiercely protecting itself from white death; and the Convent*, an embezzler's mansion later converted to a school for Indian girls and now a refuge for lost women like Mavis, who transcend death differently. The sons of the town's founding fathers have not experienced a local death since they picked up and moved in mid-century; people have died only outside Ruby. In the Convent, Consolata Sosa* has the power to raise the dead, race* takes a different tone, and Mavis's children and the Mother (Mary Magna*) sometimes seem alive. When several of Ruby's men think they have killed the women, including one who is white, there are no bodies to be found. *Paradise*'s questions become not only what death and paradise are, but also what happens in the movement from one to the other, their relation in life, time, and beyond. There is no simple answer. With African American spiritual foundations, *Paradise*'s questions about death become a means of experiencing what living in the face of death really means—including how much hope it holds—for those who have experienced America's death-filled racial history. *See also* Flying Africans, Myth of; Violence.

Karen E. Waldron

## Denver, Amy (*Beloved*)

Amy Denver is the eighteen-year-old runaway daughter of a white indentured servant who comes upon Sethe Suggs* lying in a field following the latter's escape from Sweet Home*. Abused and exhausted, Sethe has all but resigned herself to death* when Amy happens along. Amy assists her both in getting to the Ohio River and in her delivery of her fourth child, a daughter whom Sethe names Denver*. Amy's strongest desire is to reach Boston, where she can acquire some velvet. Though a temporary bond between the two women—based on common fugitive status and gender—is established, the barrier of race* (and all that implies in the slaveholding South in 1855) remains. After helping Sethe, Amy departs for Boston, afraid to be caught in daylight with an escaped slave and her child. Amy is an excellent example of a Morrison character who defies easy categorization as absolutely good or absolutely evil. *See also Beloved.*

Lovalerie King

## Deweys, the (*Sula*)

Three little boys who are adopted by Eva Peace*. The boys are not blood relations, but because of their common name, they come to resemble each other so closely that people can no longer tell them apart. The Deweys stop growing at the height of four feet, and are dependent upon Eva and, later, Sula Peace* for their subsistence. *See also Sula.*

Douglas Taylor

## Dick and Jane Story, Use of

*See Bluest Eye, The.*

## Disability

Morrison's first five novels feature a striking cluster of women with physical disabilities or congenital anomalies, each of whom functions as a pariah figure. *The Bluest Eye* * has the crippled mother of Pecola Breedlove*, Pauline Breedlove*. *Sula* * has the one-legged Eva Peace* and her facially birth-marked daughter, Sula*. *Song of Solomon* * has Pilate Dead*, who is born without a navel. *Tar Baby* * has the blind washerwoman Marie-Therese Foucault*. *Beloved* * has the limping Baby Suggs*; the one-armed Nan, who is Sethe Suggs's* early caretaker; Sethe, who is marked with a severely scarred back; and Sethe's unnamed mother, whose body bears the brand of slavery* and whose mouth is permanently twisted from the frequent punishment of the bit. Each of these disabilities, these bodily markings or wounds, is the etching of history* onto the corporeal self; these women's bodies and spirits have been literally shaped by the institutions, injustices, and resonating, devastating consequences of racism and sexism. In figuring these women as disabled, Morrison suggests that their validation, power, and identity* derive from being literally different from the cultural norm. Their political and psychological resistance to the dominant racist, sexist, ableist order is manifest in bodies that refuse to comply with the oppressive and exclusionary standards that order demands. By connecting physical being with individual history and culture, these disabled women define the self in terms of its uniqueness rather than its conformity to the norm.

All these disabled women function similarly, except for Pauline Breedlove, whose opposition to the others clarifies Morrison's message. These women are excluded from the cultural center because they are disabled, Black, poor, female, and (sometimes) old; yet they are not diminished, victimized, or demoralized. Their disabilities and anomalies are the imprints and the judgments of social stigmatization—rejection, isolation, lowered expectations, poverty, exploitation, enslavement, murder, rape. Excluded from most privileged categories but empowered in the narrative, Morrison's pariah figures explore the potential for being and agency outside culturally sanctioned spaces. The prototype for them all is Eva Peace, Sula's matriarchal, amputee grandmother. Like all the pariah women, Eva—who may have sacrificed her leg for insurance money— literally constitutes herself with a free-ranging agency whose terms are tragically circumscribed by an adversarial social order. Eva's disability augments her power and dignity, inspiring awe and becoming a mark of superiority. Eva is a goddess/queen/creatrix character, rich with mythic allusions and proportions, even though she is by dominant standards just an old, Black, one-legged woman who runs a boardinghouse. An alternative Eve, she is a trickster* whose asymmetrical legs suggest presence in both the material and the supernatural worlds, and signal empowerment rather than inadequacy. Eva is a goddess of the flesh, grounded in physical existence—nurturing, eating, defecating, dying, and demands of earthly survival. Her enduring body is both her distinction and her ultimate resource.

In contrast to Eva, Morrison denies Pauline Breedlove the authority, dignity, or quasi-supernatural powers of Eva, Therese, or Pilate. Instead of enabling, Pauline devastates. By internalizing the dominant judgment of inferiority, Pauline betrays her family, racial community*, and self. Embracing the decree of ugly and the role of the ideal servant without question or defiance robs her of the powers and community that Morrison bestows on the other disabled women. Bereft of a sustaining community of other Black women, Pauline is seduced into self-loathing, squandering her potential by finding praise and satisfaction in keeping a rich white family's house and loving their blue-eyed, blond-haired girl instead of her own daughter. With no sources of resistance, Pauline accepts disability as imperfection and idealizes white physical beauty as virtue. These sins against Blackness, femaleness, and self destroy her daughter, Pecola. Pauline is Morrison's sympathetic study of the violations and perversions of potential perpetrated by racism, sexism, and ableism. What Morrison withholds from Pauline is one of her chief emblems of empowerment: the inclusive, woman-centered, Black home* where she might have reigned as a priestess of the flesh.

With these disabled women figures, Morrison rejects assimilation or condescending tolerance. Instead, she aligns these heroic pariah figures— accentuated by the cautionary tale of Pauline—with the paradigm of outsiderness, the disabled figure. In doing so, she redefines difference from the norm, transforming it from lack, loss, or exclusion into a form of mythic empowerment. *See also* Approaches to Morrison's Work: Feminist/Black Feminist; South, Influence of; Trauma; Violence.

References: Michelle Fine and Adrienne Asch, eds., *Women with Disabilities: Essays in Psychology, Culture, and Politics* (1988); Rosemarie Garland-Thomson, *Extraordinary Bodies: Figuring Physical Disability in American Culture and Literature* (1997); Susan Wendell, *The Rejected Body: Feminist Philosophical Reflections on Disability* (1996).

Rosemarie Garland-Thomson

## Divine (*Paradise*)

*See* Truelove, Pallas/Divine (*Paradise*).

## Domesticity

Until recently, most critical attention to domesticity as a central motif in the novel has ended with examination of the didactic "domestic novel" of the nineteenth century. Reflecting the ideology of separate spheres and woman's place as moral and spiritual guardian of her household, the nineteenth-century domestic novel idealized home* as a virtuous space set apart from the greedy, corrupt, and aggressive public realm. Like many of her twentieth-century counterparts, however, Toni Morrison represents home not as a place safe from the corrupting influences of the outside world, but as a complex and potentially dangerous space in its own right. In Morrison's fictional world, domestic tasks indeed have the potential to sustain life, convey love, and express joy and devotion. At the same time, however, home is a place vulnerable to corruption and violence* both from within and from without. Morrison represents home neither as utopia nor as dystopia, but as a space offering complex possibilities of salvation or ruin.

In all of Morrison's fiction, home is a clearly matriarchal space. In *The Bluest Eye**, her depiction of the MacTeer family's domestic life centers on the two female children*, Claudia* and Frieda*, and their efforts to understand the world around them by observing their mother and her friends as they care for children, share domestic chores, and gossip. Men live on the periphery of this almost exclusively female world; Claudia and Frieda's father receives only brief mention in the novel as he struggles grimly to keep the house warm during a bitter Ohio winter. In *Sula**, the Peace household includes several generations of women; men are transient and peripheral figures, absent husbands and fathers, hangers-on and drifters. Similarly, in *Song of Solomon**, Pilate*, Hagar*, and Reba Dead* share an exclusively female household that men find threatening and strange; they peer through the windows and sneak about at night in order to get a glimpse of this potent and mysterious world. In *Beloved**, when Sethe Suggs's* house is haunted by the ghost of her dead child, male characters respond helplessly. Stamp Paid, Sethe's loyal, longtime friend, literally stands on the doorstep of her home, unable to understand the voices and relationships within; her lover, Paul D*, flees in fear and horror. While Morrison does not villainize these ineffectual male characters—both Stamp Paid and Paul D are rendered sympathetically—she portrays them as clearly outside of and apart from the domestic lives of women.

Morrison's novels give detailed attention, and thus weight and importance, to domestic tasks as a way of sustaining a meaningful life. In *The Bluest Eye*, the MacTeers live just on the edge of poverty, and domestic ritual is all that preserves the household from ruin. Morrison does not sentimentalize either poverty or domestic practice; life for a poor Black family in Lorain, Ohio*, in 1941 is cold, dirty, and cruel, and Mrs. MacTeer's response to Claudia and Frieda's troubles often seems cruel as well. Because childhood illnesses bring unanticipated worry and expense, she reacts not with tenderness but with anger when one of the children comes home sick. Morrison nonetheless portrays the torturous treatments with liniments and foul-tasting medicines as a means of preserving life, saving children from the ever-present threat of illness and death*. In *Beloved*, similarly, Morrison uses domestic tasks as a way of holding family* and community* together. When Sethe escapes from slavery* and arrives at her mother-in-law's house in free Ohio, Morrison describes the scene as a domestic paradise in which Sethe is free, for the first time, to feed and care for her family. Baby Suggs's* home serves as a way station for escaped slaves and their families where she feeds and cares for the community, and Sethe enters joyfully into this domestic life. Even when the house is later haunted and Paul D urges her to leave, Sethe refuses to run again. In *Beloved*, therefore, freedom is largely defined in domestic terms.

In virtually all of Morrison's novels, domestic tasks serve not only as expressions of love and a means of physical sustenance, but also as potentially transformative and transcendent rituals. In Morrison's fictional world, women living without men often inhabit a liminal, mystical world outside of history* and time. In *The Bluest Eye*, Claudia and Frieda learn from overhearing the women's talk over their chores that domestic life is full of mysterious rituals and fraught with secret meanings to be deciphered. It is a communal life, shared primarily by women, whose collective responsibility is to sustain the lives of husbands and children. Morrison's lyrical description of the women's tasks as they snap beans, boil sheets, and perform the dozens of domestic rituals that sustain life, transforms those tasks into sacred rites. Similarly, in *Beloved*, Baby Suggs's caretaking is not merely physical, but also spiritual; she is not merely a mother figure to the community, but a preacher of healing and salvation. Morrison also elevates Sethe's brief period of domestic happiness to mythic status by limiting its length to the twenty-eight days of the moon's rotation around the earth and of a woman's menstrual cycle. Performing domestic tasks to preserve life is therefore not merely a physical, mundane practice, but a spiritual and transcendent one as well.

Domestic life in Morrison's work is not inherently spiritual or salvific, however; its saving qualities are vulnerable to corruption. Poverty and violence threaten domestic life in *The Bluest Eye*, as Morrison shows by juxtaposing the saving power of home for the MacTeer family with the dissolution of the Breedloves, a family living without community or domestic ritual. Through the degeneracy of the father, Cholly Breedlove*, his wife and children have ended up "outdoors"—a condition partly physical but mainly spiritual. Everything about the Breedloves' domestic life proclaims their despairing spiritual condition: they live in a bleak, abandoned storefront furnished with a couch bought new but delivered with a great tear across its back; their kitchen serves as a daily battleground for the parents' fights; and Pecola Breedlove*, sharing a bedroom with her parents, interprets the sounds of their lovemaking as "terrible." Pecola's mother, deprived of any hope for an ordered and sustaining domesticity in her own home, abandons caring for her own children and uses the home of her wealthy white employers to create the domestic order she craves. Morrison shows that a domesticity performed as servitude, and to the detriment of care for one's own children, lacks any spiritual dimension.

In several of Morrison's texts, a primary function of the home is to protect girl children from sexual violence. In *The Bluest Eye*, when Frieda MacTeer is assaulted by a male boarder, the MacTeers' response is fierce, loyal, and swift as they run the offender out of town with a shotgun.

Although even a loving home can therefore be vulnerable to infiltration by evil, the power of familial support preserves Frieda's life and saves her from the long-term ramifications of this violation. In a parallel scene, Morrison demonstrates Pecola Breedlove's utter lack of family cohesion or support when her father, a victim of poverty and sexual abuse himself, rapes and impregnates her. Rather than rushing to protect her daughter, Pauline Breedlove* beats her when she finds her collapsed on the floor. Morrison implicates not only the family here but the entire neglectful community of women who fail to intervene or care for Pecola, instead gossiping about her as the child deteriorates into madness.

Even as she illustrates the potential horrors of home life, however, Morrison also creates the possibility for redefining home. While Pecola is abused by her own family, she is lovingly embraced by a household of prostitutes* who live above the Breedloves and who offer Pecola far more charity and familial care than she receives in her own home. Although they are social outcasts, these women share a communal life of stories, conversation, and mutual care, and extend an almost maternal sympathy toward the essentially motherless Pecola. Similarly, in *Song of Solomon*, the female household of Pilate, Hagar, and Reba forms an alternative to the traditional but lifeless household of Macon Dead*, who has symbolically killed his family through his materialism, cruelty, and hatred. Although impoverished and disordered, Pilate's house offers Milkman a vision of a more spiritually meaningful life than his own affluent family can provide.

The most dramatic corruption of domestic life in all of Morrison's fiction occurs when mothers are driven to kill their own children. In *Sula*, for example, Eva Peace* burns her beloved son Plum* in his bed when he arrives home from World War I mentally broken and addicted to drugs. Morrison clearly defines Eva as a loving mother. Like *The Bluest Eye's* Mrs. MacTeer, however, she is not the nurturing, playful mother her children might have desired; rather, she shows her love for them simply by keeping them alive through dark years of poverty. When Plum's drug addiction and the effects of war destroy him mentally, Eva creeps into his room to hold and rock him as she weeps, then sets him on fire in his bed.

In Morrison's *Beloved*, the legacy of slavery is what makes home vulnerable to corruption. The clearest reminder of that potential for corruption is found in the ironically named Sweet Home*, the plantation where Sethe suffers horrific abuses, including the stealing of her mother's milk by the slave owners' nephews*. Morrison's neo-slave narrative* illustrates the horrors of slavery not so much for the individual as for families, and specifically for the mothers who tend them. The impetus that keeps Sethe alive during her horrific flight from Sweet Home is the need to get milk to her still-nursing baby. Her twenty-eight days of freedom are marked not only by the joys of communal life but also by the freedom to nurse and care for her children. When her former owner arrives with a slave catcher to recapture her and her children, Sethe tries to kill all four children but succeeds only in murdering her crawlingalready? daughter. Morrison casts this horrific violence as a desperate act of mother love, a slave mother ushering her child into the only safe place she could imagine. Rather than judging Sethe's action, Morrison judges the community that condemns and shuns Sethe for the next eighteen years. Only when the women of the community finally arrive to rescue Sethe from the ghost of the baby girl that has taken control of her house is the community redeemed.

While Morrison is thus an inheritor of the nineteenth-century domestic novel, establishing home as a matriarchal realm and ascribing values to domestic life that distinguish it from the external, public world, Morrison's portrait of domesticity is far less idealized and more complex than that of her predecessors. The values of caretaking, nurturing, and sustaining life are not uncomplicated or "natural" for her female characters; they must be cultivated, practiced, and protected fiercely. Feeding one's family in Morrison's text may mean being willing to cut off a leg for the insurance money; housekeeping may require a willingness to live with a vengeful ghost; keeping one's children safe may mean being willing to kill them. *See also* Motherhood; Spirituality.

References: Lori Askeland, "Remodeling the Model Home in *Uncle Tom's Cabin* and *Beloved*," *American Literature* 64: 4 (December 1992); Jeanette Batz Cooperman, *The Broom Closet: Secret Meanings of Domesticity in Postfeminist Novels by Louise Erdrich, Mary Gordon, Toni Morrison, Marge Piercy, Jane Smiley, and Amy Tan* (1999); Michael Hogan, "Built on the Ashes: The Fall of the House of Sutpen and the Rise of the House of Sethe," in *Unflinching Gaze: Morrison and Faulkner Re-Envisioned*, ed. Carol A. Kolmerton, Stephen M. Ross, and Judith Bryant Wittenberg (1997); Giavanna Munafo, "'No Sign of Life': Marble-Blue Eyes and Lakefront Houses in *The Bluest Eye*," *Lit: Literature Interpretation Theory* 6: 1–2 (April 1995).

Kristina K. Groover

### Dreaming Emmett

*Dreaming Emmett*, Toni Morrison's only play, premiered at the Marketplace Theatre in Albany, New York, on January 4, 1986. Commissioned by the New York State Writers Institute, the play was produced to commemorate the first nationwide celebration of Martin Luther King's birthday.

Unfortunately, no print or video version of the play exists for public viewing, and thus details about the drama must be drawn from a handful of newspaper accounts and reviews. Requests to secure a script from the playwright have been denied, and the play's producers—the Albany Capital Repertory Theatre—confirm the fact that, after the 1986 production, Morrison collected every record of the play and had it destroyed.

We do know that Morrison conceived of the play two years before she received her invitation from the Writers Institute. Her desire was to "see a collision of three or four levels of time through the eyes of one person who could come back to life and seek vengeance. Emmett Till became that person" (qtd. in Croyden 6H). As Till emerged as the centerpiece of the drama, however, Morrison did not attempt to write a historically accurate play. "I like to make up stuff," she told Margaret Croyden of the *New York Times.* "I take scraps, the landscapes of something that happened, and make up the rest: I'm not interested in documentaries. I'm not sticking to facts. What is interesting about the play is the contradiction of fact. *Dreaming Emmett* is really about that" (16). In a summary of the play Croyden, who interviewed Morrison a week before opening night, writes:

The characters and the action shift back and forth in time and place, and there is a play within a play. The nonlinear story involves an anonymous black boy who was murdered. In a dream state he suffers the pain of remembering his death* 30 years before. Seeking revenge and a place in history,* he summons up the perpetrators of his murder, as well as his family and friends, all to be characters in the dream. But his ghosts refuse to be controlled by his imagination; all see the past in their own way, as the boy doggedly searches for a meaning to his death and thereby his life. At one point he is challenged by a member of the audience, a black woman who rejects his dream and provokes a confrontation on sexual issues. (6H)

According to Stephen J. Whitfield, the confrontation that closes the play gives it a "feminist perspective" (119). Tamara, the Black woman in the audience who challenges Till, condemns the slain boy for "his attraction to white women and for his indifference to Black women" (120). As Whitfield notes, this condemnation is delivered in "a voice that compels recognition as Morrison's own" (120).

*Dreaming Emmett* received mixed reviews, but this alone does not account for Morrison's unwillingness to make a script or video available. Perhaps one day she will change her mind. Until then, one resists the temptation to speculate.

References: Margaret Croyden, "Toni Morrison Tries Her Hand at Playwriting," *New York Times* (December 29, 1985); Harlow Robinson, "Dreams of a Prophetic Past: Novelist Toni Morrison Tries Her Hand at

Playwriting," *American Theatre* 2 (January 1986); Stephen J. Whitfield, *Death in the Delta: The Story of Emmett Till* (1988).

Christopher Metress

## Dupres, Lone (*Paradise*)

Title character of one of *Paradise's** nine sections, and named "Lone" because she was found that way during the trip from Louisiana and Mississippi to Haven, Oklahoma*, Lone serves (after her adopted mother Fairy DuPres dies) as Ruby, Oklahoma's* only midwife until the hospital in Demby, the nearest town, ninety miles away, begins to admit Blacks. Lone, a Christian who also "practices," befriends Consolata Sosa* and teaches her the power of "stepping-in" to people to save them. While gathering medicinal herbs in the dark before the rains come, Lone overhears the men of Ruby planning to raid the Convent*. Convinced that the men mean no good, Lone is able to persuade some of Ruby's remaining citizens to go to the Convent to prevent the violence*. They arrive too late, in time to witness the death* of the women. *See also Paradise.*

Julie Cary Nerad

# E

## Editor, Morrison as

Toni Morrison's career as an editor began in the mid-1960s when she edited textbooks for a publishing house in Syracuse, New York. Later, she became a senior editor at Random House in New York City. Her move proved particularly fortuitous and timely; for almost two decades, she nurtured the careers of a number of Black American writers. The works she edited range in genre from fiction and poetry to autobiography and "how-to" books. In other manifestations of her career as an editor, she has collected and introduced two volumes of essays on social criticism, and she has reintroduced works by other Black writers, including James Baldwin, Toni Cade Bambara, and Huey P. Newton.

When Morrison became a senior editor at Random House (in 1965 or 1968, depending on the source), she was assigned almost exclusively to Black writers. Her significance in this capacity during what has come to be described as a new renaissance period in African American letters is evidenced by the following impressive list of fiction, poetry, and nonfiction published under her direction: Toni Cade Bambara, *Gorilla, My Love* (1972), *The Seabirds Are Still Alive* (1977), *The Salt Eaters* (1979), *Those Bones Are Not My Child* (1999); Wesley Brown, *Tragic Magic* (1978); Chinweizu, *West and the Rest of Us: White Predators, Black Slaves and the African Elite* (1975); Lucille Clifton, *Generations: A Memoir* (1976); Bill Cosby, *Bill Cosby's Personal Guide to Tennis Power* (1975); Angela Y. Davis, *Women, Race and Class* (1981); Henry Dumas, *Play Ebony, Play Ivory* (1974), *Jonoah and the Green Stone* (1976), *Rope of Wind and Other*

*Stories* (1979); Leon Forrest, *There is a Tree More Ancient Than Eden* (1973), *The Bloodworth Orphans* (1977), *Two Wings to Veil My Face* (1983); Middleton A. Harris et al., *The Black Book* (1974); James Haskins, *The Cotton Club* (1977); George Jackson, *Blood in My Eye* (1972); Gayl Jones, *Corregidora* (1975), *Eva's Man* (1975), *White Rat* (1977); Nettie Jones, *Fish Tales* (1984); June Jordan, *Things I Do in the Dark* (1977); Rudy Lombard, *Creole Feast [Master Chefs of New Orleans]* (1978); James A. McPherson, *Railroad: Trains and Train People in American Culture* (1976); Muhammad Ali, *The Greatest* (1975); John McCluskey, *Look What They Done to My Song* (1974); Huey P. Newton, *To Die for the People* (1972); Barbara Chase Ribaud, *From Memphis and Peking* (1974); Quincy Troupe, *Giant Talk: An Anthology of Third World Writings* (1975); and Ivan van Sertimer, *They Came Before Columbus* (1976).

The list is impressive in terms of sheer numbers, but more important in terms of the variety of genres and subgenres represented therein, and even more important in its inclusion of so many authors and texts of enduring significance and popularity. For example, Toni Cade Bambara's two most famous works of fiction are included: the short-story collection *Gorilla, My Love* (which has been reprinted many times), and *The Salt Eaters*, a novel Random House editors saw as experimental, but nevertheless brought Bambara the American Book Award, the Langston Hughes Society Award, a Medallion Award, and a Zora Neale Hurston Society Award. Bambara echoed earlier African American writers (including W.E.B. Du Bois) and joined the many voices of her contemporaries in her commitment to art that also served a social purpose. Certainly, one finds abundant evidence of Morrison's dynamic relationship with Bambara, and Gayl Jones as well, in the common themes, issues, and narrative strategies exhibited in their respective works of fiction. Morrison scholars are also well aware that the author/editor came across the story of Margaret Garner* while editing *The Black Book**. Garner became the model for Sethe Suggs*, the protagonist in the Pulitzer Prize-winning *Beloved**.

Thus, in some ways yet to be revealed, the benefits of Morrison's work as editor have perhaps been reciprocal. No doubt her experiences at Random House enhanced her personal and professional development as an author. It was during that time that Morrison completed and published her first four novels. She has since published three additional novels and garnered some of the most prestigious literary awards (including the Pulitzer and Nobel prizes) for her efforts—guaranteeing her place in world literary history. After leaving Random House in 1983, she was named Albert Schweitzer Professor of the Humanities at the State University of New York at Albany.

Morrison is currently Robert F. Goheen Professor of the Humanities at Princeton. Her successes in the literary world have allowed her to branch out into other areas of editing, including the collecting of two very well-received volumes of essays on social criticism. *Race-ing Justice, En-Gendering Power: Essays on Anita Hill, Clarence Thomas, and the Construction of Social Reality** features thought-provoking essays by some of America's foremost legal scholars, historians, and social critics, including A. Leon Higginbotham, Jr., Paula Giddings, Patricia J. Williams, Manning Marable, Homi K. Bhabha, Wahneema Lubiano, and Cornel West. Morrison's opening essay, "Friday on the Potomac," invokes two famous literary characters—Defoe's Friday from *Robinson Crusoe* and Melville's Babo from "Benito Cereno"—to talk about the charade and spectacle surrounding the Hill-Thomas hearings.

Another Morrison-edited collection, *Birth of a Nation' Hood: Gaze, Script, and Spectacle in the O.J. Simpson Case*, includes essays and commentary by Ishmael Reed, Kimberle Crenshaw, Ann duCille, and a number of scholars who contributed to the Hill-Thomas collection. Morrison's opening essay, "Dead Man Golfing," again invokes Melville's Babo to explore the question of how—in the white mind—a Black man can go from being an affable, self-effacing pet to a raving, murderous monster in a matter of moments. The essays in both volumes give voice to a variety of perspectives on America's continuing drama of racial politics, and on its continued fascination with matters concerning race* and sex*.

Finally, Morrison's outstanding credentials permit her to maintain the in-print status, or to bring back into print, important works by deceased writers whose enduring value in Black American (and American) culture is unquestioned. They include *James Baldwin: Collected Essays* (1998); *James Baldwin: Early Novels and Stories* (1998); Toni Cade Bambara's *Deep Sightings and Rescue Missions: Fiction, Essays, and Conversations* (1999); and *To Die for the People: The Writings of Huey P. Newton* (1995), a project for which Morrison initially served as editor in 1972. With the recent resurgence of interest in Baldwin's work (several new volumes of criticism have appeared in the past two years), it is perhaps more important than ever that the original works be readily available for new generations of scholars.

Morrison's role as editor continues to develop and expand alongside her remarkable and extraordinary literary career. The ripple effect of her presence at a major publishing house during such a significant historical moment will continue to be felt for a very long time. The enduring cultural significance of works by Ali, Bambara, Clifton, Dumas, Jones, Troupe, Jordan, McPherson, and so many of the other writers she nurtured is immeasurable. In 1996, she wrote the introduction for a new release of the Mark Twain classic, *The Adventures of Huckleberry Finn*. The new volume is based on Twain's recently discovered original manuscript, which contains passages not published in previous versions of the novel. Though it is usually overshadowed by her outstanding contributions in fiction and criticism, Morrison's powerful presence as an editor must not be underestimated when considering her significance as a literary figure.

Note: The list of Morrison-edited works at Random House was provided by Rene Boatman, assistant to Toni Morrison, Department of Humanities, Princeton University.

Lovalerie King

## Ella (*Beloved*)

Formerly enslaved woman who operated the Underground Railroad station that assisted Sethe Suggs* and her children to successfully arrive at 124 Bluestone Road*. She is a very practical person, knowledgeable about herbal medicines. She would not refer to herself as an intellectual, nor would she be inclined to rely solely on divine intervention for the answers to life's problems. Under slavery*, she had spent her puberty as the sex* object for a father and son who used her in such a way as to turn her permanently against sex. She measured life's atrocities against what they had done to her. The experience killed her desire to love or be loved. Love, according to Ella, was a disability*. She had once given birth to something she described as a pup, fathered by one of her abusers, and refused to nurse it. As much as she abhors Sethe's act, she is even more appalled when she learns that Sethe's dead child has come back and is abusing the mother. Ella leads a group of chanting and praying women to Sethe's house for the exorcism of Beloved*; she knocks Sethe down and effectively forestalls the latter's misdirected ice-pick attack on Mr. Bodwin*. *See also Beloved.*

Lovalerie King

## Eloe (*Tar Baby*)

Son's* hometown, an all-Black town that has not really changed since he left. The return to Eloe allows Son to get back in touch with his history* and his past. Eloe is the bedrock of Son's existence and the center of his consciousness. It is portrayed as the authentic home of Blacks. The fact that Jadine Childs* doesn't fit in despite the hospitality of Son's family* and friends is evidence of her inauthenticity. Unfortunately, the return to Eloe hastens the failure of Son and Jadine's relationship because it exposes the real and perceived differences between them. *See also Tar Baby.*

Nicole N. Aljoe

# F

## Fairly, Oklahoma (*Paradise*)

Fairly is the all-Black town that rejected as too poor and too Black the original nine families on their trek from Louisiana and Mississippi after the overthrow of Reconstruction governments. These families went on to establish first Haven, and later Ruby, and named their rejection at Fairly the "Disallowing." Each Christmas, Ruby, Oklahoma's*, school-children reenact a conflation of the Disallowing and Christ's birth story, representing their mission as holy and Haven, Oklahoma's*, forefathers as martyrs. The Disallowing solidifies the fierce pride of the original families already wounded by the inaccurate white depictions of Black political corruption during Reconstruction and establishes an intense distrust and disapproval of light-skinned Blacks. *See also Paradise.*

Julie Cary Nerad

## Family

Toni Morrison's fiction clearly portrays the importance of family and kinship in African American culture. Her novels depict a variety of family structures, many of them alternatives to the traditional nuclear family. The need for African Americans to create alternative family structures stems from the systematic destruction of families under the slave system. Slavery*, Morrison shows us in *Beloved**, is extremely hostile to families. Slavery separated parents from their children*; these parents were themselves legally unable to marry, and often were unable even to live together. Slavery separated families, sometimes deliberately, sometimes capriciously. Nonetheless, different alternative family units developed because the concept of family is so important. Family provides individuals with a sense of identity*, community*, and history*. The result is that throughout her novels, Morrison demonstrates to the reader that there are many ways to be a family, and shows characters seeking to create some sense of family within their communities.

The families represented in much of Morrison's fiction are matriarchal. Morrison's only short story, "Recitatif"*, is a perfect example. The two main characters, Twyla and Roberta, are each the only child of a single mother. *Sula* and *Beloved*, too, have at their centers matriarchal families. Despite the prevalence of matriarchal families in her fiction, Morrison does not present them as ideal. In fact, these matriarchal family structures are often at odds with the larger society. Such is the case in "Recitatif," in which the two girls meet at an orphanage where they have been placed because their mothers are "unfit." In *Sula*, the Peace family is viewed suspiciously by the community of the Bottom*. *Beloved* presents a more extreme example. The community first abandons Baby Suggs* and Sethe Suggs* by not telling them that schoolteacher* has come to bring the escaped slave Sethe back to the plantation. After Sethe murders her crawlingalready? daughter, the community ostracizes her and her other daughter, Denver Suggs*, ignoring 124 Bluestone Road*. In *Paradise*, the Convent* functions as a matriarchal pseudo family, with Consolata Sosa* at the head. The men of Ruby, Oklahoma*, suspicious of this all-female household, break into the Convent and murder the women.

Nevertheless, Morrison's characters find stability in kinship, even when the family is at odds with the larger society, or when individual family members are at odds with each other. For example, in *Sula*, Eva Peace*, Hannah, and Sula Peace* are a strong matrilinear network despite their conflicts with each other, as are Baby Suggs, Sethe, and Denver (and—during part of the novel—Beloved*) in *Beloved*. When the larger community ostracizes these families, they have each other to turn to for support.

Morrison's portrayal of several generations of women living together is related to her belief in the importance of the "ancestor* figure" in African American culture. Morrison's "ancestor figures" are primarily responsible for naming in the novels. They also pass down culture and language. Such "ancestor figures" abound in Morrison's fiction and include M'Dear in *The Bluest Eye**, Ajax's* "conjure* woman" mother and Eva in *Sula*, Pilate Dead* and Circe* in *Song of Solomon**, Marie-Therese Foucault*, the swamp-haunt in *Tar Baby**, Baby Suggs in *Beloved*, and Consolata in *Paradise*. These women serve as guides to history (particularly racial memory) and as storytellers. Stories are important to families because they create a sense of shared history.

Morrison's first novel, *The Bluest Eye*, investigates the ways that family values, gender, and community shape both individual and cultural identity. The novel contains different examples of family structures. While the Breedloves and the MacTeers represent "traditional" nuclear families, the prostitutes* who live above the Breedloves' storefront home are a type of pseudo family. Some of the families portrayed in the novel are more successful (functional) than others, and through the novel Morrison investigates what makes a successful family.

The Breedloves are the most obvious example of a dysfunctional family, and their name is highly ironic. The Breedlove family members do not love themselves or each other. Cholly Breedlove*, the father, does not know how to be a good parent, because his own father abandoned him and his mother died when he was young. Like Cholly, Pauline (Polly) Breedlove* also did not have a close family in her childhood. Pauline points out that she never had a house. Perhaps the most tragic aspect of Pecola Breedlove's* life is that she is, essentially, motherless. Her biological mother, Polly, does not nurture her, preferring instead to care for her employer's little blond daughter. Thus, Pecola does not have someone to teach her self-love and self-confidence. Seeking a maternal figure, Pecola visits the prostitutes' apartment regularly, but they are poor surrogate mothers. Pecola does not find many good examples of mothers in her community. Like Pauline Breedlove, Geraldine also cannot adequately love and nurture her son. The result is that the little boy assaults Pecola with his mother's cat, the only creature she does love.

While Claudia MacTeer*, the narrator, relates the horrors of Pecola's childhood, she also reveals that her own family life was less than ideal. The ideal family is represented by the "Dick and Jane" story that begins each section of the book. Claudia mentions the verbal attacks her parents made on them, such as the screaming fit her mother had when Pecola drinks all the milk. Claudia also points out that parents talk at them, and we see Mrs. MacTeer lose her patience on more than one occasion. Compared to the Breedloves, however, the MacTeers are clearly committed to their children. They appear to succeed in making a decent family life. For example, while Pauline slaps Pecola and chooses the white girl over her own daughter, Mrs. MacTeer takes Pecola in (even when doing so is financially difficult for the family). Furthermore, whereas Pecola's father rapes her, Mr. MacTeer nearly kills a boarder who sexually assaults his daughter Frieda*. While the MacTeers are not perfect, they have instilled a healthy sense of self in their daughters, who are able to resist the white baby-doll images constantly thrown at them. *The Bluest Eye* shows the effect of racism on Black families.

The male characters in Morrison's novels often contrast sharply with the strong maternal figures. These male characters generally fail as patriarchal figures. Cholly Breedlove is an obvious example of the failed patriarch whose actions place the family "outdoors" and who rapes his own daughter. Many of Morrison's mothers are overly indulgent of their sons, which results in infantilizing and emasculating them. This can be seen in *Sula*, in which the childish names given to the male characters—BoyBoy, Chicken Little*, Plum*, and Tar Baby*—reflect their childish behavior, such as leaving their families and becoming addicted to alcohol or drugs. The alternative to this "overmothering" is neglect, exemplified by Eva's treatment of the three "Deweys"*. The Deweys are three boys whom Eva takes in to raise. They are not brothers, yet Eva treats them as if they are indistinguishable; she gives them the same name. She provides for their material needs, as a mother would, but does not acknowledge their individuality. As a result, their physical and mental development are stunted and it becomes impossible to tell them apart.

In *Sula*, Morrison uses the rift created by Sula Peace's and Nel Wright's* life choices to represent the conflict between traditional marriage and family, on the one hand, and independence, on the other. Neither Sula nor Nel comes from "traditional" families. For one thing, their fathers are absent. Moreover, they do not have conventional relationships with their mothers. Sula's mother, Hannah, admits that she does not like her daughter. Sula overhears this comment and is hurt.

This rejection goes far in explaining why Sula later watches her mother burn to death* without offering help. Nel's mother, Helene Wright*, is not particularly "maternal" or nurturing, either. She forces Nel to try to change the shape of her nose so that it fits in with the idea of beauty she has gained from white society. Given that Sula and Nel lack supportive mothers, the strength of their friendship during their adolescent years can be explained as an attempt to "mother" one another. Sula's rejection of both her mother (Hannah) and her grandmother (Eva) leaves her without an "ancestor figure," which also leaves her without a center. When women deny their mothers in Morrison's novels, as they often do, the result is a loss of self or center.

*Song of Solomon* presents a family within the context of a hundred years of American history. In it, Morrison redirects her investigation of family, marriage, and community to focus on the perspective of African American men. The female characters are not as clearly drawn in this novel as in Morrison's other works.

Milkman Dead*, the main character in the novel, seeks to understand how his family history and his race affect him. Macon Dead* (Milkman's father) views family as merely another reflection of material wealth, and he is incapable of giving and receiving love. Milkman feels pressured to accept his father's love of ownership of things. Like his father, he views the family itself as an annoyance. He cannot distinguish between his mother and his sisters, for instance, and he relates to his mother with thoughtlessness and indifference. Eventually, however, Milkman rejects his father's perspective and comes to embrace spirituality* over material goods.

The epigraph to *Song of Solomon*, "The fathers may soar/And the children may know their names," points to the importance of knowing family (which Milkman Dead comes to understand when he goes to seek his forefathers). Although this conception of family seems to exclude females, mothers are important in this novel. This is seen in Pilate's obsession with carrying her name around with her, because she does not want to forget her connections to family, history, and tradition.

Morrison returns to the dynamics of mother-daughter relationships in *Tar Baby*. One of the central characters of the novel is Jadine Childs*, who is in the midst of an identity crisis. She must decide what direction her life should take, and is considering a marriage proposal from a white Frenchman. She escapes to the island where her aunt, Ondine Childs*, lives to sort out her life and seek Ondine's advice. Ondine tells her that a girl has to learn how to be a daughter before she can learn to be a woman. The situation illustrates Morrison's belief in the power of family and, in particular, the value of strong maternal relationships. Jadine's problem is that she has missed out on the important mother-daughter relationship, and it is too late for her, as a grown woman, to claim it. Furthermore, Ondine is not an adequate substitute, partly because she does not know her niece very well. Even though she believes strongly in the need for loving connections between parent and child, Ondine rejects Jadine because she and her husband, Sydney Childs*, fear she will not bury them when they die.

In *Beloved*, Morrison presents the argument that the greatest horror and tragedy of slavery is the way that it separates and destroys families. Morrison depicts slavery's attempt to subvert notions of family and kinship. Sethe, the central character, does not know or remember her own mother, having been raised by the plantation's wet nurse. Sethe's children do have a sense of family at Sweet Home* when Mr. Garner* runs it. However, when he dies and schoolteacher takes over, Sethe is brutally reminded that her children do not actually belong to her. The catalyst for Sethe's decision to escape Sweet Home is when schoolteacher's nephews* physically assault her and take from her breasts the milk that is supposed to be for her crawlingalready? baby. This act denies her daughter the nourishment she needs; perhaps more important, it sends Halle Suggs*, the father of her children, into madness.

Once Sethe escapes Sweet Home and unites with her children, she attempts to create a new family with her mother-in-law, Baby Suggs. However, slavery destroys this family unit, too. Sethe kills her baby daughter in order to prevent the slave catchers from returning her to Sweet Home. Baby Suggs dies soon after, and Sethe's older sons leave home as soon as they are old enough. Later, Sethe again attempts to construct an alternative family when Paul D Garner* returns and moves in with Sethe and Denver. Slavery is indirectly responsible for the failure of this quasi-traditional family, too. When Beloved (presumably the ghost of Sethe's dead daughter) shows up, she comes between Sethe and Paul D, first by sleeping with Paul D and then by demanding Sethe's undivided attention. However, once Beloved is driven off by the community, Paul D returns, and the novel indicates that he and Sethe will try again to construct some version of a family unit.

*Paradise* depicts the pseudo family created in the Convent. The Convent functions as a family unit, but the larger community of Ruby, Oklahoma, views this pseudo family as a threat to its stability. With *Paradise*, Morrison creates in the Convent yet another all-female version of family, with Consolata Sosa as the maternal figure. These women have, for the most part, come to the Convent seeking an alternative to their dysfunctional traditional families. The alternative offered in the Convent is more nurturing and successful than what they had known in the outside world. However, their success is threatening to the patriarchal, traditional structures valued by the men of Ruby. Partly in order to put down this threat, some of the men storm the Convent and murder its inhabitants.

After the Convent women are shot and killed, the novel shows them interacting with the families they left behind when they came to the Convent. Mavis Albright* has breakfast at a diner in New Jersey with her daughter Sally. Gigi (Grace Gibson*) visits her father, who is working on a chain gang in prison; Seneca* meets the woman who abandoned her (Jean) in a parking lot; and Pallas Truelove* and her baby "appear" to her mother. Consolata (who seems to be of the spirit world to begin with) is the only character who does not have such a meeting after her death.

In all of Morrison's fiction, families emerge as essential to an individual's sense of well-being and identity. When an individual is denied family, he or she instinctively creates alternatives to fill the need. If those alternatives fail, then the individual suffers from isolation, madness, and/or loss of identity. When an individual rejects his or her family, that individual also experiences grave consequences. As Morrison so aptly illustrates, one of the greatest crimes a person, society, or system can commit is to destroy a family. *See also* Motherhood.

Reference: Cynthia A. Davis, "Self, Society, and Myth in Toni Morrison's Fiction," *Contemporary Literature* 23 (Summer 1982).

Lisa Cade Wieland

# Faulkner, William, Influence of

Superficial connections are easy to make between William Faulkner and Toni Morrison: both won the Nobel Prize for literature; both examine the South as a focus of their work; Morrison even wrote part of her master's thesis on Faulkner. Faulkner's influence on Morrison would seem clear. Yet Morrison has claimed on several occasions that she does not resemble Faulkner, which is true in that she does not merely mimic her predecessor. Morrison revisits his works in tribute to his artistic genius, but also in combat with his cultural values and beliefs. Morrison's novels exist in an intertextual relationship with Faulkner's work that allows us to move beyond a linear notion of influence to a more complicated understanding of the interplay between the two authors' works.

Morrison revisits themes that obsessed Faulkner throughout his career, engaging them from the perspective of African American culture. Perhaps the most important theme they share focuses on the effects of race* on individual and communal identity*. Faulkner's novels portray racial identity and its formation in the crucible of social relations. *Light in August*, for example, presents Joe Christmas as a man of indeterminate racial identity. As a result, others assign him race based on visible markers such as skin color and then through knowledge of his possible ancestry. Joe internalizes this debate as well, alternately viewing himself as white, then Black. Race for Faulkner, then, is a fiction imposed upon individuals in social interaction, but it is a marker written on top of one's identity, which is already within a person. Morrison accepts race's fictional status as primary and critiques its use as a means of enforcing social separatism and inequality. Where Joe Christmas accepts his fate in an existential manner, Sethe Suggs* chooses to kill her child rather than let her endure another day in the dehumanizing life of a slave.

Morrison's strong stance against racism and its horrors further defines her against Faulkner's ambivalent stance. Raised in a Southern culture that strictly demarcated racial boundaries, Faulkner writes as an early twentieth-century white male immersed in racial turmoil that he notes but cannot avoid. He also marks how white males are at times unconscious of their own offenses and privileges. Morrison registers less the ignorance of specific deeds committed than the unawareness of a systemic racism in which one is—as white—complicit with a range of brutalities.

Racism finds a challenge from these authors in the specter of miscegenation, or mixed-race relations. Faulkner uses miscegenation as a means to explore racial prejudice in his community. *Absalom, Absalom!*, for example, figures miscegenation in the character of Charles Bon, a Black man who appears white. Bon represents the fear of tainted bloodlines that would undermine the strict Southern racial hierarchies, and thus he is murdered to prevent contamination. Similarly, Joe Christmas (*Light in August*) is unable to join any community* because of his dubious parentage. Though there is no strong evidence of mixed-blood parents, the mere possibility alienates Joe from everyone around him and leads to his lynching. Faulkner thus represents a culture obsessed with notions of skin color and its (in)visibility.

Morrison similarly examines the obsession with race in American culture, but from an African American viewpoint. *The Bluest Eye** depicts the African American community's preference for the lighter-skinned Maureen Peal (a product of miscegenation) over the darker Pecola Breedlove*, revealing the internalized racialist hierarchy based on visible skin color. *Jazz's** Golden Gray*, the product of a miscegenative union between a privileged white woman and a Black slave, allows Morrison to explore racial prejudice in a manner similar to Faulkner's. Both authors suggest that United States culture is always and already mixed, and that the horror miscegenation produces is one based on a false ideology of racial purity. Faulkner and Morrison use their mixed-blood characters to ask for recognition of the falsity of racial categories. Morrison and Faulkner argue through their novels that America is a nation of many bloods, and that the repression of that fact is what leads to the social problems between racial groups. Yet where Faulkner's mixed-blood characters never receive that acceptance (only death*), Morrison's characters do achieve some form of recognition: Lestroy (Hunter's Hunter*) accepts Golden Gray as a son, while Joe Trace* manages to reconcile with Violet Trace* and create his family* anew. Morrison rewrites Faulknerian tragedy, bringing a sense of hope through recognition and reconciliation.

As part of that recognition, Faulkner and Morrison sustain an engagement with history*. Both writers focus on the past's effects on the present, and both reveal the construction of the past through historical narrative. Yet Morrison extends Faulkner's revisionist historical perspective to include African American viewpoints in a more thoroughgoing fashion, particularly in terms of Black females. Whereas Clytie is silent in *Absalom, Absalom!*, Circe* speaks in *Song of Solomon**, relating the histories of Blacks and whites. Further, while an omniscient white male narrator dominates *Absalom, Absalom!*, Morrison's *Jazz* consciously moves beyond that authoritative voice to a more inclusive communal narration.

Content is not the only point of confluence for Faulkner and Morrison. Narrative experimentation is also a hallmark of both writers. With their multiple narrators, disjunctive time sequences, and nonlinear storytelling, Faulkner and Morrison explore the limits of narrative fiction as a means of representation and communication. Their craft speaks to an engagement with each other and with American letters regarding the art of fiction. In *The Sound and the Fury*, for example, Faulkner experiments with multiple narrative styles embodied in different narrators as a means of exploring consciousness and its relation to time. *Absalom, Absalom!* extends this experimentation, using letters, conversations, and embedded stories to present the narrative. All these formal modifications are present in Morrison's novels as well. *The Bluest Eye* uses multiple narrators to present Pecola's quest. *Song of Solomon* incorporates myths* and stories told by a variety of characters to propel the story, and its protagonist, forward. *Beloved** certainly resembles *Absalom, Absalom!* in its radical experimentation with narrative form, and *Jazz* and *Paradise** continue that pattern. Both novelists display a deep understanding of their craft and a desire to extend the boundaries of narrative fiction in exciting ways.

Of course, one could trace a variety of themes and structural devices through Faulkner's and Morrison's works. The important point is that Morrison's treatment of such themes, whether conscious or simply the product of a shared culture, engages with Faulkner's novels and rewrites them in productive ways. Her connection to Faulkner is one of active incorporation, not passive reception. Faulkner's and Morrison's novels speak to one another across time, providing an ongoing critique of U.S. culture and its anxieties, fears, hopes, and dreams. *See also* History; Narrative Voice; South, Use of; Whiteness.

References: Carol A. Kolmerten, Stephen M. Ross, and Judith Bryant Wittenberg, eds. *Unflinching Gaze: Morrison and Faulkner Re-Envisioned* (1997); Patricia McKee, *Producing American Races: Henry James, William Faulkner, Toni Morrison* (1999); Philip Weinstein, *What Else but Love? The Ordeal of Race in Faulkner and Morrison* (1996).

David E. Magill

## Felice (*Jazz*)

Identified by the narrator of *Jazz* as another young woman with four marcelled waves in her hair, Felice is incorrectly perceived as a potential source of trouble, an error that propels the narrative. Instead, she becomes the lifeline who enables Joe Trace* and Violet Trace* to establish a larger sense of community*. A symbolic orphan, whose parents are separated from her by their work, she becomes the Traces' figurative daughter and an independent woman in her own right when she rejects Dorcas Manfred's* legacy of anger, deception, and dependence. *See also* Jazz.

Caroline Brown

## Fleetwood, Save-Marie (*Paradise*)

Title character of the last of *Paradise*'s nine sections and never a presence in the novel until her burial, Save-Marie is Jeff and Sweetie Fleetwood's youngest child who, like all the Fleetwood children, is bedridden. Four months after the raid on the Convent*, Save-Marie's death* (she is the first of Ruby, Oklahoma's* original settlers to die within the city limits since 1953) symbolizes an end of the "compact" between God and the original families of Ruby. *See also Paradise.*

Julie Cary Nerad

## Flying Africans, Myth of

Images of individual or collective flight as resistance to New World chattel slavery*, or as transcendence of dehumanizing constraints and restrictions in general, figure prominently in Black American literature and folklore*. Some critics have suggested, however, that images of flight alone do not signal the liberation or transcendence associated with the myth of the flying Africans; merely invoking the myth does not mean that transcendence is achieved. A basic story that incorporates the myth of the flying Africans tells of newly enslaved Blacks who, upon arriving at Ibo Landing in South Carolina and sensing the nature of things, turn and fly (or walk) back to Africa. Blacks who jumped over the sides of slave ships are said to have taken flight. Flight signals spiritual rebirth in freedom, so the question of whether those who take flight to escape oppression survive in a physical sense is less important than the fact that they are no longer oppressed. The most obvious use of the myth of the flying Africans in Toni Morrison's work is as a structuring device in *Song of Solomon*\*, but Morrison invokes the myth in most, if not all, of her novels.

In the Pulitzer Prize-winning novel *Beloved*\*, for example, passages used to describe Sethe Suggs's* most desperate act invoke the myth of the flying Africans. As schoolteacher* and his slave catchers approach 124 Bluestone Road* to carry Sethe and her children* back into slavery, Sethe is described as a giant, protective bird who gathers her children in her wings and attempts to remove them from harm's way. She is not allowed to complete her act of transcendence, however, and she ends up trying to explain to the angry ghost of the one daughter she manages to kill what it was she had in mind. The myth is nevertheless invoked here and in other scenes in *Beloved*, including the images of failed flight in the skating episode, and indeed in several characters' failed flights from Sweet Home*. Interestingly, though Sixo* is captured and killed during that his failed escape attempt, we learn through the memories of Paul D

Garner* and Sethe that, like Pilate Dead* in *Song of Solomon*, he had managed throughout to resist and transcend the limitations of the master narrative. In a significant scene, Morrison illustrates Sixo's ability to resist the master's restrictive language when schoolteacher attempts to label Sixo's act of securing food as theft.

In *Sula**, as Eva Peace* makes her way toward her son's room to end his drug-addicted life, she is depicted as a giant heron. Plum* imagines that the arm sprinkling kerosene over him is the giant wing of an eagle bestowing a blessing or salvation. The novel contains a number of other images of flight (or failed flight), including Sula Peace's* flight from the Bottom*, her return on the Cincinnati Flyer, Ajax's* wish to be a pilot, and Eva's flight from her upstairs window in a futile attempt to save the burning Hannah, whose fiery flight ends in a sizzling death. Chicken Little* "flies" over the water during Sula and Nel Wright's* adolescent game. All these images of flight notwithstanding, none of them signals the level of success that transcendence implies.

In *The Bluest Eye**, Morrison makes the overriding influence of the master narrative readily apparent by using parts of it to open the book and to frame pertinent chapters throughout. Here, as in other works, the ability to transcend the limits of the master narrative is tied to the achievement of self-knowledge and the ability to locate value in Black experience. By the time she is a pregnant adolescent, Pecola Breedlove* has endured a lifetime of negative reinforcement and abuse at almost every turn— from the larger society, from certain members of the Black community*, from many of her peers, and, most significantly, from her parents. A general failure to transcend the limitations of the master narrative's influence is manifested in the extreme self-hatred the Breedloves exhibit. Driven mad by a combination of all the negative forces in her life, Pecola longs for the blue eyes that she believes will right everything in her world. She is finally reduced to spending her days emulating a bird whose wings will not lift her in flight. Like the half-dead bird that Claudia* and Frieda MacTeer* could not save, Pecola is too far gone to resist, let alone to transcend, the narrative that allows her to exist only as a negative entity.

Perhaps the most direct parallel to the myth of the flying Africans in Morrison's corpus is found in *Song of Solomon*. Centered on Macon (Milkman*) Dead, Jr.'s, quest for identity, *Song of Solomon* begins with a North Carolina Mutual Life Insurance agent's leap (and attempted flight via homemade wings) from the roof of No Mercy Hospital*, and ends with Milkman's own giant leap toward self-knowledge, or freedom from an endless quest for Western materialism. Significantly, Milkman's leap takes place once he stops trying to define his self-worth in terms of material things and develops a rich sense of community. Just before he takes the leap that ends the novel, Milkman finally realizes that his now dead Aunt Pilate Dead* (pilot) had long been able to fly without leaving the ground. Throughout the story—which is saturated with references to flight and flyers of varying kinds—Pilate is the family* member who most obviously lives on a transcendent spiritual plane; she is a flying African because she is not constrained by the limitations of the master narrative. The end of the novel suggests that Milkman has finally learned that important distinction.

In the language of the final passages of *Song of Solomon*, Morrison makes apparent certain parallels to the flight motif in *Tar Baby**—in Son's* "jumping" ship and being reborn into the island's natural setting and, even more significantly, in his ultimate identification with the figures of the free-riding horsemen of the Isle des Chevaliers*. Son's "descent" into nature and away from materialism parallels Milkman's changing quest from the pursuit of material wealth to the pursuit of self-knowledge through a series of natural experiences. Like *Song of Solomon*, *Tar Baby* ends on an ambiguous note; however, like Milkman, Son seems poised for freedom and transcendence. In these and other Morrison works, the myth of the flying Africans is invoked to examine the potential that exists for self-knowledge and self-actualization, both of which are tied to the capacity to locate value and authority in Black experience. *See also* Ancestor; Folklore; Myth.

References: "All God's Chillen Had Wings," in *The Doctor to the Dead: Grotesque Legends and Folk Tales of Old Charleston*, ed. John Bennett (1943); Paula Barnes, *Tradition and Innovation: Toni Morrison and the Flight Motif in Afro-American Literature* (2000); Charles Chesnutt, "Sis' Becky's Pickaninny," in *Collected Stories of Charles W. Chesnutt*, ed. William L. Andrews (1992); "The Flying Africans," in *A Treasury of Afro-American Folklore*, ed. Harold Courlander (1976; repr. 1996); Georgia Writers' Project, *Drums and Shadows: Survival Studies Among the Georgia Coastal Negroes* (c. 1940; repr. 1973); Virginia Hamilton, "The People Could Fly," in *The People Could Fly: American Black Folktales*, ed. Virginia Hamilton (1985); Grace Ann Hovet and Barbara Lounsberry, "Flying as Symbol and Legend in Toni Morrison's *The Bluest Eye, Sula*, and *Song of Solomon*," *CLA Journal* 27: 2 (1983); Zora Neale Hurston, "The Last Slave Ship," *The American Mercury* 44: 243 (1944); Julius Lester, "People Who Could Fly," in *Black Folktales*, ed. Julius Lester (1969); Kenneth Porter, "Blacks and White Mores: The Flying Africans," in *Primer for White Folks*, ed. Bucklin Moon (1945); Kenneth Porter, "The Flying Africans," in *Primer for White Folks*, ed. Bucklin Moon (1945); Gay Wilentz, "If You Surrender to the Air: Folk Legends of Flight and Resistance in African American Literature," *MELUS* 16: 1 (1989–90).

                                                              Lovalerie King

## Folklore

For African Americans the common bond of the folk is formed initially in the bitter experience of the Middle Passage from the western coast of Africa to the New World. The African captives who endured this perilous journey into human bondage carried with them key aspects of their indigenous culture: music*, myth*, metaphysical systems of order, and forms of performance. Many of these aspects of their original culture endured despite their extended period of captivity. In their post-captivity experiences, this bond of the folk, based on unique aspects of their African culture and their New World experiences, is further reinforced by legalized racial segregation from the European majority. The cultural experiences of the descendants of these initial African captives who survived the Middle Passage continue to be characterized by a constant group struggle to gain acceptance into the mainstream of American life.

Alan Dundes says in *Folklore Matters* that the term "folk" can apply to any group of people whatsoever who share at least one common factor, and that what is important is that a group formed for whatever reason will have some traditions to call its own; an ethnic group is simply one type of folk (11). In his *A Treasury of Afro-American Folklore* Harold Courlander expands on Dundes's definition of folklore in a more culturally specific way:

African American folklore is myths, tales, recollections, songs and other orally transmitted lore of the various, sometimes disparate (so-called) Negro cultures in the New World. It includes narratives and traditions unique to particular communities as well as those that are shared by many or all, and it contains themes of European as well as African origin. (6)

Given Dundes's and Courlander's definitions of the folk and African American folklore, it should not surprise anyone when the argument is made that the essential core of the African American literary tradition is deeply rooted within its folkloric culture. Important texts by contemporary critics of African American literature, including Houston Baker's *Blues, Ideology, and African-American Literature* and Henry Louis Gates's *The Signifying Monkey: A Theory of African-American Literary Criticism*, acknowledge the fact that the folk roots of this tradition serve as its defining linchpin. Baker and Gates argue that the oral tradition* of the blues and the trickster* figure provide the basis for theorizing about African American literature. In the introduction to his text, Gates says, "*The Signifying Monkey* explores the relation of the black vernacular tradition to the Afro-American literary tradition. The book attempts to identify a theory of criticism that is inscribed within the black vernacular tradition and that in turn informs the shape of the Afro-American literary tradition" (xix).

Additionally, Trudier Harris says in *Fiction and Folklore: The Novels of Toni Morrison* that Houston Baker makes the point that the "blues matrix" is a method of understanding the narrative voice* of African American literature (10). Baker's "blues matrix" is a constantly evolving synthesis of African American vernacular language, and he designates it as an important repository of African American folklore. It becomes a metaphor not just for the folklore itself but for the entire folk culture: a worldview of an entire people (Janifer 156). Further, Keith Byerman asserts in *Fingering the Jagged Grain: Tradition and Form in Recent Black Fiction* that contemporary Black writers have shaped a technically sophisticated body of literature by combining the methods of modern fiction making with the materials of folk culture (1). Like Baker's "blues matrix," Byerman focuses on the "performative" (4) spontaneous aspects of Black folk culture, as well as a variety of folk forms and characters.

Toni Morrison's literary career is illustrative of this vital link between the African American folk and formal literary traditions that Byerman describes. She published her first novel, *The Bluest Eye**, some twenty years after Ralph Ellison's *Invisible Man* (1952), but Morrison's first novel is very much like Ellison's masterpiece because it continues an African American folk tradition without completely abandoning Western conventions. Just as Ralph Ellison called on all Black writers to do in "Change the Joke and Slip the Yoke," so her fiction reaches the point where "Western culture and African American folkways and traditions do not appear to pull in opposite directions, but to say the same thing in different vocabularies and reinforce insight with insight" (49). Dinitia Smith remarks in her *New York Times* article "Tragedy, Domesticity and Folklore" that Morrison's novels have the arc of Greek tragedy, yet they are filled with domestic details, street talk, and folklore (E1).

However, *The Bluest Eye* does not simply collect and retell folktales and reiterate folk beliefs and practices. Harris argues that Morrison's novels do not simply replicate the dynamics of folk communities by showing how people interact with each other to shape tales, legends, rumors, and folk beliefs. Harris's contention is that in many of her novels—*Sula**, *Song of Solomon**, *Tar Baby**, and *Beloved**—Morrison manages to simulate the ethos of folk communities and to saturate her novels with a folk aura intrinsic to the texturing of the whole:

A single folk belief or superstitious practice can reflect an entire community's attitude towards a character or involvement in a particular event. For example National Suicide Day* in *Sula* (1974) is not an isolated imposition of a ritual upon a novel. It is a dynamic event that reveals the whole community's attitude towards Shadrack*, his attitude towards death*, and the place of death in war and in the demise of one's community*. (*Fiction and Folklore* 11)

Harris emphasizes that Morrison, through careful portrayal of such nuances of folk beliefs and practices, is able to show folklore in process rather than as a static force. Clenora Hudson-Weems says, "She is a powerful fiction writer whose work abounds in mystical occurrences—conjurations, superstitious manifestations and spiritual visitations. She artistically interweaves the physical and spiritual worlds in an African continuum so characteristic of true African Americaness" (134). Barbara Christian argues in *Black Feminist Criticism: Perspectives on Black Women Writers* that Morrison's primary means of invoking these beliefs and practices is reversal of the so-called expected truth (52), most particularly the unnatural inversion of truth contained within ideas of physical beauty and romantic love (57).

In *The Bluest Eye* and in most of her later novels, Morrison establishes a pattern where she presents a dialectic of values that forces her characters and her readers to look at alternative ways of being Black, or being female or male, and of being human. For example, Pecola Breedlove's* fantasy about becoming a Black child with beautiful blue eyes is actually a fairy tale in reverse. In this reversal, though, the ugly duckling does not become a beautiful swan, the North is not a freer place for Blacks, and for some Blacks isolation within their own insanity may be preferable to their integration into the "melting pot" of mainstream America. Pecola and her mother's quest for white values is just as devastating as the racism they have been forced to endure because of their obvious Blackness and lack of knowledge about the seduction and betrayal of Black people by white culture.

In *Sula*, when the protagonist returns to her Medallion, Ohio*, neighborhood called the Bottom*, looking ten years younger than the rest of the women her age, the community* is immediately suspicious of her because of her difference. When their suspicions are connected to their rumors, she is made into a witch through the evolutionary process in folklore where rumor becomes solidified as legend. Harris says this process usually takes several generations, but Morrison's skill enables her to accomplish it in her novel in a matter of weeks (12). Morrison reinforces the folkloric elements of this novel by giving it a fairy-tale structure that is complete with ballad formulas and African American jokes and music. Kimberly Mazur says in "A Womanist Analysis: Triple Oppression in the Early Fiction of Toni Morrison" that despite being surrounded by the Civil Rights movement and pretending to be changing economically and socially, the Bottom and its residents, who actually live on a hill (the bottom of heaven), are essentially unchanged (23).

Just like the other residents of the Bottom, Sula Peace* is unchanged by the passage of time while she is away. However, when she returns, she is damned for not conforming to the norms established for the women of the community. Sula refuses to become a homemaker and baby maker, and seeks sexual gratification in nontraditional ways. Barbara Lounsberry and Grace Hovet maintain in "Principles of Perception in Toni Morrison's *Sula*" that she ignores the ownership principle of marriage and operates on the principle that sex is noncompetitive and nonthreatening. She also rejects traditional employment (128). They insist that her non-conformity eventually makes her into a pariah because she longs for independence, knowledge, and self-gratification. Morrison endows her with a significant birthmark on her eyelid that is symbolic of her original powers of perception. Others characters in the novel, though, see this birthmark (depending upon their individual perception of her) as a rose, a tadpole, a rattlesnake, her dead grandmother's ashes, or simply a scary black thing (129).

Susan L. Blake says in her article "Folklore and Community in *Song of Solomon*" that the title of Morrison's third novel is a variant of a well-known Gullah folktale. In this folktale a group of African slaves in the New World rise up one day from the field where they are working and fly back to Africa (77). When we encounter Milkman Dead*, the protagonist of *Song of Solomon*, he is searching for his freedom and identity*, but not by traveling the traditional route for African Americans. He does not pursue the North Star of freedom while fleeing slavery or sharecropping in the cruel South. Harris says Morrison reverses this piece of African American folklore by having Milkman searching for his identity while traveling from north to south on a type of Odyssean journey (12). Through Milkman's character Morrison forces us to confront the difficulties of various economic levels within the Black community, its violence*, grotesque characters, bizarre actions, and biblical allusions. In her article "Memory and Mass Culture," Susan Willis tells us that Milkman's journey of discovery from north to south is a process of reclaiming his family's* history* of post-emancipation Blacks. He learns to relinquish all of the commodity trappings and egotistical practices that defined his bourgeois life as cloistered and ignorant (186).

On his journey of discovery Milkman is made aware of the difference in the values espoused by his materialistic father, Macon Dead*, and his earthy Aunt Pilate Dead*, and he must determine which worldview represents progress for him. To Macon Dead, the richest Black man in his Michigan town, progress means strictly material progress gained at the expense of human beings. Mr. Dead advises his only son to own things. To Pilate, who, despite being born without a navel, develops into an independent, resourceful, and courageous Black woman, progress means going out of one's way to help others, even those who are not family. She is representative of the folk and family consciousness that she demonstrates by listening to her father's ghost and befriending her brother's wife and son.

Milkman eventually progresses from his father's values to his aunt's values as he discovers his family's true history in the South. His journey into the South eventually evolves into a positive quest because he starts out looking for gold but ends up seeking his family's legacy. Blake says that by basing Milkman's identity quest on a folktale, Morrison calls attention to one of the central themes of her fiction, the relationship between individual identity and community. She argues that folklore is by definition the expression of community and of the common experiences, beliefs, and values that identify a folk as a group (77). Thus the Gullah tale of the flying Africans*, including Milkman's own great-grandfather, represents a common dream, a common disappointment, and a group identity (78).

Morrison's fourth novel, *Tar Baby*, takes its title from an African American folktale in the Br'er Rabbit cycle, but it is different from her other novels. It is set in the contemporary period, and much of its action takes place not in the Midwestern United States but in the Caribbean. According to Keith Byerman, its setting, the fictional Isle des Chevaliers*, is a perverse Eden that is an exotic example of the flawed "garden" (208), and it features the major European American characters Valerian* and Margaret Street*. Terry Otten notes in *The Crime of Innocence in the Fiction of Toni Morrison* that the little community of wealthy homes where the Streets live with their Black servants, Sydney and Ondine Childs*, had been built by Haitian laborers. They built it above a swamp they called Seine de Ville (witch's tit) that was formed when the white invaders rerouted the river and displaced it to end twenty leagues from the sea (64). Although this island seems idyllic, the land is rotting and haunted by demons.

Just as she did with the myth of the flying Africans in *Song of Solomon*, Morrison offers us a revised rendering of Tar Baby's folktale. Her protagonist Jadine Childs* plays the role of the tar baby and develops a romantic interest in Son*, a bluesy traveling man from Eloe*. To Jadine, the presumed richness of African American oral and family traditions and Son's attraction to them mean little compared to her education at the Sorbonne and modeling the latest fashions in Paris and New York. Once Son comes into contact with her, he runs the risk of having his own values negatively transformed to hers. Jadine is unable to respond to the needs of anyone but herself, and she is unable to reclaim "ancient properties" that would link her more to African than to European American values. Her adoption of these values is so obvious that an African woman who sees her on the street in Paris spits on her in disgust (*Song of Solomon* 68).

Morrison generated her fifth novel, *Beloved*, from a newspaper article she discovered while editing *The Black Book**, a scrapbook of African American history. In a sensational case, Margaret Garner*, a runaway slave, killed her daughter rather than allow her to be returned to slavery*. In Morrison's version of this story her protagonist, Sethe

Suggs*, kills her child to keep her from being returned to slavery, but she is freed and ostracized even from her own Black community. Students of African myth and culture explore the relationship between the West African concept of ancestor* worship and the mythic core of the novel. *Beloved* is the first work of a trilogy that includes Morrison's latest novels, *Jazz** and *Paradise**. *See also* Conjure; South, Influence of; Spirituality.

References: Houston A. Baker, *Blues, Ideology, and African American Literature* (1984); Susan L. Blake, "Folklore and Community in *Song of Solomon*," *MELUS*: 7: 3 (Fall 1980); Keith E. Byerman, *Fingering the Jagged Grain: Tradition and Form in Recent Black Fiction* (1985); Barbara Christian, *Black Feminist Criticism: Perspectives on Black Women Writers* (1985); Harold Courlander, ed., *A Treasury of Afro-American Folklore* (1996); Alan Dundes, *Folklore Matters* (1989); Ralph Ellison, "Change the Joke and Slip the Yoke," in *Mother Wit from the Laughing Barrel*, ed. Alan Dundes (1990); Henry Louis Gates, Jr., *The Signifying Monkey: A Theory of African-American Literary Criticism* (1988); Trudier Harris, *Fiction and Folklore in the Novels of Toni Morrison* (1991); Clenora Hudson-Weems, "Toni Morrison's World of Topsy-Turvydom: A Methodological Explication of New Black Literary Criticism," *Western Journal of Black Studies* 10: 3 (Fall 1986); Raymond E. Janifer, "The Black Nationalistic Aesthetic and the Early Fiction of John Edgar Wideman," Ph.D diss., The Ohio State University (1996); Barbara Lounsberry and Grace A. Hovet, "Principles of Perception in Toni Morrison's *Sula*," *Black American Literature Forum* 13: 4 (Winter 1979); Kimberly A. Mazur, "A Womanist Analysis: Triple Oppression in the Early Fiction of Toni Morrison," M.A. thesis, Shippensburg University of Pennsylvania (1999); Terry Otten, *The Crime of Innocence in the Fiction of Toni Morrison* (1989); Dinitia Smith, "Toni Morrison's Mix of Tragedy, Domesticity, and Folklore," *New York Times* (January 8, 1998); Susan Willis, "Memory and Mass Culture," in *History and Memory in African American Culture*, ed. Genevieve Fabre and Robert O' Meally (1994).

Raymond E. Janifer

## Foucault, Marie-Therese (*Tar Baby*)

The blind former nursemaid who now works as a washerwoman for Valerian and Margaret Street*, Marie-Therese is considered a witch because she is able to commune with nature and has second sight. She claims Son* as one of the blind race of Black horsemen and is instrumental in ensuring that Son joins them at the end of the novel. In contrast to Jadine Childs*, Marie-Therese has not lost her ancient properties. In fact she is the keeper of history* and is the center of Black female authority in *Tar Baby*. *See also Tar Baby*.

Nicole N. Aljoe

# G

## Garner, Margaret

The model for Sethe Suggs* in Morrison's *Beloved**, Margaret Garner was born June 4, 1833, at Maplewood, the 297-acre northern Kentucky plantation of John Pollard Gaines, then a well-to-do lawyer and farmer, and later a state senator, colonel in the Mexican War, U.S. congressman, and second governor of the Oregon Territory. Garner was the name of Margaret's husband Robert, the slave of Gaines's neighbor John Marshall. The archive does not reveal if Margaret's parents Priscilla and Duke went by a last name.

Maplewood's twelve to fourteen slaves chiefly produced hogs and sheep for the Cincinnati market, seventeen miles north. They labored in a neighborhood (called Richwood) of large plantations with a total slave population running around 50 percent, three times the Kentucky average and significant because it allowed for the development of a more extensive (and resistant) slave subculture. Gaines himself was often absent from the plantation, leaving its management to his wife, Elizabeth, and the eldest of his twelve children, residents of the sizable "big house" constructed when Margaret was an infant. We also know from the record that, beginning at age five, "Peggy" (to her owners) worked in the Gaines household, first as "babysitter" of toddling Gaines children, later as general household servant and caretaker of Gaines's aging mother. We also know that when Margaret was seven, the Gaines family took her to Cincinnati, a sojourn on free soil that would figure importantly in her 1856 fugitive slave trial.

The September 1850 census recorded Margaret as a seventeen-year-old "mulatto" slave, and just below, Margaret's five month-old boy (Thomas), also a "mulatto." Around these bare facts, archived information unfolds the story of a single year in Margaret's biography. Notable, first, is Margaret's "mulatto" identity*: Duke and Priscilla are both listed as "black"—like all other Maplewood slaves—and so this "light brown" girl must have been the product of an interracial union, probably coercive. In 1849–50 Margaret herself must have been facing similar coercion; during that year John Gaines accepted appointment as governor of the Oregon Territory and sold Maplewood to his younger brother Archibald, a moody, violent, and grieving widower. Concurrently, Margaret became pregnant by Robert, nearly a year younger. By any standard, theirs was an exceptionally early union, and it was probably designed to stave off Gaines's advances. During the next five years Margaret bore a second, light-complexioned boy (Samuel), perhaps also by Robert; then she bore two girls (Mary and Priscilla) whom newspapermen would describe as "nearly white." Even in 1856 these signs were taken as pointing to Margaret's sexual victimization and Gaines's probable paternity. Additionally, she herself claimed that Gaines beat her, once leaving a scar on her cheek.

These conditions galvanized a decision to flee, and the Garners were aided by other circumstances. In Cincinnati, Margaret had a free Black cousin, Elijah Kite, whom Robert Garner had visited in 1855 after taking a drove of hogs to market. Then the winter of 1855–56 froze the Ohio River to a depth of six inches, forming an "ice bridge" for northern Kentucky slaves desiring freedom. So on Sunday night, January 27, 1856, Robert Garner stole a six-shooter and a horse-drawn sleigh from his master, loaded his mother and father aboard, then picked up Margaret and her four children from Maplewood. In a boldly executed plan Robert sped north, eluding slave patrols and finally abandoning the sleigh in Covington, on the Kentucky side. The fugitives walked over water, then the two miles to Kite's cabin, there to await Underground Railroad assistance. But Archibald Gaines was in close pursuit, and by Monday morning he and several U.S. marshals had the cabin surrounded. When the fugitives refused to surrender, the marshals burst in, Robert fired his pistol (wounding one deputy) and "fought like a lion." After subduing him, the slave catchers found three wounded Garner children and the body of two year-old Mary, nearly decapitated when Margaret cut her throat.

There followed the longest, most dramatic fugitive slave trial of antebellum U.S. history, with every Northern newspaper spotlighting the mother who would kill her children rather than yield them up to Southern slavery*. The Garners' attorney, the well-known Quaker abolitionist John Jolliffe, futilely argued that Margaret's 1840 sojourn on free soil emancipated her (and thus, her offspring), and that the 1850 Fugitive

Slave Act was unconstitutional. The federal commissioner ruled in late February that the seven surviving Garners should be returned to their Kentucky masters. His order was carried out on February 29, Archibald Gaines having promised to return Margaret to Ohio authorities on a murder warrant. Ohio abolitionists planned to convict Margaret for Mary's death, using the trial to showcase Margaret's victimization and slavery's horrors, and later to secretly pardon Margaret and speed her to Canada. A suspicious Gaines never fulfilled his promise. After a series of evasive maneuvers, he shipped the Garners first to Arkansas, then leased them for a year in New Orleans, and finally sold them to an acquaintance, D.C. Bonham, owner of Willow Grove plantation in Issaquena County, Mississippi. There Margaret died of typhoid fever in the late summer of 1858. Robert escaped and served in the 71st Colored Infantry during the 1863 siege of Vicksburg. In an 1870 newspaper interview, he remarked that Margaret's surviving boys, Thomas and Samuel, were still farming in Mississippi. *See also Beloved*; Suggs, Sethe.

References: Levi Coffin, *Reminiscences of Levi Coffin, the Reputed President of the Underground Railroad* (1876); Steven Weisenburger, *Modern Medea: A Family Story of Slavery and Child Murder from the Old South* (1998); Cynthia Griffin Wolff, "Margaret Garner: A Cincinnati Story," *Massachussetts Review* 32 (1991); Julius Yannuck, "The Garner Fugitive Slave Case," *Mississippi Valley Historical Review* 40 (1953).

Steven Weisenburger

## Garner, Mr. and Mrs. (*Beloved*)

The Garners owned Sweet Home* and the enslaved population whose labor they exploited there. The Garners (primarily represented by Mr. Garner's philosophy) believed that their type of benevolent slavery*— which provided for certain "privileges"—was superior to other forms of slavery. Garner referred to the men he enslaved as "men" instead of "boys," and for this he was ill-regarded among his peers. Those enslaved at Sweet Home felt that Garner's death was related to his philosophy of slavery. Morrison's drawing of this character and his particular liberal brand of slavery demonstrates that regardless of whether a master was considered kind or unkind, slavery was still slavery. Mrs. Garner, to her credit, does not punish Sethe Suggs* for stealing fabric to make herself a wedding dress, gives Sethe a pair of earrings, and speaks to schoolteacher* about having allowed his nephews* to abuse Sethe. Generally, Morrison portrays her as a kinder-than-most, but nevertheless typical, plantation mistress whose operating space was confined to the domestic sphere. She becomes an invalid following her husband's somewhat mysterious death. *See also Beloved.*

Lovalerie King

## Garner, Paul D (*Beloved*)

Since Paul F is sold shortly after Garner's* death, and Paul A is hanged during the escape attempt from Sweet Home*, Paul D Garner is the last of the Pauls* alive at Sweet Home. After being forced to witness the torture and death of the rebellious Sixo*, Paul D is manacled, shackled, collared, and fitted with a bit. Later he is sold, and after trying to kill his new owner, is put to work on a chain gang in Alfred, Georgia. He escapes and roams from place to place. In all his experiences Paul D has learned to love everything just a little bit, in case he has to give it up. In 1873, he comes upon Sethe Suggs* at the house at 124 Bluestone Road*. After driving off the spirit of the baby ghost, he and Sethe begin a romantic relationship. The ghost returns in the flesh and gradually drives Paul D off the premises—seducing him along the way. When Paul D learns about the worst of Sethe's past, he makes the mistake of telling her that she acted like something less than human in killing her child. His romantic relationship with Sethe is, in essence, disrupted by the insistent presence and full weight of the ghost of slavery*. The novel's ending suggests that Paul D and Sethe will have a chance to resume their relationship; in the end, he returns to 124 Bluestone Road. *See also Beloved.*

Lovalerie King

## Geography

Throughout the body of her work, Toni Morrison regularly focuses on geographical and physical settings. All seven novels, and much of her nonfiction writing, embody a profound sense of place, with the geographical situations often taking on the status of character. For example, in *Beloved*, 124 Bluestone Road* certainly commands as much attention as many of the humans who inhabit Morrison's books. Likewise, places in other novels—the Bottom*, the Convent*, Eloe*—are deeply familiar to Morrison's readers. Within her fictive world, Morrison steeps her characters in their settings, resulting in literature that could exist nowhere else.

In addition, Morrison's works emphasize not only where the action takes place, but also a considerable preoccupation with the very concept of geography. That is, we learn how towns are born, what histories their names reflect, the way the streets are arranged. Or, as in *The Bluest Eye*, we discover that women can be named for countries or identified by their

Southern places of origin. Morrison imbues her writing with a direct awareness of place, often emphasizing influences of the American South*, even within the urban North. Overall, Morrison's milieu embraces geography as a powerful influence, literally and symbolically.

*The Bluest Eye*, the only novel so far that Morrison has set in her hometown of Lorain, Ohio*, brings to life that steel town on Lake Erie. In her first novel, Morrison presents the layout of the town, the placement of the MacTeers' home and the Breedloves' storefront. The experiences of the characters reveal the divisions between the richer whites' manicured lakefront homes and the cinder-strewn environs of the poorer, often Black, folks. The idea of home* security becomes clear through its absence: when the Breedloves are evicted—put outdoors—Pecola Breedlove* temporarily lives with Claudia* and Frieda Breedlove*. Pecola's family home is never safe, for it is the site of her rape by her father, Cholly*, and her subsequent descent into madness. And Frieda is molested within her own more upright home by their boarder, Mr. Henry. Morrison shows the futility of seeking a safe place through the eradication of disorder attempted by some of the more geographically oriented characters, those proper ladies from Mobile, Alabama; Meridian, Mississippi; and Aiken, South Carolina. These women's direct antitheses also have geographically based names; the three prostitutes* who befriend Pecola are named China (she also appears in *Sula**), Poland, and Miss Marie, who is otherwise known as the Maginot Line (a failed fortification line in World War II France).

*Sula* also reveals a geographical bent, with the opening scene detailing the genealogy of the Bottom. Resonating with Morrison's description of the non–Dick and Jane houses in the first pages of *The Bluest Eye*, Morrison's second novel introduces its readers to the perverted racist joke that has created this place. As the community of African Americans pushed out of Medallion, Ohio*, the residents of the Bottom must live in the hills, where growing crops is hindered by the steep topography. Eventually, this neighborhood comes to embody a richness that can nurture an unconventional young woman like Sula Peace* or give Nel Wright* the courage to resist her mother's attempts to mold her into an impossible white ideal. The negativity associated with the Bottom's creation, in other words, becomes inverted, for it turns out to be a relatively positive place to live. Yet that opening scene reveals also that this neighborhood will eventually be obliterated by an encroaching white-owned golf course. The geography of *Sula* also encompasses the river, the place where Chicken Little* dies, as well as the mighty tunnel, itself the site of tragic loss of life. Each geographical focus, therefore—including the distant New Orleans Sundown House feared by Helene Wright*—possesses the bittersweet quality often characteristic of Morrison's fiction.

In her third novel, *Song of Solomon\**, Morrison intensifies this already pronounced preoccupation with geography. Here, in an unnamed Michigan city on the shore of Lake Superior (inexplicably said to be not far from Pennsylvania), the opening scene involves a delineation of the city's mapping, including its leaders' attempts to redefine what the Southside people insist on calling Doctor Street. The renamed Not Doctor Street\* joins No Mercy Hospital\* in an environment of eccentrically named places and people, not the least of which is the geographically based Macon Dead\*. This novel's focus on place also appears in the Southern source of the Dead family, Shalimar, Virginia, which Milkman Dead\* discovers on a quest with a far different motivation. Furthermore, Pilate Dead\*, Macon's sister, who lives on the other side of the tracks from his respectable home, prizes as one of her few possessions a geography book.

*Tar Baby\** involves a very different geographical setting, for most of the action occurs on a fictional Francophone Caribbean island named Isle des Chevaliers\*. Morrison describes this mythical place as being near Dominique, which could possibly be a French-inflected name for Dominica, in the southern Caribbean. But because the houses are built by workers brought in from Haiti, the area may have more in common with the Dominican Republic. Wherever Morrison imagines it to be, this is a magical place where trees yell and rivers have their hearts broken by human development. The island's sentient geography frames the story, with Son\* swept along by a willful ocean at the beginning and claimed by the horsemen and respected by the trees at the end. While on the island, the otherwise confident Jadine Childs\* is haunted by a vision of an African woman in Paris who makes her question her own authenticity. The main white characters also evoke geography, in part through their names suggesting place: Valerian *Street\** and his wife Margaret\*, who is often referred to as a faded beauty queen from Maine. Beyond the island setting, *Tar Baby* also involves Philadelphia, New York, Paris, and Son's legendary hometown of Eloe, Florida, all places Morrison instills with powerful influences over the hearts and minds of her characters.

This concentration on geographical and psychological setting becomes more pronounced as Morrison's works progress, culminating in the trilogy of *Beloved\**, *Jazz\**, and *Paradise\**. These novels profoundly illustrate the tensions between her characters' geographical expectations and emotional realizations. For each of these works, the characters' Southern origins reveal bittersweet combinations of poignant beauty and intense pain. Whether the characters in these novels end up in the North or the West, their new homes also prove to be problematic.

In *Beloved*, the ambiguities of geography occur everywhere the characters exist. Whereas the South\* evokes the horrors of slavery\*, life in the North is not free, either. For Sethe, just thinking of Sweet Home\*, the plantation in Kentucky, reminds her simultaneously that it was the site of unspeakable atrocity and violence*, and where she was together with Halle Suggs* and her children* in a place of sylvan beauty. Likewise, Alfred, Georgia, is where Paul D Garner* and his fellow prisoners are terribly abused—sexually, mentally, and physically. Nevertheless, he is amazed by its unabashed natural splendor, finding himself moved by Alfred's trees, stars, and flowers. Morrison depicts Cincinnati, Ohio, a city beyond the realm of slavery, as the refuge Sethe and her children attain against all odds, as well as Baby Suggs's* destination. Yet it is also where schoolteacher* and his nephews* track the runaways to return them to the terror of enslavement. More specifically, 124 Bluestone Road becomes both the site of togetherness, reunion, and love and a place of capture, haunting, and death*.

Ambivalent contrasts abound in *Beloved*: between the North and the South, between slavery and freedom, and, through its emphases, on borders and rivers. The Ohio River particularly fulfills this situation, for it is the division between slave state and free, as well as the site where Sethe gives birth to Denver*, another geographically named character. When Baby Suggs crosses the river into free territory, after Halle buys her freedom, she realizes for the first time that her body, particularly her beating heart, belongs to her. This geography of the in-between also evolves abstractly in the novel, as Morrison merges the realm linking life and death with the place where Beloved* originates and also with the slave ships of the Middle Passage.

Morrison informs *Jazz* with its own emphasis on borders and on divisions between the North and South through the primary settings of Vesper County, Virginia, and the City—unnamed, but clearly New York. As a novel of the Great Migration* tradition—rather than *Beloved*'s slave narrative orientation—*Jazz* emphasizes the profound distinctions between the rural South and the urban North during the early years of the twentieth century. Violet* and Joe Trace* change dramatically within these settings, and the narrator holds the City responsible for the problems they encounter. Whereas Harlem*, which Morrison maps out in some detail, becomes their racial sanctuary, in keeping with the historical Harlem Renaissance, the resulting disconnection from their Southern ancestral roots brings trouble for Violet and Joe. Also within the City, Dorcas Manfred* tries to get Joe to take her to a dance club named Mexico*. The characters may perceive themselves as stronger and more daring in the City, but Joe kills Dorcas there, and Violet desecrates the corpse at her funeral, events that leave the living utterly bereft.

Within the South, these characters experience racial violence, in which greedy whites run many African Americans, including Violet and Joe, from their land (this dispossession parallels a related event of land seizure in *Song of Solomon*). Yet the ambivalence abides, for this region is also where Joe experiences a profound love of hunting in the woods, along-side his mentor, Hunter's Hunter*, and it is also where Joe and Violet are born, and where they work, meet, and marry. Also inhabiting these Vesper County woods is Wild*, simultaneously a source of fear and Joe's quarry in his search for parental validation. A parent's absence in the South also haunts Violet, for her mother, Rose Dear*, commits suicide in a well. Furthermore, Golden Gray* of Baltimore* seeks out Vesper County in his search for his father, an ambivalent quest involving issues of race*, identity*, and privilege.

In *Paradise*, rather than drawing these more familiar distinctions between the North and the South, Morrison differentiates racist Reconstruction Louisiana from the possibility of all-Black towns in Oklahoma. In addition, once they travel to this more western setting, the Old Fathers and their families encounter the surprising stain of intraracial discrimination, for the darkness of their skin color prevents them from being accepted in towns these other African Americans have already established. Years after this Disallowing, in the contemporary setting of the novel, the geographical contrasts of note become those between Haven* and Ruby*, and then between Ruby and the Convent. Because its residents are preoccupied with a desire for absolute safety, Ruby becomes a bastion of self-righteousness, as Deacon* and Steward Morgan* and the other leaders seek to delimit the town's identity along rigid, color-struck, tradition-bound lines.

The men regard the Convent as dangerous, a foil, the perceived "evil" against which they define themselves. Therefore, the ensuing violent conflict between the men of Ruby and the Convent women—which frames the main action of the novel—becomes inevitable. The distance between these two places is seventeen miles, which Morrison reveals in her opening lines, again immediately drawing attention to the novel's geographical circumstances. Interestingly, Morrison gives another instance of her cartographic focus via Seneca's* self-mutilation; she cuts her arms and thighs, forming wounds she regards as maps, complete with streets and intersections. The in-between realm of ambiguity also appears more metaphorically in this novel, through the door/window that Anna Flood and Richard Misner* perceive after the Convent women have disappeared. Amid the potent positionings of *Paradise* (the title itself is evocative of a significant idealized location), this more conceptual perspective of ambiguous geography opens infinite possibilities. As Morrison has said in several interviews, she ends her novel with references to travel in order to emphasize the crucial nature of human beings creating and recognizing the potential for paradise while still here on earth.

Furthermore, Morrison's nonfiction and other creations also frequently involve geography. Her 1993 Nobel Prize address* sets up its story within a context where struggling people journey, including those escaping enslavement. Within this parable, the blind woman and the children evoke familiar Morrisonian themes of exile and homelessness, thereby echoing her geographical concerns. *Playing in the Dark: Whiteness and the Literary Imagination\** also involves these issues, most notably in the opening paragraphs, which plot a course for American literature in cartographic terminology. In all of Toni Morrison's work, these concerted geographical orientations abound, providing reference points for her readers and sometimes safe havens for her characters. *See also* History.

References: Melvin Dixon, *Ride Out the Wilderness: Geography and Identity in Afro-American Literature* (1987); Farah Jasmine Griffin, *"Who Set You Flowin'?" The African-American Migration Narrative* (1995); Lawrence R. Rodgers, *Canaan Bound: The African-American Great Migration Novel* (1997).

Kristine Yohe

## Ghost Story, Use of

Scholars have for some time regarded most of Toni Morrison's stories as being within the genre of magical realism\*, and indeed the supernatural seems to pervade her works. The most celebrated supernatural element of her stories would surely be the ghost who makes her eponymous presence felt in *Beloved\**. The novel's ghost borrows heavily from familiar spectral traditions, but there are many unique aspects to the ghost as well.

The novel informs its reader from the very beginning that the setting will be fantastic. The first chapter quickly and successfully blurs the lines between animate and inanimate, conscious and otherwise. In this sense, the novel follows old strategies of horror, transgressing boundaries in ways that could never be called natural. The novel seems to encourage a reading of these opening pages that unsettles the reader, a feeling that comes back to haunt the narrative when Sethe Suggs\* and her two daughters are getting along so well.

But if we can say that *Beloved* follows a path similar to those of other ghost stories, we must be careful to point out that it is not really the same path at all. For example, the structure of the narrative is quite different from the structure of most ghost stories. The traditional story featuring any kind of monster usually follows a pattern of a chaotic force infiltrating a secure space, followed by the introduction of a detective figure who investigates all the mundane explanations available, eventually names the terror for what it is, and finally initiates the appropriate pro-

cedures for destroying the monster. However, *Beloved* has no clear detective figure, and the space this ghost invades has been anything but
stable for some time. Furthermore, and though the reason that Beloved*
chooses to leave Sethe's house is not perfectly clear, it is doubtful that
the women who cannot even enter Sethe's yard have really exorcised
Beloved. In some sense, their hodgepodge of religious activities mirrors
the Western tradition of Catholic-style exorcism, but theirs is an exorcism without teeth: the ghost is not driven away by their exorcism, or at
least not by it alone.

The novel declines to answer many questions, and among those questions is one to which the traditional ghost story demands an answer:
Just whose ghost is Beloved? Is she the ghost of Sethe's slain daughter?
Most of the novel would support this reading. For example, she recalls
events which only that daughter would have witnessed, and the way she
acts as an incarnate being seems to be a direct response to the baby's
short life and gruesome death. However, powerful moments in the narrative encourage the reader to think that perhaps Beloved is the ghost
of one or more of the slaves who died in transit to the Western Hemisphere. The novel's dedication, one of the few elements of the novel we
can rely on to express the author's intentions without disguise, reinforces such an interpretation. In fact, it is never quite clear whether
Beloved has to fit just one of these definitions. Perhaps she is all of these
things and more, but if so, she is both recalling and transcending the
traditional ghost.

Another tradition of the ghost story, dating at least from the writings
of Henry James, suggests that the ghost (or hallucination thereof) must
originate in the protagonist's own psychological instability, or at least
from her own wrongdoing. In this sense the story is more traditional, in
that Beloved seems to be the reincarnation of the child Sethe slew. However, no contemporary reader would argue that Sethe's crime takes place
in a vacuum. Since Sethe is the one who is haunted, the traditional ghost
story would seem to indicate that it is Sethe who is being repaid, but since
Sethe is only trying to keep her daughter from a life of slavery*, is she
the one at fault, or is schoolteacher*, her master? Or is Mr. Garner*, her
previous and remarkably humane owner, at fault? Further, if Beloved is
not just the reincarnation of Sethe's daughter, but a vengeful spirit born
of the miseries of the many individuals who perished at sea during the
Middle Passage, why is she haunting Sethe at all? Wouldn't it be more
appropriate for her to haunt members of the white community who benefited from slavery, or even members of the African communities who
assisted the slave trade?

And of course in this context the "traditional ghost story" refers to the
traditional *Western* ghost story. African understandings of the supernatural assume a different set of traditions, and these traditions often

contradict European-informed ideas about ghosts. For example, ghost stories told within the African tradition often insist that the natural and the supernatural intertwine. Such a tradition would apply well to *Beloved*, which opens with a mundane family* that has to learn to live with the daily terrors of what appears to be a fantastic visitor. Further, Beloved's immense power to drag Sethe back into the past, and indeed her presence as a reincarnation of the dead, blurs the neat divisions of time, again echoing African traditions. This power serves the narrative well, as Beloved and Paul D Garner* struggle to make the present Sethe live in the past or present, respectively.

Finally, Beloved the ghost and 124 Bluestone Road* the haunted house work splendidly to foreground one of the novel's most powerful themes: possession. Throughout the novel, a central issue is possession: who belongs to whom, who has a claim on whom, and who owns what. Just as the spirit (who seems to fit the description of a poltergeist until she takes on flesh after Paul D casts her out) possesses the house, Sethe is possessed by her past, in which she was possessed by schoolteacher, Mrs. Garner, Mr. Garner, and perhaps even Halle Suggs*. In its subtler moments, the novel even interrogates family ties, asking troubling questions about the nature of familial love and the uncanny kind of love that could survive slavery. Introduced as it is in the opening words of the novel, ghostly possession becomes a powerful insight into the heart of *Beloved*. *See also* African Myth, Use of; Conjure; Gothic Tradition; Romantic Tradition.

Joe Sutliff Sanders

## Gibson, Grace/Gigi (*Paradise*)

In too-high heels and too-short skirt, Gigi, title character of one of *Paradise*'s nine sections, steps off the bus in Ruby, Oklahoma*, in 1971, hoping to find two trees entwined in love and some unbeatable rhubarb pie. Her boyfriend Mikey, arrested during the Oakland riots, has told her of two rocks making love forever in the desert just outside Wish, Arizona, and they are to rendezvous there on April 15, after he is paroled. But Gigi, a girl really named Grace from Alcorn, Mississippi, finds no lovemaking rocks, and on her way to anywhere else, a stranger's tale of two trees that might do brings her to Ruby; she arrives at the Convent* the day Mother (Mary Magna*) dies. Finding Consolata (Connie) Sosa* alone, drunk, and almost passed out on the kitchen floor, Gigi misses her ride to Demby and ends up staying at the Convent. Fond of sunbathing naked and wearing few clothes, Gigi immediately garners the disapproval of the more conservative Mavis Albright*, but attracts the attention of Coffee (K.D.) Smith*, only nephew of Ruby's important Morgan family. Their two-year, turbulent affair ends when the Convent women banish K.D. for beating Gigi, whose sexual attention then turns to the childlike Seneca*. Free-spirited, sensual, and liberated, Gigi had been abandoned by her mother, has a father on death row, and is haunted by the image, from the Oakland riots, of a beautiful Black boy spitting blood into his hands. Understanding that she has not approved of herself in years, Grace exorcises these images in Connie's "loud-dreaming" sessions. Grace is one of the three women shot down in the grass; however, we see her again, dressed in a black T-shirt and camouflage pants, packing a gun: first at a lake, visiting her father, who has received a permanent stay of execution, and presumably twice more, once as a passenger in a car and finally in a parking lot, helping Seneca clean her bleeding hands. *See also Paradise.*

Julie Cary Nerad

## Gigi (*Paradise*)

*See* Gibson, Grace/Gigi (*Paradise*).

## Gothic Tradition

Toni Morrison's nonfictional work *Playing in the Dark: Whiteness and the Literary Imagination*, which focuses on the presence of blackness in nineteenth-century American literature, gives an accurate though perhaps inadvertent description of her own Gothic paradigm in her novels. Morrison questions why nineteenth-century American writers, trying so desperately to break with the English tradition, would appropriate the Old World Gothic form. She then explains the power of darkness and race* in Gothic terms: all that was terrifying and unknown about the New World experience, with its vast uncharted wilderness, became part of the Gothic legacy from Europe. Additionally, for Morrison, the concept of the racialized Other became important because it represented the lure of freedom and the fear of enslavement, part of the contradictory experience of the American democracy. The European Gothic derived its power from the concept of the "sins of the fathers," an obvious biblical allusion to the curse of the past, and like its American successor, it could find sustenance only in the dusty and moldy terrain of the past. The burden of the histories—and its choking hold on the present—informed American Gothic, and it would be surprising if Morrison, with her background in American literature (a master's degree in English from Cornell) would not have felt some residual effects of reading Hawthorne and Faulkner*, two masters of the Gothic mode who are able to depict terrifying landscapes fraught with the dangers and perils and lure of darkness. Indeed, it is not coincidence that part of Morrison's master's degree thesis concerned itself with the greatest Southern Gothic writer, Faulkner, who also implicated race with the sins of the fathers and the darkness of American history*.

Obviously, Toni Morrison is interested in recounting ghost stories* as a way to access history and to understand an oppressiveness of the past so that a possibility for future equality and freedom can exist within gender and race relationships. It is not as if the ghosts can be exorcised completely, but they need to be brought out of the darkness of the past and of their hiding places, so that they can be contended with. Even as the narrator asserts in *Beloved** that it was a story not to pass on—somewhat disingenuously, after recounting an epic ghost story—the reader knows that this is most definitely a story to pass on, lest history repeat itself. One of the objectives of the Gothic is to reveal an oppressive power dynamic so that the empowered and disempowered can both escape from a vicious and stultifying cycle of history. There are many ghosts that need to be exorcised in the Morrison oeuvre—*Beloved**, most obviously, so that Sethe Suggs* and Paul D Garner* can imagine a future. Similarly, Joe* and Violet Trace* in *Jazz** need to come to terms with the ghost of Dorcas Manfred* after Joe murders his young lover in a fit of rage; here, though, the ghost of Dorcas resides more in their minds than in actual life, as real spirit, as was the case in *Beloved*.

Such psychological ghosts haunt all the protagonists in all the major works: for example, Sula Peace* is haunted by Chicken Little*, whom she inadvertently kills; Shadrack*, the passive accomplice in Sula's crime, is haunted by a battlefield of dying men in war-torn 1917 France; Pecola Breedlove* in *The Bluest Eye** is haunted by her newly fashioned self (brought about by the spells of the wizard figure, Soaphead Church*) in the psychiatric ward. Such doomed characters, like Poe's Gothic heroes, are confined within the abyss of self and cannot purge themselves of the oppression they witness and experience because they are too self-possessed, from a Gothic perspective. The ghosts emanate from themselves rather than from an encounter with others; indeed, the Morrison characters who cannot redeem themselves, who cannot experience a catharsis through a loving connection with another individual, are damned to an eternal haunting of their own minds.

If the Morrison ghosts are not manifestations of a disturbed psyche, they are often beneficial spiritual guides whose purpose is to bring the characters to a clearer sense of their history. Thus, in *Tar Baby**, images of big-breasted, maternal women haunt Jadine Childs* when she is in the Caribbean, urging her on to an understanding of the past. The group of singing women who exorcise the ghost of Beloved from Sethe's life includes mothers, dead and alive, among them the spirit of Baby Suggs*.

There are also folkloric associations with the ghosts, especially in their relation to an African past. Thus, for example, mythological blind African horsemen, the ghosts of escaped slaves, greet Son* on the Caribbean island in *Tar Baby* after Jadine has run off to Europe. Milkman Dead* in *Song of Solomon** is guided by the spirit of Shalimar of Solomon, his paternal great-grandfather, who, according to the folk song that Pilate Dead* taught him and that the children of his ancestral village sing, was able to escape slavery* and fly back to Africa like an eagle. Indeed, *Song of Solomon* is the most Gothic of Morrison's novels, in the traditional English (eighteenth-century) sense. As a quest story, it has all the underpinnings of a Gothic framework: a cursed or dysfunctional family*, the protagonist's need to free himself from a tyrannical father, betrayal and the righting of family wrongs, the search for the ancestral home, the use of magic (the evocation of the spirit of Shalimar) to guide the protagonist to the family legacy in a mysterious and hidden place (the gold in the cave). The traditional Gothic haunted house is present in many of Morrison's works: for example, the spiteful 124 Bluestone Road*, home* of Sethe, which Beloved haunts, or the Convent* mansion in *Paradise**, where the mystical and ghostlike women reside, and which is attacked by the uncomprehending men of the community*.

The fabulous or miraculous quality of Morrison's Gothic is akin to the magical realism* of Isabel Allende's or Laura Esquivel's ghost stories, and in all three cases, these women writers evoke the ghosts in order to connect their protagonists with their histories. Indeed, though *Song of Solomon* has the trappings of traditional "pure" eighteenth-century Gothic, Morrison's brand of Gothic is more thoroughly modern, for she rejects the resolution of the traditional Gothic plot. Morrison does not finally allow the realm of the rational to supersede or transcend the realm of the intuitive or the spiritual, and ultimately, though one may lay one's ghosts to rest, it is necessary to re-create their stories in order to understand one's own place in the universe. *See also* Approaches to Morrison's Work: Psychoanalytic; Ghost Story, Use of; History; Romantic Tradition.

References: Katherine Piller Beutel, "Gothic Repetitions: Toni Morrison's Use of Echo," *West Virginia Philological Papers* 42–43 (1997–98); Wesley Britton, "The Puritan Past and Black Gothic: The Haunting of Toni Morrison's *Beloved* in Light of Hawthorne's *The House of the Seven Gables*," *Nathaniel Hawthorne Review* 21: 2 (1995); Ellen J. Goldmer, "Other(ed) Ghosts: Gothicism and the Bonds of Reason in Melville, Chestnutt, and Morrison," *MELUS* 24: 1 (1999); Deborah Horvitz, "Nameless Ghosts: Possession and Dispossession in *Beloved*," *Studies in American Fiction* 17: 2 (1989); Linda Krumholz, "The Ghosts of Slavery: Historical Recovery in Toni Morrison's *Beloved*," *African-American Review* 26: 3 (1992); Franny Nudelman, "'Ghosts Might Enter Here': Toward a Reader's History," in *Hawthorne and Women: Engendering and Expanding the Hawthorne Tradition*, ed. John L. Idol, Jr., and Melinda Ponder (1999); Barbara Hill Rigney, "'A Story to Pass On': Ghosts in the Fiction of Black Women Writers," in *Haunting the House of Fiction: Feminist Perspectives on Ghost Stories by American Women Writers*, ed. Lynette Carpenter and Wendy K. Kolmar (1991); Liliane Weissberg, "Gothic Spaces: The Political Aesthetics of Toni Morrison's *Beloved*," in *Modern Gothic: A Reader*, ed. Victor Sage and Allan Lloyd Smith (1996).

Monika Elbert

## Gray, Golden (*Jazz*)

The illegitimate son of Vera Louise Gray*, the Southern aristocrat exiled from her family's plantation for carrying a Black child, and Henry Lestory/LesTroy (Hunter's Hunter*), the Black slave with whom she has a covert relationship. Golden, whose hair and eyes reflect his ambiguous racial heritage, grows up as Vera's adopted son. Vain, spoiled, and arrogant, he sets off on a patricidal voyage of discovery from Baltimore to Virginia upon discovering the truth. There he encounters first Wild*, a pregnant Black forest dweller, whom he helps to rescue when she knocks herself unconscious, then his father, who delivers Wild's unwanted baby, Joe Trace*. Rather than sympathizing with Golden's haughty indignation, Hunter tells him to accept adult responsibility and choose his own identity*.

One of the most elusive segments of *Jazz*, the Golden Gray episode can also be viewed as the unidentified narrator's active rumination on both artistry and identity. Golden seems to reject his African heritage. Yet the narrator, in constructing Golden's character and what may be the historical narrative behind Joe and Violet Trace's* present moment, fundamentally embraces the complexity that is the identity and the artistic process which permit communication in the form of literary production. *See also Jazz*.

Caroline Brown

## Gray, Vera Louise (*Jazz*)

A Southern aristocrat disinherited by her family* for her clandestine relationship with a Black family slave and subsequent impregnation by him. The biological mother of Golden Gray\*, she never informs him of his true heritage, presenting herself, instead, as his adoptive mother. When he demands to know the truth, she locks herself in her room and refuses to communicate. *See also Jazz.*

Caroline Brown

## Greek Mythology, Use of

Although direct references to Greek mythology are relatively rare in Morrison's novels (especially in comparison to biblical allusions), one does occasionally find them. The most common direct allusions are character and place names or brief descriptive metaphors. The "Elysian Fields" in *Sula\** ironically names the street on which Helene Wright's\* mother's house sits, a house she prefers to escape rather than a desirable heaven. *Paradise\** includes a Pallas\*, who in one scene becomes the very image of the warrior goddess Pallas Athena by wearing a long, flowing dress and wielding a sword. In *The Bluest Eye\**, the narrator's father is portrayed as a Vulcan guarding the flames as he adjusts doors and windows to regulate the heat in the house. At Old Jimmy's funeral, the deceased is described as a tragic hero; the mourners, as the strophe and antistrophe of a Greek chorus.

The preceding examples are quite brief, but there is one extended direct allusion to Greek mythology in the novels. *Song of Solomon\** chronicles Milkman Dead's\* "odyssey." The allusion is made apparent by the presence of the character Circe\*, who in the Greek *Odyssey* is the goddess who enchants Odysseus's shipmates by her song and a lavish feast that turns them into swine. Odysseus, made immune to her magic with Hermes's help, rescues his crew by sleeping with the enchantress. She then provides vital information on how to continue his journey home, specifically, how to get to Hades in order to consult the dead prophet Tiresias.

Morrison's Circe is also surrounded by animals, the weimaraners belonging to her now dead white employer. Unlike the Greek Circe, this one is not singing songs, weaving beautiful tapestries, or laying out banquets; she remains alive only to see through to its final destruction the home\* of her hated employer. But she is an enchantress. Even at her frail old age, Milkman feels compelled to climb the steps to embrace her. The smell of the dogs' waste in the rest of the house is replaced by a sweet ginger smell in the room where Circe sits. She gives Milkman directions to his own Hades, the dark cave where he believes he will find gold. He finds nothing, but like Odysseus's sojourn in Hades, Milkman's trip to the cave is the first step in the real purpose of his journey—to find his way home.

This is perhaps the most important parallel between *Song of Solomon* and *The Odyssey*, the quest itself. Odysseus leaves the site of the Trojan War as a warrior. As he travels home and undergoes numerous trials, his warrior self is broken down, and he returns to Ithaca with nothing that he started with, no conquered treasure from Troy or any of his adventures on the journey, nothing except his desire to be home and his newfound understanding of what "being home" means.

Milkman, too, returns home, not with the gold he seeks but with new realization about his connections to people and a place. Most important, he learns his family's real name. He leaves his father's house in Michigan, ashamed of himself for playing what now seems like a juvenile trick on his aunt Pilate Dead*, and with his sister Magdalena's* charge that he has been using people all his life. The gold is his chance at redemption, to return home a conquering hero. When he finds no treasure in the cave, he continues his journey to Virginia, the place where his grandparents lived, a small, isolated town called Shalimar that cannot even be found on the AAA map. The people of Shalimar, many of them named Solomon*, resent Milkman's rich, city ways, and put him through tests of strength and skill, including a nighttime coon hunt.

As he sits alone in the middle of wild and unfamiliar woods, he comes to the realization that nothing he has—his expensive clothes, his father's money, or anything it can buy—will help him out there. Like Odysseus, he is stripped down by his trials to the bare essentials and must rebuild himself as something new in order to reach his goal. He manages to elude Guitar Baines's attempt to kill him in the forest and continues his new search, now for his family's* past rather than for gold. He discovers the story of his family, a great-grandfather who could fly but dropped his youngest son as he attempted to fly away (shades of Daedalus and Icarus). This son was Jake*, Milkman's grandfather. The story, like that of Odysseus, is even immortalized in a song—the children's* nursery rhyme that Milkman heard as he watched them play. It is his song, the song that tells the story of his heritage. Milkman does eventually return to his father's house as a hero, not for bringing back the legacy of the gold, but the true legacy of their name.

The most interesting uses of Greek mythology, however, are evocative rather than direct. One example is a fascination with the feminine trinity, groups of women living together in threes and set apart from the everyday world. The three Graces, the three Fates, the three Furies, the three Gorgons, the three virgin goddesses, the nine Muses (three squared), and many other feminine trinities from Greek mythology elicited powerful emotions in those, especially men, who encountered them—fear, hatred, awe, gratitude, and occasionally love. The Gorgons turned men who saw them to stone; the Muses inspired great acts of artistic creation. Morrison's trinities tend to be set apart and inspire powerful emotions as well.

In *The Bluest Eye*, the prostitutes* China, Poland, and Miss Marie live together in an apartment in the same building as Pecola Breedlove*. They are set apart not only by their profession but by their profound hatred of men. They inspire strong emotions: Pecola is attracted to them because they treat her well; others are repelled by their profession and their reputation for having committed unspeakable acts, especially Miss Marie, who was thought to have killed someone by cooking the person in lye (invoking another theme favored by Morrison and Greek mythology: Medea). *Song of Solomon* presents us with Pilate, Reba*, and Hagar Dead*, who live apart from society in a house with no electricity or other comforts, and support themselves by selling bathtub liquor. Pilate even has an element of the divine about her, having been born with no navel. In *Beloved*, Sethe Suggs*, Denver Suggs*, and Beloved* form a trinity that drives Paul D Garner* and everyone else away. The Medea theme is strongly invoked in *Beloved*, too, with Sethe killing her daughter in order to keep her from slavery*. (Medea kills her children out of revenge, to save them from becoming outcasts, or to make them immortal; interpretations of her act vary widely.) In *Paradise* we have the three squared—nine chapters, named after nine women, who are set apart, living in an abandoned convent*. They inspire enough suspicion and fear in the nearby town that they are eventually hunted down by the men of that town.

What develops through the progression of Morrison's novels from earliest to latest is the level of destruction visited upon the trinities. They are women set apart, seemingly without need of, and sometimes with active hatred of, men. They are perhaps best compared to the Gorgons, who turned men to stone. Perseus destroys one (Medusa), thus neutralizing the power of the trinity and the accompanying fear of it. Paul D "exorcises" Beloved from Sethe's house and returns it (and Sethe and Denver) to the realm of society. Milkman (although indirectly) is the cause of Hagar's death and the source of Pilate's newfound joy in knowing she has her father's bones, rather than some white man's. He restores her connection to family (meaning him and their shared paternal ancestors; Reba and Hagar, her daughter and granddaughter, disappear from the novel at this point). *Paradise* multiplies the number of women and the hatred and violence* visited upon them, in order to return things to "normal."

In general, Morrison's use of Greek mythology is subtle and suggestive rather than direct. Her allusions, even the fairly obvious comparisons such as Milkman and Odysseus, invite the reader to tease out implications, rather than figure out one-to-one symbolic correspondences.

Catherine S. Quick

## Greene, Jude (*Sula*)

Nel Wright's* husband, his name suggests the New Testament figure of Judas. Jude marries Nel out of rage at his inability to secure a job building the New River Road. He is determined to take on what he perceives to be the role of a man in society at all costs. He also wants somebody to care about his hurt. Jude leaves the Bottom* for Detroit after Nel catches him and Sula Peace* having sex*. Nel has no further contact with him, and he does nothing to help raise his children*. *See also Sula.*

Douglas Taylor

# H

## Harlem, New York (*Jazz*)

Destination of thousands of Black migrants from countless rural towns and villages throughout the Southern United States; also a destination for scores of Caribbean immigrants. Harlem, fueled by massive Black migration* and a strong postwar economy, clubs that served bootleg alcohol, and white patronage of the arts, symbolized African American political and cultural confidence, and fed the movement that became the Harlem Renaissance. Harlem is where Joe* and Violet Trace* settle, and becomes the focal point of the rising action in *Jazz**. *See also Jazz.*

Caroline Brown

## Haven, Oklahoma (*Paradise*)

Precursor of Ruby, Oklahoma*, and original site of the Oven*, Haven is the all-Black town founded in 1890 by nine families who had trekked from Louisiana and Mississippi after Reconstruction ended and after being rejected by the all-Black town of Fairly, Oklahoma*, for being too poor and too Black. Zechariah "Big Papa" Morgan chose the site of the town based on his divine visions of a traveling man who guided them to the spot. After sixteen months of negotiating with and working for a family of "state Indians" who owned the land, the group finally purchased the land. Haven's imminent failure after World War II inspired the "fifteen families" to move farther west and establish Ruby. *See also Paradise*.

Julie Cary Nerad

## History

Toni Morrison's works are replete with history, with a purpose. Each novel invokes specific historical details that remind—or teach—readers about slavery's* legacy, the removal from Africa, particular locations and kinds of Black community* North and South*, labor conditions, music*, foods, religious beliefs, stories, and the rich texture of rural and urban African American culture. Morrison's novels also make clear that African American and minority history defines American history, providing its shape and feel. With novels that remember and recover specifically Black history, Morrison gives depth and complexity, as well as subjective ownership, to historical periods ranging from the Middle Passage, slavery, and the founding of all-Black communities to the Great Migration* of the 1920s, 1940s Ohio (her home state), the 1960s and Black Power, and the formation of the 1980s Black middle class. Details of clothing and context, rather than appearance, create her often specifically historical characters. Personages like Booker T. Washington and Hitler are often subjects of conversation, and Morrison frequently uses the technique of dating sections by year: 1919, 1937, 1963, and so on.

But Morrison narrates historical context and the years that particular community events happened in order to explain the present's need for and relation to the past. Morrison focuses on a kind of history that is oral and aural, known in African American lives and communities, and on a reality in which years do not signal merely a time line of external events. She does not let readers forget the pain of what happened historically, the consequences of specific events, or the white culture's obsession with Blackness, because these form the contexts of the lives Morrison explores. Historical facts, contextual specifics like Afros, bone buttons, milk cans, and a big Packard; deeply evocative renditions of individual experience; and sometimes painstakingly researched details convince readers of the truth of the history Morrison portrays.

Each of Morrison's novels and other works, such as *Dreaming Emmett** and *Playing in the Dark: Whiteness and the Literary Imagination**, presents a different aspect of African American history, although certain both general and specific events reappear throughout, like the massive Black migration from South to North, the Depression, and the murder of Emmett Till. Morrison acknowledges the importance of history and its rereading in her scholarly work and discussions of writing. But she makes it clear that much of the history she uses is oral, fragmented, contained in music, tales, folk culture, art—from memory*, song, or silent places. Morrison's historical details signal a Black narrative, the storytelling that is part of her African American experience, and the novel's potential to express the living relation of past and present for Black people, whether they recognize specific historically imagined characters and a historic structure in the fiction or not.

Morrison grounds each retelling of historical impact within a Black community. For example, *The Bluest Eye** takes place in Lorain, Ohio*, and opens with a reference to personal history as the narrator Claudia MacTeer* reflects on her childhood in the 1940s. Claudia recalls the movies of Jean Harlow, the vulnerability of Black people in the South, the candy Mary Janes, and the unique names of the community's prostitutes*: Poland, China, Miss Marie. Other historical elements include the specificity of clothing, the ways Black people take care of each other, and the novel's sense that there is more knowledge to be gained than Claudia had access to at the time. *The Bluest Eye* invites the reader to research, to ask questions and discover more. The Maginot Line, the fights between the Breedloves, Claudia's mother wrapping her in Vicks-coated flannel, and a father who keeps the fire burning like a Vulcan graphically convey what must be learned about the texture of one community's history and values. Similarly, the Dick and Jane framing story, along with the idealization of Shirley Temple and dolls with blue eyes, dramatize the overpowering presence of the standards of white culture, white beauty, and white success in the 1940s—their power, literally, to kill mind and memory, to destroy Pecola Breedlove*, Soaphead Church*, and the story.

With *Sula**, Morrison invokes the World War I of Shadrack's* past, the Depression, and what follows by inventing the town of Medallion, Ohio*, where the hill land was not considered valuable and so became the Black community called the Bottom*. Although Sula is primarily about the place and community that make Sula Peace's* and Nel Wright's* friendship possible, Shadrack's experience of World War I structures the novel. The plot begins with Shadrack's confrontation with *it*, the unbearability of what he saw and participated in on the fields of France in December 1917. Shadrack's experience of war acts as the text's specific reminder of racism and the historical treatment of returning Black veterans, but also and more generally what it means to be a throwaway person. As the novel moves through the lives of Nel and Sula, from the background of Medallion in the early twentieth century through the 1930s to the 1960s, products like Nu Nile and Strawberry Crush and *Liberty* magazine, and Nel's encounter with signs saying COLORED ONLY on the train to New Orleans, operate side by side with frequent references to years. The 1911 after which Eva Peace* does not set foot on the stairs, the 1917 when Plum* went to war, and the 1922 when Sula and

Nel are twelve keep historical events in mind while positioning the reader to understand them from Medallion's perspective. Shadrack's National Suicide Day* operates as a kind of Greek chorus claiming there is always this one form of response to history's madness. However, Shadrack, like Pecola, signals the effects of racist culture but also the reasons to return, as Sula does in 1937, to the Bottom. And as the Bottom moves through its own history, the narration laments what is past. There has always been the promise, the hope, of a brighter day, but it has never truly come, and much has been lost: the sense of place, the value of work, and the meaning of shared survival. Thus *Sula* not only rewrites history but also starts to value it in new ways, by recognizing the sustaining qualities of Black communities as the past's treasure.

*Song of Solomon** reaches farther back into African American history with its legend of the Black man who flies back to Africa. Milkman Dead* must recover a family history that moves from slavery to freedom, through the Depression and Herbert Hoover's presidency, from Virginia to Pennsylvania to Michigan. *Song of Solomon*'s sense of its characters' histories gets built through constant references to the year this or that happened, as well as to phenomena like racial-uplift groups, the shooting of Irish in the streets, the railroads, wars men lived through, the first Black doctor in town, and the TB sanatorium. Particularities of African American history are specificially invoked as well, through stories, music, and naming. Macon Dead* got his name from the ignorance and/or malice of a drunk white man at the Freedman's Bureau who asked him who his father was—"dead"—and where he was born, then wrote everything down in the wrong places. Quaker schools, the soldiers in 1918, Winnie Ruth Judd, Hitler, Sam Shepard axing his wife, Emmett Till, and the murder of four girls in a Birmingham church all appear as memory, parts of someone's life, subject of conversation, or lived event. Not only does the novel in this way re-create the history of a Black family; it rewrites the experience of World Wars I and II, the Depression, and lynch mobs from the perspective of Black people who live, see, and analyze their power dynamics. The attentive reader cannot help but reconstruct and experience the presence of African American and Indian blood everywhere on the land Milkman travels in searching for his own history.

*Tar Baby** moves to a different historical setting, with a location that emphasizes the economic structure of American race* relations. The novel tells the Caribbean story of slave history as the rape of the natural world conducted by forced labor in the cocoa, rum, and sugar trades. Within the first few pages readers must experience the connections between the Caribbean and Philadelphia, between cane fields and candy factories. References to Joan Fontaine in *Rebecca*, *The Search for Tomorrow*, and industrious Philadelphia Negroes emphasize that the popular culture of the past is its economic culture, dependent on a specific class system and racial hierarchy. References to Caribbean exoticism, the humiliations of immigrant life, and what the dream of U.S. citizenship represents—leisure suits—form the background texture of the drama between a wealthy white couple, their Black servants, and the next generation. While Son* has come from Eloe*, an all-Black town in Florida, has memories of Baltimore, and sees Isle des Chevaliers* haunted by Black, naked, hard-laboring men, Valerian Street* sees the same island as founded by Napoleonic chevaliers. There are at least two histories for every past, every place, as with the story of the tar baby and briar patch, depending on whether one is Black or white. Frequent references to years, locations, and past events weave these histories together and shape them as the forces that create the conflict between Jadine Childs* and Son. As the characters try to make each other see history differently, the reader must also engage with multiple dimensions of historical narrative, and questions about how the twentieth century can bring them together.

Morrison becomes more explicitly historical with *Beloved**, investigating not just the general qualities of African American memory but also how people experience specific events. A neo-slave narrative*, *Beloved* opens a historical trilogy of novels that extends the investigation of Black consciousness back to the Middle Passage, documenting not only Morrison's careful reading of slave texts but also how slavery necessarily lives in the present. Morrison's retelling invokes unbearable trauma*, in which it is not clear whether death* or life is preferable, and either could be imposed at any moment. With *Jazz** and *Paradise**, *Beloved* spans the African American experience, defining the shape and rhythms of culture and exploring the nature of life, death, suffering, survival, community, and love when the past *is* trauma. Making use of its setting (Cincinnati, Ohio, in 1873), *Beloved* highlights the diversity of experiences and responses to the slavery its characters encountered eighteen years before. Ohio was a free state; the Ohio River, from Kentucky the path to freedom. There were abolitionists in Ohio, as well as the Underground Railroad, newly formed communities of free Blacks, and jobs in meatpacking factories. But there were also the Klan and the Fugitive Slave Law, living memories of slavery past and present for Sethe Suggs*, Paul D Garner*, Baby Suggs*, and Stamp Paid, as well as the lost Halle Suggs*, Sixo*, and Howard and Buglar Suggs*. Denver Suggs*, born during her mother's escape, and Beloved*, killed by her mother to protect her from slavery, are as important as Sethe and Paul D; each carries a vital aspect of the experience that must be remembered. Paul D, speaking of the coffle and the bit, of working on the chain gang; Denver of paying a nickel a month to learn to read with slates; Beloved on what it was like in that dark place; and frequent movement from Kentucky to Ohio, south to Georgia and Alabama, north to Delaware—all tell a piece of the story of the Middle Passage and beyond, requiring the reader to feel, from the inside, the consequences of the way the United States was built—on the backs of Blacks, the poor, and Redmen.

*Jazz* continues the African American saga, narrating the Great Migration of the 1920s, the Black nationalist movement, the return of African American soldiers from World War I to economic racism, and the Harlem* that included both Marcus Garvey and hooch joints. Morrison challenges readings of the Harlem Renaissance as the celebratory rebirth of Black culture by highlighting the struggles associated with the music, the city, the constant reinventing of oneself, and the profound class shifts as a generation moved from hard, outdoor physical labor to waiting tables, hairdressing, and selling cosmetics. Again, Morrison gets inside the history: the reader feels the drums on Fifth Avenue, hears the cold silence, understands Alice Manfred's* sense of the threat of lowdown, below-the-belt music, as well as the music's appeal, its promise of the only possible future for a girl like Dorcas Manfred*, whose only past is her parents' violent deaths in East St. Louis. Historical details manifest in clothing, food, specific records: the marcelling iron and Victrola; Cleopatra products; the *Age*, the *News*, and *The Messenger*. The novel takes specific events—the 1919 procession of veterans of the 369 Regiment on Fifth Avenue, the East St. Louis riots, the development of Harlem's jazz clubs—and takes readers inside them with characters who watched, who felt the music or the fire, who experienced these events as the defining present.

With its musical metaphor, *Jazz* shows movement generating infinite possibilities. Joe* and Violet Trace* move from Vesper County, Virginia, where both have been physical laborers, to New York City. There is no why, no specific dream or hope; the focus is on how their lives change and what is left behind. Joe's history becomes his means of explaining how he shot Dorcas, trailing without intending to kill, yet responding instinctually to a series of losses: of his mother, hunting, a father, physical labor, his wife (when she starts sleeping with a doll). "What does the reinvented life cost?" is the question of the novel for all characters: not only Joe but also Violet, who thought she did not want children* because her mother eventually just gave up; Alice, who remembers only her husband's teeth are left; even Felice* and Dorcas. Dorcas cannot reinvent herself; she's the Beloved who signals that it's not all triumph or even survival. The most important work of reinvention is the reader's, who must revisit the history of Harlem and face the real losses now that these characters' stories have been told.

*Paradise*, like *The Bluest Eye* and *Sula*, is a novel of profoundly Black community. But it also, with *Beloved* and *Jazz*, forms the third part of Morrison's historical trilogy by representing the kind of all-Black town that got created by determined free Blacks in the South, in the Midwest, even in Oklahoma. There's a dead young woman in this text as well, and her name becomes the town's when returning veterans move the town after World War II. As with *Beloved* and *Jazz*, the history in *Paradise* consists of more than just the rich, evocative texture of period details and cultural memory, though the novel effortlessly weaves in such signals of historical time. Years, when invoked, have a specific political as well as personal context; 1963 marks John F. Kennedy's assassination; 1968, the summer of riots and the deaths of Martin Luther King and Bobby Kennedy. Readers must not only get inside these events but also must feel them as if they were being lived by runaway Black women, a town trying to keep out not only white racism but Black power, and a privileged white girl whose world makes no sense at all.

*Paradise* contains a history written and destroyed, a history that needs to be rewritten, the history of town and world seen through competing African American spiritualities. The primary questions of the novel are about immanence and history: whether paradise is now or to come; how the spine of the Civil Rights movement was made up of ordinary people; the sacrificing of fathers and mothers, past and present. With Richard Misner's* decision to stay in Ruby, the novel reclaims even the behavior of a town acting like white people as worthy of redemption. *See also* Approaches to Morrison's Work: Historical; Community; Flying Africans, Myth of; Identity; South, Influence of; Violence; Whiteness.

Karen E. Waldron

## Home

Home occupies both a literal and a conceptual space in Toni Morrison's fiction. Morrison's interest in home can be understood through the prism of American history*. As a result, home is rarely an uncomplicated space of sanctuary. Rather, Morrison probes in her literary imagination the idea of America (and often the American South*) as a dislocated home place for African Americans. The South is critical in her work because for many African Americans, the South represents a place of beginning. Although most of her novels are not set entirely in the South, its landscape frequently recurs as a familial or ancestral location, or is embedded as a memory* of home. As a result, Morrison's characterization of home does not always offer peace and serenity. Indeed, the domestic is not impervious to societal ills, such as racism and sexism. In fact, these forms of violence* are frequently replayed in this domestic arena with disastrous consequences. Often, though, it is not geography* that signals home, but identity*. There are characters in many of Morrison's novels who foster the best elements of home, regardless of the conditions of their households.

Thus, it is not always North or South that defines home; instead, certain characters transcend temporal and social divisions in order to become spaces of home for themselves and others.

In Morrison's first novel, *The Bluest Eye**, the larger setting of home is Lorain, Ohio*. This is an important beginning of literary homes in Morrison's canon because she was born and raised in Lorain. Thus Ohio not only represents a personal connection to Morrison's own life but also, as she has remarked on many occasions, it is an important state in our national past. Juxtaposed to the South (as a border to Kentucky) and the North (as a border to Canada via Lake Erie), Ohio is a complex geographic site. During the antebellum period, the Ohio River was a demarcation line between freedom and enslavement, and thus became a symbol of freedom for escaping enslaved peoples.

*The Bluest Eye*, perhaps more than any of Morrison's subsequent novels, can be understood by tracing the various arenas of home. The novel begins with descriptions of two homes: the MacTeers' and the Breedloves'. Although both families are poor and reside in modest dwellings, it is clear that the MacTeers' house is a place of warmth, love, and community*. By contrast, the Breedloves are dispossessed. The family* enjoys little if any sense of camaraderie, and the shabbiness of the storefront house and dilapidated furnishings symbolize their own feelings of unworthiness and despair. As a result, the youngest member of the household, Pecola Breedlove*, lives a desperate life in which she forever yearns for safe harbors. Although she receives temporary shelter in the home of the MacTeers, she is not of that environment and is perpetually exiled in her search for family and love.

Pecola also receives some kind of emotional safety in the home of the three prostitutes*: China, Poland, and Miss Marie. The configuration of their lives provides a counternarrative to socially assembled constructs of home. First, these are unmarried women who are not bound to the domestic in the roles of mother/wife/caretaker. Choosing how to earn their money and live their lives, the women are not susceptible to social mores and are thus able to offer love and support to this young, lost girl. However, Pecola does not join this triad, and instead continues her emotional journey to selfhood and belonging. Circumscribing her journey even further is the Dick and Jane myth*. This children's* primer story is the overarching symbol in the novel and represents the seemingly perfect image of home and happiness that Pecola must confront each day. This story does more than negate Pecola's home life; it negates her very existence. Her race* and class distance her from the fairy-tale world of Dick and Jane and their domestic bliss to such an extent that she desires blue eyes so that she may finally find a home, not merely with Dick and Jane but with herself. Despite the fact that in her madness she convinces herself that she has attained blue eyes, and thus a sense of home, her tragic life reminds the reader of the destructive consequences of perpetual displacement.

Like *The Bluest Eye*, *Sula*\* is set in Ohio, in the fictional town of Medallion\*. The first few pages of the novel identify the import of home in terms of community and neighborhood. In *Sula*, the African American population resides in the Bottom\*, an ironically named hillside community that has its beginnings in exploitation. An enslaved man was tricked by his master into acquiring this unfarmable terrain, believing that it was fertile valley land. Thus, historical forms of exploitation underlie the characters' displacement. Moreover, binary divisions, such as this spatial geography epitomizes, occur throughout the novel. Most obviously, Nel Wright\* and Sula Peace\*, the two female protagonists, bespeak this kind of separation and complementation.

Nel's and Sula's childhood homes mark the division: Nel inhabited a home that was predicated on cleanliness, whereas Sula lived in a house imbued with disorder. However, neither home provided sanctuary for the young girls. As an adult, Sula audaciously bucks traditional female rules of behavior, and leaves town after Nel's wedding. Notably, it is Nel's assumption of the mantle of housewife that provides the catalyst for Sula's years of wandering. Here, Morrison indicates that the options for the creation of home can be limiting and stifling for women. When Sula returns and literally displaces her grandmother—forcibly placing her in a nursing home—the community casts her as a pariah and she is without a sense of harborage or fellowship. By contrast, Nel, an upstanding member of the community, has worked hard to create a conventional home life for her husband and children. However, Sula engages in a brief affair with Nel's husband, Jude Greene\*, and punctures this facade of domesticity\*. Rejecting any sense of home life, Sula does not conceive of her behavior as a betrayal.

As expected, the women are estranged for many years. However, by the end of the novel, after Sula's death, Nel recognizes that although she is of the community, her true home—her place of sanctuary, belonging, and identity—is found within her friendship with Sula. Ending the novel thus, Morrison questions the sanctions surrounding homemaking and its prosaic rules regarding matrimony and family structure. Morrison posits that such constructs have the potential to damage genuine spaces of sanctuary.

Morrison continues her critique of middle-class affectedness in her third novel, *Song of Solomon*\*. The protagonist, Milkman Dead\* (Macon Dead III), lives an emotionally void life with his two sisters; his father, Macon Dead II\* (the richest businessman in town), and his mother, Ruth Foster Dead\* (the daughter of the town's only African American doctor). Despite the material advantages that this family enjoys, the Dead house is just that—an empty edifice that is bereft of nurturing and fellowship.

Milkman's father, so concerned with appearances of wealth and pomposity, forbids his family to visit or even acknowledge his sister, Pilate Dead*. Juxtaposed to Macon's home is Pilate's; she is a bootlegger who lives on the outskirts of town. Her home is antithetical to her brother's, absent as it is of indoor plumbing and any kind of modern amenity. Further, the facade of middle-class respectability, on which Pilate's brother relies, is fully absent in this dwelling. Pilate's home life resembles the triad of independent women in *The Bluest Eye*, for Pilate lives with her adult daughter Reba* and her granddaughter Hagar*. Despite the paucity of material goods, Pilate's home, a decidedly female space, becomes a site of safety, love, and protection for all who enter, including, at different times, Ruth and Milkman.

Indeed, Milkman's living in Pilate's dwelling place marks his first move into a space of community and healing. For Milkman to fully embark on this journey to home, he must leave his lakeside Michigan community and travel to the ancestral homeland of the American South. Although his flight is initiated by the hope of materialistic gain, as Milkman travels to sites of family and culture, he begins to realize that his alienation is not solely a result of his family's dissonance, but is part of a disconnection from heritage and ancestry; in short, a forgetting of home. As a result, it is only when he is on ancestral ground that he begins to reclaim his cultural identity, which includes an understanding of slavery* and the intergenerational effects of this trauma*. Thus, by the end of the novel, Milkman becomes Pilate's heir; he surrenders himself to the complications of home, recognizing that love and violence do coexist in this landscape of heritage, yet he emerges fortified by an awareness that the creation of a liberating space of home is predicated on the knowledge of family, history, and community.

Unlike the promise of home in *Song of Solomon*, in *Tar Baby** home is a less stable affair where domestic hierarchies are erected only to be unmasked and dismantled. Moving the location of her fourth novel to a fictional Caribbean island, Isle des Chevaliers*, Morrison considers the politics of homemaking as a wealthy white candy manufacturer and his wife resituate a plantation economy, complete with domestic servants and field hands. Setting the novel in a secluded island community, where the big house and servants' quarters are neatly intact, recalls not only the spatial geography of antebellum plantations but also reflects Caribbean colonial history. Despite the seemingly rigid polarization of home, Morrison confounds this construction, for it is in this domestic arena where family secrets unfold and identities converge, resulting in a destruction of racial stratification and a restructuring of home.

In *Beloved**, Morrison returns to American soil to probe the meaning and creation of home in the face of slavery. The cataclysmic event in *Beloved* is an escaped enslaved woman's mercy killing of her daughter to prevent her from becoming re-enslaved. Although Sethe Suggs* is shunned as a pariah for committing this horrifying act, it is not until Sethe and the community recognize the pain and devastation of their lives under slavery—which this murder epitomizes—that the creation of home ever can be realized. As a result, memory becomes the ultimate site of home.

Through flashbacks and recollections, the novel chronicles the different settings of home for Sethe. She was enslaved on a Kentucky plantation, known as Sweet Home*. This ironically named plantation underscores Sethe's dissociation from home. In fact, it was at Sweet Home that a pregnant Sethe was physically and sexually abused. Traumatized by this unspeakable act of violence*, Sethe fled, and after a harrowing journey, she arrives at 124 Bluestone Road*, her mother-in-law's home in Cincinnati, Ohio. Not only is Baby Suggs's* home a restorative location for Sethe, but like Pilate in *Song of Solomon*, Baby Suggs is herself a site of home for the larger African American community. Baby Suggs's largesse is most evident in the Clearing*, a wooded area in which she preaches love and dignity to a newly freed population. Retreating to this uncharted territory, Baby Suggs enables the community to feel at home in their skin and in their souls. Recognizing that slavery attempted to negate their humanity, she encourages the community to create what they have been systematically denied: a shelter, a protected place, in which to grow, flourish, and simply be. Notably, this arena of home is not confined to a domicile, but is an outside dwelling, which not only signifies the expanse of home but also problematizes the notion of home as that which merely can be purchased and owned. Instead, *Beloved* reveals the multiple ways in which home can be imagined and achieved.

Despite Baby Suggs's inability to sustain her own vision of the domestic after Sethe's infanticide*, the novel begins and concludes with the conditions of 124 Bluestone Road. The import of home as a place reflective of yearnings and memories is signaled by the narrative construction of the novel; the opening lines of the three sections of *Beloved* personify 124 as a station that chronicles Sethe's, and by extension the community's, suffering and recovery*. As a testament to this reclamation of self and history, home becomes a locus of memory and a place of belonging. Indeed, by the end of the novel, Morrison allows the reader to recognize what Baby Suggs could not: that home, although not resistant to cultural and social harms, is a locale capable of continual renewal and re-creation. Indeed, by the end of the novel Sethe, with the help of her loved ones, is encouraged to envision the possibility of creating a future.

The desire to realize a better future is amplified in *Jazz*. The Great Migration*, a mass exodus of nearly four million African Americans from the South to the North after the Reconstruction period, is the primary thrust of *Jazz* and an implicit theme in most of Morrison's previous novels. Indeed, many of Morrison's characters are from the South and bring that ethos to their lives in the North. This is true of *Jazz*, the story of Joe* and Violet Trace*, who leave the South to move to the "City," which, while not named as such, suggests New York's Harlem*. Although Morrison's prose captures the excitement and vibrancy of Harlem, this novel does not merely pay tribute to the Harlem Renaissance. Instead, Morrison directly engages with the climate of terror in the post–Reconstruction period. Drawing migrants away from a locus of family and cultural history, the City is not a utopian space of home; rather, the migrants, desperately looking for a place of protection, are dislocated in this seeming landscape of freedom. Years later, Joe and Violet find themselves alienated in a strange land. Although neither makes a return trip home, as does Milkman in *Song of Solomon*, Joe and Violet participate in ritual acts of remembrance that allow them to mourn their disconnection from the home space of the American South. Joe and Violet's dissociation from a geographic home is mediated by a metaphoric site of home, namely, jazz*. Jazz becomes an important setting of home for the new migrants because its enabling cadence offers meaning and gives expression to their lives. Moving through chords of pain, sorrow, and healing, jazz provides the expressive language of home.

Morrison's most recent novel, *Paradise**, moves away from the South–North dyad, and relocates the reader to the West, in the all-Black fictional towns of Haven* and Ruby, Oklahoma*, the first of which was founded by nine families searching for a safe place to reside after the Civil War. This novel highlights the polarities of home through gender and space; Ruby is a town founded and governed by men, whereas the Convent* (located on the outskirts of town) is a home inhabited solely by women. The Convent is a haven for displaced women seeking refuge. Like so many female spaces in Morrison's oeuvre, the Convent is an unconventional household that proves to be a threatening force to the patriarchs of Ruby. Under the guise of protecting their hometown, nine men of Ruby raid the Convent. This unprovoked attack does not result in the safeguarding of the town and its history, but unravels the hierarchy of the community's governance and undermines the community's status as a secure and protective home.

While Morrison certainly critiques patriarchy as a form of domination, this novel does not resituate a matriarchal home space. Rather, an unspecified paradise marks the final domain. In keeping with the complexion of home in Morrison's canon, even this paradise, this heavenly home, is not a utopia, but is fraught with earthly concerns. As such, it is only through communal strivings that this paradise, though imperfect, promises to be a home accessible to all. *See also* Ancestor; Approaches to Morrison's Work: Postcolonial; Children; Magical Realism.

References: Lori Askeland, "Remodeling the Model Home in *Uncle Tom's Cabin* and *Beloved*," *American Literature* 64: 4 (December, 1992); Catherine Carr Lee, "The South in Toni Morrison's *Song of Solomon*: Initiation, Healing and Home," *Studies in the Literary Imagination* 31: 2 (Fall 1998); Carol E. Schmudde, "Haunting of 124," *African American Review* 26: 3 (Autumn 1992).

Anissa Wardi

## Hunger

The novels of Toni Morrison are replete with references to hunger. Beyond the literal, physical hunger that occupies an important position in many of her characters' life stories, there are other types of hunger, or appetites, to be accounted for: sexual appetites, for instance, and metaphorical hunger for things like memory*, history*, and voice. Also important to a discussion of hunger in Morrison's work are scenes of eating and images of food that, when focused on critically, take on a greater significance, beginning to appear less like themes and more like functional parts in her narratives that help define her writing.

Physical hunger is frequently presented not necessarily in terms of class but in terms of racial power struggle—whether it be through questions of strength and voice (in *Song of Solomon**, Milkman Dead* finds that hunger energizes him, while in *Beloved**, Denver Suggs* finds that it silences her), the hunger of slaves on a homestead (in *Beloved*, for example, when schoolteacher* no longer allows the Sweet Home* men to have guns, they are no longer able to supplement their diet with game) or the hunger of slaves on the run. Hunger for food reveals much about familial ties as well, especially a woman's identity* as mother. In *Beloved*, we are told of the strength of Sethe Suggs*, a mother determined to reach her hungry children and nurse them; and in *Song of Solomon*, physical hunger offsets psychological hunger, we learn of a mother's own hunger to feed her child—Ruth Dead's* continued suckling of her son that earns him the nickname Milkman.

Travelers and mourners are two of the hungriest character types in Morrison's novels. Many of the wayward women who end up at the Convent* in *Paradise** are convinced to stay on because their travels have made them hungry and Consolata Sosa* offers them something to eat—but also because they are hungry for themselves, and the rituals that she leads them through reveal to them their hunger to know and accept themselves. In Morrison's work, there are many scenes of hungry travelers being offered the hospitality of strangers, and there are many scenes in which the proper hospitality of neighbors is shown: for example, Stamp Paid feels that, after he has words with Ella*, he has to eat a piece of something she has cooked in order to let her know that he holds no ill will toward her (*Beloved*); and Pilate Dead* makes sure that she always offers something to eat to anyone who enters her house before they begin talking (*Song of Solomon*).

The portrayal of emotional or psychological hunger in Morrison's novels often works so that the relationship of a character with food takes on some of the hidden fears and anxieties of the character's being or history. These moments of desire, or psychological hunger, usually take precedence over the physical. In *Song of Solomon*, for instance, Milkman is unable to eat the breakfast served to him in Shalimar because his real hunger originates from his desire to learn more about his family* history.

Sexual appetite is also spoken of in terms of hunger. In *Beloved*, there is a scene in which white guards line up in front of kneeling Black prisoners and force them to perform oral sex* on them, referring to it as giving them their "breakfast." Jadine Childs*, in *Tar Baby**, reflects on how she has had to reign in her "hunger" in order not to be dominated by any man. Also in *Tar Baby*, there is the interplay between sex and hunger when Margaret Street* finds Son in her closet and believes that he is there to rape her; however Son chides her about this assumption, telling her that it is hard for a person to think about sex when he is on the verge of starvation.

Images of food and eating in the novels of Toni Morrison serve to qualify the private relationship between husband and wife, as well as to express public ties to the community*. The importance of the space of food exchange between a wife and her husband can be found, for instance, in *Sula**, when the narrator mentions, indicating the very hot weather, that it is the type of weather in which women might consider putting ground glass in their husbands' food to seek revenge for ill treatment, and that it was so hot and the husbands so hungry that they would wonder about it but eat it anyway. *Beloved* shows us how food mediates ties to the community: The feast—started by a tub of blackberries picked by Stamp Paid—that angers the community against Baby Suggs and Sethe because it is considered too generous, and thus prideful, is countered by the accumulated feast—the baskets left on their yard—provided by the community when they learn from Denver that Sethe is in trouble and that the household has no more food. This charity from the community feeds the relationships in it: between the church members who conspire to help by cooking and leaving the food, but especially between Denver and the community she has been isolated from.

The fact of being in a situation where you know little about other members of your family who have been separated from you, a situation in which many of Morrison's characters find themselves, heightens one's relationship to food memories and allows characteristics of a person, such as favorite foods, to begin to embody their memory. Denver, in *Beloved*, holds onto the detail that she is told regarding the father she has never seen: that he loved soft fried eggs. Milkman, in *Song of Solomon*, always thinks of Pilate as the woman who made him his first perfect soft-boiled egg. This phenomenon explains why Pauline Breedlove*, in *The Bluest Eye*, feels like she doesn't belong in her family: because, among a longer list of grievances, nobody cares about her food preferences.

Many times descriptions of types of people are offered through descriptions of the foods they eat or of their relationship to food. Northerners are described by Guitar Baines* as interested in the fancy presentation of food instead of the food itself (*Song of Solomon*). The bland processed food eaten by the white people in whose house Macon Dead* and Pilate are hidden by Circe* causes them to revolt against it and informs their decision to leave; they depart after the morning when Pilate cries for fresh cherries, the kind she enjoyed on her father's farm, when given cherry jam from a jar (*Song of Solomon*). Associated with Pilate's wish for fresh cherries is the shooting of Macon's father, the account of which includes, along with the shooting, the fact that the white men who shot him ate the peaches from the trees in his orchard, the violation of eating the beautiful peaches embodying the killing, which was motivated by the desire for his land and the successful farm he had made of it (*Song of Solomon*).

Food and hunger in Morrison's novels are used to mark and define relationships, and they often mediate or inform politics of race*. Consider the fiasco in *Tar Baby* when Margaret attempts to cook Christmas dinner and have the help, Ondine and Sydney Childs*, join her and her husband at the dining room table—racial tension becomes unbearable and awful secrets, hidden in the family for years, surface. In these novels, characters reveal ways of thinking about their relationship to the world around them through food, through their reactions to hunger, and through the types of hunger they experience.

Lynn Marie Houston

## Hunter's Hunter/Henry Lestory/Lestroy (*Jazz*)

Golden Gray's* biological father, Hunter becomes Joe Trace's* father figure and mentor, rescuing the infant when he is abandoned by Wild*, his unresponsive mother. Hunter delivers the tiny Joe, finds an adoptive home for him with the Williams family, then teaches him how to hunt and trap. When confronted by Golden Gray with the news of his paternity, Hunter tells him that he was never informed of Vera Louise Gray's* pregnancy and, as a Black man and a slave, had no power to assist her in any case. Furthermore, Golden must now choose his own identity* and claim adult status rather than waste time feeling sorry for himself. *See also Jazz.*

Caroline Brown

# 1

## Identity

In 1865, slavery\* was abolished in the United States. Yet, for the next 100 years and more, African American men and women found themselves still struggling to secure freedom and to understand what such freedom means. Using various settings, Toni Morrison delves into the lives of African American women, examining how they cope with poverty, rape, incest, beliefs regarding beauty, and numerous forms of oppression. In exploring these survival techniques, Morrison questions how African Americans struggle to establish a self they can call their own and call free. In order to survive, Morrison's characters need to choose whether to exist in the shadows, submerging their identities, or to fight back, proving that they have a self worth respecting. Morrison says that one of her foremost concerns is exploring how we learn to live our lives fully and well. In order to discover how to live wholly, Morrison's novels focus upon issues of self and cultural identity through the lives of African Americans.

Morrison emerged on the American literary scene in 1973 with *The Bluest Eye*\*. Early on, the narrator states that when it comes to Pecola Breedlove's\* story, since it is so difficult to understand "why" such things happen, we must instead examine "how" they happened. Ultimately, in explaining Pecola's descent into insanity, the novel tells us why such tragedies occur. In her desire for blue eyes, which she associates with beauty and acceptance, Pecola sets herself up for disappointment. As she details this loss, Morrison exposes how the culture in which Pecola lives creates the false standards of beauty she strives for, and how these standards, based upon white norms, affect all the African American women and men in the novel. Claudia MacTeer* accurately pinpoints the time when the female self is threatened in childhood after Maureen Peal announces her cuteness to them. Claudia, her sister Frieda*, and her friend Pecola at a very young age encounter prejudice that molds their insecurities about their identities. Maureen, a mixed-blood child with yellow coloring, appeals to white sensibilities because she is cute and dressed to perfection. Her wealth enhances her outer image and inflates her inner image, causing her to put down the three young girls who, without money or looks, will never be seen as cute.

This feeling of being lesser, coupled with a lack of understanding, leads Pecola to dream of having blue eyes because blue eyes are owned and valued by the white world. With these eyes, she believes that she will be beautiful and recognized by others. Claudia, on the other hand, responds to the feeling of being lesser by fighting back. Through observing Pecola and the African American culture's treatment of Pecola's family, Claudia recognizes the dangerous results of alcohol, poverty, child abuse, and intraracism. She sees how such things drag a person down to a point of near selflessness. In essence, then, *The Bluest Eye* critiques the white beauty myth* while also critiquing the Black community's* intraracism as they internalize feelings of otherness, of degradation and loss of identity. Those internalized feelings create the story of what happens to Pecola and Claudia, and the contrast between Claudia's survival and Pecola's loss of self.

Set in a Midwestern community called the Bottom*, Morrison's *Sula*  follows Nel Wright* and Sula Peace* from childhood to adulthood and illustrates Morrison's ideas regarding the formation of women's identities. Morrison questions the ways in which the self has been used in narrative through her critique of "such concepts as 'protagonist,' 'hero,' and 'major character' by emphatically decentering and deferring the presence of Sula, the title character" (McDowell 80). While the title suggests Sula is the central protagonist, her presence is missing as we meet everyone but Sula. Even more interesting is Morrison's blurring of self and other revealed through Sula and Nel's friendship. These two young girls come together out of emotional needs. For example, Nel grows up in a stifling household; under her mother's hand, she becomes obedient and nonimaginative. Sula, on the other hand, lives in a house where no rules or expectations exist. As a result, Nel finds imagination in Sula's chaotic household, while Sula finds peace in Nel's ordered household.

Moreover, the two find themselves joined in their discovery that they need to create themselves, for they are neither male nor white. As the narrator indicates, the two use each other to grow; furthermore, the two young girls become women affected by their childhood experiences— Sula's overhearing of her mother's declaration that though she loves her daughter, she does not like her; Nel's realization that she is a "me" and separate from her mother's overbearing hand; and the two girls' complicity in the death* of young Chicken Little*. While this event causes Nel to become even more unimaginative and conservative—following the path given to her by her mother and the community as she marries and becomes a mother—Sula, by contrast, loses all sense of responsibility to her self and to the community. She leaves Medallion, Ohio*, returning only to wreak havoc on Nel's life. The reader journeys with both women as Morrison asks her readers to decide for themselves which woman has successfully found her self.

Sula suggests that she has been the more successful of the two, for she claims her self as she lies dying, telling Nel that she has lived fully. Nel angrily asks Sula what she has to show for her life, to which Sula replies that she has her self. However, Nel views Sula as lonely. Yet Sula asserts that her loneliness is a choice she made, while she suggests that Nel's aloneness comes from others. Here, Morrison comments on the need for agency in self-definition, suggesting that while Sula's choices may have negatively affected those around her and shortened her life, Sula has lived fully, claiming her self. Nel learns about agency as she gradually understands that her choices have been formed by those around her rather than by her actions.

With *Song of Solomon**, Morrison turns her focus to an African American man, Milkman Dead*, as he explores his family* heritage and moves from innocence to self-awareness and communal knowledge. Such an exploration succeeds when Milkman delves into traditional African American history*, mythology, and culture, and "discovers, understands, and respects these traditions" so that he then "discovers the meaning of his name, his own life, and his familial past" (Mobley 95). As a result, we trace the story of Milkman Dead questing for his identity, and we discover he can fulfill his quest only by coming to an understanding of not just his personal past but also his culture's past.

*Song of Solomon* is also about the power of naming and identity. In "The Language Must Not Sweat," Morrison focuses upon how Africans lost their names through the institution of slavery, which in turn created a loss of connection with their ancestry. In order to secure an identity, Morrison believes African Americans need to acquire names of their own choosing. She explains that Milkman needs to learn his own name and the meaning of that name, for it will give him power. Early on, we discover that the name "Dead" originated as a mistake written down by a drunk Yankee soldier. Immediately, Morrison points out that Milkman's family did not choose their name, a lack which immediately disconnects them from their past. In making this distinction, Morrison exposes the significant difference between being given and consciously choosing a name. This difference is most apparent through the actions of Pilate Dead*, Milkman's aunt. At the age of twelve, Pilate ripped her name out of the family Bible and placed it in a brass box she then hung from her left ear. With a conscious act, Pilate controls her name and carries it with her; on the other hand, Milkman was handed his names first by his parents, who named him Macon, Junior, and second by the community, who named him Milkman after discovering that his mother still nursed him at the age of four.

In addition, Milkman acquires his identity from the forceful influence of his father, Macon Dead*, who teaches Milkman that the most important thing in life is earning money and owning things. Owning things, for Macon, means that you will own not only others but also yourself. Macon has bought into the white, capitalist culture where identity results from material possessions. Milkman believes his father, yet he eventually realizes that he needs more in his life, and he sets off on a journey to the South*, where he struggles to reconstruct his family's history and understand his identity. Along the way, Milkman discovers the emptiness of his father's materialism and accepts Pilate's truth—the sense of self-identity that Pilate carries hung from her ear. As he rides a bus south, Milkman reflects upon the names that have been passed down in his family, along with the names of famous African Americans in history and music* until he ends with general names that cover a broad range of people. This action situates Milkman within a larger continuum of the African American community (O'Shaughnessy). Milkman lives the communal truths he has learned with a woman named Sweet* as he enters into a relationship where he both gives and receives. A new man, Milkman freshly understands that his identity does not derive from material acquisitions; instead, his sense of self originates from his relationships with others and his individual and communal history.

Set in the Caribbean, *Tar Baby** centers around Jadine Childs*, a young Black woman educated in France, and Son*, an uneducated Black refugee. Jade's light skin color alienates her from Black culture; however, her upbringing plays a larger role in shutting her off from her cultural heritage. Sponsored by a white man, Valerian Street*, Jadine studied art history at the Sorbonne in Paris, modeled, and traveled the world. Yet these privileges prevent her from discovering her sense of self. Caught in limbo between the Black and white worlds, Jadine longs for freedom, but she has no past to draw upon for direction that will allow her to integrate with Black culture or her self. Her lack of direction creates an overwhelming insecurity in her sense of self. This insecurity overtakes her contemplation of marriage when she wonders if she is Black enough for her new mate, especially when she wants to leave her skin color behind at times and just be known for her self.

Jadine, however, does not know how to be "just me," questing for that "me" in her involvement with Son. While finding love in Son's embrace, she remains haunted by dreams of Black women condemning her white, imitative lifestyle. This condemnation fills Jadine with fear, serving to submerge any chance of her establishing an independent identity. Jadine realizes that her safety comes from the white world. This realization pushes her to turn her back on the women ghosts and, in doing so, reject the past—a rejection that forces her to give up Son and sacrifice her chances of becoming whole. Yet Jadine's final appearance in the novel suggests that she realizes the dangers of her choice, as she returns to Paris with the desire to start over and battle with her demons. Jadine understands she no longer needs to dream of safety, for her own identity provides her the safety she seeks. As such, the novel's ending implies that Jadine will struggle to find her self within Black culture. Jadine appears to be learning to validate the beauty, strength, and history of Black women and culture; in doing so, she has found the key to establishing a solid identity.

In her fifth novel, *Beloved**, Morrison examines the effects of slavery upon an African American woman's identity. The telling of *Beloved* is dominated by Sethe Suggs's* act of infanticide* and Morrison's desire to know what causes a woman to give up her self. Throughout the novel, Sethe lacks a clearly defined self. For example, she continually refers to herself in the third person when retelling the story of Denver Suggs's* birth (Keizer). More important, she views her children* as her best thing, the one part of herself that slavery has not harmed. Yet, this identification becomes suffocating as Sethe allows Beloved* access to her self, to emotionally and physically drain Sethe of her individuality. It is up to Denver to rescue her mother from self-disintegration. Unless she leaves the house and gets a job, Denver knows her family will disintegrate and her mother will die. Her establishment in the community helps Denver mature into an independent adult, and she "rediscovers what is perhaps the most successful strategy for adult development: she replaces the solitary maternal bond with a larger community of adults and opens herself to an empathetic network of fellows" (Mathieson 15–16). In doing so, Denver learns to differentiate her self from her mother and to counteract Sethe's disintegration.

Denver's maturation illuminates the lack of differentiation between Sethe and Beloved. Beloved's immaturity and Sethe's failure to set boundaries result in Sethe's self-sabatoge. Beloved's childish demands, as well as Sethe's guilt, prevent either woman from distinguishing herself as a separate being. The disastrous results of Sethe's efforts is her own loss of identity. Meanwhile, Denver's discovery of self-identity is the catalyst that creates the return of the community into Sethe's life. The women of the Black community expel Beloved through a symphony of voices. Reminiscent of Baby Suggs's* admonition for the members of the Black community to love themselves, the Black women's voices urge Sethe to return attention to her self. With the added strength of these women, as well as Denver's watchful eye, Beloved is expelled and Sethe returns to the living. Morrison concludes *Beloved* with the admonition that Sethe's story should not be passed on, for Sethe and Beloved's story is a dangerous one of self-sabotage. Sethe's thick love denies Beloved life, and her own life as well. Through Denver's emergence as an autonomous adult, the expulsion of Beloved, and the return of Paul D Garner* and the Black community, Sethe's chance for selfhood emerges. As Barbara Schapiro explains, "the free, autonomous self, *Beloved* teaches, is an inherently social self, rooted in relationship and dependent at its core on the vital bond of mutual recognition" (209). *Beloved* illustrates the need of human beings to differentiate self from others and to claim that self; after all, as Denver learns, there is a self to protect if one is to survive in this world.

Morrison's sixth novel, *Jazz*\*, covers familiar territory: love, what is it to be a man or a woman, the importance of relationships, the role of the community in the identity and survival of the individual, and women's friendships. What is most interesting about *Jazz*, however, is Morrison's ambiguous narrator. As readers, we never discover the narrator's name, gender, age, or race*, for Morrison wants readers to create their own interpretations of her works. Here, she does so by creating a narrative presence who is the voice of African American history, the voice of the local neighborhood, and the voice of the African American community (Lesuinne). Readers must construct the narrator's identity and question the narrator's reliability in telling the stories of Joe Trace*, Violet Trace*, and Dorcas Manfred*. In involving readers in the process of telling and interpreting the stories, Morrison forces them to confront the ways in which we create and re-create our own identities and stories—how we know who is who, and how we define people's identities by having to define our selves in the process.

As the novel concludes, the narrator reflects upon the stories that have been told, most specifically the story of Joe and Violet's marriage. Joe's affair with Dorcas, whom he killed rather than lose, irrevocably altered all three people's lives. The novel details how the affair came about and, more important, how Joe and Violet picked up the pieces of their lives afterward. Violet searches endlessly for a way to release her pain, to understand her place and her identity in the urban environment she inhabits. She longs for love, and late in the novel she learns that to come into her self, she must open herself up to the world and people around her. Furthermore, the narrator realizes that we are all searching for our selves, trying to understand our own stories that we create. The narrator understands that s/he needs to figure out what is missing in his/her life and then find a way to replace what is missing. This understanding is revealed even more clearly in the closing paragraph as the narrator points out that the remaking of self in the novel is done by both the narrator and readers alike. With *Jazz*, Morrison has created a novel in which the very process of creating and knowing self is enacted upon readers and by readers.

Once again, with *Paradise*\*, we encounter Morrison's primary concerns, among them women rebelling against the patriarchy, the dangers of intraracism, and people's desire to be free and safe. The novel creates two locales—Ruby, Oklahoma\*, and the Convent\*. In Ruby men lead the community, while in the Convent women reign. *Paradise*, ostensibly, sets out to explain how the men of Ruby came to attack the women of the Convent. At the same time, the novel critiques the false belief that a separatist Black community will be free of oppression. In Ruby, a small all-Black town in Oklahoma, people believe that they will be protected from white oppression. However, *Paradise* reveals that oppression does not always originate from the influences of white culture. The separatism enforced by the town creates an atmosphere of social exclusion; moreover, the atmosphere forces the excluded group, which finds itself in Ruby, to define "its own nature, goals, and values. But its processes of definition inevitably involve the creation of an 'other'—'them' as opposed to 'us.' Naturally, good qualities appear in us; evil qualities in them. The world is defined in absolute terms, with no middle ground, only binary opposites" (Kubitschek 181). What results in *Paradise* is a commentary on how a place can be the cause of its own destruction, a destruction that stems from the community's founding members' efforts to impose their identities, values, and beliefs on the townspeople.

While the novel does not delve directly into issues of self-identity as previous novels do, *Paradise* does indeed illustrate the dangers of people trying to control other people by creating an identity and way of believing for the place in which they reside. As a result, Ruby becomes a place where the men in power decide who can live in the town and who cannot. Ultimately, in exploring how these men wreak havoc upon the women of the town and the Convent, Morrison's novel asserts that artificially imposed separations create as many troubles as culturally created separations. The people of Ruby learn that, like the town, they cannot live divided on the basis of polar oppositions and beliefs about good/evil, white/Black, love/hate, and more. The warning found in *Paradise* is that people need to define the places they live in as a group, for if a few take control of a community's identity, disintegration of the place and the people in it is sure to follow. Moreover, who is excluded defines a place and a community as much as who is included.

Toni Morrison's novels, in some shape or form, handle how identities, both individual and communal, form, sustain, and/or destroy themselves. From her critique of white cultural myths and intraracism in *The Bluest Eye* to the close examination of two women's lives in *Sula* to the larger discussions regarding the influences of African American history upon

African American identities in the present found in her later novels, Morrison provides readers with a well-rounded evaluation of the challenges and successes to be found when the self is revealed and sustained by both an individual and the community in which the individual resides. In doing so, Morrison provides a blueprint for her readers to follow as they attempt to enact the creation of their own selves while investigating the influences of history, relationships, and place upon their understanding of those selves. *See also* Ancestor; Family.

References: Carolyn Denard, "The Convergence of Feminism and Ethnicity in the Fiction of Toni Morrison," in *Critical Essays on Toni Morrison*, ed. Nellie Y. McKay (1988); Genevieve Fabre, "Genealogical Archaeology or the Quest for Legacy in Toni Morrison's *Song of Solomon*," in *Critical Essays on Toni Morrison*, ed. Nellie Y. McKay (1998); Arlene R. Keizer, "*Beloved*: Ideologies in Conflict, Improvised Subjects," *African American Review* 33: 1 (1999); Missy Dehn Kubitschek, *Toni Morrison: A Critical Companion* (1998); Thomas LeClair, "'The Language Must Not Sweat': A Conversation with Toni Morrison," *New Republic* (March 21, 1981); Vernique Lesoinne, "Answer Jazz's Call: Experiencing Toni Morrison's *Jazz*," *MELUS* 22: 3 (1997); Barbara Offutt Mathieson, "Memory and Mother Love in Morrison's *Beloved*," *American Imago* 47: 1 (Spring 1990); Deborah E. McDowell, "'The Self and the Other': Reading Toni Morrison's *Sula* and the Black Female Text," in *Critical Essays on Toni Morrison*, ed. Nellie Y. McKay (1988); Marilyn Sanders Mobley, *Folk Roots and Mythic Wings in Sarah Orne Jewett and Toni Morrison* (1991); Gloria Naylor and Toni Morrison. "A Conversation," *The Southern Review* 21: 3 (1985); Kathleen O'Shaughnessy, "'Life life life life': The Community as Chorus in *Song of Solomon*," in *Critical Essays on Toni Morrison*, ed. Nellie Y. McKay (1988); Barbara Schapiro, "The Bonds of Love and the Boundaries of Self in Toni Morrison's *Beloved*," *Contemporary Literatrue* 32: 2 (1991); Valerie Smith, *Self-Discovery and Authority in Afro-American Narratives* (1987).

Jeannette E. Riley

## Infanticide

The seminal event in Morrison's novel *Beloved*\* is Sethe Suggs's\* murder of her daughter to save her from a life of slavery\*. This action, at once an indictment of slavery and an exploration of maternity, shapes the entire novel as the narrative spirals around the actual infanticide, seemingly unable to confront this unspeakable deed head-on. A startling disruption of the normative maternal function, commingling the mother's nourishing milk with the child's blood, the murder of Beloved* places maternal power at the forefront of the novel and forces the reader to consider complex issues of identity*, responsibility, and morality. Loosely based on the story of Margaret Garner*, a fugitive slave who killed one child, wounded two others, and sought to murder a fourth to prevent them from being recaptured by the slave owner, *Beloved* forces a direct confrontation between Sethe's dual identities as slave and mother, two categories that blur the lines of selfhood. Historically, motherhood* has often been connected with violence*; the ultimate symbol of the "good mother"—the pelican who mutilates herself to feed her children* with her blood—suggests the ambiguity of the figure. Add to that Sethe's role as slave, and motherhood in the novel becomes doubly conflicted.

Infanticide has existed at all times and in all societies. Although judged by Darwin as one of the most important checks on population growth, infanticide seems to occur most commonly in oppressive cultures where female agency is closely monitored and controlled. In early modern England and America, infanticide came to be associated almost exclusively with unmarried, sexually active women—the "looser sort," women who killed their newborn babies to "avoid their shame*." Such shame cultures, while not openly encouraging murder, at least tacitly seemed to condone it, especially when the child was conceived out of wedlock. Documented cases of infanticide within marriage are far more unusual and difficult to explain. Although sometimes linked with witchcraft and other forms of malevolent nurture, more frequently, married mothers who killed their children did so not in an attempt to avoid the shame of motherhood or out of spite, but rather out of their sense of duty as mothers. Because married women were generally not committing infanticide to maintain their reputations, their actions more clearly indicted patriarchal definitions of domesticity* and motherhood, and necessitate a more thorough examination of the motivations behind their crimes. The very existence of infanticide, then, calls patriarchal systems into question, and represents a clash of maternal and paternal power. It is just this clash of ideologies that Morrison so effectively chronicles in her depiction of Sethe's murder of her daughter in *Beloved*.

The infanticide in *Beloved* (technically a filicide, since the child is more than a year old) is all the more compelling because such occurrences apparently were rare in slave society. Despite the fact that mortality rates were higher for slave children than for whites, there is no real evidence to suggest that the practice of infanticide among slave mothers was widespread. Nonetheless, proponents of slavery often used infant mortality statistics to justify their treatment of slave mothers as little more than brood mares and stereotyped them as at worst murderous and unnatural, as at best careless and unloving. Recent scholars dispute this idea, arguing instead that many infant deaths were likely the result of sudden infant death syndrome (SIDS). Although tales of heroic mothers who murder their children to save them from slavery occur occasionally in antislavery tracts from the period, it is hard to know the true incidence of these actions. There are few documented cases of infanticide among slave mothers, and their motives are even more difficult to ascertain. Evidence presented in several court hearings in Virginia in the 1850s, for instance, suggests that the motivation for killing newborns was similar to that in other Western cultures—to avoid the shame of illegitimacy. Nonetheless, court records do reveal at least a few instances of salvific infanticide: an Alabama slave killed her child because her mistress was abusing it, and another killed her child to prevent it from being sold.

Abolitionist writings offer two explanations for the infanticidal slave mother. The first of these, depicted in Elizabeth Barrett Browning's poem "The Runaway Slave at Pilgrim's Point" (1848), presents the mother murdering her child because she identifies it with her oppressive master: "Why, in that single glance I had/Of my child's face, ... I tell you all,/I saw a look that made me mad/The master's look. ... " The mother's action here seems almost Medea-like in its revenge on the father, but the mother gains at least a measure of sympathy because her actions reveal the master's sexual exploitation of his slave. Morrison represents this type of infanticide with her portrayal of Sethe's mother, who rejects the children fathered by her white owners, and with Ella, who refuses to nurse her white baby and causes its death through neglect.

The second explanation for infanticide is more sympathetic and is described in works such as Mary Livermore's "The Slave Tragedy at Cincinnati," a poem published in *The Liberator* in 1856, and in Harriet Jacobs's *Incidents in the Life of a Slave Girl* (1861). In these works the slave mother contemplates killing her child to free it from the tyranny of slavery. The most famous actual instance of this kind of child murder is that perpetrated by Margaret Garner, whose story was memorialized in poetry, plays, and novels in the nineteenth century, then disappeared into the pages of history until Morrison revived it with *Beloved*. Although romanticized by philosophers and writers as a heroic act (see, for instance, *The History of Women, from the Earliest Antiquity to the Present Time* [1779], where William Alexander portrays such killings as humanitarian acts of compassion), infanticide remains problematic in these texts and certainly in Morrison's novel. At once a form of resistance to slavery—a way for mothers to redefine their infants as their own rather than as commodities to be used by the slave owners—it is also a kind of acquiescence to the slave system that classifies human beings as property. Therein lies the true tragedy of Morrison's novel; no matter how hard Sethe tries to free herself from the horrors of slavery, she is thoroughly defined by its mindset and its violence*. *See also* Stowe, Harriet Beecher, Influence of.

References: James Berger, "Ghosts of Liberalism: Morrison's *Beloved* and the Moynihan Report," *PMLA* 111: 3 (1996); Eugene D. Genovese, *Roll, Jordan, Roll: The World the Slaves Made* (1976); Steven Weisenberger, *Modern Medea: A Family Story of Slavery and Child-Murder from the Old South* (1998); Deborah Gray White, *Arn't I a Woman? Female Slaves in the Plantation South* (1985).

Susan C. Staub

## Isle des Chevaliers (*Tar Baby*)

The island on which the main action of *Tar Baby* takes place. The English translation is "the island of the horsemen." According to Marie-Therese Foucault* and Son*, the horsemen are Black slaves who were struck blind at the sight of the island. *See also Tar Baby*.

Nicole N. Aljoe

# J

## Jake (*Song of Solomon*)

Macon Dead, Sr., father of Macon Dead II*, and grandfather of Milkman Dead*. He was a slave who, upon emancipation, was mistakenly named Macon Dead by a drunken Yankee officer. He owned his own farm in Virginia and was brutally murdered in front of his children after refusing to give up his land to whites. He was the youngest child of Ryna and Solomon*, and married Singing Bird*. *See also Song of Solomon*.

Fiona Mills

## Jazz (1992)

*Jazz* is the second novel of Toni Morrison's trilogy that began with *Beloved** and ended with *Paradise**. All three works, historical in scope, are centered around the unclaimed Beloveds, those bruised and battered Black girls and women simultaneously on the margins and at the core of American history* and culture. *Jazz*, like the other novels, functions as an ensemble piece, panoramic in scope and ambition. However, it both becomes the textual manifestation of the music* after which it is named and chronicles the era during which jazz* became the hallmark of African American achievement. What further distinguishes the novel is Morrison's appropriation of another artistic commodity, James Van Der Zee's photograph, published in *The Harlem Book of the Dead*, of an unidentified dead woman who rests, silenced, in her coffin. Refusing to name her assailant, suspected of having been her lover, she slowly bled to death from a gunshot wound. Her image was captured for posterity by her grieving family*. Morrison's novel is a literary counterstatement to Van Der Zee's earlier visual statement, her interpretation of the mystery of the young woman's identity* and experiences. Rather than a lovely, opaque enigma, she becomes Dorcas Manfred* and speaks from the dead. Yet it is not Dorcas alone who speaks; it is a community* of people marginalized by custom and lost to the passage of time.

Although the Harlem* Renaissance, even at its most neglected, has provoked continuous interest and is, in fact, in the process of being recuperated as a focus of intense academic and artistic scrutiny, it has typically been the social elite—prominent professionals, the political leadership, the intellectuals, artists, and entertainers—who have represented the larger era. The narratives of ordinary people, workers often migrating to the metropolis from small towns and rural regions, are all too frequently eclipsed by the better-known and more exhilarating accounts of the luminaries. Still, in his photographs, Van Der Zee honors the lives of both the celebrated and the anonymous, portraying all with the dignity and artistry allowed by his vision. Though commonly posed in mannered positions, sporting borrowed finery and surrounded by props, the substance of their lives—from their social and religious affiliations, to their family bonds, group aspirations, and individual dreams—is represented with obvious respect and affection. Morrison returns to examine these individual lives that are constantly sandwiched between the more ostentatious Harlem Renaissance and the Jazz Age. Her vehicle for doing so is the music that has loaned the era its name, yet that at the time was surreptitiously enjoyed or barely tolerated, if not held in outright contempt, by the Black bourgeoisie, who scorned its vulgarity and licentiousness. However, jazz, with its passion, speed, and cultural vitality, did capture the pulse of the African American masses. And Morrison's novel reincorporates the music into Van Der Zee's visual testaments. Her text proceeds where the uplift of the Harlem Renaissance necessarily left off.

While jazz, with its nonsequential cycles, functions as the novel's medium, its melody is the scandalous trio, composed of adulterous husband, aggrieved wife, and younger woman, at the heart of the novel. From this initial arrangement, the enigmatic narrator interjects variations, which erupt and seek resolution against the chaotic harmony of Harlem of the 1920s; the novel, the perpetual elaboration of this original melody, becomes, like jazz itself, a chronicle of rhythmic and emotional innovation and the manifestation of the African American movement into the modern moment. Though bound by the narrator's contrapuntal harmony, which repeats and remixes its particular philosophical stance throughout, the text, like jazz, it is destabilized by the ruptures and distinct rhythms of the various characters' unexpected solos. As such, the narrative not only advances; it is in continuous regression. These shifting tempos and combinations allow the emergence of secrets, of the past, unshared and abandoned. Jazz becomes the process through which the past and present touch, that space in which order collapses and reinvention is possible.

The core of *Jazz* revolves around Joe* and Violet Trace*, for whom the reclamation permitted by jazz appears elusive. Caught within an unfulfilling marriage and the melodrama of erotic compulsion and simmering resentments, both are lost to the siren call of Dorcas, Joe's dead mistress, whose face stares at them, frozen in a borrowed photo placed by Violet in the couple's parlor. Not only has each partner rejected the other in favor of Dorcas, they have both rejected themselves as individuals. Dorcas, young, near-white, superficially attractive, cosmopolitan yet immature, becomes the standard against which all else is judged—and found lacking. After his murder of her, Joe falls into a self-absorbed melancholy. Violet, increasingly manic, makes a brief attempt at adultery with a younger man, then abandons it for the dogged pursuit of the mystique that even in death surrounds her rival. In order to move beyond this space, each must exorcise those demons that have permitted them to internalize Dorcas's image as their reality, to crave her body as their own.

Within this process, the past becomes a metaphorical orphan, suppressed and abandoned. The novel's emotional entanglements and erotic obsessions, seemingly a by-product of the now, of the clash of need, impulse, and changing values, are even more profoundly the intrusion of the past into the present, which becomes a metaphor for the larger African American community. Jazz represents the movement through which Violet and Joe each reclaim this past, that which both have, in a sense, rejected for the glamour and security represented by the City. Fractured people, individuals whose behavior diverges from their conscious intentions, they must reconcile the dichotomy between their internal and external worlds and discover constructive ways to integrate the discordant elements of their fragmented beings into a whole. In doing so, they must first fall into those cracks, those psychic fissures, manifested as harmonic stops and severed melodies, that serve as the foundation of the music and, by extension, of the novel.

For Violet and Joe this process takes very different forms, becoming a reflection of the multiplicity that is jazz. Yet for both spouses, new songs, based on the active reinterpretation of that which was passively received, can thus emerge. Although a destructive process, Violet's song contains, like jazz, the possibility for renewal within its structure. It begins with Violet's psychological alienation, expressed as a turbulent division between the urban Violet and her rural, assertive, younger self. Noisy and frantic, this break is manifested in an antisocial hysteria, her descent into an unkempt and aggressive egotism. Violet disrupts Dorcas's funeral and is brutally ejected. In a rage following the humiliation of the funeral, she releases her birds, pampered domestic pets, in the middle of winter. Later, she attempts to possess Dorcas through an intrusive quest, which ultimately leads her to shamelessly invite herself into the life of the teenager's bereaved aunt.

Before the commotion of her very public breakdown at Dorcas's funeral, Violet is trapped within a persona that is of decreasing personal significance. Her life is divided into work and marriage, both of which confer status and safety. Trapped within the rage and sorrow of a life that has passed her by, she anesthetizes herself to avoid feeling either. The result is a psychic split between her social self and private other, between superego and id. Violet's "cracks," her minor transgressions before the funeral, are the means by which her subconscious sabotages the facade that has replaced a substantive self. Interestingly, Joe's betrayal does not create this submerged self; it merely permits its escape. This self, who had earlier sat down in the street, disoriented and uncommunicative, is also the self who, driven by maternal longing, impetuously plotted to steal an infant left in its care. This renegade self is Violet, hexed by loneliness and the unresolved conflicts of the past. With Dorcas's death, her recognition of the depth of the lie with which she was willingly complicitous causes an acrid revolt.For Violet to liberate herself from this self-constructed prison, she must allow herself to be reborn through the disruption symbolized by the jazz process. The violence of the funeral, the frenzy with which she drove away her domesticated pets, and the rebellious nonproductivity of mental disorder produce a chaos, rich and discordant. Yet they also release Violet from her mechanical parroting of normalcy, her going through the motions of respectability.

After complaining of a headache and requesting a place to sit down, she finds her way to the door of Alice Manfred*, Dorcas's aunt. Staid, class-conscious, and wary of the shabbiness Violet represents, Alice had resisted Violet's written requests to meet. However, once Alice does let "Violent," Violet's appellation within the larger community, into her structured home and tidy life, both are permanently changed. Their interaction is the manifestation of the jazz structure. The two clash and challenge one another, each convinced of the correctness of her beliefs. Yet they bond through talk and simple acts of sharing in the form of directed activity. Each accepts the other's presence and is subtly altered in the process. Their friendship becomes a duet, odd and unsentimental. This is an especially important process for Violet, who has begun to live largely in her own mind, consumed by the aimless quest for vengeance and the neat explanation that will supposedly balm her wounded spirit. Alice allows Violet to redefine femininity through a model of platonic bonding. For Violet, orphaned by her mother's suicide and her father's being chased from the South* due to his radical politics, Alice becomes a maternal presence, mending her clothing, giving her tea, providing her a space to sit and while away the time. But Alice is also her equal, a sister and a friend. Though theirs is an unconventional friendship, noncommittal and brusque, it also represents a safe space away from the sexist demands and racial violence of the larger society. In this space, Violet finds someone who accepts her idiosyncrasies and is willing to interact with her on her often peculiar terms.

And it is this past from which Violet cannot escape. Distanced memories over which she has no control and which dominate her waking moments, its variations, hard and incessant, or soft and quizzical, are played and replayed by her stunned consciousness. Central to them is Rose Dear*, her mother. As Rose Dear is lost to the sorrow and silence of depression and humiliation at the hands of white creditors, ending her life four years later at the bottom of a well, so Violet cannot lift herself from the anger and shock of Joe's deception. As she had done as a child, Violet once again watches passively as her life unravels. Although she attempts to lash out, her actions are unfocused. She rages at the symptoms and leaves untouched the underlying disorder, the love, capricious and irate, starved and hungry for more. She thus attempts to hurt the dead Dorcas but avoids Alice's gruff suggestion of questioning Joe about his motives for fear of what he might say. Feeling unfulfilled in her life and rejected within the marriage, she envisions happiness coming either from a baby or from a younger, lighter, more voluptuous Violet. Unable to find beauty or worth in herself, her attitude, whether dazed withdrawal or a silent but hostile recrimination, is merely a manifestation of this impotence.

Yet even as there is a movement to growth in the form of owning and admitting the depth of her rage, Violet is unable to shift the initial paradigm. The narrative's tone is unchanged and its variations adhere to the same theme. Violet remains furious that someone took what she assumed was hers. Beneath this possessive wrath is an insecurity of her value apart from the value Joe bestows on her, both by his affection and by the symbolism of his presence as a spouse and a man.

However, even as Violet fixates on her memories of her beloved grandmother, True Belle*, and the racially ambiguous, economically privileged Golden Gray*, the mixed-race child who was True Belle's ward, her narrative twisting from third person to first and back again, she finds a way out of them. This takes the form of an abrupt, jazz-inspired shift allowed by her recollection of her experience with Alice earlier that day. Alice had curtly informed Violet that Joe could possibly cheat on her again. Violet perhaps cannot control the variables affecting her life, but she can find something within the marriage worth saving. Implicit in this is the fact that Violet must invest in herself, loving both herself and others freely, with few expectations and conditions. While Alice castigates the wheedling Violet, her attention strays from the task at hand and she burns her ironing. Even as she yells in frustration, however, she laughs. Violet joins her. Both lose themselves in the fullness of the moment, comical and joyous.

Sitting in a café, Violet focuses on her first memory* that is not filled with rancor and self-pity. Once again it is of True Belle, who saved Rose Dear, Violet, and her siblings from dispossession and poverty. Rather than with tears, though, it was with the hope and generosity of laughter. Violet later recalls laughing with Alice, tickled by both the irony of the burning iron and the retrospective absurdity of her behavior at the funeral. When she looks outside the window of the café, she notes that it is spring, a time of rebirth and regeneration—her divided consciousness reunifying into a single identity. Although Violet cannot change the past, she can alter her response to it. As a result of reorienting her perspective, she can become the primary agent of her own contentment. In having sought out Alice, and investing in the tart honesty of her friendship, she regains access to both True Belle's grace and the wonder that is her own life. As with jazz, beauty emerges from the intersection of convention and innovation; transformation itself arises from conflict; and love, fluid but endlessly nourishing, permits the rebirth of the soul.

A similar dynamic occurs in relation to Joe's psychic rupture after his murder of Dorcas. Like Violet, he must return to the past in order to transform the present. Unlike Violet, Joe's journey is configured as a descent into the heart of jazz, which is the blues, his distress manifesting itself as a depression, solitary and torpid, a figurative cave within which he has interred himself. He is trapped not only within his guilt but also in his self-indulgent memories of the murdered girl. Grieving for Dorcas—and himself—is his way of keeping her alive, of possessing her even in death. Thus, healing and transformation will involve letting her go. However, this is not simply by finding a way out of the morass of his depression. It is through accepting his complicity and using the resulting regression as an instructive tool to better comprehend his motivations. Therefore, by re-enacting his hunt for Dorcas, he journeys back to the past, back to the literal cave/metaphorical womb of the maternal. As much the search for his lost mother, Wild*, as for his child-lover, both of whom have abandoned him, it provides insight and catharsis.

Joe and Violet's narratives are a study in contrasts, yet both incarnate the instability of those imprisoned within their own perspectives. Violet's voice veers almost haphazardly, the force of her will permitting her to abruptly seize the word that weaves itself, unquoted, into the art of the ongoing narrative. Joe's solo, reasonable and methodical, is exclusively contained within quotation marks, a controlled composition that never quite touches—that, in fact, refuses to acknowledge—the rage at its core. However, when his words abut those of the larger narrative, what emerges is an antiphonal exchange that provides a haunting mental collage. This sequence juxtaposes Joe's conscious rationale behind his pursuit of Dorcas, written in the first person, with the narrative's objective, third-person chronicle of his earlier searches for his mother, who abandoned him as a newborn. In the process it reveals the inextricability of the two women in Joe's mind and the tragedy that is inevitable when love becomes possession.

And there is always a possessive—in fact, a predatory—element to Joe's conception of Dorcas. From the moment he sees her, his mind devours her image. Soon after, as a guest at her aunt's house, where he is selling his Cleopatra cosmetics to the assembled members of a woman's club, he covertly seduces her. Finally, he stalks her. She is the object of his pursuit, to be pleased, indulged, and controlled. Dorcas is far from an innocent led astray, but rather an enthusiastic participant in the intrigue, relishing the clandestine nature of their liaison. Nevertheless, for Joe, despite his insistence otherwise, her function is that of an icon, a charm who permits him renewed youth. And it is this connection to his youth that links Dorcas to Wild for Joe, becoming the undercurrent of his search. The hoof marks symbolized by Dorcas's facial acne link her to the untamed Wild, who abandoned Joe in his infancy. Whether the prior search occurs in the realm of Joe's subconscious or is simply being recounted by the mysterious narrator, the two women inevitably merge into one. As Joe moves from borough to borough seeking Dorcas, he stealthily moved through the Virginia bush. As he follows the sooty twang of guitars, so he had known the music of the earth; both mislead him. He eventually locates Dorcas in the arms of Acton*, a younger man, vain and swaggering, at a dance with harsh lights and free-flowing alcohol.

He never finds Wild, but he does discover her cave, timeless and serene, with walls that change from gold to fish-gill blue, and the remnants of other people's lives for furniture. A home* at once orderly and uncultivated, it deepens her mystery, further removing her from Joe, an intruder. Joe's three months of unquenchable tears appear to be as much for Wild as for Dorcas, and much more for himself than for either woman. He thus feels the wound that throbs at the core of his existence, yet can neither identify nor heal it because he has not opened himself to the possibility. However, for Joe as for Violet, transformation is made possible through the dynamic created by community. When Felice*, Dorcas's friend, enters their lives in search of her mother's ring, which unbeknown to her was buried with Dorcas, she brings the possibility of the joy signified by her name into their lives. Though the narrator first views her as a threat, the reincarnation of Dorcas with her marcelled hair and youthful voracity, this assumption is proven incorrect, becoming an example of an error that forces the narrator's improvisation beyond the expected.

What emerges is the reconfiguration allowed by the jazz structure. Players change, the melody shifts, and a new energy is created. Calls change, as do responses. This synthesis begins with talk, the figurative touching of souls, and the intimacy of nonsexual bonding outside of the conjugal union. Both Joe and Violet increase Felice's confidence through their attentiveness and respectful acceptance of her developing opinions, which, in turn, grants her the courage to confront her own fears and let go of her anger at Dorcas, symbolized by the ring that was buried with her. Felice, who becomes their figurative daughter, brings to Joe and Violet the joy of nonjudgmental camaraderie and the freedom that the truth, no matter how painful, represents, permitting them to share and mature.

The image of the trio both opens and closes the novel, yet it is an ensemble reconfigured. The three, all symbolically orphaned, have found a home with each other; the dynamic of friendship evokes the patterns of jazz performance. As jazz strains coming through an open window from a neighbor's home fill the apartment with joy, its cultural expressivity becomes a point of pride, a space of affirmation. Ultimately, it allows the reclaiming of the love assumed lost, which materializes in reconfigured combinations of the solo, the duo, and the trio. Reflecting the constantly shifting patterns, spontaneity, and exuberance of jazz, it is transformed into the manifestation of self-love, romantic love, and platonic love. What thus becomes possible is the creation of harmony, not necessarily resolution or closure, from the tumult of psychic cacophony.

*Jazz* examines the myriad ways in which love becomes transfigured within interpersonal relationships, effecting concrete change both within and between individuals. Through the Violet-Joe-Dorcas trio and its reconfigurations, love is posited as an abstract yet powerful force that can permit either chaos or transcendence. It re-creates, from the lives of its various characters, the movements of jazz as performance; the reader, as auditor, is witness to the virtuosic display, removed yet bound by the very process of reading. However, while the novel re-creates the rhythm and configurations of jazz performance through the dynamic of the trio, it also invites the reader to participate in jazz as a creative process, an ongoing, ever-evolving endeavor. Through the presence of the narrator as self-conscious artist, what Morrison captures in the metaphor of the talking book, the abstract and intangible process that is creativity becomes an active manifestation of love. *See also* Baltimore, Maryland; Gray, Vera Louise; Hunter's Hunter; Malvonne; Mexico; Music; Narrator of *Jazz*/Talking Book; Virginia.

References: Elizabeth M. Cannon, "Following the Traces of Female Desire in Toni Morrison's *Jazz*," *African American Review* 31: 2 (Summer

1997); Angels Carabi, "Interview with Toni Morrison," *Belles Letters: A Review of Books by Women* 10: 2 (Spring 1995); Carolyn M. Jones, "Traces and Cracks: Identity and Narrative in Toni Morrison's *Jazz*," *African American Review* 31: 3 (Fall 1997); Veronique Lesoinne, "Answer Jazz's Call: Experiencing Toni Morrison's *Jazz*," *MELUS* 22: 3 (Fall 1997); Roberta Rubenstein, "Singing the Blues/Reclaiming Jazz: Toni Morrison and Cultural Mourning," *Mosaic* 31: 2 (June 1998).

Caroline Brown

## Jazz

Despite the gap implicit between an aural art form and the printed word, wave after wave of new readers have noticed similarities between the fiction of Toni Morrison and jazz music*. The similarities characteristically center around the style of both dialogue and narration, but they are not necessarily limited to just those elements. There has been much critical debate, especially in the 1990s, over why or even whether Morrison's works should be considered through the lens of a jazz aesthetic. As many scholars correctly point out, William Faulkner* and James Joyce employed strategies similar to Morrison's, especially in their famous styles, suggesting that perhaps these strategies are a modernist invention now so widely used that there is no point in labeling them "jazz" or otherwise. Unlike those authors, however, Morrison has made clear both her affection for jazz and the influence of the genre on her writing. The most readily apparent allusion to the musical tradition in her fiction is, of course, the title of the novel *Jazz*\*, a work that, interestingly enough, never mentions the word "jazz" anywhere in its text. The invisible but almost tactile presence of jazz in this work has provided justification for many scholars to look for a similar presence elsewhere in Morrison's oeuvre.

Morrison herself has noted on several occasions that her approach to writing is similar to the jazz musician's approach to composition. In particular, Morrison is eager to point out the necessity of producing a work that seems to have been created easily. At least one scholar has insinuated that this mark of excellence in art is not unique to jazz (indeed, the European Renaissance was fond of the same illusion, calling it *sprezzatura*), but the analogy between the two is peculiarly appropriate for jazz, since its greatest works have historically elicited criticism that it is all spontaneous, that no discipline is necessary for its creation. Morrison's careful research and detailed historical settings, which play so easily on the page, are in many ways similar to the seemingly endless hours of practice and revision necessary for musical excellence, and jazz is notorious for the difficulty of its polyethnic traditions.

In particular, critics find themselves drawn to Morrison's style when discussing the influence of jazz on her fiction. The most notorious example might be the use of verbal "riffing," which most accurately means "brief repetition," but has been used by many scholars to mean "varying repetition." Therefore, when one character echoes a word used by another character, repeats it, reinterprets it, or even turns it around to mean something other than what the original speaker intended, a jazz interpretation of the passage might consider the second character's lines to be a series of riffs off the words of the first. Other jazzlike elements of Morrison's style include call and response (perhaps more accurately considered to be an aspect of the spiritual tradition than of jazz) and apparent improvisations in dialogue.

However, the hallmarks of a jazz aesthetic in Morrison's work have implications for more than her written style. Many critics have used the jazzy style of her books to tie her art directly to an African tradition. Most such efforts come from an understanding of jazz as a direct descendant of African musical styles, which is not precisely accurate, since jazz sprang to life far from the shores of Africa and has been performed with non–African instruments, lyrics, and sensibilities of time for at least the vast majority of its history*. Still, many writers have found an empowering interpretation of Morrison's work through the uniquely African elements of jazz music. The most fruitful intersections of ethnicity, jazz, and Morrison's work come from an understanding of jazz as a distinctly (though of course not exclusively) African American art form. For example, the novel *Jazz*, which is in many ways a novel about the migration of Black Southerners to the North, centers itself around not African culture or conflicts, but around the difficulties and triumphs of descendants of Africans who identify themselves as citizens of the United States. In the novel, allusions to jazz strengthen the differences between urban and rural, modern and past, community* and individual. Therefore, jazz itself becomes a wonderfully appropriate metaphor for the tensions within the novel.

The use of jazz aesthetics in Morrison scholarship has slowed to a trickle since the 1997 publication of Alan Munton's "Misreading Morrison, Mishearing Jazz: A Response to Toni Morrison's Jazz Critics." Munton traces the urge to map jazz aesthetics onto literature back to Henry Louis Gates's highly influential *The Signifying Monkey: A Theory of African-American Literary Criticism*, then on to its first formal application to Morrison, Anthony J. Berrett's article "Toni Morrison's Literary Jazz." Munton's article demonstrates a keen understanding of the history and terminology of jazz, and he uses that acumen to tear into the jazz critics. His argument seems to have three goals: drawing attention to the sloppy use of jazz terms in jazz criticism, the "Africentric" habit of turning jazz into a monoracial art form, and the utter destruction of all previous arguments for a jazz aesthetic in literary scholarship.

Still, readers with all manner of academic pedigrees continue to investigate the obvious relationship between jazz music and Toni Morrison's fiction. Many point out the similarities in the African American experience and the history of jazz as an appropriated commodity in the culture. Others discuss the open-ended nature of many of Morrison's narratives, which they say recall the lack of closure in jazz compositions. Munton's arguments aside, there seems to be a strong jazz impulse in the fiction of Toni Morrison, an impulse that continues to excite her readers.

References: Anthony J. Berrett, "Toni Morrison's Literary Jazz," *College Language Association Journal* 32: 3 (March 1989); Alan Munton, "Misreading Morrison, Mishearing Jazz: A Response to Toni Morrison's Jazz Critics," *Journal of American Studies* 31: 2 (1997); Alan J. Rice, "Jazzing It Up a Storm: The Execution and Meaning of Toni Morrison's Jazzy Prose Style," *Journal of American Studies* 28 (1994).

Joe Sutliff Sanders

# K-L

## K.D. (*Paradise*)

*See* Smith, Coffee/K.D./Kentucky Derby (*Paradise*).

## L'Arbe de la Croix (*Tar Baby*)

The name of Valerian Street's* home* on the Isle des Chevaliers*. The house is as much a character as the people. It seems to have a mind of its own. It is constructed out of the jungle, and nature—in the form of ants, the tiles that keep popping up, and the greenhouse—keeps seeking to claim its own desires. In the end, nature reasserts its primacy. The house is also a series of contradictions, reminiscent of the relationships within. This is conveyed in the name "Tree of the Cross," a site of Christian martyrdom and transcendence. *See also Tar Baby*.

Nicole N. Aljoe

## Lestory, Henry (*Jazz*)

*See* Hunter's Hunter/Henry Lestory/Lestory (*Jazz*).

## Lorain, Ohio (*The Bluest Eye*).

Morrison's birthplace, and also the setting for her first novel, to date the only novel she has chosen to set in her hometown. *See also The Bluest Eye*.

Gena Elise Chandler

# M

---

### MacTeer, Claudia (*The Bluest Eye*)

Claudia MacTeer functions as a central character in *The Bluest Eye**.
While Pecola Breedlove* is the story's protagonist, Claudia lends a voice
to Pecola and narrates the other characters' lives. Thus, this is Claudia's
story as well, for as she tells readers the story of Pecola and the others,
she tells her own story as well. As a nine-year-old child meeting Pecola
for the first time, and a grown woman looking back on the events of her
childhood, Claudia recounts the occurrences that lead to that fateful year
of 1941 when Pecola is pregnant with her father's baby. In essence, though
the voice of the story is that of a child, the reader has a chance to return
with an adult Claudia in her memory*, trying to make sense of the sense-
lessness of the past. The young Claudia, in her childhood innocence, refuses to accept the standards of a world that would label her as ugly and
unlovable simply because of her skin color. While her parents have long
accepted the ways of the world, Claudia has made her own world and her
own ways despite her detractors. She cannot understand what it is about
white baby dolls, little white girls, and white movie starlets that makes
them so lovable and her not lovable. In her attempt to make sense, she
dissects and dismembers the dolls, trying to learn what they are made of
and what makes them so special. She does not see the ugliness in Pecola
herself or any Black girl simply because she is Black. In fact, Claudia is
ambivalent toward images of whiteness* in all forms, particularly seen
in her rejection of white baby dolls and little white girls (i.e., Shirley Temple). She has no desire to reflect or appear in these images, and she resents being told by others that she must do so.

Thus, like a child unable to comprehend the incomprehensible, she shows disinterest in and disregard for all white images. In adulthood, Claudia is better able to understand those images and their pervasive effect on her as an adult. She has lost that childhood optimism which helped her to look upon those images as not better than herself. She now understands that she, too, has been a victim of those images and that they have destroyed a very powerful part of her life—her innocence—just as they destroyed Pecola's. Claudia is left with a lingering bitterness and a distrust of love that speaks to her inability to really love—accept—Pecola after her fall into madness. More important, she mourns the loss of innocence, and it is in innocence that humans gain the ability to love.

Gena Elise Chandler

## MacTeer, Frieda (*The Bluest Eye*)

Frieda is Claudia MacTeer's* older sister and friend to Pecola Breedlove*. Her voice is literally spoken through Claudia, but she, like all of the characters in the text, struggles to find love and acceptance in a world that views love and acceptance impossible for those who are Black. Frieda also seems to assume the role of surrogate mother to both Pecola and Claudia in the text. Frieda is the one to whom Pecola and Claudia turn initially to get answers to their questions. When Pecola begins to menstruate, Frieda is the one who recognizes her plight and handles the duty of managing Pecola's menstrual flow. She calms Pecola's fears and turns her seeming ugliness into something potentially beautiful—Pecola's ability now to have a baby. Likewise, it is Frieda who takes the brunt of the punishment when her mother mistakenly accuses the three girls of "playing nasty" in their attempt to hide Pecola's menstruation.

Frieda, in essence, is the foil to Claudia and Pecola. In contrast to Claudia, she represents the transition from childhood innocence and rejection of things not understood, to adolescent acceptance of and reconciliation with the things that seemingly cannot be changed. While she, too, is assailed by images of whiteness*, she is old enough now to be so used to the images that she has learned, though wrong, how to accept them. She and Pecola both covet the Shirley Temple cup, while Claudia still has enough innocence and rebellion to loathe it. Frieda has the love and acceptance of her younger sister to comfort her in what the world sees as ugliness. Pecola represents the converse—what happens to one who does not have a support system, like a sister or family*, to remind her that, despite what the world may think or say, she is still beautiful and loved.

Frieda, however, is not unaffected by the world or left unscarred by it. Just as the seasons into which the book is divided mark the changes, deaths\*, and rebirths that occur through the year in nature, so Frieda, like Claudia and Pecola, experiences disillusionment and loss of innocence as she matures from a child into a young woman. Her innocence is lost when Mr. Henry, the boarder living in the MacTeer house, tries to convince her she is beautiful by attempting to molest her. Frieda, who once seemed blind to the same destructive forces that caused Pecola to withdraw and Claudia to rebel, is violently shocked back into reality. She is reminded of her loss of innocence and understands a little better the world around her and the difficulties in finding love. *See also The Bluest Eye.*

Gena Elise Chandler

## Magical Realism

The term "magical realism" refers to the amalgamation of realism and fantasy in art, film, and literature. In the magical realist text, characters encounter elements of magic and fantasy with the same acceptance that they meet those settings and figures commonly associated with "reality" and "fact."

The magical realist label originated in 1924 when German art historian Franz Roh applied the expression *magischer realismus* to post–Expressionist paintings that combined realism with an emphasis on expressing the miracle of existence. Scholarly concensus, however, points to exiled Cuban novelist Alejo Carpentier as the key figure in establishing the link between Latin American fiction and the phenomenon that he called *lo real maravilloso*. In his classic 1949 essay, "On the Marvelous Real in America," Carpentier sought to differentiate Latin American magical realism from European Surrealism by highlighting the distinction between the arbitrary—even contrived—alteration of reality that characterized the work of the Surrealists, and the organic representation of the Latin American weltanschauung in *lo real maravilloso*. For Carpentier, magical realism mirrored an understanding throughout the Caribbean and Central and South America of a more permeable boundary between the real and the fantastic than was commonly accepted in North America and Europe.

Postcolonial scholar Brenda Cooper explains that "magical realism arises out of particular societ[ies]—postcolonial, unevenly developed places where old and new, modern and ancient, the scientific and the magical views of the world co-exist" (216). This notion, that magical realism arises out of those colonial and postcolonial moments which create a substantial population of subjects whose interests may be counterhegemonic, explains the contradiction between the relative absence of magical realist texts produced in Europe—and by Euro-American writers in Canada and the United States—and the growing proliferation of such texts in

Africa, Asia, and Latin America—and among European, Canadian, and
U.S. authors of African, Asian, and Latin descent. The refusal of the magical realist text to respect Western, postindustrial notions of the division
between reality and fantasy invests it with a powerful potential to destabilize the cultural hegemonies that contribute to the privileging of "first
world truths" over "third world myths."

Within Anglophone literature, novelists of the African Diaspora—especially African, Afro-Caribbean, and African American writers—have
used elements of myth* and magic to remember, express, and account
for those experiences which Western notions of history*, reality, and
truth have failed to address. For writers of the African Diaspora, the incorporation of mythic and magical elements exposes the role of social
construction in maintaining the white-over-Black hierarchy; resists
meanings for Blackness developed in the service of that hierarchy; and,
finally, achieves a new and emancipatory vision of Blackness that privileges the interests of people of African descent. Postcolonial scholar Jane
Campbell argues that this specific use of magical realism "constitutes a
radical act, inviting the audience to subvert the racist mythology that
thwarts and defeats Afro-Americans, and to replace it with a new mythology rooted in the black perspective" (x).

African American novelist Toni Morrison deploys magical realism to
the very ends, and with the very same effect, that Jane Campbell describes. Morrison's novels probe the depths of African American history
and experience, digging past those stereotyped images developed in the
service of white supremacy—images like the Black brute, the thug, the
sapphire, the sambo, the tragic mulatto, the mammy, the coon—to uncover those roles, relationships, and experiences which the hegemonic
culture has shown little interest in exploring. Morrison focuses on those
experiences which the Euro-dominant majority, in its disinterest, has
failed to develop means of representing. She enters these spaces, moments, and experiences with a freedom shared by many Black writers of
the postmodern period. Released from the bonds of accommodationist
protest and subsequent nationalist rage that limited their literary forebears, Morrison and her contemporaries (authors such as David Bradley,
Octavia Butler, Charles Johnson, Gloria Naylor, and Randall Kenan) pursue their own questions about African American history and experience,
creating prose fiction narratives that privilege their own concerns as U.S.
Black authors.

Morrison's strategic and emancipatory introduction of magical realism (as a tool for constructing a counterhegemonic Blackness of unlimited possibility) is evident, to varying degrees, in all of her fiction, but
two of her novels, *Beloved** and *Song of Solomon**, stand out as particularly strong examples of the trend. The epic scope of these works links
them with those Latin American novels (*100 Years of Solitude, El Reino*

*de Este Mundo*, and others) so closely associated with the development of popular and scholarly interest in the magical realist trend. It also points to the usefulness of magical realism to writers whose interest is in narrating histories that have, because they were not written down, become what book critic James Woods has called "a necessary superstition—a myth, made of oral tellings and retellings" (45). In *Song of Solomon*, magical realism becomes a tool for demonstrating how, transmitted orally over several generations, these "necessary superstitions" are not only encountered as real by the communities that have preserved them, but—when shared with the broader community of Morrison's readers—also become part of a more widely accepted understanding of that which is possible and true.

Developed to preserve and protect those moments and experiences which the historical record has overlooked, necessary superstitions become the backbone of Morrison's novel, where they function as the bridges on which protagonist Milkman Dead* crosses over from the urban decadence of the Northern city of his youth to a powerful encounter with the mystery of his ancestral legacy in the rural American South*. In *Song of Solomon* magic becomes a metaphor for, and measure of, one's retention of those Africanisms—especially African folk beliefs—which slavery* sought to diminish. In this novel the major characters can be divided between those who live ignorant of the depth and breadth of their history and those who have had the privilege of encountering it firsthand. Those who resist or simply have no access to their own family* histories appear trapped within small, unimaginative lives, their dreary days circumscribed by Western notions of possibility and truth that limit the meanings and value of Blackness. Characters who have maintained a connection to the power and mystery of their own ancestry are depicted as empowered women subjects whose experience of a reality that transgresses conventional limitations on time, space, and plausibility is evident in the magic and mystery that shape their lives and permeate their surroundings. Among the major characters Pilate Dead*, Milkman's aunt, and Circe*, the ancient midwife and crone, retain the strongest connections to history. With the aid of their astonishing wisdom and power, Milkman sets out on a journey that expands his sense of the real sufficiently to allow him to recuperate the magic that is his family legacy. Milkman's access to magic seems metaphorical, his recovery of those gifts celebrated in the myth of flying Africans* of his slave ancestors a symbol of the spiritual emancipation that marks the end of his quest. But Morrison teases her readers with the possibility that his magic is literal, born out of the protagonist's recovery*, generations hence, of a capacity for flight acknowledged throughout African and African American folklore*, but simply unfathomable within constraints of Western thought.

In *Beloved*, Morrison challenges the same line between fact and fantasy that she subverts in the magical realist text of *Song of Solomon*. *Beloved* differs from *Song of Solomon*, however, in its use of a Black woman's journey as the lens through which to manipulate this boundary. In *Beloved*, Morrison's omniscient narrator witnesses the conditions of slave motherhood* and slave womanhood through the eyes of the protagonist, Sethe Suggs*. Alongside the narrator, Morrison's readers experience the tragedy of Sethe's transition from slavery to freedom, a shift marked by her now famous decision to kill her own daughter rather than permit her to suffer the plight of a woman enslaved. As difficult as it is to conceive of the complex interaction of fear and love that results in Sethe's tragic act of infanticide*, Morrison finds the conventional language of domestic violence* sufficient to capture the drama and horror of this crucial moment. The scene in which Sethe murders the title character, her infant daughter Beloved*, requires the author to convincingly depict a Black woman acting out of a temporary sociopathy, driven by fear and desperation. Patricia Hill Collins and others have noted the widespread tendency throughout Europe and North America to portray Black motherhood as sociopathic, and Morrison is able to draw upon this popular construction of the relationship between Afro-diasporic identity* and women's reproduction (an impression essential to maintaining prevailing racial hierarchies) in describing this dreadful moment.

It is only once Morrison steps away from the spectacle of the murder to depict Sethe's sadness and grief that the language and imagery of white supremacy, in which the Black-mother-as-sociopath is presented as "real" and "true," and that was so useful in her portrayal of the aberrant Black mother, begin to fail the author. As she probes the depth and texture of Sethe's grief, it becomes more and more apparent that the protagonist's crime, however hideous, was driven more by her compassion and love for the girl child Beloved than by deviance and fear. Morrison's embrace of the magical real in depicting Sethe's longing and grief is simultaneously a rejection of the systems of meaning that, in privileging controlling images like the Black-mother-as-sociopath, have no interest or investment in representing African American mothers' compassion and love.

Beloved's return from the dead as an unruly and mischievous ghost can be read as a metaphor for the Black mother's lingering sorrow for a child lost to the intolerable brutality of slavery, a symbol dramatic and vivid enough to counteract the conspicuous absence of conventional realist language to account for that specific brand of despair. Beloved's eventual incarnation, a full two decades after her death* and burial, as a fully embodied child-woman depicts the persistence and intensification of Sethe's grief over time, counter to the more widely held belief that grieving inevitably gives way to acceptance. Complicated by her equal and related grief over the loss of her own humanity, Sethe's sorrow presents a new vision of both Blackness and womanhood, and Morrison's language of metaphor—rife with conjurings, hauntings, and ghosts—seeks to articulate an experience of motherhood and loss rendered unspeakable by representations of womanhood and childhood that fail to take into account the perversions of slavery. *See also* African Myth, Use of; Ancestor; Approaches to Morrison's Work: Postcolonial; Memory; Oral Tradition.

References: Jane Campbell, *Mythic Black Fiction: The Transformation of History* (1986); Brenda Cooper, *Magical Realism in West African Fiction: Seeing with a Third Eye* (1998); Wendy B. Faris and Laura Parkinson Zamora, eds., *Magical Realism: Theory, History, Community* (1995); James Wood, "The Color Purple," review of *Paradise*, by Toni Morrison, *New Republic* (March 2000).

Ajuan Maria Mance

## Magna, Mary/Mother (*Paradise*)

A Sisters Devoted to Indians and Colored People nun who "steals" the abandoned and sexually abused nine year old Consolata (Connie) Sosa* from dirty city streets (presumably in Brazil), "adopts" her, and brings her to Christ the King School for Native Girls, a.k.a. the Convent*, in 1925. After the school loses its funding and its clientele of Arapaho Indian girls, the aging Mother and Connie remain at the Convent, selling produce, pies, bread, and, most famously, "purply black" hot peppers and hot pepper relish to travelers and locals. Mother, glowing bright white from Connie's "stepping-in," dies in 1971. *See also Paradise.*

Julie Cary Nerad

## Malvonne (*Jazz*)

Joe* and Violet Trace's* neighbor in their Harlem* apartment. A cleaning woman with access to others' secrets, Malvonne has the potential to be the novel's unidentified narrator, although it later seems unlikely. She rents a room in her apartment to Joe, where he pursues his clandestine relationship with Dorcas Manfred*. Malvonne then betrays the confidence to Violet. *See also Jazz.*

Caroline Brown

## Manfred, Alice (*Jazz*)

The aunt of the murdered Dorcas Manfred*. Trapped within her own notions of respectability, Alice attempts to stifle her niece's developing sexuality*, which hastens Dorcas's rebellion. However, her friendship with Violet Trace* permits her to face her fears and disappointment related to her own sexuality and potential victimization within a racist and sexist society. This allows her to mature emotionally. *See also Jazz.*

Caroline Brown

## Manfred, Dorcas (*Jazz*)

The teenager with whom Joe Trace* has an affair and whom he later shoots to permit his continued possession of her in life and in death. Dorcas is many things: a wounded child who lost her parents to violent racism and unnecessary death*; a scheming woman; a freethinking, happy-go-lucky girl; a self-serving friend; a sensuous nihilist trapped within her limited expectations of womanhood. She is based on an actual homicide victim who refused to name her assailant, suspected of having been her boyfriend; the original woman, still unidentified, was captured by James Van Der Zee, the Harlem* Renaissance-era photographer. Morrison borrows the motif to give words to the silenced casualty of what appears to have been misogynistic violence*, in the process implicating the victim herself. *See also Jazz.*

Caroline Brown

## Masculinity

In her various novels, Toni Morrison has identified masculinity as a key concern for African American culture. Her fiction takes as one of its tasks exploring the possibilities for Black men to imagine a different conception of masculine identity*, one that focuses on communal values over individual competition and rejects violence* as a necessary ingredient. Morrison always recognizes that masculinity is not a biological given but a social invention, as is race*. Morrison represents a plurality of masculinities in her fictions, and she also notes the ways that gender, class, and race are discursive categories that structure the practice of manhood.

Morrison's fiction reflects anxieties of African American men regarding their identities, tensions rooted in the dehumanizing treatment accorded them in slavery*, and the continued debasement directed at them through individual and structural racism. Morrison critiques such treatments throughout her work as a cause for Black masculine anxiety.

*Beloved's\** Paul D Garner\*, for example, has difficulty asserting his manhood when facing white racists who demean him and when confronted by Black women like Sethe Suggs\* and Beloved\* who, in his mind, steal his strength through sexual desire. Morrison interrogates the myths of dominant notions of masculinity, suggesting alternative means for African American men to establish their manhood while also reflecting their frustration at disempowerment. She rejects notions of manhood based on economic success or property attainment, focusing instead on more personal philosophies and blurring gender lines. Morrison thus critiques both the racist patriarchy that denies Black men their masculinity and the individual men who accept such patriarchal definitions of manhood and use them to evade communal responsibility. She takes issue with the adoption of white definitions of manhood by African American men, a model that she portrays as individualist, competitive, misogynist, and destructive. Morrison's fiction, then, becomes a treatise on a manhood rooted in community\*, cooperation, equality, and constructive behavior. Morrison ultimately supports not the individualism of Anglo modernism but the collectivism of African American life, the individual as always and already part of the community.

Morrison reveals the frustrations of African American men and the violence that often functions as a self-defining tool for them. This violence, as Morrison shows us, is often directed at women in a spectacle that divides the community across gender lines. For example, Cholly Breedlove\* is caught in the act of having sex\* by white hunters and forced to continue at gunpoint. He later denigrates the females of his household, directing his anger and violence against them because he cannot do otherwise. This violence destroys his home\* psychologically. *Tar Baby's\** Son\* rapes Jadine Childs\* in an act of masculine aggression against the lighter-skinned female, thus representing the interlocking mechanisms of race and gender oppression. *Jazz\** also represents violence against women in Joe Trace's\* shooting of his lover. *Paradise\**, where the men of the community come together to murder the women of the Convent\*, provides a powerful critique of such actions. Male solidarity comes at the cost of women's lives, and the rationales for inciting such violence are based in irrational anxieties about feminine power. Morrison uses these characters as a means of demonstrating the violent gender divide in African American culture.

We similarly see the use of violence to mark Black manhood in *Song of Solomon\** as well, when Guitar Baines\* and Milkman Dead\* join the Seven Days\*, a group that kills white persons as vengeance for lynchings and other culturally legitimated murders of African Americans. The group sees these retaliations as a means of reclaiming Black subjectivity and exacting vengeance against white culture. Violence becomes a means of negotiating the political space of America, where Black men are disenfranchised. It replaces tenderness and love for Guitar, becoming his means of interacting with the world. Yet even as Morrison reflects these feelings, she provides an alternative. Milkman, who initially joins the Seven Days and participates in its rituals, moves beyond violence and comes to find his identity. As a result, Morrison critiques the decision of many African American men to resort to violence, suggesting that it damages the community it seeks to help.

Song of Solomon focuses on Milkman's search for manhood. As he travels, he must discover how to be a Black man, creating an identity that will integrate with the African American community. As a young boy, Milkman does not consciously realize the privileges accorded to males; rather, he accepts them as given, disrespecting his sisters as the weaker sex. Only when his sisters rebel and inform him of his actions does he realize his mistake. Milkman's journey to manhood travels through, and over, females and their bodies. Ruth*, Lena*, Pilate*, Hagar*, and Reba Dead* define Milkman's masculinity as much as his dealings with other men do. They inform him of his privilege as a male, removing his ignorance, and they shape his identity through their actions. Song of Solomon argues that the problem of masculinity does not belong solely to males; it is a community issue.

When Milkman arrives in Shalimar, Virginia, he meets other men who test him in a series of African American rituals by which he must prove his manhood. Morrison replicates tribal rituals within the context of American individualism. Success means communal acceptance; failure means communal rejection. They assault him verbally, insulting and degrading him in the tradition of the dozens. The fight and the hunt in which he partakes provide further means for Milkman to demonstrate his ability to compete with the other males. Morrison depicts these rites of passage, but she also critiques them as barriers erected to divide African Americans into strict gender dichotomies. She sees these tests of individual prowess as contributing to the individualist beliefs that undermine African American unity. Milkman's success comes when he gives up individualistic notions of manhood and embraces the community and its definitions of identity through language and communal mythos. His acceptance of his ancestral mythos, as evidenced by his final ambiguous leap, signifies his movement away from individualist notions of identity and toward the communal model.

Beloved likewise fixates on Black manhood and its construction in a culture with slavery as its legacy. Paul D struggles to define his masculinity through white norms, but comes to realize that he must find alternative definitions with Sethe. Beloved questions traditional masculine models of self-ownership, contradicting those humanist ideals against a legacy of slavery and its notion of Black selfhood as the property of another. The slave owner Mr. Garner* teaches his slaves to be a particular type of Black men; he gives them physical prowess but no individual agency. Paul D learns from Garner that manhood is asserted through aggression and violent behavior. But since slavery defined Black men as property, not as men, Paul D recognizes that without his freedom, he is less than a man. His troubled manhood brings him to ask Sethe to bear his child as a means of legitimating his masculine identity.

Morrison profoundly destabilizes notions of Black manhood in her fiction, for she reveals that all traditional identity structures are differential, based in a notion of another. Thus, Black manhood results from the repudiation of women and whites. Stamp Paid (slave name Joshua) allows his wife to be raped by the master's son in order to gain freedom. The master's son asserts his manhood through such rape while signaling that Joshua can never be a man in American culture. Slavery denied manhood to Black males while objectifiying Black women and using them as a means by which to assert white manhood. Morrison shows, however, that this notion of pure identity is a white fantasy, providing instead the reality of a communally constructed identity.

In addition, Morrison is keenly aware of the need to disrupt biological notions of gender. As a result, she demonstrates through several characters that females can adopt masculine traits, and vice versa. Morrison describes Sula Peace* as a masculine character on several occasions. Her assertiveness and sexual aggression cast her as masculine, interrupting simplistic biological notions of gendered behavior. *Tar Baby*'s Jadine also takes on many typically male characteristics. *Beloved*'s Sethe, though feminine in many respects, is often connected to war imagery, a traditionally masculine domain. She is isolated from the female community and must be more assertive and forthright, again traditionally defined masculine characteristics. In addition, Paul D takes on many characteristics normally associated with the feminine. His empathy and his willingness to show emotion become traits men can share as well. Morrison demonstrates through her main characters the arbitrary nature of gender characteristics. Gender blurring in this manner demonstrates the fluidity of identity and its arbitrary connection to biology.

Morrison's fictions depict a plurality of masculine identity formations, reflecting the anxieties for African American men living in a culture that has refused to accept their masculine identities. Yet Morrison does not validate all possible formations. She critiques the violent responses of Black men to oppression, particularly when that violence is directed toward the Black community. She also disrupts reductive biological notions of gender, placing traditionally feminine qualities in her male characters in order to blur gender lines and stress the commonality of human beings. Morrison redefines Black manhood in her texts, producing a more egalitarian model that disrupts traditional individualist beliefs and reasserts the social dimensions of identity. *See also* Ancestor; Myth.

References: Elizabeth Ann Beaulieu, "Gendering the Genderless: The Case of Toni Morrison's *Beloved*," *Obsidian II: Black Literature in Review* 8: 1 (Spring/Summer 1993); Herman Beavers, "The Politics of Space: Southernness and Manhood in the Fictions of Toni Morrison," *Studies in the Literary Imagination* 31: 2 (Fall 1998); Philip Weinstein, *What Else but Love? The Ordeal of Race in Faulkner and Morrison* (1996).

David E. Magill

## Medallion, Ohio (*Sula*)

Fictional town that serves as the setting for the novel's action. *See also Sula.*

Douglas Taylor

## Memory

Memory is a powerful force in Morrison's novels. Its power comes from its ability to shape experience. Morrison's novels reveal a concern for African American history* and cultural memory. Morrison maintains that, through memory, we keep in touch with our ancestors*. When an individual does not remember the past (his or her ancestors), it is dangerous. Morrison illustrates this in her second novel, *Sula**, in which Sula Peace* attempts to "make" herself by cutting herself off from her history (her family* and the community*). Her most dramatic actions are watching her mother, Hannah, burn to death, then leaving the Bottom* for several years and, when she returns, sending her grandmother, Eva Peace*, to a nursing home. Sula's actions result in personal failure. She dies, never having really succeeded in changing the community.

Keeping in touch with one's ancestors occurs through reconstructive memory. Memory, for Morrison, is a conscious, deliberate act. Remembering is a creative process, not an effort to find the truth. Morrison's fiction bears witness to the need for a usable past. For African American artists like Morrison, the past and the present are interdependent. Morrison's fiction revives, in order to pass on, mythic truths that create connections between individuals and the past, specifically the traditions of Black American and Africa. She "forces" the reader's memory because of her belief that those who do not remember the past are in danger. Knowledge of the past, gained through memory, is a necessary basis for constructing the future.

While an editor at Random House in the 1970s, Morrison anonymously edited *The Black Book**, a collection of African American historical documents that chronicles the lives of ordinary African Americans. The book contains diverse and unusual primary sources, such as bills of sale from slave auctions, pictures, newspapers, and musical scores. These sources enable Morrison to present some of the people and material that had been left out of history textbooks. The work, then, helps to make the past part of the memories of contemporary society.

Like other writers of the African Diaspora, Toni Morrison uses memory as a main narrative structure in her novels. Through memory, Morrison can reconstruct those voices of oral history which are absent and/or silenced in written versions of history. The settings of Morrison's novels are significant because place has the power to evoke memories. The power of place is particularly evident in Morrison's third novel, *Song of Solomon\**. Milkman Dead\* must travel to the South\*, where his great-grandfather lived, in order to understand himself and his ancestry. Morrison relied on her own memories of family stories about the Reconstruction to tell Milkman's story. She adapts the African American myth\* that enslaved Africans in the South escaped by flying (literally) back to Africa. Thus, Morrison takes on the role of the griot, albeit a modern one. The novel itself, then, serves as a cultural artifact that preserves the myth by keeping it a part of cultural memory. At the same time, *Song of Solomon* provides an overview of American history as it affects a single family.

Morrison draws on and creates cultural memory in her writing. The Margaret Garner\* story was the inspiration for *Beloved\**, the myth of the flying Africans\* is the backdrop for *Song of Solomon;* and the well-known tar baby story serves as the springboard for Morrison's fourth novel, *Tar Baby\**. Stories serve as catalysts or prompts to unlock memories. Whereas Sula deliberately tries to deny her past and memories, in *Tar Baby*, Jadine Childs\* has no cultural memory. She is unconnected to the past, and therefore in danger. When Jadine moves from Paris to Isle des Chevaliers\*, she is seeking out her extended family, Sydney and Ondine Childs\*, in order to develop a sense of who she is and where she comes from before moving forward with her life. However, Sydney and Ondine cannot give Jadine cultural or family memory, despite their blood relationship to her. They are not "ancestors," and Jadine has never spent much time with them. She does not have a history with them, or shared memories, and she cannot create these things once she is grown. Thus, Jadine cannot take her place in the line of history.

Of all of Morrison's novels, *Beloved* is the most focused on memory. *Beloved* is created out of the scraps and fragments of Morrison' s own memories of the Margaret Garner case, specifically, and slavery\*, in general. The novel is Morrison's attempt to bring forward into literature the unbearable memory of slavery so that African Americans and society can move on at last.

*Beloved's* plot is constructed to mirror the way that memories unfold. The plot emerges in nonlinear fragments as different characters remember their experiences and share them with the reader and/or each other. Since many of these memories have been repressed for a long time, the process of uncovering them is slow and painful. The recognition of the past involved in memory requires the effort of the entire community, and cannot be accomplished by one individual. Like the central character, Sethe Suggs*, readers of the novel must engage in the act of creative reconstruction. They have to piece together the fragments and different accounts in order to find coherent meaning for themselves. However, the narrative always foregrounds the subjectivity of any memory created. Morrison's narrative approach to memory in *Beloved* and in her other fiction allows the novel to go back and forth between the past and the present, and blurs the distinction between them.

In *Beloved*, Morrison uses memory to show the reader the hidden side of slavery. The novel illustrates the relationship between history and memory. History provides the exterior view of slavery, and memory is the personal, interior view. Throughout her novel, Sethe tries to forget her experiences as a slave at Sweet Home* plantation, but memories keep surging up and frustrating her attempts.

Morrison uses the term "rememory" instead of "memory" in *Beloved*. This term underscores that to "re-member" is to put together, or creatively reconstruct, the pieces of something. However, rememory does not depend on just one individual's subjective reconstruction. Morrison establishes a community of rememberers whose consciousnesses overlap at times, and at other times remain independent. Rememory also depends on place, as well as a cyclical notion of time. Rememories represent racial memory. Forgetting is called "disremembering," which is the opposite of remembering, and implies an almost conscious choice. For much of *Beloved*, Sethe struggles to resist "rememories" by "beating" back the past and claiming to "disremember," but fails.

In *Beloved*, Morrison investigates the role of individual and cultural memory in relationships. Paul D Garner* keeps his memories locked up inside him and does not want to acknowledge them. However, the narrator points out that in order to make a life with Sethe, Paul D must put his memories next to hers. Paul D is as devoted to keeping his memories dead as Sethe is to keeping her memory of Beloved* alive.

Throughout *Beloved* the narrator reminds us that the story is not one to pass on. On the one hand, the phrase suggests that the *Beloved* tale should not be repeated and should not happen again. On the other hand, it also suggests that the story is one not to pass up. By repeating the warning at the end of the novel, Morrison implies that while this story should not be repeated, it should be remembered. *Beloved* deals with the tension between remembering and forgetting. Beloved, the "ghost" of Sethe's crawlingalready? baby, is the physical manifestation of Sethe' memory. As long as Sethe cannot put her memories in the past (and acknowledge their role in the present), they will haunt her.

*Jazz\**, Morrison's next novel after *Beloved*, continues the project of *Beloved* by telling the stories of three individuals in order to tell the story of a people. In this case, Morrison provides brief yet detailed glimpses into the lives of African Americans in the rural South after emancipation. Like *Beloved*, *Jazz* is a story reconstructed from bits and pieces of memory and stories. Specifically, the plot derives from two real tales Morrison remembered hearing. Since individuals and societies construct memory from images, all "rememories" are such "reconstructions," simultaneously complete and incomplete. *See also* Recovery.

Lisa Cade Wieland

## Mexico (*Jazz*)

The nightclub where Joe Trace* agrees to take Dorcas Manfred* on an illicit rendezvous. *See also Jazz*.

Caroline Brown

## Migration

In keeping with the historical emphasis on mobility evident throughout much of African American culture, migrations, trips, and travels of all sorts pervade the action within Toni Morrison's works. The Middle Passage, the Underground Railroad, the Great Migration—these momentous mass relocations set the tone for much of the history* of Black people in the United States. In each of Morrison's novels, her characters undergo journeys that often resonate with these historical precedents, and she frequently depicts characters traveling between the American South* and the North. While engaging in physical movement, these characters also experience emotional and psychological journeys, which Morrison asserts can be equally, if not more, important, no matter what the ultimate destination. Repeatedly, Morrison demonstrates that inward exploration often overlaps with exterior travels, resulting in essential growth and greater possibilities not otherwise possible. Geographical relocation alone will not suffice.

In *The Bluest Eye\**, Cholly* and Pauline Breedlove* meet in Kentucky, after she has moved there with her family* from their home* in Alabama, and he has traveled from Georgia. The couple eventually decides to marry and press further north to Ohio. Echoing many other early twentieth-century African Americans seeking better possibilities in the industrial North—such as Morrison's own parents, who also came from Alabama and Georgia—Cholly and Pauline settle in Lorain, Ohio*, where he finds a job in the steel mills and she eventually does domestic work. But when loneliness sends Pauline to seek refuge in movie theaters, she takes a dangerous emotional journey, resulting in a destructive shift in cultural values, whose legacy contributes to her daughter Pecola's* subsequent downfall. Other more materially successful Lorain residents, such as Geraldine, have migrated there from Southern cities like Marietta, Georgia, Aiken, South Carolina, Newport News, Virginia, and Mobile, Alabama—bringing their conservative sensibilities with them. One other local inhabitant, an odd, somewhat delusional, even perverted man whom everyone calls Soaphead Church*, grows up in the West Indies, travels to the United States for his education, and eventually settles in Lorain. For all of the characters in *The Bluest Eye*, then, their physical migrations are unable to overcome fundamental psychic difficulties.

Compared with the rest of Morrison's novels, *Sula** has a more fixed setting, focused primarily in the Bottom*, a neighborhood outside of fictional Medallion, Ohio*. Nevertheless, this novel also includes important journeys, as well as shorter trips. After its opening gives the history of the Bottom, *Sula* provides Shadrack's* background, which takes him from Medallion to World War I France, where he experiences great trauma* and even madness, and then back to Medallion. Once he returns home, Shadrack establishes the annual National Suicide Day*, his own bizarre parade through town, which years later will be the occasion to lead several Medallion residents on a momentous trek to their tragic end in the tunnel.

The two other important physical journeys in *Sula* are taken by Nel* and Helene Wright* and by Sula Peace* herself. Evoking the proper Southern women of *The Bluest Eye*, Helene strives above all to be proper, fighting hard to forget her New Orleans mother, a Creole woman she considers disreputable. Eager to leave that perceived taint behind, Helene readily marries and joins the tide of Southerners on the Great Migration, settling in Medallion, where she seeks to impose her strict propriety on her daughter, Nel. Years later, when Helene's grandmother is ill, Helene and Nel take the train back to New Orleans, a trip Nel will always remember because it reveals her mother's essential weakness and steels Nel to avoid a similar fate.

Sula's own migration occurs offstage, and all we learn is that in her ten years away from Medallion, she has gone to college in Nashville and traveled elsewhere. Sula's return home, however, assumes mythic proportions, for it is accompanied by flocks of robins. Nevertheless, her travels away from Medallion seem to allow Sula to come back with a vengeance, as she promptly sends her grandmother, Eva Peace*, to a nursing home, enabling Sula to indulge her personal whims, including a fleeting affair with Nel's husband, Jude Greene*. The novel ends with Nel much later embarking on her own belated emotional migration, which occurs while she is walking away from visiting Sula's grave. Nel realizes that perhaps she has judged her childhood friend too harshly, that perhaps Sula has always recognized the necessity of the internal journey that Nel only now begins to understand.

In *Song of Solomon**, physical migrations and journeys become much more central. While it is set in an unnamed Northern/Midwestern city on Lake Superior, the plot involves Pilate* and Macon Dead's* move there from their father's farm in Pennsylvania, as well as Milkma Dead's* momentous trip south. Indeed, in the opening scene, Mr. Robert Smith* announces his impending flight from the top of the hospital across Lake Superior. Other journeys, large and small, include Macon's pretentious Sunday drives, Ruth's* bus rides to her father's grave, Guitar Baines* stalking Milkman while on the hunt with local men in Virginia, and Hagar Dead's* driven nonstop venture to try to buy the beauty that will win Milkman's affection. But it is Milkman's journey back in time, back to the source of his familial heritage, that has the greatest significance. Consistent with Morrison's proclivities, his geographical movement enables substantial emotional growth. Although Milkman leaves his Northern home to travel south initially for a selfish reason—he is seeking what he believes is gold hidden in a cave—what he actually discovers is far more valuable. Symbolically, Milkman sheds his materialistic outer coverings, such as his watch and dress shoes, and arrives at a much deeper appreciation for what is really important, such as his family. And these corresponding physical and personal expeditions converge when Pilate joins him in Virginia, Guitar's subsequent murder of her the catalyst for Milkman's own prodigious leap. This novel, therefore, opens with a failed flight and ends with what seems to be the most powerful flight of all, as Milkman leaps into the air, his ultimate journey transcending any earthly restrictions.

*Tar Baby** has the most exotic primary setting of Morrison's works, the Caribbean Isle des Chevaliers*, to which each of the main characters has traveled some distance. The novel begins with Son's* long swim, taking him from the ship job he abandons and resulting with his stowing away on board the small sailboat operated by Jadine Childs* and Margaret Street*. Within the world of *Tar Baby*, the older characters—Ondine and Sydney Childs*, Margaret, and Valerian Street*—remain fixed on the island. But Jadine and Son are more mobile, traveling to New York City, to Eloe*, Florida, back to New York, and then back to the island. By the end of the novel, Jadine is en route to Paris, where, she hopes, she will no longer need to constantly seek safety, yet her ultimate destination is uncertain. In *Tar Baby*'s final pages, magical Marie-Therese Foucault* facilitates Son's definitive and final journey to join a realm of mythic import. After traveling from the larger island of Dominique in a boat piloted in the dark by blind Marie-Therese, Son crawls ashore at Isle des Chevaliers, gradually finding his way and finally running off into what seems to be a legendary existence. Marie-Therese hopes, Morrison asserts, that he will forgo chasing the unworthy Jadine and instead merge with the stampeding island horsemen and embrace his own profound fate.

While Morrison's first four novels involve characters traveling between influential settings, the next three focus even more on geographical migration and its attendant emotional implications. In *Beloved**, *Jazz**, and *Paradise**, Morrison's characters leave their Southern homes in search of better lives in the North and West. Yet their quests for some sort of Promised Land are futile, for the relocations prove only to be different, not necessarily better.

Within *Beloved*, Sethe Suggs's* escape/migration from Sweet Home*, Kentucky, to Cincinnati, Ohio, echoes and revises the slave narrative tradition; the journey itself becomes a powerful metaphor, for it is simultaneously an escape and the scene for Denver Suggs's* birth. Paul D Garner* also migrates northward to Delaware by following nature's signs, such as the North Star, the spring flowers, and the moss on trees. Baby Suggs*, too, travels to the North, her departure actually sanctioned after her son Halle* buys her freedom. However, for each of these characters, the North fails in its billing as a place of refuge because the Promised Land turns out to be yet another site of horror. Along these migratory lines, we also see Beloved* herself undergoing a monumental metamorphosis; she transforms herself into a living being and travels what she describes as a great distance before arriving at 124 Bluestone Road*. This home outside Cincinnati becomes the destination for each of *Beloved*'s main characters, with Paul D arriving there after his self-proclaimed seventeen-year walk. Paul D's earlier trip taking him further south from Sweet Home—on the way to the hellish prison camp in Alfred, Georgia—reveals another migratory emphasis, as he recalls that his sense of physical control diminishes the farther south he travels. Morrison also demonstrates that even shorter journeys can be significant, as Denver's fearful venture out of the yard of 124 becomes her own and her mother's only chance for survival.

Furthermore, it is the physical incursion into the yard of 124 by schoolteacher* and his confederates that sets much of the novel's most powerful action into motion. Because of this invasion, to which Baby Suggs takes particular offense, Sethe believes that another essential journey is in order, this time between the land of the living and the domain of the dead. Again focused on seeking a safe place, as so many Morrison characters are, Sethe perceives the transition from life to death* as preferable to allowing her children to be remanded to what she views as the living hell of slavery*. In other words, rather than return from the relatively free North to the enslaved South, Sethe prefers to take her children and herself to what she describes as the far shore of existence, where they can be together with her late mother. Once the townswomen banish Beloved's presence to its rightful place, Sethe feels lost and hopeless. But by the novel's end, Sethe begins to realize, with the help of Paul D, that internal exploration and recovery* actually are possible, and that she can finally leave the past behind and embark on a journey into the future.

Literal and metaphorical journeys into a troubled Southern past also inform *Jazz**, Morrison's most direct Great Migration novel. This work gives great attention to Joe* and Violet Trace's* train journey from agricultural Virginia* to Harlem* not long after the turn of the century. Indeed, their very name, "Trace," suggests migration along tracks, paths, and roads. Also invoking the Harlem Renaissance tradition, *Jazz* presents Violet and Joe initially regarding the City, as Morrison calls it, as enthralling. Not only do they find it relatively easy to earn money, but they also manage upward mobility within this Northern setting, eventually landing a spacious apartment and satisfying jobs. Yet, Harlem eventually fails in its promise. Violet becomes mentally unstable after moving there, feeling trapped and confused, and Joe, too, loses his way, ultimately committing murder while on a hunting trek within this urban environment. However, by the end of *Jazz*, once Violet and Joe participate in their own fundamental emotional explorations, the Promised Land's enticements may just be beginning to come true.

In addition to Violet and Joe, others figure in the novels focus on geographical migration. Golden Gray* sets off on his own expedition southward, traveling from Baltimore* to Vesper County, Virginia, in search of his father. Interestingly, this is the same county that Joe traverses in his own parental search—yet Golden easily stumbles upon the otherwise elusive Wild*, and Joe comfortably bonds with Golden's quarry, Henry Lestory, otherwise known as Hunter's Hunter*. Years earlier, his mother, Vera Louise Gray*, and True Belle*, her servant and Violet's grandmother, made their own important migration from Vesper County to Baltimore to enable them to hide Golden's birth. Each of these journeys is steeped in identity* exploration and provides pivotal insights into the characters' lives.

*Paradise**, Morrison's seventh novel, embodies another migrational history, in which African Americans from the deep South relocated westward to build all-Black towns in Oklahoma and Kansas. The Old Fathers of *Paradise* flee from bigotry and violence in postbellum Louisiana and Mississippi, making a long trek to Oklahoma, where they hope to live in some of the African American towns already established. Along the way they attract more followers, but they also experience painful exclusion, as they are denied sanctuary by those they had expected to welcome them. The very circumstances that accompany the travelers' decision on where to found Haven, Oklahoma*, their first settlement, involve an almost mythical figure of a man who eventually leads them to the site.

Yet after the influences of the twentieth century encroach, the community leaders feel compelled to retreat farther west. The earlier seminal event of rejection, the Disallowing, determines the trajectory the settlers eventually take; rather than stay in Haven, they seek out an even more remote, and they hope safer, setting, traveling onward to what will become Ruby, Oklahoma*.

The townsmen, especially the twins Deacon* and Steward Morgan*, define Ruby by what it is not—specifically, the Convent*, seventeen miles away. Smug in their self-righteousness, the Ruby men believe visiting the Convent represents a dangerous foray into depravity. The very distance between Ruby and the Convent becomes a transitional space for significant physical and emotional journeying as each of the main characters in *Paradise* traverses this route, the men usually driving and the women often walking. Drawn to and yet repelled by each other, the residents of the Convent and the citizens of Ruby seem bound to travel these seventeen miles repeatedly—the most profound trip being the hunt on which the townsmen embark when they drive to the Convent to kill the women.

Furthermore, Deacon and Steward define the threat they believe the Convent represents in terms of another formative journey—when they accompany their father and uncles on a tour of the African American towns in the state. Echoing an earlier journey around Oklahoma and Kansas that their forebears took before the twins were born, this second trip also includes all-Black towns, many of which have failed in the intervening years. Their wounds still smarting from the Disallowing, the Morgan men seem almost to appreciate the hardships some of the other towns experience. While visiting one of the more prosperous communities, young Deacon and Steward see nineteen proper African American women who leave a lasting impression on the boys, resulting in their later horror at what they perceive to be the lawlessness of the women in the Convent.

These women have traveled great distances to reach the Convent, although their origins are somewhat indeterminate. The novel does reveal that Consolata Sosa* has come to Oklahoma all the way from Brazil; Mavis Albright*, from Maryland; Gigi (Grace Gibson*), from Alcorn, Mississippi, as well as San Francisco; and Seneca* from endless journeys, most recently from Indiana and Wichita, Kansas.

Throughout *Paradise*, these large and small journeys are numerous, from Deacon's barefoot walk, to Billie Delia Cato's* relocation from Ruby to Demby, to Anna Flood's return to Ruby from Detroit. Morrison further reveals her interest in metaphysical journeying here, which the physical mobility seems to prompt. Deacon's unusual walk through Ruby parallels his newfound interest in truth-telling; the Convent women's final journeys of forgiveness and healing follow their flights from the site of murder, as well as their own potential traversals between life and death. The final scene of *Paradise* also evokes migrations and mobility of all sorts, as Morrison alludes here to homecoming, flowing ocean waves, and ship voyages.

Toni Morrison's fictional writings embrace migrations, travels, trips—journeys both physical and emotional. While one may cause the other, she seems to say that neither is adequate alone. Morrison's own personal history reflects this migratory sensibility; her parents participated in the Great Migration, moving to Lorain, Ohio, from Georgia and Alabama, thus enabling their daughter, it seems, to understand and appreciate North, South, and the significant space for journeying in between.

References: Melvin Dixon, *Ride Out the Wilderness: Geography and Identity in Afro-American Literature* (1987); Farah Jasmine Griffin, *"Who Set You Flowin'?": The African-American Migration Narrative* (1995); Nicholas Lemann, *The Promised Land: The Great Black Migration and How It Changed America* (1991); Nell Irvin Painter, *Exodusters: Black Migration to Kansas After Reconstruction* (1976); Lawrence R. Rodgers, *Canaan Bound: The African-American Great Migration Novel* (1997).

Kristine Yohe

## Misner, Richard (*Paradise*)

The young reverend, an outsider who comes to Ruby, Oklahoma\*, in 1970, is mistrusted by Ruby's citizens and resented for his efforts to motivate the youth to participate in the Civil Rights movement. After the attack on the Convent\* women, Misner sees, or feels, a spiritual window in the air outside of the Convent. Although Misner has no answers either to solve the mysteries of the Convent or to give to Deacon Morgan's\* introspective musings, he emerges as a spiritual and political hope for Ruby when he decides to stay in the divided town while giving the eulogy for Save-Marie Fleetwood\*. *See also Paradise.*

Julie Cary Nerad

## Mister (*Beloved*)

"Mister" is the name of a rooster at Sweet Home\* whose freedom Paul D Garner\* envies. Paul D had assisted in Mister's birth, having helped him out of his shell after the hen had walked away with the other chicks and left him trapped inside his shell. Sethe Suggs\* and Paul D describe the rooster as hateful and able to best every other animal in the yard.

After Paul D is captured, shackled, and manacled, he watches Mister strutting around the yard and realizes that the rooster is more "man" than he ever was. Mister is one of the objects upon which Paul D focuses as he meditates on the meaning of manhood. *See also Beloved*; Garner, Paul D; Masculinity.

Lovalerie King

## Morgan, Deacon (*Paradise*)

Born in 1924, Deek is grandson of Zechariah "Big Papa" Morgan, founder of Haven, Oklahoma*, twin of Steward*, husband of Soane*, and head of one of the "fifteen families" who established Ruby, Oklahoma*. In 1954, already married and father of two boys, Deek has a short but passionate affair with Consolata (Connie) Sosa* that he ends ostensibly because Connie bites his lip and licks his blood while making love. But he also ends the affair because their relationship is a threat to Ruby's social structure; Deek is one of the respected "fathers" of the community. Looking for an explanation for the loss of his sons in Vietnam (both die in 1968) and for the changes in Ruby, Deek cannot reconcile his patriarchal life view and his ideals of stability and morality with Connie and the rest of the Convent* women; they are a threat to his authority and the community* he has worked to build his entire adult life.

Along with Steward, Deek leads the raid on the Convent in an attempt both to erase the perceived challenge of the matriarchal community and to eliminate his own lingering guilt over his long-ago affair. However, during the raid, when the unarmed Connie enters the room and addresses a vision only she sees, Deek attempts to deflect his brother's aiming arm. Although he is not physically stronger than his twin, he is the morally stronger of the two. After Steward murders Connie, a rift opens between the brothers. Unlike Steward, Deek begins to understand that the isolated and unchangeable new "haven" they had attempted to create and tried to uphold through patriarchal control and violence* was impossible. As he walks barefoot to Richard Misner's* house in a reenactment of his grandfather's 200-mile barefoot walk from Louisiana to Mississippi, the reader understands that Deek will find what he never knew to look for. *See also Paradise*.

Julie Cary Nerad

## Morgan, Dovey (*Paradise*)

As wife of the prominent Steward Morgan* and sister to Soane Morgan*, Dovey is one of Ruby, Oklahoma's* leading (but childless) women who, over the years, grows increasingly restless and helpless until she meets her "friend," a mysterious man who first appears to her just after a wave of butterflies, and never tells her his name. Except for one dream, her friend's visits stop after Steward leases Dovey's private space—a repossessed house at the edge of town—to his newly married nephew. Dovey and Soane are the only witnesses to Steward's shooting of Consolata Sosa* at the Convent, and the sisters' disagreement over which husband is responsible leaves an irreparable rift in their relationship. *See also Paradise.*

Julie Cary Nerad

## Morgan, Soane (*Paradise*)

Wife of Deacon Morgan* and sister to Dovey Morgan*, Soane taught the schoolchildren of Ruby, Oklahoma*, before Patricia Best Cato*. Knowing her husband Deek is having an affair with Consolata (Connie) Sosa*, a beautiful, green-eyed woman who lives at the Convent*, Soane walks the seventeen miles there and demands that Connie help her abort her child. However, Soane has no intent of aborting the child; rather, she uses that excuse to show herself and her sexual relationship with her husband to Connie. After Connie refuses to help her, Soane loses the child during the walk back to Ruby and understands the miscarriage as God's punishment. Ten years later, Soane develops an unexpected but deep and long-lasting friendship with Connie because Connie "steps-into" and saves her son Scout after he falls asleep driving a truck. On her way to help prevent the slaughter of the Convent women, Soane understands that she has truly forgiven Connie but wonders whether she has ever forgiven Deek. Her sons Scout and Easter died in Vietnam, and Soane has been unable to read their final letters; she finally wonders whether that refusal has been a way to punish Deek for his unfaithfulness. Soane gains insight into both herself and her husband after she witnesses Steward's murder of Connie, and Deek's too-late attempt to stop him. Unthinkingly, Soane implies to Dovey that the blame should rest on Steward. The brief exchange between the sisters changes their relationship forever. *See also Paradise.*

Julie Cary Nerad

## Morgan, Steward (*Paradise*)

Born in 1924, Steward is the twin of Deacon*, husband of Dovey*, and head of one of the "fifteen families" who established Ruby, Oklahoma*, Steward and Dovey are unable to have children*, so the patriarchal

Steward places all his expectations of the future on his nephew K.D. (Coffee Smith*). Steward loves his wife, the history* of his family*, the memory* of his sister Ruby, his bank, his position in the community*, and, perhaps most of all, his idea of what is Right. Rasher than his twin and conservative in matters of race*, Steward cannot tolerate the changing youth in Ruby, nor can he accept the menless women at the Convent*; for him, both are signs of failure, disintegration, and loss of control. Thus it is Steward who kills the "white girl" in the first line of the novel and who shoots Consolata Sosa* in the head despite, or perhaps because of, his brother's cautioning hand. *See also Paradise.*

Julie Cary Nerad

## Motherhood

In her efforts to plumb the depths of human emotion, Toni Morrison returns again and again to that most fundamental of personal relationships—the tie between mother and child. Motherhood is at the very core of human experience, and to truly grasp our capacity for love, for grief, for pain, for survival, one must take the full measure of motherhood, as Morrison does. Motherhood, in one form or another, is central to all of her novels. She is able to take historically and culturally African American interpretations of maternity and strip away the socially imposed limitations on that motherhood, thereby exposing the universal humanity of that experience. In so doing, she dissolves the boundaries of the maternal role, creating an ever-widening, intergenerational definition of the concept of mothering.

Motherhood in *The Bluest Eye** is hard work, a heavy load of economic and moral responsibility with few redeeming moments of tenderness or affection. Both of the mothers in this novel—Mrs. MacTeer and Pauline Breedlove*—are supremely pragmatic in their motives toward their daughters. Theirs is a motherly love hardened by necessity; their first responsibility toward their daughters is to keep them alive, their second, to teach them to fend for themselves. The broader implications of fending for themselves are the ability to survive in a hostile world, to maintain personal integrity in the face of the dominant white culture, and to grow up to be decent, acceptable citizens.

But Pauline Breedlove is functioning on the fringes of society; in the white home where she is employed as domestic help, she is just that— the help. The little white girl she cares for has access to a nurturing, maternal side of Pauline that her own children never see; even Pecola* calls her mother "Mrs. Breedlove," an impersonal, distancing name that emphasizes the difficulty of this mother-child relationship, while her white "daughter" calls her by an affectionate/demeaning first name. But while

Pauline has a double identity* as a mother, she has no support network within her own community*—the Breedloves are accepted by no one. They live in white culture only as domestic help; in Black culture, as an example of what not to become, of sloth and laziness steeped in violence*, poor taste, and alcohol. Pecola's mother has no community in whose ways she can train her daughter. In her inability to protect her daughter from her drunken husband, Mrs. Breedlove fails in her maternal duty; not only does Pecola get pregnant when her father rapes her, but when she miscarries, her tenuous hold on sanity is broken, and she is rendered forever incapable of attaining the status of decent, acceptable citizen.

Mrs. MacTeer, on the other hand, is constantly aware of her responsibility toward Claudia* and Frieda*, ever vigilant that they might stray from the narrow path of moral decency and cultural acceptability that she believes will keep them safe in life. She is aware of her place in her social world, and is willing to sacrifice tenderness and mercy toward her daughters in order to ensure that they maintain that standing while surviving the delicate game of interfacing with the dominant white culture. They are taught to fear prostitutes*, to despise laziness, and to scorn those who are outside of their culture's accepted margins. Even as she berates Claudia for an inconvenient illness, she nonetheless clearly loves her daughter, but has no emotional energy available for open demonstrations of that affection. Throughout this novel, emotional comfort is an unheard-of luxury in a world where survival is a daily struggle.

In *Sula**, Morrison explores the intergenerational effects of maternal relationships. Eva Peace* embodies matriarchy—holding court from her wagon-throne, never leaving her bedroom but ruling her little kingdom well within her divine right as mother and grandmother. Nel Wright*, like Sula Peace*, comes from a line of women fending for themselves; her mother, raised by her grandmother, has rejected her own mother's life of prostitution, instead embracing the virtue of the Catholic Church and life as a small-town pillar of decency. Like her mother, Nel chooses a seemingly traditional life with a husband and children*, but when her husband, Jude Greene*, is seduced by Sula, Nel loses him as well as her lifelong best friend.

In Eva, Morrison examines both the pragmatic and the affectionate sides of motherhood. When Eva's husband abandons her in the dead of winter, leaving her destitute with three children to feed, Eva has no choice but to rise to the occasion; we are never entirely sure what happened to her leg, but it is clear that the loss of that leg is what enables her to survive financially and raise her children to adulthood. But throughout the novel her single-minded insistence on survival is tempered by unabashed love for her children; Plum*, particularly, is her acknowledged favorite. Eva's murder of her grown son, when she discovers his opium addiction, foreshadows Sethe's Suggs's* refusal to allow her children to be destroyed by slavery* in *Beloved**—Eva will end Plum's degradation herself, rather than allow him to kill himself with drugs.

Eva's matriarchal dynasty is short-lived; her eldest daughter, Hannah, who lives with her, burns to death (with daughter Sula looking on); years later, Sula dies of a prolonged illness, pathetically alone, having institutionalized her grandmother and alienated everyone else in town who might care about her, particularly Nel. Sula leads a supremely narcissistic life. She has no regard for anyone's feelings; she does exactly what she pleases, without thought for convention or public disapprobation. Her betrayals of the three most important women in her life (Nel, Eva, and Hannah) indicate her lack of balancing superego. But Nel's more traditional life choices don't shield her from the repercussions of Sula's selfishness; even after she loses her husband to Sula, Nel's sense of herself as peacemaker and protector prompts her to take responsibility, unbidden, for the ill Sula, as well as the dead Sula. Both women struggle throughout the novel to establish identities for themselves independent of their female/maternal lineage, but both ultimately fail; the complex dynamics of mother-child relationships are too strong, too much a part of who they are, for either of them ever to be totally divested of that inheritance.

In *Song of Solomon**, Morrison creates a mother character who has achieved a level of financial and social security that affords her the luxury of a more complex and affection-based relationship with her children. As in Morrison's previous novels, the presence of an abusive husband complicates Ruth Dead's* life; while Cholly Breedlove's* decisive act is to rape his daughter, and BoyBoy chooses to leave Eva, Macon Dead* just stays and torments his wife and children. Ruth's love for her son is her only act of open defiance against Macon; she tricked him into getting her pregnant a third time, years after he had lost all sexual interest in her, and then fought to keep the baby he wanted her to lose or abort. Milkman Dead's* very existence is the hard evidence of Ruth's maternal instinct, and she turns to that relationship for what little validation and pleasure she can eke out of life.

On the other side of town, Macon's sister, Pilate Dead*, holds sway in a very different household; she raised her daughter, Reba*, alone, and the two women have now raised Reba's daughter, Hagar*, again without the benefit or burden of male input. Hagar grows up indulged and protected; Pilate is an eccentric, but strong and capable, woman, levelheaded and wise. Pilate and Reba both dote on Hagar, but she loses her heart to Milkman, and comes completely unhinged when he jilts her.

Pilate and Macon both live their lives under the shadow of their adored father's death; as children, they witnessed his murder and found themselves alone in the world. The novel hinges on their struggle to truly understand and come to terms with what happened to him, and to themselves, on that farm in Pennsylvania; throughout, Pilate is driven by visits from her father's ghost, convinced that he is urging her to atone for her sins and honor his memory*. Milkman pieces together a history* of his grandparents that neither Macon nor Pilate knew, and reveals that the dead grandfather's visits were not about himself, but about his wife's memory; Macon, Sr., urges Pilate to honor her mother, which she has never been able to do because her mother died a few minutes before Pilate's birth. This is clearly a quest novel; for each character the quest takes a slightly different form, but for all it is about understanding, honoring, and justifying the past. For Pilate and Macon, and their respective families, the most elusive part of that past is the memory of their dead mother, Singing Bird*.

In *Beloved*, Morrison creates her most complex portrayal of motherhood; even the novel's title is a testament to Sethe's dubious legacy of love and blood. Having escaped from slavery at great personal cost, when Sethe sees her owner and tormentor coming to recapture her and her children, she attempts to kill her children to keep them from having to live through the cruelty that she has experienced at schoolteacher's* hands. She succeeds only in killing her toddler daughter, and schoolteacher is sufficiently horrified that he abandons his mission. Throughout the novel, Sethe's mothering is intertwined with her memories of her own mother, who was separated from her by the cruelties of slavery, and with the mothering and memories of her mother-in-law, Baby Suggs*. The ghost of Beloved*, who appears as the flesh-and-blood incarnation of Sethe's traumatized psyche, is also an amalgam of generations of African and maternal suffering under the inhumanity of the slave trade. The novel revolves around Sethe's accommodation of first the invisible baby ghost, and later the physical girl who appears, Beloved's ghost returned to life. When faced with the person that her beloved daughter could have been, Sethe relinquishes her own right to endure and live, and her obligation to mother her remaining child. Sethe's entire identity is a part of, and a reaction to, her mothering, and the reality of motherhood in the face of life's injustices threatens to annihilate her.

Sethe has four children, but her sons, Howard* and Buglar Suggs*, pick up and leave early in the novel, unable to cope with the intensity of the ghost-child who haunts their home; significantly, the result of their departure is a truly matriarchal family unit. When Baby Suggs dies, Sethe is left alone to support the weight of her past, her grief, her ancestral legacy, and her adolescent daughter's needs. Paul D Garner*, the last of the men with whom she survived the atrocities on the plantation, reappears and attempts to support and nurture Sethe, but his arrival only complicates the relationships between the mother and her two daughters, one living, one not. Sethe's ultimate catharsis, the exorcism of

Beloved's human ghost, can be accomplished only by the women of the town, when they come out to support Sethe at Denver Suggs's* behest. Symbolically, Sethe is unable to support the weight of her motherhood alone; yet again Morrison is pointing out, among other things, the importance of community-based mothering. The novel is ultimately homage to the strength of women everywhere who, collectively, enable the world's children to live and thrive and, by extension, sustain the very existence of humanity, no matter what the exigencies of life and survival.

In *Tar Baby**, Morrison examines, for the first time, the relationship between a white mother and her son; significantly, Margaret Street* is the only mother in any of Morrison's novels who maliciously abuses her child, with no better excuse than her own psychological disturbances. Interestingly, this is the only actual mother-child relationship in the book, and we never meet Michael; it is his refusal to visit that fuels some of the animosity between Margaret and Valerian Street*. Margaret clearly is mentally ill, but Ondine Childs's* exposure of the woman's intermittent but intentional torture of her young child, years prior, reveals the depth of dysfunctionality in this miserable little family.

Jadine Childs*, Ondine's and Sydney Childs's* orphaned niece, and Son*, her lover, are more of Morrison's motherless children. We know that Jadine was orphaned when she was twelve and was raised by her aunt and uncle, who financed her exclusive boarding school education. Son, who goes by various aliases, almost as if protecting his true name/identity, seems to have only a father. Both of these characters are aimless, rootless, narcissistic, and ultimately alone in the world. Jadine is self-conscious of her status as an orphan, and while she welcomes the emotional dependence of her relationship with Son, she has no intention of relinquishing her financial and social independence. Son simply feels no concrete obligation to anyone other than himself. Having killed his wife, he is a fugitive from the law, but believes that he is punishing himself by living with his guilt. He has an idyllic memory of the nobility of Eloe*, the small Florida town where he was raised, but nothing strong enough to hold him or stop his worldwide wandering.

Ondine, the cook and wife of the Streets' butler, has a troubled relationship to motherhood. Having no children of her own, Ondine has raised her brother-in-law's daughter, only to watch her succeed in the world and come back to visit as a guest of Margaret, where she is expected to wait on Jadine like the servant that she is. At the same time, Ondine has witnessed the abuse of Michael, and while she seals her own complicity by not revealing Margaret's abuse until years later, when it is far too late, she also admits to trying to help the boy by giving him the mother love that Margaret couldn't. At the end of the novel, Ondine feels that the mothering she has done throughout her life has been without recompense; perhaps it is her substitute status in the lives of Jadine and

Michael that allows Morrison to point out the truly sacrificial nature of motherhood.

In *Jazz**, two of the primary driving forces of the novel stem from motherhood unfulfilled: Violet Trace's* inability to become a mother, coupled with the memory of her own mother's suicide, and Joe Trace's* inability ever to know his mother. As in Morrison's other novels, an understanding of the present is always an exercise in untangling the knotted threads of history, and in this novel we see an entire cast of characters attempting to compensate for their lack of an enduring sense of being rooted in a stable network of maternal relationships. Neither Violet nor Joe can find comfort in a mother or a child; this lack of lineage forces them to find other ways of coping with life's challenges. Violet has few, if any, resources. She is mentally unstable, and ultimately her marriage provides the safety net that keeps her sane and functional. Joe is clearly searching for a mother figure; the image of his whispering to a wild woman in a cornfield, hoping she is his mother, frames the book. Dorcas Manfred*, Joe's lover, is more a child than a mother figure, and cannot really meet his psychological needs. In the final scenes of the novel, it is their shared history that enables the Traces to hold their marriage together—each is lacking a matriarchal lineage, so they create their own history, marital rather than maternal. Clearly, in this particular novel, the characters' lack of stability, of rootedness, represents the sense of disorder that plagued the Jazz Age culture as a whole; motherhood, or the lack thereof, becomes an allegory for a much larger cultural condition.

In Morrison's seventh novel, *Paradise**, the motley group of women who live at the Convent* represent a matriarchal rejection of the patriarchal "paradise" of Ruby, Oklahoma*. It is this insubordination that brings down upon them the wrath of the town's male old guard, and though the town's wise woman (poignantly named Lone DuPres* in honor of her discovery as an abandoned/motherless infant in the wilderness) tries to save them, she is too late, and the women are sacrificed. The symbolic leader of the Convent is a woman whom Consolata (Connie) Sosa* (the oldest resident, and mother figure to the women who gravitate there) calls Mother (Mary Magna*); she is actually an ill and aged nun who dies early in the novel.

The Convent actually was, at one time, a community of nuns running a school for Native American girls; it gradually becomes a shelter for various lost and hunted women who struggle to heal their wounds and nurture each other in an entirely female environment. For almost every one of the women at the Convent, motherhood is the background on which emotional battles are waged: for one, it is the accidental suffocation of her twin babies that fuels her escape from an abusive husband; another runs away from home when her boyfriend falls in love with her mother, and later gets pregnant, most likely after being raped. Another was just a child when her mother, whom she thought was her sister, walked out of their apartment and never returned. For all these women, the distinction between mother and daughter is unclear; the line between self/identity and mother love is blurred. Each is unable to create order from her own emotional chaos, but with Connie's help, the women support each other in their journeys toward wholeness and independence.

By contrast, in the town of Ruby (even the name has maternal significance), Black women have achieved the ironically incapacitating status of the white ideal of subordinate, subservient motherhood: they have no voice, no independent thought, no power. When any one of the women needs a truly supportive female community, she finds that community at the Convent. At the end of the novel, it is the women of the town who try to prevent the massacre of the Convent women, and it is the town's marginal women, Patricia Best Cato* (daughter of an outside woman) and Lone DuPres, who are able to look objectively at this piece of Ruby history and understand the male pride and arrogance that led to such senseless cruelty. But the town's female voices have all been silenced; neither Pat nor Lone speaks of what she knows to be true.

Throughout her novels, Morrison dissects, examines, and re-examines the archetypal images of motherhood, ruthlessly challenging traditional definitions of mothering. She examines the intergenerational impact on the human psyche of motherhood as both a presence and an absence. Writing out of a tradition in which mothers are the keepers of history— the oral tradition*—Morrison inextricably links the mother's role with the role of history. To lose, or dishonor, or ignore one is to lose the other. And these are the primal relationships of humanity. We are nothing outside of history; likewise, without mothers, we would not exist. *See also* Approaches to Morrison's Work: Feminist/Black Feminist; Domesticity; Family; Home; Infanticide.

References: Patricia Hill Collins. "The Meaning of Motherhood in Black Culture and Black Mother/Daughter Relationships," *Sage* 4: 2 (1987); Carole Boyce Davies, "Mother Right/Write Revisited: *Beloved* and *Dessa Rose* and the Construction of Motherhood in Black Women's Fiction," in *Narrating Mothers: Theorizing Maternal Subjectivities*, ed. Brenda O. Daly and Maureen T. Reddy (1991); Stephanie A. Demetrakopoulos, "Maternal Bonds as Devourers of Women's Individuation in Toni Morrison's *Beloved*," *African American Review* 26: 1 (1992); Karen E. Fields, "To Embrace Dead Strangers: Toni Morrison's *Beloved*," in *Mother Puzzles: Daughters and Mothers in Contemporary American Literature*, ed. Mickey Pearlman (1989); Marianne Hirsch, "Maternal Narratives: 'Cruel Enough to Stop the Blood,'" in *Reading Black Reading Feminist: A Critical Anthology*, ed. Henry Louis Gates, Jr.

(1990); Barbara Offutt Mathieson, "Memory and Mother Love in Morrison's *Beloved*," *American Imago* 47: 1 (Spring 1990).

Lisa C. Rosen

## Music

When describing her childhood, Toni Morrison frequently mentions the music that was always playing at home or the fact that her mother sang both jazz and opera. If this is the reason for Morrison's understanding of music, she has also passed it on; one of her sons is a musician and sound engineer. Her many credits include the libretto for *Honey and Rue*, a song cycle composed with André Previn for the Black soprano Kathleen Battle, and the musical *New Orleans*, concerning the origins of jazz* in that city's Storyville. Her most engaging relationship to music, however, may be the way she translates it into the written word

Morrison uses music as both a structural and a symbolic element in her work. Music often carries information about community* knowledge, aesthetics, or perspectives. Toni Morrison often discusses the power of music and the way it functions in culture in discussions of her craft. She sometimes refers to music as an ideal art form. In her "Rootedness: The Ancestor* as Foundation," an essay excerpted from an interview with Eleanor Traylor, she details elements of music (Black music in particular) that sustain its power. Morrison argues that traditionally, music has been the primary art form of healing for Black people. Because of the changing place of Black music as a commodity in American culture, she asserts, music can no longer do this work alone (Evans 340.)

Morrison sees the novel as another form that can mirror what happens with Black music, and perhaps take that work further. In creating her works, she attends to the participatory nature of music—the way it makes listeners respond through singing or dancing. Morrison aims for her fiction to touch those same nerves, to make readers not only speak back to the text, but also recognize their responses as part of the text (Evans 341).

She continues this line of thinking about music in "Living Memory," an interview with Paul Gilroy. Once again, Morrison mentions the way art, especially music, has been a source of healing and sustenance. She contemplates the "intricacy" and "discipline" involved in making the work of music, particularly of improvisational music, seem effortless. Here she also states her aim to mirror in her writing this seamless stitching together of available information that is so often achieved in music. She strives, Morrison says, to parallel the tension between what information is given in the music and what is left up to the imagination that exists in exchanges between composers or performers of music and their audiences (Evans 181).

Much of what Toni Morrison learns from music is incorporated into her fiction, but it also informs her analysis of others' works. In her critical monograph *Playing in the Dark: Whiteness and the Literary Imagination\**, Morrison examines tropes and structural problems regarding Black presence in literature by white American writers. Before beginning this project, however, Morrison attends to the moment of a French writer's memoir in which the author first recognizes her own madness.

The event takes place in a club, while listening to Louis Armstrong. Overwhelmed by the music—specifically Armstrong's improvisation—the author (Marie Cardinal) describes running into the street, screaming that she is going to die. Morrison argues that moments of self-awareness such as these are often sparked by interactions with Black people or Black figurations in literature not written by Blacks. She calls attention to the fact that Cardinal's reaction is not simply to Louis Armstrong's Black body, but specifically to jazz and its structure. Morrison comes away from the passage with the notion that what she calls the "cultural associations" of jazz are as meaningful as its "intellectual foundations." It may be useful to think of the "cultural associations" of jazz as the ways in which jazz operates in culture as a symbol of Blackness or of the city, while the "intellectual foundations" are the structural base and logic of the music.

Symbolic and structural elements of music appear throughout all of Toni Morrison's fiction in one way or another. Music figures most prominently, however, in her three works in which the title refers to the musicality of the work. These works are the novels *Jazz\** and *Song of Solomon\** and her only short story, "Recitatif\*." In each of these works, the idea of music, or a genre of music, appears at the outset to offer readers a way in which to approach (their participation in) the text.

"Recitatif" takes its title from a vocal style commonly found in opera. "Recitatif" may be so named in order to foreground the events of the story in the way that a recitatif would in opera. In this story, the reader is privy to four reunions between a Black woman and a white woman (Twyla and Roberta, perhaps respectively) who lived together in an orphanage for part of their childhood. Although readers know that one character is white and the other is Black, Morrison does not give us physical descriptions or direct references to either character's race\*. Music appears throughout the story, but each time the music carries more than one cultural association.

As a result, music sets the tone of the context for several exchanges, indicating the way in which each character invests in or responds to a raced community. For example, when Twyla and Roberta meet in an upscale grocery store, Twyla repeatedly notes that classical music is playing over the loudspeaker as she thinks about the expensive prices of the food or the expensive clothes on Roberta. Twyla is made uncomfortable by the cultural associations of classical music. The music is a symbol of upper-class culture, and perhaps also of whiteness*.

Sometimes the music underscores the ambiguous relationships of genres and musicians and their cultural associations. When Roberta tells Twyla that she is to meet with "Hendrix," Twyla inquires what she is doing now. What is the reader to take from Twyla's failure to understand that Roberta's "Hendrix" is Jimi Hendrix? Is Twyla referring to Nona Hendryx? If so, what does her lack of knowledge about Jimi Hendrix and Roberta's lack of knowledge about Nona Hendryx say about each musician as a cultural figure? Depending on the time period, each figure could play a different role in the characterization of Twyla and Roberta as Black and white figures.

Among the musical styles mentioned in the story, however, "recitatif" seems to carry the most ambiguous cultural associations of all. The vocal style called "recitatif" (or "recitative") is designed for singing the narration of events in an opera and often precedes an aria. The complexity of the aria presents the opportunity for soloists to demonstrate their expertise, while the recitatif is composed to follow the simple rhythms of natural speech. An aria gives detailed information about a character or the moment, whereas the main purpose of the recitatif is to give the audience the other necessary information in the form of dialogue or narration.

How is "Recitatif" related to the recitatif? A reader may experience each of the five sections of the story as a "recitatif" from an opera missing its other parts. The dialogue and narration foreground the plot. Readers must imagine the rest.

One may even read the positioning of this story in relation to Toni Morrison's other works. "Recitatif" (1983) appeared in print between *Tar Baby** and *Beloved**, the first novel in Morrison's trilogy that includes *Jazz* and *Paradise**. "Recitatif" can be read as one narrative passage foregrounding the story of race in America, preceding the aria, *Beloved*. However, it may be that after "Recitatif," Morrison mirrored the tension between operatic vocal styles in *Beloved* with its many narrated chapters followed by detailed, introspective passages from the perspectives of Sethe Suggs*, Beloved*, and Denver Suggs*. However readers read the "recitatif" of "Recitatif," Morrison makes good use of the cultural associations and intellectual foundations of all of the music in the story.

In *Song of Solomon*, these elements of music are part of the plot. One of the central threads of the story is a song, the words of which are transformed throughout the novel. While the melody and structure of the song remain the same in different places and time periods, the names of the people mentioned change. The reader learns the way a particular family* history* and Black community memory* change over time and region. The song stands, among other translations of oral culture into print, as a representation of the routes through which community knowledge passes.

As Wahneema Lubiano argues, while a particular story is being told in vernacular culture, the *ways* of distributing information throughout a community are also passed on (95, 96.) In the case of *Song of Solomon*, the process of passing on these different kinds of knowledge occurs in different forms of oral storytelling. The names of places and characters, for example, carry histories informed by other, similar-sounding words. Places and people are renamed by a community's insistence on remembering them by events in their lives or their desires. Finally, both children* and adults sing songs that preserve community lore.

There is also the aural story that nature tells, especially in Shalimar, where memory is kept in the way characters listen to their terrain. Ryna's sorrow is remembered not only through the song (of Solomon*), but also through the sound of the wind whipping through the landscape. Morrison uses music as only part of the soundscape in which a system of remembering one's relationship to the events in one's community is rehearsed. The memories conserved include not only details about a story (i.e., Solomon left behind his wife and son Jake*) but also the feelings of the community in which the story took place.

Part of the value of understanding music as part of a whole host of vernacular elements in this work is that it allows the reader to distinguish which relationships are particular to music. Perhaps the most important distinction is that music allows the song to travel away from the place of its origin and gives the information a greater context. While the patterns for naming and renaming places and people in the text are passed down across time, these aural histories do not tend to travel far from their places of origin. The primary force propelling music from person to person is not the need to pass information or even to judge one's relationship to a place or event. Because music travels casually along lines of those who share an aesthetic, the context for songs extends far beyond the particular places in which other kinds of memory are contained.

Once a song is separated from its original context, the lyrics can change. If the information articulated in the song sometimes points in different directions (Solomon becomes Sugarman, Jake becomes Jay), what remains is the melancholy mood of the song—the blues. The sadness of the singers' "Don't leave me here" resonates throughout the book. This mood, appropriately, propels the plot of *Song of Solomon*. The sadness of having been left is partially responsible for Macon Dead's* miserliness, Ruth Dead's* loneliness, Milkman Dead's* selfishness, even for Pilate Dead's* misunderstood message from the dead.

One of Morrison's goals for her fiction is to relay the mood of a musical form. She has acknowledged the desire to depict the feelings of "dislocation" evident in spirituals for the writing of *Beloved*. In *Jazz*, she wanted to create a syntax that gives the illusion of jazz improvisation, but also to portray the "reckless, romantic" gestures of the form (Pici 374.)

Each chapter of *Jazz* can be read as a solo taken by a different instrument. The first sentence of each chapter responds directly to some word, phrase, or idea from the last sentence of the chapter before it, as if in response to the last musical phrase of a preceding solo. The distinct syntax and rhythm in the language of each chapter support this idea. The repetition of phrases creates the effect of a riff. Like a response to the last musical phrase of the preceding solo, the first sentence of each chapter responds directly to some word, phrase, or idea from the last sentence of the chapter before it (Pici 390.)

Even the first word of the novel refers to the cultural associations and intellectual foundations of jazz. The word "Sth" has been read as the sound of sucking teeth, often made in judgment on some person or event in African American communities. This word has also been read as fanfare—the first sounds a musician (particularly a horn player or percussionist) makes to announce that he or she is to take over the next solo. Whether the reader reads the word as the sounds of people or instruments, or simply pronounces the "s," the sound produced may resemble the sound of a cymbal.

Toni Morrison has also incorporated the illusion of one of jazz's most characteristic elements, improvisation. For Morrison, this property of the novel is most evident in the final chapter. One form in which improvisation appears is the narrator's surprise. In *Jazz*, Morrison's narrator begins telling the story without knowing exactly how it will end. It does have expectations, however. The narrator tells the reader that it expects Felice*, Joe Trace*, and his wife Violet* to act together in the same way that Dorcas Manfred*, Joe, and Violet do. When the story is set up in the same way, however, the song plays differently. Joe, Violet, and Felice interact in ways that the speaking voice of the text does not expect.

Music has a stronger presence, structurally and symbolically, in *Jazz* than in other printed texts by Toni Morrison. It is therefore fitting that the narrator of the book calls attention to the limitations of being an aural text in a printed form. In a direct address to the reader, the narrator of *Jazz* "speaks" about the way a book works and a reader reads. In addition to the appreciation this "character" feels for the reader, it expresses the longing to do what music (or any aural text, any aural being) can do that a book cannot—to say what it has to say *out loud. See also* Oral Tradition.

References: Mari Evans, ed., *Black Women Writers 1950–1980: A Critical Evaluation* (1984); Wahneema Lubiano, "The Postmodern Rag: Political Identity and the Vernacular in *Song of Solomon*," in *New Essays on Song of Solomon*, ed. Valerie Smith (1995); Nicholas F. Pici, "Trading Meanings: The Breath of Music in Toni Morrison's *Jazz*," *Connotations* 7: 3 (1997–98); Danielle Taylor-Guthrie, ed. *Conversations with Toni Morrison* (1994).

Mendi Lewis Obadike

## Myth

Because people organize knowledge into narrative structures, particularly those captured in myths and fairy tales, Toni Morrison views fiction as indispensable. The variety and significance of myth in her novels illustrates how this theory governs and shapes Morrison's own work—from the myth of the flying Africans* underpinning *Song of Solomon** to the Br'er Rabbit fable she revises in *Tar Baby**. Morrison draws upon an apparently limitless repertoire of myths, appropriating classical, Christian, and African traditions to portray twentieth-century wounds and the love that potentially heals them. Morrison also mines contemporary myths from popular culture, particularly those perpetuating the troubling and often disruptive Western beauty standards exploded in *The Bluest Eye** and the happily-ever-after stories of men and women in love tested and strained in *Sula**, *Tar Baby*, *Beloved**, and *Jazz**, among others. Finally, the myth of the pleasures offered in the Garden of Eden holds a particular force for Morrison, as she consistently alludes to and then dismisses this fantasy in several reimagined guises. These guises range from the tainted and colonized beauty of the Caribbean in *Tar Baby*, to a perfect Harlem* at once promised and revoked during the 1920s in *Jazz*, to the perpetually unstable place of harmony and serenity established by the 8-rock people of *Ruby, Oklahoma**, in *Paradise**.

Myths explain why things are the way they are—why the world is as it is and why things happen the way they do; Morrison's novels exemplify this truism. Several of her novels, such as *The Bluest Eye* and *Paradise*, open by describing the aftermath of a trauma*, implicitly promising to explain how and why the trauma occurred. On the first page of *The Bluest Eye*, a child's voice immediately betrays the novel's secret, that Pecola Breedlove* was carrying her father's baby. Similarly, Morrison opens *Paradise* with a description of the crime that also closes her narrative frame: nine men attack the Convent* women as punishment for shattering Ruby's fantasies of happiness. Morrison, in other words, exploits the form and content of myths by treating her novels as a basis for explaining the troubling ways of the world. In so doing, she also revises the familiar, if unacknowledged, mythic content deeply informing our values and beliefs.

Morrison's interest in magical realism* also reflects her indebtedness to myth. Just as ancient myths deploy supernatural stories to explain what is beyond rational comprehension, Morrison's novels provide the quality of truth that can be accessed only through magic, exaggeration, and fantasy. Pilate Dead's* birth without a navel and Beloved's* ghostly appearance at 124 Bluestone Road* eighteen years after her death* are two examples of the supernatural stories underlying primary characters' lives in Morrison's fiction. The supernatural outcomes of Morrison's novels also borrow mythic elements, thus resisting the demand for closure associated with realist narrative: How does Beloved disappear without a trace? How can the Convent women of Ruby survive the ambush? Does Milkman Dead* really ride the air to be free? The answers are insignificant compared with the questions these supernatural tales elicit. While using the mythic structure to signal an explanation of the inexplicable, and simultaneously using supernatural elements to reinforce ambiguity, Morrison effectively raises questions in each of her novels about the mythic content lurking beneath our consciousness. Written during the explosion of racial strife in America from 1965 to 1969, *The Bluest Eye* exposes dominant racial assumptions—or myths—about beauty, as well as what Morrison calls the "gaze" condemning young African American girls, the most silenced victims of racial tension. Clutching her Shirley Temple cup and blue-eyed baby dolls amid the insistent repetition of the Dick and Jane primer, the myth of middle-class American happiness disintegrates, literally, before Pecola Breedlove's eyes.

The novel opens with a general description of "the" private, pretty house and "the" happy family, making such fairytales appear to be available to everyone—the very basis of the American Dream. But as *The Bluest Eye* progresses, such dreams are exposed as elusive myths, particularly for the Breedlove family, reduced to living in a storefront under the watchful eye (or gaze) of the community*. At every turn, the novel lays bare the danger of embracing such myths, from Pauline Breedlove's* adoration of the white, middle-class family for whom she works, to her satisfaction from watching idealized Hollywood film stars, to her equation of Blackness and what she perceives as "ugliness" in her daughter, herself, and her husband. The most striking effect of internalizing this myth, however, is Pecola Breedlove's self-splitting, resulting in the belief that Soaphead Church* has, in fact, granted her cobalt blue eyes.

The "who will play with Jane?" query fundamental to the mythic Dick and Jane primer cuts to the heart of a second tragedy of *The Bluest Eye*. Pecola is rejected by nearly everyone, except perhaps Claudia* and Frieda MacTeer* and the triad of prostitutes* at the margins of society, Furylike in their associations with vengeance and retribution. Pecola's rejection takes on full force when her father, the also-victimized Cholly Breedlove*, at once embraces and rejects her by impregnating her. In her victimization, Pecola Breedlove resembles Philomela, an ancient mythical figure who was raped and subsequently tortured with voicelessness.

Northrop Frye famously views novels' plots as recurrences of basic mythic formulas and associates elemental forms of myth with seasonal cycles of spring, summer, autumn, and winter. Likewise, the turning of the seasons provides the structural basis for *The Bluest Eye*. Beginning with the autumn and the new school year, the novel progresses through winter, spring, and finally to summer—storm season, the child narrator reports, both literally and figuratively. *The Bluest Eye*, then, draws on the structure of myth by linking seasonal changes with such narrative events as the departure and return of Persephone from Hades. In other words, *The Bluest Eye* turns ideas as seasons themselves turn, and in this turning, challenges the promises offered by a Dick and Jane primer mythology and the Western myth that the bluest eyes are the most beautiful.

*Sula* opens in a spirit similar to that of Morrison's first novel, with the promise of explaining through a folk anecdote how the text's current situation came to pass. The first pages provide a rich description of a community in the hills—paradoxically referred to as the Bottom*, thanks to its beginnings in a "nigger joke." Morrison's narrator provides the insider's story for the origins of the Bottom by complicating the trickster* myth. Traditionally a trickster figure, both oppressed and driven by appetite, dupes others but is ultimately duped himself. In *Sula*'s opening, the identity* of the trickster figure is unclear after the narrator reveals that Blacks settled the Bottom high in the hills because a farmer promised freedom and desirable land to a former slave. Rather than reward the man's hard work with fertile land in the bottom of the valley, however, the farmer proclaims the merits of the land in the hills by explaining that it is the bottom of heaven. After the expectant landowner presses the farmer for the hilly land, the farmer happily concedes, eventually reversing the traditional equation of trickery with the oppressed.

A trickster figure in her own right, Sula Peace* is named after a failure in spirit or an alteration of proper conditions according to the African Babangi language. Defying assumptions about how Black women ought to behave, she is accompanied by an ominous flock of robins; she is a wanderer, an anarchist, a disruptive femme fatale. According to African myth, a plague—like the family-shattering plague Sula embodies—lifts only with the community's sacrifice, as indicated by the accidental deaths at the tunnel on National Suicide Day*. Not only a trickster figure, Sula's character strikingly resembles Queen Jezebel of the Hebrew Bible. Other characters in the novel interpret Sula's prominent stemmed-rose birthmark as the mark of evil, recalling Jezebel's aggressive rule over Israel in the ninth century B.C.E., establishing her mythic reputation as a beautiful temptress and the embodiment of feminine evil.

Sula's own indiscretions include seducing her best friend Nel Wright's* husband, Jude Greene*, in a scathing inversion of the modern-day fairy-tale romance Nel deeply values. Traditionally, water and fire have mythic powers of purification; however, in *Sula* these natural elements are deathly in their excess. This excess is omnipresent in Sula's past, as she takes joint responsibility for the drowning death of Chicken Little* in her childhood and watches her mother, Hannah, burn to death simply because she is interested.

Before the burning death of Hannah Peace, the three generations of Peace women lived on the outskirts of the Bottom as pariahs. Like the three female prostitutes of *The Bluest Eye*, they resemble the chorus in Greek tragedy, the Furies, and the Fates, who spun, measured, and cut the stories of people's lives. Like these women, World War I veteran Shadrack* is an outsider and source of confusion and mystery to people of the Bottom. With the desire to see his own face in a toilet bowl, Shadrack appears as Narcissus, the beautiful youth in Greek mythology* who refused all love and was punished for this indifference by falling in love with his own image in a pool. Similarly, the novel's heroine ultimately dies alone, unable to recognize the reflection of her other half embodied by Nel.

*Song of Solomon* draws not only on the romantic quest narrative, but also on the African American and classical European myths of men who could fly. Although many readers associate Morrison's flying characters with the classical Greek figures Daedalus and Icarus, who attempt freedom with wings and candle wax, Morrison suggests that her novel's meaning draws on the specific myth about Black people who could fly. She explains that this particular myth was a part of her life's folklore*, grounded in spirituals and gospels proclaiming the ability to fly to freedom as a gift. In *Song of Solomon*, this gift manifests at the pinnacle of Milkman Dead's search for his past, as he discovers that his great-grandfather was a part of a flying African tribe. In a forceful rejection of the oppression of slavery*, the flying African, Solomon* Sugarman, flew home to Africa.

Revising the contemporary myth of the fragmented African American family, Morrison connects two biblical myths: Solomon, who in his quest for freedom unintentionally left behind his son, and Hagar, the namesake of Pilate's granddaughter, Hagar Dead*, in *Song of Solomon*. Traditionally, the Hagar myth derives from the book of Genesis, where Sarah orders her slave Hagar to procreate with Sarah's husband, Abraham. After Hagar bears a son named Ishmael, Sarah conceives a son named Isaac. As a result, Sarah casts away Hagar and Ishmael, leaving them to wander the wilderness of Beersheba, consoled only by the voice of God telling her that he will make Ishmael a great nation. In *Song of Solomon*, this great nation is established by Morrison's trademark trilogy of female outcasts led by Pilate, a proud and spiritual survivor.

During his heroic quest, Milkman visits the supernatural world of Circe*, known in Greek myth as a puzzling goddess of rare cruelty and strange kindness who, despite her skill in the arts of Hecate, is powerless to challenge the Olympians. Her greatest strength, perhaps, is her blatant rejection of Zeus's law of hospitality: she changes her guests into beasts without risking retribution. According to Homeric myth, Circe wore her hair braided to control fate and the forces of creation and destruction, for in many folk-magic spells, tying and untying knots has the power to bind and release energy. Circe, the rescuer of Macon Dead* and Pilate after their father dies, is Milkman's necessary guide to "Hades" before Pilate joins the search.

Finally, many of the members of the Dead family possess names and character traits grounded in African or European myth. Macon Dead, Jr., for example, resembles Anaanu, the trickster spider who fakes his death in order to disenfranchise others at night; by privileging material wealth, both Anaanu and Macon Dead give up their positions in the world and their families. Macon's sister Pilate, who carries her name in writing in her ear, is named after "Christ-killing" Pontius Pilate, and Macon's daughter First Corinthians Dead* is named after Paul's first letter to the Corinthians, which attacks ambition, pride, and vanity, qualities paradoxically portrayed through Macon's capital-seeking success as well as Milkman's ultimate search in the South for racial heritage and pride.

In *Tar Baby*, Morrison returns to the African origins of Joel Chandler Harris's Br'er Rabbit folk tale by reintroducing Black women's spiritual and creative heritage. According to Morrison, the "tar baby" myth transcribed in Southern folklore originates not only in African trickster tales of Anaanu, but also in the ancient African "tar lady," considered a powerful mythical symbol of Black womanhood because of her power and creativity in binding things together. According to Morrison, a tar pit was a sacred place because tar comes out of the earth and has the power to build things, such as African pyramids and the boat, according to Hebrew mythology, that Moses' mother built to carry him down the Nile.

In the Southern appropriation of this myth, however, the tar lady possessing the capacity to suture things becomes a tar baby who, in the hands of the trickster figure, traps wrongdoers. According to Harris's Uncle Remus story, Br'er Fox places a tar baby in the road to catch Br'er Rabbit. After both insulting and striking the decoy, Br'er Rabbit becomes stuck in the tar. *Tar Baby*'s Son* changes a detail of the tale when telling it to Jadine Childs*, explaining that white farmers place a tar baby in the road in order to prevent Br'er Rabbit from eating their cabbages. Morrison's intentional ambiguity about her novel's own elusive tar baby shows the complexity of both the evolution of myths and the perspectives of characters in contemporary fiction. The tar baby here is transformed back into the tar lady, as in the figures of the striking African woman Jadine sees in the grocery store and the swamp women who watch while Jadine literally tries to free herself from a tar pit. Yet Jadine herself functions as both a tar lady and a tar baby; this culturally savvy and attractive Sorbonne-educated model embodies for Son both the artistic African woman and the threatening, seductive temptress.

Both Eloe*, Florida, and the Isle des Chevaliers*, near Dominique, represent potentially Edenic briar patches for characters in *Tar Baby*. For Son, Eloe's small population, consisting primarily of old family and friends, provides a misleading safe haven which seduces him into thinking that it is the only possible place to settle down with Jadine. Conversely, the Isle des Chevalier, an idyllic paradise originally lush and fruitful, was eventually overdeveloped through Haitian labor supported by European capital. In reality, this island is the site of complicated racial tension on many levels: between Euro-American Valerian* and Margaret Street*, and Sydney and Ondine Childs*, the Black servants with whom they live; between Sydney and Ondine and the indigenous Gideon-called-Yardman and his apparently interchangeable wife Marie-Therese Foucault*, and, in a complicated triangular relation, between Europe-educated Jadine, her aunt Ondine, and their patron-mistress Margaret. In this novel ending with the folktale mantra "Lickety-split," all characters are portrayed in a weblike tangle of tar and ladies inspired by both myths of tricksters and dueling beliefs about racial pride and uplift.

The name of Sethe Suggs*, the haunted heroine of *Beloved* who kills her baby daughter in an attempt to protect her from slavery, resembles Lethe, the personification of oblivion, daughter of Eris, and river in the underworld from which souls could drink to forget their past lives before being reborn. The four horsemen (schoolteacher*, one nephew, one slave catcher, a sheriff) who approach 124 Bluestone Road to recapture Sethe and her children signal the coming of the Apocalypse as foretold by Saint John in Revelation. The predicted war, conquest, famine, and death, all borne out through the course of *Beloved*, accompany Sethe's murder of Beloved. Both borrowing from the historical story of Margaret Garner* and inverting the mythic story of Medea, who killed her children for the love of a man, Morrison here displays the qualities of "too-thick love" described in *Sula* and the "graveyard love" described in *Song of Solomon*.

Through a pastiche of gothic horror embodied by an eighteen-year-old ravenous ghost, African-based beliefs about the powers of community, the myths of slavery portrayed by events at the ironically named Sweet Home*, and a rejection of Southern paternalism, *Beloved* revises the stories about motherhood* and romantic love among slaves by blurring the distinction between past and present as indicated by their rememories. Named after the chorus in the biblical Song of Solomon,

Beloved traverses the Middle Passage to get to 124 Bluestone Road—traveling not only distance but also time in search of her mother.

Perhaps the novel least explicitly interested in mythic sources for its narrative base, *Jazz* takes up the power of jazz* music* on levels of both form and content. Like *The Bluest Eye* and *Paradise*, it opens in traditional mythic form by providing the entire plot on its first pages—middle-aged Joe Trace* killed his teenage mistress Dorcas Manfred*, and at the funeral, Joe's wife, Violet*, tried to slash Dorcas's face—as well as a promise to explain the details and motivations behind an inexplicable, in this case devastating, situation. Set in Harlem* during 1926, the height of the Harlem Renaissance, Morrison's plot recaptures the history* of Harlem to show how its creative energy is indebted to African American performers. At the turn of the twentieth century, life for African Americans in Northern neighborhoods like Harlem gained mythic status; in the North, the lore conveyed through letters and train gossip indicated that African Americans would not experience the racism pervasive in the South* and they would be able to achieve unknown pleasures, liberties, and higher wages. As *Jazz* demonstrates, Harlem did offer African Americans many artistic and cultural opportunities; however, this electric and promising neighborhood also erupted with untold jealousy, violence,* passion, and malaise.

Motivated by Morrison's interest in why ideas of paradise necessarily involve exclusion and why, in mythic representations of paradises, women are threatening interlopers in a "haven" dominated by men, *Paradise* exploits the myth of a homogeneous Eden. *Paradise*'s master narrative is told by patriarchal Zechariah, who, like Moses, leads his people from a land that rejected them to a utopia free of the complications of racial tension. Suturing the Old Testament story of Exodus with the New Testament story of Joseph and Mary's journey to Bethlehem, Zechariah here represents the prophet Zachariah who kept the torch of Mosaic law burning, preached zealously, and embodied the symbols of piety and righteousness. According to the myth of Zachariah, most of his kinsmen possessed neither spirit nor true faith; after being seduced, they committed evil deeds, deeply worrying Zachariah. The tension between the Old Fathers who founded Haven, Oklahoma*, and the second generation of Ruby, is palpable in their disagreement over the motto inscribed in the Oven*; for the second generation, it is a difference between fearing authority and becoming authority figures themselves—a tension at the heart of the myths of Eden, Oedipus, and the prophet Zachariah.

Finally, like many Morrison novels, *Paradise* resists closure and resolution. The citizens of Ruby are unsure of what really happened when the nine 8-rock Ruby men ambushed the outsiders seeking solace in the Convent*, although they know that when they went back to look, there were no bodies. Even the Cadillac was gone. The return of the Convent women seems at once earthly and unearthly—idyllic and apocalyptic. In a final gesture toward magical realism and supernatural gothic, Piedade's* song offers solace, though there is so much work to do "down there" in *Paradise*. *See also* African Myth, Use of; Conjure; Ghost Story, Use of; Gothic Tradition; Romantic Tradition.

References: Cynthia Y. Davis, "Self, Society and Myth in Toni Morrison's Fiction," in *New Casebooks: Toni Morrison*, ed. Linden Peach (1998); Carolyn Denard, "Mythical Consciousness of Morrison and Faulkner," in *Unflinching Gaze: Morrison and Faulkner Re-Envisioned*, eds. Carol A. Kolmerten, Stephen M. Ross, and Judith Bryant Wittenberg (1997); Trudier Harris, *Fiction and Folklore: The Novels of Toni Morrison* (1991); Anne Bradford Warner, "New Myths and Ancient Properties: The Fiction of Toni Morrison," *The Hollins Critic* 25: 3 (1988).

Aimee L. Pozorski

# N

## Narrative Voice

As is the case with other Black women writers, Toni Morrison's concern with voice in her fiction is intimately connected with questions about the nature of language. Feminist linguists point out that Western language and literature are culturally determined. In the case of American literature, this culture is patriarchal and white. Morrison's experiment with narrative voice and language in her fiction provides possible alternatives to this patriarchal, Western way of telling stories. Morrison helps develop a feminine, African American language in her fiction. She creates a feminine linguistic and narrative "wild zone" that is a subversive alternative to phallocentric language. The best example of the feminine "wild zone" is in the section of *Beloved** where Stamp Paid hears 124 Bluestone Road* (the house) narrate. As a male, Stamp Paid cannot understand this language, and cannot enter the zone. Throughout Morrison's novels, women are the main storytellers, as well as singers. Morrison suggests that African American feminine language is musical. Morrison recreates this musical language in the narratives, most dramatically exemplified in *Jazz**.

Morrison's attention to narrative voice leads her to attempt to capture in writing African American speech and storytelling patterns. She has said that she wonders what makes a book "Black." One answer is that Black language is a distinctive feature of Black literature. Morrison believes it is important to represent the storytelling voice of the griot in her stories so that the reader can hear it. Her use of narrative voice in her novels has several effects on the reader. First of all, the narrative voices are lyrical storytellers, and their narratives replicate the African oral storytelling tradition* of the griot. Morrison often employs multiple narrative voices in a single text. Having more than one narrative voice tell a story recalls the call-and-response pattern found in the African American tradition. Additionally, this multiplicity of narrators represents the sense of community* so important in Morrison's fiction. At the same time, the reader is involved in the creation of meaning in the text, and thus experiences this sense of community for himself or herself.

Even though the novels are written texts, Morrison's narrators are oral storytellers because of the way they relate the story to the reader. By emphasizing oral storytelling, Morrison highlights the impossibility of clear resolutions because to some extent stories necessarily are products of the individual storyteller. Therefore, when readers see the limitations of a narrative voice, they understand that the notion of finality is subjective. Instead of giving her readers clear, definite endings, Morrison urges collaboration between the writer, the narrator, and the reader.

Morrison uses a variety of narrative styles and techniques to create this collaboration and to relate character to theme, shape to focus, voice to effect. She uses innovative narrative techniques, such as incorporating frames, like the Dick and Jane primer sections of *The Bluest Eye**. Morrison sometimes uses chapters as parentheses, as in *Jazz*, and at other times to signal a change in narrative voice or perspective (as she does in *Beloved* and *Paradise**, for example). In *The Bluest Eye* and *Sula**, Morrison uses chapter headings more traditionally to signal a change in time. In some cases, Morrison's narrative technique intentionally misdirects the reader. More common is the technique of having the narrator(s) provide fragments out of which the reader slowly builds episodes of the story. In *The Bluest Eye* and *Beloved*, Morrison relies on the perspective of a child to narrate the story. The narrative structure of each novel works with the story line to create the desired effect. Morrison has stated repeatedly that her objective is to present a narrative voice that seems to be speaking to the reader, and she is highly conscious of using techniques that create this storytelling effect. One technique is to have the narrator meander away from the main plot. Another is to reveal the story casually, effortlessly. Even when the narrator's identity is a mystery (as it is in *Jazz* and *Paradise*, for example) the narrator needs to appear "real" (genuine) to the reader. The texts of all of Morrison's novels are "writerly" (according to Roland Barthes's distinction) rather than "readerly," in that they involve the reader in the creation of meaning.

The Dick and Jane structure of *The Bluest Eye* shows the extreme contrast between the fictional tale of how things should be, and the reality presented in the novel. In addition to the Dick and Jane primer divisions, Morrison divides the story according to the seasons. This complicated narrative structure forces the reader of *The Bluest Eye* to be active, and Morrison is successful in drawing the reader in.

In contrast, *Sula*'s narrative structure is much simpler and more traditional because it follows a chronological format. Instead of using complicated narrative techniques, Morrison reserves complexity for the character of Sula Peace* herself. However, the story that the narrator relates is not just Sula's story; it is the story of the Bottom* and its inhabitants—Shadrack*, Nel Wright* and her parents, and the Peace family. The narrator relates as much about these people, the Bottom community, as she does about Sula. Sula never narrates herself. Instead, she becomes a sign or symbol who is constructed out of the collaboration of reader and narrator. Sula's story is intertwined with these other stories and is revealed incrementally by the narrative voice. The narrative pattern of *Sula* demonstrates that life itself is nonlinear and does not follow a progressive pattern.

In terms of its narrative form, *Beloved* is a postmodern novel primarily because of the linguistic play found throughout the novel. Morrison employs both oral and written discourse, shifts narration from third-person omniscient to interior monologue, and repeats words and phrases. This narrative style evokes the oral tradition*. The shifting narrative voice reminds the reader that stories are told by one person to another.

The narrative of *Jazz* is told rapidly and with fragments. In addition to the mysterious female narrative voice, there is a "written" narrator who refuses to explain or connect these fragments. In terms of narrative technique, *Jazz* is composed of "rhythmic paragraphs" that mimic a musical score—a jazz* piece. Morrison models her narrative strategy on the progression of a jazz solo in order to show how improvising a single detail can alter the nature of what is expressed. Just as a jazz score relies on improvisations of a single detail, so Morrison's narrative strategy in *Jazz* is to represent the continual process of change experienced by African Americans by constantly changing the narrative style.

Whereas the narrative voice of *Jazz* initially seems confident and omniscient, as the novel progresses, she expresses doubts and frustration at her limitations. She confesses her own unreliability as a storyteller. The narrator's comments can be seen as a humorous undercutting of the conventions of narration, but they also show her revising her own interpretation of the narrative, just as she invites readers to revise theirs at will. *Jazz* ends with the narrative voice urging the reader to make (and remake) his/her own interpretations of the narrative. Both *Jazz* and *Beloved* resist closure; in fact, these novels underscore the artificiality and even "danger" of closure, because once a story is closed, it is possible to forget it. Stories and histories stay alive only when they are remembered and retold.

Throughout her novels, Morrison frequently employs narrators who are somewhat anonymous and whose purpose seems to be to relay information or emotion. Even when characters from the story take over the narration, they often seem fragmented, undefined, and somewhat indistinguishable from the larger community (as we see in *Sula* and *Paradise*, for example). Morrison repeatedly has maintained in interviews that her fiction is not autobiographical. Just as "Toni Morrison" can't be found in her novels, so her narrators are frequently anonymous transmitters of information and feeling, rather than distinct personalities or characters.

The narrative voice of *The Bluest Eye* is polyphonic. The seasonal sections use first-person narrative, Claudia MacTeer*. However, even when Claudia narrates (which is often) there are two "I"s: Claudia the youngster who experiences the events as they happen, and Claudia the adult looking back on these events. Claudia most often presents herself as a child. Nonetheless, the reader is aware from her narrative voice and language that the narrator actually is an adult working through memory*. Even so, Claudia doubts her ability as a narrator and her ability to remember correctly. At the end of the novel, she worries that she has assembled lies in the name of truth. In addition to Claudia, Morrison uses an omniscient narrator at times. In the opening lines of *The Bluest Eye*, this narrative voice replicates the pattern of Black women gossiping in the backyard. The narrative voice has what Morrison terms a "back fence connotation" that creates a sense of intimacy between the reader and the story, who seem to be sharing a secret. The narrative technique of creating intimacy between reader and text is necessary to prepare the reader for the terrible details of the story that follows, a tale of rape, incest, and racial self-hatred. In the primer scenes, Morrison's narrator assumes an authoritative stance, particularly when she relates to the reader the values and lifestyles of the women of Mobile, or describes the history of the Breedloves' apartment.

Morrison provides alternatives to the third-person narrator of *The Bluest Eye*. Although these narrators have their own limitations, they stand as important contrasts to the "omniscient" voice of the primer sections. Soaphead Church's* narrative section consists exclusively of a formal letter to God, chastizing him for his treatment of Pecola Breedlove*. Pecola's narrative section consists of a dramatic, schizophrenic dialogue between Pecola and the second self she creates out of her imagination.

In *Sula*, the narrative voice and perspective usually is limited to the consciousness of a single character. However, at times it shifts to reveal the thoughts and feelings of the community. *Song of Solomon* uses the narrative perspective of the male protagonist (as the novel's title indicates), Milkman Dead*. However, throughout *Song of Solomon*, different voices tell many stories about the relationships of characters, and of the past and the present. Pilate Dead* is the best storyteller, due to her status of "culture bearer." Pilate's storytelling teaches Milkman (and, through him, the reader) how to listen, and how to be a story-teller. *Tar Baby* has a different narrative style. The narrative of this novel is structured according to the "call-and-response" pattern found in African American culture. The narrator acts as a chorus, pointing out the action and its meaning, but avoiding passing judgment on the characters.

Morrison's narrative voice is much more complicated and mysteri-ous in *Jazz*. In this novel, Morrison uses a narrative voice that emu-lates the improvisational techniques of jazz in order to tell the story. The narrative voice of *Jazz* is both detached from and involved in the story. As in *The Bluest Eye*, the novel opens with a gossipy female tone ("Sth") that invites the reader to share a secret. In fact, throughout the narrative, the voice is seductive. The reader, however, is never certain to whom this voice belongs. The narrator speaks from somewhere above and beyond the City. It is clear that she likes the City, but she doesn't seem to be a resident of the community. She says that she does not have muscles, so she can't defend herself, and remarks that she observes ev-erything about everybody in order to try to figure things out. The nar-rator sometimes seems to be a disembodied voice, while at other times she seems human.

As the narrative progresses, the narrator contradicts herself, and seems to change throughout the story. At times she seems omniscient, but at other times it is obvious that she is limited, or even incorrect. She has a ubiquitous line of vision that distinguishes her from the characters she observes, and, despite her fallibility, she knows and sees more than they do. At times, she appears to be a character in the story, while at other times she seems apart from it. A sense of chaos and instability is the result for the reader, who also must participate actively in the narrative. The narra-tive voice in *Jazz*, then, may very well be the voice of narrative itself.

In *Paradise*, Morrison employs a narrative voice who seems omniscient. The voice begins by stating that they, the men of Ruby, Oklahoma*, shoot the white girl first when they storm the Convent*. However, throughout the course of the narrative, the authority or omniscience of the narrator is called into question. Either the voice is limited or she is playing games with the reader, for she never directly reveals which of the women killed is the white girl.

In many of her novels, Morrison makes use of shifting conscious-nesses, multiple narrative voices and perspectives, and the technique of free indirect discourse in which the narrative slips and slides from one consciousness to another without clear indication. The multiple story-tellers and voices change constantly and without warning. The reader must be attentive to all of these voices in order to create meaningful connections.

Morrison has stated that using multiple narrators in her fiction enables her to give credibility to various and significantly different voices, which replicates the complexity and polyvocality of African American culture itself. Morrison's incorporation of multiple narrative voices also challenges Western (patriarchal, white, linear) plot-driven narrative, and replaces it with circular, nonauthoritarian narrative.

Additionally, Morrison's use of multiple perspectives allows her to depict many subjects and themes, and to have various individuals comment upon the central character of the novel. Morrison uses multiple narrators to represent the call-and-response pattern of the African American oral tradition. The narrative voices speak to and comment on one another. This technique can be found in many of Morrison's novels, but perhaps most dramatically in *The Bluest Eye*, *Sula*, *Beloved*, and *Paradise*.

Morrison primarily uses omniscient narrators. Sometimes, as in *The Bluest Eye*, there is a first-person narrator (Claudia), but her narration coexists with the omniscient narrator. By using multiple narrators, Morrison underscores that her novels are stories of communities, not just individuals. Claudia's use of "we" throughout her narrative is a sign that she includes herself and the reader in the victimization of Pecola. The reader is included in the community, which is both good and bad. Similarly, in *Paradise*, Morrison's narrative technique creates a sense of community. Morrison uses multiple narrative perspectives to tell us the story of Ruby's history, and draws the reader into this community, making him or her somewhat complicit in the violence* and intolerance that culminate in the massacre at the Convent. While the narrative perspective in many of these novels seems stable, the subjects that the narrator relates are disordered, violent, and troubling. This creates additional tension for the reader.

In *Beloved*, the plot develops as various characters add their perspectives and stories in their attempt to explain to themselves and to each other what happened and why. This indirect way of uncovering the plot places the reader in a situation similar to that of the characters.

Throughout all of Morrison's fiction, the reader can hear a lyrical, musical quality in the narrative voice(s) she creates for each tale. Her ability to combine form and function, to use narrative voice and technique to complement and enhance the plot of the tale, places her in the tradition of William Faulkner* and Virginia Woolf*. However, her ability to replicate the African American storytelling tradition represents her departure from her predecessors, and shows her unique contribution to African American literature. *See also* Approaches to Morrison's Work: Feminist/Black Feminist; Narrator of *Jazz*/Talking Book.

Reference: Martha J. Cutter, "The Story Must Go On and On: The Fantastic, Narration, and Intertextuality in Morrison's *Beloved* and *Jazz*," *African American Review* 34: 1 (Spring, 2000).

Lisa Cade Wieland

### Narrator of Jazz/Talking Book (*Jazz*)

Jazz* is presented as a self-contained stylistic device that functions both inside and outside of the narrative's perimeters. Not only does the jazz idiom structure the text, but, flamboyantly self-referential, it speculates about the unwinding action even as it incorporates itself into it. In the process, jazz becomes its own enigma, an object of beauty, tantalizing and impenetrable; while it beguiles, it simultaneously denies access. A textual puzzle that entices, then eludes, it materializes as jazz itself, immersing the reader in its polyphony. Yet it is not simply jazz as a musical form or a poetic device; it is jazz personified as a separate character, what Morrison herself characterizes as a talking book. Materializing in the slippery presence of the disembodied narrative voice* that is admittedly without muscles, the narrator observes the ensuing events, perhaps inventing them as well, becoming the reader's guide into the essence of jazz, its composer/conductor/ performer. *See also Jazz.*

Caroline Brown

### National Suicide Day (*Sula*)

Holiday established by Shadrack* as a means of controlling and exorcising the chaos and death he experiences during World War I. National Suicide Day falls of January 3 of each year. *See also Sula.*

Douglas Taylor

### Neo-Slave Narrative

The autobiographical slave narratives authored by African Americans during the eighteenth and nineteenth centuries form a cornerstone of Black arts and letters. In the twentieth century—and particularly in the wake of the Civil Rights movement and Black Power activism of the 1960s and early 1970s—African American writers have evidenced a keen interest in returning to the thematic concerns and literary conventions of these foundational texts in novels that scholars have come to term neo-slave narratives. From the mid-1960s to the present, such prominent authors as David Bradley, Octavia Butler, J. California Cooper, Ernest

Gaines, Charles Johnson, Gayl Jones, Ishmael Reed, and Sherley Anne Williams, among others, have crafted neo-slave narratives. These novels have taken such forms as historical fiction focused on the era of slavery*; irreverent, politically engaged satire; speculative fiction that posits an ancestral presence which significantly shapes the lives of twentieth-century characters as an enduring legacy of slavery; and personal odysseys narrated by protagonists themselves, much in the manner of actual slave narratives.

Building upon the precedent of Arna Bontemps's *Black Thunder* (1936) and *Drums at Dusk* (1939), the interest of contemporary authors in the neo-slave narrative as a literary form was inaugurated by the publication of Margaret Walker's *Jubilee* in 1966. Significantly, Walker availed herself of substantial oral and written historical documentation of Black voices in order to tell a story of the struggle from slavery to freedom from an African American point of view. In fact, literary projects such as Walker's helped to spur a radical reshaping of the historiography of slavery to include similar voices during the early 1970s. Yet, as Ashraf Rushdy has capably demonstrated, the emergence of an intensive interest in neo-slave narratives also owed much to specifically contemporary concerns, chief among which were issues of self-definition. Well aware of the potential social and political damage to be wrought by such acts of cultural misappropriation and misrepresentation as white author William Styron's deeply flawed *The Confessions of Nat Turner* (1967) and the 1965 Moynihan Report's allegations of African American familial pathology as a legacy of slavery, African American authors seized upon the form of the neo-slave narrative as a way of asserting narrative control over Black cultural representation and, often, issuing biting social commentary regarding America's failings on this front to date. The scholarship of Elizabeth Beaulieu adds to this contextual framework the important observation that African American women authors have evidenced particular interest in the experiences of enslaved mothers—again, figures charged with crucial historical *and* contemporary significance. Toni Morrison is no exception in this regard.

While slavery serves as an essential historical background for the action of several of Morrison's novels—most notably *Song of Solomon** and *Paradise**—*Beloved** is her only work to date that falls squarely within the conventions of the neo-slave narrative genre. In *Beloved*, Morrison interweaves the fabric of her rich writerly imagination with threads drawn from the history of slavery, specifically the case of an escaped slave mother named Margaret Garner*. Like Garner, Morrison's protagonist, Sethe Suggs*, attempts to murder her children* rather than see them returned to slavery. It is, of course, the daughter whom Sethe successfully murders, Beloved*, who returns to haunt the family's home at 124 Bluestone Road*, on the outskirts of Cincinnati. In the tradition of slave narrative author Harriet Jacobs, Morrison thus calls attention both to the vulnerability of nominally free African Americans in the northern United States (owing especially to the nation's various nineteenth-century Fugitive Slave laws) and to the special dilemmas of Black mothers not fully in possession of their own children.

Through the flashbacks of Sethe and Paul D Garner* to their experiences at the ironically named Sweet Home* plantation in Kentucky, Morrison's novel also dramatizes several crucial themes voiced in slave narratives: acts of extreme physical and psychological violence* against enslaved persons; the ever-present threat of forced separation from family* and loved ones; the tenuous recognition of slave marriages by slaveholders, even relatively "sympathetic" ones; the vulnerability of enslaved women, in particular, to sexual violation; and the enormous privations and perils involved in an attempt to escape from bondage to "free" territory. To the conventions of its historical antecedents, Morrison's neo-slave narrative adds at least three key elements: (1) supernatural qualities centering around the re-embodiment of Beloved; (2) an exploration of Sethe and Denver Suggs's* relative ostracism with respect to other African Americans in and around Cincinnati, which provides a window onto tensions within Black communities themselves vis-à-vis the haunting legacy of slavery; and (3) through the four sections in the middle of the novel in which the women of 124 Bluestone Road speak "unspeakable thoughts, unspoken," Morrison expands her neo-slave narrative to encompass not only slavery in the U.S. context per se, but the Middle Passage transport of Africans to the Western Hemisphere as well—a subject that echoes her dedication of the novel to the "Sixty Million and more" believed to have perished in the course of the Atlantic crossing.

Morrison's objectives in exploring this thematic terrain in her neo-slave narrative are manifold. Not least would seem to be the way in which historical African American mothers—and specifically the actions of a figure like Margaret Garner—are to be presented to contemporary readers. In this sense, the character of schoolteacher*, with his pseudo-scientific studies of the alleged human and animal characteristics of the Sweet Home slaves, would seem to stand in allegorical relationship to such twentieth-century figures as Styron, Moynihan, and historian Stanley Elkins—toward whose dubious modes of representation neo-slave narratives such as Morrison's clearly are intended to serve as a countervailing voice. Further, as several critics have noted, the novel's ambiguous closing refrain about not passing on the story suggests both Morrison's concern with the difficulty Americans have evidenced in confronting the realities of slavery's traumatic history and, simultaneously, the refusal of such narratives of slavery simply to go away. Indeed, Morrison's novel would seem to comprise an Ellisonian fingering of the jagged grain of this history*, exploring at once its most intimate and harrowing dimensions as a means of gaining mastery over the memory of slavery and the form of its contemporary representation. *See also* Approaches to Morrison's Work: Feminist/Black Feminist; Approaches to Morrison's Work: Historical; Memory; Recovery; Trauma.

References: Elizabeth Ann Beaulieu, *Black Women Writers and the American Neo-Slave Narrative: Femininity Unfettered* (1999); Frances Smith Foster, *Witnessing Slavery: The Development of Ante-bellum Slave Narratives* (1979); Deborah E. McDowell and Arnold Rampersad, eds., *Slavery and the Literary Imagination* (1987); Ashraf H. A. Rushdy, *Neo-Slave Narratives: Studies in the Social Logic of a Literary Form* (1999).

Stacy I. Morgan

## Nephews, The (*Beloved*)

Schoolteacher's* teenage nephews. Under schoolteacher's direction, they participate in the torture-death of Sixo*. They forcibly "milk" Sethe Suggs* and, later, they beat her as punishment for reporting the abuse to Mrs. Garner*. Followers whose ability to reason is somewhat lacking, they buy wholesale into schoolteacher's theories and do his bidding. *See also Beloved.*

Lovalerie King

## Nobel Prize Address

The Nobel Prize committee, describing her as one "who in novels characterized by visionary force and poetic import, gives life to an essential aspect of American reality," awarded Toni Morrison the Nobel Prize in literature in 1993. This award came after several others in Morrison's career. She was nominated for the National Book Award in 1975 for *Sula*, earned the National Book Critics' Circle Award in 1977 for *Song of Solomon*, and won the Pulitzer Prize in 1988 for *Beloved*. Morrison was the first African American woman to receive the Nobel Prize in literature.

For her Nobel speech Morrison chose to focus on the familiar parable of the old, blind, and wise Black woman who is questioned by a group of children*. Seeking to test the old woman's knowledge, the children ask her one question: whether the bird they hold in their hand is alive or dead. The old woman ambiguously replies that the answer is in their hands. This recounting of the story begins Morrison's speech. The rest of her talk speculates on the ambiguity of the old woman's answer and the possible implications of the children's question.

The speech has three distinct sections as Morrison moves from a discussion of the expected to one of the provocative. The first section takes the task of assigning meaning to the metaphors of the story. Interestingly, the bird becomes language; the woman, a writer. The woman's answer, then, is a comment on dead language. Morrison speaks in this section of the oppressive nature of language when it becomes unyielding and narcissistic, allowing neither the quest for knowledge nor the exchange of ideas. The responsibility for this stagnation lies with those who use language for their own selfish ends. The children in this instance are not interested in creation, but rather in whether or not the old woman can crack what is ultimately a dead code. This reading of the metaphors coincides with popular readings of the children as presumptuous and intrusive.

The second section of the speech, maintaining the metaphor of the bird as language, considers the possibility that the bird is not dead, that the children do not bring the woman oppressive language, but rather the possibility of creativity. This section starts with a reading of the biblical story of the Tower of Babel. Instead of lamenting the lack of a unifying language that would have allowed the builders to reach heaven, Morrison celebrates language that questions, creates, and illuminates. This view of language as living sheds new light on the old woman's response to the children. The children search for a definitive answer, for a precise definition of language, and the old woman responds that the power is in their question, in their desire to know.

The third section shifts attention away from the old woman and her answer and focuses instead on the children and their question. In this view the children are desperate to be taken seriously, resorting to a trick to be heard. The shift makes up the rest of Morrison's speech as she quotes from the children's pleading with the old woman. Morrison gives voice to the children and validates their curiosity, putting a new twist on an old tale that usually dismisses them. As she does in her fiction (e.g., *Beloved*'s reworking of a story from a newspaper clipping), Morrison takes what seems very straightforward (the children are somehow disrespectful in their interruption of the serenity of this old woman) and reveals the unexpected—the children have not come to the old woman to play a trick, but rather to seek knowledge, sincerely, from one presumed to know.

Morrison speaks of the deep silence that follows the old woman's answer to the children (the tale, after all, usually ends with her reply). The children fill this silence with their own pleading, with their desire to know and understand how to use language. In Morrison's version of this tale, the children eloquently follow the old woman's answer with another question. This time there is no trick, only pleading for the wisdom the old woman is presumed to have. The children seek the power of language not to abuse it, but rather to bring order to the chaos, meaning to the unknown.

The children, in fully articulating their question, also articulate the answer and Morrison's view of how language shapes reality. We know the world through the shapes and shades that language provides. The children—metaphors for young artists, writers of color, marginalized peoples everywhere—come to the old woman longing to know how to use language, how to create, how to make meaning of the world around them. To this rearticulation of the question, the old woman gives a new answer. The children are rewarded for their curiosity, and Morrison shows us how language can reshape our knowledge of the world.

Conseula Francis

## No Mercy Hospital (*Song of Solomon*)

Alternate name for Mercy Hospital, a charity hospital in the city's northern end. As with Not Doctor Street*, the African American community* has renamed this place. This misnomer accurately reflects the irony inherent in naming a hospital "Mercy" that refused to admit African Americans until 1931. Significantly, Robert Smith* commits suicide by jumping from one of the hospital's cupolas while, simultaneously, Ruth Dead* goes into labor (with Milkman*) on the hospital steps and is admitted as the hospital's first Black patient.

Fiona Mills

## Not Doctor Street (*Song of Solomon*)

Alternate name for Mains Street, where the only Black doctor in town, Dr. Foster, lived and worked. Members of the African American community* referred to the street as "Doctor Street" until city legislators posted official signs disclaiming this misnomer. However, the Black community still refused to call it Mains Street and, instead, took to calling the street "Not Doctor Street."

Fiona Mills

# O

## 124 Bluestone Road (*Beloved*)

124 Bluestone Road is the present-moment address of the house provided to Baby Suggs* by the Bodwins* when she was released from slavery* in 1848. Located on the outskirts of Cincinnati, Ohio, it is a twenty-eight-day refuge for the newly escaped Sethe Suggs* and her children*, the site of a huge celebratory gathering, and the place where Sethe kills her daughter. Sethe took over the house—haunted by the dead child's ghost—after Baby Suggs died. *See also Beloved*; Ghost Story, Use of; Home; Sweet Home.

Lovalerie King

## Oprah's Book Club

When in the fall of 1996 media superstar Oprah Winfrey selected Toni Morrison's *Song of Solomon** as the second novel to be featured in the worldwide reading initiative she called Oprah's Book Club, the then nineteen-year-old text was revitalized. It sold approximately a million copies after the telecast.

Since then, Oprah has chosen two other Morrison novels for dinner and an informal causerie, namely, *Paradise** (broadcast March 6, 1998) and *The Bluest Eye** (broadcast May 26, 2000). Oprah also acquired the film rights to *Beloved**. For ten years Oprah struggled to bring Sethe Suggs's story to the silver screen; the film appeared in 1998 with Oprah

in the starring role and Danny Glover playing Sethe's partner, Paul D
Garner*. Oprah also has procured the film rights to *Paradise*.

What Oprah Winfrey and her book club ultimately did was to thrust
Toni Morrison and her oeuvre into a wider public domain, a feat neither
the Pulitzer nor the Nobel Prize managed to do. Certainly the Pulitzer
and the Nobel are two of the most coveted accolades among the literati.
These honors signify that one has made a most notable contribution to
one's field, and that this contribution has served humanity. One's work
is thereby regarded as distinguished, and the honoree gains recognition
among his or her peers. However, public recognition generally is limited
to a small audience.

Some readers initially interested in reading Morrison deemed her work
too difficult. Her texts challenge the reading process such that they frus-
trate some readers, causing them to abandon her work. Morrison's novels test the lay reader's intellect and make them question their ability to
follow story line, plot, and character development. Her participation in
Oprah's Book Club gave the public the opportunity to experience the
Pulitzer Prize winner and Nobel laureate firsthand. Oprah's telecast
soothed our feelings of reader anxiety and gave us permission to admit
that Morrison challenges the way we read books.

During her appearances on Oprah's show, Morrison smiled warmly at
the audience's reactions to her work. She seemed pleased that readers re-
acted to her stories with difficulty. She mentioned during the Oprah dinner that it is not her intent to make reading easy, for the writing process
is very meticulous. Every word on the page is special because it is chosen exclusively for the one who holds the book; in this way Morrison invites each reader to participate actively in the reading process.

Oprah's Book Club introduced to a wide audience stories about African
Americans that are rich with history*, multilayered, and excruciatingly
dense. Even the names of the characters are peculiar: Milkman Dead*,
Guitar Balnes*, Pecola Breedlove*, Cholly Breedlove*, Soaphead
Church*, Sethe Suggs*, Buglar Suggs*, crawlingalready?, Baby Suggs*,
Pilate Dead*, schoolteacher*, and Lone DuPres*. These appellations are
in and of themselves "characters" that serve to embellish the person
behind the name as well as the narrative within which they move. The
characters who populate Morrison's novels do strange, sometimes incomprehensible things: a mother and daughter live with a sad ghost; a
daughter lies naked in the bed with her dead father, his fingers in her
mouth; an old woman finds comfort lying on her back on a cold kitchen
floor; a Black girl wishes for blue eyes; and a band of African American
men invade a convent, carrying shotguns. Weird things happen: trees
grow breasts and beckon a confused young woman to suckle them; a
crazed World War I veteran founds and celebrates National Suicide Day*;
a mother burns her son to death*; a man flies (or does he?); women in a

convent are "murdered" in cold blood, yet rise from the dead and walk among the living; a father, in a drunken stupor, rapes his preadolescent daughter in the name of "love." Oprah's Book Club provided an open forum for a discussion of Morrison's literary Black community. Moreover, given Oprah's worldwide viewing audience, Morrison's appearances on the show furthered discussion of African American literature on an international scale.

Ever since Oprah Winfrey announced in the fall of 1996 that she planned to start America reading, her book club has revolutionized the publishing industry. Her monthly selection inspires her studio audience and 14 million television viewers to patronize booksellers such as Barnes and Noble, Borders Books, Scribner's, and the online bookselling giant Amazon.com; the economic impact on Oprah Book Club authors' sales has astounded authors and publishers alike. Oprah's clarion call made the talk show a viable medium to promote and sell books. Moreover, Oprah's Book Club has rescued obscure and/or struggling authors and given them a voice on national television.

When Toni Morrison appeared on Oprah's show, audiences watched and read. Toni Morrison is now a household name, and her participation in the Oprah Book Club catapulted her to a level of fame that a Hollywood movie based on a novel could not generate. Certainly, *Beloved* made it to the silver screen; however, it was Morrison's appearances on Oprah's show that sent publishers scrambling to reprint her novels and readers flocking to buy her books. *See also Beloved*, Film.

Kwakiutl L. Dreher

## Oral Tradition

The African American oral tradition includes folktales, such as the trickster* tales of Br'er Rabbit, High John de Conquer, and Stagger Lee, and other tales of both heroes and common people passed down from generation to generation within families and through communal storytelling situations. Although the African American oral tradition retains significant connections to African oral forms, it is a dynamic and live form of cultural expression, not a static collection of tales, and also includes sermons, toasts, and the lyrics to spirituals, work songs, chants, blues, and rap songs. Taken as a whole, the oral tradition is a rich source of cultural beliefs and values, and conveys the knowledge that African Americans have accumulated for how to survive and endure in America.

Zora Neale Hurston, a noted African American writer and anthropologist, characterizes the oral traditions of African Americans in her short essay, "Characteristics of Negro Expression," and in her longer work, *Mules and Men*, in which she records numerous storytelling sessions.

Hurston emphasizes the presence of audience participation in call and response, an antiphonal form in which the main speaker shares the act of storytelling with the audience. Often, oral tales end without a clear resolution and invite the audience to participate in considering the moral implications of the tale. Other important structural features of the oral tradition include nonlinearity, repetition, and the complex use of metaphor and imagery.

Toni Morrison's writing draws heavily on the African American oral tradition, in a variety of ways. We can categorize these connections under two main headings: thematic and structural. Morrison makes the oral tradition a theme within her tale by incorporating whole tales, by depicting the act of telling stories and preaching sermons, and by exploring and developing the cultural beliefs that the oral tradition conveys, including beliefs about the supernatural. She also structures her novels using many of the features of oral tales, including call and response, nonlinearity, and the jazzlike repetition and improvisation of core images. Morrison's work emphasizes the dynamic nature of the oral tradition, its emphasis on creation and change; it also needs to be understood as being in a creative and dynamic relationship to the oral tradition, rather than as reductively incorporating static tales.

Admittedly, Morrison most obviously uses the oral tradition when she incorporates or refers to familiar folktales, such as the Gullah myth of flying Africans* in *Song of Solomon**, or the classic Br'er Rabbit tale in *Tar Baby**. While these tales offer Morrison a cultural framework, her novels might also be thought of as signifying upon or re-envisioning the meaning of these tales. In *Song of Solomon*, Milkman Dead* must decode what at first appears to be a meaningless children's* jump-rope chant in order to learn about his ancestors* and to understand his present situation. This chant tells the story of Milkman's enslaved great-grandparents, who produced twenty children before the father, Solomon*, flew back to Africa and the mother, Ryna, grieved to death. Importantly, in order to decode this tale, Milkman, who has grown up in the North, immersed in middle-class culture, must learn to listen well to others and to trust their tales; in the process he learns much valuable information from the personal stories that he hears from his distant relatives and others in the community* where his ancestors lived. The final scene, in which Milkman is atop the cliff from which his grandfather jumped or flew, trusting the air, can be read not only as repeating the specific image of flying from the tale, but also as emphasizing the value of knowledge transmitted through the air—that is, oral tales.

*Tar Baby* at first seems to follow the shape of the classic trickster tale, with Son* playing the part of Br'er Rabbit, stealing from the more powerful Valerian Street*, being trapped by the tar baby in the form of Jadine*, and finally becoming free by returning to the "briar patch," or home field in which he is comfortable. Both Son and the narrator explicitly refer to the tar baby tale to emphasize these connections. But as Trudier Harris has pointed out, Morrison leaves room for other connections as well, which complicate the meaning. Jadine could be read as a trickster, or Br'er Rabbit figure, as well, with Son as the tar baby by whom she is entrapped; arguably, Jadine is freer at the end of the novel than Son, but she also finally dismisses the idea of a briar patch that can provide shelter. By allowing these multiple readings, Morrison incorporates the ambiguity and amorality of classic trickster tales while preventing a reductive connection between her work and the folk tradition.

In addition to incorporating particular tales, Morrison thematizes the oral tradition as a whole within her work, depicting the act of telling stories, of preaching sermons, and of signifying as a means of community building. By engaging her characters in various acts of storytelling, Morrison is able to explore the complex function of the oral tradition in African American culture. For instance, when Baby Suggs* preaches in the woods in Beloved*, Morrison evokes the history of African American preachers who imbued Christianity with the communal ethos of African American folk culture, and dramatizes the interaction between sermon and response, showing how the congregation collaborates in shaping the message. The complex storytelling sessions involving Denver Suggs*, Sethe Suggs*, and Beloved* also reveal the ways in which the audience calls forth stories and helps to shape them, and they highlight the way in which narrating traumatic events can help to give those memories meaning for both narrator and audience. In The Bluest Eye*, Morrison explores the isolation and loss of cultural resilience that follows from this lack of storytelling, as Pecola Breedlove* is overwhelmed by the story of white superiority that she internalizes through reading books. But Morrison does not simplistically idealize the oral tradition; in both Beloved and Sula*, communal storytelling takes the form of gossip that results in isolation for Sethe and for Sula Peace*, the objects of that gossip.

On another level, Morrison's work is an extension of the oral tradition because it explores cultural traditions and beliefs about ancestors, the supernatural, and good and evil that stem from that tradition. The conjurers who inhabit these novels, such as M'Dear in The Bluest Eye, Ajax's* mother in Sula, and Pilate Dead* in Song of Solomon, act as cultural resources, figures who store the accumulated knowledge of the community. As conjurers, they have a store of knowledge about both the natural and the supernatural worlds, and can use herbs, roots, and other materials to at least partially heal those who have been hurt by living in this world, though they have the ability to hurt others as well. These conjurers are sometimes accepted and sometimes shunned by the larger community, and occupy a position that is neither entirely good nor entirely evil. This moral ambiguity is also characteristic of the oral tradition; in African American folk belief, good and evil are accepted as integrally linked rather than as polar opposites. Thus even when the community believes a character like Sula to be evil, they do not try to destroy her or run her out of town. In *Paradise\**, Morrison explores the destruction that follows from trying to separate good from evil, to create a paradise by limiting who can belong to the community.

Morrison's later novels, most notably *Beloved* and *Paradise*, allow the supernatural a greater role. While critics disagree on how the character Beloved should be interpreted—as Sethe's baby daughter's ghost come back to life, as the supernatural return of the spirit of a slave from the Middle Passage, or simply as a young woman who has escaped from being locked up for years by a white man—the characters in the novel understand her to be a ghost, and the community as a whole acts on this belief in order to exorcise her and save Sethe. They continue the belief conveyed through the oral tradition from its African origins, that spirits interact with the living. In *Paradise*, Mavis Albright\*, Gigi (Grace Gibson\*), Pallas Truelove\*, and Seneca\* continue to interact with their families after they have been shot and their bodies have disappeared, and Consolata Sosa\* is able to bring Deacon Morgan's\* son back to life after he has died. Following Africanist spiritual beliefs, the line between living and dead is not absolute in these novels. Morrison's development of patterns of thought conveyed through the African American oral tradition challenges Western culture's insistence on sharp distinctions between the material and the spiritual worlds, and attempts to draw the reader into a worldview that understands both as interactive with and integral to the whole.

While the thematic connections are perhaps easiest to see, the structural connections have more recently drawn scholars' interests. Morrison herself discusses the form of her novels as emanating from a type of oral storytelling common in kitchens and on porches, in which the participation of the audience is essential to the performance, and she frequently discusses her work as inviting the reader into the text. Often, the reader must actively construct the meaning of the novel by sorting through and evaluating information gained from the characters' individual stories. These stories often conflict, not only in perspective but also in factual detail, and Morrison rarely provides a neutral omniscient narrator to help the reader judge which perspective to believe. This happens, for example, in *Song of Solomon* when Macon Dead\* and his wife Ruth\* tell their son Milkman quite different stories of how their marriage disintegrated, and in *Beloved*, when we learn about Sethe's murder of her baby through the perspectives of Baby Suggs, schoolteacher\*, and Stamp Paid before learning about it from Sethe's perspective. The interior monologues near the end of *Beloved*, in which Denver, Sethe, and Beloved each speaks her own story, show how multiple first-person stories become intertwined into a complex harmony of voices, so that the narration offers a dialogue rather than a monologue, and meaning is communally constructed from the perspectives of many individuals. In *Jazz**, Morrison creates an omniscient narrator who is not an objective knower but instead a developing character, who speaks directly to the reader and who understands herself to be unreliable, changing the story of Golden Gray*, for instance, as the novel progresses and then self-consciously commenting on this fact.

Through these narrative techniques, Morrison develops narrative as always stemming from embodied perspectives, and though her novels are written literature, they evoke the storytelling experience of live performances. By structuring her novels in accord with the oral tradition, Morrison critiques the literary tradition of omniscient perspectives that leads readers to accept master narratives and the idea that there can be a universal perspective on history and reality. *See also* African Myth, Use of; Ancestor; Conjure; Folklore; Ghost Story, Use of; Narrative Voice; Spirituality.

References: Alma Jean Billingslea-Brown, *Crossing Borders Through Folklore: African-American Women's Fiction and Art* (1999); Trudier Harris, *Fiction and Folklore: The Novels of Toni Morrison* (1991); Marilyn Sanders Mobley, *Folk Roots and Mythic Wings in Sarah Orne Jewett and Toni Morrison* (1991); Maggie Sale, "Call and Response as Critical Method: African-American Oral Traditions and *Beloved*," *African American Review* 26 (Spring 1992); Jeanne Rosier Smith, *Writing Tricksters: Mythic Gambols in American Ethnic Literature* (1997).

Suzanne Lane

## Oven, The (*Paradise*)

Built in Haven, Oklahoma*, in 1890 for communal cooking, the Oven became a symbol of the patriarchal community's unity and a testament to the fact that none of the community's women ever cooked in a white kitchen. After World War II, when the men came back to a failing Haven, they decided to disassemble the Oven and rebuild it in Ruby, Oklahoma*. For a time, the round, brick Oven served as both a cookplace and a reminder of what Haven stood for; however, after the convenience of modern appliances, the Oven ceased to be a functional part of the community and began to serve primarily as a hangout for Ruby's youth. Outside of Ruby, the Civil Rights era dawns and the Oven again becomes the primary but contested site of representation for the community's spirit:

upon the five-foot-by-two-foot iron plate forged by Deacon Morgan*
and Steward Morgan's* grandfather are engraved words that divide
rather than unite the community. Is the motto "Beware the Furrow of
his Brow," as Esther Morgan claimed from her "finger memory," a memory made from passing her fingers over the letters while she was too
young to read? Or is it "Be the Furrow of His Brow," as the more politically active youth in Ruby claim? Although Patricia Best Cato*, the unofficial town historian, suggests that the youths' interpretation is more
accurate than the elders suspect (it is others who need to beware his
power, not those within Ruby), the debate becomes one that encapsulates
the power struggle between generations: the former is a message of patriarchy, tradition, patience, and separation; the latter, a message of democracy, change, empowerment, and involvement. The Black fist with
red fingernails painted on the Oven and the tilting of the Oven's foundation signal the political change that has entered Ruby by the 1970s.
*See also Paradise.*

Julie Cary Nerad

# P

## *Paradise* (1998)

*Paradise* is Toni Morrison's seventh novel, the last in a trilogy that includes *Beloved*\* and *Jazz*\*, which focuses, respectively, on the three primary sociocultural movements or moments in African American U.S. history: slavery\*/Reconstruction, the Jazz Age/Great Migration\*, and the Civil Rights/Black Power movement. *Paradise* is divided into nine sections, each bearing the title of a female character in the novel, that weave past and present, tale and experience, memory\* and supposition into a story that gradually unfolds and constructs the complex historical, moral, and political life of a small group of people. The novel opens in the early morning hours of a July day in 1976 with the murder of a girl identified only as white. Nine men, who go unnamed in the beginning section "Ruby," invade the Convent\* and, with loaded guns and coiled rope, cautiously tour the rooms to gather evidence of the women's unnatural practices. After a short battle with the women, who are armed only with common household items, the men finally complete their mission: they shoot the remaining four women, one between the eyes and the last three running through the early-morning mist in a futile attempt at escape. And so the reader opens the story of five haunted and hunted women, and of Ruby\*, an all-Black town in Oklahoma.

In 1976, Ruby has a population of 360 and no need for a jail, bus stop, café, or gas station. The drugstore looks like a regular house and, on either end of the town, the pavement stops just past the last of Ruby's buildings. Located ninety miles from the nearest town, Ruby is a closed community, suspicious of "outsiders" and participant in a deal with God: no one dies in Ruby. The slaughter at the Convent, located seventeen miles and a world away from Ruby, is both the end of this covenant and the beginning of a new one. Despite its geographic and moral separation from the patriarchal Ruby, the lives of the two are deeply intertwined, and it is their relationship that becomes the focus of the novel.

The town of Ruby was founded in 1951 by the "fifteen families": Deacon* and Steward Morgan*, William Cato, Ace Flood, Aaron Poole, Nathan and Moss DuPres, Arnold Fleetwood, Ossie Beauchamp, Harper and Menus Jury, Sargeant Person, John Seawright, Edward Sands, and Roger Best. But the history of Ruby begins before its founding. With few exceptions, these "new fathers" are descendants of the "nine families" (Blackhorse, Morgan, Poole, Fleetwood, Beauchamp, Cato, Flood, and two DuPres) who had established the all-Black town of Haven, Oklahoma*, in 1890. On an exodus from Louisiana and Mississippi after the overthrow of Reconstruction governments, the nine families are rejected by the all-Black, but light-skinned, town of Fairly, Oklahoma*, an act dubbed "the Disallowing," for being both too poor and too Black. Later designated by Patricia Best Cato*, Ruby's unofficial town historian, as "8-rock" for the shade of black found deep in coal mines, it was their dark skin color that not only caused their rejection at Fairly, but also prevented them from finding jobs in the Redemption South and kept them poor. The narrative of the Disallowing solidifies the fierce pride of the original families, already wounded by the inaccurate white depictions of Black political corruption during Reconstruction and establishes an intense distrust and disapproval of light-skinned Blacks as well as whites. Consequently, a reverse hierarchy of skin color—from dark to light—governs first in Haven and later in Ruby. Illustrating the significance of the rejection, each Christmas, Ruby's schoolchildren reenact a conflation of the Disallowing and Christ's birth story, representing their mission as holy and their Haven forefathers as martyrs.

Their sense of difference and ordained purpose is further strengthened in the town's consciousness by the narrative of Haven's divine founding. Leading the band of 158 wanderers, Zechariah "Big Papa" Morgan chose Haven's site based on his religious visions of a traveling man who guided them to the spot. After sixteen months of negotiating with and working for a family of "state Indians," the group finally purchased the land and promptly built a large, round, brick communal Oven. Though its primary purpose was to provide food for the community, the Oven also served as a symbol (perhaps ironically, due to the associations between an oven and the womb) of the patriarchal community's unity and a testament to the fact that none of their women ever cooked in a white kitchen. The tight-knit, self-sufficient community prospered until the

1940s, when the outside world intruded and threatened its traditional, exclusionary existence.

Returning from World War II, Haven's men find the town failing financially and, in their eyes, morally, and they decide to move farther into Oklahoma to begin anew as their fathers and grandfathers had done sixty years before. The town they establish 240 miles west of Haven remains nameless until 1954, when Ruby Morgan (sister of two of the town's most prominent men) dies because no (white) hospital will admit her for treatment, a reenactment on an individual level of the Disallowing. Thus, the town is not only named for a dead woman, the first person buried there, but also as a reminder of the racism and segregation its founders attempted to escape. Having served their country and come home to increased white prejudice and racism, the disillusioned men establish Ruby out of a protective impulse to isolate themselves; however, their efforts are ultimately futile because even in the middle of nowhere, they cannot escape the sociopolitical changes sweeping the United States in the 1960s and 1970s.

One of the primary struggles in the novel results from the efforts of Ruby's youth to resist the repressive and isolationist policies of their parents' generation. Encouraged by Reverend Richard Misner*, the lately-come and youngest of Ruby's three ministers, the younger generation begins by 1970 to take up the Black Power movement as its own. Their new political consciousness, one that signals an involvement with the world outside Ruby, creates a rift in Ruby's traditional, patriarchal social structure, and this growing division manifests itself in an argument over the Oven.

When the new fathers established Ruby, they brought with them and rebuilt brick by brick by Oven, Haven's communal and symbolic center. Initially, the Oven served as both cook place and reminder of what Haven represented; however, as more of Ruby's homes acquire modern appliances, the Oven ceases to be a functional, unifying part of the community. Instead, it begins to serve primarily as a hangout for Ruby's youth, who appropriate the Oven as their own space within the confines of the restrictive town politics and morality. When someone paints a Black fist with red fingernails on the side of the Oven, the festering derision explodes into open division and initiates a disagreement over the words of the Oven's "motto," a now-incomplete message engraved on a five-foot-by-two-foot iron plate forged by Big Papa Morgan. Ruby's older generation, including Big Papa's twin grandsons Deacon and Steward Morgan, believe the motto says "Beware the Furrow of his Brow." They base their belief on Esther Morgan's ancient "finger memory," made from passing her fingers over the letters while she was too young to read, and they understand the motto as a warning from God to be moral, obedient to tradition, and righteous. The more politically active youth, however, argue (itself an affront to their elders) that the motto reads "Be the Fur-row of His Brow," and serves as an empowering instruction to do God's work against white racism. Patricia Best Cato believes a compromise: the youth's interpretation is more accurate than their elders suspect because Haven's founders may have meant the motto as a warning to outsiders, both whites and the lighter-skinned Blacks who disallowed them.

Regardless of the motto's original message, the debate becomes one that encapsulates the power struggle between Ruby's generations: the first is a message of patriarchy, tradition, patience, and separation, and the second a message of democracy, change, empowerment, and in-volvement. And it is the tilting of the Oven's foundation near the end of the novel that signals the sociopolitical changes and violence that have entered Ruby by the mid-1970s. Unable to accept the inevitable chal-lenge of the younger generation to their patriarchal authority, however, the men of Ruby need someone to blame. Although—or perhaps be-cause—many of Ruby's citizens visit the Convent in times of trouble (Arnette Fleetwood to self-abort a baby, Menus Jury to suffer through the delirium tremens, Billie Delia to escape an abusive mother, Sweetie Fleetwood to find a haven from always-sick children), the Convent and its women, who live free of patriarchal restrictions, become the scapegoat for Ruby's growing turbulence.

Never an actual convent, the Convent was originally an embezzler's mansion, decorated throughout with sexually explicit objects: bathroom fixtures, doorknobs, and ashtrays shaped like genitalia; paintings of cop-ulating couples or women in positions of subjugation; dark, mysteri-ous rooms whose original purposes are now unknown. After having thrown one grand orgy in the not-quite-completed mansion, the em-bezzler was arrested, and the land was leased to the Catholic Church. The Sisters Devoted to Indians and Colored People came to the Con-vent in 1925 to establish Christ the King School for Native Girls, also known as Sisters of the Sacred Cross School for Arapaho Girls, and quickly destroyed, hid, or painted over the sexually explicit decor. By 1953, demand for the school had dwindled to nothing, and all of the sis-ters were reassigned except the aging Mother Mary Agnes (Magna Mary*) and her unofficially adopted daughter Consolata Sosa* (Con-nie), whom she "stole" from dirty city streets (presumably in Brazil) at the age of nine, abandoned and sexually abused. The two women re-main at the Convent and sell hot pepper jelly and pies to Ruby's citi-zens and occasional travelers. But as early as 1954, still inhabited by nuns and not yet seen as a threat by Ruby's men, the Convent shows itself as a place of female subversiveness.

At the age of thirty-nine, a still-beautiful, still-green-eyed Connie has a short but intense love affair with Deacon Morgan, a married father of two and already one of Ruby's most prominent men at the age of twenty-nine. Deek ends the affair after Connie bites his lip and licks his blood while making love; her behavior, he tells himself, is that of an animal. But more accurately, he ends the affair because their relationship, encapsulated by that one action, is a threat to Ruby's social structure: Deek cannot reconcile his patriarchal life view, his ideals of stability and morality, with Connie's deep, unrestrained passion. Unaware that the affair is over, however, Deek's wife, Soane*, decides to confront Connie and walks the seventeen miles to demand that Connie help her abort her child. Having no intent of actually aborting the child, Soane uses the request as an excuse to show herself and her sexual relationship with her husband to Connie. Connie refuses to help her and, during the walk back to Ruby, Soane loses the child and believes the miscarriage is God's punishment for her deceit. More than ten years later Connie and Soane develop an unexpected but deep and long-lasting friendship because Connie, using her gift for healing, revives Soane's son Scout after he falls asleep at the wheel of a truck. The relationship between the two women is one of the primary narrative representations of the connections between Ruby and the Convent: both women give love to the same man and life to the same child. However, the similarities between the women are obscured for Ruby's citizens by differences of convention: the one is redeemed in marriage within the confines of Ruby; the other, a whore unrestrained in a never-was Convent that by 1976 is seen as the ultimate threat to the patriarchal community of Ruby.

With the arrival of Mavis Albright* in 1968, the Convent begins to transform once more, this time into a safe haven for wayward women, some on the run from men or the law, some searching for something or someone. Regardless of what brings them to the Convent, the women stay without financial obligation or moral restriction, and without intending to. The twenty-seven-year-old fugitive Mavis arrives after accidentally suffocating her newborn twins by leaving them in the car while she ran into the store for some weenies. Believing that her abusive husband and three surviving children are trying to kill her, Mavis steals her husband's Cadillac and begins driving west, picking up hitchhikers to help fund the journey, until she finally runs out of both gas and money near the Convent. Almost immediately after entering the Convent, Mavis begins to hear the laughter of Merle and Pearl, her dead twins, and she finds herself staying without ever deciding to. Having the aging Connie to look after, the ghostly presence of the ever-growing twins, and the aggressive, nighttime, sexual dream-visits of a strange man, Mavis lives an uneasy mixture of reality and fantasy, but is safe from both her husband and the law.

The second of the Convent women, Gigi (Grace Gibson*), steps off the bus in Ruby in 1971 in too-high heels and a too-short skirt, hoping to find two trees entwined in love and some unbeatable rhubarb pie. Her boyfriend Mikey, arrested during the Oakland riots, has told her of two rocks making love forever in the desert just outside Wish, Arizona, and they are to rendezvous there on April 15, after he is paroled. But Gigi, a girl really named Grace from Alcorn, Mississippi, finds no lovemaking rocks and, on her way to anywhere else, a stranger's tale of two trees that might do and a bus bring her to Ruby; the road she walks takes her to the Convent the day Magna Mary dies. Finding Connie alone, drunk, and almost passed out on the kitchen floor, Gigi misses her ride to Demby and remains at the Convent. Fond of sunbathing naked and wearing few clothes, Gigi immediately garners the disapproval of the more conservative Mavis when she returns with now-unneeded medicine for Magna Mary, and her behavior attracts the attention of K.D. (Coffee Smith*), only nephew of the important Morgan family. Their two-year, turbulent affair ends when the Convent women banish K.D. for beating Gigi, whose sexual attention then turns to the childlike twenty-year old Seneca*, who arrives at the Convent in 1973.

Mavis believes that Seneca arrives just in time to save Mavis and Gigi from killing each other. Seneca's boyfriend, Eddie Turtle, has been convicted for the hit-and-run death of a child, and Seneca has been unsuccessfully attempting to get money for his defense from his mother when the rich and beautiful Norma Keene Fox finds her in a Wichita bus station. After three weeks of being Fox's "personal assistant" and sexual play toy, Seneca is paid five hundred dollars and sent on her way, confused and afraid to return to Eddie. She is hitching rides to nowhere in particular when, from the back of a pickup truck, she sees the weeping, uncombed, coatless Sweetie Fleetwood walking down the road through an approaching blizzard. Sweetie reminds her of another crying Black woman she saw when she was five, just after her mother (whom she thought was her sister) abandoned her in their government housing apartment, leaving only a scrawled note written in lipstick that she could never read, first because she was too young and then because, smeared by tears and sweat from being stored in her shoes, it had become unreadable. Shipped from one foster home to another after being sexually abused by a foster brother, Seneca grows up trying only to please those around her. She develops an early association between wounds (usually small cuts) and sympathy, and thus regularly cuts herself with a razor, making fine, straight "roads" that flood with blood and look surgical in their precision. Having no one and no place to go, Seneca stays at the Convent, attempting the impossible task of keeping peace between Mavis and her new roommate/sexual partner, Gigi, and making the newcomer Pallas Truelove* feel at home.

Pallas, presumably the "white girl" whom Ruby's men shoot first, arrives at the Convent in 1975, sixteen years old and pregnant. Leaving behind her father and her senior year of high school, the wealthy Pallas (also called Divine, which is her mother's nickname) runs away with Carlos, the high school janitor (who fancies himself a sculptor) to visit her estranged artist mother. After a few months of bohemian lifestyle and lots of pot, Pallas sees her mother and Carlos making love in the grass under the stars. Trying to escape the wounding memory, she wrecks her car and is then chased by two men into a swampish lake. Hiding in the darkness, only her face above the black water, Pallas hopes the soft fingers around her legs are harmless bottom grass and friendly fish. After the men abandon their search, Pallas, traumatized and unable to talk, hitches a ride in a pickup truck with Mexican workers who leave her at a church shelter in Demby. However, believing the girl has been sexually abused, the Mexican woman in the truck soon returns and takes her to the Demby Clinic. Billie Delia Cato*, who works in the clinic, finds her in the alley outside, standing over her own vomit, and takes her to the Convent, where after several days she begins to speak again. Pallas briefly goes home to her father, only to return to the shelter of the Convent, where in 1976 she delivers a baby boy.

Thus, in 1975, five haunted women are living at the Convent. The aging Connie, now almost blind and living among and from old bottles of wine in the cellar, longs for the release of death and an escape from the bickering, lost women who surround her. However, on one of her occasional trips to the garden for fresh air, she encounters a strange young man with long, cascading brown hair who asks with a wry smile for a drink, floats when he moves, and insists Connie knows him. After the encounters with the stranger begin, Connie marshals the women into a new sense of purpose and life. They clean themselves, shave their heads, begin to work together, and listen to Connie's stories of Piedade*, a beautiful singing woman who becomes a maternal figure of paradise embodied. Connie instructs the women to paint images of themselves, their pasts, and their fears on the basement floor and walls, and begins to lead them in sessions of "loud-dreaming" that allow them to exorcise the ghosts that haunt them by telling their stories to each other.

Mavis must come to terms with her guilt over the death of the twins and her fear of abusive men. Grace, understanding that she has not approved of herself in years, must exorcise the image of a blood-flower spreading on a young Black boy's clean white shirt, a memory from the Oakland riots. Seneca's "loud-dreaming" allows her to transfer her cuts from her own body to her traced image, and to let go of the desolation she felt when she understood her sister/mother was never coming back. Pallas releases the hated and haunting vision of her mother and Carlos and the memory of entwining tendrils in the dark water. When Soane Morgan sees the women again, just before the attack on the Convent, she recognizes them as women who are no longer haunted. Thus, as they dance in the predawn rain of a July day in 1976, letting the clean water wash away their fear and pain, they are holy women.

But nine of Ruby's men believe them anything but holy, and gather at the Oven to lay their plans: Sergeant Person, looking to control more of the Convent land he now has to lease; Arnold and Jeff Fleetwood, wanting someone to blame for the sick Fleetwood children and Arnette's never-seen baby; Wisdom Poole, hating the women for their connection with Billie Delia, who was loved by two Poole brothers; Harper and Menus Jury, needing to eliminate the witnesses to Menus's drying out; K.D. (Coffee) Smith, taking revenge on the women who had thrown him out; and, leading the pack, Deek and Steward Morgan, one looking for explanation and absolution from his guilt, and the other not needing either. Despite their own unspoken personal motives, all the men are looking for someone to blame for the changes in Ruby. The Convent women, unhampered by patriarchal convention, not bound by the laws and traditions of Ruby, are the ultimate outsiders, and thus a threat to the community the men have worked their entire adult lives to build. As the women dance, the men gather their weapons, prepare for battle, and engage in a ritual of eating rare steak, singed on the fire and washed down with liquor. And the people of Ruby? While gathering medicinal herbs in the dark before the rains come, Lone DuPres*, Ruby's aging and no-longer-needed midwife, overhears the men of Ruby planning their raid and attempts to warn the dancing women, who pay her no heed. After considerable effort, she is finally able to persuade some of Ruby's remaining citizens to go to the Convent to prevent the violence*. However, despite Lone's efforts, the people of Ruby arrive too late, in time only to witness the aftermath of the raid. When they get there, the men have invaded the Convent, and while searching for their prey, they find what they knew they would—justification. Strings of baby booties hanging above a new but empty crib. An unreadable letter written in smeared bloodlike red. Drawings of a mother with fangs, and fish in dark water. The men take these things for signs of deviltry rather than the remnants of an exorcism of fear, hatred, self-doubt, and trauma*. They have no other way to interpret the painted sounds and chalk demons born from the women's loud dreaming. Although the women put up a fight with a butcher knife, boiling chicken stock, a skillet, a cue stick, an alabaster ashtray, and a gilt picture frame, the men are too many, and as the women run through the still-misted grass in an attempt to escape, they are shot down by Sargeant, Wisdom, Coffee, Deacon, and Steward.

But it is Steward Morgan alone who kills the white girl in the first line of the novel. Steward loves his wife, his family's history*, the memory* of his sister Ruby, his bank, his position in the community, and perhaps most of all his idea of what is Right. Rasher than his twin and a hard-core race conservative, Steward above all others cannot tolerate the changing youth in Ruby, nor can he accept the menless women at the Convent; for him, both are signs of failure, disintegration, and loss of control. A man who never forgets anything, Steward remembers how close one Convent woman came to ruining his twin brother's life twenty two years before. Thus, it is also Steward who shoots Connie in the head despite, or perhaps because of, his brother's cautioning hand. During the raid, when the unarmed Connie enters the room and addresses a vision only she sees, Deek attempts to stop his brother's aiming arm. Although Deek is not physically stronger than his twin, he is the morally stronger of the two. After Steward murders Connie, a rift opens between the brothers. Unlike Steward, Deek begins to understand that the isolated and unchanging new "haven" they had attempted to create and tried to uphold through patriarchal control and violence was impossible, that they had become what their grandfathers hated: those who attack and destroy others who are different, for being different. Walking barefoot to Reverend Misner's house in a reenactment of both his grandfather's 200-mile barefoot walk from Louisiana to Mississippi, and the seventeen-mile walk to the Convent so many in need of help had made, Deek hopes to find what he never before knew to look for.

Although all five women are shot, when the only mortician in Ruby, Roger Best, returns to the Convent, there are no bodies and Mavis's Cadillac is missing. Later, when Reverend Richard Misner and Anna Flood visit the Convent to see for themselves that the women are gone, they see, or rather feel, an opening in the air (he sees a door; she, a window) that leads to some other place. Although Misner has no answers to the mysteries of the Convent women and the mysterious passageway to somewhere else, or to Deacon Morgan's introspective musings, he emerges as a spiritual and political hope for Ruby. Misner decides to stay in the more-than-ever divided town while giving the eulogy for Save-Marie*, the youngest of the Fleetwood children and never a presence in the text until her burial. Four months after the raid on the Convent, Save-Marie's death (she is the first of Ruby's original descendants to die within Ruby's city limits since 1953) symbolizes an end of the "compact" between God and the original families of Ruby. When the (now only presumably) slaughtered women's bodies disappear, many bicker over competing versions of the raid, yet some of Ruby's citizens understand that God has given Ruby another chance, a new covenant that can be successful only if they are willing to change. Having once taken refuge at the Convent, Billie Delia Cato is one of the few who befriended the Convent women and is the only character who is not puzzled by their disappearance; she believes the women have left, only to return prepared for a battle with Ruby, with men, and with all the forces that haunted them. And indeed, the reader does see each of the women again. Mavis has a brief, somewhat surreal encounter with her now-grown daughter,

Sally, in a country inn restaurant before disappearing into the crowd. Grace, dressed in a black T-shirt and camouflage pants and packing a gun, appears first at a lake, visiting her father, who has received a permanent stay of execution, and again helping Seneca clean her bleeding hands in a stadium parking lot. Seneca's sister/mother Jean approaches her, mis-remembers their old address, and doesn't know for certain that the woman is Seneca until they are separated once again. Pallas appears again at her mother's, dressed in a long, flowing rose madder and umber skirt, sword in hand, baby carried on her chest, and looking for a pair of shoes she had left behind. She rides off in a car full of women. The novel closes with an image of Consolata, sitting at the ocean's edge with her head in Piedade's lap, in *Paradise*.

References: Geoffrey Bent, "Less Than Divine: Toni Morrison's *Paradise*," *Southern Review* 35: 1 (Winter 1999); Katrine Dalsgard, "The One All-Black Town Worth the Pain: (African) American Exceptionalism, Historical Narration, and the Critique of Nationhood in Toni Morrison's *Paradise*," *African American Review* 35: 2 (2001); Kristin Hunt, "Paradise Lost: The Destructive Forces of Double Consciousness and Boundaries in Toni Morrison's *Paradise*," in *Reading Under the Sign of Nature: New Essays in Ecocentrism*, ed. John Tallmadge and Henry Harrington (2000); Justin Tally, "Toni Morrison's (Hi)stories and Truths," in *FORECAAST: Forum for European Contributions to African American Studies Lit* (1999); Peter Widdowson, "The American Dream Refashioned: History, Politics and Gender in Toni Morrison's *Paradise*," *Journal of American Studies* 35: 2 (2001).

Julie Cary Nerad

## Patsy/Thirty-Mile Woman (*Beloved*)

Patsy is Sixo's* lover who lives on a plantation seventeen miles from Sweet Home*. Sixo's peers at Sweet Home call her Thirty-Mile Woman because Sixo must walk over thirty miles round-trip to see her. Paul D Garner* reveals to us Sixo's explanation that he appreciated Patsy's ability to take all the pieces of him and give them back in the right order. Seen through Sixo's eyes, Patsy is an extraordinary character, but one who gets very little narrative space. When Sixo and Paul D are discovered during the escape attempt, Patsy manages to avoid capture. She is pregnant with Sixo's child, to whom Sixo gleefully refers, just before he is killed, as Seven-O. *See also Beloved*.

Lovalerie King

## Pauls, the (*Beloved*)

Paul A, Paul D, and Paul F are all brothers bred (or perhaps manufactured is a better word, since no mention is made of their having parents) at Sweet Home*. They came to adulthood within the confines of Sweet Home. The suggestion is that there must have been Pauls B, C, and E at some point. The Pauls' collective perceptions of themselves vis-à-vis the world was created, conditioned, and honed under Mr. Garner's* special philosophy of slavery. They had been reared to serve perfectly and contentedly; prior to schoolteacher's* arrival, they were not beaten, they had plenty to eat, and Garner even allowed them to use guns for hunting. He told them that they were men, and they believed him. Garner's death and schoolteacher's new rules turned their "safe" little manufactured world upside down. Paul F is sold for the money needed to keep Sweet Home afloat, and Paul A is hanged during the collective escape attempt. Paul D is sold after a foiled escape attempt. *See also Beloved.*

Lovalerie King

## Peace, Eva (*Sula*)

Sula Peace's* grandmother. Eva has only one leg. It is rumored that she allowed her missing leg to be cut off by a passing train in order to collect insurance money with which to take care of her family after her husband BoyBoy abandoned her. Eva has a large, disorderly house over which she plays matriarch to a host of tenants and family members. *See also Sula.*

Douglas Taylor

## Peace, Sula (*Sula*)

Daughter of Hannah Peace and childhood friend of Nel Wright*. Sula grows up in the expansive house of her grandmother, Eva Peace*. Her distinguishing physical features include a birthmark shaped like a stemmed rose, over one of her eyelids, and a left forefinger slightly shorter than it should be as a result of her cutting it off at the tip to scare the Irish boys who harass her and Nel on their way home from school. Sula is deeply and negatively impacted by three events that happen in quick succession at a crucial moment in her life: she overhears her mother, Hannah, comment that she loves Sula but does not like her; Chicken Little*, a boy from the neighborhood, drowns after Sula accidentally swings him into a river; and Hannah Peace, her mother, burns to death before Sula's eyes while trying to light a yard fire. *See also Sula.*

Douglas Taylor

## Piedade (*Paradise*)

The mystical, singing Black woman/goddess and safe harbor for Consolata Sosa* (Connie) both before and after the slaughter at the Convent*.
In the final year at the Convent, Connie tells the no-longer-haunted
women about Piedade's beaches and her soothing songs, and it is Piedade
who nestles Connie's head in the final scene of the novel. In Portuguese,
the word means "compassion"; Piedade is also a northern area of Rio de
Janiero, Brazil. *See also Paradise.*

Julie Cary Nerad


## Plato, Use of

In the "Allegory of the Cave" (Book VII of the *Republic*), Plato describes
human beings "living in an underground, cavelike dwelling, with an entrance a long way up. . . . They've been there since childhood, fixed in the
same place, with their necks and legs fettered, able to see only in front of
them, because their bonds prevent them from turning their heads
around. Light is provided by a fire burning far above and behind them.
. . . Do you suppose . . . these prisoners see anything of themselves and
one another besides the shadows that the fire casts on the wall in front
of them? How could they, if they have to keep their heads motionless
throughout life?" (514a–b). Plato provides us with an image of ignorant
humanity trapped in the shadowy depths of illusion. The rare individual
escapes the limitations of the cave and, through a long, tortuous, intellectual and emotional journey, discovers a higher realm, a true reality.
As a result of this enlightenment, however, the freed individual is frequently misunderstood and outcast by those who prefer to remain in the
dark cave. In *The Bluest Eye**, Toni Morrison underscores Pauline
Breedlove's* story with Plato's "Allegory of the Cave." Traces of this allegorical imagery can also be found in Morrison's depiction of the sugar-
brown Mobile girls in the chapter titled "Winter."

In "Toni Morrison's Allegory of the Cave: Movies, Consumption, and
Platonic Realism in *The Bluest Eye*," Thomas Fick suggests that "it is a
mistake to think of the cinema only as cultural shorthand for twentieth-
century escapism; its appearance in *The Bluest Eye* serves to recall an
older and more intellectually distinguished precursor. The cinema functions . . . precisely like the famous cave in Plato's *The Republic*" (14).
Pauline Breedlove finds solace from her world in the movie theater. The
images she hypnotically watches on the screen take the place of Plato's
hand-carried objects; a movie projector, the place of his fire; and an audience, the place of his prisoners. This movie audience willingly looks to
escape their reality and submerge themselves in Hollywood fantasy. Con-

versely, Plato's prisoners do not choose to escape into the cave; they are unwillingly chained in the darkness from childhood and grow to believe in the shadows because they know nothing else. In "Eruptions of Funk: Historicizing Toni Morrison," Susan Willis notes that "Polly Breedlove lives a form of schizophrenia, where her marginality is constantly confronted with a world of Hollywood movies, white sheets, and blond children. When at work or at the movies, she separates herself from her own kinky hair and decayed tooth" (265). When she is in the dark theater, the harshness of Pauline's outside world disappears and she can content herself with the shadows, the illusions—she is no longer flawed. There the black-and-white movie images shine through and come together, making a magnificent whole. Whether submerging herself in the falsity of cinema or the white world in which she works, Pauline continually looks to escape her reality. The shadows on the cave wall, like the images on Pauline's movie screen, look very real, and the prisoner is attached to the illusion because it constitutes his world—it gives meaning to his existence. Once thrust out of that existence, the prisoner's truth, like Pauline's, reveals itself. But whereas the freed man embraces his newfound reality, Pauline runs back into the cave; she, like the remaining chained prisoners, hides among the black-and-white images on the screen.

Like Plato's prisoners who know of no other home but the cave and its shadows, Morrison's sugar-brown Mobile girls know only of Mobile and their shadow-filled existence. Described as hollyhocks whose roots are deeply planted in the ground and whose heads can do no more than indifferently nod in the wind, these women are fixed in place. Like the prisoners who refuse to abandon the cave, the sugar-brown Mobile girls prefer to remain deeply rooted in the ground and, as a result, have come to accept illusion as reality; change is threatening. These brown-skinned women are taught to fight change, emotion, and truth; they are taught to fight what Morrison has termed the "funk." These girls look to destroy the "funk," to battle it until it dies. In *Flash of the Spirit*, Robert Farris Thompson traces the etymology of the word "funk" and notes that "the slang term 'funky' in Black communities originally referred to strong body odor, and not to 'funk,' meaning fear or panic. The Black nuance seems to derive from the Ki-Kongo *lu-fuki*, 'bad body odor,' and is perhaps reinforced by contact with *fumet*, 'aroma of food and wine,' in French Louisiana. But the Ki-Kongo word is closer to the jazz word 'funky' in form and meaning, as both jazzmen and Bakango use 'funky' and *lu-fuki* to praise persons for the integrity of their art, for having 'worked out to achieve their aims'" (104). In Platonic terms "funky," or "funk," is the "integrity" of one's art.

Knowledge of reality, according to Plato, is a great intrinsic good. A life in which we know the truth about what exists is far superior to one in which we remain ignorant of the fundamental realities of the universe. For Plato, the achievement of one's aims is to know reality; it is the single most important thing an individual can attain, and without it, the soul is lost—like the souls of the chained prisoners, like the souls of the sugar-brown Mobile girls, and like the soul of Pauline Breedlove. Like Plato's prisoners, these women look to fight the funk, to fight reality all the way to the grave because they are secure and comfortable in and with the life and world they know—the only life they have known. Change of any kind is threatening. Like the freed prisoner who returns to the cave and attempts to share his enlightenment with the others, the "Funk" is fought against and threatened with death if it dare go near any of them. Morrison's sugar-brown Mobile girls look to destroy the funk in the same way the remaining prisoners look to destroy the newly enlightened man.

There is no figure in *The Bluest Eye* who ascends from darkness and emerges into the light, who finds enlightenment and chooses it over the shadows, as one of Plato's prisoners ultimately does. What we do find in Pauline Breedlove and the sugar-brown Mobile girls is the same unwillingness to step outside of the cave that Plato's prisoners display when they are given the opportunity, an unwillingness driven by fear and a need to exist within a false, albeit familiar, construct because it is easier to do so—because it is comfortable and safe—rather than emerge from the cave and face the painful light of the sun. *See also Bluest Eye, The.*

References: Thomas H. Fick, "Toni Morrison's Allegory of the Cave: Movies, Consumption, and Platonic Realism in *The Bluest Eye*," *JMMLA* 22 (1989); Plato, "The Allegory of the Cave," in his *Republic*, trans. G.M.A. Grube (1992); Robert Farris Thompson, *Flash of the Spirit: African and Afro-American Art and Philosophy* (1984); Susan Willis, "Eruptions of Funk: Historicizing Toni Morrison," in *Black Literature and Literary Theory*, ed. Henry Louis Gates, Jr. (1984).

Traci M. Klass

## Playing in the Dark: Whiteness and the Literary Imagination (1992)

In *Playing in the Dark: Whiteness and the Literary Imagination*, Toni Morrison focuses her attention on what she calls the Africanist presence in American literature, a term she uses to describe the centrality of Blackness (even in texts where African Americans are absent as characters) in the literature in which all of the dramas of American national identity* have been and continue to be played out. Throughout *Playing in the Dark* Morrison makes the case that Africanism in American literature has positioned American identity and the reader of American literature as white. To the extent that writers are also readers, whiteness* marks the imaginations of American writers and informs the writerly struggle to create language that breaks free of images premised on familiar racial narratives. However, the focus of Morrison's critique is not the distorted, false representation of people of color. Rather, in her readings of Edgar Allan Poe, Willa Cather, Ernest Hemingway, and Mark Twain, among others, Morrison makes the case that American Africanism is central to the narrative strategies that have made possible the invention of a coherent American, white identity. In this book Morrison is concerned with the effects of American Africanism on the minds of white writers and readers.

Morrison locates the beginning of writing *Playing in the Dark* in the context of questions raised during her three William E. Massey lectures at Harvard University, and she dedicates the book to her students at Princeton with whom she explored questions about the limits of the imaginative act of writing in a society founded on contradictory notions of both individual freedom and racial hierarchy. In such a context, what can writing mean for an African American writer such as herself? What can it mean for writers and readers to take responsibility for their art and for the values they use to create and communicate a world through literature? And, finally, what does it mean for a writer to present herself or himself as unraced in a racial state? These are some of the questions Morrison considers in *Playing in the Dark*.

By making visible the Africanist presence in American literature and its role in the invention and maintenance of white/American identity, Morrison shows how race* is the condition for the very possibility of American literature and that race, like gender, needs to be central, rather than peripheral, to the study of American literature. Morrison rejects the canonical view of American literature and the imagination as unfettered by the ideological and material realities of race in the United States, and points out some factors that have silenced discussion of race in the criticism of U.S. literature. One factor is the mainstream American belief that bringing up the subject of race is both impolite and racist, as if the bodily differences marked as racial differences are themselves horrible and unmentionable. The ideological and practical implication of this barrier is the normalization of whiteness against a demonized Blackness.

Another important contribution to literary criticism and the understanding of racialization and whiteness in *Playing in the Dark* is the way Morrison directs her critique of American Africanism at the perpetrators of racism rather than at its victims. As Morrison contends, when discussions of race in literature are confined to African American, Native American, Latin American, and Asian American literatures, critics are able to ignore and deny the extent to which the invention of the Africanist presence in American literature is really a sustained reflection on the fears and desires of the white self. American identity and the identity of American literature have been created on the back of the Africanist presence, and for Morrison this truth has interestingly complex consequences for writers and readers of American literature.

Morrison's *Playing in the Dark* appeared in 1992, in the midst of canon debates on U.S. college and university campuses. Progressive students and faculty in Women's Studies, African American Studies, Lesbian and Gay Studies, Latin American Studies, Asian American Studies, Native American Studies, and other area studies programs were critiquing the Eurocentrism and maleness of the Western literary canon and advocating a multicultural curriculum. Conservative faculty and students perceived multiculturalism as an unjustified politicization of education, an education that they argued ought to prioritize texts and values that reflected a "universal," "human" condition. The National Association of Scholars opposed multiculturalism and the view that issues of race, gender, and sexuality* are crucial components of education in a culturally diverse world. In 1987 Allan Bloom published *The Closing of the American Mind,* in which he argued for the central place of the Western canon in education. And in *Telling the Truth: A Report on the State of the Humanities in Higher Education* (1992), Lynne Cheney, then chair of the National Endowment for the Humanities (1986–1993), claimed that multicultural, feminist, and poststructural criticisms of universal truth have falsely politicized the humanities.

In *Playing in the Dark,* Morrison challenges these criticisms of feminist and anti-racist influences on the study of literature by pointing out that all studies of literature are political. Even denials of the centrality of race reflect a cultural hegemony in which "American" and "human" mean "white." Morrison acknowledges that some literary critics are proud of their ignorance of African American literature. What surprises Morrison is that these literary critics remain unconcerned about the presence of race in the canonical literature they read and support. Because Americans do not live in a world without race, race matters to any serious study of American literature and identity.

*Playing in the Dark* has profoundly influenced many scholars in feminist theory, critical race theory, and disability studies. Feminist and critical race theorists who seek to understand the narratives of race and gender informing the construction of whiteness have benefited from Morrison's discussion of the construction of whiteness in American literature. And scholars in disability studies have explored parallels between her critique of the Africanist presence and their articulation of a "disability presence" in literature that constructs normalcy. Undoubtedly, Morrison's *Playing in the Dark* will continue to enrich and complicate our understanding of cultural hegemony, American literature, and American identity. In *Play-*

*ing in the Dark,* as in her edited collection *Race-ing Justice, En-gendering Power* (also published in 1992), Morrison demonstrates how narratives of race can both obscure and illuminate the realities of race and racism in the United States.

References: Allan Bloom, *The Closing of the American Mind* (1987); Lynne V. Cheney, *Telling the Truth: A Report on the State of the Humanities in Higher Education* (1992).

Kim Q. Hall

## Plum/Ralph (*Sula*)

Eva Peace's* youngest child and only son. When he is a child, Eva saves his life by removing the hardened stool from his rectum during a bout of severe constipation. Later, Eva takes Plum's life by setting him on fire after he returns from World War I addicted to heroin. *See also Sula.*

Douglas Taylor

## Prostitutes China, Poland, and Miss Marie (*The Bluest Eye*)

Outsiders in the community due to their profession, the three prostitutes who befriend Pecola Breedlove* nevertheless ascend to middle-class status as a result of their associations with many of the well-to-do men of Lorain, Ohio*. Their apartment is a haven of sorts for Pecola, because they accept her for who she is; they are the only people who make her feel beautiful and loved. *See also Bluest Eye, The.*

Gena Elise Chandler

# R

## Race

In a 1983 interview, Toni Morrison recalled that watching her father dominate in a racial conflict with another man allowed her to witness pride and assertion in such encounters, dynamics that recur throughout her work. In both her fiction and her nonfiction, Morrison represents conflict and domination to illustrate how language, power, and race are implicated with one another in canonical American literature as well as in American society at large.

Morrison forcefully illustrates how race functions as a metaphor crucial to American literature and culture. Her work consistently demonstrates the difficulty of escaping racially inflected language that perpetuates unspoken messages of racial domination. "Race talk," she suggests, has become the gratuitous, pop-culture insertion of racial signs that serve no function but to debase Blacks. Following the philosophical work of Frantz Fanon, Morrison's writing documents how Black feelings of inferiority result from the values of America's white patriarchal system: a system she calls the "master narrative" that perceives Blacks as objects of contempt. Many of Morrison's characters, most notably *The Bluest Eye*'s\* Pecola Breedlove\*, embrace this value system along with the consequent sense of inferiority that stems from dominant racial stereotypes and whites' projections of racist shame.

As Morrison frequently asserts in both her fiction and her nonfiction, in order fully to understand and appreciate the canonical literature of the United States—from Herman Melville and Nathaniel Hawthorne to

William Faulkner and herself—one must grasp both the vocabulary and the perspective of reading race between the lines. Until relatively recently, Morrison argues, critics neither had motivations nor developed a discourse for interpreting literary racial constructs in widely regarded texts of the nineteenth and twentieth centuries. For example, Melville's use of darkness as a symbol that projected the new country's guilt about slavery* in such novels as *Benito Cereno* and *Moby Dick* remained largely overlooked. Morrison's three-dimensional African American characters reflect her keen interest not only in promoting a deeper understanding of how race functions in American literature, but also in reclaiming through critical language the presence of African Americans in the history and culture of the United States.

Morrison introduces *Playing in the Dark: Whiteness and the Literary Imagination** by describing her response to Marie Cardinal's memoir, *The Words To Say It*, connecting Cardinal's madness, or "possession," with the cultural associations of jazz*. In making this connection, Morrison began to understand how Black artists facilitate discovery or change in literature they had not written. Particularly, Morrison explores the relationship between Cardinal's breakdown and the internalization of socially constructed attitudes about race.

The Cardinal vignette introduces three major stages of Morrison's interest in race: how Black characters and images function in literature; what assumptions underlie such figures; and—the primary focus of *Playing in the Dark*—the sources of Black imagery and their effects on our overall literary imagination. In a section titled "black matters," Morrison argues, using as a test case Willa Cather's *Sapphira and the Slave Girl* (among others), that the long-standing difficulty of critical discourse in recognizing an African American presence in canonical American literature reinforces the belief that the fundamental qualities of U.S. national culture derive from an idea of "Americanness" completely free of African and African American culture. And yet, as Morrison argues, values such as individualism, struggles with morality, and good versus evil emerged directly in response to the Africanist presence in the United States: states united superficially through the denial of such a presence, which was perceived as threatening to the new country's cohesion.

Finally, by examining the racial vulnerability, exclusion, and hierarchy at the root of U.S. literary history and culture, Morrison seeks not only to provide a closer look into Blacks' imaginations but also to examine the effects of racist ideology on the "masters" of these narratives. In other words, Morrison asks, how can the Africanist presence in American literature self-reflexively contribute to the national literary imagination? Ultimately, she concludes that it would be impossible to extricate Africanist characters and histories from what we consider canonical American literature because its ethos depends wholly upon the Africanist presence it has for so long denied.

A precursor to *Playing in the Dark*, "Unspeakable Things Unspoken: The Afro-American Presence in American Literature," first appeared in *Michigan Quarterly Review* in the winter of 1989. Its original title was "Canon Fodder" because it seriously engages the canon debates contemporary with its publication. By taking on such debates, Morrison reinforces how the presence of African American literature and awareness of its culture both reinvigorate literary scholarship in the United States and raise scholarly standards. As Morrison argues, since serious scholarship has begun to move away from denying the African American presence in literature, African American writers must increasingly recognize themselves as the subjects of their own narratives—both to witness and to participate in their own experience—rather than to be imagined as objects for scrutiny. Additionally, Morrison asserts, we must seriously engage with literature written by and for African Americans in order to examine origins and assumptions previously overlooked in "raceless" literature.

Morrison argues that studying African American literature can facilitate a greater understanding not only of literature in general but also of sociology. She suggests that undertaking this project requires developing a theory of literature accommodating African American literature based on its culture, history, and artistic strategies; examining the foundational nineteenth-century works of the American canon to uncover the "unspeakable things unspoken"—how African Americans inspired literary choices, language, and structure; and considering both contemporary and noncanonical literature for similar influences, regardless of how they are categorized or esteemed by literary critics.

Morrison finds an example of such "unspeakable things" in Herman Melville's *Moby Dick*, a novel in which Melville illustrates his own recognition of the emergence of whiteness* as an ideology in the United States. Melville stages this recognition as the battle between the white whale (the ideology of race) and Ahab, who lost to this ideology a treasured body part, family*, society, and his place in the world. In other words, according to Morrison, Melville's writing is not as interested in depicting white people as it is in dramatizing idealized whiteness. Through this example, Morrison demonstrates how critical inquiry reveals where and why American literature may insist on its antithesis to Blackness, as well as how language reveals what is absent: a presence assumed not to exist.

Morrison concludes "Unspeakable Things Unspoken" with an analysis of her own novels, demonstrating how she uses language—and, in turn, how language uses her—to illustrate qualities other than skin color, subject matter, and ethnicity that constitute African American writing.

She concludes that she utilizes language to demonstrate a particular vulnerability of crucial aspects of African American culture, calling on others to do the same.

In *Playing in the Dark*, Morrison explains parenthetically that "Recitatif"*—the only short story she has ever written—experimentally removes all of the racial codes from a text featuring two characters wholly dependent upon racial identity*. By refusing to specify the race of her two primary characters, Twyla and Roberta, and simultaneously describing them with particular racially identified characteristics such as hair texture, clothing choices, body type, diet, musical interests, and political investments, Morrison arbitrarily switches racial coding and consistently tests readers' fundamental assumptions about race. Ultimately, "Recitatif" becomes an experiment in language, as Morrison considers whether a story can be written without the linguistic short cuts habitually employed in American literature to categorize and to stereotype its characters.

In her afterword to the 1993 edition of *The Bluest Eye*, Morrison recalls a girl she knew in elementary school who wanted blue eyes, associated blue eyes with beauty, and believed that beauty could be performed, rather than simply beheld. *The Bluest Eye*, Morrison explains, is her own attempt both to understand how racial self-loathing motivated the young girl's wish and to portray the gaze of the "master narrative" underlying such self-condemnation. Through Pecola Breedlove, Morrison investigates how a vulnerable child might internalize and embrace damaging racial stereotypes with the potential to destroy her. As she does so, Morrison's prose is simultaneously race-specific and race-free: using "quiet as it's kept" as an insider's phrase to open the novel, for example, Morrison establishes a sense of inclusion versus exclusion and exposes the devastation of racial divisions in 1965–69, the time frame during which she wrote the novel.

Pecola's sense of racial identity and her understanding of what constitutes beauty emerge powerfully through interactions with characters such as Mr. Yakabowski and Maureen Peal. Mr. Yakabowski, the shop owner who sells Pecola candy, actually fails to see Pecola for who she is even when she stands before him, and betrays to her his disgust with her Blackness. Maureen Peal, known as Meringue Pie to the girls who envy her, enchants the school and possesses the "thing to fear"—"beauty" by her community's standards—yellow skin, brown hair, green eyes, and enviable wealth.

Seeing themselves through white culture crystallized in the "Black e mo" chant and the Shirley Temple cup, the Breedloves lose their own sense of identity, further positing the inadequacy of white mythology for African Americans. Racialized identity and racial construction both oppress and disembody these characters, as illustrated through Cholly

Breedlove's* emasculation, Pauline Breedlove's* earnestness, Pecola's wish, Soaphead Church's* desire to help her, and Geraldine MacTeer's obsession with "funk." In *The Bluest Eye*, whiteness appears not as a racial category but as the norm against which all other races are measured. In other words, as in *Moby Dick*, whiteness appears in this text as an ideal rather than a race. Only Claudia MacTeer*, it seems, rejects such an ideal, hating Shirley Temple, for example, for all that she represents.

Set in the hills of Medallion, Ohio*, *Sula's* Bottom* is a lost community of Blacks, the result of a joke a white farmer played on his slave. Organizing themselves around local holidays such as National Suicide Day*, the people in the Bottom find unity only through excluding the two characters brave enough to transgress social norms: Shadrack*, a World War I veteran, and Sula Peace*, a biologically Black character who chooses "Blackness" as a culture and a way of life. Afraid neither to watch her mother's burning to death nor to seduce the husband of her best friend, Sula, along with her mother and grandmother, openly question loyalty in a community rooted in white values. Sula's best friend, Nel Wright*, and Nel's mother, Helene Wright*, on the other hand, are outstanding citizens by Medallion's standards: conservative, religious, and impeccable. Despite their impeccability, however, they, too, experience awkward moments that underscore the racial tensions pervading the novel. Traveling south in November 1920, Helene and Nel accidentally enter the whites-only section of a train and face public humiliation at the hands of an unforgiving conductor. This event permanently marks Nel, as she witnesses the inexplicable power of her mother's coquettish, transgressive smile; she loathes the soldiers' posthumiliation leers; and she realizes the defining power of the custard-colored skin concealed beneath her mother's dress.

In "Unspeakable Things Unspoken," Morrison acknowledges that while writing *Sula*, she consciously wrote both for and out of Black culture while simultaneously considering the position of white culture. Like the domination by Morrison's father during a confrontational racial encounter, Morrison's characters consistently reclaim their dignity and subtly assert personal authority. Helene's contentious smile, Shadrack's narcissistic gaze in the water of a toilet bowl, and Sula's sacrifice of her left forefinger all offer models for rejecting white hegemony, facing racist bullies, and maintaining a sense of peace. Finally, while visiting Sula's grave at the end of the novel, Nel finds written in concrete the answer to what Medallion ultimately wished for: the Peace family name recorded on each gravestone like a chant, signifying neither people nor words, but wishes.

Set against the backdrop of red, white, and blue, *Song of Solomon* begins with the flying leap of an agent for North Carolina Mutual Life, an insurance company owned by and dependent upon Blacks. The agent's flight, like Solomon's* flight before him and Milkman Dead's* flight after him, seeks freedom from the impositions and the injustices of racism in the United States.

From the beginning, *Song of Solomon* establishes racial binaries embodied by characters at odds with one another. For example, Macon Dead*, metaphorically dead from internalizing white racism and middle-class shame, opposes his sister Pilate Dead*—a bootlegger and a pariah, proud and self-reliant in her appreciation for the past. Similarly, Macon's son Milkman represents middle-class assimilation, while his friend and foe Guitar Baines* dramatizes lower-class Black nationalism. As an activist in the Seven Days* terrorist organization, Guitar advocates revenge killings as payback for white America's murderous acts, prompting a conflict between the two men not resolved until they meet in Shalimar, Virginia, during a fruitless race to find gold.

The Black history that Pilate wears in her earrings and that Milkman seeks for himself crucially depends upon oral tradition*: a tradition perpetuated by the children* of Shalimar; the truth revealed in the Sugarman song; spirituals promising freedom; and the life stories of the people Milkman encounters on his quest. As Milkman travels from north to south, facing Circe* and a bobcat hunt in the process, he symbolically sheds Western values through his loss of materials and materialism alike. Like his graveyard-lover Hagar Dead*, who literally buys into the Anglo beauty myth with brand-name accessories and mango, red, and blue makeup, Milkman struggles to find not only his roots but also sources of love. And just as Hagar's makeup washes away in a downpour, so is Milkman disarmed of the values threatening his identity. Not until he flies off of Solomon's Leap*—with the "tar" of Guitar's name echoing in the hills, paving the way for *Tar Baby*—can Milkman Dead offer up his life, having rediscovered its meaning and recognized all he is leaving behind.

As Morrison explains in "Unspeakable Things Unspoken," an interest in masking and unmasking drives *Tar Baby*, as it both underscores and explores the gap between the mask and the person who hides beneath it. Interested in how characters experience inter- and intraracial tensions, as well as class conflicts, *Tar Baby* traces the failed love affair between Jadine Childs* and Son*. Raised in the United States, educated in Europe, and vacationing on Isle des Chevaliers*, Jadine is a Black woman who feels obligated to confess that she hates hoop earrings, does not have to straighten her hair, and does not particularly like Charles Mingus. Conflicted by what constitutes whiteness and Blackness, Jadine wants to be categorized as neither white nor Black, but as her singular self completely separated from the pressures of racial denomination. Associated with European beauty standards after posing for a magazine cover, Jadine is haunted by the image of a Black woman she sees in the grocery store who both represents Black pride and makes her feel inauthentic.

Jadine's relationship with Son is dramatized by the contrasting cities in which they choose to live: Jadine chooses New York for personal advancement and the sophisticated culture of white society, whereas Son chooses his hometown, Eloe*, depicted through stereotypes of primitivism and nature as "pure" Blackness. The masquerade of New York society set off by the purity of Eloe allows *Tar Baby* to construct whiteness as the sign of contamination and difference—a dramatic reversal from other canonical American literature.

Ultimately, the relationship between Jadine and Son fails because of class warfare and cultural differences, undercutting the myth* that Black men and women experience everything identically because of their shared heritage of discrimination, racism, and slavery. *Tar Baby* explores but refuses to resolve the racial and class divisions it depicts. It is unclear in the end whether Marie-Therese Foucault* leads Son to an awakening or to his death, just as it is unclear how much Jadine gains or gives away as she decides to return to Europe. *Tar Baby* begins with an epigraph from 1 Corinthians declaring: "there are contentions among you," and ends having revealed these contentions without pretending to relieve them.

As Morrison explains in "Unspeakable Things Unspoken," *Beloved** begins with the three numbers of a street address, which is surprising in a novel about former slaves, who generally owned nothing—certainly not property in the aftermath of the Civil War. Beginning in medias res, *Beloved* forces readers to experience the disorientation of the novel's characters: slaves who were kidnapped without explanation from one place, and delivered in the dark to another.

*Beloved* locates the effects of racial categorization and racial tension in a very specific historical context: the years of slavery her characters endured on Sweet Home* plantation as well as their relative freedom later, in rural Ohio. Located on the interstices of history* and memory*, *Beloved* apparently lacks both structure and conventional temporal organization because traumatic memory exceeds the boundaries of both. Circling the subject of slavery, *Beloved* undermines the racial categories dependent upon an understanding of Blacks as animals and property by contrasting the animalistic treatment of slaves at Sweet Home with the Black community's humanity, exemplified by Baby Suggs's* sermons in the clearing and Paul D Garner's* tobacco-tin heart.

*Beloved* memorializes a mother's determination to protect her baby from a life of slavery and portrays the cultural memory of infanticide* with a ghost threatened by extinction through forgetting. As Amy Denver* forcefully articulates, dead things hurt when coming back to life, especially the horrific memories of a baby's death. The infanticide depicted in *Beloved* is based on the story of Margaret Garner*, a woman embraced by abolitionists invested in her sentence: if her baby were considered human, she would have been tried for murder; however, her baby was considered property, making Garner guilty only of stealing goods. In the end, after the community's exorcism of a ravenous baby ghost, the trace of this ghost disappears. Yet it is unclear how much of her story is recalled, begging the haunting question: How can history be remembered if it is not to be passed on?

Like *Jazz's** subject matter, the music* of its title is simultaneously improvisational, sexual, political, and expressive of the tensions between private and public, past and present. *Jazz* represents music as a medium for conveying Black culture: the experience of its differences and similarities, and of the complexity of African American identity not otherwise portrayed in mass media. In many ways, jazz in this novel operates as the central expressive element of Black culture, contributing crucially to the production of Black culture and individual identity.

*Jazz* is set in "the City" of lightness and dark, using chiaroscuro to reveal how whites project their own darkness onto dark background, where figures stand out as distinctive because of significant contrasts. This city houses the Black public sphere, where double consciousness complicates the differences within African American culture, as well as the divisions between white and Black culture. Concluding with the image of two people whispering with each other under the covers, *Jazz* illustrates how visual media are inadequate for representing African American experience, for the musical media of Black cultural expression emphasize originality over fidelity, as well as the possibility of unity through the cacophony and syncopation that jazz embodies.

*Paradise** famously begins with the claim that the white girl in the Convent* was shot first, but refuses to reveal the racial identities of the women who sought asylum there. Like "Recitatif," written fifteen years before, *Paradise* highlights Morrison's interest in how characters might resist racial encoding. By refusing to assign a racial category to the women of the Convent, Morrison wanted readers to attempt to identify these characters racially until they realized that race is the least reliable information for defining or understanding them.

The "paradise" of *Paradise*—Ruby, Oklahoma*—depends upon the fantasy that only a community inhabited by a single race and necessarily excluding others can offer peace and prosperity. The events that *Paradise* depicts illustrate how racial prejudice is not a biological requirement, but rather serves a social purpose. Through the legacy of Ruby's dark-skinned people and the racial discourse of Fairly, Oklahoma's*, rejection of them, Morrison shows how this "Disallowing" works to form Ruby's sense of its own group identity. As the dark-skinned leaders of Ruby perpetuate the rejection of the Fairly people by turning on the light-skinned pariahs seeking safety in the Convent, they demonstrate how racial categories are implicated by the social factors leading to exclusion and violence*. In *Paradise*, as in many of Morrison's novels, racial discourse does not function

to label the physical traits of her characters, but rather to reveal the social forces dependent upon racial encoding to justify exclusion, injustice,
suffering, and violence. *See also* Approaches to Morrison's Work: Historical.

References: J. Brooks Bouson, *Quiet as It's Kept: Shame, Trauma, and
Race in the Novels of Toni Morrison* (2000); Patricia McKee, *Producing
American Races: Henry James, William Faulkner, Toni Morrison* (1999);
Timothy B. Powell, "Toni Morrison: The Struggle to Depict the Black
Figure on the White Page," in *Toni Morrison's Fiction: Contemporary
Criticism*, ed. David L. Middleton (2000); Philip M. Weinstein, *What Else
but Love?: The Ordeal of Race in Faulkner and Morrison* (1996).

Aimee L. Pozorski

## Race-ing Justice, En-gendering Power: Essays on Anita Hill, Clarence Thomas, and the Construction of Social Reality (1992)

In July 1991 President George H.W. Bush nominated Clarence Thomas
to the U.S. Supreme Court, and the Senate confirmation hearings following his nomination sparked much public controversy about sexual
harassment and the politics of race* and gender in the United States. At
first, many African Americans expressed reservations about Thomas's
nomination. While they supported an African American nominee as a
replacement for Justice Thurgood Marshall, they were critical of
Thomas's history* of opposing affirmative action and welfare, an opposition that fueled his public attack on the "laziness" of his sister, Emma
Mae Martin, as a welfare recipient. Many African Americans who had
fought to secure the benefits of full citizenship for people of color wor-
ried that Clarence Thomas's presence on the Supreme Court would further erode civil rights victories.

Nonetheless, these concerns about Thomas's conservative political history disappeared from the confirmation process and mainstream media
commentary when Anita Hill, a professor of law who had worked for
Thomas in the 1980s, testified that Clarence Thomas had sexually ha-
rassed her while he was her supervisor. At once media spotlight and public discussion became riveted on the bodies and sexualities* of two
African Americans, one man and one woman. And as Clarence Thomas's
qualifications took a back seat to the Senate committee's concerns about
Anita Hill's credibility, the academic and nonacademic publics became
embroiled in debate concerning race and gender power. In response to
Hill's testimony, Thomas portrayed himself as a victim of racism despite

his long history of denying the persistence of harmful effects of racism in the lives of African Americans. In other words, Thomas was critical of affirmative action proponents who argued that racism continued to have negative effects on opportunities for African Americans; however, during the Senate confirmation process, Thomas made the fact of his Blackness in a racist society an issue for the Senate and public to consider in making their judgments about the truth of Hill's accusations and his qualifications for the U.S. Supreme Court. The Senate confirmed Clarence Thomas's appointment to the Supreme Court in October 1991 by a vote of 52–48, but the controversy sparked by the representations of Hill and Thomas in the hearing was far from over.

Toni Morrison's *Race-ing Justice, En-gendering Power* was one of a number of publications appearing after Thomas's confirmation hearings. It is a Morrison-edited collection of essays by A. Leon Higginbotham, Jr., Andrew Ross, Manning Marable, Michael Thelwell, Claudia Brodsky Lacour, Patricia J. Williams, Gayle Pemberton, Nell Irvin Painter, Carol M. Swain, Homi K. Bhabha, Christine Stansell, Nellie Y. McKay, Margaret A. Burnham, Wahneema Lubiano, Kendall Thomas, Cornel West, Kimberly Crenshaw, and Paula Giddings. In her introduction Morrison states her desire to contribute to a new conversation about race and gender as they shape the lives of men and women of all races, and each contributor furthers that conversation by focusing on the interrelatedness of race and gender in the representation of both Clarence Thomas and Anita Hill. For Morrison and her contributors, the Anita Hill/Clarence Thomas controversy is yet another text in which Black bodies are the battleground for the establishment of white American male identity and the protection of white and patriarchal privileges.

Each essay addresses at least one of the many questions and outrages generated by the media spectacle of Thomas's confirmation and what many feminists came to understand as Anita Hill's burning at the stake (*Race-ing Justice* 161): How could Catherine MacKinnon, a feminist, legal scholar, and lawyer, overlook Thomas's anti-woman and anti-Black history in her initial support of him (*Race-ing Justice* 255)? How could so many African Americans support Thomas, given his opposition to victories of the Civil Rights struggle such as affirmative action? How could Anita Hill's testimony of sexual harassment be dismissed? Why couldn't the all-white-male Senate committee understand Hill's delay and reluctance to come forward? What does African American support for Clarence Thomas indicate about Black leadership (*Race-ing Justice* 391)? The essays in Morrison's book show how the answers to these questions are found in understanding how dominant narratives of race and gender erase Black women's experience of both racism and sexism by conceptualizing all Black people as male and all women as white (*Race-ing Justice* 403).

When racism is conceived as distinct from sexism, Black male conservatives who have consistently opposed efforts to promote the welfare of a majority of African Americans are, nonetheless, able to win the sympathies and support of African Americans, other people of color, and anti-racist white people by claiming to be the victims of white racism. This is precisely what Clarence Thomas achieved in his infamous description of the Senate's questioning of him in response to Hill's charge as a "high-tech lynching." Morrison and her contributors convincingly argue that Clarence Thomas's confirmation was a setback rather than a victory for African Americans, and that Anita Hill was the victim of both racism and sexism in Thomas's confirmation hearing. In her introduction, Morrison portrays Thomas as a contemporary version of Friday in *Robinson Crusoe*, a man of color who is "rescued" into an adversarial culture and repays the debt by killing members of his culture when ordered to do so because he no longer understands the language of his culture of origin.

The essays in Morrison's *Race-ing Justice, En-gendering Power* share the view that an articulation of the racial dimensions of sexism and the gendered dimensions of racism remained glaringly absent in the media focus on Thomas and Hill. Thus, the new conversation to which Morrison hopes to contribute must look to the inextricable connections between racism and sexism in the experiences of women of color. Only then will the national conversation about race and gender move beyond conceptualizing the harms of racism and sexism as mutually exclusive.

There have been many other media spectacles focused on race and gender since the publication of Morrison's *Race-ing Justice, Engendering Power* in 1992, most notably the O.J. Simpson trial and the intervention of the Supreme Court in the 2000 presidential election. In the latter, Clarence Thomas joined a majority of the Supreme Court in halting a recount of Florida votes and proclaiming George W. Bush, the son of former President George H.W. Bush, the new president of the United States, a move that many claim prevented many African American votes in Florida from being counted. Toni Morrison's book on the Clarence Thomas/Anita Hill controversy continues to be a useful guide and an intelligent voice for understanding the complexities of the 1991 Senate confirmation hearing and current media spectacles highlighting the intersecting dynamics of racism and sexism. *See also* Masculinity.

Kim Q. Hall

## "Recitatif"

"Recitatif," Toni Morrison's only short story, appeared in print in 1983 as part of Amiri and Amina Baraka's anthology *Confirmation*. It is an experiment in avoiding race* as a means of representing character. The story also deals with the issues of individual and family*, and the relationship between the past and the present. The title alludes to the musical term recitatif, a vocal performance in which a narrative is sung rather than spoken. This story is like a musical performance because the plot itself is a "song" that reconstructs the past for the reader.

"Recitatif" traces the relationship of two women, one Black and one white, who meet as children in an orphanage. The characters' names are Twyla (the narrator) and Roberta. However, the narrative never reveals the race of either character.

The two girls meet in the early 1960s when they are sent to "St. Bonny's" because their mothers are declared unfit. Twyla reveals that her mother likes to dance too much, and Roberta claims that her mother is sick. Both girls understand that there must be deeper reasons for being sent there, but they share an unspoken pledge not to probe further. The girls initially respond negatively to each other because of their racial difference. However, these concerns fade as they are left to themselves. Twyla tells of one visitors' day when both girls' mothers came. Not long after that visit, the girls return to their homes. Before they separate, Twyla relates in some detail seeing Maggie, one of the orphanage workers, who appears to be hard of hearing, pushed down by the older children. The incident disturbs her, so much so that it remains part of her memory* of the brief time she lived at St. Bonny's.

Years later, Twyla is waiting tables at a Howard Johnson's when Roberta comes in with two men. Twyla describes them as hippies, and learns that they are on the way to a Jimi Hendrix concert. Even though Twyla and Roberta recognize each other, their conversation is brief. Roberta does not want to relive old memories with Twyla, and Twyla feels embarrassed by her job.

After Twyla marries and has children, she meets Roberta once again in an A&P in an exclusive neighborhood. Twyla is decidedly working-class, but Roberta is financially well-off, having married an IBM executive. The meeting is cordial, and the friends enjoy catching up over coffee. As they recall their days at St. Bonny's, Twyla mentions remembering when Maggie fell down. Roberta corrects her and states that the older girls pushed Maggie. Roberta accuses Twyla of blocking the bad memory, which upsets Twyla, and reminds her of how Roberta snubbed her in Howard Johnson's. Roberta brushes it off, blaming it on the racial tension of the time.

The story shifts to the fall of the same year, and Twyla describes the racial strife that has come to the town because of forced busing. Her son is to be bused across town, but angry mothers are picketing the school. Roberta is one of the pickets, and the two women face off over the issue. Morrison never makes clear, however, which side of the issue each woman takes. Instead, as the conflict goes on, the women's picket signs become more personal and take the place of conversation between them.

Years later, when the children have grown, Twyla and Roberta meet again. Again, Roberta brings up the Maggie incident and tells Twyla that she really believed Maggie was Black, and that the violence against her was racially motivated. Roberta confesses wanting to participate in the assault, even though she did not. The story ends with Roberta crying with frustration that they will never know what really happened to Maggie.

The frustration Roberta and Twyla experience over the Maggie incident parallels the frustration readers experience as they try to determine the racial identities of the characters. The narrative continually frustrates any attempt to figure out the race of each character, and causes readers to examine their own assumptions about race. *See also* Music.

Lisa Cade Wieland


## Recovery

Set against a background that blends a realistic past with supernatural elements and folklore*, Toni Morrison's novels can be said to constitute an imaginative history of African Americans. They trace events from slavery* to the Great Migration*, through a Jazz Age Harlem* and postwar Ohio, through the Civil Rights movement to contemporary times. Along this sweep of history* readers encounter ghosts, modern-day tar babies, flying Africans, and, more commonly, characters left fragmented and traumatized by the world around them. Morrison's fiction documents these characters' attempts to put their lives back together again, to claim a sense of self that they lost or that they never had to begin with. Her work, therefore, offers lessons in recovery: the wounded struggle to heal, the forgotten seek a voice, discredited ways of knowing and being compete for recognition, and neglected stories of the past move toward center stage. Recovery may in fact be the most common theme in her writing.

Morrison frequently discusses her work in terms of recovery. In a 1988 interview with Christina Davis, she explains that official versions of history have erased or distorted the African American experience, so that Black people now face the task of setting the record straight by recovering the stories, the voices, the very presence of African Americans within a national consciousness. In "Rootedness: The Ancestor as Foundation," Morrison describes how the novel functions as a means of restoring that presence by providing the mythological and archetypal stories through which cultures define themselves. This process of self-definition, Morrison says, is a form of healing, with contemporary novels serving a purpose akin to music's* role in the African American community*.

In Morrison's fiction, then, recovery has several meanings and raises several questions. The term refers primarily to the reconstruction of an insufficiently acknowledged African American past and its rich traditions in myth* and storytelling. Historical recovery, in turn, should foster healing: restoring the presence leads to restoring the soul. For characters in her novels, however, such healing never comes easily. The past may exist as something to recover from more than to revisit; it may be something inaccessible, that characters can never truly know or understand, or mythic histories may offer insufficient antidotes for real problems in the present. Morrison's novels set the terms for recovery and consider its limits, reminding readers that easy solutions to life's difficult problems rarely exist. Yet recovery is also a necessary, driving force in her work, despite the complexities that it presents. Those who remain cut off from their pasts or their traumas* find themselves unable to cope with the present, especially when their troubles come to haunt them—and they usually do—in unexpected ways.

Critics such as Trudier Harris, Jill Matus, and Nancy J. Peterson have examined the role of history and healing in Morrison's fiction, noting how she creates narratives that run counter to official histories and traditional ways of knowing the past. She tells stories that might otherwise go untold, incorporates elements of folklore and myth, and asks readers to fill in the gaps of her nonlinear, sometimes ambiguous plots. In doing so, Morrison's work reexamines our most fundamental notions about the way American history and culture are constructed, and asks whether these constructions offer nourishing, sustaining environments in which everyone might grow. Whether the past is something that characters must recover or recover from in order to heal, it forms an elemental part of who they are in the present and where they will go in the future. Their struggles offer lessons that all readers might heed.

In three of Morrison's novels—*Beloved\**, *Jazz\**, and *Paradise\**—the past is a trauma that characters must recover from, and they rely upon violent, but not always successful, means of doing so. Her most poignant work, *Beloved*, recounts the psychological horrors of slavery* that linger in the mind long after physical freedom has been obtained. For Sethe Suggs*, an escaped slave, those horrors reach their nadir when she murders her own baby girl rather than have the child taken back to the plantation, ironically named Sweet Home*. The daughter's ghost continues to haunt Sethe, breaking up her family, driving away the community, and eventually leading Sethe to the brink of death* herself. Only when the townspeople come together to exorcise Beloved's* ghost can Sethe, along with her Sweet Home friend Paul D Garner*, begin the recovery process. The novel's ending suggests, however, that while the ghost of the past may be forgotten, it is never completely gone, and its potential for emotional destruction might be held only temporarily at bay. In addition to telling the story of Sethe (one based upon the actual account of Margaret Garner*, an escaped slave who similarly murders her child), *Beloved* acts as a meditation on communal healing. Its epigraph mentions the millions of African Americans who were enslaved, and the novel also charts the ways in which a culture learns to survive during and after a holocaust. One of its primary characters is Baby Suggs*, Sethe's mother-in-law, who teaches escaped and freed slaves to love themselves through her impromptu sermons in the woods. Both her story and Sethe's recall a historical moment that our nation has yet to fully come to terms with, suggesting that healing will happen only—if it happens at all—when our national ghosts are recognized for what they are and for the harm they continue to do.

*Paradise* and *Jazz* take African American history forward, into the Great Migration of families from the Reconstruction and Jim Crow South, where rights and freedoms enacted by federal law rarely materialized in fact, to Western and Northern states, where opportunities seem endless. While characters in these novels seem to be functioning normally and successfully in their new locations, their premigration experiences continue to boil under the surface, leading them to destructive acts. As in *Beloved*, these novels show what happens when wounds of the past go untended rather than heal successfully. In *Paradise*, inhabitants of an Oklahoma town find their refuge from whites unraveling under the pressure of class and skin-color prejudice. Town fathers exert an enormous amount of control, trying to eliminate difference and prevent change. They insulate themselves from outsiders, carefully monitor who marries whom, and begin to blame a nearby commune of women for anything that goes wrong. Rather than maintain order, their efforts lead to tensions that eventually erupt in a violent outburst at the women's house on the outskirts of town. The supernatural also makes an appearance in this novel's ambiguous ending: Are the women killed, do they escape, do they live on as ghosts, and, most important, does their exorcism in any way help preserve Paradise?

Set during the Harlem Renaissance, *Jazz* also takes an act of violence as its central event. After Joe Trace* murders his much younger lover, Dorcas*, his wife Violet* is driven by jealousy to mutilate the girl's corpse. Because of past losses—caused in part by the disruption of families* and turmoil of life occasioned by slavery and events after the Civil War—Joe and Violet cannot cope with the possibility of loss in the present. Like Sethe and the townspeople of *Paradise*, they resort to drastic means to prevent further violence* against their souls. The novel ends with Violet and Joe returning to Dorcas's picture on the mantle, trying to understand where they have been and, by implication, where they might go. These three novels, often seen as a trilogy, offer readers important history lessons: although recovery as a process is often complicated and incomplete, traumatic events of the past must be confronted if one is to move forward into the future. Attempting to ignore or bury problems leads only to their coming back to haunt, sometimes literally.

*The Bluest Eye** and *Sula** cover African American experience in mid-twentieth-century, where individuals lived farther away from the traumas of slavery and Reconstruction, but still felt the negative effects of social marginalization. In these novels, the past is not as much the problem for characters as prevailing cultural norms; however, like *Beloved*, *Paradise*, and *Jazz*, they show how individuals and communities can be driven to drastic means while attempting to heal. *The Bluest Eye*, Morrison's first novel, examines how aesthetic standards derived from white culture can be detrimental to Blacks. Because the Breedlove family believe themselves to be physically ugly, their lives descend into existential ugliness. The mother, Pauline*, rejects her own family in favor of her white employer's home and children; the misguided attempts of the father, Cholly*, to compensate for his perceived shortcomings as provider result in his raping their daughter Pecola*, and Pecola believes that having blue eyes will deliver her from poverty and abuse. She is a child whom no one can save: not the stable, loving MacTeer family who take her in, not the prostitutes* who accept her for herself, not Soaphead Church*, a minister and pedophile whose attempt to make her believe that she has blue eyes finally drives her over the edge of sanity. The novel is framed by the voice of Claudia MacTeer*, near in age to Pecola, who mourns the loss of the child whom she compares to a flower planted in bad soil, and who strives to find meaning in a story that ostensibly has none.

*Sula* similarly tries to recover the dignity of people who do not seem to count within the culture at large. Residents of the Bottom* inhabit the rocky hillside land rejected by white people in the valley. They look to Sula as a scapegoat for their woes because of her unconventional lifestyle, while Sula looks to her friend Nel Wright* for comfort and stability. When Sula has an affair with Nel's husband, loses her friend, and ultimately dies alone, the Bottom residents are at a loss. Turning their attention to Shadrack*, a shell-shocked veteran of World War I, they eventually follow him to an ironic and tragic end. In celebration of National Suicide Day*, he leads them into a tunnel that collapses, leaving the town virtually deserted and open again to whites, who decide that they prefer hillside homes after all.

While *The Bluest Eye* and *Sula* castigate white culture in general for practices and values that traumatize Blacks, *Tar Baby** and *Song of Solomon** focus on two particular institutions: traditional nuclear families and middle-class respectability. Both of these novels, set in contemporary times, bring Morrison's examination of African American experience into the present moment and posit recovery of history and myth as cure for modern spiritual backruptcy. *Tar Baby*'s Margaret* and Valerian Street*—white, well-off, and relatively self-sufficient on their West Indian plantation—live with their servants Ondine and Sydney Childs*, characters described as well-bred Philadelphia Negros. The Streets' outward show of success, however, masks a dysfunctional household with a history of child abuse at its core. The novel's revelations are set in a motion by the return of Jadine Childs*, Ondine and Sydney's niece, whom the Streets have helped toward a modeling career, and the arrival of Son*, who stows away on Margaret Street's boat but is later invited into her family's home*. Son eventually saves himself from these characters' superficial respectability through supernatural means: running from his obsession with Jadine, he becomes absorbed into the island itself, apparently joining the legendary French cavaliers who haunt it.

Milkman Dead*, in *Song of Solomon*, experiences a similar fate, and his story stands as one of Morrison's clearest statements on the possibilities for historical and psychic recovery. As Milkman's last name suggests, he is emotionally and culturally stunted. His family, although traditional and successful, is trapped in a cycle of anger and resentment. Milkman has no ties to his past or to any person, with the exception of his aunt, Pilate Dead*, who lives with her daughter Reba* and her granddaughter Hagar*, and whose immediate family offers a spiritually nourishing counterpart to Milkman's own. (Similar multigenerational trios exist in *Sula* and *Beloved*, indicating Morrison's belief that "traditional" family may be defined differently from the father-mother-two-children norm.) Only by seeking out his family's history can Milkman grow. He returns to his father's and Pilate's birthplace, ostensibly looking for gold, and learns there the story of his great-grandfather Solomon*, a legendary figure who escaped slavery by flying away. By reconnecting with his roots, Milkman very literally learns to stand tall (a limp he has had since childhood mysteriously disappears), learns how much he loves Pilate, and learns how to understand—if not to forgive—his parents' shortcomings. The novel's end also leaves him presumably learning, like Solomon, how to fly.

As in several Morrison novels, however, this ending poses problems. Is Milkman's flight literal or metaphorical? Does it represent healing or escape? Morrison's ambiguity is most likely deliberate. The goal of her fiction is not so much to document a character's recovery as to engage readers in the process of revising their own understanding of the history, myths, and traditions they have been given. They must decide for themselves what happens and, therefore, how to interpret the act. Morrison's art is that of the storyteller, who depends upon listener participation to create meaning, and who transmits culture in ways often more profound than those who delineate our official versions of history. *Song of*

*Solomon*, in fact, is framed by a very real past: the modern Civil Rights movement as a background reminds the audience that the struggle to claim the voice, and a rightful place in history, is more than a rhetorical issue within the pages of a book. The answers that Morrison provides are never easy, but the questions she asks are always compelling. *See also* Approaches to Morrison's Work: Historical; Flying Africans, Myth of; Ghost Story, Use of; Memory.

References: Christina Davis, "Interview with Toni Morrison," *Presence Africaine* 145 (1988); Trudier Harris, *Fiction and Folklore: The Novels of Toni Morrison* (1991); Nancy J. Peterson, "'Say Make Me, Remake Me': Toni Morrison and the Reconstruction of African-American History," in *Toni Morrison: Critical and Theoretical Approaches*, ed. Nancy J. Peterson (1997).

Julie Buckner Armstrong

## Rekus (*Sula*)

*Sula* Peace's* father and Hannah Peace's husband. Rekus is a "laughing man" who dies when Sula is three years old. *See also Sula*.

Douglas Taylor

## Romantic Tradition

Toni Morrison's art defies easy classification. One may find her novels categorized within several literary contexts at once: the modernism of writers such as William Faulkner*, the postmodernism of Thomas Pynchon, the magical realism* of Gabriel García Márquez, Zora Neale Hurston's Black vernacular, or Alice Walker's African American feminism. Compounding this difficulty is Morrison's own disdain of attempts to pigeonhole her writing into any canon. Literary critics, nevertheless, continue to locate within her richly allusive texts affinities to a variety of writers and traditions. Within the past few years, Morrison has been examined alongside practitioners of American literary romance, Nathaniel Hawthorne in particular, with comparisons made between *Beloved** and *The Scarlet Letter*, as well as *Song of Solomon** and *The House of the Seven Gables*. Morrison has also emerged as a leading critic of the genre; her *Playing in the Dark: Whiteness and the Literary Imagination** examines connections between race* and romance, through writers such as Edgar Allan Poe and Herman Melville.

"Romance" is a term that defies easy classification. What critics refer to as American literary romance has roots in classical epics and medieval quest narratives, where heroes journey through otherworldly landscapes, encounter dramatic adventures, and pursue clearly defined goals. Similar elements occur in Milkman Dead's* search for gold in *Song of Solomon*. Other related modes include the gothic* fictions and historical romances of the eighteenth and early nineteenth centuries, echoes of which may be found in *Beloved*, where the past comes back to haunt the present in a very literal way. The romance also shares linguistic and ideological roots with the romantic movement, where the tension between William Wordsworth's idealism and Lord Byron's skepticism manifests itself as a Hawthornian or Melvillian inquiry into what human beings can know for certain. Morrison's work participates in this inquiry too, constantly calling into question established truths, stereotypes, and constructions of history*. Perhaps the most often quoted definitions of the term come from Hawthorne, who opposed his romantic mode of writing to the novel's realism in a series of prefaces to his published works. Romance, Hawthorne notes, blends the "Actual" and the "Imaginary," allowing writers to experiment with the "possible" rather than confine themselves to the "probable." In other words, writers of romance do not attempt to mirror the customs, manners, and codes of a recognizable world as much as they work within the realm of symbol, myth*, or allegory.

This definition, as Hawthorne outlines and critic Richard Chase later clarifies, would distinguish between a realistic novel of manners by a writer such as Jane Austen and works such as *Moby Dick* and *The Scarlet Letter*. Emily Miller Budick summarizes more recent criticism on this topic, which asks whether romance constitutes an evasion of socioeconomic and political realities or just a different way of examining them. *The Scarlet Letter*, for instance, does not offer readers a glimpse into Puritans' daily lives as they might actually have lived them, but it does engage political questions relevant to both Hawthorne's time and our own: What does it mean to be a member of a community*? How does one decide what to believe from a range of competing perspectives and interpretations? What is the relationship of the past to the present? These questions concern Toni Morrison, too, and she asks them in each of her novels.

*Song of Solomon* closely resembles what Hawthorne would call "romance." In this work, Morrison juxtaposes the "actual" world of Milkman Dead to the "imaginary" realm of myth occupied by his great-grandfather Solomon*, who supposedly escaped slavery* by flying away. Milkman, as his surname implies, is spiritually and emotionally dead, with no direction to his life and unable to find a meaningful, nourishing connection to his family, his friends, or his past. Partially to escape this situation, and partially because he thinks that he may find hidden gold, Milkman returns to his father's birthplace, where he learns more about his family* history and especially the story of Solomon—a kind of "gold" very different from what he expected. Milkman's spiritual guide along the way is his aunt Pilate Dead*, who also stretches the limits of the possible with her almost magical powers and her mysterious lack of a navel. Although Milkman's journey does reveal a certain amount of sociopolitical reality (his family's past is a microcosm of African American history from slavery to migration* to the North to a contemporary return to roots), the novel is more accurately an imaginative, and skeptical, engagement with what it means to be both Black and American. Like *The Scarlet Letter, Song of Solomon* explores tensions between the individual and the community*, and between competing versions of truth and history.

Morrison continues to ask probing questions about America as well as its literature in her criticism. *Playing in the Dark*, a collection of lectures given at Harvard University, investigates the mostly white, mostly male canon of American literature to find recurring examples of what she calls the Africanist presence at work. The book's second section, "Romancing the Shadow," is particularly important for understanding American literary romance. Here, Morrison argues that romance does not evade history and reality, but instead offers a very real exploration of contradictions inherent in American society. Most obviously, the early romancers' investigations of individual free will emerged within the context of slavery: classic writers Hawthorne and Melville both completed their best work during the 1850s. The romantic tensions between guilt and sin, light and dark (as noted by Richard Chase) are revealing, too. What might Americans feel guilty of, Morrison asks, and what lies behind our best writers' obsession with what Melville called "the power of blackness"? Morrison also asks readers to pay careful attention to the ways in which African American characters and the color black itself are used to advance plots, create tone, or shape themes, and her reading of Poe's *The Narrative of Arthur Gordon Pym* outlines how the Africanist presence is often used as an "Other" against which writers define such terms as "white," "free," "individual," and "American."

Since the early nineteenth century, romance has been viewed as a form with particular possibilities for America. For Hawthorne, it was a means of distinguishing his own, and his nation's, writing from a European literature that leaned toward realism. For contemporary critics, Morrison included, romance is a means of exploring certain American issues or problems. Although her fiction draws its strength from a variety of sources in addition to the romantic tradition, she has become increasingly recognized as one of our foremost practitioners of it. *See also* Flying Africans, Myth of.

References: Eberhard Alsen, ed., *The New Romanticism: A Collection of Critical Essays* (2000); Emily Miller Budick, *Engendering Romance: Women Writers and the Hawthorne Tradition, 1850–1990* (1989); Richard Chase, *The American Novel and Its Tradition* (1990).

Julie Buckner Armstrong

## Rose Dear (*Jazz*)

Violet Trace's* mother, whose name symbolizes her emotional fragility. Deserted first by her mother, who, as a slave, was forced to move to Baltimore with Vera Louise Gray*, then by her husband, whose radical politics forced him to abandon his family and move from the South, Rose Dear becomes severely depressed. Although rescued by True Belle*, her mother, who returns from Virginia to care for her daughter and five granddaughters, Rose Dear eventually commits suicide by hurling herself into the recesses of a well, which haunts Violet, now herself symbolically orphaned. *See also Jazz.*

Caroline Brown

## Ruby, Oklahoma (*Paradise*)

The primary setting of *Paradise*, Ruby (population of 360 in 1976) is an all-Black town in Oklahoma with no need for a jail, bus stop, café, or gas station. Ruby was founded in 1951 by the "fifteen families," descendants of the "nine families" who had established the all-Black town of Haven, Oklahoma*, in 1890. Returning from World War II, many of Haven's men found the town failing and decided to move farther into Oklahoma to begin anew, as their fathers and grandfathers had done sixty years before. They established Ruby 240 miles west of Haven and 90 miles from the nearest town of Demby, but they brought with them the communal center of Haven, the Oven*, and rebuilt it. The new town remained nameless until 1954, when Ruby Morgan (sister of two of the town's most prominent men) died because no (white) hospital would admit her for treatment. Thus the town was named not only for a dead woman, but also as a reminder of white racism and segregation. Except for a few people, all of the original citizens of Ruby are coal black, a shade designated "8-rock" by Patricia Best Cato*, the unofficial town historian. The original nine families of Haven were also "8-rock," and it was their dark skin color that not only prevented them from finding jobs in the South after the overthrow of Reconstruction governments but also caused them to be rejected by the all-Black but light-skinned town of Fairly, Oklahoma* (an act dubbed "the Disallowing"). Consequently, a reverse hierarchy of skin color—from dark to light—governs within the city limits.

When the town begins to struggle with a generational division fostered by the Civil Rights movement, symbolized by the tilting foundation of the Oven, nine men attack the Convent*, the home of five no-longer haunted women that is located seventeen miles outside of Ruby, in July 1976. When the (presumably) slaughtered women's bodies disappear, the citizens understand that God has given Ruby another chance, a chance that can be successful only if they are willing to change. *See also Paradise.*

Julie Cary Nerad

## Ryna's Gulch (*Song of Solomon*)

Ravine where the wind sounds like a woman howling. Supposedly the howling is that of Ryna, Solomon's* wife, who screamed out loud for days after he flew away and left her behind to care for their twenty-one children. It is in this valley that Guitar Baines* hides, and shoots and kills Pilate Dead*. *See also Song of Solomon.*

Fiona Mills

# S

## Schoolteacher (*Beloved*)

Schoolteacher is the name that Sethe Suggs* and her peers bestow upon Mr. Garner's* brother, who takes over management of Sweet Home* following Garner's death. So named because he is constantly taking notes, schoolteacher personifies scientific racism, out to prove his belief that Blacks are subhuman and that slavery* is their manifest destiny. After he took over at Sweet Home, he initiated a series of cruel practices that forced the enslaved population to plot a mass exodus. He supervised the capture and torture-death of Sixo* during the latter's escape attempt. He ordered Sethe's forced "milking" and her subsequent beating; under the full force of the Fugitive Slave Law, he tracked Sethe and her children to 124 Bluestone Road*, creating the circumstances that culminated in Sethe's attack on her own children*. In short, schoolteacher's cruel form of slavery led ultimately to the total depletion of Sweet Home's enslaved population. *See also Beloved.*

Lovalerie King

## Seneca (*Paradise*)

A childlike twenty-year-old, Seneca, title character of one of *Paradise*'s nine sections, arrives at the Convent* in 1973. Her boyfriend, Eddie Turtle, has been convicted for the hit-and-run death of a child, and Seneca has been unsuccessfully attempting to get money for his defense from his mother when the rich and beautiful Norma Keene Fox finds her in a Wichita bus station. After three weeks of being Fox's "personal assistant" and sexual toy, Seneca is paid $500 and sent on her way, confused and afraid to return to Eddie. Hitching rides to nowhere in particular, she sees the weeping, uncombed, coatless Sweetie Fleetwood walking down the road through an approaching blizzard, and remembers another crying Black woman she saw when she was five, just after her mother (whom she thought was her sister) abandoned her in their government housing apartment, leaving only a scrawled note written in lipstick that she could never read, first because she was too young, and then because, smeared by tears and sweat from her shoes (where she kept it), it had become unreadable. Shipped from one foster home to another after being sexually abused by a foster brother, Seneca grows up trying only to please those around her. She develops an early association between wounds (usually small cuts) and sympathy, and thus regularly cuts herself with a razor, making fine, straight "roads" that flood with blood but look surgical in their precision.

Having followed Sweetie to the Convent and having no place else to go, Seneca stays, attempting the impossible task of keeping peace between Mavis Albright* and her roommate/sexual partner, Gigi (Grace Gibson*). Seneca's "loud-dreaming" and ritual painting on the basement floor allow her to transfer her cuts from her own body to her traced image. Seneca is shot down in the grass while attempting to escape the men of Ruby, Oklahoma*, but later appears to the reader in a stadium parking lot with a friend (presumably Gigi) rinsing her cut hands with beer. Her sister/mother Jean approaches her, misremembers their old address, and does not know for certain that the woman is Seneca until they are separated once again. *See also Paradise.*

Julie Cary Nerad

## Seven Days, The (*Song of Solomon*)

A politically motivated group of African American men who avenge the deaths of Blacks killed by whites. Guitar Baines*, Porter, and Robert Smith* belong to this group. *See also Song of Solomon.*

Fiona Mills

## Sex/Sexuality

One of Morrison's many important contributions to African American literary history is her groundbreaking treatment of sex and sexuality. Morrison was one of the first Black American writers to explore and depict sexuality's full spectrum of possibility, its capacity to express love, hate, joy, sadness, compassion, lust, and even longing for spiritual transcendence. For Morrison, sex is as much a part of life as birth and death*, and she treats it the same way that she approaches all aspects of human relationships—without sentiment or censure. Although many contemporary readers might take this attitude for granted, to fully appreciate the significance of Morrison's treatment of this subject, we must first locate her work in the larger historical context of Black American history*.

Since the inception of the African American literary tradition in the eighteenth century, Black authors have always carried the burden of representing the race*. Black writers were obliged to present African Americans in the best light possible in order to combat racist stereotypes, including the belief that peoples of African descent possessed animal-like, uncontrolled libidos. An awareness of this stereotype contributed to a history of Black writing that was often quite conservative in its treatment of sexuality. When writers such as Claude McKay, Nella Larsen, and Langston Hughes dared to address sexuality openly during the Harlem Renaissance, they were often condemned by Black critics for seeming to pander to and perpetuate white racist stereotypes.

The pressure to produce positive images was as powerful as ever in 1970 when Morrison published her first novel, *The Bluest Eye**, which details the psychological disintegration of a little girl after she is raped by her father. Morrison knowingly broke the taboo of speaking openly about such a dark issue, as she insisted on producing fiction that described every aspect of the Black community*—including good and bad experiences. Morrison presents rape in this work as symptomatic of American race relations. Pecola Breedlove's* rape is partly the result of her father, Cholly*, having been "raped" by white men when he was a teenager; these men surprise Cholly while he is having sex with a girl in the woods, and then force him at gunpoint to continue. Morrison tells us that Cholly hated the girl who was his sexual partner because she had witnessed his failure, and that he later transfers this shame and hatred to Pecola, another girl whom he cannot protect from the destructive forces of a racist American society. Rape has equally devastating effects in *Beloved**, especially when Sethe Suggs* has her milk stolen by schoolteacher* and his nephews*. Halle Suggs*, Sethe's partner, is psychologically destroyed after he watches this act from the rafters of the barn; here again Morrison is attuned to the enormous psychic cost borne by Black men who feel unable to protect Black women from sexual violation. The threat of rape sets the action of *Tar Baby** in motion, but here Morrison deliberately toys with the myth* of the Black male rapist; the ordered white household of L'Arbe de la Croix* is turned upside down when Son*, the protagonist, is found sitting in a white woman's closet.

Overall, however, Morrison sees sexuality in positive terms, as a vital means of connecting with oneself and with others. Morrison reserves some of her most lyrical passages for her descriptions of lovemaking, such as Pauline Breedlove's* memory of better times with Cholly in *The Bluest Eye*. Pauline achieves a prismatic ecstasy—one of june bugs, berry juice, lemonade, and rainbows—one of the few moments of pure joy in what is otherwise a relentlessly dark novel.

Some of Morrison's *least* sympathetic characters are the ones who dislike sex, such as Helene Wright* in *Sula*\*, Geraldine in *The Bluest Eye*, and Jadine* in *Tar Baby*. Helene is harsh and rigid, and she spends her life trying to compensate for her origins as a prostitute's daughter by meeting the world with an attitude of severity and domination. Geraldine represents a type of African American woman that Morrison describes as obsessed with controlling the uncontrollable messiness of sexuality, nature, and human emotion. Jadine deals with the loss of her mother as a child by becoming a cold adult who manipulates men in passionless relationships. All of these characters share a capacity for cruelty, snobbery, and racial self-loathing. Morrison uses their negative attitude toward sexuality as an index to their sense of alienation.

In stark contrast are Eva*, Hannah*, and Sula Peace* in *Sula*. All three of these women are wholly unashamed of their sexuality. Hannah, Sula's mother, has a constant stream of different partners, and Sula inherits her mother's free-spirited attitude toward sex. Morrison explicitly links Sula's sexual aggressiveness with her lust for life, her desire to do and experience everything. However, Morrison also knows that sexual freedom can come with a high price. When Sula returns to her hometown after her travels, her irreverent attitude and actions frighten and upset the community, who then use her sexual libertinism as an excuse to ostracize her. Morrison makes this point even more clearly in *Paradise*\*, where several men from Ruby, Oklahoma*, a small Black community, murder a group of unmarried women living together on the outskirts of town for (allegedly) torturing children, promiscuity, and lesbianism. The citizens of Ruby demonize the Convent* women as a way of dealing with the internal strife developing in the community between the different generations.

In *Paradise*, Morrison also explores the relationship of sexuality and spirituality*—Christianity in particular. The Convent itself was originally a Prohibition-era bootlegger's pleasure cove, and its explicitly erotic decor, including obscene statuary and phallic door fixtures, survived despite the efforts of nuns, who lived there after the original owner abandoned the house, to destroy them. The fusion of sexual and spiritual longing is clearest in Consolata Sosa* (Connie), who transfers her all-encompassing love of Christ to one of the townsmen, Deacon (Deek) Morgan*. At one point she bites his lip, unconsciously performing the rite of the Eucharist on her lover. Morrison reinforces the connection between sexuality and spirituality at the novel's end when Consolata introduces the Convent women to a female god, Piedade*, a divinity that one critic has compared to the female god described in the Gnostic gospels, a god reminiscent of antiquity's highly sexual fertility gods.

John Charles

## Shadrack (*Sula*)

Shell-shocked African American veteran of World War I who returns to the Bottom* to found National Suicide Day*. Shadrack's name is taken from the book of Daniel in which three Jews—Shadrack, Meschach, and Abednego—are sent to the fiery furnace by King Nebuchadnezzar for refusing to worship the king's gods and, miraculously, survive. *See also Sula.*

Douglas Taylor

## Shakespeare, William, Use of

*See Tar Baby* (1981).

## Shame

"Shame is a multidimensional, multilayered experience," observes shame theorist Gershen Kaufman. "While first of all an individual phenomenon experienced in some form and to some degree by every person, shame is equally a family phenomenon and a cultural phenomenon. It is reproduced within families, and each culture has its own distinct sources as well as targets of shame" (191). Describing herself as living in "a present that wishes both to exploit and deny the pervasiveness of racism," and in a society in which African Americans have had to "bear the brunt of everybody else's contempt" (xiv; Angelo 256), Morrison focuses attention on the ubiquity and complexity of shame—the so-called master emotion in the African American experience. In the classic shame scenario, the individual feels exposed and humiliated—looked at with contempt for being unworthy, flawed, or dirty—and thus wants to hide or disappear in an attempt to protect against feelings of painful exposure.

At once an interpersonal and intrapsychic experience, shame derives from the sufferer's "vicarious experience of the other's scorn," and indeed central to the shame experience is the "self-in-the-eyes-of-the-other" (Lewis 15). In her novels, Morrison dramatizes the painful sense of exposure that accompanies the single shame event, and she also depicts the devastating effect of chronic shame and internalized racism on her characters' sense of individual and social identity*, describing their socially produced feelings of self-loathing and self-contempt, their feelings that they are, in some essential way, inferior, defective, and/or dirty. Examining the individual, familial, and cultural impact of racial shame, Morrison's novels expose to public view the painful collective and private shame suffered by Black Americans in our race-conscious American society.

That Black shame derives from the vicarious experience of white scorn becomes evident in *Beloved*'s* description of the formative and "dirtying" power of racist practices and representations. Despite her proud demeanor, Morrison's ex-slave character, Sethe Suggs*, is a woman tormented by humiliating memories of schoolteacher's* contemptuous treatment of her. A practitioner of the nineteenth-century pseudoscience of race*, schoolteacher asks Sethe and the other Sweet Home* slaves questions and takes measurements of them, then writes down his observations in his notebook. Viewing the slaves as animalistic—that is, as fundamentally and biologically different from white people—schoolteacher is intent, as he makes his inquiries, on documenting their racial inferiority.

Although Sethe initially thinks that schoolteacher is a fool, she is humiliated when she overhears him instructing his nephews* on how to describe her as a member of a lower race by listing her human traits on one side of the page and her animal traits on the other. The contemptuous racist discourse of schoolteacher engenders feelings of self-contempt in Sethe, who feels dirtied when she is suddenly made aware of schoolteacher's profound disgust for her race, and when schoolteacher's nephews subsequently milk her like an animal, one boy sucking on her breast and the other holding her down, while schoolteacher watches and records his observations. The fact that Sethe remains distressed by these humiliating moments of exposure years later reveals the magnitude of the shame she feels on learning of her designated role as the contemptible and degraded racial inferior.

When Sethe slits the throat of her child with a handsaw, she commits her act of rough love to keep her children from being dirtied—that is, shamed—by whites. Her act grows out of her awareness that whites not only can work, kill, or maim the slaves but also can dirty them so much that they cannot like themselves anymore or forget who they are. Sethe wants to protect her children* from the dehumanizing forces of slavery and the dirtying power of racist discourse. While whites might dirty her, Sethe determines that they will not dirty her children, the best part of her and the part that is clean. And no one, she resolves, will ever list her daughter's traits on the animal side of the paper.

If in *Beloved* Morrison describes how slavery and white contempt dirty the slaves, in *The Bluest Eye*\* she depicts the damaging impact of racial shame on the lives of the poor and Black Breedloves. Living in a racist society that tells them Black is ugly and finding support for their racial ugliness in every billboard, movie, and glance, the Breedloves internalize the contempt directed at them from the shaming gaze of the dominant white culture and believe that they are, in fact, ugly. *The Bluest Eye*, in its unremitting focus on the self-hatred of the Breedloves, points to the pernicious effects of white contempt and internalized racism. And in depicting the racial shaming of Pecola Breedlove\*, *The Bluest Eye* dramatizes an extreme form of the shame vulnerability suffered by Black Americans in white America.

Intent on revealing the terrible damage that racial contempt can cause in a child, Morrison shows the impact of learned cultural shame on Pecola. What Pecola learns from her parents—that, like them, she is ugly—is confirmed by the unfriendly gaze and insulting speech of others. In the gaze of the white storeowner, Mr. Yacobowski, for example, Pecola senses racial contempt. In his glazed, vacant look—his inability to see her—Pecola senses his distaste for her Black skin. Pecola is also shamed by a group of Black boys who circle her in the school playground, holding her at bay. Their feelings of learned self-hatred and hopelessness become expressed in their angry, insulting speech as they dance around Pecola, who, for their own sake, they treat with scorn. By humiliating Pecola, as the narrative makes clear, the boys express their deep-rooted contempt for their own Black identity\*.

In another scene that points to the role of intraracial shaming in the construction of a stigmatized racial identity—the encounter between Pecola and Geraldine—*The Bluest Eye* focuses attention on the color-caste hierarchy and the link between class and shame within the African American community. To a middle-class woman like Geraldine, a lighter-skinned "colored" person of order and precision, lower class, dark-skinned Blacks like Pecola are dirty and disorderly "niggers." When Geraldine looks at Pecola—who has a torn and soiled dress, muddy shoes and dirty socks, and matted hair—she feels that children like Pecola are everywhere. Dirty, smelly, and disgusting, such children sleep six in a bed, their urine mixing together as they wet their beds. Where they live, flowers die and tin cans and tires blossom. Like flies, such children hover and settle. Openly expressing her contempt, Geraldine uses shaming words to reinforce Pecola's feeling that she is a disgusting and worthless human being.

Feeling utterly flawed and dirty, Pecola defends herself by withdrawing and hiding; squeezing her eyes shut, she even imagines the physical disappearance of her body. Remarking on the connection between shame and the wish to hide or disappear, shame theorist Leon Wurmser explains that the purpose of hiding is "to prevent further exposure and, with that, further rejection, but it also atones for the exposure that has already occurred" (54). "If it is appearance (exposure) that is central in shame, disappearance is the logical outcome of shame … ," writes Wurmser (81). Rejecting her despised Black identity, Pecola imagines that she can cure her ugliness—that is, her racial shame—only if she is miraculously granted the same blue eyes that little white girls possess. As Morrison describes the racial self-loathing of Pecola, she dramatizes the devastating impact of racial contempt on her shame-vulnerable character who has so internalized white contempt for her Blackness that she desires blue eyes so others will love and accept her.

In novel after novel Morrison draws attention to the damaging impact of white racist practices and learned cultural shame on the collective African American experience. Just as Morrison shows how Sethe is "dirtied" by slavery and schoolteacher's racist discourse and how Pecola feels racially flawed because she lives in a culture that views Black as ugly, so in *Song of Solomon** she shows how the shame-haunted Hagar Dead* comes to see herself as a racially spoiled Black underclass woman and how the middle-class Milkman Dead* is burdened by the "shit" of inherited family and racial shame; in *Sula**, how the uninhibited and rebellious Sula*, who insists that she likes her own dirt, hides her abiding sense of shame under a defiant display of shamelessness; in *Tar Baby**, how the elitist Jadine* confronts her deep-seated shame anxiety about her racial identity in her ultimately failed love relationship with Son*, whom she initially sees, through the lens of inherited racist stereotypes, as a racially inferior and uncivilized underclass man; and in *Paradise**, how the 8-rock people of Ruby, Oklahoma*, are shaped by their collective, and humiliating, memory* of the Disallowing, the dismissal of their dark-skinned ancestors by light-skinned Blacks, who shunned the 8-rock people because they viewed dark skin as a racial "stain." Also investigating the class tensions and divisions within the African American community, Morrison deals with the sensitive issue of the color-caste hierarchy as she repeatedly brings together dark-skinned, lower-class and light-skinned, middle-class characters, such as Pecola and Geraldine in *The Bluest Eye*, Son and Jadine in *Tar Baby*, and Pilate* and Ruth Dead* in *Song of Solomon*, or as, in *Paradise*, she focuses on the color prejudice of the dark-skinned people of Ruby toward light-skinned Blacks.

While Morrison is intent on representing Black pride in her novels— such as Milkman's discovery of his "golden" racial heritage in the myth of the flying Africans* in *Song of Solomon*, or Violet* and Joe Trace's* sense of expansive Black pride and self-ownership as they train-dance their way to Black Harlem* in *Jazz**, or the pride the people of Ruby take in their utopian all-Black town in *Paradise*—she also shows how the humiliated memories and experiences that result from living in a racist society reverberate in the lives of her characters. As she stages scenes of inter- and intraracial shaming in her novels, Morrison uses her fiction to aestheticize—and thus to gain narrative mastery over—the painful race matters she describes. An author who has earned the pride of place among contemporary American novelists, Morrison explores the collective and private shame of African American life in a complex art form that conveys, but also aesthetically contains and controls, intensely painful feelings of racial shame. *See also* Approaches to Morrison's Work: Psychoanalytic; Trauma.

References: Bonnie Angelo, "The Pain of Being Black: An Interview with Toni Morrison," in *Conversations with Toni Morrison,* ed. Danielle Taylor-Guthrie (1994); J. Brooks Bouson, *Quiet as It's Kept: Shame, Trauma and Race in the Novels of Toni Morrison* (2000); Gershen Kaufman, *Shame: The Power of Caring* (1980; 3rd ed., rev. and enl., 1992); Helen Block Lewis, "Introduction: Shame—the 'Sleeper' in Psychopathology," in *The Role of Shame in Symptom Formation,* ed. Helen Block Lewis (1987); Andrew Morrison, *The Culture of Shame* (1996); Donald Nathanson, *Shame and Pride: Affect, Sex, and the Birth of the Self* (1994); Leon Wurmser, *The Mask of Shame* (1994).

J. Brooks Bouson

## Singing Bird (*Song of Solomon*)

Jake's* wife, mother of Macon Dead* and Pilate Dead*, and Milkman Dead's* grandmother. She is part Native American. Her name is the last word to cross Jake's lips. *See also Song of Solomon.*

Fiona Mills

## Sixo (*Beloved*)

Present only in the memories of Sethe Suggs* and Paul D Garner*, Sixo is the most apparent symbol of physical resistance in *Beloved*. He is described as being very dark-skinned and very resistant to the rules of slavery*, even the "liberal" rules of Sweet Home* under Mr. Garner's* regime. Having been brought to Sweet Home as an adult, Sixo provides a stark contrast to the brothers Paul*, because he never accepted willingly the premise that he was destined to be a slave. Born and raised in Africa, Sixo needed no white man to tell him that he was a man. He asserted his humanity in a number of ways, most obviously by refusing to use farm animals as sexual surrogates and by resisting slavery in numerous ways. He helped Sethe look after her children, especially after schoolteacher* increased the demands on her time. He walked over thirty miles to visit his lover, Patsy*. Associated with trees among which he danced at night, Sixo represents an African ideal of manhood. Under New World slavery he was the quintessential rebel, and his presence disrupted the smooth operations of the system. Along with Halle Suggs*, he planned the escape from Sweet Home. He negated certain principles of schoolteacher's scientific racism, and thus he was doomed. A powerful, larger-than-life character, Sixo was both very strong and very gentle. The story details two major confrontations between Sixo and schoolteacher. The first ends in Sixo being beaten, and the second ends in his being put to death during the 1855 escape attempt when schoolteacher finally realizes that he will never be a willing slave. *See also Beloved.*

Lovalerie King

## Slavery

Although permeating Morrison's novels, the contradictions and horrors of slavery are most clearly visible in *Beloved**. This particular text details the range of torments that white masters frequently inflicted upon their slaves. A selection of such cruelties would include that slaves regularly carried weights of up to 100 pounds; picked okra and other crops while carrying babies on their backs; and were lashed by young white boys, sons and grandsons of the masters.

Slave children* were perhaps at the greatest disadvantage, for as youngsters they had little opportunity to demonstrate proficiency at any household task or otherwise endear themselves to their employers. As a case in point, *Beloved*'s Baby Suggs* relates how her various owners were apt to suddenly take away her children. Two of Baby Suggs's daughters vanish so quickly that she cannot even say good-bye to them; furthermore, she also suffers the disgrace of having one of her sons traded for lumber, a human life bartered for building materials.

Six different men father Baby Suggs's eight children; masters treated female slaves as both physical and sexual property. Slave women could be taken by white men at any time, and even a female slave's marriage to a male slave did not prohibit a white man from taking liberties with her. In fact, demanding sexual services of female slaves was such a common occurrence that slaves noted the rare times when they were not ill-used. Baby Suggs notes that while she lived at Sweet Home, no one actually impregnated her. Mr. and Mrs. Garner*, Baby Suggs also observes, went against the norm and never studded (as one would stud an animal) their male slaves or bred the female slaves.

Just the same, slavery was a reality at Sweet Home*, and the Garners' plantation was not without its injustices. One example is the actual naming of the slaves: Mr. Garner calls Baby Suggs "Jenny" because that was the name on her sales ticket when he bought her. Throughout the years Mr. Garner never inquired as to her real name, and Baby Suggs answered to Jenny, never knowing why her new owners chose to call her that.

Only when she leaves Sweet Home does Baby Suggs reveal to Mr. Garner that she received her name from her husband. Mr. Garner advises her to keep her "white" name on account of "Baby Suggs" not being suitable for a mature freed slave woman. This battle over names and naming is one that Morrison introduces in *Song of Solomon**, when Macon (Jake) Dead*, a former slave, gets his name upon registering with the rather incompetent Freedman's Bureau. Jake's aversion to slavery passes down through his descendants, including the character Milkman*.

Milkman's interchanges with his friend Guitar Baines* demonstrate not only the injustice of whites' naming of slaves, but also the injustice of slave status and slave mentality. Milkman claims that Guitar's reactionary politics emulate those of Malcolm X, who wants white people to know that African Americans do not accept their slave names. Guitar, though, claims that slave names do not bother him, but slave status does. He wants neither to be an actual slave nor to feel as if he were; consequently, Guitar feels that his random murdering of a white person (in response to every random murdering of an African American) is an action that changes his slave status.

What comprises slave status continues to be of critical interest in *Jazz** with True Belle*, a slave who becomes a free woman. Because of her position as a slave, she observes things, including the fact that her mistress, Vera Louise Gray*, becomes pregnant by a slave. True Belle eventually leaves her own family* to follow Vera Louise when her parents disown her. During this time, white women who gave birth to nonwhite infants commonly deposited the children at the Catholic Foundling Hospital; Vera Louise kept the child, an act very much against the norm.

The relationship between Vera Louise's child and the child's father sheds light on public thought about slavery. When Vera Louise's child, Golden Gray*, confronts his father, Henry Lestory (Hunter's Hunter*), who had been unaware that he fathered this son, the two men engage in a dialogue about what slavery, race*, and color mean in their society. Golden defends his mother's actions, claiming that had Vera announced that he was nonwhite, he could have been enslaved. Lestory claims that Golden need not necessarily have been a slave, but instead could have been raised as a "free nigger." Golden, still ardently defending his mother's actions, claims that he wants to be a free man rather than a free slave; Hunter answers by stating that all men want to be free.

Slave status is continually explored in *Beloved*, where Baby Suggs is property and has a price (the property and price of slaves being knowledge with which another slave, Paul D Garner*, is well familiar); accordingly, Mr. Garner will not merely release or free her. Instead, he demands that someone buy her, a duty performed by another slave, for the only person to make an offer to buy her is her youngest son, Halle*.

To buy his mother's freedom, Halle works for neighboring plantation owners on Sundays for five years. After this period, he has earned enough to procure his mother from Mr. Garner. Halle is twenty-five at this time, and his mother is sixty. Due to her son's extraordinary sacrifice, Baby Suggs has approximately ten years of freedom; however, after leaving Sweet Home, she never sees any of her children again. Her freedom means abandoning the one child she has known the longest.

Baby Suggs's freedom, coming at so high a cost, means little to her when she looks back upon how she has already suffered as a slave. Baby Suggs suspects that the Garners had their own special type of slavery. Despite the fact that Mr. Garner listened to his slaves and did not consider deferring to their opinions to be depriving himself of authority or power, he nevertheless treated the slaves as if they were paid labor, teaching them only what he and his wife wanted known.

Although Baby Suggs never went hungry and was never cold, and taking into consideration that Mr. Garner allowed someone to buy her freedom, she knows that Mr. Garner will keep Halle and will still be renting out her son, perhaps even after she dies. She ultimately spends her final years unhappy and depressed, despising white people and eventually confining herself to her bed.

Life for another female slave, Sethe Suggs*, in *Beloved*, is more woeful than that of Baby Suggs. When Sethe informs her mistress, Mrs. Garner, that she wishes to marry, the woman smiles and soon laughs. Wedding ceremonies were not an option for slaves, and no slaves were truly married in the legal sense that white people were wed, a fact that Baby Suggs acknowledges to Mr. Garner when she leaves his plantation. Though Sethe and Halle ape white conventions by having a type of wedding, Morrison is careful to show that slavery is an institution which not only denies African Americans basic necessities but also continually mistreats them. Without Baby Suggs at Sweet Home and upon Mr. Garner's death, the slaves suffer much more than they had in years past. Mr. Garner is replaced by a white man the slaves call schoolteacher*, who brings his two nephews* with him. The nephews, with schoolteacher's approval, capture the pregnant Sethe and lecherously take her milk. In addition, schoolteacher beats her so badly that her back bleeds, becoming infected and permanently scarred.

As terrible as slavery is, *Beloved* shows that escape from slavery is possible. Sethe secretly sends her three children away from Sweet Home and she, in the late stages of pregnancy, soon follows. However, her freedom is temporary; schoolteacher searches for her and discovers her where-abouts. Four horsemen (schoolteacher, a nephew, a slave catcher, and a sheriff), representing the four riders of the Apocalypse from the book of Revelation, quietly travel to Sethe's home to capture her and her four children.

Yet in this pivotal scene in the novel, the men do not get to return schoolteacher's "property" to him; schoolteacher's appraisal of Sethe's value drops so low that he deems her not even worthy to be a slave. The men discover Sethe in a shed, attempting to kill her children so they would not have to return to a life of slavery. Weighing the balance between watching her children grow up as slaves (as Baby Suggs watched her own children grow up as slaves until all but one were sold away from her) and, even worse, slaves under schoolteacher's rule at Sweet Home, and suffering quick deaths at the hands of their mother, Sethe opts for the latter. She succeeds in murdering only her elder daughter.

For the second time, then, schoolteacher loses his slaves, and he now has no hopes of reacquisition. Confronted with Sethe's incredible car-nage, schoolteacher decides that she and her offspring are ruined, gone wild due to the mishandling of his nephews. (Of interest is that he does not blame himself and his beating of her.) Schoolteacher relinquishes his claims upon her, and Sethe is taken to a rat-infested jail with her younger daughter, whom Sethe is still nursing.

Males as well as females suffered the ills and injustices of slavery. Being a slave did not stop *Song of Solomon*'s Macon (Jake) Dead from having one of the best farms in Montour County, but being an African Ameri-can allowed white people to take his farm and to murder him in front of his two children. In *Beloved*, schoolteacher sells Paul D, another slave at Sweet Home, to a man named Brandywine. After Paul D attempts to kill his new owner, Brandywine does not slay the slave; instead, Brandywine sells Paul D to work on a chain gang in Alfred, Georgia.

Morrison's depiction of the life of a slave who works on the chain gang is perhaps one of the most fear-inspiring passages in all her oeuvre. The slaves dwell in an underground ditch, each man in a box five feet by five feet. Three white men are in charge of the forty-six slaves. The daily life of the slaves commences when the men wake to a rifle shot; they leave their cages only after the white men unlock the cage doors. Upon exit-ing their cages, the men chain themselves to each other. While chained, the slaves kneel down so that selected slaves may be forced to provide oral sex for the guards. Those slaves who attack are shot; after satisfying the guards, the slaves then toil for the entire day.

Just as the guards' treatment of the slaves is appalling, so is the slaves' habitation. One day a rainstorm appears and lasts for over a week. The ditch, swollen with water, begins to cave in on itself; the slaves, chained to each other, narrowly escape from the uncontrollable mud. As a result of their escape from death*, the slaves also manage to flee from the white men. The runaway slaves later meet some Cherokees who remove the slaves' connecting chain; this action is one that both literally and figuratively frees the men. No longer chained to each other by the white men's chain, the former slaves gain possession of their own lives and freedom.

Thus, the slave Paul D becomes a free man like those in Morrison's later novels. In *Paradise*, the future founders of Ruby, Oklahoma*, experience difficulty with other African Americans. These future founders, like the "Negro homesteaders" with whom they quarrel, are free men who were former slaves; nevertheless, the homesteaders think that the future founders do not have enough money to reside in communities surrounding the Negro homesteaders. As a result of the conflict, this new group of African Americans establishes Ruby, believing that for ten generations they fought to close the gaps between free versus slave, rich against poor, and white against Black.

Just as these two groups of African Americans experience discord, so Ruby's younger generation believes that former slaves would not tell African Americans to continually live in fear of God; they impart their dissatisfaction with such a view to the older generations of Ruby. During such an exchange, one Morgan brother resents hearing his grandfather being labeled an ex-slave, as if that were the summation of his grandfather, who was also an ex-lieutenant governor, an ex-banker, and an ex-deacon, among other things. However, Beauchamp maintains his conviction that African Americans born during slavery were only slaves, any other accomplishments being void and nil.

What Beauchamp suggests is that slavery is mentally overwhelming; one does oneself a disservice if one attempts to separate an African American from his or her history, no matter how insufferable that history may be. In the same novel, Patricia Best Cato* asks Richard Misner* whether his interest in Africa is due to its not having a history of slavery, thereby being the type of fantasy that Beauchamp's comment suggests. Misner and Patricia fail to come to an understanding; Misner asserts that he desires to rid his community* of slave mentality, while Patricia is firm that her past, Misner's past, and indeed her community's past, *is* slavery.

The history*, fact, folklore*, and fantasy of what is and was slavery explode within Morrison's *Tar Baby*. When Son* first looks from the boat and sees the land of Dominique, he sees little of the land that 300 years prior had caused slaves to be struck blind. According to this folk history, as retold by Gideon (Yardman), slaves on board a doomed ship could not see how or where to swim, and were therefore at the mercy of the waters. They floated or swam and ended up on the island along with some horses that had survived the waters and come ashore. Some of the slaves were only partially blinded, and were later rescued and returned to slavery. However, the totally blind slaves somehow hid and produced a race of people, no longer slaves, who were also blind.

In conclusion, Toni Morrison's works depict slavery as a vile institution, and her dramatizations of just how evil slavery was, serve as a reminder and as a caution for race relations in today's society. Her readers' consideration of slavery enforces an awareness of humankind's sometimes appalling behavior. *See also Beloved*; Death; Neo-Slave Narrative; Violence; Whiteness.

William S. Hampl

### Smith, Coffee/K.D./Kentucky Derby (*Paradise*)

K.D. is the son of Ruby Morgan and the "Army buddy" the Morgan twins gave their sister to, and the only surviving Morgan child in Ruby, Oklahoma\*. After impregnating and abandoning Arnette Fleetwood (an act unheard of in Ruby), and a two-year, turbulent, abusive affair with Gigi (Grace Gibson\*) at the Convent\*, K.D. marries Arnette in 1974 and attempts to assume his role within Ruby as the next generation of Morgan patriarch. K.D. participates in the attack on the Convent\* women. *See also Paradise.*

Julie Cary Nerad

### Smith, Robert (*Song of Solomon*)

A North Carolina Mutual Life Insurance agent and member of the Seven Days\*. The novel opens with his suicidal leap from No Mercy Hospital\*. *See also Song of Solomon.*

Fiona Mills

### Smith, Ruby (*Paradise*)

Title character of one of *Paradise*'s nine sections, Ruby, sister of Deacon\* and Steward Morgan\* and mother of K.D.\* is the first member of the original nine families to die in the town and the first person buried there; thus, she is the source of the town's name. Ruby, already a mother and war widow in 1950, grows ill on the trip from Haven, Oklahoma\*, to the then-unnamed town of Ruby. After improving briefly, her health again deteriorates, and in 1953 Deacon and Steward take her first to the

Demby hospital, then to the Middleton hospital, seeking treatment. Because she is Black, she is refused treatment, and dies in the hospital waiting room while the nurse tries to contact a veterinarian to examine her. *See also Paradise.*

Julie Cary Nerad

### Solomon (*Song of Solomon*)

Jake's* father and Milkman Dead's* great-grandfather. He was an African slave who literally flew back to Africa, leaving his wife and twenty-one children behind in Virginia. He becomes a legendary figure, and young children sing a cryptic nursery rhyme about him. *See also* Flying Africans, Myth of; *Song of Solomon.*

Fiona Mills

### Solomon's Leap (*Song of Solomon*)

Double-headed rock located on a cliff named after Solomon*, Milkman Dead's* great-grandfather, who literally flew back to Africa, leaving his wife, Ryna, and twenty-one children behind. Pilate Dead* and Milkman return to this place to bury the remains that Pilate has been keeping in a sack in her living room. While they are doing so, Guitar Baines* shoots and kills Pilate. The novel ends with Milkman's ambiguous leap off this cliff, into the arms of Guitar. *See also* Flying Africans, Myth of; *Song of Solomon.*

Fiona Mills

### Son/William Green (*Tar Baby*)

Son is the representation of the authentic Black man in *Tar Baby**. Closely connected to Black cultural values, he is in complete opposition to white cultural values. Son is also associated with nature. While hiding, his return to nature is symbolized by his dreadlocked hair, his lack of ease in New York City, and his ability to cure Valerian Street's* plants. Son romanticizes his past and Black culture. Unable to exist in the future, through Marie-Therese Foucault's* machinations he joins the Black horsemen—effectively returning to live in the past. He is also connected to the trickster* figures of Br'er Rabbit and Caliban. *See also Tar Baby.*

Nicole N. Aljoe

## Song of Solomon (1977)

Like many of her fictional works, Toni Morrison's *Song of Solomon* is infused with mythology and concerns itself with finding and preserving a sense of community* within African American life. In a break from Morrison's traditional foregrounding of female characters, *Song of Solomon* centers around a male protagonist, Milkman Dead*, and his search for identity* as well as a connection to his ancestors* and the larger African American community. Not incidentally, Morrison's third novel, with its captivating synthesis of the classical Greek myth* of Icarus and the African American Gullah myth of flying Africans*, also exemplifies the significance of folklore* in her fiction.

*Song of Solomon* opens with the captivating suicidal leap of Robert Smith*, a North Carolina Mutual Life Insurance agent, off the roof of No Mercy Hospital* and the simultaneous birth of Milkman Dead, the son of Macon Dead Jr.*, a middle-class African American slumlord who prevails tyrannically over less fortunate members of the Black community in Morrison's fictional Midwestern town. With her opening line, Morrison establishes the novel's main themes of mercy, community, and identity for her readers. Mercy and community are particularly important for Morrison in this novel. As she states in her essay "Unspeakable Things Unspoken," much of the novel is about the search for mercy—something that few, if any, characters exhibit or experience. Not only is the white community, as exemplified by its ironically named Mercy Hospital (referred to as No Mercy Hospital by the Black community for its refusal to admit African American patients), incapable of mercy, but many members of the Black community, most notably Macon Dead and, initially, Milkman himself, engage in similarly unmerciful behaviors. Accordingly, Milkman's indoctrination into the African American community is as much about his search for identity as it is about his ability to become merciful toward others.

Throughout *Song of Solomon*, most palpably via her incorporation of the folk song of Solomon*, Milkman's long-lost ancestral grandfather, Morrison insists that archetypal folk tales and stories are vital to the preservation of the African American community. In this novel, she traces the progression of Milkman from a young African American male ignorant of the value of such stories to an enlightened listener who, ultimately, becomes the bearer of the same stories. *Song of Solomon* also addresses the need for African Americans to know and embrace their ancestral roots and become responsible within their own communities. Morrison also emphasizes the importance of basing one's individual identity on these larger issues.

Morrison incorporates a number of classical archetypes in this novel, including biblical allusions, Greek mythology, Western quest myths, and traditional African American folktales. Many critics have argued that Morrison uses the quintessential archetype of man's quest for self-knowledge as the basis of her story. Critic A. Leslie Harris maintains that Milkman's development in many ways parallels the phases of the classic mythic hero as enumerated by Joseph Campbell in *The Hero with a Thousand Faces*. Indeed, Morrison has incorporated some of these archetypal elements into her work, thus lending *Song of Solomon* a certain universality. Other critics, such as Linden Peach, point out the book's decidedly African ontology, given its adaptation of a traditional Gullah folktale about African slaves who, upon arrival in America, flew back to Africa and its emphasis on non–Western values. Scholar Linda Krumholz concurs with Peach by broadening the list of literary allusions in the novel to include comparisons to Mwindo and Kambili stories, both of which are African epics.

These critical interpretations strengthen the contention that Morrison's novel is more than a mere mirroring of the traditional Western quest story. Significantly, in *Song of Solomon* Morrison manipulates classic Western myths, specifically that of Icarus and the traditional heroic quest, to promote communal responsibility and respect for one's cultural heritage within the African American community. This is exemplified by her inclusion of the supernatural and African American folklore, her celebration and critique of African American male flight, and her emphasis on community throughout the novel. More significant than her story's resemblance to classical myths is her adaptation of such archetypes, rendering them uniquely her own while privileging African American values and sensibilities over the traditional Western ones depicted in the original myths. As such, Morrison uses this novel to preserve African American history* and culture.

Throughout *Song of Solomon*, Morrison emphasizes the necessity of individuals caring for and remaining connected to the African American community. Although much of the novel focuses on Milkman's search for identity, paralleling the traditional heroic quest, the importance of his journey lies not in his creation of a separate, individual identity, but rather in his discovery of an undeniable link between his individuality and the larger Black community. Here, Morrison's adaptation of the quest myth differs markedly from Western privileging of individuality over communal responsibility. Her deviation lends itself to non–Western positions of interpretation. *Song of Solomon* does not celebrate Milkman as the rugged individualist, as do most epics about heroic quests. Significantly, Linda Krumholz contends that it is not until Milkman loses his overwhelming self-centeredness, learns about his ancestral heritage, begins to see his place in relation to his past, and makes amends with those in the African American community whom he has hurt that he becomes a hero.

Violence* and racism are also key elements in this novel, as demonstrated by the Seven Days*, a group dedicated to avenging the murders of Blacks by whites. For every African American killed at the hands of whites, the members of this group ritualistically kill a white person in exactly the same manner. The group is so named because each of the seven members is responsible for avenging the deaths of African Americans who are killed on a specified day of the week. The novel explores the explosive effects of rage—a direct result of racism—within the African American community and the violence to which it often leads. This violence is ultimately self-destructive as evidenced by Robert Smith's suicide on the novel's opening page. Since Smith is a member of the politically motivated Seven Days, his suicide is emblematic of Black rage. Smith's individual frustrations experienced as a Black man living in an oppressive, white-dominated culture incite him to end his life. He believes that his only recourse in a world in which African Americans have no representation in the justice system is suicide. Guitar Baines*, Milkman's best friend and also a member of the Seven Days, explains the frightening reality of this predicament to the politically oblivious Milkman by contending that the Seven Days exist because of the lack of access to legitimate means of justice for African Americans. This reality becomes too much for Smith to bear, and he commits suicide believing that, as a Black man, he would never experience justice.

Toni Morrison includes an abundance of references and occurrences specific to Black culture in *Song of Solomon*. Along with her fictional re-creation of historical events that irrevocably impacted African Americans, such as the death of Emmett Till, she also focuses intensely on the folk element of the Black community. This is most apparent in her inclusion of characters such as Pilate Dead* and Circe*, whose supernatural knowledge and folk magic establish them as ancestral figures. These women function as preservers of Black culture and serve as spiritual guides for the wayward Milkman. Both possess supernatural physical characteristics. Pilate has no navel, and Circe, although everyone in town presumes she is dead, continues to live in the house in which she worked as a servant over fifty years ago, while its walls literally deteriorate around her. Both Pilate and Circe practice folk magic, use natural medicine to heal people, and clairvoyantly predict events in Milkman's life. Not coincidentally, Milkman assumes Circe is a witch when he first meets her. Nevertheless, Pilate and Circe are instrumental in teaching Milkman about his family's* past and enabling him to define himself in relation to his heritage. Such figures, the novel suggests, possess monumental importance for African Americans living in a Eurocentric society. Morrison's depiction of Circe and Pilate, both of whom represent the folk element of the Black community, as essential in Milkman's journey of self-discovery evidence her desire to privilege folk beliefs in her writing.

   Significantly, *Song of Solomon* includes the names of familiar characters in the Western literary canon. Although Circe and Pilate, whose
names are found in two of the best-known books in world literature, may
be familiar to readers, Morrison's characters possess entirely unique characteristics and personalities that reflect African American sensibilities. In
this novel, Circe, best known as Odysseus's guide to the underworld, delivers both Macon and Pilate as babies, and hides and protects them after
their father is brutally murdered. Only years later, when she guides Milkman through the confusing history of his grandparents' past, does she
parallel her Greek namesake. Morrison's character is nothing like Homer's
goddess, steeped as she is in Black folk culture, as illustrated by her practice of natural healing, apparition-like appearance, and unusual longevity.
Moreover, Circe, due to her long-suffering position as a servant in a rich
white household after the end of slavery*, symbolizes the thousands of
African American women who endured similar hardships. In a similar instance of co-opting a familiar character's name, Morrison reinvents the
personality of Pilate, renowned in the Bible as the man who condemned
Jesus to death. Against Circe's advice, Pilate's father, Macon Dead, Sr., insists on this name for his baby daughter. Morrison's Pilate, though, is the
antithesis of Pontius Pilate due to her representation of strength, loyalty
to one's family, and dedication to the Black community. Unlike the biblical Pilate, who was responsible for Christ's death, Morrison's character
goes to extreme lengths to love and protect her family members, even taking a bullet that was intended to kill her nephew, Milkman.
   Many critics have discussed *Song of Solomon*'s similarity to the classic mythological archetypes, specifically the quest motif. This is most apparent in Milkman's journey to his father's Virginia homeland in search
of a sack of gold hidden by his father years ago. Although Milkman's
Southern journey resembles larger Western heroic myths, its main purpose vastly differs from that of journeys undertaken by other protagonists. During his exploration of the South, Milkman uncovers his Black
heritage. In so doing, he discovers his own identity. His journey is not
about finding the gold or even about proving his manhood by undergoing and surviving a perilous solo journey à la Odysseus. Rather, Milkman's journey is about his gradual acquisition of an identity, and its
emergence and dependence upon his connection to the greater African
American community. Pilate accompanies Milkman during the latter part
of his journey, as do other members of the African American community. Milkman's contact with people such as Circe, King Walker, Sweet*,
and Susan Byrd is crucial, for it enables him to learn about and appreciate his cultural heritage and, consequently, himself. As always, Morrison
insists on inextricably linking the individual to the community. Milkman can know himself only when he knows the names and stories of his
ancestors, which he learns while on his journey.

Toni Morrison continues to deviate from the traditional heroic quest with *Song of Solomon*'s celebration of feminine rootedness in one's ancestry and communal responsibility. This replaces the traditional glorification of masculine independence and singularity prevalent in Western heroic myths. Although men control the Dead household, throughout her novel Morrison emphasizes the inherent stagnation and danger present within a male-dominated household devoid of a sense of its heritage and cooperation. It is only women who possess a willingness to preserve their cultural roots and, subsequently, the African American community. The Dead women illustrate the severe price to be paid for this, since Macon's mental and physical abuse has reduced the female members of his family to lifeless beings with no sense of themselves. For instance, Macon's wife, Ruth Dead*, is a timid shell of a woman who relies on the presence of a water stain on her dining room table to assure her of her own existence. She has allowed herself to be dominated by her husband and has, in turn, ignored her daughters in favor of doting on her only son, Milkman. Her unnatural attachment to Milkman is manifested in her insistence on nursing him beyond his fourth birthday. Similarly, Macon's daughters, First Corinthians Dead* and Magdalena Dead*, live as though scared of their own shadows, their growth stunted by his domination. Milkman follows his father's example and has little to do with his sisters and his mother. Unfortunately, neither sister progresses beyond her frightened temperament to stand up to the Dead men who demean and ignore them.

Milkman's abhorrent treatment of his sisters and Ruth exemplifies his behavior toward women in general. Consequently, he must overcome this type of selfish behavior in order to understand his cultural roots and establish a connection with the African American community. He views women as objects to be used and discarded once they are no longer worthwhile. His nineteen-year relationship with Hagar Dead*, his cousin, exemplifies his self-centeredness. When she demands a more mature, committed relationship from him, he writes her off with a casual Christmas card. Initially, he even regards Pilate, who later becomes his mentor, in this manner as he robs her house in the middle of the night without the slightest hint of remorse. His behavior toward women symbolizes his self-centeredness and disregard for the larger community that surrounds him. Throughout *Song of Solomon*, Morrison insists upon the need for Milkman to correct his former transgressions against women and embrace their instruction in order to successfully complete his quest for self-identity. Consequently, Milkman must depend on the guidance of Circe and Pilate in order to uncover his ancestral roots and construct his identity in relation to the larger African American community.

Given the dichotomy that Morrison establishes between Macon and Pilate, Milkman becomes caught between their contradictory lifestyles.

Macon represents the achievement of individual desires to the detriment of the surrounding community, while Pilate embodies individual responsibility to the community. Macon's behavior as a slumlord epitomizes his lack of concern for the Black community as well as his all-consuming desire to attain the respect of the white middle class. He has no empathy for the hardships that his Black tenants face while contending with prejudice and discrimination, and instead concerns himself only with taking their money. He has removed himself completely from the African American community and rejected their cultural values in his haste to assimilate into the white middle class. Over the course of the novel, though, Milkman's choice becomes clear as he gradually rejects Macon's selfish lifestyle centered on ownership in favor of Pilate's unwavering attachment to her heritage that she literally carries around with her in a sack.

Toni Morrison's additional intention of rendering her writing political in *Song of Solomon* is most apparent in the scenes that take place in the barbershop. Here, history and fiction intersect. Unlike Macon, the men who hang out at the barbershop truly have their finger on the pulse of the Black community. Their experiences as Black men living in a white society lend undeniable wisdom to their words of advice. These men witness and experience racial injustice on a daily basis and engage in heated debates concerning race* politics within the seclusion of the barbershop. For instance, Railroad Tommy cautions Milkman not to bother trying to integrate into white society, which directly contradicts Macon's vain attempts to do so. He wisely understands that to try and do so will only bring heartbreak. It is better to entrench oneself in the Black community and seek support and understanding there. In keeping with the political nature of the barbershop conversation, Morrison includes a remarkably realistic discussion about the actual 1956 murder of Emmett Till in her novel. News of Till's death instantaneously triggers memories of similar experiences of injustice in each of the men in the barbershop. The death of Till provides a common link between them since they have all experienced racial injustice. Milkman, on the other hand, due to his political and social ignorance, does not share this bond and remains isolated from them. In comparison to the Seven Days and the men in the barbershop, Milkman is pathetically out of touch with the Black community.

Morrison's incorporation of the supernatural and folklore into *Song of Solomon* is also a political act. Through her use of signifying, Morrison creates an alternative way of naming and knowing that privileges African American values. Morrison's insistence on the authenticity of supernatural events, beginning on page 1 with Mr. Smith's failed attempt to fly across Lake Superior, including Pilate's lack of a navel, and ending with Milkman's ambiguous life-affirming leap, forces readers to suspend their disbelief and accept as fact that which the Western world, with its basis in empiricism and rationality, considers to be untrue. In so doing, she promotes and gives credibility to a unique way of knowing that is primarily African American. She offers an alternative to Western individualistic ideologies by rewriting the typical heroic quest myth. As such, she insists that those ideologies do not work for African Americans.

Although Morrison's novel begins with Milkman's complete isolation from the Black community, *Song of Solomon* ends with his open embrace of an African American heritage, as illustrated by his final leap away from the body of his spiritual guide and mentor, Pilate, into the arms of Guitar, his communal brother. By the end of the novel, Milkman has come full circle in his appreciation of the stories he has been told concerning his family's legacy. He no longer floats blindly through life, oblivious to everything and everyone around him. His journey to his ancestral homeland has enabled him to understand the importance of the names of people, places, and things, and to connect them back to himself. Now he truly understands the significance of knowing one's heritage. Milkman has also come to understand the crucial support that his family, both living and dead, give him. He now understands that, although he may be physically unaccompanied, he is never truly alone because of his inextricable link to his family and the African American community. Thus, his journey has made him cognizant of the integral part that his ancestry plays in the construction of his individual identity.

Morrison demonstrates this through his transition from a passive listener to the stories of his family's past to an active bearer of important historic information as he relates the stories he has heard about his grandparents to his aunt Pilate at the end of the novel. He has become like Circe, Susan Byrd, Reverend Cooper, and, of course, Pilate in his ability to preserve his cultural heritage in the stories that he now possesses and can pass on. Consequently, Milkman's journey, sparked as it was by an individual desire, is ultimately about a young man's alienation from and reimmersion into the African American community, and his acceptance of his responsibility to respect and preserve his heritage. *See also* African Myth, Use of; Dead, Reba; Jake; Myth; Not Doctor Street; Ryna's Gulch; Singing Bird; Solomon's Leap.

References: A. Leslie Harris, "Myth as Structure in Toni Morrison's *Song of Solomon*," *MELUS* 7: 3 (1980); Linda Krumholz, "Dead Teachers: Rituals of Manhood and Rituals of Reading in *Song of Solomon*," *Modern Fiction Studies* 39: 3–4 (1993); Catherine Carr Lee, "The South in Toni Morrison's *Song of Solomon*: Initiation, Healing and Home," *Studies in the Literary Imagination* 31: 2 (1998).

Fiona Mills

## Sosa, Consolata/Connie (*Paradise*)

In 1925, at age nine, the homeless Consolata, title character of one of *Paradise's* nine sections, was "stolen" from the streets of (presumably) Brazil by Mother Mary Agnes (Mary Magna*) and taken to Oklahoma to live with the Sisters at the Christ the King School for Native Girls, known locally as the Convent*. At the age of thirty-nine, Connie meets Deacon (Deek) Morgan*, age twenty-nine and one of the most prominent men in Ruby, Oklahoma*. After their short but intense love affair, the married Deek abruptly ends the relationship. Shortly afterward the school closes, but Connie and Mary Magna continue to live alone at the Convent and sell hot pepper jelly to travelers and Ruby's citizens. After saving the life of Deek's son Scout by "stepping into" him, Connie becomes lifelong friends with Soane Morgan*, Deek's wife. Connie's life changes again when Mary Magna dies in 1971, by which time wayward women have started making their home at the Convent. By 1975, an aging and almost sightless Connie longs for the release of death* and an escape from the bickering, lost women who surround her—until she sees a strange young man with long, cascading, brown hair in the garden. After their encounters begin, Connie starts to tell the women of Piedade*, a beautiful singing woman, a maternal figure of paradise embodied, and leads the women in sessions of "loud-dreaming" that allow them to exorcise the ghosts that haunt them. During the attack on the Convent by nine of Ruby's men, Connie is shot in the head by Deek's twin brother, Steward*. Although Soane and Lone DuPres* both see her dead, Connie's body disappears with the rest of the Convent women. We see her once more in the novel, sitting at the ocean's edge with her head in Piedade's lap. *See also Paradise.*

Julie Cary Nerad

## South, Influence of

The influence of the South on Toni Morrison's fiction comes from the history* and literature of the region as well as Morrison's own heritage. The daughter of Southern parents, Morrison heard their stories of Southern racism. Morrison's fiction bears traces of the historical contexts of the shadow of slavery* in the postbellum South: the Great Migration* north, the return south, and the consequent preservation of Black townships. More profound in her novels is the intricate reworking of the literature of the American South. Although she is noted for her literary kinship with William Faulkner*, Morrison's oeuvre stretches beyond Faulkner's vision of the South to reveal an African American perspective not fully defined in other works of Southern fiction.

The child of a Georgia-born father and an Alabama-born mother, but born and raised in Lorain, Ohio*, Morrison inherited two distinct views on the South. Her mother left the South and never returned, while her father made frequent visits from Ohio. Both parents told stories of the South, yet it was the disparity of her mother's hatred of the place and her father's tolerance of it that kept Morrison's attention. Upon her own visit to the South, Morrison found both her mother's and father's visions of the South to be accurate, and those visions helped seed her imagination to better communicate the historical realities of the place. While the settings of Morrison's novels are not in the geographic region generally accepted as the South, their settings border that region which history records as the focal point of many of the African American conflicts in American history. Even the Southern view of slavery contrasts with the more progressive, but also problematic, Northern view. The agrarian mode of existence is also central in the South of the literary imagination, and stems from the history of the South. These elements, as well as the primary movement of African Americans in the twentieth century from the South to the North in the Great Migration, are recognized in Morrison's fiction. Moreover, the challenge of African Americans in the post-slavery South appears in *Paradise**. While none of Morrison's novels is meant to be a work of historical fiction, the narrative trajectories of her works bear traces of historical shifts in populations and attitudes about the meaning of place.

The central historical experience of African Americans in the South most specifically influences Morrison's trilogy *Beloved**, *Jazz**, and *Paradise*. *Beloved*'s chronicle of slavery and freedom begins the historical survey by showing the brutality of slavery as an institution in pre–Civil War Kentucky. One subtext of *Jazz* is the diaspora from the South to the North and the period historically centered on the Harlem* Renaissance. The third work, *Paradise*, explores the other side of the exodus by focusing on those African Americans who remained in the South and claimed territory and land as their own, separate from the white society that had enslaved them. Although *Paradise* may be an interrogation of the exclusive idea of utopian societies, the patriarchy governing the town of Ruby, Oklahoma*, is strongly reminiscent of the patriarchal literary South created by the Fugitive Group of poets from Vanderbilt University.

Allen Tate, John Crowe Ransom, Robert Penn Warren, and Donald Davidson, the Fugitive Group's most prominent literary members, went on to become the central figures in the publication of the Agrarian Movement's utopian manifesto, *I'll Take My Stand*, in 1930. The Fugitives used their poetry and prose to create an ideal vision of a South that was moving away from its historically agarian heritage to become a more industrialized region. Like the men of Ruby, the Fugitive Group sought to propagate a utopian vision of the South in order to maintain the vision of history they embraced. The consequent Southern literature of the early twentieth century echoes this rural, gothic* setting, and only later did critics begin to separate the geographic reality of the South from the literary ideal created by the Fugitives. *Paradise* follows the same pattern of exploding utopian misconceptions by showing the problematic results of imposing an unachievable ideal onto a town.

Toni Morrison's fiction also shows the influence of Zora Neale Hurston's fictional and anthropological works, which chronicle the all-Black township of Eatonville, Florida. In addition to her model of an all-Black township, Hurston's records and those of other scholars preserve the Southern, African American vernacular and the intricately woven folklore*, songs, and beliefs brought from Africa and adapted to fit the situation and setting of slavery in the South. These influences, as well as many of the call-and-response patterns indicative of secret slave communications adopted by the African American Protestant churches, are present in Morrison's novels such as *Song of Solomon** and *Tar Baby**.

While a number of critics write about the relationship of the literature of Toni Morrison to that of William Faulkner, there is far more in the history of Southern literature to illustrate an influence of the South upon Morrison. Her African American literary ancestors* and peers Ralph Ellison, Richard Wright, Ernest Gaines, and Alice Walker, as well as her literary heirs such as Randall Kenan, all expand the place of African Americans in a Southern setting. In opposition to the early works of modern Southern literature, Morrison's focus on the African American gives voice to a marginal group of people and fills out the experience of an otherwise predominantly white historical and literary South. *See also* Geography.

References: Carol A. Kolmerten, Stephen M. Ross, and Judith Bryant Wittenberg, eds., *Unflinching Gaze: Morrison and Faulkner Re-Envisioned* (1997); "Toni Morrison and the American South." *Studies in the Literary Imagination* 31: 2 (Fall 1998); Twelve Southerners, *I'll Take My Stand: The South and the Agrarian Tradition* (1977; orig. pub. 1930).

F. Gregory Stewart

## Spirituality

Christian allusions, symbols, and images permeate much of the fiction of Toni Morrison. Many of these references are obvious and conventional: characters bearing biblical names, forthright discussions of humanity's relationship to God, characters wrestling with the consequences of sin and guilt and searching for redemption, the role of the church, and religious practices in the daily life of the community*. But as with just about any theme or other fictional element with which Morrison works, she takes these conventional references and molds them into surprising and more complex forms. While she does draw heavily from the language, history*, and practices of the Western Judeo-Christian tradition, she complicates and enhances that tradition by incorporating sources from other cultures, including most notably religious practices and folklore* traditions associated with Africa.

In *Playing in the Dark: Whiteness and the Literary Imagination**, Morrison argues that scholars of American culture have for too long failed to recognize the influence of African cultures on the development of the unique practices and beliefs by which the United States has come to be identified. She argues that any investigation of American culture that does not take into account the pervasive influence of African traditions is fundamentally flawed because of its denial of what must be regarded as an inextricable element of the American experience. A superficial reading of Morrison would suggest that she is interested in this African influence because her fiction deals primarily with the lives of African Americans. A closer examination of her work, however, reveals that she develops these characters within the larger framework of American culture, investigating their capacity for surviving in a complex society that oversimplifies itself by marginalizing that which makes it complex. Gazing intensely into the heart of American history, Morrison cannot overlook the atrocities and injustices perpetrated upon African Americans by a culture obsessed with racial oppression and separation, but for her, the stories of her characters involve much more than their battles with the clearly visible demons of racism. Much of the difficulty of their journey hides behind more subtle guises, in the customs of their own communities that have become infused with the destructive elements of the dominant white society, leading them to doubt or even forget the traditions that sustained their ancestors*.

While Morrison demonstrates that these guises can take many forms, including sexism, predatory business practices, and fashion trends, the guise that dominates much of her first novel, *The Bluest Eye**, and to which she returns time and time again, is that of Christianity, especially as it is practiced within the white, European tradition. Pauline Breedlove* of *The Bluest Eye* is perhaps the best example within Morrison's fiction of an African American character searching for solace within the traditions of the white community. Pauline pulls away from the Christian church of her childhood and its African-inspired rhythms and rituals to a church that fulfills her desire to be like the white movie stars she emulates. Both her name and her religious evolution suggest the influence of the teachings of St. Paul upon her beliefs, teachings that have often been manipulated by the dominant forces within white culture, from slave masters to segregationists, to uphold the status quo. Instead of focusing on the current needs of her community, and specifically her family*, Pauline is more interested in the promises of an afterlife and the escape it offers from the drudgery of her earthly existence. Consequently, she lacks the compassion or the common sense to deal adequately with the crises ripping apart her family. She sees Christ as a judge of the sins of fallen humanity, exemplified by Cholly*, her self-destructive husband. She feels nothing but contempt for Cholly and relishes the thought that some day he will have to pay for his many transgressions. According to Pauline, Christianity is not about the possibility of redemption or the building of a community; it is all about the self, the individual soul, imprisoned within a flawed body, that is trying to rise above the filth which threatens to drag it back to earth.

Pauline's movement toward a Pauline-based theology and its focus on the self proves to be especially destructive for her daughter, Pecola*. With her mother modeling the roles she has drawn from the dominant white culture, Pecola, who suffers from a wholly inadequate sense of self, is left without any significant knowledge of her African American heritage. And when she looks to the cultural practices favored by her mother, she is consistently met with indifference, from the blank stare of Mr. Yacobowski to the uncaring eyes of the Anglicized Jesus hanging in Geraldine's home. Ultimately she falls victim to Soaphead Church*, whose loathing of the physical world transcends even her mother's. Though they never appear together in the text, Pauline and Soaphead unwittingly become the dual catalysts that ignite Pecola's self-destruction. While their belief in transcendence offers them a sense of self-worth and power, it is necessarily limited by its isolation of the self from the physical world. Such a belief system cannot sustain a family, much less a community, especially one that historically has been marginalized.

This transcendent model, based primarily upon the traditions of European Christianity, proves to be woefully inadequate for most of Morrison's African American characters. The community is a central, unifying element in much of her fiction, and a community must necessarily look to the physical in order to understand what ultimately holds it together. Much can be made of community spirit and pride and other abstractions, but without the unity brought about by the daily struggle to provide the physical necessities of life, a community would lack any practical basis for holding itself together. It is within this physical community that Morrison's characters primarily find their redemption and their salvation, not through the isolated actions of a transcendent self.

In *The Bluest Eye*, Cholly, a character seemingly beyond redemption because of his sexual abuse of his daughter, understands that love cannot be transcendent, that it must be present in the actions of the guardian, friend, or lover. He does not find solace in escape, but rather through an embracing of the real, a stance modeled for him by his Aunt Jimmy and Blue Jack. Thus even his abuse of Pecola can be seen, as Morrison's narrator suggests, as a manifestation of his love for her and his desire to reconnect her to the physical world. The Bottom* community in *Sula** is also representative of the redemptive possibilities within the physical community, as are the various communities encountered by Milkman Dead* in his journey to uncover his heritage. In *Beloved**, Sethe Suggs* and Paul D Garner* understandably try to transcend their horrific past, and at times find themselves isolated from each other and from their communities, but it is only their coming together and their sharing of their shared past that allows them to move forward.

Even though Morrison often places transcendence and physicality at odds in her fiction, she also finds inventive and intriguing ways to pull them together. Ghosts or spirits, prevalent in *Song of Solomon**, *Beloved*, and *Paradise**, are associated with the transcendent, but Morrison deftly connects them to the physical, moving beyond the popular notion of ghosts as otherworldly and ethereal entities, and presenting them as apparently material beings. The ghost of Beloved*, for example, is gluttonous in her desire for the physical, gorging herself on food and satisfying her sexual urges with Paul D. Morrison also employs names of characters and places that suggest a blending of the transcendent and the physical. In *Song of Solomon*, there are three generations of men named Dead, of whom one is actually dead, though he also appears as a ghost who exhibits physical qualities. In *Tar Baby**, the Caribbean estate of Valerian Street* is known as L'Arbe de la Croix*, a name directly pointing to the material substance upon which Christ was crucified but which also, in some Christian traditions, has come to symbolize the transcendence of Christ over the physical boundaries of human existence.

As the Christian cross suggests, the crux of Christianity lies in this meeting of the transcendent and the physical, in the birth of a transcendent and infinite God into a physical and finite human body. However, as Morrison reveals through her fiction, the Christian traditions of the West, frequently invested with large doses of Platonic philosophy, have tended to view the transcendent as primary and the physical as an inferior representation, forever to be relegated to the realm of the undesirable. Given her aversion to such thinking, Morrison must look outside these Western traditions to find a way to reconnect the transcendent to the physical. And it is within the rich folk and religious traditions of African and African American cultures that she finds the essential resources for this task.

Many of Morrison's allusions to African and African American folklore are quite obvious, such as the myth of the flying Africans* in *Song*

*of Solomon* and the title of *Tar Baby* and its numerous references to
the Br'er Rabbit folktale. These explicit references certainly add significant layers of meaning to her texts and connect her stories to traditions that transcend the boundaries of her settings. It is in her less
explicit allusions, however, that we find some of Morrison's most intriguing reflections on the complex roots of African American culture.
One such reference, presented unforgettably in *Sula\**, is her discussion
of the fourth face of God. Playing off the Western Christian notion of
the Trinity, Morrison suggests that God has a fourth face, one that accounts for the existence of evil and suffering in a universe ruled by a
supposedly omnipotent and benevolent deity. This idea reflects a theological position prevalent within numerous African religious and folk
traditions. Within orthodox Western Christianity, theologians for centuries have developed tortured arguments to explain away the apparent paradox of the existence of evil in the face of an all-powerful and
good God, and have been reluctant to compromise the belief in God's
sovereignty in any way. But this has not been the case in many African
traditions, where there seems to have been a greater willingness to accept the idea of God's fallibility. And numerous African folktales depict
God as a thoroughly humanized, and at times almost comical, character.

In contrast to the judgmental Pauline Breedlove, several of Morrison's
characters, reflecting this belief in God's fourth face, do not see evil and
sin as something to be sequestered and ultimately destroyed. The characters in Morrison's fiction who manage to find their way productively
through whatever wretched maze life has constructed, do so not by ignoring or by attempting to eliminate evil but through improvisation and
endurance. Morrison's concept of the fourth face suggests that neither
the nature of God nor the direction of life is ascertainable or under-
standable. It does not, however, condone a passive acceptance of pain and
injustice. Sethe in *Beloved* perhaps best exemplifies this attitude of endurance in spite of overwhelming suffering. She continues to battle her
inner and outer demons, not in hopes of some day finding relief in a
blessed afterlife but simply because she has come to expect so little from
her fellow humans or her God. One might characterize her stance as an
updated version of stoicism, but unlike the practitioners of this philosophy, she lacks any confidence in an ordered universe. Given so little with
which to work, Sethe manages to piece together a remarkable testament
to her stamina and wisdom. Within this most impoverished of characters, dehumanized in ways almost beyond our comprehension, we find a
philosophy of life as complex as the incomprehensible world with which
she struggles.

This philosophy of life rests upon a foundation somewhat akin to the
Christian doctrine of original sin: the crime of innocence. Morrison explicitly discusses this phenomenon in *Tar Baby*, but she introduces it

into much of her fiction, including most notably *The Bluest Eye, Sula,* and *Beloved.* Morrison characterizes innocence as a crime because it prohibits one from beginning the process of grappling with the vagaries of life, including problems created by injustice and oppression, and those inexplicable difficulties which can be attributed to God's fourth face. Consequently, Morrison's characters do not fall from a state of innocence but rise above it, thereby recognizing that life offers no promises of an otherworldly peace, just a maze of perpetual challenges that will test strength and endurance and character. *See also* African Myth, Use of; Ghost Story, Use of.

References: Allen Alexander, "The Fourth Face: The Image of God in Toni Morrison's *The Bluest Eye," African American Review* 32 (1998); Deborah Guth, "'Wonder What God Had in Mind': *Beloved's* Dialogue with Christianity," *Journal of Narrative Technique* 24: 2 (1994); Lauren Lepow, "Paradise Lost and Found: Dualism and Edenic Myth in Toni Morrison's *Tar Baby," Contemporary Literature* 28: 3 (1987); Vashti Crutcher Lewis, "African Tradition in Toni Morrison's *Sula," Phylon* 48: 1 (1987); Terry Otten, *The Crime of Innocence in the Fiction of Toni Morrison* (1989).

R. Allen Alexander, Jr.

## Stowe, Harriet Beecher, Influence of

When Toni Morrison's novel *Beloved\** was published in 1987, author Margaret Atwood was among the first to connect it to *Uncle Tom's Cabin,* written by Harriet Beecher Stowe more than century earlier. In her review for the *New York Times,* Atwood asserts that Sethe Suggs's\* quest to get herself, her milk, and her unborn babe across the Ohio River to freedom "makes the ice-floe scene in *Uncle Tom's Cabin* look like a stroll around the block." Since then, comparison of the two novels has interested many students of Morrison. The originality of Morrison's best-known and most respected novel has never been in question. Rather, commentary has been focused on appreciating the ways Morrison's novel "talks back" to Stowe's.

Most critics praise Morrison's revision of Stowe's perspective. For instance, some, like Lauren Berlant, praise Morrison's nonsentimental treatment of slavery's\* legacy. Others, like Harryette Mullen, value her authentic Black position. And still others, such as Lori Askeland and John N. Duvall, appreciate her dismantling of patriarchal authority. However, many critics, Nancy Armstrong and Cynthia Griffin Wolff among them, are also fascinated with the similar sensibility impelling these two novels by women of different race\* and time.

Certainly a general point of interest among critics is the degree of parallel between *Uncle Tom's Cabin* and *Beloved*. For instance, they share common settings. Sethe flees from Sweet Home* in Kentucky, and her passage to freedom in Cincinnati, Ohio, is across the Ohio River. Similarly, Eliza flees from the Shelby Plantation in Kentucky and crosses the river to find refuge at the Byrds' home in Ohio. In both cases the danger of the Ohio River crossing emblemizes all the dangers faced by desperate runaway slaves.

Some critics focus on the larger similarity: their treatment of slavery as inherently evil. For instance, both make this point by having the slaves belong to benign masters, whose unanticipated changes in fortune drastically alter the slaves' lives. Mr. Shelby faces bankruptcy, so he must sell Tom and Eliza's son Harry; Mr. Garner* dies suddenly, so schoolteacher* takes control of the Sweet Home "men" and Sethe. Also, in both stories the evil of slavery is linked to patriarchy by having caring white women who are nevertheless powerless to stop the abuse of slaves; Mrs. Shelby is too ignorant of finances, and Mrs. Garner is too sickly. Both authors show that everyone—be they white or Black, master or slave—is victimized by slavery. And further, they equally demonstrate the absolute individual need for connection—to family* and to community*—which is denied to slaves.

The parallel given the most attention, however, is between Stowe's Eliza and Morrison's Sethe, both mothers who flee to save their children from slavery. Rather than see her toddler son sold, Eliza flees across the Ohio ice floes with him in her arms. Pregnant and with milk-laden breasts for her crawlingalready? baby, Sethe flees, giving birth to Denver Suggs* on the Ohio before crossing.

Interestingly, when we consider not just Sethe's crossing but her desperate act of infanticide* as well, we see analogues to other female slaves in Stowe's novel. In order to communicate the horrifying inhumanity of slavery, Stowe depicts women suffering a variety of outrages. Perhaps most noteworthy is Cassy, whose desire to avenge a life of sexual enslavement and the loss of two children transcends any moral compunction. Her story combines the horrors suffered by Sethe and Beloved*. And then there is Emmeline, the fifteen-year-old slave bought to replace Cassy in concubinage. The tale that inspires these two to retreat to the attic to "haunt" Legree also echoes Beloved's story. Another minor character reinforces the desperation of Eliza and Cassy. Lucy is a slave being transported on the same riverboat as Tom. When her child is secreted from her in the night, she commits suicide. The aged alcoholic Prue, who drinks to forget her painful past, also provides a variation on this theme. Stowe provided numerous archetypes for Morrison to work with, and the real atrocities of slavery provided Stowe's archetypes.

While one can note that Morrison is revising Stowe to some degree, one must also note the fact that both writers were overtly employing factual incidents. Stowe set the precedent of documentation when she published her *Key to Uncle Tom's Cabin*, providing factual analogues for the horrific events that occur to her characters. And Morrison continued the tradition, documenting the horrendous account of Margaret Garner*, an escaped slave who killed one of her children* in an attempt to kill all rather than see them returned to slavery. Morrison has discussed Garner's tragic story as the inspiration for *Beloved*. But she has also made it very clear that she did not desire historic accuracy as much as a catalyst for her imagination.

Critics have been somewhat at odds about the significance of the similarities between the real woman, Stowe's women, and Morrison's women, primarily because the chronology foils easy connection. Stowe's story, with all its prefiguration of Morrison's, was written four years before the infanticide of Margaret Garner, which we know prefigured *Beloved*. So while both women used real incidents and while Morrison's echoes of Stowe seem clear, we cannot establish a direct chain from Garner to Stowe to Morrison. However, perhaps the linkage between these two novels and history is not one slave woman's aberrant experience. It is the unspeakable experiences suffered by multitudes of women— women like Margaret Garner; like Eliza, Cassy, Emmeline, Lucy, and Prue; like Sethe and Beloved. What both Harriet Beecher Stowe's and Toni Morrison's uses of factual material show us is that slavery is an abomination, impelling other abominable acts and the burden of their history*.


References: Nancy Armstrong, "Why Daughters Die: The Racial Logic of American Sentimentalism," *Yale Journal of Criticism* 7: 2 (1994); Lori Askeland, "Remodeling the Model Home in *Uncle Tom's Cabin* and *Beloved*," *American Literature* 64: 4 (1992); Margaret Atwood, "Haunted by Their Nightmares" (review of *Beloved*, by Toni Morrison), *New York Times Book Review* (September 13, 1987); Eileen T. Bender, "Repossessing *Uncle Tom's Cabin*: Toni Morrison's *Beloved*," in *Cultural Power/Cultural Literacy*, ed. Bonnie Braendlin (1991); Lauren Berlant, "Poor Eliza," *American Literature* 70 (1998); John N. Duvall, "Authentic Ghost Stories: *Uncle Tom's Cabin, Absalom, Absalom! and Beloved*," *The Faulkner Journal* 4: 1–2 (1988); Harryette Mullen, "Runaway Tongue: Resistant Orality in *Uncle Tom's Cabin, Our Nig, Incidents in the Life of a Slave Girl*, and *Beloved*," in *The Culture of Sentiment: Race, Gender and Sentimentality in Nineteenth-Century America*, ed. Shirley Samuels (1992); Angelita Reyes, "Using History as Artifact to Situate

*Beloved's* Unknown Woman: Margaret Garner," in *Approaches to Teaching Toni Morrison*, ed. Nellie Y. McKay and Kathryn Earle (1997); Cynthia Griffin Wolff, "'Margaret Garner': A Cincinnati Story," in *Discovering Difference: Contemporary Essays in American Culture*, ed. Christoph K. Lohmann (1993).

Jane Atteridge Rose

## Street, Margaret (*Tar Baby*)

Wife of Philadelphia candy king Valerian Street* and mother of Michael. Margaret's secret abuse of Michael as a child is revealed during the time frame of the novel. *See also Tar Baby*.

Nicole N. Aljoe

## Street, Valerian (*Tar Baby*)

Philadelphia candy king who retires to the Isle des Chevaliers* and imports his entire household to the island. He is incredibly selfish and capricious—a Prospero-like character who seeks to control nature and humanity. Valerian does not realize that his actions have consequences for himself or for others. His sense of entitlement and power are shaken when he finds out that his wife Margaret* abused their only son. *See also Tar Baby*.

Nicole N. Aljoe

## Suggs, Baby (*Beloved*)

Baby Suggs, also called Grandma Baby, is the spiritual center of Morrison's *Beloved*. She was mother to Halle Suggs*, mother-in-law to Sethe Suggs*, and grandmother to Howard and Buglar*, and Denver Suggs*, and the child known as Beloved*. Sexually exploited under slavery*, she had given birth to eight or nine children over the years, but she arrived at the Garners'* plantation in Kentucky (Sweet Home*) in 1838 with Halle, the only child she had been allowed to keep. When Halle purchased his mother's freedom after having hired out his time off on Sundays, Baby Suggs moved into a house on the outskirts of Cincinnati provided to her by the abolitionist brother and sister Quakers, the Bodwins*. This would eventually become 124 Bluestone Road*. When Sethe managed to free herself and her children from slavery in 1855, they joined Baby Suggs, who had become a spiritual leader and preacher; then Baby witnessed an event that finally crushed her seemingly indomitable spirit—

her daughter-in-law driven to infanticide*, her precious grandchild put to death at the hands of its mother. Though her physical body fails in 1865, she remains in the memories of those who knew her; she is the ancestor* who provides the spiritual impetus that Denver needs at a critical moment in 1875. *See also Beloved.*

Lovalerie King

## Suggs, Denver (*Beloved*)

Denver is the fourth child and second daughter of Sethe* and Halle Suggs*. Named for the young white woman, Amy Denver*, who came to Sethe's aid during her escape, Denver represents the future for the free Black community*. When the novel opens, eighteen-year-old Denver is living a stunted, stifling, reclusive existence with her mother and the ghost of her slightly older sister in the house at 124 Bluestone Road*. Her brothers have run off, and Baby Suggs* is dead. She is not happy when Paul D Garner* arrives. Denver has long since given up going to school, after being driven from the school yard amid taunts about her mother's horrendous deed and subsequent incarceration. She is a little strange from having lived such a sheltered life. Though she was born free, literally on the Ohio River, she suffers indirectly from the trauma* of slavery*. She is the first to recognize Beloved* as her sister returned from the dead. A naturally bright young woman, she also recognizes that the demanding ghost will never be satisfied, and thus takes the initial step that results in the successful communal exorcism of the greedy ghost. Denver represents the future. *See also Beloved.*

Lovalerie King

## Suggs, Halle (*Beloved*)

Halle Suggs is the only one of her children that Baby Suggs* was allowed to keep. With his mother, he goes to live at Sweet Home* in 1838. In 1848, he earns enough money to purchase her freedom, effectively buying a wife, because his mother's replacement is Sethe Suggs*; a year after her arrival, Sethe chooses him from among the available young men enslaved at Sweet Home. Along with Sixo*, Halle plans the collective escape from Sweet Home. Possessed of a sensitive and generous nature, Halle is not prepared to deal with the worst that slavery* has to offer, and he is completely undone when he witnesses the brutal "milking" of his wife at the hands of schoolteacher's* nephews*. He is lost forever to those who long for his presence—his children*, his mother, his wife, and his friends. The last word we have on Halle comes from Paul D Garner* when he arrives at 124 Bluestone Road* in 1873. He had last seen Halle back in 1855, sitting on the stoop, smearing clabber all over himself. *See also Beloved.*

Lovalerie King


## Suggs, Howard and Buglar (*Beloved*)

Howard and Buglar are the two oldest children of Sethe* and Halle Suggs*. Tired of living with the constant anxiety of wondering what their resident ghost will do next, they flee 124 Bluestone Road* in 1864. At age thirteen, they had lived for almost ten years with the knowledge that their mother tried to kill them. In 1875, they are still absent and silent. *See also Beloved.*

Lovalerie King


## Suggs, Sethe (*Beloved*)

Sethe Suggs is the traumatized protagonist of Morrison's fifth novel, *Beloved**. In the present moment of the story (1873–1875 Ohio), Sethe's past comes to haunt her in the form of the daughter (now a young adult) whom she killed some twenty years before. In 1848, thirteen-year-old Sethe had arrived at the Garners'* plantation in Kentucky (Sweet Home*) as a replacement for Baby Suggs*, whose freedom had been purchased by the man who would become Sethe's husband and the father of her four children. After giving birth to her fourth child during her escape to freedom, Sethe experiences full freedom for the first time in her life. Twenty-eight days later, schoolteacher*, whose brutality had precipitated the full-scale escape among the enslaved population of Sweet Home, arrives to carry Sethe and her children* back into slavery. Sethe's unsuccessful attempt to thwart schoolteacher's efforts by killing her children and committing suicide ends in one child's death and Sethe's incarceration. When she is released from jail, she returns to the house at 124 Bluestone Road*, determined to endure life in stoic fashion, even after it becomes obvious in 1864 that the house is haunted by the ghost of her dead daughter. A visit from Paul D Garner*, an old friend from the Sweet Home days, sets into motion a series of life-shattering and transforming events, including the return of her daughter from the dead. The ghost wants to consume Sethe, and once Sethe recognizes her daughter, she is willing to submit totally. *See also Beloved.*

Lovalerie King

## Sula (1973)

Sula, Toni Morrison's second novel, was published in 1973. Its epigraph, "Nobody knew my rose of the world but me. ... I had too much glory. They don't want glory like that in nobody's heart," is taken from Tennessee Williams's *The Rose Tattoo* and refers to the stem-and-rose-shaped birthmark of the novel's main character, Sula Mae Peace*. The epigraph also foreshadows the animosity she will encounter from the inhabitants of the Bottom*, the African American neighborhood in Medallion, Ohio*, in which Sula grows up alongside her best friend, Nel Wright*.

*Sula* begins with an elegiac evocation of the Bottom, describing the manner in which neighborhood landmarks are being cleared away to accommodate suburban development, and explaining the origins of the Bottom's name as a "nigger joke." According to the narrator, the Bottom was given its name by a white farmer who promised his slave a piece of bottom land in exchange for the performance of some difficult chores. After the chores were completed, the farmer thought better of the deal and deceived the slave into thinking that the difficult-to-farm, hilly part of his property was the bottom land the slave had been promised, since, from God's perspective, it was the bottom of heaven.

The first chapter of the novel follows Shadrack*, a shell-shocked twenty-two-year old African American veteran of World War I. Morrison uses the single yet devastatingly effective image of a soldier whose body continues running after his face and head have been shot off to illustrate the trauma* of Shadrack's wartime experience. This trauma will manifest itself in a number of ways when Shadrack returns home. While recuperating in a Veterans Hospital, Shadrack begins to hallucinate that his hands expand to enormous proportions. When a male nurse attempts to feed Shadrack, Shadrack attacks him and is placed in a straitjacket. Rather than continue his treatment, the hospital releases him on his own recognizance with $217, a suit of clothes, and some discharge papers. As is the case with many mentally ill people today, it is not long before Shadrack is reinstitutionalized—this time in jail. In what could be read as an ironic revision of Professor Woodridge's dictum in Ralph Ellison's *Invisible Man* to not waste time on the uncreated conscience of one's race*, but rather focus on the uncreated features of one's face, Shadrack, while jailed, discovers the features of his face in the light reflected off the water of a jail cell toilet bowl. After he is released, Shadrack returns to Medallion and, in an attempt to forge some sort of order out of the death and chaos he has experienced, decrees January 3 of each year National Suicide Day*.

In a novel named after its ostensible protagonist, it may seem strange that so much time is devoted to the tribulations of a World War I veteran. Some critics, however, have suggested that Shadrack's World War I experience is symbolic of the historical experience of African Americans vis-à-vis Western culture in general. For her part, Morrison says she needed a familiar madness to serve as a foil for Sula's eccentricity.

Even the following chapter, "1920," does not focus on Sula, but on Nel Wright, Sula's soon-to-be best friend, as she travels to New Orleans to attend her great-grandmother's funeral. Nel travels with her mother, Helene Wright*, a light-complexioned Creole woman from New Orleans. Helene's grandmother, Cecile, raised her, because she did not want her growing up in the brothel where her mother worked as a prostitute. When Helene was old enough, she married Wiley Wright*, a ship's cook, and escaped what she viewed as her shameful past by going to live with her husband in Medallion. In Medallion, she made a new life for herself by joining the most conservative church in town and becoming a respected mother and housewife. If it were up to her, Helene would never return to the place of her upbringing, but she feels compelled to do so when she learns that her grandmother is ill.

Prior to this trip, Nel's identification with her mother is complete. But when she sees her mother capitulate to a racist train conductor by smiling at his verbal abuse, a fissure opens up in their relationship and Nel, for the first time, is led to contemplate her own selfhood. Interestingly, the novel suggests that Nel's relationship with Sula, to whom we are finally introduced, is both the result of Nel's newfound independence and a substitute for its greater development.

Morrison spends time on Sula's family* background in the next chapter, but beyond a mention of the early and unintentional education she receives about sexual matters by observing Hannah, her pleasantly promiscuous mother, Sula is noticeably absent. Instead, Morrison introduces us to a host of lesser characters—BoyBoy, Tar Baby*, Plum*, and the Deweys*. It is as if because Sula, the central character, has no center, Morrison's narrative is forced to expand outward in imitation of the circles of sorrow that play such an important role in the novel's conclusion. Following this line of thought, perhaps, the Bottom itself is *Sula's* richest character, and Eva Peace's* house is, if not its center, at least a hub of its activity.

Another hub of the Bottom's activity is Carpenter's Road, the small business sector of the Bottom where Edna Finch's Mellow House, the Time and a Half Pool Hall, Reba's Grill, the Elmira Theater, and Irene's Palace of Cosmetology are located. It is also the part of town where men, young and old, congregate to spend time in each other's company and flirt with the women who pass by. Here Sula and Nel seek and find confirmation of their budding sexuality*. The stares they receive from the men on Carpenter's Road are among the incidents that mark the young girls' coming of age. The other events include a confrontation with a group of Irish boys whom Sula scares away by cutting off a fingertip, Sula's overhearing her mother say that she loves her but does not like her, and a small boy, Chicken Little*, slipping out of Sula's hands into a river and drowning. Although Sula is the person most directly involved in these events, she is not the only one upon whom they have an impact. Unfortunately, the ambiguity between the roles of spectator and participant is lost on Nel, and she grows up thinking that these events have little or no bearing on who she has become. The closeness of Sula and Nel's relationship and the interrelatedness of their destinies have led some critics to suggest that the novel has a dual protagonist, Sula/Nel. Morrison has commented that if Sula and Nel were a single person, they would be complete. Their incompleteness is demonstrated by their failure to accept responsibility for Chicken Little's death. Later, as if mirroring Nel's passive interest in the dying Chicken Little, Sula watches from her grandmother's back porch as her mother burns to death while trying to light a fire in the yard.

It is hard to say whether the dream that Eva Peace has of a wedding ceremony in which the bride is attired in a red gown is, as she interprets it later, a foretelling of Hannah's death or of Nel's wedding. Nel's wedding represents a death for Nel and for Nel's relationship with Sula. In Sula's eyes, Nel is the closest thing she has to an other and a self, and although she does an excellent job of disguising her pain, Sula is hurt by Nel's decision to marry, viewing it as a kind of betrayal. Jude Greene*, Nel's groom, asks Nel to marry him not out of love, but out of rage at his inability to secure a job building the New River Road and a determination to take on what he perceives to be the role of a man in society. The narrator suggests that Jude also wants somebody to care about his pain. After the ceremony, Nel watches Sula leave the church with just the hint of a strut and take the main road out of town, not to be seen again for ten years.

When Sula returns to the Bottom, she is accompanied by a plague of robins, and everything she does seems calculated to shock. She sends her grandmother to a nursing home for indigent white women, she sleeps with Nel's husband, and she wounds the egos of the men in town by terminating her short-lived affairs with them without offering any suitable explanation for her loss of interest. Soon rumors begin circulating that Sula sleeps with white men; that she pushed Teapot, a five-year-old boy, down her front steps; that she caused Mr. Finley to choke on a chicken bone; that she does not look her age; that she had no childhood diseases; that mosquitoes refuse to land on her; and that the mentally ill Shadrack treats her with an inordinate amount of respect. In short, the neighborhood brands Sula a witch and makes her the scapegoat for its ills and misfortunes. Ironically, this has a positive effect on the residents of the

Bottom, in that it causes them to band together against the perceived threat in their midst.

The only inhabitant of the Bottom who accepts Sula, at least for a time, is Ajax*, and this is partly because Sula reminds him of his conjure* woman mother. Ajax and Sula become lovers, and each time Ajax visits Sula, he brings her a gift. Ajax differs from the other lovers Sula has had because he listens to her and is not threatened by her intelligence and strength. Uncharacteristically, Sula begins to feel possessive toward him. One day when Ajax comes to visit Sula, he sees that she is wearing a green ribbon in her hair and has cleaned the house in preparation for his visit. Taking these as signs that she is going to ask for a more serious commitment from him, he ends their relationship.

A year later, Sula falls ill and is bedridden. Nel, still hurt by what she views as Sula's betrayal, goes to check on her. After she gets Sula some medicine from the drugstore, they enter into a conversation about the way that Sula is living and has lived her life. Finally, Nel gets up the courage to ask Sula why she "took" her husband, Jude, if they were friends. Sula replies that she did not kill him; she just had sex with him, and she cannot understand why Nel could not just get over it if they were such good friends. As Nel leaves, Sula asks her how she knows which one of them is the good one, and suggests that maybe she has been a better friend to Nel than Nel has been to her. Shortly afterward, Sula dies.

Many critics have commented upon the small amount of space Sula takes up in a novel that bears her name. We do not meet her until the end of the third chapter (the second, if you take the first section to be a prologue), and she dies two chapters before the end of the novel. Morrison says that she had Sula die before the novel's close because she wanted readers to miss her.

The residents of the Bottom are far from missing Sula. If anything, they are jubilant at the news of her death*, and seem to have expectations of it ushering in a new era for the neighborhood. They are supported in their belief by several developments: the announcement of a tunnel-construction project that they hope will employ Black workers, the relocation of Eva Peace from the ramshackle house to which Sula had sent her to a more upscale nursing home, and the downpour of freezing rain that coats the Bottom with a layer of beautiful silver ice. However, it is not long before the positive moral effect that Sula had over the inhabitants of the Bottom loses its strength, and people begin to return to their selfish and mean-spirited ways. Life in the Bottom takes such a sour turn after Sula's death that when Shadrack comes through the neighborhood on January 3, tolling his bell for the commencement of National Suicide Day, the townspeople, for the first time ever, join him in his celebration. But things get out of hand when they come face-to-face with the tunnel at which the men had hoped to find

work. The tunnel becomes a symbol of all the dashed hopes of the previous year, and the people begin to destroy it with great vigor. In a reversal of the biblical story of the parting of the Red Sea, the walls of the
tunnel collapse and the townspeople are drowned in torrents of freezing water that pour in from the river.

The last chapter of the novel is told from Nel's point of view. It takes
up the elegiac tone of the novel's opening section, contrasting what the
Bottom used to be with the historical change of "1965," the year of the
Watts Rebellion and the beginning of the Black Power movement (symbolized by the "new look" the young people are said to have). Nel is a
member of a church circle that goes around visiting seniors. At the time
of narration, it is Nel's turn to visit the nursing homes. The last home
she visits is Sunnydale, Eva Peace's new residence. Eva is senile now, and
her comments are composed of both sense and nonsense. When she asks
Nel about her role in the drowning of Chicken Little, Nel is shaken, and
tells Eva that she is confusing her with Sula. Eva replies that there was
never any difference between the two of them and suggests that, at the
very least, Nel is complicit for having watched.

After leaving Eva, Nel goes to the colored part of the cemetery in
Beechnut Park, where Sula is buried, and is overtaken by memories of
her once best friend. Upon leaving the cemetery, Nel has an epiphany.
She realizes that for many years she thought she had been missing Jude,
when in actuality it was Sula she missed. Nel also realizes for the first
time in her adult life that the girlhood friendship between her and Sula
had been the most important relationship in her life.

Although Morrison's novel is named *Sula*, in many ways it is Nel who
embodies the traits of a traditional protagonist. Nel's realization at the
novel's end signals the possibility of change. At the very least, it has already led her to an awareness of the porous boundaries between good
and evil, and to an understanding that good is always complicated and
contaminated by evil's presence.

This is the meaning that Sula's life has for Nel, and the reason why
readers are not always able to instantly identify with Sula. By presenting us with a character who lacks many, if not most, of the attributes we
have come to expect of heroes (wisdom, self-awareness, generosity, and
willingness to sacrifice herself for the greater good of the community*),
Morrison causes us to question what a Black woman hero coming of age
in the 1930s and 1940s might look like. The question is not too different
from the one raised by Harriet Jacobs about Black women's sexuality in
the nineteenth century. In both cases, the answers are complicated and
differ from what we might expect. And yet Sula is not entirely lacking
in heroic attributes—she is fearless, has a great sense of adventure, and
is willing to risk public censure in order to live her life the way she sees
fit. While our society praises men for these attributes, they are often

considered troubling in women. *Sula*, the book and the character, does an excellent job of challenging this double standard. *See also* Rekus.

References: Rita A. Bergenholtz, "Toni Morrison's *Sula*: A Satire on Binary Thinking," *African American Review* 30: 1 (1996); Maggie Gale-house, "'New World Woman': Toni Morrison's *Sula*," *Papers on Language and Literature* 35: 4 (1999); Phillip Novak, "'Circles and Circles of Sorrow': In the Wake of Morrison's Sula," *PMLA* 114: 2 (1999); Maureen T. Reddy, "The Tripled Plot and Center of *Sula*," *Black American Literature Forum* 22: 1 (1988); Karen F. Stein, "Toni Morrison's *Sula*: A Black Woman's Epic," *Black American Literature Forum* 18: 4 (1984).

Douglas Taylor

## Supernatural, Use of

*See* Ghost Story, Use of.

## Sweet (*Song of Solomon*)

A prostitute with whom Milkman Dead* has an affair while in Virginia. Their affair is significant in that it is the first time Milkman gives of himself to another person. *See also Song of Solomon.*

Fiona Mills

## Sweet Home (*Beloved*)

The role played by Sweet Home, the Kentucky plantation where *Beloved*'s Sethe Suggs* meets her husband and has the first three of her four children*, is central to understanding the events that later occur at 124 Bluestone Road*. Long before Sethe kills her young daughter, meets the incarnation of that daughter in the figure of Beloved*, and loses her sanity, she arrives at Sweet Home a naive young girl. A beautiful place owned by the benevolent Garner* family*, Sweet Home represents a sort of Eden for Sethe. There she experiences love and knows protection for the first time. There she bears her first three children and creates a life with her husband. It is at Sweet Home that Sethe first discovers who she is. Yet it is also at Sweet Home that that identity* is destroyed forever.

The paradoxical nature of Sweet Home, a place where beauty and ugliness, good and evil, coexist uneasily underscores the central moral question of the novel: Are Sethe's actions to be condoned or condemned? By highlighting both the wonderful and the terrible aspects of Sweet Home, Morrison demonstrates both the complex forces that go into the making of Sethe's psyche and the impossibility of easy answers.

As a young woman, Sethe believes in the goodness of human nature. She believes that the male slaves at Sweet Home really are men, as Mr. Garner claims. After Mr. Garner's death* and schoolteacher's* arrival, however, Sethe learns to doubt her own senses. Schoolteacher, a man trusted by Mrs. Garner to oversee the farm, teaches his nephews* that Sethe and her children are animals, and are to be treated as such. On Sethe's final day at Sweet Home, as she is trying desperately to find her husband, Halle*, so they can flee together, schoolteacher beats her so badly that he carves a scar in the shape of a tree on her back, and then watches as his nephew nurses her. This scar, an indirect reference to the tree in the Genesis story of Eden, reminds Sethe not only of the evil done to her at Sweet Home but also of the paradise she previously considered it. Sethe loses more than her innocence at Sweet Home; she also loses the sense of security she needs to survive emotionally.

Full appreciation of Sethe's actions cannot occur without an examination of both the evil wrought at Sweet Home and the seductive grip it continues to exert over the lives of its former slaves. Despite everything that has happened to them, Sethe and Paul D Garner* cannot forget the terrible beauty of the place and the sense of belonging it gave them. The interaction between the yearning for their lost innocence and the repugnance that this longing gives them constitutes the novel's core. *See also* Approaches to Morrison's Work: Ecocritical; *Beloved*; Slavery.

Elizabeth Ely Tolman

## Tar Baby (1981)

Morrison's fourth novel, *Tar Baby*, is often considered one of her most problematic and controversial works. Its controversy stems from the rather wide and complex web of aesthetic and thematic issues that Morrison explores. Not only does she comment on relationships between Blacks and whites, men and women, parents and children*, the urban and rural, and between class groups, but she also exposes the sometimes difficult and complicated relationships between Black men and women. This complex allegorical novel spent four months on the *New York Times* bestseller list and solidified Morrison's reputation as a masterful novelist. Overflowing with her now legendary lush language and imagery, *Tar Baby* dramatizes the multiple dilemmas of identity*, feminism, and the tangled connections between history* and the present.

*Tar Baby* is Morrison's first novel located outside Ohio; set in contemporary society, it is her first to feature white characters. The central narrative concern of the novel is the romance of Son* and Jadine Childs*. Son, a young Black drifter, escapes from a commercial fishing boat and ends up hiding in the luxurious vacation home, L'Arbe de la Croix*, belonging to retired Philadelphia candy king Valerian Street*. After Son is discovered hiding in Margaret Street's* closet, rather than call the police, Valerian capriciously invites him to stay. The invitation upsets the small community* at the house, including Sydney and Ondine Childs*, the butler and cook, and their niece, the beautiful Black model Jadine, who has joined them on the island for a respite. Son's presence exacerbates the already delicate balance of power in the Street household and finally reveals the instability of its foundation. Son and Jadine's relationship eventually fails, succumbing to the very different perspectives each has about life, Blackness, and relationships. The novel's fantastic ending and the reordering of the power relationship at L'Arbe de la Croix raise more questions than answers.

Morrison uses a number of aesthetic tools to convey her message of the inherent complexity of all relationships. Primary among these is the novel's use of the allegorical form that allows for an engagement with large abstract issues. For example, Morrison stages the symbolic battle for the definition of Black American society through the characters of Son and Jadine. Seen from this perspective, Son represents a version of Blackness that opposes white cultural and capitalistic values, and is connected to nature and the historical Black South*; Jadine personifies a contemporary Blackness that has embraced feminism and white cultural values, is not connected to the past (Jadine is an orphan), and is more concerned with succeeding according to the rules of capitalistic society. The failure of their relationship can be interpreted to mean that Black American society is in trouble because of these differences, or that Black American society should not be interpreted as essentially monolithic. Although Morrison raises and engages both of these possibilities, the narrative thrust of the novel seems to agree with the first interpretation and censures the last. We see this most clearly in the allegorical conclusion of the novel, where Jadine returns to what the novel has classified as her inauthentic life of independence and material success in Paris, while Son achieves union with the authentic Black past personified by the blind horsemen.

In addition to allegory, Morrison uses magical realism* and fantasy to great effect. The use of fantasy is articulated in the novel's setting on a Caribbean island. Indeed, the most dazzling scenes are those that linger over the sheer hallucinatory effect of life in the tropics. As Jadine points out, islands exaggerate things; the sun and the landscape conspire to facilitate feelings and actions of excess. This excess makes the setting of the novel operate as a character, just as the people in the novel do. This is conveyed most spectacularly in the descriptions of the daisy trees, which move around and are as much concerned with the relationships between the characters as we are. Butterflies, ants, copperhead snakes, and fish are also important participants in and viewers of the dramas unfolding before them on the island. Even the very earth of the island has agency, as it pushes out its covering of handmade Mexican tiles, asserting its desire for freedom. More than mere personification, Morrison acknowledges that nothing is as simple or straightforward as it seems. Take, for example, her treatment of the myth* of the blind horsemen. For Valerian, the blind horsemen are French chevaliers—upright in spotless uniforms, riding in formation across the hills, backed by the sparklingly clear and strict Napoleonic Code. For Son, the horsemen are barefoot and blind escaped slaves, tired and exhausted from their long years of riding. These distinctions highlight their very different perspectives and places within the chain of power and history.

Morrison enhances this ambivalence by incorporating aesthetic influences from a variety of sources. At the center of the novel is the folk image of the Tar Baby, popularly derived from one of Joel Chandler Harris's Uncle Remus tales, "Tar Baby" (1879). The Uncle Remus tales have been interpreted as allegories of slave life, with Br'er Rabbit representing the Black slave and Br'er Fox the white master. In the Harris story, Br'er Fox, to catch Br'er Rabbit, constructs a human figure made out of sticky tar or pitch, a tar baby. When he encounters the tar baby along the road, Br'er Rabbit ends up hitting it because he thinks it has disrespected him. The more he struggles, the faster he is stuck. Because he is a trickster* figure, Br'er Rabbit is able to maneuver his escape and run away, lickety-split, lickety-split. Son makes this same sound when Marie-Therese Foucault* maneuvers his escape from Jadine.

Consequently, many read Jadine as the tar baby and Son as Br'er Rabbit. Like Uncle Remus's tar baby, Jadine was constructed by white society and ends up trapping Br'er Rabbit/Son. The fact that Jadine is immersed in tar after their picnic on the beach—the first time it becomes clear that Son is desirable—would seem to be unambiguous evidence that Jadine is the tar baby. However, if we consider that for Morrison, the tar baby also represents the ability of the Black woman to hold her community together, then viewing Jadine as such becomes more complicated, for she does not hold her community together. Other than Son, Sydney, and Ondine, she has very little interaction with the Black community. In addition, Jadine "abandons" the Black community at the end of the novel to return to Paris. Also, after she falls in the tar, she struggles mightily to escape its blackness, and after she does escape, she makes sure that she has cleaned every bit of it from her body. Finally, it is important to consider that the trickster figure itself is often an ambivalent character—it triumphs through deception that can be innocent or evil. Br'er Rabbit is caught by the tar baby because he believes he is superior to it, just as Son falls in love with Jadine because he thinks he can teach her the right way to be Black by forcing his dreams of Eloe* into hers.

Morrison does not confine herself to using African American cultural references but casts a wide net. Most spectacularly, *Tar Baby* incorporates elements of Shakespeare's play *The Tempest* and is concerned with similar questions regarding colonialism, capitalism, imperialism, and power. Like Prospero, Valerian has created an island paradise for himself by manipulating nature and people. Not only does Valerian control everything on the island, but everyone in the household of L'Arbe de la

Croix is in his debt; he monetarily supports his wife, employs Sydney and Ondine, has paid for Jadine's schooling and continues to support her monetarily, and, because he invited Son to stay rather than call the police and has arranged for him to get a visa, Son is also in his debt. Further, like Prospero he is surprised when everyone revolts against his caprice and control. Although the meteorological storm in the novel does not happen on the island, it mirrors the emotional storm that sweeps through L'Arbe, exposing Margaret's secret abuse of her son, Michael. The storm changes everything, cleansing so that all secrets are exposed. Additionally, Son, like Caliban, is portrayed as a child of nature. He saves Valerian's plants and helps them grow. Jadine, like Ariel, is formed by white cultural values and exists, uncomfortably, in between. In the end, like Prospero, Valerian is weakened. By incorporating or alluding to *The Tempest*, Morrison calls attention to the breadth of her influences. A truly American writer, Morrison incorporates influences from Black and white culture.

In addition to these aesthetic issues, the novel explores related thematic issues such as the state of the Black community and definitions of Blackness. Written in the late 1970s, during the rise in numbers of the Black middle class, *Tar Baby* has been called a cautionary tale about contemporary Black life. In her attainment of feminist independence and material success, Jadine has divorced herself from the bedrock of essential and authentic Blackness. However, inasmuch as Morrison comments on the dangers of contemporary Black aspirations of "making it," the novel also negatively comments on those who would "romanticize" the Black experience through Son's character. On the run for eight years, his memories of Eloe and New York City sustain him in his absence from them. However, as becomes clear when he returns, these memories are not borne out by the reality. New York has become a city full of crying Black women, and Black men who walk on tiptoe willfully ignore the cries of Black women. Eloe is not the romantic, essential, unquestionable bedrock of Black culture. As Jadine points out, Eloe may be an all-Black town, but whites who live elsewhere run it. Son romanticizes Eloe, until Jadine's photos provide a contradictory image of Eloe as slow, stupid, and backward.

Through exchanges like these, Morrison uses the relationship of Son and Jadine to engage with the issue of class in the Black community. Blacks are supposed to be a cohesive community. Situating the novel outside of the familiar U.S. borders allows Morrison to explore cultural divisions that do, in fact, exist. She includes Blacks from diverse backgrounds and experiences: Jadine, the orphaned "new" Black woman without connections to history; Son, the authentic Southern Black man; Sydney and Ondine, middle-class, striving Philadelphia Negroes; and the Caribbean natives, Marie-Therese and Gideon. These differences raise questions about the nature of Blackness and whether it is essential and inborn or something one must learn, as Gideon says of Jadine that she has to choose Blackness. Although Morrison seems to be interested in interrogating the myth of the cohesion of the Black community—of all of the Black characters, Jadine is the only one to argue for a new definition of Blackness that does not rely on dualistic thinking and white opposition—Son's redemption and Jadine's banishment reinscribe the notion of a singular, authentic Blackness.

In addition to these concerns with race and class, like Morrison's earlier novels *Tar Baby* is also concerned with relationships and love. Of the three couples in the novel, one is a success, another is failing but ends well, and the last fails. Relationships fail in the novel when differences are foregrounded and neither party is willing to compromise. Sydney and Ondine's successful relationship is based on mutual acceptance and trust, compromise and fluidity. They come from similar backgrounds, have similar goals, interests, and perspectives about each other, the world, and what it means to be Black. Neither has more power or control in the relationship. On the other hand, Valerian's marriage to Margaret begins to fail because of his excessively patronizing attitude toward her. Valerian has all the power and control in their early relationship because Margaret comes from a lower class. He does not see her perspective, nor does he see her as an equal. Furthermore, Margaret does not see herself as Valerian's equal, but rather as his trophy. She thinks that Valerian married her only for her looks, and now she must do all she can to retain them. The power dynamic within their relationship changes when Valerian has to relinquish control over his island paradise and the community at L'Arbe de la Croix, becoming physically dependent on Margaret. At this point Margaret realizes that she makes important contributions to their relationship other than her beauty. Finally, like Valerian and Margaret, Jadine and Son are from two different class groups. This seems unimportant at first, since they are both Black, but slowly it begins to undermine their relationship. Despite their racial similarities, they turn out to have very different ideas about relationships, the world, gender roles, race*, and each other. Neither is willing or able to compromise or agree on anything. The relationship fails, and both are at fault because neither is willing to relinquish control or to consider the other's perspective as valid.

As a novel, *Tar Baby* has an epic feel—not in length but in structure, influences, and thematic concern. Morrison relies on dialogue and imagery to convey her message, and incorporates a wide variety of cultural influences and references. Just as Milton stages his battle for good and evil in Paradise, Morrison stages a battle for Blackness on a colonial island paradise. In the end the novel seems to shy away from the potential of epic, which raises large and abstract questions and leaves them answerable only by the reader, by seeking solace in safety. In *Tar Baby* Morrison asks the question "What is Blackness?" and answers conclusively, shutting the door on any other possibility, that only those with true and authentic properties shall know. *See also* Approaches to Morrison's Work: Postcolonial; Isle des Chevaliers.

References: Krishnamoorthy Aithal, "'Getting Out of One's Skin and Being the Only One Inside': Toni Morrison's *Tar Baby*," *American Studies International* 34: 2 (1996); Madelyn Jablon, "*Tar Baby*: Philosophizing Blackness," in *Approaches to Teaching the Novels of Toni Morrison*, ed. Nellie Y. McKay and Kathryn Earle (1997); Dorothea Drummond Mbalia, "*Tar Baby*: A Reflection of Morrison's Developed Class Consciousness," in *Toni Morrison*, ed. Linden Peach (1997); Marilyn Sanders Mobley, "Narrative Dilemma: Jadine as Cultural Orphan in *Tar Baby*," in *Toni Morrison: Critical Perspectives Past and Present*, ed. Henry Louis Gates, Jr., and K. Anthony Appiah (1993); Malin LaVon Walther, "Toni Morrison's *Tar Baby*: Re-Figuring the Colonizer's Aesthetics," in *Cross Cultural Performances: Differences in Women's Re-Visions of Shakespeare*, ed. Marianne Novy (1993).

Nicole N. Aljoe

## Tar Baby (*Sula*)

Very light-complexioned, possibly white, tenant of Eva Peace*. The people of the Bottom* originally refer to him as "Pretty Johnny." Eva gives him the nickname "Tar Baby" out of fun and meanness. Tar Baby is from the hill country and has a beautiful singing voice, which he sometimes uses at Wednesday-night prayer meetings to sing what seems to be his favorite song, "In the Sweet By-and-By." The residents of the Bottom have little respect for him, because he spends most of his time trying to drink himself to death with cheap wine. *See also Sula*.

Douglas Taylor

## Trace, Joe (*Jazz*)

It is Joe's murder of Dorcas Manfred*, the teenager with whom he carries on an adulterous relationship, that precipitates the narrative that is *Jazz*. Born to an unidentified forest-dwelling woman, simply called Wild*, who rejects him after his birth, Joe longs for the adoring feminine gaze lost at birth. As a result, he attempts to regain unconditional maternal love in Dorcas's arms, shooting her when she demands her independence, taunting and humiliating him in the process. Through his nonsexual bonding with Felice*, Dorcas's friend who becomes a surrogate daughter, he learns to freely give and receive affection, further deepening his own bond with and appreciation for Violet*, his wife. After having spent a lifetime continually reinventing himself in order to survive as a Black man in a hostile environment, Joe is able to grow into his own adulthood and emotional maturity. *See also* Jazz.

Caroline Brown

### Trace, Violet (*Jazz*)

When Violet discovers the identity of the dead girl with whom her husband, Joe Trace*, had been carrying on an affair, she attends the funeral in order to slash the dead girl's face with a knife. Apprehended in the process of attempting to assault the corpse, she is thrown out of the church. When she returns home, she releases her pampered birds that parrot loving endearments, forcing them to fend for themselves in the harsh winter snow. So ends her own parroting of normalcy. When Violet reemerges, her search for the power behind Dorcas Manfred's* mystique begins, and she questions everyone about the murdered girl. Finally ending in the home of Alice Manfred*, Dorcas's bourgeois, grief-stricken aunt, the quest forces Violet to confront the demons in her own past. This includes the suicide of Rose Dear*, her mother; Violet's own rejection of motherhood*; and her current maternal longing, which hides her dissatisfaction with herself. Fundamental to this is the ghost of Golden Gray*, the blond, mulatto child for whom her grandmother cared and who becomes the standard of beauty against which it is impossible to compete. Dorcas becomes the reincarnation of Golden, and Joe's infidelity symbolizes the fact that both have rejected their blackness for an alien model. However, through Alice's friendship, honesty, and laughter, Violet confronts the pain of her past. In choosing laughter—her grandmother's model for survival, which is ultimately more complex and freeing than tears—she allows herself to move on from anger and victimization. *See also* Jazz.

Caroline Brown

### Trauma

"The ordinary response to atrocities," writes trauma specialist and psychiatrist Judith Herman, "is to banish them from consciousness. Certain violations of the social compact are too terrible to utter aloud: this is the meaning of the word unspeakable" (1). As Toni Morrison incorporates troubling scenes of violence* and death* in her art, she reveals that, as trauma theorists have shown, trauma can result not only from a single encounter with life-threatening violence but also from a prolonged exposure to physical danger or abuse. Exploring the catastrophic historical traumas suffered by African Americans, Morrison represents the unspeakable horrors of slavery* in works like *Beloved**, and the terrors of the postslavery years and of racist and urban violence in works like *Song of Solomon**, *Jazz**, and *Paradise**. She also depicts, in novel after novel, the trauma of defective or abusive parenting or relationships and the Black-on-Black violence that exists within the African American community* in her jarring descriptions of child and spousal abuse, incest and infanticide*, self-mutilation and self immolation, suicide, and murder.

Persistently and insistently, Morrison focuses on inter- and intraracial violence in her fiction, even at the risk of alienating some of her readers. In her first novel, *The Bluest Eye**, Morrison describes the progressive traumatization of Pecola Breedlove*, who is rejected and physically abused by her mother and raped by her alcoholic and unpredictably violent father. Ultimately damaged beyond repair, Pecola ends up living in the dissociated world of the severely traumatized individual, where she converses with her alter identity*, her only "friend." Directing attention to the traumas of African American life in *Sula**, Morrison describes a world where whites are equated with the uncontrollable evils of life and where Black survival may come at the terrible cost of self-mutilation. From the opening account of Shadrack's* traumatic war experiences through depictions of Eva Peace's* and Sula Peace's* self-mutilation, Eva's setting fire to her son, Plum*, Chicken Little's* drowing, Hannah's fiery self-immolation, and the mass drowning of many members of the Bottom* community, Sula calls attention to the unexpected violence of African American life in scenes that evoke the dissociated world of the trauma victim—jarringly violent but also highly visual scenes that recall the "sensory and iconic forms of memory*" associated with trauma, memories that focus on "fragmentary sensation, on image without context" (Herman 39, 38).

In *Song of Solomon*, the search for African American roots leads to the recovery* of painful family* memories of white supremacist persecution and violence. Central to the family and cultural heritage of the Dead family is the traumatic and formative story of how Macon* and Pilate Dead*, as adolescents, witnessed the murder of their father, an emancipated slave, who was killed by the white men who stole his land. Imitating the racist violence perpetrated by whites against African Americans, Milkman Dead's* friend, Guitar Baines*, is a member of a terrorist organization that carries out revenge killings against whites. In a troubling scene of Black-on-Black violence, a deranged Guitar hunts down Milkman, intent on killing him, and he kills Pilate, who is presented as a wise woman of the folk and a natural healer. Despite the positive rhetoric of the closure, which describes Milkman's epiphanic moment of racial flight and pride in his Black roots, the fact that Milkman leaps into the waiting arms of Guitar suggests that this moment of heroic flight can also be read as a suicidal and nihilistic gesture.

If *Song of Solomon* looks back in part to the traumatic legacy of slavery, *Beloved* bears witness, in a sustained and unrelenting way, to the horrors of the slave experience. In dramatizing the humiliations and traumas the slaves were forced to endure at the hands of their white oppressors, Morrison describes, with almost clinical precision, the effects of trauma on her ex-slave character, Sethe Suggs*, who remains haunted by her traumatic "rememories"—that is, her uncontrolled remembering and reliving of the emotionally painful experiences she suffered as a slave. In describing Sethe's diminished life, a life plagued by haunting rememories that become concretized in the ghost, *Beloved* presents what Judith Herman calls the "dialectic of trauma," the oscillation of "opposing psychological states"—those of intrusion and constriction—which is "perhaps the most characteristic feature of the post-traumatic syndromes." In the aftermath of a traumatic experience, the individual "finds herself caught between the extremes of amnesia or of reliving the trauma, between floods of intense, overwhelming feeling and arid states of no feeling at all" (47). Because of the constant interruptions of the trauma, Herman explains, the traumatized individual is unable to resume the usual course of her life, and what would normally be a safe environment may end up feeling dangerous because the trauma survivor cannot know for certain that she will not confront some reminder of the trauma.

Caught up in the dialectic of trauma, Sethe lives a constricted life as she attempts to avoid reminders of and forget her past as a slave, and reestablish some control over her inner life. But Sethe's troubled past returns to haunt her in the form of the ghost of her dead daughter, the crawlingalready? baby Sethe killed by slitting her throat with a handsaw to prevent the slave catchers from returning her to slavery. The unpredictable intrusions of the ghost convey not only the experience of intrusive memory—an "abnormal form of memory, which breaks spontaneously into consciousness"—but also the "involuntariness," the "driven, tenacious" and "'daemonic' quality" of traumatic reenactments in intrusive phenomena (Herman 37, 41). Sethe's haunted house, like the psychic world inhabited by the trauma victim, is a dangerous and unsafe place where there is a loss of predictability and control.

When Paul D Garner* finds his way to 124 Bluestone Road*, he seemingly ousts the ghostly presence from Sethe's trauma-haunted house. But the past is not so easily forgotten, and thus Beloved*, the embodiment of the ghost and the rememoried past, comes to life. Returning from the dead as a physically traumatized and emotionally abandoned child in an adult body, Beloved recalls descriptions of abused children* with her expressionless and empty eyes, her failed memory, and her disintegration anxiety—she fears that she will fly apart and end up in pieces. Beloved, who "disremembers" everything, initially reminds Paul D of the homeless, dazed ex-slaves he saw wandering the roads after the end of the Civil War. Beloved also represents the sexually abused slave woman, for both Sethe and Stamp Paid think that perhaps Beloved has escaped from the clutches of a white rapist, and Beloved herself describes her sexual abuse by white men, who called her "beloved" in the dark and "bitch" in the daylight. She also comes to embody the collective suffering and psychic woundedness of those who survived the torments of the slave ships, only to be victimized by slavery.

Pointing to the terrible emotional costs of slavery's disruption of the mother-child bond, Beloved is a greedy ghost that needs a lot of love, and as the murdered child magically returned from the dead, she is desperately needy for Sethe's love and attention. When Sethe identifies Beloved as her dead but resurrected daughter, she thinks she can lay down her burdened past and live in peace. Instead, Sethe becomes involved in a deadly battle as she finds herself obsessing on and literally being taken over by the past. Wanting to make up for the past, Sethe strives to satisfy the insatiable Beloved, and the more Beloved takes, the more Sethe tries to justify the past. In a repeated drama, Sethe attempts to make amends for the infanticide and Beloved makes her pay for what she has done. Overtaken by the past, Sethe begins to waste away.

Illustrating the potentially healing communality of those who have survived a common traumatic experience, Beloved describes how thirty women from the community gather at 124 Bluestone Road and drive out Beloved with their shout-song. One of the unaccounted-for victims of slavery, Beloved is intentionally forgotten like a bad dream, for remembering her seems unwise. Beloved's story is not one to "pass on," the narrative insists. Yet, as critics have often commented, this repeated injunction is profoundly ironic, given the fact that in Beloved, Morrison has "passed on" the story of slavery and memorialized the lives of the forgotten "beloveds" unrecorded in history but living and lingering in the African American collective memory and cultural imagination.

Continuing in Jazz and Paradise the fictional reconstruction of the African American historical and cultural legacy that she began in Beloved, Morrison tells the story of the migration* of the ex-slaves to Black Harlem* in Jazz and to Oklahoma in Paradise. Both novels look to a traumatic past of white persecution, as Morrison describes the escape of Jazz's Joe Trace* from his hometown in Virginia, which is burned to the ground by whites, or the desire of the 8-rock people in Paradise to live in a separatist community where they are safe from the random and organized violence of whites that swirls around them. Yet even as both novels describe the trauma of white racist violence, they also are centered around disturbing scenes of Black-on-Black violence. In Jazz, Morrison tells the story of the fifty-year-old Joe Trace's murder of his eighteen-year-old lover, Dorcas Manfred*, while in *Paradise* she describes the violent massacre of five women by nine Black men—men who imitate the white man they think they have outfoxed by demonizing and scapegoating those they find unworthy and different.

Intent on staging scenes of inter- and intraracial violence in her novels, Morrison seems driven to speak the unspeakable. If Morrison deliberately evokes the oral quality of gossip through her use of narrative fragments in the repeated but constantly interrupted telling of her characters' stories, she also is an author caught up in the desire to tell and not tell, which typifies our culture's approach to trauma and also recalls the way trauma victims tell their stories. In *Beloved*, for example, the narrative tells and retells in a circuitous way the story of the infanticide just as Sethe circles around the subject when she tries to explain to Paul D why she killed her infant daughter. The opening passage of *Jazz*, which is meant to jolt readers, describes Joe's murder of Dorcas, and then the unfolding narrative circles around this central act of violence, looking into the trauma-ridden pasts of the characters in an attempt to explain why the murder happened. In a similar way, *Paradise* opens with a dramatic description of a horrific crime—the attack on the Convent* women by nine men of Ruby, Oklahoma*—and then the narrative slowly and circuitously spirals around this violent event in an attempt to make sense of the present by looking at the past lives of both victims and perpetrators.

If in Morrison's novels we find evidence of the desire to bear witness to the trauma that exists in the lives of African Americans, in Morrison's insistent aestheticizing of violence we also find evidence of her desire to artistically repair the racial wounds she has exposed. Counteracting depictions of white oppression and Black violence, Morrison's novels dramatize the potentially healing power of the sense of safety and connection offered by the African American community and by what Morrison calls the African American ancestors*: wise and benevolent elder figures like Pilate in *Song of Solomon*, Baby Suggs* in *Beloved*, and Lone DuPres* in *Paradise*. Morrison, then, seems intent on effecting a cultural cure through her art. Yet the tenuousness of that cure is revealed not only by her repeated depictions of the intergenerational transmission of victimization but also by her constant restagings of scenes of violence in each successive novel as she confronts in her fiction the historical legacy of slavery and the painful collective and private traumas suffered by Black Americans in the race-divided American society. *See also* Approaches to Morrison's Work: Psychoanalytical; History; Race; Shame; Whiteness.

References: J. Brooks Bouson, *Quiet as It's Kept: Shame, Trauma, and Race in the Novels of Toni Morrison* (2000); Judith Herman, *Trauma and*

*Recovery* (1992); Jill Matus, *Toni Morrison* (1998); Naomi Morgenstern, "Mother's Milk and Sister's Blood: Trauma and the Neoslave Narrative," *Differences: A Journal of Feminist Cultural Studies* 8: 2 (1996); Laurie Vickroy, "*Beloved* and *Shoah*: Witnessing the Unspeakable," *The Comparatist* 22 (1998).

J. Brooks Bouson

## Trickster

Toni Morrison is highly skilled in the use of trickster figures and a master trickster herself. As a character in a story, the trickster is a complex literary figure most often found in ethnic literature, a figure whose shape is most often determined by its cultural context. However, the trickster can also be the author who, as the storyteller, may purposely outwit or mislead the reader in order to create a specific, final narrative effect.

In folklore* the trickster figure is usually an animal such as a rabbit, coyote, or monkey, that represents an underling and uses its skill and cunning to outwit a superior—that is, a smaller, often weaker creature besting a larger, more powerful adversary. Tricksters are also found in mythic belief systems such as the Greek and Roman versions of the tale of Prometheus, who steals fire from Mount Olympus to save humankind, and Hermes, who was born of a deception and is the gatekeeper and guide to the Underworld. The most common trait among trickster figures is that each is a model of nonconformity used to outwit, disrupt, or comment on conformity and the agents of conformity. The kind of verbal labyrinth created by the trickster figure, both as character and as storyteller, is a primary, cultural defense against such racial and human problems as have been inflicted on African Americans since the first event of slavery*.

Trickster figures tend to fall under two categories: the folkloric character, such as Anansi, Br'er Rabbit, and Iktuma, and the trickster as religious deity, including Hermes, Loki, and Esu. As a folkloric hero, the trickster manipulates the nature of the world either for personal gain or for magnanimous reasons. As a god, the trickster dwells comfortably in a realm between concepts, categories, and rigid dogma as the embodiment of individuality, satire, parody, irony, indeterminacy, magic, ambiguity, sexuality*, chance, uncertainty, and contrasting dualities, such as disruption and reconciliation, betrayal and loyalty, closure and disclosure, encasement and rupture, represented as a single figure (Gates 6). Every trickster, regardless of any type of distinction, exposes norms, ideology, and categorization as static, and therefore flawed, arbitrary human constructs.

Practically, the trickster deity is the most powerful among the god figures. She rules communication so much that, for example, in the Fon religion of West Africa, none of the gods can communicate without Legba
acting as interpreter. It is said that Esu Elegbara (Esu), the trickster deity
of the Yoruba, carries a calabash full of *ase*, the substance the supreme
deity used to create the universe. African trickster tales were brought to
the United States by slaves, who were separated from family*, forbidden
to speak their own languages, compelled to do hard labor, and kept illiterate. In the African archetypal pattern, the trickster manipulates the
larger animals not only to obtain food or to survive, but also to satisfy
other fundamental human cravings: power, status, wealth, and sexual
prowess. Also common in African tradition, the trickster often proves to
be as cruel and merciless as his or her opponent is. These tales became a
way for an oppressed people to express and endure their pain. Although
the stories were recounted out of sorrow and pain, they transcended the
environment and turned many an unbearable day or event into one of
smiles, chuckles, and, sometimes, laughter. In this way, the slave became
the trickster who confounded the oppressor. These same methods were
also translated into real-world actions when slaves began escaping and
used various trickster maneuvers to convey information about the route
of the Underground Railroad that often led slaves to freedom in Northern states and Canada. For decades, these myriad stories were the medium
in which African Americans instinctively sought protection and reas-
surance from a hostile world and uncertain life.

The works of Toni Morrison reflect more than her mastery of folkloric figures, most especially that of the trickster; her stories also exhibit
her ultimate skill of author as trickster. In an important critical study,
*Fiction and Folklore: The Novels of Toni Morrison*, Trudier Harris discusses Morrison's novels as a series of reversals, inversions, and sub-
versions of well-known folktales and the rhetorical strategies of the folk
narrative. According to Harris, in *The Bluest Eye** Morrison inverts the
lesson of "The Ugly Duckling"; in *Sula** she subverts the traditional
fairytale structure; in *Song of Solomon** she reverses the Odyssean
journey; in *Tar Baby** she subverts the tales of "Snow White" and
"Sleeping Beauty"; and in *Beloved** she reverses and undermines the
traditional ghost story*. In *Writing Tricksters*, an equally important critical text on the subject of tricksters in ethnic literatures, Jeanne Rosier
Smith observes that for Morrison, "the trickster offers a way to challenge traditional versions of African American female identity and imagine new alternatives" (29).

However, perhaps more important is the fact that Morrison does not
simply blur the common designs of certain story patterns; instead, she
continues to confound and confuse—in true trickster fashion—the

familiar narrative models by replacing the European American archetypes with African and African American folkloric paradigms. In doing so, Morrison completes a perfect act of duplicity and becomes the ultimate author-as-trickster-figure.

The Morrison novel that most obviously incorporates the trickster figure is *Tar Baby*. The title alone compels a comparison with the famous folktale of the same name, a story that features Br'er Rabbit first as trickster, then as victim, and finally, depending on the cultural version, as the one who escapes or who is eaten. Son* is Morrison's adaptation of Br'er Rabbit in *Tar Baby*, but she makes more subtle uses of the tale as well. It is necessary to note that the ending of the white American version of the Tar Baby* story differs significantly from that of the African American. In the popular version of the slave's tale, Br'er Rabbit becomes completely stuck to the tar baby built by the animals he has attempted to trick and, at the very least, is totally at their mercy, whereas he is clearly able to free himself and escape in the white version. The Tar Baby tale influences the psychology of the narrative structure of Morrison's novel and becomes the central trope as certain of the characters confront personal versions of the "tar baby" as psychic traps.

In addition, the motif of "masks" is an important thread in the figurative fabric of many African American stories, including *Tar Baby*. Masks, emotional and psychological, function as variations of the trickster device. Morrison explains that a "mask sometimes exists when Black people talk to white people" (Ruas 218). A smile or laughter acts as a veil that allows white people to see or hear the respect and acquiescence they expect from Black people and masks the true, private feelings of rage, hate, and scorn felt by the Black people for the whites—in turn, the Black people become trickster figures, masking their true feelings and desires. However, in the end, one point Morrison makes about this "masking" is that it turns on the trickster by privileging the expectations of the whites over the voices of the Blacks, thereby tricking the trickster. On the other hand, Henry Louis Gates, Jr., points out the "multiplicity of meanings" encoded in African American folklore (19). Such reverberation of meaning allows Morrison to question not only the "family" arrangements at work in the household of Margaret* and Valerian Street* but also the values taught to Jadine Childs* that deny her the cultural roots she seeks. Usually the silence that accompanies such masking does not challenge cultural domination, but rather helps to perpetuate it. However, in African American folklore the mask, a sign of the trickster, is considered a subversive strategy that enables survival at the same time that it critiques structures of domination. Moreover, the trickster figure generally has a mental agility that most often eases his passage through many a treacherous and dangerous world, usually in spite of, as well as at the expense of, the more powerful, dominant adversary. In *Tar Baby*, Morrison's inversion of the elements of masking demonstrates how the use of masks can fool the trickster and, rather than protecting the wearer, become a barrier.

Other tales that circulated during the time of slavery and the century that followed focused on the myth of flying Africans*. Such stories recount the belief that native-born Africans brought to the colonies had a special power, a secret word that, when uttered, allowed them to lift themselves from the burden of slavery and fly home to Africa. Later, African Americans came to view this tale as an allegory suggesting that although they are bound by shackles of bigotry and inequality, their spirits can never be enslaved by the dominant culture. Achieving such freedom is truly a trickster's coup. In *Song of Solomon*, Morrison elaborately blends the folktale of the flying people with the contemporary, ongoing, African American quest for cultural identity, made more difficult for Black children* because their fathers are so often absent—having "flown away" from the family. During the decades of slavery, the concept of family* was virtually nonexistent for the Africans and their descendants. The men were merely sires and the women breeders of more slaves. However, Morrison presents the modern flight of Black fathers as strong, adventurous events; for although the fathers may fly away, they leave their children with the need to remember, to sing, and to continue the story— family roots are defined by memories, songs, and oral history. This reaffirmation of history* in *Song of Solomon* and its connection to the present is an example of Morrison the author as trickster, signifying on the reader's assumptions and expectations, turning an apparent negative into a positive model.

In *The Bluest Eye*, the trick is on Pecola Breedlove*, a young Black girl whose acceptance of the dominant culture's definition of ideal beauty— blue-eyed, blond, "Barbie"—is what destroys her. In this novel, Pecola, the Ugly Duckling—dark-eyed, brown child—does NOT grow up to be a lovely, *white* swan.

With *Sula*, Morrison has created a main character whose "complete disregard for societal values, suggests her affinities to the trickster" (Smith 115). Ironically, Sula's* social role is clearest at the time of her death*; the friction she caused served as adhesive, keeping the community* together. Jeanne Rosier Smith notes, "The community's response to Sula highlights the anarchic trickster's crucial role in maintaining a system of social relations. ... Without Sula's scorn to 'rub up against,' even motherhood* becomes meaningless" (117).

*Beloved* is one novel seldom mentioned in discussions of the trickster tradition and Toni Morrison, but not because it does not contain such elements. This novel is arguably the most powerful and complex of Morrison's works: it portrays social injustice, corruption, guilt, despair, secret sin, alienation, and retribution—all underscored by a chorus of timeless voices. The trickster motif is everywhere, subtly applied, as if a curtain of gauze though which the reader views the narrative events. Trudier Harris declares, "In her amorality, Beloved* shares kinship with some of the tricksters of tradition—ever guided by personal desires. ... Such figures are recognizable by the power they wield. ... With her supernatural dimension, Beloved has no obvious limits" (160–61).

In the African American literary tradition, it is the female trickster, more often than the male, who employs linguistic trickery and ironic layering of meanings, as well as the one who articulates and subverts prevailing models of femininity, family, and community. A fundamental element of Morrison's style is her strong trickster aesthetic, which she augments with a powerful sense of what it means to be African American. Toni Morrison weaves details, memory, dreams, history, and tropes into stories so rich in texture that identifying a single thread is an impossible task. Behind the mask of the author, deep within the fabric of her complex narratives, we find Toni Morrison, storyteller and trickster extraordinaire. *See also* African Myth, Use of; Conjure; Ghost Story, Use of; Narrative Voice; Oral Tradition.

References: Henry Louis Gates Jr., *The Signifying Monkey* (1998); Trudier Harris, *Fiction and Folklore: The Novels of Toni Morrison* (1991); Charles Ruas, *Conversations with American Writers* (1985); Jeanne Rosier Smith, *Writing Tricksters: Mythic Gambols in American Ethnic Literature* (1997).

Cynthia Whitney Hallett

## True Belle (*Jazz*)

Violet Trace's* maternal grandmother. A slave deeded to Vera Louise Gray* when the latter is expelled from Virginia for her taboo pregnancy with a Black child, True Belle is forced to desert her own family and live in Baltimore. There she functions as the primary caretaker of Golden Gray*, becoming his first true love (which reveals the complexity of the bonds between white children and their Black caretakers). Although Golden is emotionally bound to True Belle, she will always remain a possession for him, fundamentally tied to providing for his many needs. On the other hand, True Belle, in her adoration of Golden, performs a disservice to her own kin by bringing tales of the mixed-race child to the rural Violet, who becomes enamored and forever measures herself against his privilege. *See also* Jazz.

Caroline Brown

## Truelove, Pallas/Divine (*Paradise*)

Title character of one of *Paradise*'s nine sections, and presumably the white girl whom the men of Ruby, Oklahoma*, shoot first when they raid the Convent*, Pallas arrives at the Convent in 1975, sixteen years old and pregnant. Leaving behind her father and her senior year of high school, the wealthy Pallas ("Divine" is her mother's nickname) runs away with Carlos, the high school janitor (who is "really" a sculptor), to visit her artist mother, whom she hasn't seen in years. After a few months of bohemian lifestyle and lots of pot, Pallas sees her mother and Carlos making love in the grass under the stars. Trying to escape the memory*, she wrecks her car and is chased by two men into a swampish lake. Hiding in the darkness, only her face above the black water, Pallas hopes the soft fingers around her legs are only bottom grass and friendly fish. After escaping the men, a mute, dirty, traumatized Pallas hitches a ride in a pickup truck. Believing the girl has been "bothered," the Mexican woman in the truck takes her to the Demby clinic, where Billie Delia Cato* finds her in the alley, standing over her own vomit. Billie Delia takes her to the Convent. After some months, Pallas briefly goes home to her father, only to return to the Convent. Delivered of a baby boy, Pallas's "loud-dreaming" allows her to exorcise the hated and haunting vision of her mother and Carlos, and to rid herself of the memory of entwining tendrils in the dark water. Although Dovey Morgan* and Lone DuPres* both confirm that Pallas is dead after the attack on the Convent, her body disappears with the others. However, we see her again at her mother's, dressed in a long, flowing rose madder-and-umber skirt, sword in hand, baby carried on her chest, looking for a pair of shoes she had left behind. She rides off in a car full of women. *See also Paradise.*

Julie Cary Nerad

## Twain, Mark, Influence of

Since its inception, American literature has dealt with themes of journey, search for identity*, and ascertainment of one's place in society. Mark Twain (1835–1910) in particular made these themes his own, exploring them in *The Adventures of Huckleberry Finn* and *The Tragedy of Pudd'nhead Wilson*, as well as in his short story "A True Story." Likewise, Toni Morrison's fiction embraces these thematic structures. *Song of Solomon*, *Beloved**, *Jazz**, and *Paradise** all include transformative journeys in which characters, and subsequently the readers, search for identity. Both authors consciously propel their readers toward what is often an unwelcome confrontation with the impact of racism on American society.

In Twain's *The Adventures of Huckleberry Finn* we have two journeys running parallel—Huck's and Jim's—that take us along on their search for freedom and a final sense of identity. While Huck seeks to leave his abusive father behind, he in fact finds himself on a trek of discovering who he truly is, as well as something even more profound. Along the way, Huck's journey takes us toward a greater understanding of the issues characterizing the antebellum South*, issues that eventually tore the country apart in the Civil War. Jim, who shortly after the novel begins makes the perilous decision to run away rather than remain a slave, initiates a journey to freedom, a quest that in the novel's latter portion shifts from the literal desire for individual freedom to that of the freedom of choice and identity.

These characters take readers along on their journey of discovery and revelation so that we can appreciate the sensitivity, the dilemma, and the crisis of identity that they themselves experience. Twain takes us on their journeys to compel us to confront the wound of race* and lack of identity from which America still suffers. He tackles this theme again and boldly moves on to the forbidden issue of miscegenation in *The Tragedy of Pudd'nhead Wilson*. Once again Twain's primary character is a slave, not a runaway like Jim, but a slave mother named Roxana, or Roxy. When confronted with the threat of being separated from her son, Chambers, after both of them are sold down the river at the whim of her master— and with no opportunity to express herself and certainly no choice— Roxy, like many other enslaved mothers, elects to kill herself and her son in order to become free of the abhorrent reality of being enslaved.

While preparing for the murder/suicide, Roxy devises another plan that essentially undermines the South's entire mythology of slavery*, intelligence, and environment. Roxy switches the identity of her natural son with that of her master's child, effectively undercutting established notions of prejudice, conviction, and convention.

In both of these novels by Twain, the audience is left with more questions than answers. Although race is a key theme in each of the works, it is not the overriding one. The pervasive theme, underscored by the journey motif, is one of identity and relevance—self-worth in an American society that values neither for some individuals.

Like Twain, Morrison strives to engage her characters and her readers with issues that they (and we) would much rather avoid. Her narratives allow us to work ourselves into the fiction so that we can understand the characters and the situations in which they find themselves. With Twain's and Morrison's characters, what we can be certain of is that the journey has had a profound impact on them as well as on those around them. But as to the ultimate impact or long-lasting effect of the journey, we cannot be certain. And more important, we are left with the question, Are we supposed to have this satisfaction at the conclusion of the novels? As with

Twain's Huck, Jim, and Roxy, so Morrison's Milkman Dead* in *Song of Solomon*, Sethe Suggs* in *Beloved*, Violet Trace* in *Jazz*, and the women as well as the inhabitants of Haven, Oklahoma*, in *Paradise* all are searching for identity and relevance. Each of them is on a quest that is most definitely still in progress as the novels conclude.

Milkman searches for two answers—his identity as a man and his identity as an African American male. He needs to understand himself in the larger society of men and women, as well as in the society of African American men. And as with Twain's Roxy, Morrison compels her audience to identify, or consubstantiate, with Milkman and his dilemma.

Similarly, Sethe's journey in *Beloved* begins before the novel starts and continues beyond its conclusion. We are literally riveted to every page, every image, every word and thought that Sethe, another enslaved mother, utters, for her literal and psychological wandering represents the journey motif at its most effective. Like Twain's Roxy, Sethe seeks freedom for herself and her children*. And like Roxy, Sethe's angst and rage against the degradation of the institution itself, as well as the race perpetuating that prejudice, emerges clearly.

What Twain and Morrison do so well with this motif is to engage the imaginations and emotions of the audience fully and completely. A similar reading experience based on the journey motif develops in *Jazz* and *Paradise*. As the characters are left to wrestle with profound issues, so are we. Sensitive topics such as race, identity, relevance, and self-worth reel in our minds, and will not simply vanish when the reading experience ends; these issues, though they are fundamental, remain troublesome.

No African American man or woman in other popular fictional works by white authors in Twain's time was given voice or presence—much less identity and relevance. With *Huck Finn*, Twain portrays a man who seeks freedom to be visible, to unite with his family, and simply to be. In *Pudd'nhead Wilson* we see a woman seeking ultimate freedom for herself and her son who realizes along the way that mother love alone cannot guarantee a happy ending. In each case these characters exercise their right to voice themselves regardless of the consequences, even to the extent that they employ what might be identified as the rhetoric of silence which many persons of color adopt as a means of actually exerting voice and controlling a rather tenuous situation.

Like Twain, Morrison renders characters who are essentially marginalized by a country that refuses to allow them voice, presence, and place. Whereas Twain's setting places his characters directly within slavery, Morrison's characters should be beyond these issues and themes, but they are not. Like their Twain counterparts, Morrison's Milkman, Sethe, Violet, and the characters of *Paradise* have all suffered marginalization and invisibility at the hands of a society that would rather not have them. They must make their own meaning and find their own voices in spite of their social and racial position. As with the journey motif, all of these individuals are still in the process of asserting their voices as the novels conclude, and the readers are left with the task of continuing the dialogue, regardless of the obvious discomfort.

What Twain and Morrison bring to American fiction that few other American authors do is the compulsion to look again at characters, their values, and the situations they encounter as we revise the way in which we read and understand fiction, particularly American fiction. We are fundamentally transformed by the reading experience and likely will never be the same again, as we are not meant to be. Great fiction compels us to act upon what we read, and both Twain and Morrison capture voices that we do not hear enough in situations we would rather not confront, even now.

Jocelyn A. Chadwick-Joshua

# V

## Violence

Violence in Toni Morrison's works serves a dual function: on the one hand it can lead to knowledge of self in a historical context, and on the other hand to self-annihilation. While those who escape violation and trespass celebrate integrity and dignity, those who commit violent acts, whether intentionally or not, often have internalized the lessons of racist hatred too well and have appropriated white ideals of beauty, community*, worth, and love. The trope of violence that informs Black life from the antebellum period well into the twentieth century is counterbalanced by dreams and folklore*; dreams foreshadow violence and suggest the moral complexity that underlines those who commit violent acts, and folklore serves to undermine white realism with the traditions and myths* of Black culture. The tension between fleeing the past and taking flight toward, literally and figuratively, the future has roots in Toni Morrison's earliest full-length work, The Bluest Eye*, and is developed in subsequent works.

Written from the point of view of nine-to-twelve-year-old Claudia MacTeer*, whose voice alternates between that of adolescent and that of grown woman, The Bluest Eye challenges the Dick and Jane fable learned in childhood readers, to the detriment of Black children in rural Ohio in the 1930s. Claudia comes to renounce the lies perpetrated in these readers because her parents have instructed her in their deception and instilled in her a sense of self-worth, pride, and the value of Black life and culture. The young Pecola Breedlove*, who counters Claudia, learns an entirely different and violent message. From her mother, Pauline Breedlove*, Pecola cultivates a disdain for herself because she is not white, and from her father, Cholly Breedlove*, who rapes her, she learns the unspoken lesson that the Black female body is to blame for the ways that it is violated. Pecola's desire for blue eyes, which leads to madness, is framed as a destructive message of the espousing of white ideals and the subsequent inability to comprehend that these ideals are achieved through Black powerlessness and racist attitudes, which have a historical root.

Violence and violation of the Black female body are mirrored in folklore, and Claudia remembers 1941, the year that Pecola's incestuous child is stillborn, as the year the marigolds would not bloom. Not only do violence and premonition occur in the strange phenomena of Nature, but names and naming prove ominous. Pecola's surname is Breedlove, signaling an irony that she is born into a family which breeds something other than love, namely, a violent contempt for Black beauty and Black life. Counter to the Breedlove family is the MacTeer family, whose children*, Claudia and Frieda*, have the protective love of their parents to caution against sexual trespass. As a result they learn to value their own beauty and to rage against Maureen Peal, the light-skinned girl of affluent parents who shows up at school with new clothes and money in her pocket. They rage against her not because of who she is but because of the white values she represents.

The theme of violence as a current that runs through Black female relationships—between mother and daughter, sisters, and friends—is further developed in *Sula**. Sula Peace* is the daughter of a free-loving mother, Hannah, and the granddaughter of Eva Peace*, a woman who is believed to have lain down on railroad tracks after her husband deserted her, sacrificing a leg for insurance money. This narrative largely focuses on the intimate relationship between girlhood friends, Sula and Nel Wright*. Much as their households differ—Sula's mother is free in her sexuality, while Nel's mother is prim, proper, and repressed—the childhood friends differ. Yet without the other, each is incomplete.

Violence and dream are embedded in *Sula* in ways that comment on the struggle for self-actualization in a climate of racial hatred that exiles Blacks to the Bottom* and complicates their interpersonal relationships. The hills of Medallion, Ohio*, are nicknamed the Bottom because a white landholder, wishing to occupy the fertile Ohio valley, man's duped an illiterate former slave into believing the rocky hillside was the Bottom of Heaven, the space closer to God, and hence better land for cultivating. Yet nothing will grow here. The men, who can find no self-sufficiency in the land and no work in the town, tend to flee the Bottom. Economic disenfranchisement wreaks havoc on Black households, and the violence done is apparent in the absence of men within the family unit. In fact,

Nel's husband, Jude Greene*, deserts her following Sula's return to the Bottom after a ten-year absence, which coincides with the couple's wedding anniversary. When Sula takes Jude to bed, not because she has designs on him but because she can, her friendship with Nel is severed. But Sula is unapologetic. In her long exodus from the Bottom, and in her free and easy sexuality that parallels her mother's, she has learned lessons about intimate relationships that are lost on Nel. What she finds through education and city life is that no matter where she goes, the position of Black men and women is riddled with the violence of racist hatred. Men and women are everywhere the same, but friendship between women, she learns too late, cannot be easily duplicated or repaired.

When Sula, the woman with the rose birthmark that stems above her eye—a marking that Morrison borrowed from Nathaniel Hawthorne's short story "The Birthmark," in which the main character meets a fate that Sula's parallels—dies, the Bottom's inhabitants breathe a sigh of relief. Her death*, much like her life, proves ominous. Her passing, which follows a hard winter of starvation, is followed by National Suicide Day*, a holiday established by Shadrack*, a World War I veteran who has gone AWOL. On one particular day of the year, Shadrack marches through the streets with a cowbell, inviting Bottom folks to kill themselves because it is easier than living in a world that disdains Blackness. When the Bottom folks finally parade behind Shadrack, their joining him is as much mockery as it is relief from the pall Sula has cast over the community, for Sula is the pariah in their midst and her passing leaves them with no ominous force by which to gauge their own conduct and construct their own lives. He leads them down to the white valley and to the entrance of the tunnel whose construction, begun in 1927, was rapidly abandoned. Abandoned, this project failed both to provide Blacks with work as builders and to connect the Bottom to commerce in the nearby areas. When the tunnel suddenly collapses in a quick January thaw, the inhabitants meet painful death through suffocation. On this violent note of irony and ineffectualness, the figurative made manifest, the novel ends.

Shadrack cannot predict the deaths of so many Bottom people, yet he has witnessed violence and death from the beginning. He has done so both in the war and in his bearing silent testimony to Nel and Sula's drowning of Chicken Little* when the women were young girls. Baiting the stammering Chicken Little with the promise of vision, Sula lures him to the river's edge, swings him around, and, losing her grip mid-flight, releases him into the muddy water that soon swallows him. Whereas Sula has protected Nel in the past (saving them both from the taunts of the Irish boys who block their direct path homeward from school by cutting off the tip of her finger), now Nel "covers" for Sula. She encourages Sula to confront Shadrack with what he saw, but his answer of "always" suggests he has seen everything and nothing at the same time. And so the secrecy, begun by witnessing violence in girlhood, begins.

As in Morrison's other works, violence breeds violence. Chicken Little's death is followed by Eva's burning of her heroin-addicted son Plum*, whom she rescued at birth by sacrificing her last bit of lard, lovingly but violently shoving it up his anus, to pull from him the hard stools of his constipation. Later she throws herself from her third-story window when she sees Hannah, her daughter whose dress caught fire while she was canning, twitching to her death. What Eva cannot comprehend is that Sula watched her own mother dance and burn, fascinated by motion, much as she was in Chicken Little's drowning. Yet no one character clearly perpetrates evil here. Instead, blame and responsibility must be understood as a consequence of the post–World War II era in which many claims were made on behalf of equality but few were fulfilled.

Much as *Sula* throws into relief the nature and origin of friendship, kinship, and physical relationships, and argues for violence as both intimacy and rupture, Morrison's third novel, *Song of Solomon**, explores the tension of violence that unites and divides friends, lovers, and family* members. Here, violence threatens to reveal the ugliness behind the poorly knit divides between Blacks who have property and money, those who do not, and the whites who render them nameless, or literally misname them. Again, an unlikely friendship is at the core of the novel, this time between two men, Guitar Baines* and Milkman Dead*. Both are present (Milkman in utero) at the death of Mr. Robert Smith*, a low-level Black insurance agent who collects policy premiums and who yearns to sprout wings and fly. That Mr. Smith believes himself capable of such flight is sheer lunacy. However, as Morrison urges, we must focus on the desire rather than its improbable actualization. When Mr. Smith throws himself off the cupola of No Mercy hospital*, where Blacks are not allowed entry, Guitar watches. From this opening moment of violent self-destruction, the novel is full of distraction and tension.

A violence in misreading others' actions informs the text, perpetuating further trespass and urging secrecy that does no good. For instance, in cultivating his future father-in-law's favor, the man who courts Milkman's mother, Macon Dead*, misreads his importance as a man of property. His wife's father accepts Macon as suitor only because his daughter's own affection toward him seems out of proportion. When Macon Dead finds his wife, Ruth, naked, or in what she later argues is a "slip" (pun intended), sucking the fingers of her dead father, his desire for his wife, which has root more in his infatuation with middle-class standards, becomes disgust with her as a body. And when Milkman learns that his name was given to him by his father's lackey, Freddie, who steals up to the family window one day and observes Ruth nursing Milkman far past infancy, he, too, begins to wish his mother ill.

Violence occurs in this novel both within the family—the suggested violence of incest and trespass, of bodies revealed and concealed at inappropriate moments—and within the community. Milkman falls in love with Hagar Dead*, but he cares little that the woman he beds is his cousin. Yet, in the ordering of nature that concurs with cultural concepts of appropriate sexual behavior, no good can come of this relationship. When the thwarted Hagar tries to kill Milkman because he has forsaken her, we read not only the violence of trespassing against natural order but also the pain that ensues when intimacy sours, love abandons, and worlds divided, clash. The parting of lovers, cousin to cousin, mirrors the rupture between sister and brother, Pilate Dead* and Macon. Death takes on a force and presence here: Macon wishes his sister Pilate, who is an embarrassment to him because she takes no stock in material possessions and disgraces his "name" by living vicariously, dead; Ruth wishes her son's cousin dead; and Pilate protects both granddaughter and nephew from the complicated wrath of others' murderous intentions, to which she herself is not immune. The violence of self-interest clashes with preservation of the community, and this violence is further played out in the friendship between Black males, Milkman and his friend Guitar.

When Guitar joins the Seven Days*, a group that avenges whites' random violence against Blacks by acting out in kind, Milkman stalls in affirming his friend's actions. Milkman, whose disdain of Hagar, it can be argued, urged her own death, proves mute on the point of noninvoked hatred, or murder for the sake of murder. That Hagar despises him because he rejected her, and therefore wants to kill him, he can understand, but that Guitar would blindly buy into a militant Black ideology without weighing actions and deeds, cause and consequence, he cannot. What Morrison confronts here is the espousing of ideology without thinking through the consequence of belief. From her vantage point, the Black Power movement of the 1960s gave rise to a certain militant separatist agenda that had harmful consequences. In *Song of Solomon*, Guitar is the product of such an inchoate movement, and is victimized by it. When Milkman sets off to hunt for the gold that his father believes the dead body of the hunter he killed as a child shielded, and that Pilate supposedly later stole, Guitar stalks him in his quest. Whereas Milkman's initial quest for gold rapidly becomes secondary to his search for family origin, Guitar's hunt of Milkman begins with something akin to Black solidarity, but ends as a material chase as well as one of personal vengeance, brother turning against brother. Guitar stalks Milkman and accidentally shoots Pilate; Milkman leaps after her. At this instant, much like Mr. Smith at the beginning of the novel, he flies to his death—his flight invoking both African lore and mythic transcendence.

Violence and chase, running to and away from one's inheritance, a desire to learn one's origins and affirm one's "people"—and at the same time an apparent disdain for this knowledge—is further played out in Morrison's fourth novel, *Tar Baby**. Set largely in the island of Dominique, the novel opens with the appearance of a mysterious stranger, Son*, who has sought refuge on a ship after murdering his wife, whom he found in bed with another man. When Son's hunger for land becomes a preoccupation, he throws himself overboard, believing he is near enough to shore to reach it by swimming. But the current betrays him, and he must seek safety on a neighboring boat, the *Queen of France*, which docks at des Chevaliers*, an island named after the fabled blind African horsemen who fled white colonizers, seeking asylum in its hills.

Violence occurs through the clashing of beliefs and the difference in class and race* prejudices. Son falls in love with Jadine Childs*, the light-skinned "tar baby" of the novel's title. Jadine is the orphaned niece of Ondine and Sydney Childs*, a Black couple Son accuses of "Uncle Tom'ism" because they serve to a fault both Valerian Street*, heir to a large candy factor that made its fortune on the backs of Blacks in sugarcane plantations, and his wife Margaret*, a woman haunted by memory and disturbed by her adult son Michael's seeming abandonment of her. Jadine is the product of a European and white upbringing that Valerian has largely funded. In love with white ideals and material possessions, with things that are dead and bear no life, Jadine's refusal of Son's advances—which are threatening in their crude sexuality* and violent nature, for he, too, fears her and all that she stands for—is an initial disavowal of her Blackness. Son's espousal of Black community and life fly against her principles of upward mobility, cultivated through her assimilation of white, materialist values.

When it becomes apparent that Margaret abused her only child, Michael (who has no voice in the narrative), by violently pinpricking and burning him as an infant, the seemingly sound and cultivated relations between those who serve and those who are served, founded on race as well as class differences, explodes. Margaret accuses Ondine, who witnessed these violations, of culpability and appeals to her as a woman of feeling. Ondine defends herself and reminds Margaret of the gulf between their positions. What results from this confrontation is a reordering of power structures, though not their resolution. After Margaret's crime is revealed, her millionaire husband becomes senile and helpless. He has been deceived and lied to by his wife, and the knowledge that he failed to shield his son from harm emasculates him. Power positions are reversed. Margaret now revels in her position as caretaker of her ailing and elderly husband. Servant becomes master. Butler Sydney drinks the master's wine and assures that there will be no returning to the States, to Valerian's residence in Philadelphia, because he and Ondine are happy in Dominique. Master is at the mercy of servant, husband is now dictated to by wife, yet as the narratives close, all characters occupy positions of exile.

Much as Sula and Nel's relationship is predicated on a desire for the "other" to complete the self, so, too, is Son and Jadine's relationship. Only here, argue for the purity of their positions. Neither can find any room for the other within their value systems, but it is at Jadine that Morrison levels the most damning critique. In choosing white position and status over her Black heritage, Jadine has, in essence, sold her soul to the highest bidder. Chasing Jadine down, Son returns to the Isle des Chevaliers and is taken in by the mythic blind African riders who inhabit the hills, forever resisting colonization. The tension here lies in the idea that Son must flee to a mythic past in order to reclaim himself and, by having him do so, Morrison asks us to examine the potential for self-actualization and the establishment of Black community in a world that argues for divide.

*Beloved** further develops the idea that violence ensues when the past is denied or disallowed. In this novel, Morrison considers the legacy of slavery* and its inheritance for both Blacks and whites. Again, oral tradition* as well as fable and folklore work to counter violation and make a plea for integrity and dignity in a world that demeans Black culture. Set in Ohio in the antebellum period and the years that follow the Emancipation Proclamation, the novel traces the then-pregnant Sethe Suggs's* escape from slavery. Sethe gives birth on the banks of the Ohio River before crossing to freedom, and it is Amy Denver*, a young white woman who is herself an exile, who facilitates Sethe's passage and treats the whip marks that cover her back. White cruelty is countered here by the bonds between women and the difficult relationship between mother and child. When white bounty hunters come for Sethe and her children, Sethe kills her crying infant. This act, Morrison urges us to understand, is not so much one of unfelt infanticide* as a rebuke against slavery. Sethe would rather her infant, Beloved*, be dead than sold into the hands of white slave masters who abuse Black women for sport and pleasure.

Dream is invoked here to counter violence and give it context. Beloved returns to Sethe to make her confront her own past, and yet her preoccupation with doing so harms Sethe's relationship with her very real daughter, Denver Suggs*, who accuses her mother of loving the dead more than the living. What Sethe does not communicate well to Denver is that African American women must reconcile themselves to the violence of the past before they proceed with the business of living. Because slavery and its legacy infringe on current and past relationships, there is an insatiability for touch, intimacy, understanding, and closure that cannot be easily had. That is, fusion of African past with living presence is necessary in healing old and existing wounds. What is yearned for here, as is evidenced in Morrison's earlier works, is a sense of "rootedness" and identity* that can occur only after historical loss has been reconciled with personal trespass and everyday struggle.

In *Beloved*, the material reality of social and racial oppression argues for a relationship between kinfolk, living and dead, to heal past wounds and ensure family survival. The struggle between living and dead takes on murderous tones when the ghost of Beloved threatens to strangle Sethe, literally and figuratively. The stranglehold that the dead have over the living is further developed in Morrison's subsequent work *Jazz*\*, which opens with Violet Trace\* slashing at the face of Dorcas Manfred\*, who has been shot dead by Violet's husband, Joe\*. Joe serves no jail time for his crime of passion, and much of the narrative concerns itself not so much with the violence of these acts but with the events that lead up to them and allow for them, as well as for the healing that follows.

Joe and Violet have migrated from the South to the North, and this is Morrison's first work to use the urban environment as a backdrop. Lured by the promises of opportunity and freedom, Violet and Joe find that Harlem\* in the 1920s does not disappoint. Yet there is an undercurrent that runs through the lives of its inhabitants which threatens old order with new, and this is the current of music, particularly jazz\*. With its improvisation, dynamic construction, and threat of longing, jazz urges new roles and new ways of self-expression that cannot be contained in the given order. Much as the music "breaks out" of given modes of expression, the characters are subject to improvisational patterns of understanding and relating to one another. Much as the music\* of jazz is committed to change, the characters find that to survive in the urban environment in which they are transplanted, they, too, must be committed to change. Perhaps this is why Alice Manfred\*, Dorcas's aunt, receives Violet in her house, taking in the woman who robbed her niece's funeral of dignity and grace by desecrating the corpse with a knife. What Alice and Violet, whom the community nicknames Violent, have in common is the sense of disembodiment and loss. Much as Violet wonders what happened to her lost youth, Alice, fearful that she has violated her own convictions, wonders what happened to her girl-self who promised not to raise a child in the suffocating atmosphere of Black female propriety that her own parents used to rein in ambition.

Violence is this novel is healed in these unlikely friendships, and in the seemingly impossible but well-wrought reconciliation between husband and wife. Tragedy is not random here; it has a historical and socioeconomic root in the Black community and in Black relationships that counter white culture, creating an argument for itself as center rather than margin. In essence, though the adults view jazz as a sexual threat to young Black men's and women's conduct, it emerges here as a language that offers its listeners a wider emotional frame in which to contextualize their lives and argue for the power of forgiveness to heal violent rupture.

Whereas *Beloved* invokes the slave narrative to trace the escape of Blacks from the South to the North, *Jazz* uses improvisation to narrate the struggles Blacks had in adapting to the change from a rural to an urban environment. *Beloved* includes images of burnings—the master's whip tears open the flesh on Sethe's back—and in *Jazz*, Violet leaves a hot iron on a blouse's lapel, burning it beyond repair and marring it with a print of a Black ship that resembles the slave ships of white colonizers.

*Paradise** is the last part of the narrative trilogy that begins with *Beloved*. Morrison's most recent novel further comments on the relationships between men and women, women and women, mother and child, "seared" into our personal and collective histories, by referencing canonical literature. The title recalls the last part of Dante's *Divine Comedy*. For if Beloved speaks to Dante's "Inferno," and *Jazz* to "Purgatory," then *Paradise* is a reply to "Paradiso." As in Morrison's earlier works, this text contains characters who will not die and who school the living in tradition and myth, teaching them timeless human lessons about moral frailty and fragility as well as the tenacity of relationships, human and otherworldly.

*Paradise* opens with a violent death, the death of a white girl. The men who are culpable come from the all-Black town of Ruby, Oklahoma*. As an all-Black community founded during the collapse of Reconstruction, when Blacks were betrayed by promises made but never realized, Ruby was believed a haven for Black families. Yet the town proves exclusionary, priding itself on tradition and dark skin color free of the "taint" of miscegenation. The 1970s children of its founders prove dissatisfied with custom and practice, and espouse a freer sexuality and morality. Those who do not fit the town's parameters are ostracized to a place that becomes known as the Convent*. When the men of Ruby attack the Convent, it is less clear whether their murderous rage is motivated by a sense of warped moral propriety that the Convent women somehow trespass against the town's values, or whether it is motivated by financial interest, for the Convent now occupies a sizable tract of real estate.

Because the narrative develops more as sketch than plotted narrative and gives us only a limited glimpse into the characters' consciences, it relies on inference to decode actions and consequences. The women of the Convent—Mary Magna*, Consolata Sosa*, Grace Gibson*, Seneca*, and Pallas Truelove*—either have betrayed their families or been betrayed by them. Collectively, their worlds are littered with the violence of abuse, neglect, sexual trespass, alcoholism, and a compassion for others, but an inability to exercise any compassion toward themselves. What Morrison critiques here are the mechanisms of opposition and fragmentation that lead, as they do in *The Bluest Eye*, to madness, literal and figurative. When exclusion is used to keep certain individuals from the community, havoc and further destruction ensue.

As she develops as a writer and establishes herself as a key literary figure, Morrison continues to address the legacy of slavery and meditates on the price of power for both those who wield it and those who are denied it. Her novels celebrate acts of creativity, the power of forgiveness, and the pain that comes from self-examination. She cautions that in forging new and viable identities, violence is inevitable. It is our acts of interpretation that possess, much as literature itself does, the power to situate violence in a socioeconomic and historic context. This involves not only recognizing violence as moral ambiguity but also understanding the role violence plays in the formation of identity. *See also* Approaches to Morrison's Work: Feminist/Black Feminist; Approaches to Morrison's Work: Historical; Approaches to Morrison's Work: Psychoanalytical; Flying Africans, Myth of; History; Trauma; Whiteness.

References: Henry Louis Gates, Jr., and K. A. Appiah, eds., *Toni Morrison: Critical Perspectives Past and Present* (1993); Missy Dehn Kubitschek, *Toni Morrison: A Critical Companion* (1998); Katherine McKittrick, "'Black 'Cause I'm Black and Blue': Transverse Racial Geographies in Toni Morrison's *The Bluest Eye*," *Gender, Place Culture: A Journal of Feminist Geography* 7: 2(June 2000); Vincent O'Keefe, "Reading Rigor Mortis: Offstage Violence and Excluded Middles 'in' Johnson's *Middle Passage* and Morrison's *Beloved*," *African American Review* 30: 4 (Winter 1996); Katy Ryan, "Revolutionary Suicide in Toni Morrison's Fiction," *African American Review* 34: 3 (Fall 2000).

Jennifer Driscoll

## Virginia (*Jazz*)

State where both Joe Trace* and Violet Trace* are born and raised. The point of origin of the narrative that becomes *Jazz*, including where True Belle* and Vera Louise Gray* come from; where Golden Gray* discovers Wild* and Hunter's Hunter* delivers her baby; and where Violet lives with Rose Dear*, her mother, who later commits suicide. *See also Jazz.*

Caroline Brown

# W

## Whiteness

Toni Morrison is concerned in part with individual white persons who perpetrate acts of violence* and terror, yet she is more interested in the abstract notion of whiteness as a political formation supporting white supremacy. As a system of power, whiteness uses skin color as a means for legitimizing certain ideals as normative, thereby defining nonwhite as marginal. It produces notions of unequal difference based on arbitrarily chosen characteristics. Whiteness in this abstract form secures dominance by being defined a priori as neutral, normal, and unremarkable. Morrison, then, in her fiction and her criticism, pursues the project of making Blackness legitimate. She disrupts the false opposition of Black and white from both sides of the binary, revealing the disturbing power of whiteness and suggesting strategies for the physical and psychological regeneration of African American cultures and traditions.

Morrison's scholarly work is where she describes this project in overt terms. "Unspeakable Things Unspoken: The Afro-American Presence in American Literature," an essay that appeared in *Michigan Quarterly Review* in 1989, introduces Morrison's commitment to defining whiteness as an ideology. She sees the canon as the domain of white male cultural purity, though she admits to recent discussions that have included race* as a factor. She then reads *Moby Dick* as Melville's recognition of the moment when whiteness became ideology, when it went beyond individual identity* to become a powerful and exclusionary force. In this reading, Ahab becomes the individual white male trying to slay the monster

devouring America: white maleness, or the belief system of white superiority. Thus, Morrison argues that whiteness is a demon that haunts
whites as well as Blacks.

*Playing in the Dark: Whiteness and the Literary Imagination** continues this trend. Here she reveals the Africanist presence in American
literary texts, a presence that, she argues, manifests as a means of defining whiteness. Whiteness, as Morrison sees it, is an idealization, not an
individual identity, naturalized as a defense against fear. Her goal is to
open the canon to Blackness by demonstrating its appearance in canonical literature previously considered beyond questions of race. In so
doing, she exposes the power of whiteness's invisibility. Her fiction also
pursues this project, each work exploring the connection between white
and Black culture as she demonstrates the structural implications of
whiteness in American culture. Her disruption of whiteness works
through the constant assertion of Blackness as a positive identity, not a
secondary definer of white, as well as through the exposure of whiteness's workings and its alignment with other identity markers such as
gender, sexuality, and national identity.

Morrison's novels critique whiteness in its abstract forms, recognizing
its manifestations in both individual acts of prejudice and structural racist
formations. Morrison recognizes the effects of racist acts in propagating
demeaning visions of Black identity. She reveals the power of individual
racism to abstract or degenerate Blackness, implicitly defining whiteness
as a beneficial identity. Cholly Breedlove*, forced to have sex at gunpoint
by racist white hunters, cannot escape the psychological ramifications of
that trauma*. It haunts him and his family. The Seven Days* group in
*Song of Solomon** is a specific response to lynchings by white racists.
The terrible murders compel the group of Black men to retaliate against
the white community with equal murders in an escalating cycle of violence. *Beloved*'s* schoolteacher* uses rational science to redefine the slave
from a human being into an abstract commodity. This revision allows
him to perpetrate his horrible acts without guilt. The power of whiteness, as Morrison depicts it, lies precisely in its abstraction of Blackness
as well as its abstraction from responsibility. Individual whites claim no
responsibility because they did not commit the horrible acts of slavery*.
But such denial ignores the complicity of all white persons in a system
of privilege and power from which they benefit.

Bodwin*, the landlord of 124 Bluestone Road* and Denver Suggs's*
boss, represents this ideal of abstracted whiteness. Certainly he is a good
man, as he aids Blacks throughout the novel and will support Denver's
education financially. Yet Sethe Suggs* sees him only for his whiteness,
misidentifying him as the malignant schoolteacher and attacking him
with an ice pick. On one level, Bodwin is no different. He represents the
innocently ignorant white man for Morrison, that white man who does

not recognize his privilege and his complicity. Sethe's vision of him, however, changes our picture as well. She sees the whiteness (and therefore the implicit power to denigrate her as an object) that is invisible to others because of her life experience.

Thus, Morrison shows us another key assumption of whiteness: its nonraced status. *Beloved*'s white people are not evil monsters. Yet the invisible normativity of civilized whiteness is constantly brought into being against the high visibility of Blackness, defined as savagery. "Race," so Morrison shows us, means "colored" in American culture; to be white is to be without race. Sethe's actions bring whiteness into racial consciousness and force us to stare at it uncompromisingly. Whiteness, then, involves much more than prejudiced individuals. Morrison opposes the structural racism that grants whiteness institutional power and defines white identity as a valuable property. Blackness, in this system, has no intrinsic value. We see the implications of white supremacy reflected in such institutions as slavery (*Beloved*), consumer culture (*The Bluest Eye**  and *Jazz**), and the complex system of property and business embodied in white U.S. capitalism present in all her novels.

One issue that Morrison repeatedly returns to is the incorporation of white ideals into Black subjectivity. White culture depends in part on its imagery for maintaining power. Thus, Morrison's critique focuses on cultural media as a structure reproducing white and Black identities in a fashion that ensures current power relations and homogenizes Blackness. Morrison argues against a desire for whiteness by demonstrating the devastating effects of cultural media's inculcation of white culture into the African American psyche. Desire becomes whitewashed, leaving African Americans alienated and outcast. *The Bluest Eye* is Morrison's most overt critique of this phenomenon. It examines the problems of physical aesthetics and its racialist bias in American culture through the character of Pecola Breedlove*. Morrison exposes whiteness's assumption of the norm by juxtaposing the "aberration"—Blackness—against the conventional representations of "normal" white personhood—advertisements, movie actresses, toys. The Black community in the novel, faced with constant waves of racist images, assimilates those ideals and then directs its hatred toward Pecola Breedlove. The group projects their learned negative characteristics, incorporated from a wider set of cultural media that rejects Blackness as tainted or deformed, onto Pecola. Faced with such hatred in the community* as well as in her own family, Pecola desires whiteness in the form of the blue eyes she believes will bring her love and respect. This desire to be white erases Blackness as acceptable, yet that desire is made to seem natural.

*The Bluest Eye* confronts the widespread psychological damage wrought on African Americans (particularly females) by their immersion in white cultural media's institutional racism. In Morrison's view, the internalization of racist self-images has immeasurably damaged the Black community. Yet *The Bluest Eye* goes beyond a simple reversal of the individual white/Black dichotomy; instead, Morrison argues that the problem exists on a cultural level. She reveals the internalization of such racist notions of personal beauty in the Black community as well as the propagation of such standards across multiple venues. Thus, much like *The Black Book**, Morrison's first novel explores the manifestation of abstract principles of identity in the material world. *Song of Solomon* presents Black self-hatred as well and portrays two tactics employed against it: externalized violence, as exemplified in Guitar Baines's* actions, and internalized self-definition through cultural traditions, as shown in Milkman Dead's* journey. Morrison supports the latter strategy, arguing against the violence consuming African American culture.

*Jazz* presents another version of the desire for whiteness. Violet Trace* hears the stories of Golden Gray* and her desire turns in that direction, toward the abstract person over the concrete individuals in front of her. She idealizes the lighter-skinned Gray, and this feeling isolates her. She cannot accept herself as she is, but always dreams of a different, and in her eyes better, Violet. This turning of desire away from Blackness toward whiteness, Morrison argues, happens as white desires become promulgated in America as "normal" desires. The disguising of particularized white desires as universal or normative suggests that everyone should share them, minimizing the differences of particular racial heritages that might lead to different wants. Instead, everyone is placed within the context of whiteness.

As a result, Morrison suggests, whiteness inculcates itself through a heightening of these desires in consumer culture. Morrison shows that African Americans internalize such notions and begin to reproduce the desire for whiteness themselves by imagining it as superior. For example, Violet spends her life holding onto the image of Golden Gray and living up to its ideal. At the end of *Jazz*, however, she decides to create herself anew, to see herself in a different image. Alice Manfred*, on the other hand, cannot change. She continues to see herself through white eyes, denigrating herself because of her perceived inability to match their ideals. The incorporation of whiteness into Black ideals of personhood also appears in *Beloved*. Paul D Garner* must work throughout the novel to escape his internalized white notion of himself as a person and become something else. He must reject slavery's ideals of Blackness and create different definitions of Black personhood.

*Beloved* moves beyond the individual level, revealing the pernicious effects of whiteness on American culture. Whiteness haunts this novel just as thoroughly as Beloved* herself does, for whiteness is the ideology behind slavery. Morrison wrote *Beloved* as a means of exploring the wounds created by slavery, and in a sense the novel is a photo negative of traditional historical accounts of slavery. It takes as its viewpoint not the top-down white position but the Black position underneath, reversing the story to tell it from a slave's point of view in the immediate post-bellum period. As a result, whiteness does not stand out in the novel as a primary focus, but it haunts the edges. It drives slavery's horrors through the negation of Blackness as personhood. To be a person meant being white. Beloved's return haunts Sethe precisely because it is a return of slavery's horrors in the body of her deceased daughter, a daughter she killed rather than allow her to become the property of a white man.

Sethe's actions, while shocking to our modern sensibilities, take on a different tint when viewed from the world of the slave mind-set. Her action declares personhood for herself and her child through the taking of agency, of power, and, because it is so shocking, highlights the drastic means necessary to move beyond white definitions of Blackness as property, into an alternative definition with agency. Violence becomes necessary for Sethe individually just as the violence of the Civil War becomes necessary for the United States corporately to cleanse itself of the horror of slavery.

*Sula* also represents the cultural problems inherent for the Black community. Morrison portrays the development of African American community within a society that places economic and cultural conditions under white supremacist control. Shadrack* and Plum*, veterans of World War I, stand alone, rejected by the country they fought for. The Bottom* is a group of people striving to maintain their identity through tradition and togetherness. Yet their rejection of Sula leads them to disaster. The novel asserts a belief that the African American community must come together as a whole in order to survive in white American culture.

Morrison constantly portrays whiteness as a property, a commodity with value that implicitly marks Blackness as having no value. Morrison's project, then, is to give Blackness a value outside the traditional capitalist notions of property and labor. *Tar Baby**, with its setting in the Caribbean, focuses on colonialism and its relationship to racial cultures. While the white owners have nothing but good intentions at heart, Morrison reveals their benevolence to have a darker side. The conflicted multiracial household suggests that even the kindest owners are bound within a complex social system of property and business that undermines their goodness. *Tar Baby*'s Valerian Street* is a white character with the power of property behind him, similar to *Beloved*'s Bodwin. Valerian's whiteness, the identity that enables him to gain property, is itself a property protected and supported by law. He buys items constantly, including people, whom he treats as trinkets; objects and subjects are the same to him. He often wastes things, throwing them into the corner to gather dust. Morrison indicts white capitalism as wasteful through this characterization, portraying it as a system that dismisses Black persons as trinkets to be used and discarded. Yet she also depicts capitalism's valuation of whiteness as an ideal identity. Valerian can act as he does because he works within a larger cultural system of exchange that overly values whiteness.

While the depiction of racism's effects is a crucial part of her project, Morrison also decenters whiteness by disrupting its binary logic of biological and cultural superiority. Multiracial characters provide one means for Morrison to destabilize whiteness. The logic of whiteness depends on a binary notion of race rooted in unequal difference. Morrison's characters, however, are often not so easily classified. Their unstable racial identity undermines the strict logic of binary difference that supports white superiority. Golden Gray, for example, is one character who makes the split between Black and white less easy to make. His name indicates his ambiguity: he is golden and gray, not white or Black. Standing in between two races, Golden Gray looks white but has African American ancestry. As a result, he upsets the easy binary of white/Black distinction. When Gray learns of his heritage, however, he finds the revelation overwhelming. Raised as white, he sees his Blackness as a taint, reflecting the internalized notions of race that American culture provides. Morrison thus reveals whiteness's insupportable logic but also recognizes the material effects of this belief system on Black psyches.

Morrison's fiction supports African Americans who take control of their identities by claiming subjectivity against white definitions. In *Beloved*, for example, the white slave owners take the power of denying or affirming subject status through the practice of naming slaves. The slaves resist, however, by naming themselves. *Beloved* presents many such resistances to white supremacy. Paul D, for example, refuses to believe the white culture's representation of Sethe even as he doubts his own knowledge of her in light of her actions. And certainly Sethe's murder of her own child can be seen as the ultimate act of resistance, embodying as it does not only a condemnation of slavery but also an assertion of property rights and individual autonomy for Sethe. To kill the beloved child is to claim a mother's right to decide what is best for her child, a right denied to slaves in antebellum culture. Children were often sold away from parents, seen as more property. Yet Sethe claims ownership of that property in a radical act of slave revolt.

This action is what Morrison proposes for African American life: to reject white definitions of Blackness and affirm positive notions of African American identity. The result if this does not happen is insanity, as in the case of Pecola Breedlove, or death. And when one does claim subjectivity, as Milkman does in affirming his heritage, spiritual rebirth ensues. *Song of Solomon* represents another space for Morrison to decenter whiteness and re-create Blackness as affirmation and presence instead of negation and absence. Morrison locates the survival of African American culture in its return to history.

Certainly Morrison's engagement with history is one means by which she seeks to engage whiteness. Traditional histories, Morrison implicitly shows us, reveal the tracings of whiteness through the exclusion of African American stories as well as their emphasis on certain logic-based forms of evidence. Morrison's later novels rewrite history as a means of dispelling white mythos. Morrison inserts different accounts as a means of delegitimating the official histories of American culture, histories that are whitened by the exclusion of African American viewpoints. She chooses to restore history's color. *Beloved, Jazz,* and *Paradise** all engage the question of historiography on a fundamental level, and all present alternative histories for America rooted in African American viewpoints. Morrison's return to history, started with her earliest work as editor and continued throughout her fiction, inserts Blackness into historical discourse, asserting its centrality in U.S. culture.

Morrison's novels affirm Blackness over and against the oppressive cultural power of whiteness. But this is not to say that she sees the abolition of whiteness as the only step for African American success. *Paradise* is her statement against the myth of Black unity with no white oppression. *Paradise* begins with the death of a woman identified by her race. As the novel unfolds, the reader pieces together parts of the mystery and comes to realize that the men of Ruby, Oklahoma*, have killed the women living in the Convent* because of their perceived threat to the community. The Convent represents a space of multicultural harmony as well as feminine sanctity that causes anxiety for the males of Ruby. The death of a white woman indicates that her whiteness did not save her; she had been Blackened by her association with African Americans. But the white woman was only one of five to die. The novel portrays a Black community not at peace with itself. The women's deaths come about as the result of a town divided not only by race but also by gender. Whiteness is an ideology of purity and an arbiter of power. The delegation of power, however, is uneven and influenced by gender. As *Paradise* powerfully reveals, Morrison does not want to romanticize Blackness but, instead, to negotiate realistically positive visions of African American identity that incorporate all types of Blackness. Through such self-definition, as well as the disruption of whiteness as a nonnative identity, she fights for a more egalitarian society. *See also* Approaches to Morrison's Work: Historical; Identity.

References: Wahneema Lubiano, "Toni Morrison (1931–)," in *African American Writers*, ed. Valerie Smith (1991); Patricia McKee, *Producing*

*American Races: Henry James, William Faulkner, Toni Morrison* (1999); Michael Nowlin, "Toni Morrison's *Jazz* and the Racial Dreams of the American Writer," *American Literature* 71: 1 (March 1999); Philip Weinstein, *What Else but Love? The Ordeal of Race in Faulkner and Morrison* (1996).

David E. Magill

## Wild (*Jazz*)

The untamed, cave dwelling biological mother of Joe Trace\*, who rejects him at birth. A mysterious presence in *Jazz* who has no past or future, there is some question as to her identity\*. In interviews, Morrison has suggested her connection to the murdered toddler who is reincarnated in *Beloved*\*. Morrison has called Wild a type of Beloved, who lives in the same era, moves within the Ohio-Virginia region, and also is pregnant. *See also Jazz.*

Caroline Brown

## Woolf, Virginia, Influence of

British novelist (1882–1941) and the subject of Morrison's master's thesis, "Virginia Woolf's and William Faulkner's Treatment of the Alienated" (Cornell University, 1955, under the name Chloe Ardellia Wofford). Morrison analyzes one novel each by Woolf and Faulkner\*, *Mrs. Dalloway* and *Absalom, Absalom!*, demonstrating differences in their approaches to fictionalizing contemporary problems of alienation. She concludes that since Woolf sees alienation and detachment as necessary if modern existence is to be made tolerable for those who are alone, hers is the more pessimistic viewpoint.

When Toni Morrison wrote her thesis, few African American literary role models had been published. In addition, interest in the writings of Virginia Woolf had been in decline since the 1930s. During the 1950s, Woolf's works were the topic of only thirteen dissertations nationwide (in contrast to 365 in 1999). At Cornell during the same period, most graduate theses and dissertations in English literature focused on writers within the canon, specifically male British writers of the seventeenth through nineteenth centuries. Why Morrison chose a modern female writer whose works were not ordinarily studied or readily available as a subject for her thesis will probably remain unknown. Barbara Christian points to the publication in English of Eric Auerbach's *Mimesis* in 1953, with its seminal analysis of *To the Lighthouse*, as a likely source for Morrison's discovery of this writer from a world significantly unlike her own. Perhaps one of her instructors paid special attention to Woolf. Whatever the source of her interest, Morrison demonstrates in her own writing certain narrative approaches and themes that could have been influenced by her early study of selected works by Virginia Woolf. Both novelists share an interest in characters who feel isolated from society, a desire to experiment with language and narrative form, and a feminist worldview.

In "Virginia Woolf's and William Faulkner's Treatment of the Alienated," Morrison notes Woolf's respect for the sanctity of an individual's private self and free will. She shows how alienation assists those characters in *Mrs. Dalloway* who are solitary to triumph over their existential predicaments. In her struggle for self-knowledge, Clarissa Dalloway exemplifies the kind of personal detachment that makes modern existence tolerable. Morrison contrasts what she sees as Woolf's bleak, pessimistic viewpoint with Faulkner's search for a more positive outlook, and uses Clarissa and her "double," Septimus Warren Smith, as examples of different kinds of estrangement. She is struck by Woolf's creation of these parallel lives in *Mrs. Dalloway*, and later adopts similar techniques in using pairs of characters to parallel one another or to create together a wholeness that any solitary character might lack. The most obvious examples are found in *Sula**, with the pairing of Shadrack* and Sula*, as well as Sula Peace* and Nel Wright*. Isolation and alienation became important in her characterizations of, for example, the Peace family (*Sula*), Pilate Dead* (*Song of Solomon**), Sethe Suggs* (Beloved*), and the women of Ruby, Oklahoma* (*Paradise**), some of her notable outsiders.

In their essays, Morrison and Woolf express shared passion for the transformative nature of language. In their novels, they demonstrate the desire to depict the complex inner lives of selected characters by creating unique narrative forms. Woolf's belief that the novel of the future must focus on interior life rather than "action" and her skill in writing interior monologue must have influenced Morrison's experiments with the languages of private selves that she attempted in her first two novels, *The Bluest Eye** and *Sula*, and mastered with *Beloved*. Within the context of the consciousnesses of characters, each writer uses different narrative techniques to demonstrate how repressed memory influences and even sustains being (witness Sethe in *Beloved* and Septimus Warren Smith in *Mrs. Dalloway*). Woolf is more dependent on stream-of-consciousness techniques, but both women are able, each in a different way, to destabilize narrative authority. Their narrators share a high level of lyricism and an acknowledgment of the importance of subjective impressions. Morrison notes also in her thesis the paradoxes that time imposes on the human condition. Experimentation with the presentation of subjective time abounds in works by Woolf (e.g., *Mrs. Dalloway, The*

*Waves*) and Morrison (e.g., *Beloved, Paradise*), wherein time present and time past are inseparable.

Certainly Morrison is aware of Virginia Woolf's tendency to privilege her race* and class, whether consciously or unconsciously. Nonetheless, she must have identified with Woolf's feminist concerns, mindful likewise of what it means to be female in male-dominated societies and aware of the extent to which women characters keep life moving on in spite of their social contexts and personal alienation. They both create uncommon and complex female characters who seek understanding of their multifaceted identities and who are considered variously by the others who wrestle with their own ambiguous perceptions of those who are important to them. Such quests for identity* are especially obvious in Woolf's *To the Lighthouse* and *Orlando* and Morrison's *Song of Solomon* and *The Bluest Eye*.

While these similarities are notable, consideration of the body of works by both Virginia Woolf and Toni Morrison shows significant differences in the worlds of their novels and their personal styles. Nonetheless, Morrison and Woolf contrast the public and private selves of their characters, show the importance of self-knowledge while positing the unknowableness and ambiguity of human nature, and demonstrate palpably the relationship between war and madness. They are bound together by their mutual interest in the power of language to change perception and the importance of the subjective consciousness. While it is clear that the two writers have drawn inspiration from different sources, comparison of the novel Morrison must have studied most conscientiously, *Mrs. Dalloway*, and her own second novel, *Sula*, yields significant resemblances and a presumed influence of Virginia Woolf. *See also* Faulkner, William, Influence of.

References: Eileen Barrett, "Septimus and Shadrack: Woolf and Morrison Envision the Madness of War," in *Virginia Woolf: Emerging Perspectives*, ed. Mark Hussey and Vara Neverow (1994); Barbara Christian, "Layered Rhythms: Virginia Woolf and Toni Morrison," in *Virginia Woolf: Emerging Perspectives*, ed. Mark Hussey and Vara Neverow (1994); Ann Harris-Williams, "Woolf and Toni Morrison: Moments from the Critical Dialogue," in *Virginia Woolf: Emerging Perspectives*, ed. Mark Hussey and Vara Neverow (1994); Toni Morrison (Chloe Ardellia Wofford), "Virginia Woolf's and William Faulkner's Treatment of the Alienated," M.A. thesis, Cornell University (September 1955); Lisa Williams, *The Artist as Outsider in the Novels of Toni Morrison and Virginia Woolf* (2000).

Judith Espinola

### Wright, Helene (*Sula*)

Nel Wright's* mother. Helene's mother is a New Orleans prostitute. Her grandmother, Cecile, raises Helene. In order to distance herself from what she perceives to be her shameful past, Helene becomes obsessed with propriety. She marries Wiley Wright*, a ship's cook, moves with him to Medallion, Ohio*, and becomes a staunch member of the Bottom's* most conservative church and a manipulative and overprotective housewife and mother. *See also Sula.*

Douglas Taylor

### Wright, Nel (*Sula*)

Daughter of Helene* and Wiley Wright* and childhood friend of Sula Peace*. Nel has traveled outside of Medallion, Ohio*, only once when, as a child, she attended her great-grandmother's funeral in New Orleans. Her relationship with Sula Peace is full of girlish games, childhood adventures, and shared dreams. As Nel grows older, however, she rejects these things for a life of conformity as the wife of Jude Greene*. *See also Sula.*

Douglas Taylor

### Wright, Wiley (*Sula*)

Ship's cook, husband of Helene Wright*, and father of Nel Wright*. *See also Sula.*

Douglas Taylor

# Selected Bibliography

## PRIMARY TEXTS

### Novels

*Beloved*. New York: Knopf, 1987.
*The Bluest Eye*. New York: Holt, Rinehart & Winston, 1970.
*Jazz*. New York: Knopf, 1992.
*Paradise*. New York: Knopf, 1998.
*Song of Solomon*. New York: Knopf, 1977.
*Sula*. New York: Knopf, 1973.
*Tar Baby*. New York: Knopf, 1981.

### Literary Criticism

*Playing in the Dark: Whiteness and the Literary Imagination*. Cambridge, MA: Harvard University Press, 1992.

### Edited Collections

*Birth of a Nation'hood: Gaze, Script, and Spectacle in the O.J. Simpson Case*. Ed. with Claudia Brodsky Lacour. New York: Pantheon, 1997.
*Race-ing Justice, En-Gendering Power: Essays on Anita Hill, Clarence Thomas, and the Construction of Social Reality*. New York: Pantheon, 1992.

### Essays and Stories

"Behind the Making of *The Black Book*." *Black World* 23 (February 1974): 86–90.
*The Big Box*. With Slade Morrison. New York: Hyperion, 1999.
"Black Matter(s)." In *Falling into Theory: Conflicting Views on Reading Literature*. Ed. David Richter. Boston: Bedford Books of St. Martin's Press, 1994.

"City Limits, Village Values: Concepts of the Neighborhood in Black Fiction." In *Literature and the Urban Experience: Essays on the City in Literature*. Ed. Michael C. Jaye and Ann Chalmers Watts. New Brunswick, NJ: Rutgers University Press, 1981.

"Home." In *The House That Race Built: Black Americans, U.S. Terrain*. Ed. Wahneema Lubiano. New York: Pantheon, 1997.

*Lecture and speech of acceptance, upon the award of the Nobel prize for literature, delivered in Stockholm on the seventh of December, nineteen hundred and ninety-three*. New York: Knopf, 1994.

"The Marketing of Power: Racism and Fascism." *Nation* (May 29, 1995): 760.

"Memory, Creation, and Writing." *Thought: A Review of Culture and Idea* 59 (December 1984): 385–90.

"Recitatif." In *Confirmations: Stories by Black Women*. Ed. Amiri Baraka and Amina Baraka. New York: William Morrow, 1983.

"Rediscovering Black History." *New York Times Magazine* (August 11, 1974): 14–24.

"Rootedness: The Ancestor as Foundation." In *Black Women Writers (1950–1980): A Critical Examination*. Ed. Mari Evans. Garden City, NY: Anchor/Doubleday, 1984.

"The Site of Memory." In *Inventing the Truth: The Art and Craft of Memoir*. Ed. William K. Zinsser. Boston: Houghton Mifflin, 1987.

"Slow Walk of Trees (as Grandmother Would Say) Hopeless (as Grandfather Would Say)." *New York Times Magazine* (July 4, 1976): 104, 150, 152, 156, 160, 162, 164.

"Strangers." The *New Yorker* (October 12, 1998).

"Unspeakable Things Unspoken: The Afro-American Presence in American Literature." *Michigan Quarterly Review* 28 (Winter 1989): 1–34.

"What the Black Woman Thinks About Woman's Lib." *New York Times Magazine* (August 22, 1971): 14, 15, 63, 64, 66.

## INTERVIEWS

Bakerman, Jane. "The Seams Cannot Show: An Interview with Toni Morrison." *Black American Literature Forum* 12 (Summer 1978): 56–60.

Davis, Christina. "Interview with Toni Morrison." *Presence africaine* 145 (1988): 14–50.

Jones, Bessie W. "An Interview with Toni Morrison." In *The World of Toni Morrison*. Ed. Bessie W. Jones and Audrey L. Vison. Dubuque, IA: Kendall/Hunt, 1985.

LeClair, Thomas. "'The Language Must Not Sweat': A Conversation with Toni Morrison." *New Republic* (March 21, 1981): 25–29.

Lester, Rosemarie K. "An Interview with Toni Morrison, Hessian Radio Network, Frankfurt, West Germany." In *Critical Essays on Toni Morrison*. Ed. Nellie Y. McKay. Boston: G.K. Hall, 1988.

McKay, Nellie Y. "An Interview with Toni Morrison." *Contemporary Literature* 22 (Winter 1983): 413–29.

Naylor, Gloria, and Toni Morrison. "A Conversation." *Southern Review* 21: 3 (July 1985): 567–93.

Parker, Bettye J. "Complexity: Toni Morrison's Women—An Interview Essay." In *Sturdy Black Bridges: Visions of Black Women in Literature*. Ed. Roseann P. Bell. Garden City, NY: Doubleday, 1979.

Ruas, Charles. "Toni Morrison." In *Conversations with American Writers*. New York: Knopf, 1985.

Stepto, Robert B. "'Intimate Things in Place': A Conversation with Toni Morrison." *Massachusetts Review* 18 (Autumn 1977): 473–89.

Tate, Claudia. "Toni Morrison." In *Black Women Writers at Work*. Ed. Claudia Tate. New York: Continuum, 1983.

Taylor-Guthrie, Danielle, ed. *Conversations with Toni Morrison*. Jackson: University Press of Mississippi, 1994.

## SECONDARY SOURCES

Abel, Elizabeth. "(E)merging Identities: The Dynamics of Female Friendship in Contemporary Fiction by Women." *Signs: Journal of Women in Culture and Society* 6: 3 (Spring 1981): 413–35.

Agular, Sarah Appleton. "'Everywhere and Nowhere': Beloved's 'Wild' Legacy in Toni Morrison's *Jazz*." *Notes on Contemporary Literature* 25: 4 (September 1995): 11–12.

Agular, Sarah Appleton. "Listening to the Mother's Voice in Toni Morrison's *Jazz*." *Journal of Contemporary Thought* 6 (1996): 51–65.

Aithal, Krishnamoorthy. "'Getting Out of One's Skin and Being the Only One Inside': Toni Morrison's *Tar Baby*." *American Studies International* 34: 2 (1996): 76–85.

Alexander, Allen. "The Fourth Face: The Image of God in Toni Morrison's *The Bluest Eye*." *African American Review* 32 (1998): 293–303.

Allan, Tuzyline J. *Feminist and Womanist Aesthetics: A Comparative Review*. Athens: Ohio University Press, 1995.

Allan, Tuzyline J. "Womanism Revisited: Women and the (Ab)use of Power in *The Color Purple*." In *Feminist Nightmares, Women at Odds: Feminism and the Problem of Sisterhood*. Ed. Susan Ostrov Weisser and Jennifer Fleischner. New York: New York University Press, 1994.

Alsen, Eberhard, ed. *The New Romanticism: A Collection of Critical Essays*. New York: Garland, 2000.

Alwes, Karla. "'The Evil of Fulfillment': Women and Violence in *The Bluest Eye*." In *Women and Violence in Literature: An Essay Collection*. Ed. Katherine Anne Ackley. New York: Garland, 1990.

Andrews, Jennifer. "Reading Toni Morrison's *Jazz*: Rewriting the Tall Tale and Playing the Trickster in the White American and African American Humour Traditions." *Canadian Review of American Studies* 29: 1 (1999): 87–107.

Andrews, William L., and Nellie Y. McKay, eds. *Toni Morrison's Beloved: A Casebook*. New York: Oxford University Press, 1999.

Angelo, Bonnie. "The Pain of Being Black: An Interview with Toni Morrison." In *Conversations with Toni Morrison*. Ed. Danielle Taylor-Guthrie. Jackson: University Press of Mississippi, 1994.

Armstrong, Nancy. "Why Daughters Die: The Racial Logic of American Sentimentalism." *Yale Journal of Criticism* 7: 2 (1994): 1–24.

Askeland, Lori. "Remodeling the Model Home in *Uncle Tom's Cabin* and *Beloved*." *American Literature* 64: 4 (1992): 785–805.

Atwood, Margaret. "Haunted by Their Nightmares" (review of *Beloved*). *New York Times Book Review* (September 13, 1987): 1, 49–50.

Badt, Karin Luisa. "The Roots of the Body in Toni Morrison: A Matter of 'Ancient Properties.'" *African American Review* 29: 4 (Winter 1995): 567–77.

Baker, Houston. *Blues, Ideology, and African-American Literature*. Chicago: University of Chicago Press, 1984.

Baker, Houston. "Knowing Our Place: Psychoanalysis and *Sula*." In *Toni Morrison*. Ed. Linden Peach. New York: St. Martin's Press, 1998.

Bakerman, Jane S. "Failures of Love: Initiation in the Novels of Toni Morrison." *American Literature* 52: 4 (January 1981): 541–63.

Barnes, Paula. *Tradition and Innovation: Toni Morrison and the Flight Motif in Afro-American Literature*. New York: Garland, 2000.

Barrett, Eileen. "Septimus and Shadrack: Woolf and Morrison Envision the Madness of War." In *Virginia Woolf: Emerging Perspectives*. Ed. Mark Hussey and Vara Neverow. New York: Pace University Press, 1994.

Basu, Biman. "The Black Voice and the Language of the Text: Toni Morrison's *Sula*." *College Literature* 23: 3 (October 1996): 88–103.

Beaulieu, Elizabeth Ann. *Black Women Writers and the American Neo-Slave Narrative: Femininity Unfettered*. Westport, CT: Greenwood, 1999.

Beaulieu, Elizabeth Ann. "Gendering the Genderless: The Case of Toni Morrison's *Beloved*." *Obsidian II: Black Literature in Review* 8: 1 (Spring–Summer 1993): 1–17.

Bell, Bernard. "*Beloved*: A Womanist Neo-Slave Narrative; or Multivocal Remembrances of Things Past." *African American Review* 26 (1992): 7–15.

Belsey, Catherine, and Jane Moore, eds. *The Feminist Reader: Essays in Gender and the Politics of Literary Criticism*. Cambridge, MA: Blackwell, 1989.

Bender, Eileen T. "Repossessing Uncle Tom's Cabin: Toni Morrison's *Beloved*." In *Cultural Power/Cultural Literacy*. Ed. Bonnie Braendlin. Gainesville: Florida State University Press, 1991.

Bennett, Paula. "The Mother's Part: Incest and Maternal Deprivation in Woolf and Morrison." In *Narrating Mothers: Theorizing Maternal Subjectivities*. Ed. Brenda O. Daly and Maureen T. Reddy. Knoxville: University of Tennessee Press, 1991.

Bent, Geoffrey. "Less Than Divine: Toni Morrison's *Paradise*." *Southern Review* 35: 1 (Winter 1999): 145–49.

Bergenholtz, Rita A. "Toni Morrison's *Sula*: A Satire on Binary Thinking." *African American Review* 30: 1 (Spring 1996): 89–98.

Berlant, Lauren. "Poor Eliza." *American Literature* 70 (1998): 635–68.

Berrett, Anthony J. "Toni Morrison's Literary Jazz." *CLA Journal* 32: 3 (March 1989): 267–83.

Bhabha, Homi. *The Location of Culture*. London: Routledge, 1994.

Bidney, Martin. "Creating a Feminist-Communitarian Romanticism in *Beloved*: Toni Morrison's New Uses for Blake, Keats, and Wordsworth." *Papers on Language and Literature* 36: 3 (Summer 2000): 272–301.

Billingslea-Brown, Alma Jean. *Crossing Borders Through Folklore: African-American Women's Fiction and Art*. Columbia: University of Missouri Press, 1999.

Bischoff, Joan. "The Novels of Toni Morrison: Studies in Thwarted Sensitivity." *Studies in Black Literature* 6: 3 (1975): 21–23.

Bjork, Patrick Bryce. *The Novels of Toni Morrison: The Search for Self and Place Within the Community*. New York: P. Lang, 1992.

Blake, Susan. "Folklore and Community in *Song of Solomon*." *MELUS* 7: 3 (Fall 1980): 77–82.

Bloom, Harold, ed. *Toni Morrison*. Broomhall, PA: Chelsea House, 2000.

Bouson, J. Brooks. *Quiet as It's Kept: Shame, Trauma, and Race in the Novels of Toni Morrison*. Albany: State University of New York Press, 2000.

Branch, Eleanor. "Through the Maze of the Oedipal: Milkman's Search for Self in *Song of Solomon*." *Literature and Psychology* 41: 1–2 (1995): 52–84.

Brown, Cecil. "Interview with Toni Morrison." *The Massachusetts Review* 36: 3 (Autumn 1995): 455–73.

Budick, Emily Miller. "Absence, Loss, and the Space of History in Toni Morrison's *Beloved*." *Arizona Quarterly* 48: 2 (Summer 1992): 117–38.

Budick, Emily Miller. *Engendering Romance: Women Writers and the Hawthorne Tradition, 1850–1990*. New Haven: Yale University Press, 1989.

Burbanks, Samuel IV. "African Spiritual Culture in *Sula, Song of Solomon*, and *Beloved*." 1997. 10 July 2001. *http://www.timbooktu.com/burbanks/spiritual.htm*

Byerman, Keith E. *Fingering the Jagged Grain: Tradition and Form in Recent Black Fiction*. Anthens: University of Georgia Press, 1985.

Cadman, Deborah. "When the Back Door Is Closed and the Front Yard Is Dangerous: The Space of Girlhood in Toni Morrison's Fiction." In *The Girl: Constructions of the Girl in Contemporary Fiction*. Ed. Ruth Saxon. New York: St. Martin's Press, 1998.

Campbell, Jane. *Mythic Black Fiction: The Transformation of History*. Knoxville: University of Tennessee Press, 1986.

Cannon, Elizabeth M. "Following the Traces of Female Desire in Toni Morrison's *Jazz*." *African American Review* 31: 2 (Summer 1997): 235–47.

Carmean, Karen. *Toni Morrison's World of Fiction*. Troy, NY: Whitson, 1993.

Chadwick-Joshua, Jocelyn. "Metonymy and Synecdoche: The Rhetoric of the City in Toni Morrison's *Jazz*." In *The City in African-American Literature*. Ed. Yoshinobu Hakutani and Robert Butler. Madison, NJ: Fairleigh Dickinson University Press, 1995.

Chase, Richard. *The American Novel and Its Tradition*. Baltimore: Johns Hopkins University Press, 1957; Cambridge, MA: Harvard University Press, 1990.

Christian, Barbara. *Black Feminist Criticism: Perspectives on Black Women Writers*. New York: Pergamon Press, 1985.

Christian, Barbara. "Community and Nature: The Novels of Toni Morrison." *Journal of Ethnic Studies* 7: 4 (Winter 1980): 65-78.

Clasby, Nancy Tenfelde. "Sula the Trickster." *Lit: Literature Interpretation Theory* 6: 1–2 (April 1995): 21–34.

Coleman, Alisha. "One and One Make One: A Metacritical and Psychoanalytic Reading of Friendship in Toni Morrison's *Sula*." *CLA Journal* 37: 2 (December 1993): 145–55.

Coleman, James W. "Beyond the Reach of Love and Caring: Black Life in Toni Morrison's *Song of Solomon*." *Obsidian II: Black Literature in Review* 1: 3 (Winter 1986): 151–61.

Coleman, James W. "The Quest for Wholeness in Toni Morrison's *Tar Baby*." *Black American Literature Forum* 20: 1–2 (Spring–Summer 1986): 63-73.

Collins, Patricia Hill. *Black Feminist Thought: Knowledge, Consciousness, and the Politics of Empowerment*. New York: Routledge, 1990.

Collins, Patricia Hill. "The Meaning of Motherhood in Black Culture and Black Mother/Daughter Relationships." *Sage* 4: 2 (1987): 3–10.

Comfort, Susan. "Counter-Memory, Mourning and History in Toni Morrison's *Beloved*." *Lit: Literature Interpretation Theory* 6: 1–2 (April 1995): 121–32.

Conner, Marc C., ed. *The Aesthetics of Toni Morrison: Speaking the Unspeakable*. Jackson: University Press of Mississippi, 2000.

Cooper, Brenda. *Magical Realism in West African Fiction: Seeing with a Third Eye*. London: Routledge, 1998.

Corey, Susan. "The Religious Dimensions of the Grotesque in Literature: Toni Morrison's *Beloved*." In *The Grotesque in Art and Literature: Theological Reflections*. Ed. James Adams and Wilson Yates. Grand Rapids, MI: W. B. Eerdmans, 1997.

Courlander, Harold, ed. *A Treasury of Afro-American Folklore*. New York: Marlowe, 1996.

Croyden, Margaret. "Toni Morrison Tries Her Hand at Playwriting." *New York Times* (December 29, 1985), sec. 2: 6H, 16H.

Cumings, Susan G. "'Outing' the Hidden Other: Stranger-Women in the Work of Toni Morrison." In *Dissent and Marginality: Essays on the Borders of Literature and Religion*. Ed. Kiyoshi Tsuchiya. New York: St. Martin's Press, 1997.

Cutter, Martha J. "The Story Must Go On and On: The Fantastic, Narration, and Intertextuality in Toni Morrison's *Beloved* and *Jazz*." *African American Review* 34: 1 (Spring 2000): 61–75.

Dalsgard, Katrine. "The One All-Black Town Worth the Pain: (African) American Exceptionalism, Historical Narration, and the Critique of Nationhood in Toni Morrison's *Paradise*." *African American Review* 35: 2 (2001): 233–48.

David, Ron. *Toni Morrison Explained: A Reader's Road Map to the Novels*. New York: Random House, 2000.

Davies, Carole Boyce. "Mother Right/Write Revisited: *Beloved* and *Dessa Rose* and the Construction of Motherhood in Black Women's Fiction." In *Narrating Mothers: Theorizing Maternal Subjectivities*. Ed. Brenda O. Daly and Maureen T. Reddy. Knoxville: University of Tennessee Press, 1991.

Davis, Cynthia Y. "Self, Society and Myth in Toni Morrison's Fiction." In *New Casebooks: Toni Morrison*. Ed. Linden Peach. New York, St. Martin's Press, 1998.

DeLancey, Dayle B. "Motherlove Is a Killer: *Sula*, *Beloved*, and the Deadly Trinity of Motherlove." *SAGE: A Scholarly Journal on Black Women* 7: 2 (Fall 1990): 15–18.

DeLancey, Dayle B. "Sweetness, Madness, and Power: The Confection as Mental Contagion in Toni Morrison's *Tar Baby*, *Song of Solomon*, and *The Bluest Eye*." *Process: A Journal of African American and African Diasporic Literature* 2 (Spring 2000): 25–47.

Demetrakopoulos, Stephanie A. "Maternal Bonds as Devourers of Women's Individuation in Toni Morrison's *Beloved*." *African American Review* 26: 1 (1992): 51–59.

Denard, Carolyn. "Mythical Consciousness of Morrison and Faulkner." In *Unflinching Gaze: Morrison and Faulkner Re-Envisioned*. Ed. Carol A. Kolmerten, Stephen M. Ross, and Judith Bryant Wittenberg. Jackson: University Press of Mississippi, 1997.

Denby, David. "Haunted by the Past." *The New Yorker* (October 26 and November 2, 1998): 248–53.

Dickerson, Vanessa D. "The Naked Father in Toni Morrison's *The Bluest Eye*." In *Refiguring the Father: New Feminist Readings of Patriarchy*. Ed. Patricia Yaeger and Beth Kowaleski-Wallace. Carbondale: Southern Illinois University Press, 1989.

Dixon, Melvin. *Ride Out the Wilderness: Geography and Identity in Afro-American Literature*. Urbana: University of Illinois Press, 1987.

Dundes, Alan. *Folklore Matters*. Knoxville: University of Tennessee Press, 1989.

Duvall, John N. "Authentic Ghost Stories: *Uncle Tom's Cabin, Absalom, Absalom!* and *Beloved*." *The Faulkner Journal* 4: 1–2 (1988): 83–97.

Duvall, John N. *The Identifying Fictions of Toni Morrison: Modernist Authenticity and Postmodern Blackness*. New York: Palgrave, 2000.

Duvall, John N. "Naming Invisible Authority: Toni Morrison's Covert Letter to Ralph Ellison." *Studies in American Fiction* 25: 2 (Autumn 1997): 241–53.

Eckard, Paula Gallant. "The Interplay of Music, Language, and Narrative in Toni Morrison's *Jazz*." *CLA Journal* 28: 1 (September 1994): 11–19.

Eisenberg, Evan. *The Ecology of Eden*. New York: Knopf, 1998.

Ellison, Ralph. "Change the Joke and Slip the Yoke." In *Mother Wit from the Laughing Barrel*. Ed. Alan Dundes. Jackson: University Press of Mississippi, 1990.

Evans, Mari, Ed. *Black Women Writers (1950–1980): A Critical Evaluation*. New York: Anchor Books, 1984.

Faris, Wendy B., and Laura Parkinson Zamora, eds. *Magical Realism: Theory, History, Community*. Durham, NC: Duke University Press, 1995.

Ferguson, Rebecca. "History, Memory and Language in Toni Morrison's *Beloved*." In *Contemporary American Women Writers: Gender, Class, Ethnicity*. Ed. Lois Parkinson Zamora. New York: Longman, 1998.

Fick, Thomas H. "Toni Morrison's Allegory of the Cave: Movies, Consumption, and Platonic Realism in *The Bluest Eye*." *JMMLA* 22 (1989): 10–22.

Fields, Karen E. "To Embrace Dead Strangers: Toni Morrison's *Beloved*." In *Mother Puzzles: Daughters and Mothers in Contemporary American Literature*. Ed. Mickey Pearlman. New York: Greenwood, 1989.

Fine, Michelle, and Adrienne Asch, eds. *Women with Disabilities: Essays in Psychology, Culture, and Politics*. Philadelphia: Temple University Press, 1988.

FitzGerald, Jennifer. "Selfhood and Community: Psychoanalysis and Discourse in *Beloved*." *Modern Fiction Studies* 39: 3–4 (Fall/Winter 1993): 669–87.

Foster, Frances Smith. *Witnessing Slavery: The Development of Ante-bellum Slave Narratives*. Westport, CT: Greenwood, 1979.

Furman, Jan. *Toni Morrison's Fiction*. Columbia: University of South Carolina Press, 1996.

Galehouse, Maggie. "'New World Woman': Toni Morrison's *Sula*." *Papers on Language and Literature* 35: 4 (Fall 1999): 339–62.

Garabedian, Deanna M. "Toni Morrison and the Language of Music." *CLA Journal* 41: 3 (March 1998): 303–18.

Garland-Thomson, Rosemarie. *Extraordinary Bodies: Figuring Physical Disability in American Culture and Literature*. New York: Columbia University Press, 1997.

Gates, Henry Louis, Jr. *The Signifying Monkey: A Theory of African-American Literary Criticism*. New York: Oxford University Press, 1988.

Gates, Henry Louis, Jr., and K. A. Appiah, eds. *Toni Morrison: Critical Perspectives Past and Present*. New York: Amistad, 1993.

Gilroy, Paul. *Small Acts: Thoughts on the Politics of Black Cultures*. New York: Serpent's Tail, 1993.

Glotfelty, Cheryll, and Harold Fromm, eds. *The Ecocriticism Reader: Landmarks in Literary Ecology*. Athens: University of Georgia Press, 1996.

Goldstein-Shirley, David. "Race/(Gender): Toni Morrison's 'Recitatif.'" *Journal of the Short Story in English* 27 (Autumn 1996): 83–95.

Gravett, Sharon L. "Toni Morrison's *The Bluest Eye*: An Inverted *Walden*?" *West Virginia University Philological Papers* 38 (1992): 201–11.

Grewal, Gurleen. *Circles of Sorrow, Lines of Struggle: The Novels of Toni Morrison*. Baton Rouge: Louisiana State University Press, 1998.

Griffin, Farah Jasmine. *"Who Set You Flowin'?": The African-American Migration Narrative*. New York: Oxford University Press, 1995.

Guth, Deborah. "A Blessing and a Burden: The Relation to the Past in *Sula, Song of Solomon*, and *Beloved*." *Modern Fiction Studies* 39: 3–4 (Fall–Winter 1993): 575–96.

Guth, Deborah. "'Wonder What God Had in Mind': *Beloved*'s Dialogue with Christianity." *Journal of Narrative Technique* 24: 2 (1994): 83–97.

Hardack, Richard. "'A Music Seeking Its Own Words': Double-Timing and Double Consciousness in Toni Morrison's *Jazz*." *Callaloo: A Journal of African-American and African Arts and Letters* 18: 2 (Spring 1995): 451–71.

Harding, Wendy, and Jacky Martin. *A World of Difference: An Intercultural Study of Toni Morrison's Novels*. Westport, CT: Greenwood, 1994.

Harris, A. Leslie, "Myth as Structure in Toni Morrison's *Song of Solomon*." *MELUS* 7: 3 (1980): 69–76.

Harris, Trudier. *Fiction and Folklore: The Novels of Toni Morrison*. Knoxville: University of Tennessee Press, 1991.

Harris, Trudier. "Reconnecting Fragments: Afro-American Folk Tradition in *The Bluest Eye*." In *Critical Essays on Toni Morrison*. Ed. Nellie McKay. Boston: G.K. Hall, 1988.

Harris, Trudier. "Toni Morrison: Solo Flight Through Literature into History." *World Literature Today* 68: 1 (Winter 1994): 9–14.

Harris, Trudier. "The Worlds That Toni Morrison Made." *The Georgia Review* 49: 1 (Spring 1995): 314–30.

Hayes, Elizabeth T. "'Like Seeing You Buried': Persephone in *The Bluest Eye, Their Eyes Were Watching God*, and *The Color Purple*." In *Images of Persephone: Feminist Readings in Western Literature*. Gainesville: University Press of Florida, 1994.

Heinze, Denise. *The Dilemma of "Double-Consciousness": Toni Morrison's Novels*. Athens: University of Georgia Press, 1993.

Henderson, Mae. "Toni Morrison's *Beloved*: Re-Membering the Body as Historical Text." In *Comparative American Identities: Race, Sex, and Nationality in the Modern Text*. Ed. Hortense Spillers. New York: Routledge, 1991.

Hirsch, Marianne. "Maternity and Rememory: Toni Morrison's *Beloved*." In *Representations of Motherhood*. Ed. Donna Bassin, Margaret Honey, and Meryle Mahrer Kaplan. New Haven, CT: Yale University Press, 1994.

Hirsch, Marianne. *The Mother/Daughter Plot: Narrative, Psychoanalysis, Feminism*. Bloomington: Indiana University Press, 1989.

Holloway, Karla. "*Beloved*: A Spiritual." *Callaloo* 13: 3 (1990): 516–25.

Holloway, Karla F. C., and Stephanie Demetrakopoulos. *New Dimensions of Spirituality: A Biracial and Bicultural Reading of the Novels of Toni Morrison*. New York: Greenwood, 1987.

hooks, bell. *Talking Back: Thinking Feminist, Thinking Black*. Boston: South End Press, 1989.

Hovet, Grace Ann, and Barbara Lounsberry. "Flying as Symbol and Legend in Tony Morrison's *The Bluest Eye, Sula*, and *Song of Solomon*." *CLA Journal* 27: 2 (December 1983): 119–40.

Hudson-Weems, Clenora and Wilfred D. Samuels. *Toni Morrison*. Boston: Twayne Publishers, 1990.

Hunt, Kristin. "Paradise Lost: The Destructive Forces of Double Consciousness and Boundaries in Toni Morrison's *Paradise*." In *Reading Under the Sign of Nature: New Essays in Ecocentrism*. Ed. John Tallmadge and Henry Harrington. Salt Lake City: University of Utah Press, 2000.

Hunt, Patricia. "'Free to Do Something Wild': History and the Ancestor in *Jazz*." *Lit: Literature Interpretation Theory* 6: 1–2 (April 1995): 47–62.

Iyasere, Solomon O., and Marla W. Iyasere, eds. *Understanding Toni Morrison's Beloved and Sula: Selected Essays and Criticism of the Works by the Nobel Prize-Winning Author*. Troy, NY: Whitson, 2000.

Jablon, Madelyn. "*Tar Baby*: Philosophizing Blackness." In *Approaches to Teaching the Novels of Toni Morrison*. Ed. Nellie Y. McKay and Kathryn Earle. New York: Modern Language Association of America, 1997.

Jones, Carolyn M. "Traces and Cracks: Identity and Narrative in Toni Morrison's *Jazz*." *African American Review* 31: 3 (Fall 1997): 481–95.

Kaufman, Gershen. *Shame: The Power of Caring*. 1980. 3rd ed., rev. and exp., Rochester, VT: Schenkman, 1992.

Keenan, Sally. "'Four Hundred Years of Silence': Myth, History, and Motherhood in Toni Morrison's *Beloved*." In *Recasting the World: Writing After Colonialism*. Ed. Jonathan White. Baltimore: Johns Hopkins University Press, 1993.

Klotman, Phyllis R. "Dick-and-Jane and the Shirley Temple Sensibility in *The Bluest Eye*." *Black American Literature Forum* 13 (1979): 123–25.

Kolmerten, Carol A., Stephen M. Ross, and Judith Bryant Wittenberg, eds. *Unflinching Gaze: Morrison and Faulkner Re-Envisioned*. Jackson: University Press of Mississippi, 1997.

Koolish, Lynda. "Fictive Strategies and Cinematic Representations in Toni Morrison's *Beloved*: Postcolonial Theory/Postcolonial Text." *African American Review* 29.3 (1995): 421–38.

Krumholz, Linda. "Dead Teachers: Rituals of Manhood and Rituals of Reading in *Song of Solomon*." *Modern Fiction Studies* 39: 3–4 (1993): 551–74.

Krumholtz, Linda. "The Ghosts of Slavery: Historical Recovery in Toni Morrison's *Beloved*." *African American Review* 26: 3 (Fall 1992): 395–408.

Kubitschek, Missy Dehn. *Toni Morrison: A Critical Companion*. Westport, CT: Greenwood, 1998.

Kuenz, Jane. "*The Bluest Eye*: Notes on History, Community, and Black Female Subjectivity." *African American Review* 27: 3 (1993): 421–31.

Lee, Catherine Carr. "The South in Toni Morrison's *Song of Solomon*: Initiation, Healing and Home." *Studies in the Literary Imagination* 31: 2 (1998): 109–23.

Lee, Kyung Soon. "Black Feminism: *Sula* and *Meridian*." *Journal of English Language and Literature* 38: 3 (Fall 1992): 585–99.

Lehmann, Elmar. "Remembering the Past: Toni Morrison's Version of the Historical Novel." In *Lineages of the Novel*. Ed. Bernhard Reitz and Eckart Voigts-Virchow. Trier, Germany: Wissenschaftlicher, 2000.

Lemann, Nicholas. *The Promised Land: The Great Black Migration and How It Changed America*. New York: Vintage, 1991.

Lepow, Lauren. "Paradise Lost and Found: Dualism and Edenic Myth in Toni Morrison's *Tar Baby*." *Contemporary Literature* 28: 3 (Fall 1987): 363–77.

Lewis, Helen Block. "Introduction: Shame—the 'Sleeper' in Psychopathology." In *The Role of Shame in Symptom Formation*. Ed. Helen Lewis. Hillsdale, NJ: Lawrence Erlbaum, 1987.

Lewis, Vashti Crutcher. "African Tradition in Toni Morrison's *Sula*." *Phylon: A Review of Race and Culture* 48: 1 (March 1987): 91–97.

Lounsberry, Barbara, and Grace A. Hovet. "Principles of Perception in Toni Morrison's *Sula*." *Black American Literature Forum* 13: 4 (Winter 1979): 126–29.

Lubiano, Wahneema. "The Postmodernist Rag: Political Identity and the Vernacular in *Song of Solomon*" In *New Essays on Song of Solomon*. Ed. Valerie Smith. Cambridge: Cambridge University Press, 1995.

Malmgren, Carl D. "Texts, Primers, and Voices in Toni Morrison's *The Bluest Eye*." *Critique: Studies in Contemporary Fiction* 41: 3 (Spring 2000): 251–62.

Maslin, Janet. "*Beloved*: No Peace from a Brutal Legacy." *The New York Times* (October 16, 1998): E1, 20.

Mathieson, Barbara Offutt. "Memory and Mother Love in Morrison's *Beloved*." *American Imago* 47: 1 (Spring 1990): 1–21.

Matus, Jill. *Toni Morrison*. New York: St. Martin's Press, 1998.

Mayer, Sulvia. "'You Like Huckleberries?': Toni Morrison's *Beloved* and Mark Twain's *Adventures of Huckleberry Finn*." In *The Black Columbiad: Defining Moments in African American Literature and Culture*. Ed. Werner Sollors and Maria Diedrich. Cambridge, MA: Harvard University Press, 1994.

Mazur, Kimberly A. "A Womanist Analysis: Triple Oppression in the Early Fiction of Toni Morrison." M.A. thesis, Shippensburg University of Pennsylvania, 1999.

Mbalia, Dorothea Drummond. "*Tar Baby*: A Reflection of Morrison's Developed Class Consciousness." In *Toni Morrison*. Ed. Linden Peach. New York: St. Martin's Press, 1997.

Mbalia, Dorothea Drummond. "Women Who Run with Wild: The Need for Sisterhoods in *Jazz*." *Modern Fiction Studies* 39: 3–4 (Fall–Winter 1993): 623–46.

McDowell, Deborah E., and Arnold Rampersad, eds. *Slavery and the Literary Imagination*. Baltimore: Johns Hopkins University Press, 1987.

McKay, Nellie Y., ed. *Critical Essays on Toni Morrison*. Boston: G.K. Hall, 1988.

McKay, Nellie Y., and Kathryn Earle, eds. *Approaches to Teaching the Novels of Toni Morrison*. New York: Modern Language Association of America, 1997.

McKay, Nellie Y. "An Interview with Toni Morrison." In *Conversations with Toni Morrison*. Ed. Danielle Taylor-Guthrie. Jackson: University Press of Mississippi, 1994.

McKee, Patricia. *Producing American Races: Henry James, William Faulkner, Toni Morrison*. Durham, NC: Duke University Press, 1999.

Middleton, David L., ed. *Toni Morrison's Fiction: Contemporary Criticism*. New York: Garland, 2000.

Middleton, Victoria. "*Sula*: An Experimental Life." *CLA Journal* 28: 4 (June 1985): 367–81.

Miner, Madonne M. "Lady No Longer Sings the Blues: Rape, Madness, and Silence in *The Bluest Eye*." In *Conjuring: Black Women, Fiction, and Literary Tradition*. Ed. Marjorie Pryse and Hortense J. Spillers. Bloomington: Indiana University Press, 1985.

Mitchell, Angelyn. "'Sth, I Know That Woman': History, Gender and the South in Toni Morrison's *Jazz*." *Studies in the Literary Imagination* 31: 2 (Fall 1998): 49–60.

Mobley, Marilyn. "Jadine as Cultural Orphan in Toni Morrison's *Tar Baby*." *The South-ern Review* 23: 4 (Autumn 1987): 761–70.

Mobley, Marilyn Sanders. *Folk Roots and Mythic Wings in Sarah Orne Jewett and Toni Morrison: The Cultural Function of Narrative*. Baton Rouge: Louisiana State University Press, 1991.

Mobley, Marilyn Sanders. "Narrative Dilemma: Jadine as Cultural Orphan in *Tar Baby*." In *Toni Morrison: Critical Perspectives Past and Present*. Ed. Henry Louis Gates, Jr., and K. Anthony Appiah. New York: Amistad, 1993.

Mock, Michele. "Spitting Out the Seed: Ownership of Mother, Child, Breasts, Milk, and Voice in Toni Morrison's *Beloved*." *College Literature* 23: 3 (October 1996): 117–26.

*Modern Fiction Studies*. Special issue 39: 3–4 (1993).

Mohanty, Satya P. "The Epistemic Status of Cultural Identity: On *Beloved* and the Post-colonial Condition." *Cultural Critique*. 3: 1–2 (1999–2000): 41–80.

Moreland, Richard C. "'He Wants to Put His Story Next to Hers': Putting Twain's Story Next to Hers in Morrison's *Beloved*." In *Toni Morrison: Critical and Theoretical Approaches*. Ed. Nancy J. Peterson. Baltimore: Johns Hopkins University Press, 1997.

Morgenstern, Naomi. "Mother's Milk and Sister's Blood: Trauma and the Neoslave Narrative." *Differences: A Journal of Feminist Cultural Studies* 8: 2 (1996): 101–26.

Mori, Aoi. "Embracing Jazz: Healing of Armed Women and Motherless Children in Toni Morrison's *Jazz*." *CLA Journal* 42: 3 (March 1999): 320–30.

Mori, Aoi. *Toni Morrison and the Womanist Discourse*. New York: P. Lang, 1999.

Morrison, Andrew. *The Culture of Shame*. New York: Ballantine/Random House, 1996.

Moses, Cat. "The Blues Aesthetic in Toni Morrison's *The Bluest Eye*." *African American Review* 33: 4 (Winter 1999): 623–36.

Mullen, Harryette. "Runaway Tongue: Resistant Orality in *Uncle Tom's Cabin, Our Nig, Incidents in the Life of a Slave Girl*, and *Beloved*." In *The Culture of Sentiment: Race, Gender and Sentimentality in Nineteenth-Century America*. Ed. Shirley Samuels. New York: Oxford University Press, 1992.

Munafo, Giavanna. "'No Sign of Life': Marble-Blue Eyes and Lakefront Houses in *The Bluest Eye*." *Lit: Literature Interpretation Theory* 6: 1–2 (April 1995): 1–19.

Murray, Roland. "The Long Strut: *Song of Solomon* and the Emancipatory Limits of Black Patriarchy." *Callaloo: A Journal of African-American and African Arts and Letters* 22: 1 (Winter 1999): 121–33.

Nathanson, Donald. *Shame and Pride: Affect, Sex, and the Birth of the Self*. New York: Norton, 1994.

Neubauer, Paul. "The Demon of Loss and Longing: The Function of the Ghost in Toni Morrison's *Beloved*." In *Demons: Mediators Between This World and the Other. Essays on Demonic Beings from the Middle Ages to the Present*. Ed. Ruth Pet-zoldt and Paul Neubauer. Frankfurt, Germany: Peter Lang, 1998.

Nissen, Axel. "Form Matters: Toni Morrison's *Sula* and the Ethics of Narrative." *Contemporary Literature* 40: 2 (Summer 1999): 263–85.

Novak, Phillip. "'Circles and Circles of Sorrow': In the Wake of Morrison's *Sula*." *PMLA* 114: 2 (March 1999): 184–93.

Nowlin, Michael. "Toni Morrison's *Jazz* and the Racial Dreams of the American Writer." *American Literature* 71: 1 (March 1999): 151–74.

Ogunyemi, Chikwenye. "Womanism: The Dynamics of the Contemporary Black Female Novel in English." *Signs: Journal of Women in Culture and Society* 11 (1985): 63–80.

Olorounto, Samuel B. "Studying African-American Literature in Its Global Context," *VCAAA Journal* 7: 1 (Summer 1992): 4–12.

O'Reilly, Andrea. "In Search of My Mother's Garden, I Found My Own: Mother-Love, Healing, and Identity in Toni Morrison's *Jazz*." *African American Review* 30: 3 (Fall 1996): 367–79.

Otten, Terry. *The Crime of Innocence in the Fiction of Toni Morrison*. Columbia: University of Missouri Press, 1989.

Page, Philip. *Dangerous Freedom: Fusion and Fragmentation in Toni Morrison's Novels*. Jackson: University Press of Mississippi, 1995.

Page, Philip. "Traces of Derrida in Toni Morrison's *Jazz*." *African American Review* 29: 1 (Spring 1995): 55–66.

Painter, Nell Irvin. *Exodusters: Black Migration to Kansas After Reconstruction*. New York: Norton, 1976.

Peach, Linden. *Toni Morrison*. New York: St. Martin's Press, 2000.

Peach, Linden, ed. *Toni Morrison*. New York: St. Martin's Press, 1998.

Pearce, Richard. "Toni Morrison's *Jazz*: Negotiations of the African American Beauty Culture." *Narrative* 6: 3 (October 1998): 307–24.

Pessoni, Michele. "'She Was Laughing at Their God': Discovering the Goddess Within in *Sula*." *African American Review* 29: 3 (Fall 1995): 439–51.

Peterson, Nancy J. "'Say Make Me, Remake Me': Toni Morrison and the Reconstruction of African-American History." In *Toni Morrison: Critical and Theoretical Approaches*. Ed. Nancy J. Peterson. Baltimore: Johns Hopkins University Press, 1997.

Peterson, Nancy J., ed. *Toni Morrison: Critical and Theoretical Approaches*. Baltimore: Johns Hopkins University Press, 1997.

Pettis, Joyce. "Difficult Survival: Mothers and Daughters in *The Bluest Eye*." *SAGE: A Scholarly Journal on Black Women* 4: 2 (Fall 1987): 26–29.

Pici, Nicholas F. "Trading Meanings: The Breath of Music in Toni Morrison's *Jazz*." *Connotations* 7: 3 (1997–98): 372–98.

Plasa, Carl, ed. *Toni Morrison: Beloved*. New York: Columbia University Press, 1998.

Plato. "The Allegory of the Cave." In his *Republic*. Trans. G.M.A. Grube. Cambridge: Hackett, 1992.

Powell, Timothy B. "Toni Morrison: The Struggle to Depict the Black Figure on the White Page." In *Toni Morrison's Fiction: Contemporary Criticism*. Ed. David L. Middleton. New York: Garland, 2000.

Randolph, Laura B. "Oprah and Danny." *Ebony* (November 1998): 36–37, 40, 42.

Reddy, Maureen T. "The Tripled Plot and Center of *Sula*." *Black American Literature Forum* 22: 1 (Spring 1988): 29–45.

Reyes, Angelita. "Using History as Artifact to Situate *Beloved*'s Unknown Woman: Margaret Garner." In *Approaches to Teaching Toni Morrison*. Ed. Nellie Y. McKay and Kathryn Earle. New York: Modern Language Association of America, 1997.

Rice, Alan J. "Erupting Funk: The Political Style of Toni Morrison's *Tar Baby* and *The Bluest Eye*." In *Post-Colonial Literatures: Expanding the Canon*. Ed. Deborah L. Madsen. London: Pluto Press, 1999.

Rice, Alan J. "'It Don't Mean a Thing if It Ain't Got That Swing': Jazz's Many Uses for Toni Morrison." In *Black Orpheus: Music in African American Fiction from the*

*Harlem Renaissance to Toni Morrison.* Ed. Saadi A. Simawe. New York: Garland, 2000.

Rice, Herbert Williams. *Toni Morrison and the American Tradition: A Rhetorical Reading.* New York: P. Lang, 1996.

Rigney, Barbara Hill. *The Voices of Toni Morrison.* Columbus: Ohio State University Press, 1991.

Robinson, Harlow. "Dreams of a Prophetic Past: Novelist Toni Morrison Tries Her Hand at Playwriting." *American Theatre* 2 (January 1986): 17–19.

Rodgers, Lawrence R. *Canaan Bound: The African-American Great Migration Novel.* Urbana: University of Illinois Press, 1997.

Rodrigues, Eusebio L. "Experiencing Jazz." *Modern Fiction Studies* 39: 3–4 (Fall–Winter 1993): 733–54.

Rosenberg, Ruth. "Seeds in Hard Ground: Black Girlhood in *The Bluest Eye.*" *Black American Literature Forum* 21: 4 (Winter 1987): 435–45.

Royster, Philip M. "Milkman's Flying: The Scapegoat Transcended in Toni Morrison's *Song of Solomon.*" *CLA Journal* 24: 4 (June 1981): 419–40.

Rubenstein, Roberta. "Singing the Blues/Reclaiming Jazz: Toni Morrison and Cultural Mourning." *Mosaic: A Journal for the Interdisciplinary Study of Literature* 31: 2 (June 1998): 147–63.

Rueckert, William. "Literature and Ecology: An Experiment in Ecocriticism." *Iowa Review* 9: 1 (1978): 71–86.

Rushdy, Ashraf H. A. "Daughters Signifyin(g) History: The Example of Toni Morrison's *Beloved.*" In *Toni Morrison.* Ed. Linden Peach. New York: St. Martin's Press, 1998.

Rushdy, Ashraf H. A. *Neo-Slave Narratives: Studies in the Social Logic of a Literary Form.* New York: Oxford University Press, 1999.

Russell, Sandi. "It's OK to Say OK." In *Critical Essays on Toni Morrison.* Ed. Nellie Y. McKay. Boston: G. K. Hall, 1988.

Ryan, Katy. "Revolutionary Suicide in Toni Morrison's Fiction." *African American Review* 34: 3 (Fall 2000): 389–412.

Sale, Maggie. "Call and Response as Critical Method: African-American Oral Traditions and *Beloved.*" *African American Review* 26 (Spring 1992): 41–50.

Samuels, Wilfred D., and Clenora Hudson-Weems. *Toni Morrison.* Boston: Twayne, 1990.

Schapiro, Barbara. "The Bonds of Love and the Boundaries of Self in Toni Morrison's *Beloved.*" *Contemporary Literature* 32: 2 (Summer 1991): 194–210.

Schappell, Elissa, and Claudia Brodsky Lacour. "Toni Morrison: The Art of Fiction CXXXIV." *The Paris Review* 35 (1993): 83–125.

Sherard, Tracey. "Women's Classic Blues in Toni Morrison's *Jazz:* Cultural Artifact as Narrator." *Genders* 31 (2000).

Smith, Barbara. "Toward a Black Feminist Criticism." In *All the Women Are White, All the Blacks Are Men, But Some of Us Are Brave.* Ed. Gloria T. Hull, Patricia Bell Scott, and Barbara Smith. Old Westbury, NY: The Feminist Press, 1982.

Smith, Dinitia. "Toni Morrison's Mix of Tragedy, Domesticity and Folklore." *New York Times* (January 8, 1998): E1, 3.

Smith, Valerie, ed. *New Essays on Song of Solomon.* New York: Cambridge University Press, 1995.

Solomon, Barbara H., ed. *Critical Essays on Toni Morrison's Beloved.* New York: G.K. Hall, 1998.

Stein, Karen F. "Toni Morrison's *Sula*: A Black Woman's Epic." *Black American Literature Forum* 18: 4 (Winter 1984): 146–50.

Storhoff, Gary. "'Anaconda Love': Parental Enmeshment in Toni Morrison's *Song of Solomon*." *Style* 31: 2 (Summer 1997): 290–309.

*Studies in the Literary Imagination*. Special issue "Toni Morrison and the American South" 31: 2 (Fall 1998).

Subryan, Carmen. "Circles: Mother and Daughter Relationships in Toni Morrison's *Song of Solomon*." *SAGE: A Scholarly Journal on Black Women* 5: 1 (Summer 1988): 34–36.

Tally, Justine. "Toni Morrison's (Hi)stories and Truths." in *FORECAAST: Forum for European Contributions to African American Studies Lit*. Piscataway, NJ: Transaction Publishers, 1999.

Tate, Claudia. *Psychoanalysis and Black Novels: Desire and the Protocols of Race*. New York: Oxford University Press, 1998.

Taylor-Guthrie, Danielle, ed. *Conversations with Toni Morrison*. Jackson: University Press of Mississippi, 1994.

Thompson, Robert Farris. *Flash of the Spirit: African & Afro-American Art and Philosophy*. New York: Vintage, 1984.

Tibbetts, John C. "Oprah's Belabored *Beloved*." *Literature Film Quarterly* 27: 1 (1999): 74–76.

Travis, Molly Abel. "Speaking from the Silence of the Slave Narrative: *Beloved* and African-American Women's History." *The Texas Review* 13 (1992): 69–81.

Twelve Southerners. *I'll Take My Stand. The South and the Agrarian Tradition*. Baton Rouge: Louisiana State University Press, 1977. Original copyright 1930.

Vickroy, Laurie. "The Force Outside/The Force Inside: Mother-Love and Regenerative Spaces in *Sula* and *Beloved*." *Obsidian II: Black Literature in Review* 8: 2 (Fall–Winter 1993): 28–45.

Waegner, Cathy. "Toni Morrison and the 'Other' Reader—Oprah Winfrey and Marcel Reich-Ranicki as Mediators?" In *Holding Their Own: Perspectives on the Multi-Ethnic Literatures of the United States*. Ed. Dorothea Fischer-Hornung. Tübingen, Germany: Stauffenburg, 2000.

Walcott, Rinaldo. "Deceived: The Unreadability of the O.J. Simpson Case." *Canadian Review of American Studies* 28: 2 (1998): 177–88.

Walker, Alice. *In Search of Our Mothers' Gardens: Womanist Prose*. New York: Harcourt Brace Jovanovich, 1983.

Walther, Malin LaVon. "Toni Morrison's *Tar Baby*: Re-Figuring the Colonizer's Aesthetics." In *Cross-Cultural Performances: Differences in Women's Re-Visions of Shakespeare*. Ed. Marianne Novy. Urbana: University of Illinois Press, 1993.

Warner, Anne Bradford. "New Myths and Ancient Properties: The Fiction of Toni Morrison." *The Hollins Critic* 25: 3 (1988): 1–11.

Waxman, Barbara. "Changing History Through a Gendered Perspective: A Postmodern Feminist Reading of Morrison's *Beloved*." In *Multicultural Literatures Through Feminist/Poststructuralist Lenses*. Ed. Barbara Frey Waxman. Knoxville: University of Tennessee Press, 1993.

Weever, Jacqueline de. "The Inverted World of Toni Morrison's *The Bluest Eye* and *Sula*." *College Language Association Journal* 22 (1979): 402–14.

Weinstein, Philip M. *What Else but Love?: The Ordeal of Race in Faulkner and Morrison*. New York: Columbia University Press, 1996.

Wendell, Susan. *The Rejected Body: Feminist Philosophical Reflections on Disability*. London: Rowtledge, 1996.

Whitfield, Stephen J. *Death in the Delta: The Story of Emmett Till*. New York: The Free Press, 1988.

Widdowson, Peter. "The American Dream Refashioned: History, Politics and Gender in Toni Morrison's *Paradise*." *Journal of American Studies* 35: 2 (2001): 313–35.

Wilentz, Gay. "African Spiritual Culture in *Sula, Song of Solomon*, and *Beloved*." In *Toni Morrison's Fiction: Contemporary Criticism*. Ed. David L. Middleton. New York: Garland, 1997.

Willis, Susan. "Eruptions of Funk: Historicizing Toni Morrison." In *Black Literature and Literary Theory*. Ed. Henry Louis Gates, Jr. New York: Routledge, 1984.

Willis, Susan. "Memory and Mass Culture." In *History and Memory in African American Culture*. Ed. Genevieve Fabre and Robert O'Meally. New York: Oxford University Press, 1994.

Winfrey, Oprah. *Journey to Beloved*. New York: Hyperion, 1998.

Wolff, Cynthia Griffin. "'Margaret Garner': A Cincinnati Story." In *Discovering Difference: Contemporary Essays in American Culture*. Ed. Christoph K. Lohmann. Bloomington: Indiana University Press, 1993.

Wood, James. "The Color Purple" (review of *Paradise*). *New Republic* (March 2000): 45.

Wurmser, Leon. *The Mask of Shame*. 1981. Northvale, NJ: Jason Aronson, 1994.

Wyatt, Jean. "Giving Body to the Word: The Maternal Symbolic in Toni Morrison's *Beloved*." *PMLA* 108: 3 (May 1993): 474–88.

Yancy, George. "The Black Self Within a Semiotic Space of Whiteness: Reflections on the Racial Deformation of Pecola Breedlove in Toni Morrison's *The Bluest Eye*." *CLA Journal* 43: 3 (March 2000): 299–319.

# Index

# About the Editor and Contributors

R. ALLEN ALEXANDER, JR., is Assistant Professor of English at Nicholls State University, where he teaches courses in early American, Southern, and Louisiana literature, and the American novel. He has published essays on Toni Morrison and George W. Cable, and reference articles on Morrison, Albert Murray, W.P. Kinsella, J.F. Powers, and Tim Gautreaux.

NICOLE N. ALJOE is a Ph.D. candidate in English at Tufts University, a research fellow at the W.E.B. Du Bois Institute for Afro-American Research at Harvard University, and a Menderhall Fellow in the Department of English at Smith College. She is currently completing her dissertation, "So Much Things to Say: The Creole Testimony of Caribbean Slaves," a close examination of Caribbean slave narratives.

JULIE BUCKNER ARMSTRONG is Assistant Professor of English at the University of South Florida, St. Petersburg. A coeditor of *Teaching the Civil Rights Movement* (forthcoming), she has also published articles on Toni Morrison, Flannery O'Connor, and Carson McCullers. Her current research focuses on artistic responses to a 1918 lynching in south Georgia.

ELIZABETH ANN BEAULIEU is the director of the Women's Studies Program at Appalachian State University, where she also teaches in the Department of Interdisciplinary Studies. She is the author of *Black Women Writers and the American Neo-Slave Narrative: Femininity Unfettered* and several articles on Black literature.

SHANNA GREENE BENJAMIN is a doctoral candidate in English at the University of Wisconsin, Madison. Under the auspices of a Ford Foundation dissertation fellowship, she is completing a dissertation titled "A(unt) Nancy's Web: Tracing Threads of Africa in Black Women's Literature."

J. BROOKS BOUSON is Professor of English at Loyola University of Chicago. She has published essays and book chapters on authors including Dorothy Allison, Margaret Atwood, Saul Bellow, Emily Dickinson, Ted Hughes, Franz Kafka, Edwin Muir, Toni Morrison, George Orwell, and Christa Wolf, and is the author of three books—*Quiet as It's Kept: Shame, Trauma and Race in the Novels of Toni Morrison; Brutal Choreographies: Oppositional Strategies and Narrative Design in the Novels of Margaret Atwood;* and *The Empathetic Reader: A Study of the Narcissistic Character and the Drama of the Self*

CAROLINE BROWN specializes in twentieth-century American literature, the literature of the African Diaspora, and women's studies at the University of Massachusetts, Boston. She received her Ph.D. in comparative literature from Stanford University, and has studied and taught in Africa, Europe, and the Caribbean. Her current project is a cross-cultural exploration of madness and modernism in Black women's novels.

JOCELYN A. CHADWICK-JOSHUA is an Assistant Professor in the Graduate School of Education at Harvard University. Among the courses she teaches is a seminar on Twain, Faulkner, and Morrison. She has published extensively on Twain, and plans a book on Twain and Morrison after she completes her current book project. She consults with high school English departments around the country on how to teach Twain and Morrison more effectively.

GENA ELISE CHANDLER is a Ph.D. student in English at the University of North Carolina at Chapel Hill. Her areas of study include twentieth-century African American literature and critical theory. Her research interests examine the concept of storytelling and identity formation in African American literature through principal features of African Diasporic theory.

JOHN CHARLES is a Ph.D. candidate in English at the University of Virginia, where he specializes in American literature and the color line. His dissertation is on the post–World War II rise of the African American "white life" novel.

DEBORAH DE ROSA is Assistant Professor at Northern Illinois University where she teaches graduate and undergraduate classes in African

American literature and late nineteenth-century American literature, with an emphasis on women authors. Her current project involves assembling an anthology of nineteenth-century American women authors who used children's literature as an avenue through which to express their opposition to slavery.

KWAKIUTL L. DREHER is Assistant Professor of English and Ethnic Studies at the University of Nebraska, Lincoln. Her research interests include film and visual culture, twentieth-century American literature (1970–present), African American literature, and Black autobiography. She is currently at work on a book titled *The Black Actress 1940–1970: Lena Horne, Diahann Carroll, and Eartha Kitt.*

JENNIFER DRISCOLL is an Associate Professor of English at Marist College, where she teaches writing and composition. Her research interests include women's life-writing in the late nineteenth and twentieth centuries and discourses of the emotions. She is currently completing a project on narrative that considers how women's outrage frames their relationship to self and community.

MONIKA ELBERT is Professor of English at Montclair State University and Distinguished Scholar for the academic year 2001–02. Her recent work includes two volumes of uncollected (or lesser-known) Alcott stories and an edited collection, *Separate Spheres No More: Gender Convergence in American Literature, 1830–1930.*

KELLY NORMAN ELLIS is Assistant Professor of English at Chicago State University, where she teaches creative writing, African American literature, and women's literature. She is a founding member of the Affrilachian Poets, a band of traveling writers of color who share roots in the deep South and Appalachia.

JUDITH ESPINOLA is Professor Emeritus and consultant in interdisciplinary studies at De Anza College. She previously held teaching and administrative positions at Evergreen State College and the University of Washington, directed and performed in numerous literary adaptations, and wrote on narrative in novels by Virginia Woolf.

CONSEULA FRANCIS is an Assistant Professor at the College of Charleston in South Carolina. Her research interests include nineteenth-century American literature, Black intellectual thought, and media studies.

ROSEMARIE GARLAND-THOMSON is Associate Professor of Women's Studies at Emory University. Her work focuses on feminist theory and disability studies in the humanities. She is the author of *Extraordinary Bodies: Figuring Physical Disability in American Literature and Culture*, and editor of several collections on disability studies. She is currently writing a book on staring and one on the cultural logic of euthanasia.

KRISTINA K. GROOVER is Associate Professor of English at Appalachian State University. She is author of *The Wilderness Within: American Women Writers and Spiritual Quest*, and essays on Harriette Arnow, Kaye Gibbons, Sarah Orne Jewett, and Toni Morrison. She is currently editing a collection of essays on constructs of spirituality in women writers' texts.

KIM Q. HALL is Assistant Professor of Philosophy and a member of the Women's Studies program at Appalachian State University. She is currently editing the *NWSA Journal* special issue on feminist disability studies. She also edited (with Chris J. Cuomo) *Whiteness: Feminist Philosophical Reflections*.

CYNTHIA WHITNEY HALLETT is Assistant Professor of English at Bennett College. Her book *Minimalism and the Short Story* offers revealing analyses of stories by Raymond Carver, Amy Hempel, and Mary Robinson. With the short story central to her scholarship, Hallett has published articles on Amy Hempel, Zora Neale Hurston, Toni Morrison, Mary Robison, and Alice Walker.

WILLIAM S. HAMPL is an instructor at the Broadened Opportunity for Officer Selection and Training program at the Naval Education and Training Center in Newport, Rhode Island. His areas of interest are literary nonfiction and post-1945 female authors. His latest essay, considering the novels of Iris Murdoch, appears in *Modern Fiction Studies*.

LYNN MARIE HOUSTON is an Assistant Professor at Southeastern Louisiana University. Her teaching and research interests are in the areas of ethnic studies, cultural studies, and food studies. Some of her essays have appeared in *Journal of American and South African Comparative Studies, M/C: A Journal of Media and Culture, Postmodern Culture, Performing Arts Journal,* and *Proteus*.

JAMES M. IVORY is Associate Professor of English at Appalachian State University and the author of *Identity and Narrative Metamorphoses in Twentieth-Century British Literature* (2000).

RAYMOND E. JANIFER is Associate Professor of English and director of the Ethnic Studies Program at Shippensburg University. In addition to contributing to this volume, he has forthcoming articles in volumes including "Looking Homewood: The Evolution of John Edgar Wideman's Folk Imagination," in *Contemporary Black Men's Fiction and Drama*, and "Letter to My Daughter," in *Paperthin, Souldeep: A Collection of Personal Letters and Journal Entries of African American Men*.

LOVALERIE KING is Assistant Professor of English at University of Massachusetts, Boston, where she teaches American and African American literature. She has published on Black women playwrights, Morrison's *Beloved*, and Gayl Jones's *Song for Anninho*. She is at work on a manuscript titled "Theft, Race, and Morality: The Counter-Discourse in African American Literature," and a college textbook.

CONNIE ANN KIRK is a writer and scholar who teaches at Mansfield University. She is at work on a book about the motif of houses in American literature, which includes discussion of Morrison's *Beloved*. She is editing *The Encyclopedia of American Children's Literature*, forthcoming from Greenwood Press.

TRACI M. KLASS is a doctoral student at the University of Florida, Gainesville, and received her master's degree in English from Florida Atlantic University. Her academic interests include studies in classical literature and philosophy, literary theory, Victorian literature, Franz Kafka, and Toni Morrison. Her work on Morrison ranges from examining Platonic undertones in the novels to investigating traits and literary themes Morrison shares with the writer George Eliot.

SUZANNE LANE is Assistant Professor of English at California State University, San Bernardino. Her primary research focuses on the intersections of contemporary African American literature and folk traditions.

DAVID E. MAGILL is a doctoral candidate in American literature at the University of Kentucky. He is currently completing his dissertation, "Modern Masculinities: Race and Manhood in 1920s U.S. Literature and Culture," which explores the reformulation of Jazz Age white masculinity in response to contemporary anxieties about raced and gendered identities.

AJUAN MARIA MANCE is Assistant Professor of English at Mills College. She received her doctorate in English from the University of Michigan, Ann Arbor, and is currently at work on a study of U.S. Black women poets and self-representation.

GRACE MCENTEE is Professor of English at Appalachian State University, where she teaches nineteenth-century American literature and African American literature. Her articles and contributions to encyclopedias include pieces on Barbara Neely and Charles Johnson, as well as on African American history and culture.

CHRISTOPHER METRESS is Associate Professor of English at Samford University. His essays and reviews have appeared in such journals as *American Literary History, African American Review, Mississippi Quarterly, The Southern Review,* and *Studies in the Novel.* He recently edited *The Lynching of Emmett Till: A Documentary Narrative.*

FIONA MILLS is a Ph.D. candidate and teaching fellow in English at the University of North Carolina, Chapel Hill. Her dissertation is titled "'Chitlins con Carne': Cross-Cultural Connections in Afro-Latino/a Literature." She is currently coediting a book of collected essays on Gayl Jones.

STACY I. MORGAN is Assistant Professor in the Department of American Studies at the University of Alabama. His principal research interests include literature, art history, folklore, and performance. He is currently revising a manuscript exploring social realism in African American literature and visual art.

JULIE CARY NERAD received her Ph.D. from the University of Kentucky. Her dissertation, titled "Complicated Cords: Racial Passing, Cultural Discourses, and (National) Families," explores the role of the family and the qeustion of the passer's intent to pass in racial passing novels from 1850 to 1920. Her most recent scholarly publication, an essay on Pauline E. Hopkins's *Contending Forces,* appears in *African American Review.*

MENDI LEWIS OBADIKE is a doctoral candidate in literature at Duke University. Her dissertation is a theory of the soundscape in novels of manners by African American writers. She writes in New Haven, CT.

AIMEE L. POZORSKI is a Fellow at the Center for Humanistic Inquiry and a doctoral candidate in English at Emory University. She is working on a dissertation titled "Figures of Infanticide: Traumatic Modernity and the Inaudible Cry." She has written on avant-garde poet Mina Loy, as well as on literature of the Holocaust and the works of Toni Morrison.

CATHERINE S. QUICK is Assistant Professor of English at Stephen F. Austin State University, where she teaches courses in folklore, mythology, and world literature. Her recent research projects have focused on the rhetorical function of folkloric and mythic structures in contemporary literature.

JEANNETTE E. RILEY is Assistant Professor of English and Women's Studies at University of Massachusetts, Dartmouth. She teaches women's literature, post-1945 American literature, and literary theory. Much of her scholarship revolves around post-1945 women's literature. Riley has published articles on Eavan Boland, Adrienne Rich, and Wallace Stegner.

JANE ATTERIDGE ROSE is Professor of English at Georgia College and State University, where she teaches courses in American literature and women's studies. She has taught graduate and undergraduate courses on Toni Morrison; however, most of her scholarship focuses on nineteenth-century American women writers, particularly Rebecca Harding Davis.

LISA C. ROSEN, Ph.D., is an independent scholar living and working in Cary, NC. Her professional interests include Southern literature, particularly by women, and the role of motherhood in women's writing.

JOE SUTLIFF SANDERS is a doctoral candidate in English at the University of Kentucky. In addition to a small body of fiction, he has published criticism on various aspects of speculative fiction and narrative theory. He teaches courses on fantasy, U.S. literature, and major Black writers.

SUSAN C. STAUB is Professor of English at Appalachian State University, where she teaches Renaissance literature. Her current research focuses on representations of women, crime, and domestic violence in the early modern period. She has recently published a facsimile edition of mothers' advice books and completed a book-length study of representations of domestic violence in the street literature of seventeenth-century England.

F. GREGORY STEWART is an instructor in Literary Studies at the University of Texas at Dallas, where he is completing his doctorate. His areas of research and teaching specialization are Southern and African American literature and culture, as well as popular culture studies.

JOHNNIE M. STOVER is Assistant Professor of English at Florida Atlantic University, teaching in the areas of nineteenth- and twentieth-century American literature, African American literature, American Indian literature, and Southern literature. Current research interests include Zora Neale Hurston, Southern modernist writers, and nineteenth-century African American women's biography.

DOUGLAS TAYLOR is an Assistant Professor of English and African American Literature at the University of Texas at Austin. His Ph.D. is from the University of North Carolina at Chapel Hill, where he wrote a dissertation titled "Outlaws, Nationalists, and Revolutionaries: Masculinity, Black Power, and the African American Prison Narratives of the 1960s and 1970s."

ELIZABETH ELY TOLMAN is a visiting lecturer in Romance languages at the University of North Carolina, Chapel Hill. She has published on Brazilian author João Ubaldo Ribeiro and Cuban poet Dulce María Loynaz, and is at work on a distance education course in intermediate Spanish for health care professionals.

KAREN E. WALDRON is Professor of Literature and Associate Dean for Academic Affairs at College of the Atlantic in Bar Harbor, ME. Her specialty is nineteenth- and twentieth-century American women's and minority literatures; her published work includes essays on Fanny Fern, William Faulkner, and Leslie Marmon Silko.

ANISSA WARDI is Assistant Professor of English and director of Cultural Studies at Chatham College, where she teaches courses in African American literature. She has a recent essay in *African American Review,* titled "Inscriptions in the Dust: *A Gathering of Old Men* and *Beloved* as Ancestral Requiems."

STEVEN WEISENBURGER is a Professor of English and director of the Program in American Culture at the University of Kentucky. The author of two books and numerous articles on modern American fiction, he has also written *Modern Medea: A Family Story of Slavery and Child Murder from the Old South,* a narrative history of the Margaret Garner fugitive slave case of 1856.

LISA CADE WIELAND is Assistant Professor of American Literature and Writing at Spalding University. Her scholarly interests include Southern literature and women's literature. She has published articles on Eudora Welty and has presented at several academic conferences.

KRISTINE YOHE, Ph.D., is Assistant Professor in the Department of Literature and Language at Northern Kentucky University, where she has taught since 1997. Her teaching and scholarship focus on Toni Morrison, particularly *Beloved* and *Paradise.* Other professional interests center on Underground Railroad literature, as well as African American and Afro-Caribbean writers including Edwidge Danticat and Jean-Robert Cadet.